THE ROUTLEDGE HANDBOOK OF PHILOSOPHY OF WELL-BEING

The concept of well-being is one of the oldest and most important topics in philosophy and ethics, going back to ancient Greek philosophy. Following the boom in happiness studies in the last few years it has moved to centre stage, grabbing media headlines and the attention of scientists, psychologists and economists. Yet little is actually known about well-being and it is an idea that is often poorly articulated.

The Routledge Handbook of Philosophy of Well-Being provides a comprehensive, outstanding guide and reference source to the key topics and debates in this exciting subject.

Comprising over 40 chapters by a team of international contributors, the *Handbook* is divided into six parts:

1. well-being in the history of philosophy
2. current theories of well-being, including hedonism and perfectionism
3. examples of well-being and its opposites, including friendship and virtue and pain and death
4. theoretical issues, such as well-being and value, harm, identity and well-being and children
5. well-being in moral and political philosophy
6. well-being and related subjects, including law, economics and medicine.

Essential reading for students and researchers in ethics and political philosophy, it will also be an invaluable resource for those in related disciplines such as psychology, politics and sociology.

Guy Fletcher is a lecturer in Philosophy at the University of Edinburgh, UK. His current research is in metaethics, on moral language and moral psychology. Another strand of research is in political philosophy, on hate speech. He also has a persistent side-interest in John Stuart Mill. His book, *The Philosophy of Well-Being: An Introduction* is forthcoming with Routledge.

Routledge Handbooks in Philosophy

Routledge Handbooks in Philosophy are state-of-the-art surveys of emerging, newly refreshed, and important fields in philosophy, providing accessible yet thorough assessments of key problems, themes, thinkers, and recent developments in research.

All chapters for each volume are specially commissioned, and written by leading scholars in the field. Carefully edited and organised, *Routledge Handbooks in Philosophy* provide indispensable reference tools for students and researchers seeking a comprehensive overview of new and exciting topics in philosophy. They are also valuable teaching resources as accompaniments to textbooks, anthologies and research-oriented publications.

Also available:

The Routledge Handbook of Embodied Cognition
Edited by Lawrence Shapiro

The Routledge Handbook of Neoplatonism
Edited by Pauliina Remes and Svetla Slaveva-Griffin

The Routledge Handbook of Contemporary Philosophy of Religion
Edited by Graham Oppy

Forthcoming:

The Routledge Handbook of the Stoic Tradition
Edited by John Sellars

The Routledge Handbook of Philosophy of Imagination
Edited by Amy Kind

The Routledge Handbook of Philosophy of Colour
Edited by Derek Brown and Fiona Macpherson

The Routledge Handbook of the Philosophy of Biodiversity
Edited by Justin Garson, Anya Plutynski, and Sahotra Sarkar

The Routledge Handbook of Philosophy of the Social Mind
Edited by Julian Kiverstein

The Routledge Handbook of Collective Intentionality
Edited by Marija Jankovic and Kirk Ludwig

The Routledge Handbook of Brentano and the Brentano School
Edited by Uriah Kriegel

THE ROUTLEDGE HANDBOOK OF PHILOSOPHY OF WELL-BEING

Edited by Guy Fletcher

LONDON AND NEW YORK

First published 2016
by Routledge
2 Park Square, Milton Park, Abingdon, Oxon, OX14 4RN

Simultaneously published in the USA and Canada
by Routledge
711 Third Avenue, New York City, NY 10017

Routledge is an imprint of the Taylor & Francis Group, an informa business

British Library Cataloguing in Publication Data
A catalogue record for this book is available from the British Library

Library of Congress Cataloging in Publication Data
A catalog record for this book has been requested

ISBN: 978-0-415-71453-2 (hbk)
ISBN: 978-1-315-68226-6 (ebk)

Typeset in Bembo Std
by Swales & Willis Ltd, Exeter, Devon, UK

Printed and bound in the United States of America by Publishers Graphics, LLC on sustainably sourced paper.

CONTENTS

Contents

CONTRIBUTORS

Anna Alexandrova teaches philosophy of science in the Department of History and Philosophy of Science, University of Cambridge, UK, where she is also a Fellow of King's College. She writes on the virtues and vices of idealised modelling in economics and on the promises and pitfalls of the scientific study of well-being. She received her PhD from the University of California, San Diego in 2006 and up to 2011 taught at the University of Missouri–St. Louis. Her 2008 article "Making Models Count" won *Philosophy of Science*'s Best Article by Recent PhD award.

Erik Angner is Associate Professor of Philosophy, Economics and Public Policy at George Mason University, Virginia, USA, where he directs the undergraduate Philosophy, Politics and Economics programme.

Neera K. Badhwar is Professor Emerita of Philosophy at the University of Oklahoma, and Affiliate at George Mason University, Virginia, USA. Her research interests are in moral psychology, ethical theory and practical ethics. She is the author of *Well-Being: Happiness in a Worthwhile Life* (OUP 2014).

Anne Baril is Assistant Professor of Philosophy at the University of New Mexico, USA. She has research interests in ethics and epistemology. Her recent publications include "The Role of Welfare in Eudaimonism" (*Southern Journal of Philosophy* 2013) and "Pragmatic Encroachment in Accounts of Epistemic Excellence" (*Synthese* 2013). Currently she is writing a book in which she argues for the moral and prudential importance of epistemic virtue.

Lorraine Besser-Jones is Associate Professor at Middlebury College, Vermont, USA. She is the author of *Eudaimonic Ethics* (Routledge 2014) and the co-editor *of The Routledge Companion to Virtue Ethics* (Routledge 2015).

Gwen Bradford is Assistant Professor of Philosophy at Rice University, Texas, USA. She is the author of *Achievement* (OUP 2015).

Ben Bradley is Allan and Anita Sutton Professor of Philosophy, and chair of the Philosophy Department, at Syracuse University (USA). He is the author of *Well-Being and Death* (OUP 2009) and co-editor of the *Oxford Handbook of Philosophy of Death* (OUP 2012).

Ben Bramble recently received his PhD from the University of Sydney, Australia, and is currently a Postdoctoral Fellow at the University of Vienna, Austria. His research interests include value theory, reasons for action, well-being and moral responsibility. He is working on a monograph defending a comprehensive welfare-based theory of ethics.

Eric Brown, Associate Professor of Philosophy at Washington University in St. Louis, USA, researches and teaches ancient Greek and Roman philosophy, primarily, and is the author of *Stoic Cosmopolitanism* (Cambridge University Press forthcoming).

Stephen M. Campbell is Assistant Professor of Philosophy at Bentley University in Boston, USA, and the Well-Being category editor for the international philosophy database PhilPapers. His current research focuses on conceptual and ethical issues related to well-being, death, meaning and disability.

Sarah Conly is an Associate Professor of Philosophy at Bowdoin College, Maine, USA. She is the author of *Against Autonomy: Justifying Coercive Paternalism* (Cambridge University Press 2013) and has just completed a book for Oxford University Press, *One Child: Do We Have a Right to More?* which should appear in 2015.

Dale Dorsey is Associate Professor of Philosophy and Meredith J. Docking Faculty Scholar at the University of Kansas, USA. He works primarily on well-being, consequentialism and the normative authority of morality.

Guy Fletcher is lecturer in Philosophy at the University of Edinburgh, UK. His areas of interest are metaethics, ethics and political philosophy.

Molly Gardner has served as a Research Assistant Professor at the University of North Carolina at Chapel Hill, USA, and the Adam Smith Guest Professor at the University of Bayreuth in Germany. She obtained her PhD in philosophy from the University of Wisconsin-Madison.

Christopher W. Gowans is Professor of Philosophy at Fordham University in New York City, USA. He works in a variety of areas of moral philosophy and is author of *Buddhist Moral Philosophy: An Introduction* (Routledge 2014), *Philosophy of the Buddha* (Routledge 2003) and *Innocence Lost: An Examination of Inescapable Moral Wrongdoing* (Oxford University Press 1994).

Alex Gregory is a lecturer in Philosophy at the University of Southampton, UK. His research addresses various topics in ethics, moral psychology and metaethics, but focuses primarily on questions about desire, reasons for action and well-being.

Marco Grix is a doctoral student in Philosophy at the University of Auckland, New Zealand. His main areas of research interest are moral, social and political philosophy, with a special focus on human needs and human consumption.

Daniel Groll is an Associate Professor at Carleton College in Northfield, Minnesota, USA, and an affiliate faculty member at the Center for Bioethics at the University of Minnesota. He has written papers on autonomy, paternalism, moral disagreement and the clinician–patient relationship, which have appeared in *Ethics*, *The Hastings Center Report*, *Oxford Studies in Metaethics* and *Pediatrics*.

Alicia Hall is Assistant Professor of Philosophy at Mississippi State University, USA. Her research focuses on subjective accounts of well-being as well as interdisciplinary applications of well-being research. In addition to her work on well-being, her research interests include issues of justice in healthcare.

Jennifer Hawkins, PhD, is Associate Research Professor in the Department of Philosophy at Duke University, North Carolina, USA. She has wide-ranging interests in ethical theory, with special interests in bioethics and moral psychology. She is currently writing a book about well-being.

Allan Hazlett is Assistant Professor of Philosophy at the University of New Mexico, USA. He is the author of *A Luxury of the Understanding* (OUP 2013) and *A Critical Introduction to Skepticism* (Bloomsbury 2014), and is the Secretary of the Scots Philosophical Association. His research concerns the value of knowledge, the sources of normativity and issues in social and political epistemology.

Chris Heathwood is Associate Professor of Philosophy at the University of Colorado Boulder, USA.

Jules Holroyd is a lecturer in the Department of Philosophy at the University of Nottingham, UK. Her research addresses questions in moral psychology and social and political philosophy. In particular, she is interested in implicit cognition, responsibility and feminist philosophy.

Diane Jeske is Professor of Philosophy at the University of Iowa, USA. She is the author of *Rationality and Moral Theory: How Intimacy Generates Reasons* (Routledge 2008). Her published work focuses on issues concerning duties to friends and family, the nature of our reasons and utilitarianism vs deontology.

Guy Kahane is Associate Professor of Philosophy at the University of Oxford, UK, and fellow and tutor in philosophy at Pembroke College, Oxford. Kahane is also deputy director of the Oxford Uehiro Centre for Practical Ethics and the Oxford Centre for Neuroethics, and an associate editor of the *Journal of Practical Ethics*.

Antti Kauppinen is an Assistant Professor of Philosophy at Trinity College Dublin, Ireland. His research is focused on metaethics, in particular moral sentimentalism and practical reasoning, and normative ethics, in particular well-being and meaningfulness. He has also written about philosophical methodology.

Simon Keller is Professor of Philosophy at Victoria University of Wellington, New Zealand. He has published extensively on topics in ethics, political philosophy and metaphysics. He is the author of *The Limits of Loyalty* (Berghahn Books 2007) and *Partiality* (Princeton University Press 2013).

Richard Kim is a Postdoctoral Fellow and member of the Center for East Asian and Comparative Philosophy, City University of Hong Kong. His current research is at the intersection between contemporary moral psychology and East Asian philosophy (especially early Confucianism). He is currently working on a book project, *Conceptions of Human Nature: East and West.*

Richard Kraut is Professor of Philosophy and Charles E. and Emma H. Morrison Professor in the Humanities at Northwestern University, Illinois, USA. Among his works are *Aristotle on the Human Good* (Princeton University Press 1989) and *Against Absolute Goodness* (OUP 2011).

William Lauinger is an Assistant Professor of Philosophy at Chestnut Hill College in Philadelphia, Pennsylvania, USA. He works in ethics and the philosophy of religion, and he is the author of *Well-Being and Theism: Linking Ethics to God* (Bloomsbury Academic 2012).

Eden Lin is Assistant Professor of Philosophy at Rutgers University, Newark, USA. He received his PhD from Princeton University in 2013.

Philip McKibbin is a research assistant at the University of Auckland, New Zealand. He holds a Master of Arts in Philosophy.

Tim O'Keefe is Associate Professor of Philosophy at Georgia State University, USA. He is the author of numerous works on the Epicureans, including *Epicurus on Freedom* (Cambridge University Press 2005) and *Epicureanism* (Routledge 2010). He has also published on the Cyrenaics, Pyrrhonian skeptics, Platonic *spuria* and Aristotle's cosmology.

Jason Raibley is Associate Professor of Philosophy and Director of the Center for Applied Ethics at California State University, Long Beach, USA. He received his PhD from UMass Amherst, USA. He writes on topics in moral psychology, ethical theory, metaethics and bioethics.

Douglas Reeve completed his PhD in philosophy at University College London, UK, in 2013, on Global Poverty, Human Rights and Development.

Christopher M. Rice is an Assistant Professor of Philosophy at Lynn University, Florida, USA. He received his PhD in philosophy from Fordham University, New York, USA, in 2012.

Alex Sarch is a Postdoctoral Fellow in Law and Philosophy at the University of Southern California, USA. He received his PhD in philosophy from UMass Amherst, where he wrote his dissertation on objectivity and well-being, and then received his JD from the University of Michigan Law School. His current work lies at the intersection of moral philosophy and criminal law, with a particular focus on culpability and motivation as they pertain to legal concepts like wilful ignorance, complicity and attempts.

S. Andrew Schroeder is an Assistant Professor of Philosophy at Claremont McKenna College, California, USA. His research addresses questions in normative and metaethics, as well as more practical issues connected to ethics, health and economic analysis.

Robert Shaver is Professor of Philosophy at the University of Manitoba, Canada. He is the author of *Rational Egoism* (Cambridge University Press 1999) and, more recently, various papers on Sidgwick, Ross, Prichard, Rashdall and Bentham, non-naturalism and experimental philosophy.

Anthony Skelton is Associate Professor in the Department of Philosophy at the University of Western Ontario, Canada. His research focuses on issues in normative ethics and the history of ethics, and he is the co-editor of *Bioethics in Canada* (OUP 2013).

Valerie Tiberius is Professor of Philosophy at the University of Minnesota, USA. Her work explores the ways in which philosophy and psychology can both contribute to the study of well-being and virtue. She is the author of *The Reflective Life: Living Wisely With Our Limits* (OUP 2008), *Moral Psychology: A Contemporary Introduction* (Routledge 2015) and numerous articles on the topics of practical reasoning, prudential virtues, well-being and the relationship between psychology and ethics.

Justin Tiwald is Associate Professor of Philosophy at San Francisco State University, USA. He has published widely on issues in Chinese philosophy. Recent works include "Xunzi on Moral Expertise" (*Dao* 2012), "Sympathy and Perspective-Taking in Confucian Ethics" (*Philosophy Compass* 2011) and *Readings in Later Chinese Philosophy* (Hackett 2014), an anthology.

Jonathan Wolff is Professor of Philosophy and Dean of Arts and Humanities at University College London. His works include *Disadvantage* (with Avner de-Shalit) (OUP 2007) and *Ethics and Public Policy* (Routledge 2011).

Christopher Woodard is Associate Professor in the Department of Philosophy at the University of Nottingham, UK. He is the author of *Reasons, Patterns, and Cooperation* (Routledge 2008), and he is writing a book for Oxford University Press provisionally entitled *Taking Utilitarianism Seriously*.

INTRODUCTION

Well-being has a long-distinguished history as a locus of philosophical exploration. This should come as no surprise. Much practical philosophy is focused on the questions of how we ought to live in general, what we ought to do, or what morality requires of us. But the answer to these questions must be sensitive to the question of how it would be best for us to live. That is, what I ought to do is surely in at least some way affected by what would make my life go better or worse *for me*. To make this less abstract, think about the following cases.

First, suppose a charity collector stops me in the street and asks me to donate £2. If I am affluent then it is plausible that the effect on my well-being of donating £2 is negligible. It is close to nothing, possibly nothing. If that is so then it is plausible that I ought to donate the money. If, by contrast, I am destitute, hungry and homeless then it does not seem plausible that I ought to donate the money. This is plausibly because the cost *to me* of donating is too high. The 'currency' in which we determine these different possible costs to me, the ones we use in thinking about whether I ought to donate, is *well-being*. We are thinking about the effect on how my life goes *for me*.

Ordinary reflection on what makes a life go well reveals that a large number of things positively affect our lives, things such as pleasurable experiences, friendship, meaningful work, feeling good about ourselves, achievements and purpose, leisure and intelligence. It also reveals that a large number of things negatively affect our lives, things such as stress, worry, injury, disease, insufficient money, misery, lack of freedom, lack of self-worth. What is distinctive about the *philosophy* of well-being is its focus on the question of which things *in and of themselves* make someone's life go better or worse *for them*. It thus seeks an account of what is *fundamentally*, or non-instrumentally, good or bad for us and why.

Philosophers working on well-being give very different answers to this question. Some identify particular goods and bads, seeking to justify the view that (only) these things fundamentally affect well-being. The most famous example of this is hedonism, the view that only pleasure and pain fundamentally affect well-being. Other philosophers look for a kind of grand explanatory story, such as a story of human nature, out of which they hope to extract a theory of what fundamentally determines our well-being. One theory of this type is Aristotelian perfectionism, which is the view that human nature determines the nature of human well-being.

The philosophy of well-being is, as this makes clear, extremely important in its own right. All of our important life decisions are connected with effects on well-being, and the philosophy of well-being is therefore a major part of philosophical investigation into how to live. It is also important because our conceptions of well-being clearly underpin investigation in so many other fields. Psychology, economics, medicine and law, to name just a few, are all plausibly ultimately concerned with how to protect or promote well-being. The philosophy of well-being is thus vital to these disciplines. But this is only a part of well-being's significance beyond philosophy. A useful question to ask of *any* institution, organisation or area of study is whether it ultimately helps us to live better, or to know how to live better.

The 41 chapters within this handbook are testament to the philosophical significance of well-being. They demonstrate the array of historical traditions which have thought philosophically about the topic, the multitude of theories of well-being, the diverse range of theoretical issues connected to well-being, and the various ways in which well-being is connected to research beyond moral philosophy.

The collection is divided into six parts thus:

1. Well-being in the history of moral philosophy
2. Theories of well-being
3. Particular goods and bads
4. Theoretical issues
5. Well-being in moral and political philosophy
6. Well-being and other disciplines.

Part 1: Well-being in the history of moral philosophy

Part 1 covers historical traditions and opens with Eric Brown's paper on well-being in the Socratic dialogues. Brown summarises thinking about well-being in the local context of the dialogues before showing Socrates' commitment to a view of well-being in which, whilst other things may be non-instrumentally good for us, only wisdom (or, more strictly, wise activity) is unconditionally good for us. Brown also shows why the apparent textual evidence that Socrates had a hedonic conception of well-being is misleading.

Richard Kraut gives an outline of Aristotle's theory of eudaimonia, focusing, first, on the extent to which Aristotle is thinking about *well-being* and, second, on the most plausible interpretation of Aristotle's theory of eudaimonia, one in which well-being is attained through the flourishing of our endowment of inherent powers.

Tim O'Keefe's chapter on hedonistic theories in antiquity considers those ancient theorists who eschewed eudaimonistic or perfectionist theories of well-being in favour of theories that took pleasure to be the sole contributor to well-being. He focuses in particular on the Epicureans and the Cyrenaics and their accounts of well-being and theories of the nature of pleasure before drawing parallels with the Pyrrhonian skeptics.

Next are four chapters considering the place of well-being within certain religious traditions. Richard Kim introduces thought about well-being within Confucianism, focusing on Mencius and Xunzi and their common proposal that the best human life is that which reaches sagehood.

Justin Tiwald looks at well-being in the Daoist tradition, examining the views of human welfare that can be found or extracted from the *Daodejing* and the *Zhuangzi*. There is much to learn from this chapter about well-being in the Daoist tradition. Two significant points are that the *Daodejing* supplies objections to a desire-fulfillment conception of well-being, and suggests a certain degree of sympathy with the objective list theory, whilst the *Zhuangzi* offers a radical way of thinking about well-being and its pursuit, one that has some affinities with perfectionism but which does not cohere fully even with this theory.

Christopher W. Gowans examines Buddhist thinking and how it pertains to well-being. He makes clear some of the difficulties in doing so—the Buddhist 'no-self' teaching and the difficulty of seeing how unrecognisable as a human life the state of nirvana is described as being. One major strand to the chapter is the extent to which Buddhist thinking about well-being fits within a perfectionist, nature fulfillment, view.

William Lauinger tackles the Christian tradition, covering Augustine, Aquinas and Calvin as well as more contemporary Christian philosophy of well-being such as that of Finnis. He shows that there is no consensus among contemporary Christian philosophers about the nature of well-being.

This historical section closes with a chapter from Robert Shaver in which he covers thought about well-being in the era of Sidgwick, Moore, Prichard, Ross, Carritt, Broad and Ewing, a group of philosophers not commonly taken to have much to say about well-being. Shaver shows that these philosophers, and Sidgwick especially, had much to say of relevance to contemporary work on well-being.

Part 2: Theories of well-being

Part 2 examines particular theories, or kinds of theories, of well-being. Alex Gregory outlines the hedonistic theory of well-being, arguing that Nozick's experience machine is the most pressing issue for the view. Gwen Bradford provides an overview of perfectionist theories of well-being, one which emphasises the diversity within perfectionist theories.

Next up is the desire-fulfillment theory of well-being. Chris Heathwood brings out the wide range of objections that theory faces but also the wide range of replies it can make. Guy Fletcher provides an outline and defence of the objective list theory. He argues that the challenges to objective list theories often highlight epistemic or explanation problems faced by all theories of well-being (though not perhaps to equal extents) or the need for further refinement of the views of the sort which can also be demanded of other theories of well-being.

Christopher Woodard examines hybrid theories. He makes clear the enormous diversity of hybrid theories and how much work there is left to do. He argues that we must consider specific hybrid theories in detail because hybrid theories neither uniformly solve certain problems nor uniformly suffer standard defects.

The final two chapters of this part highlight an important choice point in theories of well-being, namely to what extent a person's well-being depends upon that person's individual nature. Alicia Hall and Valerie Tiberius encourage us to think about the ways in which theories of well-being can be subject-dependent, where such theories hold that well-being must 'fit the quirks and contours of our own lives' where this might be a matter of fitting our attitudes, our values, our physical and emotional natures, or our aptitudes and capacities. By contrast, Lorraine Besser-Jones' paper on eudaimonism distinguishes philosophical and psychological conceptions of eudaimonia but argues that each conception abstracts from the individual to the species because 'the kind of flourishing embraced by both philosophical and psychological conceptions of eudaimonism is one based on how human beings *tend* to behave and what kinds of things *tend* to enable them to function well'.

Part 3: Particular goods and bads

Part 3 examines particular things that are thought to contribute positively to well-being (and, in the case of pain, negatively) with an eye to seeing how the correct theory of the nature of these things can help us to understand their contribution (or non-contribution) to well-being. In the background here are the questions of how plausible it is that these things contribute to well-being and, if so, how (instrumentally or non-instrumentally), and why. First up are pleasure and pain. Ben Bramble examines pleasure, arguing for a felt-quality theory of pleasure, and then suggesting that it is not only the degree of pleasurableness of a given pleasure that determines its contribution to a person's well-being.

Guy Kahane's chapter looks at pain, tackling the question of which type of theory is the best account of the nature of pain and of why it is bad. He also examines views which claim that pain is not always bad, as well as some evolutionary-based reasons to be sceptical of the badness of pain.

S. Andrew Schroeder looks at the vexed relationship between health and well-being. His conclusion is that the connection between health and well-being is a mere contingent one and that reductions in health probably reduce well-being less than is commonly thought.

Diane Jeske defends a similar view with respect to friendship. She argues that the claims about friendship and well-being, such as that friendship is *essential* to a good life, exaggerate its importance, partly by relying upon an overly idealistic conception of the nature of friendship. Jeske argues that with a more plausible conception of friendship in hand we see that the connections between friendship and well-being are numerous, but contingent and causal. We are not *necessarily* better off for having friends, even if we very often are.

Virtue is the topic of the next two chapters. Anne Baril highlights the difficulty of determining whether virtue contributes to well-being. She outlines a number of different questions connected to this issue—the different ideas of virtue and the different ways in which something might contribute to well-being—before concluding, on an optimistic note, that we should not rule out the view that some degree of virtue is (not simply instrumentally) necessary for the highest degrees of well-being.

Allan Hazlett undertakes a similar task for epistemic virtues or epistemic goods in particular. His question is: what things are both epistemic and conducive to well-being (either the well-being of some salient individual or the well-being of individuals in general)? His answer is pessimistic for knowledge; he argues that we have failed to find a plausible (non-trivial) articulation of the idea that knowledge is necessary for well-being, but cautiously optimistic for other goods such as being known and being ignored.

Next up is achievement and meaningfulness, with chapters by Gwen Bradford and Simon Keller, and by Antti Kauppinen. Bradford and Keller examine achievement—both what it is and why it might contribute to well-being. They distinguish three paradigmatic features of achievement—independent value, effort and purposiveness—before discussing the reasons for thinking that achievement is necessarily or only contingently well-being promoting.

Kauppinen examines *meaningfulness*, a topic whose relation to well-being is unclear. His chapter provides a comprehensive overview of the different theories of meaningfulness in life along with a discussion of the ways in which meaningfulness and well-being may be distinct types of value.

The next chapter, by Marco Grix and Philip McKibbin, discusses needs. They argue for an understanding of what needs are, which takes them as being fundamentally connected, not to harm avoidance or survival, but rather to well-being. They then turn from this proposal to examine links between need theory and theories of well-being, arguing that each side has much to learn from the other.

Neera K. Badhwar's chapter is on happiness. She begins by noting the difficulties in tackling happiness and well-being, not least in the frequency with which 'happiness' and 'well-being' are used interchangeably. Having clarified this, she then surveys the major theories of happiness, including hedonistic theories of happiness and those theories that take happiness to be a form of emotional fulfillment or of affective and evaluative satisfaction given your own values. Having provided helpful coverage of the strengths and weakness of each proposal she then turns to how plausibly happiness is incorporated with the main theories of well-being.

Turning once more to the negative side of well-being, this section ends with Ben Bradley's chapter on well-being and death. Bradley starts by carefully distinguishing all of the different claims that might be made in saying that death is bad for us. He addresses the view that death is bad for us by being some form of deprivation and then turns to issues where well-being, death and time connect, such as posthumous harm. Finally he considers what attitudes it is rational for us to have towards death.

Part 4: Theoretical issues

In Part 4 Eden Lin examines and clarifies the debate between monism and pluralism about well-being. He makes clear exactly how to conceive of the two sides of the debate and usefully presents the main arguments of each side, clarifying their strong and weak points.

Jason Raibley details the debate between atomists and holists about well-being (roughly put, the debate between those who treat lifetime well-being as being built from discrete units of momentary well-being, and those who deny this). Raibley applies this to recent debates about whether the 'shape' of a life has some effect on overall well-being.

Jennifer Hawkins examines the putative 'experience requirement' on theories of well-being, an issue stemming from Nozick's experience machine example. Hawkins subjects the example to forensic scrutiny, detailing just what it assumes and the weak points it has, thereby demonstrating how many subtle issues are tangled together by it.

In their chapters, Anthony Skelton and Christopher M. Rice turn attention to subjects long neglected in the philosophical study of well-being: children and non-human animals. Rice considers theories of *animal* well-being, arguing that there are useful insights from animal well-being for thinking about human well-being and vice versa. Skelton points out the ways in which philosophical theories of human well-being have neglected well-being in *children*. He points out the ways in which theories of well-being generate bad results when applied to children and the failings in specific theories of chilldren's well-being.

This part of the collection closes with two chapters, one by Anna Alexandrova and one by Stephen M. Campbell, questioning the assumption that there is one single topic which theorists of well-being are investigating. Alexandrova examines the plurality of constructs used in *scientific* investigation of well-being whilst Campbell finds a similar plurality among *philosophical* discussions of well-being, despite the assumption of commonality of subject matter. These chapters outline important challenges for philosophers of well-being.

Part 5: Well-being in moral and political philosophy

This section opens with Dale Dorsey on welfarism—the view that welfare or well-being is the only thing that makes a normative difference. Dorsey carefully spells out exactly what could fall within the scope of a 'welfarist' theory along with the difficulties in providing positive, non-circular arguments for the view. He also examines the wide range of objections standardly brought against welfarism.

Molly Gardner's chapter also examines the connection between well-being and practical normativity. In particular she focuses on well-being and the 'non-identity problem', namely the problems that arise from cases where an 'action that is the condition of an individual's worthwhile existence also imposes certain constraints on the individual's prospects for well-being'. As Gardner notes, such cases raise serious questions about the connection between practical reasons and well-being. Gardner discusses two strategies for solving the non-identity problem through appeal to well-being, noting difficulties for each.

Sarah Conly examines the relationship between well-being and autonomy. She argues that realistic governmental interference is likely to do nothing significant to us as persons, in damaging or undermining our psychology, and that worries about governmental interference to promote our well-being are overblown. Whilst bad interventions are possible, there is no reason to think that a broad range of beneficial interventions are not possible.

Government intervention is a theme also in the chapter on well-being and disadvantage, by Jonathan Wolff and Doug Reeve. They examine the thought that, at least in some cases, governments should intervene to promote the well-being of the most disadvantaged. They look at the question of how to identify the least advantaged. They consider the 'separate spheres' approach, one which treats different aspects of people's lives as providing distinct realms of possible advantage/disadvantage, before defending a development of the capability approach, one incorporating work from social psychology.

Jules Holroyd's chapter is on well-being and feminism. As she points out, it is a commonplace that gender inequality damages women's interests. One question this provokes is whether this should be understood in terms of reduced well-being. Should feminists put this claim in terms of well-being at all? If so, which theory of well-being best underpins the claim? Holroyd's chapter also nicely brings out the many contributions to the theory of well-being that come from feminist thought, for example through the question of whether the correct theory of well-being could entail that well-being is something which could be attained despite gender inequality or, rather, whether well-being is 'part of what gender justice would achieve for women'.

Part 6: Well-being and other disciplines

Alex Sarch investigates the way in which well-being and law are related, via the plausible thought that law, in general or particular laws, might have the aim of promoting or protecting well-being. After looking at the law and economics movement, which claims that law should (perhaps exclusively) promote well-being, Sarch examines the role of well-being in tort law, arguing that tort law for the most part protects well-being only indirectly.

Well-being and economics is the focus of Erik Angner's chapter. Angner explores conceptions of well-being underlying contemporary welfare economics. He outlines three different approaches to welfare assessment and finds that each corresponds to a specific account of well-being: while standard economics is based on preference satisfaction accounts, the economics of happiness is based on mental-state accounts, and the social indicators/capability approach on objective-list accounts. The discussion underscores how economists both use and produce philosophy in their scientific practice.

Daniel Groll closes this volume by examining the multifaceted connections between medicine, well-being and autonomy. The first part of the chapter examines whether, and if so how, well-being plays a role in typical doctor–patient interactions and how the patient's autonomy should be treated. Does the doctor have promoting the patient's *well-being* as her goal? If so, does she have any special *expertise* on this, and is this expertise *qua* doctor? Can the doctor ever *impose* treatment upon the patient? The second part of the chapter looks at cases of doctor–patient interactions where the patient is in some way less able to exercise agency, such as through being disabled or unconscious. Groll makes clear the number of thorny issues that arise in medicine from such cases.

As these all-too-brief summaries make clear, these chapters cover a huge amount of ground both within the theory of well-being and in other areas of practical philosophy.

PART I

Well-being in the history of moral philosophy

1

PLATO ON WELL-BEING

Eric Brown

Plato's uses of well-being

To speak of well-being, as they frequently do, the characters in Plato's dialogues use several expressions interchangeably, including the infinitive phrases "to live well" (*eu zēn*), "to be successful" (*eudaimonein*), and "to do well" (*eu prattein*), as well as the related abstract nouns "success" and "doing well" (*eudaimonia, eupragia*). The concept invoked by these expressions plays two central roles in their discussions, as some characters propose that well-being is, or at least should be, the ultimate goal for both individual human action and political decision making.

The second, political role for well-being prompts disagreement. Socrates (in the *Gorgias* and *Republic*, especially), the Eleatic stranger (in the *Statesman*), and the Athenian (in the *Laws*) assert that political action—law making, judging, educating, war making, and the rest—should promote the well-being of the political community's citizens. But other characters, including Callicles (in the *Gorgias*) and Thrasymachus (in the *Republic*) maintain that politics should serve the well-being of politicians. The ensuing debates in large part concern competing conceptions of well-being. Socrates and his allies emphasize cooperative goods as opposed to the competitive trophies favored by Callicles, Thrasymachus, and their kind. Team Socrates suggests that if politicians would take the correct view of well-being, they would not see a deep conflict between their own and that of the citizens. Team Callicles and Thrasymachus suggests that if politicians took the Socratic view of well-being they would display weakness and forego some of life's greatest advantages.

The first, ethical role for well-being, by contrast, prompts no controversy. Plato's characters agree that everyone wants his or her life to go well and that, on reflection, at least, all our other goals are subordinate to this (*Euthd.* 278e, *Symp.* 204e–205a). So, Socrates regularly assumes that one should act for the sake of one's own well-being, and this "eudaimonist axiom" is readily accepted, even by those interlocutors such as Callicles and Thrasymachus who disagree sharply with Socrates about how we should live.

In contrast to Plato's characters, modern readers often take the ethical role to be more problematic than the political one. Modern political liberalism wants states to provide the conditions for the individual pursuit of well-being more than well-being itself, but many modern moral philosophers reject the eudaimonist axiom still more thoroughly. They read Socratic ethics as an objectionable egoism, incompatible with the quite reasonable thought that other beings' ends should matter to us. But these critics are insufficiently attuned to the varieties of well-being in Plato's dialogues. Unlike many of his interlocutors, and unlike his modern critics, Socrates clings to the platitudinous identification of well-being and doing well, and he insists that doing well is the same as acting virtuously (*Charm.* 171e–172a, *Cr.* 48b, *Euthd.* 278e–282d, *Gorg.* 507c, *Rep.* 353e–354a). But if well-being is simply virtuous activity, then acting for the sake of one's own well-being is simply acting so as to act virtuously, which is not objectionably egoistic at all.

This is the Socratic view of well-being that Plato favors, and the dialogues advance this view in part by rejecting several other views, sometimes because they conflict with ordinary thoughts about what makes a human life go well, sometimes because they lead to civil strife as political ends, and often because they cannot play the role that the eudaimonist axiom sets for them, to be the ultimate end that explains and justifies human action.

Naïve conceptions

In the *Euthydemus*, after they agree that everyone obviously wants to do well (*eu prattein*), Socrates and Cleinias take it to be even more obvious that we do well by possessing many things that are good for us (278e–279a). They then list the goods that apparently cause our lives to go well: material goods (riches), goods of the body (health, good looks, bodily needs), social goods (noble birth, power, honor), goods of character (temperance, justice, bravery), and goods of intellect (wisdom) (279a–c).

Socrates and Cleinias do not explicitly say what well-being *is*. They say only what role it plays for us—everyone wants to get it—and what causes it—possessing the things that are good for us. One might produce a sophisticated account of what well-being is, to explain how the things that are good for us cause our well-being. But Socrates and Cleinias do not. Still, their naïve account can suggest that well-being is simply a state caused by, and perhaps constituted by, the possession of things that are good for us. So understood, Socrates and Cleinias offer something like an "objective list" conception of well-being.[1] But their particular list leaves important questions unanswered. Is it really comprehensive? Where are pleasure and friendship? Is each of the listed goods necessary for well-being? And do they all contribute equally to well-being? Could, say, sufficiently massive wealth and power compensate for a deficit of justice? Perhaps, then, it is better to think of this *Euthydemus* passage as an introduction to a *family* of views of well-being, a family whose members differ on which goods belong on the list, how the listed goods are ranked, and so on.

Other Platonic characters also appeal to some member of this family, and, like Socrates and Cleinias in the *Euthydemus*, they insist that they are appealing to an ordinary understanding of well-being. In the *Gorgias*, Polus insists that even a child would know that someone can be unjust and successful (*eudaimōn*) by amassing great wealth and power (470c–471d). Thrasymachus makes the same claim in the *Republic*: everyone would agree that the complete tyrant, whose injustice leads to complete power and great resources, enjoys a successful life (344a–c). When Glaucon and Adeimantus worry that it might be better to be unjust than just, they are relying on what they take to be common-sense thoughts about the importance of competitive goods to well-being (364a), and when Adeimantus objects that the guardians of Socrates' ideal city would not enjoy good lives, he takes it for granted that wealth is necessary for living well (419a–420a). All these characters assume that wealth and power are necessary for well-being, and they all claim that this assumption is widespread.

But Socrates clearly rejects the assumption. He calls the conception of *eudaimonia* that drives Adeimantus' objection to the guardians' situation "foolish and adolescent" (466b). In fact, Socrates objects not merely to conceptions of well-being according to which wealth and power are necessary. He offers reasons to doubt a broad range of "objective list" views of well-being.

He advances one reason in the *Euthydemus*. After Socrates and Cleinias complete their list of the goods that are supposed to make life go well, Socrates argues first that the possession of a good would not make one's life go well unless that good benefited one, and that a good would not benefit one unless it were used (280b–e). He then argues that using a good would not benefit one unless it were used rightly, and that using a good rightly requires using it wisely (280e–281b). A large part of Socrates' reasoning here is immediately accessible to Cleinias. If we have advantages such as wealth, power, or honor, we have a greater capacity to act than if we lack these things, and it is better for us to have a greater capacity to act only if we act wisely. Wielding great power foolishly does us no good.

But Socrates pushes this reasoning beyond common sense. Because the things ordinarily thought to be good for us seem to depend in large measure on luck, the proponent of the initial "objective list" view can sum up his view by saying that good fortune makes our lives go well. Socrates insists, instead, that wisdom plays the role of good fortune (279d), that it makes our lives go well (281b). His point seems to be that the causal power to benefit, to make a life go well, cannot belong to all the initially listed goods, because most of them sometimes benefit us and sometimes harm us, depending on whether they are used wisely or foolishly (281d–e). On his view, only wisdom possesses that causal power, because only it has the power to cause wise, beneficial use, without ever causing foolish, harmful use.[2]

Socrates might have insisted that wisdom no more possesses the power to effect well-being than wealth does, because one needs both wisdom to guide the use and another set of goods to be wisely used. But he does not say this. He says that only wisdom causes well-being (281b), and that only wisdom is good for us (281e, 292b). This outstrips common sense, but it is not unintelligible. Socrates might distinguish between necessary conditions and causes (cf. *Phdo* 99a–b) and identify wealth and the other initially listed assets as mere necessary conditions of wisdom causing well-being. Just as the cobbler makes a shoe but could not do so without leather, so wisdom makes well-being but could not do so without certain advantages being present. This leaves questions about what one needs, beyond wisdom, to live well, but in the *Euthydemus*, Socrates is content to leave such questions unanswered, so long as he has convinced Cleinias that only wisdom *causes* well-being.[3]

So understood, Socrates' argument turns on some curious and contentious thoughts about causation, but his central point can be expressed in other terms. Of the goods that the "objective list" conception takes to constitute well-being, most are only conditionally good—beneficial in some circumstances (when wisely used) but not in others (when foolishly used)—whereas wisdom is unconditionally good (it never uses itself foolishly). Now, nothing in the very idea of well-being requires that it or its constituents be unconditionally good. But the idea of a goal for the sake of which one should do everything one does is different. This is the idea of an ultimate end that could fully explain and justify action, and a merely conditional good is not up to that task. When one acts with a conditional good as one's end, we can always ask, "What makes that a good end to pursue here and now?" This open question renders the justification of the action incomplete.

Socrates does not fully develop this line of thought in the *Euthydemus*, but it returns elsewhere, along with an additional set of reasons to doubt the "objective list" family of conceptions of well-being. These fuller objections are launched not directly against the naïve suggestion that Socrates and Cleinias introduce in the *Euthydemus*, but against some more sophisticated theories about what well-being is.

The Protagorean conception

One sophisticated way to develop the ordinary thought that a life goes well by the possession of good things vindicates every member of that family of views (and then some). Protagoras says that a human being is the measure of the things that are and are not, and Plato's *Theaetetus* construes this as the thought, for instance, that if the wind appears cold to Peter and warm to Paul, then the wind *is* cold for Peter and it *is* warm for Paul (151d–160e). (Actually, Socrates seems to imply that Protagoras is committed to thinking that if the wind appears cold to Peter, then the wind-for-Peter is-for-Peter cold-for-Peter,[4] but I will proceed with a slightly simplified picture in view.)

In the *Theaetetus*, Socrates addresses more than one Protagoreanism. He sometimes worries about a perfectly general version of the "measure doctrine," so that *whatever* kind of appearance we are talking about, if X *appears* F to A, then X *is* F for A. On this view, for instance, if the measure doctrine appears false to Socrates, then the measure doctrine is false for Socrates. Socrates sometimes worries about a narrow Protagoreanism that applies not to all appearances but only to sense perceptions. This would exclude the measure doctrine's appearing false, but include the wind's appearing chilly. Last, Socrates acknowledges still other ways of restricting Protagoreanism, such as applying it only to certain evaluative appearances. This suggests how someone might understand well-being in a pure subjectivist way. On such a view, what appears to me to be well-being is well-being for me.

In the *Theaetetus*, Socrates responds to Protagoreanism with a barrage of objections, some of which (such as the claim that it refutes itself: 170a–171d) target the perfectly general version and some of which (such as the distinction between sense perception and knowledge: 183b–186e) target the narrow version that concerns sense perceptions only.[5] But at least two of his objections would tell against Protagoreanism about well-being (cf. *Crat.* 385e–386e).

First, what we take to be good for us belongs to the class of our concerns about the future. Even if everyone is the measure of what *is* for him or her, we can ask whether every person is also the measure of what *will be* for him or her (178a–179b). If a layman thinks that drinking this particular concoction will make his bodily condition appear good to him and thus be good for him, his future experience might convict his thought of error. Moreover, a doctor might be the better measure of how the man's body would appear to him after he drank the concoction. In response, it will not do for the Protagorean to raise doubts about personal identity through time (cf. 166b). When I predict that X will appear F to A tomorrow, it does not matter whether I am identical with A. If X does not appear F to A tomorrow, my prediction has been shown false. The Protagorean would do better to characterize my prediction more carefully. She should say that it appears to me now that X will appear F to A tomorrow, for X's not appearing F to A tomorrow does not contradict how things appear to me now. But if I am the measure only of how tomorrow seems to me here and now, I am not the measure of how things will be tomorrow. I cannot make a genuine prediction, and this is a serious cost to the theory, given the practical importance of predictions, which Socrates' discussion makes plain. A person could, conceivably, muddle through life with nothing more than appearances of what will appear to be the case tomorrow. But if he or she *never* thinks that later appearances make a difference to the value of earlier predictions and if his or her judgments of what will appear to be the case in the future never change accordingly, then he or she will be incapable of learning by trial and error, which requires recognizing *error*. Such a creature's life will be very short or very lucky. Others could perhaps help him or her by making apparent things that will keep him or her safe. But the creature could not say that these helpers are *wise*, for the creature could not say that the helpers make the appearances better than they were before.[6]

This argument from predictions grounds a general concern that Socrates repeatedly raises, that Protagoreanism undermines the distinction between the wise and unwise. The measure doctrine takes everyone to be equally good at determining how things are, but Socrates thinks that this is a special achievement. Of course, the measure doctrine does this by collapsing the distinction between how things appear to be and how they are, and Socrates rejects this conflation. This would be Socrates' second response to Protagoreanism about well-being: it gets the ontology wrong, construing well-being as a relation between the world and the passive receptions of a human being when it is a matter of stance-independent fact for a human being to discover by active effort. Socrates maintains that we cannot even coherently represent things as being the way Protagoreans have to take them to be, because our language attributes more independence and stability to features of the world than the collapse of appearance and reality can allow (cf. 179c–183b).

Socrates encounters Protagoreanism in the *Protagoras*, too, though readers usually miss it.[7] Here Protagoras initially fails to identify courage and wisdom because he assumes that something beyond knowledge, some natural spiritedness, is required to motivate right action in the face of fear (351a–b). But Socrates gets Protagoras to identify courage and wisdom (360d–e). He argues that any motivation represents a course of action under the guise of some apparent value. To be moved by pleasure is to pursue something pleasant that one takes to be good for one. To be moved by fear is to avoid something fearsome that one takes to be bad for one (358d). So one cannot act without representing one's action as good for one, without believing that it is the thing to do. Socrates also argues that one cannot act against one's knowledge of what to do. Most people deny this, because they construe knowledge as just another mental state, just like pleasure or pain, fear or love. But Socrates argues that knowledge is a special achievement that contrasts with these other motivations. They represent what appears to be good or bad for one, whereas knowledge depends upon taking the measure of appearances and determining what is good or bad for one. Knowledge exists where how things appear to one have been fully settled in favor of how things are, and such a condition does not admit of contrary appearances that could motivate action counter to knowledge.

Much of Socrates' argument in these pages is pitched explicitly against the many, and not Protagoras, and much of it invokes a narrow hedonism about value. But Socrates' aim is to convert Protagoras from seeing knowledge as just one motivation, like fear, to seeing knowledge as something very different from other motivating mental states. He introduces pleasure and pain as two among many motivating passions, alongside fear, love, and others (352b–e). He needs to establish that all these motivating passions share a defect that knowledge lacks, and he does so by contrasting their reliance on how things appear to be good or bad with the knower's art of taking the measure of appearances and determining how things are. Thus, after Socrates has induced Protagoras to agree that courage, like the other virtues, is identical to wisdom, he summarizes his conclusion that all virtues are forms of knowledge oddly, saying "*all things* are knowledge [πάντα χρήματά ἐστιν ἐπιστήμη]" (361b1–2, emphasis mine). He is pointedly echoing Protagoras' measure doctrine, "that of *all things* a human being is the measure [πάντων χρημάτων μέτρον ἄνθρωπον εἶναι]" (*Tht.* 152a2–3). On Socrates' view, in the *Protagoras* no less than in the *Theaetetus*, Protagoreanism misconstrues measure, conflating appearance with reality, when there is a measuring art that makes its possessors wise and virtuous.

Hedonist conceptions

Protagoreanism about well-being flatters the democratically inclined, because it makes every person equally an authority over what makes her own life go well,[8] but it is not a thought that Plato's dialogues attribute to most Athenians. Yet Socrates does regularly attribute to them another sophisticated development of the naïve thought that well-being is constituted by possessing things that are good for us. This is the view that well-being consists in pleasure (or good feelings) and the absence of pain (or bad feelings), where pleasure either is or strongly correlates with the satisfaction of desire. One might again think that this is a family of views, as one might want to distinguish hedonism about well-being from a desire satisfaction view of it, and one might want to distinguish both of those from emotional well-being. But the dialogues do not sharply distinguish here. The unifying thoughts, which also tie these views to Protagoreanism, are thus: people desire just what they take to be good for them and they take to be good for them just what feels good to them. In any view animated by these thoughts, possessing what is good for us causes well-being by bringing us the pleasure of satisfied desire that *is* well-being.

The *Gorgias* dramatizes how this broad hedonism about well-being can stand behind the naïve "objective list" approach to well-being. After Socrates makes trouble for Polus' claim that a wealthy tyrant enjoys a good life despite being unjust, Callicles emerges to defend Polus. Callicles rejects Socrates' "conventional" understanding of justice in favor of a "natural" justice according to which the stronger deserve more than the weaker (483a–484c). In his view, life goes well not when one restrains one's desires with temperance and conventional justice, but when one allows one's appetites to grow as large as possible and one has the courage and shrewd judgment to satisfy those appetites and continually fill oneself with pleasures (491e–492c, 494a–b).

Socrates puts pressure on Callicles' conception of well-being in two ways. First, he suggests that the pursuit of this well-being undermines itself (492e–494a). Pleasure demands the satisfaction of one's appetites, but their satisfaction merely prompts the growth of more appetites. Second, he tries a series of maneuvers to get Callicles to concede that there is a difference between what is good for us and our pleasure (494b–499b). One maneuver is to appeal to shameful pleasures, to suggest that some pleasures are intrinsically bad for us (494b–495c). Another is to argue that, because a momentary pleasure can be felt at the same time as a momentary pain, pleasure and pain are not genuine opposites, and that because what is good for us and what is bad for us are genuine opposites, pleasure cannot be what is good for us (494e–497e). Third, Socrates argues that the presence of good things in us should make us better, but pleasure evidently does not make us better, since pleasure occurs in foolish people just as readily as it occurs in intelligent people, though it is better to be intelligent than foolish.

These maneuvers are a mixed bag, but there is something to them. If well-being is identified with pleasure and serves as the ultimate end for the sake of which a person should do everything she does, pleasure needs to be unconditionally good. It needs to fulfill what goodness fulfills without any deficit. But pleasure does not seem able to do that. Some pleasures, in some circumstances, are not good. At least, our shame prevents us from taking them to be good, and our thoughts about what something good for us does for us prevents us from taking them to be good.

Socrates assumes throughout his response to Callicles that the best account of well-being will have to be coherent (cf. 481c–482c). He takes pride in the consistency of philosophy, and derides Callicles for his inconsistencies. So it matters that Callicles' sense of shame does not cohere with his explicit theory of well-being, and it matters that Callicles' understanding of goodness and badness does not match his understanding of how pleasure and pain work in us. Socrates does not think that the evaluation of a theory of well-being can be assessed by a few isolated commitments.

Nor, it seems, does Callicles. At least, after Socrates' maneuvers, Callicles says that he never meant to deny that some pleasures are better than others (499b). But if one pleasure is better than another, not because it is more of a pleasure and not because it gives rise to more pleasure, then there must be something good for us that is intelligible apart from pleasure, some non-hedonic standard of goodness by which to adjudicate pleasures as better and worse. Socrates runs with this, and argues that the wise pursuit of the best pleasures will require a craft to pick out the better and the worse (499c–505b).

Despite Socrates' forthright rejection of Callicles' hedonism, many readers think that Plato's dialogues endorse a hedonic conception of well-being. There are three principal grounds for such suspicion.

First, Socrates seems to endorse hedonism toward the end of the *Protagoras*.[9] Readers are struck by the way Socrates introduces hedonism, abruptly and without any hint of dissent (351b–e). They are struck, too, by the way Socrates presents himself and Protagoras together as teachers of the many, drawing out of them a commitment to hedonism (353c–354e). But Socrates must shift abruptly after his first attempt to show that courage is identical to wisdom has failed (349e–351b). Protagoras has insisted that courage requires spiritedness in addition to knowledge, to overcome fear. Socrates needs a fresh start to establish that knowledge is not something that can be overcome by fear. Moreover, Protagoras has already indicated some affinity for hedonism (317c, 320c), and, as I have explained, Socrates associates Protagoreanism with hedonism. When Protagoras balks at endorsing hedonism (351b–e), Socrates offers him the chance to consider what the many would say instead of answering for himself, just as he did earlier when Protagoras balked at admitting that unjust action can be temperate (333c). This gives Socrates the chance to continue to examine Protagoras' own views, without Protagoras having to admit openly to holding those views. The delicacy of his situation is enough to explain the elaborate pretense that Socrates and Protagoras would together elicit hedonism from the many. The articulation of hedonism and the assignment of this view to the many merely enable Socrates to show what is wrong with the assumption that knowledge can be overcome by a passion. This larger purpose does not, as we have seen, require hedonism. We need not suppose that Socrates endorses hedonism in the *Protagoras*; he can use it dialectically, in an ad hominem argument.[10]

Second, in the *Republic*, Socrates offers three "proofs" that it is always better to be just than unjust, and each of these proofs seems to appeal to a broadly hedonic conception of well-being. According to the first (culminating at 577c–580c), the tyrannically constituted soul, ruled by law-less appetitive desires, is least able to do what it wants, and suffers regret about past failures to satisfy desire, neediness about present failures, and fear about future ones, whereas the justly ordered, aristocratically constituted soul, ruled by rational desire, is most able to do what it wants, and suffers least from regret, neediness, and fear. As a result, Socrates and Glaucon agree that the tyran-nical soul enjoys the least well-being (*eudaimonia*) and the aristocratic soul the most. This inference seems to identify well-being with good feelings and the absence of bad feelings. The second and third proofs are even clearer. Though they are supposed to establish the same conclusion as the first concerning well-being (*eudaimonia*) (583b), they explicitly show that the just person's aristocrati-cally constituted soul enjoys the most pleasure, more than any unjust person's soul (580c–588a). Because Socrates advances these as proofs of the thesis he plainly endorses, it is natural to suppose that he endorses the broadly hedonist conception of well-being they invoke.[11]

But this cannot be right. Socrates and his interlocutors in the *Republic* agree that well-being (*eudaimonia*) is the ultimate end "which every soul pursues and for the sake of which every soul does everything it does" (505e1–2).[12] But, in the *Republic*, Socrates explicitly rejects pleasure and good feelings as this end. In fact, he appeals to both considerations that he offers against Calliclean hedonism in the *Gorgias*.

First, he insists that pleasure is not unconditionally good, because there are intrinsically bad pleasures (505c; cf. 509a). This makes pleasure a bad fit to be what fully justifies action.

Socrates underscores this point with reflection on the Protagorean side of the broadly hedonist approach to well-being. What feels or appears good to one is not the same as what is good for one, and the ultimate end is what *is* good for one (505d).[13]

Second, Socrates argues that the pursuit of pleasure and good feelings undermines itself. This emerges as a corollary to his critique of spirited and especially appetitive desire. The critique rests on three observations. First, because good feelings arrive with the satisfaction of desire, they can come cheaply. All three parts of the human soul have their own pleasures (581c), and agents of many different kinds achieve good feelings. Next, if spirited and appetitive desires are indulged and are not held in check by countervailing commitments to what is genuinely good for one, they will grow stronger and more numerous (589a–b with 571b–572b, 416e–417a, 549a–b; cf. 602c–606d). Third, as spirited and appetitive desires grow, they increasingly conflict with each other and in other ways increasingly outstrip our ability to satisfy them, leading to the regret, neediness, and fear that characterize the tyrannical soul. This empirical critique, like the "paradox of hedonism," suggests that there is something self-defeating about pursuing pleasure directly. But because well-being, as the ultimate end, is supposed to *explain* as well as justify action, one must be able to successfully pursue it directly. So the empirical critique impugns hedonist conceptions of well-being.

Socrates' rejection of hedonist theories of well-being in the *Republic* further explains why he also rejects Adeimantus' appeal to a naïve "objective list" approach (466b, with 419a–420a). Many of the goods on the "objective list" are only conditionally valuable, and are the objects of spirited and appetitive desire. So they are problematic as ultimate ends, and, as we will see below, as constituents of the ultimate end.

We might still wonder about *Republic*'s stance on well-being. Why would Socrates invoke broadly hedonist conceptions of well-being that he rejects in order to argue for his thesis that it is always better to be just than unjust? Because he needs to. He cannot show that it is better to be just than unjust on the "objective list" conception of well-being that Thrasymachus, Glaucon, and Adeimantus have assumed. Nor can he simply invoke his own conception of well-being if, as I will suggest below, his opponents are apt to see it as question begging. The broadly hedonist conception of well-being comports with his interlocutors' views nearly enough, and it gives Socrates just enough room to argue for his conclusion. So it serves his dialectical purposes. He might even think that the hedonist conceptions are extensionally adequate representations of well-being—that well-being does in fact correlate perfectly with the presence of good feelings and the absence of bad feelings. What is clear is that he rejects these conceptions as intensionally inadequate: they do not capture the ultimate end of our rational pursuits.[14]

The third principal source for those who would attribute a hedonist conception of well-being to Plato is the *Laws*. When the Athenian argues that someone who suffers no conventional evil but is unjust does not enjoy well-being, he faces special resistance from the fact that such a person seems to live pleasantly (661d–662a). The Athenian concedes that the best life is most pleasant (662a–664c; cf. 732e–734d), and he concedes that people are motivated by pleasure to the extent that they will not be motivated to do anything that does not bring more pleasure than pain (663b). These concessions might suggest hedonism about well-being, but they should not. The Athenian says that what is good for a person and what is pleasant for her are inseparable, but not identical (663a–b; cf. 662a and 734d–e). This comports with Socrates' arguments in the *Republic*: the most just life is best and most pleasant, but well-being is not identical with pleasure.

The Socratic conception

Against Protagoras, Socrates maintains that well-being is a matter of objective fact, discoverable by the wise. Against hedonists, he maintains that well-being must be an unconditional good that one can successfully pursue directly. These arguments make trouble for many of the goods on the naïve list of what causes our lives to go well. But they make no trouble for wisdom and, especially, if we recall the *Euthydemus'* insistence on use or activity, wise activity. And in fact Socrates frequently insists that well-being—doing well, being successful—is identical to virtuous activity (*Charm.* 171e–172a, *Cr.* 48b, *Euthd.* 278e–282d, *Gorg.* 507c, *Rep.* 353e–354a), and since he also frequently insists that virtue is or at least requires wisdom,[15] he can also be taken to say that well-being is virtuous activity.

Although Socrates suggests this view in Book One of the *Republic* (353e–354a), he cannot *assume* it in the rest of the dialogue, since Glaucon and Adeimantus issue a challenge that rests on a competing conception of well-being. This helps to explain why Socrates' arguments in the *Republic* appeal, as we have seen, to a conception of well-being that he rejects and why so few readers of Plato attribute to him this clear, Socratic conception of well-being as virtuous activity.[16]

But there are also other reasons why readers miss this. First, the Socratic view seems to fit poorly with Socrates' broader understanding of value. At least apart from the *Euthydemus*, he identifies things other than wisdom as good for us, and he even insists that some such things are non-instrumentally good for us (e.g., *Rep.* 357b–358a). But Socrates can consider something to be non-instrumentally good—good regardless of what follows from it—without thinking that it is unconditionally good—good in all circumstances. A pleasantly amusing activity might be finally valuable, but not unconditionally so, because it would not be good when, say, virtue required helping someone.[17] The recognition of final goods other than virtuous activity does not entail the recognition of unconditional goods other than wise virtuous activity, and as the ultimate goal to explain and justify action, well-being must be an unconditional good.

Nevertheless, even if Socrates does not *have* to identify final goods as constituents of well-being and parts of the ultimate end, he still might do so. Even if goods other than virtue and virtuous activity are only conditionally valuable, still they might be conditionally valuable parts of an unconditionally valuable whole, and Socrates might be thought to develop this possibility in the *Philebus*.[18] But the *Philebus* addresses three questions that are not easily kept distinct: (1) What is the successful life like? (2) What things are good for a human being, by causally promoting a successful life? and (3) What is the good for a human being, the ultimate goal of action, which is the success of a successful life? Socrates plainly suggests that a successful life is a mixed life, including various pleasures and knowledge (60c–61a, cf. 22a–23a), and he plainly thinks that some pleasures and knowledge are good for a human being. But does he conclude that these various goods constitute a single unconditional good that is the success of a successful life? It seems, rather, that he means to isolate the best part of a mixed life, and to assign a special role to it (64c–d). He says that what makes a mixture of goods a successful life is what puts this mixture into a kind of unity, manifesting beauty, measure, and truth (64d–65a). This seems to locate the success of a successful life not in the various goods mixed into it, but in the wise way in which they are mixed. If this is what Socrates means, then he is not taking back his thought that the unconditional good, the ultimate goal of action, is virtuous or wise activity.

Charity might generate a third reason to doubt that Plato fully endorses a Socratic conception of well-being as virtuous activity. After all, this conception is indeterminate to the point of being uninformative. For what is virtuous activity? It certainly will not do to say that it is the sort of activity that is done for the sake of being virtuous activity. But Plato's dialogues offer two ways of identifying virtuous activity. The first is psychology. Virtue is the disposition that makes its possessor do what it essentially does well (*Rep.* 352d–354d). To give an account of the virtues of the soul, then, one must first give an account of how the soul works. An account of healthy and unhealthy psychological functioning will identify the virtues as the dispositions of healthy functioning.[19]

The second way of identifying virtue is wisdom. For Plato, virtue is or requires wisdom, and wisdom is or requires a coherent grasp of how things are. So virtue is determined not merely from the "scientific" point of view, working out an explanatory account of how, say, anger works, or love, or lust, but also from the agent's point of view, working out how these feelings, and the values they implicate, do and do not hang together with each other and with all our other attitudes. Only if we can survive Socratic examination can we begin to think that we might be wise and virtuous, and this constrains what wise and virtuous activity could be.

Of course, these methods are hard, and reasonable people can disagree about where they lead. The many followers of Socrates and Plato who embraced the Socratic conception of well-being as virtuous activity disagreed sharply about what virtuous activity is. Some, including Cynics and Stoics, took a more ascetic, but also more democratic and psychologized, view: they think that virtuous activity is available to anyone, just by the achievement of psychological coherence, and not requiring good fortune in one's external circumstances. Others, such as Aristotle, believe that virtuous activity, as the best realization of the best condition a human being can be in, is what a powerful, beautiful, wealthy, and in other ways fortunate member of a ruling elite does. On this view, humans naturally desire certain aristocratic ends, and virtuous activity is hampered, even if only slightly, by the frustration of these desires. Psychological coherence itself requires some good fortune. These debates between Peripatetics and Stoics play out possibilities left open by Plato's dialogues, as Greek philosophers tried to determine what well-being is by determining what virtuous activity is.[20]

Related topics

Aristotle, hedonistic theories of well-being in antiquity, objective list theories, perfectionism, subjectivism, hedonism.

Further reading

Plato, especially the *Euthydemus, Protagoras, Gorgias, Republic,* and *Philebus.* For alternatives to the interpretations mooted here, start with Irwin (1995) and Annas (1999).

Notes

1 On such views, see Fletcher (Chapter 12, this volume).
2 Cf. Dimas (2002); McCabe (2002).
3 Cf. Jones (2013).
4 Waterlow (1977: 33–34); Lee (2005: 44–47).
5 For the first of these, see especially Burnyeat (1976). For the second, see Cooper (1970).
6 Chappell (2004: 132).
7 Vlastos (1956) is an exception.
8 Farrar (1989) and Shaw (2015).
9 Taylor (1991) and Irwin (1995).
10 Zeyl (1980) and Shaw (2015).
11 Butler (1999).
12 Notice the terms of the challenge put to Socrates and of his answer: 347e with 352d, 358a, 361c–d, 365c–d, 545a–b, 580b–c.
13 See Kamtekar (2006).
14 Cf. *Eu.* 11a–b with Evans (2012).
15 For the identity claim, the "unity of virtues" thesis, see Penner (1973).
16 Compare, for instance, the characterizations of Socrates' conception(s) of well-being in the *Republic* by Annas (1981: 314–334) and Reeve (1988: 153–159).

17 Cf. Korsgaard (1983).
18 Cooper (1977).
19 Cf. Bradford on perfectionism (Chapter 10, this volume).
20 This chapter condenses interpretations I develop at greater length elsewhere, and I thank those who have helped with those forthcoming essays, including especially Emily Austin, Scott Berman, Erik Curiel, Matt Evans, Verity Harte, Rusty Jones, Rachana Kamtekar, Richard Kraut, Casey Perin, David Reeve, Clerk Shaw, Rachel Singpurwalla, Iakovos Vasiliou, Matt Walker, and Eric Wiland.

References

Annas, J. (1981) *An Introduction to Plato's* Republic, Oxford: Clarendon Press.

Annas, J. (1999) *Platonic Ethics, Old and New*, Ithaca, New York: Cornell University Press.

Burnyeat, M. (1976) "Protagoras and Self-Refutation in Plato's *Theaetetus,*" *Philosophical Review* 85(2), 172–195.

Butler, J. (1999) "The Arguments for the Most Pleasant Life in *Republic IX*: A Note Against the Common Interpretation," *Apeiron* 32(1), 37–48.

Chappell, T.D.J. (2004) *Reading Plato's* Theaetetus, Sankt Augustin: Academia Verlag.

Cooper, J. (1970) "Plato on Sense Perception and Knowledge: *Theaetetus* 184–186," *Phronesis* 15, 123–146.

Cooper, J. (1977) "Plato's Theory of Human Good in the *Philebus,*" *Journal of Philosophy* 74(11), 714–730.

Dimas, P. (2002) "Happiness in the *Euthydemus,*" *Phronesis* 47, 1–27.

Evans, M. (2012) "Lessons from *Euthyphro* 10a–11b," *Oxford Studies in Ancient Philosophy* 42, 1–38.

Farrar, C. (1989) *The Origins of Democratic Thinking: The Invention of Politics in Classical Athens*, Cambridge: Cambridge University Press.

Irwin, T.H. (1995) *Plato's Ethics*, Oxford: Oxford University Press.

Jones, R.E. (2013) "Wisdom and Happiness in *Euthydemus* 278–282," *Philosophers' Imprint* 13(14), 1–21.

Kamtekar, R. (2006) "Plato on the Attribution of Conative Attitudes," *Archiv für Geschichte der Philosophie* 88(2), 127–162.

Korsgaard, C. (1983) "Two Distinctions in Goodness," *Philosophical Review* 92(2), 169–195.

Lee, M-K. (2005) *Epistemology After Protagoras: Responses to Relativism in Plato, Aristotle, and Democritus*, Oxford: Clarendon.

McCabe, M.M. (2002) "Indifference readings: Plato and the Stoa on Socratic Ethics" in T.P. Wiseman (ed.) *Classics in Progress: Essays on Ancient Greece and Rome*, London: British Academy.

Penner, T. (1973) "The Unity of Virtue," *Philosophical Review* 82(1), 35–68.

Reeve, C.D.C. (1988) *Philosopher-Kings: The Argument of Plato's* Republic, Princeton: Princeton University Press.

Shaw, J.C. (2015) *Plato's Anti-hedonism and the* Protagoras, Cambridge: Cambridge University Press.

Taylor, C.C.W. (ed.) (1991) *Plato: Protagoras*, 2nd ed., Oxford: Oxford University Press.

Vlastos, G. (1956) "Introduction," in G. Vlastos (ed.) *Plato: Protagoras*, Indianapolis: Bobbs-Merrill.

Waterlow, S. (1977) "Protagoras and Inconsistency: *Theaetetus* 171a6-c7," *Archiv für Geschichte der Philosophie* 59(1), 19-36.

Zeyl, D.J. (1980) "Socrates and Hedonism: *Protagoras* 351b–358d," *Phronesis* 25, 250–269.

2

ARISTOTLE ON WELL-BEING

Richard Kraut

Does Aristotle have a theory of well-being?

"Every craft and every line of inquiry, and likewise every action and decision, seems to seek some good" (I.1 1094a1–2).[1] Thus begins Aristotle's *Nicomachean Ethics*. It starts from an observation about "some good" as the object of all human striving, and soon turns to "the good," that is, "the best good" (I.2 1094a21–22), which is then (I.4 1095a18) equated with *eudaimonia* (commonly translated as "happiness"). It is generally agreed, Aristotle notes at this point, that "living well and doing well are the same as being happy" (1095a19–20). But, he asks, what, more precisely, is this highest good? What do living well, doing well, and happiness consist in? After surveying answers that others have given to this question, he comes to the conclusion that the good he has been seeking is a certain kind of activity of the soul in accordance with virtue (I.7 1098a16–17). From that point on, the *Ethics* becomes a full-scale treatment of the virtues and several other goods (friendship and pleasure) that accompany the virtues.

It is generally assumed that in all of this Aristotle is talking about what we call "well-being." Other expressions now used to express the same concept are "welfare" and "prudential value." It is a concept that we employ when we talk about what is in someone's interest, or what benefits him, or what is to his advantage, or what is good for him. Someone's well-being or welfare, we assume, is non-instrumentally beneficial or advantageous. If someone acquires what is beneficial only when used as a means to something else, that acquisition does not by itself increase his well-being. How much well-being he has (more colloquially: how well off he is) is a matter of how he is faring with respect to what is non-instrumentally good for him. Well-being is not one benefit among others, but an overall measure of how someone is faring with respect to what is non-instrumentally good for him.

Back, now, to Aristotle: notice that the opening line of the *Ethics* says only that the object of each instance of human striving is "some good." Notice as well how lacking in specificity this claim is. Aristotle has not said here that we aim, in all that we do, at some advantage to ourselves. He does not even say that we aim at what is advantageous to *someone or other*. He has other words that are correctly translated "advantageous" or "beneficial" (*ophelimon, sumpheron*)—but his word here is *agathon*, which is properly translated as "good," but not "advantageous" or "beneficial".

Perhaps it will be said that when Aristotle says that the highest good is *eudaimonia*, and equates this with living well and doing well, he must be understood to be talking about what we call "well-being." That is of course how he is commonly interpreted. But why ought he to be read in this way? The Greek word, *eu*, that is translated "well" is simply the adverbial form of the adjective, *agathon*, and we have already observed that this is a highly generic commendatory term, as contrasted with the greater specificity of Aristotle's words for what is beneficial or advantageous to someone. If someone is doing something well, it does not immediately follow, from the meaning of those words, that he is doing what is beneficial to himself or to anyone else. Similarly for "acting well" and "living well." When it is said that someone is living well, that merely means that he is living in a good way—that he deserves to be commended for the way he is living. He is living as he ought, and as is right for him to live. But to say that he is living in a way that is in his own interest is to make a different and more specific claim—a claim that need not even be intended as a commendation. ("He is doing that only for self-interested reasons" can be a form of criticism.) By contrast, to say that someone is living in a good way is necessarily to speak with approval of his way of life.

The question I am raising can be put this way: when Aristotle's inquiry into the good culminates in the conclusion that it consists of virtuous activity (I.7 1098a16–17), should we take him to be arguing there that such activity is the most beneficial thing for someone to have? Is he arguing that virtuous activity is the highest good *of* a human being, or instead that virtuous activity is the highest good *for* a human being? The first of these claims (using "of") means that virtuous activity is the best good that any human being can possess. The second (using "for") means that virtuous activity is what benefits a human being most of all. We cannot assess the merits or deficiencies of Aristotle's argument unless we know which of these two conclusions he is trying to reach. And to do so, we have no choice but to trace the progress of his discussion of goodness throughout Book I, beginning with the first line of his treatise.[2]

Aristotle, as I have said, does not start with the observation that *advantageousness* is on everyone's mind when they act, but with the more general observation that *goodness* is on everyone's mind. Are there grounds for supposing that at some point in Book I he moves from the generic idea of goodness to the more specific idea of advantageousness? If he *has* moved from one to the other, is some fallacy involved in this transition? Should we, out of charity, read him as making no claims about the advantageousness of a virtuous life, but only claims about the goodness of such a life—because to read him otherwise would open him to the charge that he has illicitly changed the subject?

Here is one way of defending Aristotle against this charge: we can say that when he writes, in his opening line, that goodness is on everyone's mind, he is speaking elliptically.[3] What he has omitted to say, but should be taken to mean, is that every craft (etc.) aims at what is good *for someone* (*tini*). And to speak of what is good for someone is of course to speak of what is advantageous. Thus read, the *Ethics* begins with an observation about the ubiquity of advantageousness in our practical thinking. This allows us to take all of the other statements that Aristotle makes in the remainder of Book I about goodness to be elliptical statements about what is good for someone. And in this way, we can vindicate the widely held belief that Aristotle has a theory of well-being.

But there is an alternative interpretation that I think should be preferred. When Aristotle says that every craft (and so on) seems to aim at some good, we should take him to mean that when a builder (for example) makes a house, he has an answer to the question, "why are you doing that?" There is, in other words, a reason why he is building it. Saying that he is aiming at some good when he builds a house is simply a way of saying that he is doing so for some reason. Were the builder to say, "I am building this house because its coming into existence is good," that would mean: "I am building this house because there is a reason why it should come into existence." But what is that reason? He has (according to this interpretation) not yet said so. Similarly, the opening line (thus read) means that whenever we decide to act, we have a reason for acting. But no restriction has been placed in this line on what that reason is. It may be some advantage that the agent sees for himself, or for someone else. But it may be some other reason—a reason that does not advert to advantage but some other factor.[4]

What other sorts of considerations besides advantageousness does Aristotle think relevant to making decisions? He says in Book II, Chapter 3 (1004b30–32) that there are three "objects of choice" (*eis tas haireseis*): the *kalon* (what is fine, beautiful, noble), the advantageous (*sumpheron*), and the pleasant (*hêdu*); and three opposite "objects of avoidance": the shameful (*aischron*), the harmful (*blaberon*), and the painful (*lupêron*). So, according to the interpretation I am proposing, the first line of the *Ethics* leaves it open that sometimes we make decisions on the basis of pleasure but not on the basis of advantage, or on the basis of the *kalon* but not advantage. (This does not mean that, according to Aristotle, people do sometimes choose in this way—only that *his opening sentence* does not rule out this possibility.)

Here is one reason for preferring this reading to the one that says that Aristotle is speaking elliptically in his opening line: it would have been quite easy for Aristotle to say that every craft (etc.) aims at some advantage. He need only have used *sumpheron* or *ophelimon* instead of *agathon*. And yet he does not choose these words. If we read him as speaking elliptically (saying "good" where he means "good for someone"), we can offer no explanation for why he did not express himself more clearly.

Second, as we have seen, Aristotle himself points out (*NE* II.3) that there are *several* types of reasons, not just one, for making decisions: they come under the headings of the advantageous, the fine, and the pleasant. It would be strange, then, for him to write an opening line in which he asserts that all of our endeavors have just one of these (advantageousness) as their object.

Third, we can easily understand why an author might begin a treatise with a statement that presupposes as little as possible. The weaker the premise one starts from, the less vulnerable to objection it is. If Aristotle begins by taking goodness to be what practical thinking has in mind, and this means merely that when we engage in craft activities, or pursue some investigation, or make some decision, we have a reason for doing so, he makes no commitment to what sorts of reasons we have. This is as it should be—the question of what sorts of reasons we have can be postponed momentarily. By contrast, if Aristotle says nothing in favor of the idea that advantageousness lies behind all practical thinking, he is beginning with a premise that cries out for defense.

If these considerations convince us that the opening sentence of the *Ethics* adverts to reasons for action but not to advantageousness as a reason, ought we to say that even when he reaches the conclusion, in *NE* I.7, that virtuous activity is the greatest good, he means, not that it is more advantageous to the agent than anything else, but that what we have most reason to seek and sustain is such activity? That would be an implausible way to read him. Aristotle cannot be non-committal about whether it is better (more advantageous) for someone to be a good human being or a bad human being. He cannot be read to mean that although in *some* respect (e.g., the *kalon*) a virtuous life is superior to the life of someone who lacks virtue, it is not the case that the virtuous life is more *beneficial*. That would leave unanswered the question: "In that case, why should we be virtuous?"

The best interpretation, then, is one that takes Aristotle to be moving from an opening claim about goodness (not advantageousness) to a further claim about which goods *benefit* us most— and doing so without committing some logical fallacy. To read him in this way, we need only observe that every activity Aristotle mentions, after his opening line, can plausibly be understood as an endeavor that seeks some goal on the assumption that it brings some advantage to someone. He is, in other words, implicitly offering an inductive argument for a narrower and stronger claim than the one with which his treatise begins. "Health is the end of medicine, a boat of boat building, victory of generalship, and wealth of household management" (1094a8–9). In each case, it is advantageousness that motivates a pursuit. Similarly for all of his remaining examples: bridle making, horsemanship, generalship. The doctor is not aiming at pleasure (his own or that of his patient) or at something beautiful, fine, and noble. He is trying to benefit a sick individual. Similarly, each of the other activities mentioned is obviously designed to bring about some beneficial consequence.

So, Aristotle is not changing the subject, even though he begins with a claim about goodness, and then moves to claims about advantageousness. He has done something to earn the right to assert not only that we seek what we take to be good, but also that we seek what we take to be advantageous.

I suggest that, by the end of Book I, Chapter 1, all of Aristotle's further statements that employ the term *agathon* ("good") are best understood as assertions about advantageousness. For example, when he says, in the opening lines of Book 1, Chapter 2, that "the good"—that is, "the best good"— is something that we "wish for because of itself," all else being sought for its sake, we should take him to be asserting that what stands at the top of this hierarchy of ends is something that is more *advantageous* than (and in that respect, better than) everything subordinate to it. Aristotle's inductive argument has come to an end in Chapter 1; Chapter 2 tacitly adopts its conclusion, and so, although we could not understand *agathon* in terms of advantageousness in the opening line, at this point in his exposition we can and should so interpret it.[5]

What counts in favor of this suggestion is that, when we reach Book I, Chapter 3, it is clear that Aristotle is using *agathon* to advance claims about what is advantageous. Since that is the manner in which he is addressing his audience in I.3, and he has completed his inductive argument for moving from goodness to advantageousness in I.1, there is no good reason to refuse to interpret the occurrences of *agathon* in I.2 as assertions about advantageousness.

Here is the passage in I.3 that I have in mind:

> Fine things [*kala*] and just things, about which politics inquires, have many differences and variations, and so they seem to exist only by convention and not by nature. But good things [*agatha*] also have that kind of variation, because of the harms [*blabas*] that result from them for many people (1094b14–18).

Aristotle's point is that we should not move from (a) the variation of the *kalon* (what is often *kalon* in some circumstances is not) to the conclusion that (b) the *kalon* is a mere matter of convention; for if we did, we would also have to move from (c) variation in what is good (what is generally good is sometimes harmful) to the conclusion that (d) goodness too is conventional. The words *kalon* and *blaberon* are drawn from his three categories of choice-worthy goals and three opposite categories of objects to be avoided (recall the taxonomy of II.3, cited above). He is saying that that just as nothing is good (*agathon*) or bad just as a matter of convention, so nothing is *kalon* or shameful just as a matter of convention. What is significant for our purposes is his use of *agathon* as a term that expresses the concept of advantageousness. Here it is legitimate to substitute for the generic commendatory term *agathon* the more specific way in which something can be *agathon*: by being advantageous. Aristotle is now advancing claims about what is advantageous by using the term *agathon*.

This gives us sufficient reason to read his theory of goodness as a theory of well-being. When he says, in I.4, that the ultimate end that everyone seeks is *eudaimonia* (living well), we have strong textual grounds for taking him to mean that at the top of the hierarchy of goods is something that is most *advantageous* for the individual who has that good. And so, when he argues in I.7 that this is virtuous activity, we are justified in taking this to mean that such activity is not merely the good *of* a human being, but also something that is good *for* the virtuous person.

If further evidence for this interpretation is needed, it can be found by combining Aristotle's statement, in *NE* I.2, that the subject that studies the supreme *good* is political science (1095a24–27), and his later statement (VIII.9) that what political science studies is the common *advantage*.

> The political community seems to have come together from the beginning and to abide for the sake of advantage [*sumpherontos*]. For it is at this that the lawgivers aim, and justice, they say, is the common advantage [*sumpheron*]. So the other communities aim at some portion [*kata merê*] of what is advantageous [*sumpherontos*] . . . but the political community does not aim at the present advantage [*sumpherontos*], but at the whole of life (1160a11–23).[6]

Each of the subordinate disciplines and crafts mentioned in *NE* I.1 (medicine, boat-construction, military strategy, household management, bridle making, horse riding) has what is advantageous to someone as its goal; and the degree to which each of their subordinate ends is to be pursued is determined by the political leader, who regulates the city by looking to the highest goal of all—the advantage of each of the citizens. That advantage is the same for all: a happy life, or, to put it in our terms, a life full of well-being.

Eudaimonia and happiness

Now that we can be sure that it really is well-being that Aristotle is talking about, let us ask what his theory of well-being says.

As I noted earlier, Aristotle says that the highest good is *eudaimonia* and he adds that "living well and doing well are the same as being *eudaimon*" (I.4 1095a19–20). It is important not to be misled by the common practice of using the word "happiness" to render his *eudaimonia*. The Greek word is unmistakably a term of evaluation, as Aristotle's statement here indicates. It is composed of two segments: *eu*, meaning "well"; and *daimon*, which refers to a less-than-omnipotent divine being who oversees one's life. To be *eudaimon*, then, is to have, as it were, a guardian angel who is doing well in guiding one's life. Or, as we might put it, it is to be smiled upon by Lady Luck—if we personify Luck as a force that takes a personal interest in one's life. But Aristotle pays no attention, in his ethical theorizing, to the *daimon* element in the etymology of *eudaimonia*. He is guided instead by the widely accepted assumption of Greek speakers that when one asks whether someone is *eudaimon*, one is asking whether she is living well. And that of course depends on what kind of life she has. One cannot assess how well someone's life is being lived unless one knows what good things or bad things are in it.

By contrast, our term "happiness" is most often used as a description of someone's state of mind, some mood or emotion that she is feeling. One can be in a "smiley" mood, or feel a sudden joy or sense of well-being. When used in this common way, it is part of our empirical vocabulary, not a term by which we assess how well someone's life is going for her. We can criticize someone for being joyous when that response is inappropriate, or for being happy with herself when she should be dissatisfied. Even so, we do sometimes use "happy" in an evaluative context. We can say that a plant is not happy in a dark corner, meaning simply that it is not doing well there; or we can criticize someone's writing by noting his unhappy choice of words. Furthermore, happiness is often regarded not as a shallow and passing feeling, but as a uniquely valuable state of mind—something elusive and deep, and worthy of being one's ultimate end (even if it is best achieved by aiming at other goals). We should distinguish this deep and meaningful happiness from a shallow and fleeting feeling of pleasure.[7] It is, as I said, elusive: many people wonder whether they are happy in the way that matters most. In doing so, they implicitly assume that a life is not truly happy unless it is devoted to what does not merely seem good but really is so. So understood, our term "happiness" is evaluative as well as descriptive, and like the term *eudaimonia* it conveys the idea of well-being and of a healthy state of the soul.

Is *eudaimonia* a dominant or an inclusive end?

Aristotle puts good (advantageous) things into one of three categories: (a) those chosen only because of the other things they bring; (b) those chosen for themselves as well as for what they bring; (c) those that bring nothing else but are chosen only for themselves (I.7 1097a25–34). Happiness, he claims, goes into the third of these categories.

It is tempting to object: "can't one seek happiness in part because one's own *un*happiness would make one less eager or able to help others become happy?" But there is a way to interpret Aristotle that protects him against this objection: we can take him to mean that my happiness leads to no further advantage that *I* could have; it is therefore not to be sought for the sake of something else that benefits *me*. If it were desirable for the sake of some further good, that other good would be even better than happiness (I.1 1094a14–16)—and Aristotle holds that there can be no such good.

This allows some well-lived lives to be better than others; Aristotle argues, in fact, that a political life is happy in a secondary way (X.8 1178a7–9), and that it is the life devoted to philosophical theorizing that is happiest (X.7–8). In that sense, there can be something better than this or that happy life—namely, an even happier life. But there is no good, X, not identical to happiness, such that X plus happiness is better for someone to possess than happiness alone.

Because *eudaimonia* is the supreme good in this sense, it might be regarded as a composite made up of several parts. That would help explain why Aristotle thinks that one can do no better for oneself than to be *eudaimon*. Suppose we make a list of all the things rightly chosen for themselves: A, B, C, and D. To be *eudaimon*, we might say, is simply to have all of these goods. It is an inclusive end—inclusive of all intrinsic goods. It is the supreme good because nothing can be better than having A, B, C, and D. Surely it would not be better to *lack* some of these goods.[8]

Aristotle appears to be saying precisely this:

> We think happiness is most choiceworthy of all goods [since] it is not counted as one good among many. [If it were] counted as one good among many, then, clearly, we think it would be more choiceworthy if the smallest of goods were added; for the good that is added becomes an extra quantity of goods, and the larger of two goods is always more choiceworthy (1097b17–20).

But there is a different way of reading this passage, one that does not commit Aristotle to the idea that happiness is a plurality, containing all the intrinsic goods there are.[9] According to this second interpretation, Aristotle means that the supreme goodness of happiness does not consist in its simply being the best single item on a list of intrinsic goods. Its supremacy does not consist in its being better than A, better than B, better than C, and so on. For if it merely had that kind of supremacy, it might still be inferior to some combination of itself and something else. Instead, its special supremacy must consist in this fact: once you have seen that someone's life is as happy as a life can be, because it has X (the good in which happiness consists), then you are committed to saying not merely that X is better than any other single good, but also that "X plus A" or "X plus B" (and so on) do not name something better than "X" alone. The goodness of a life that is happy (the benefit to oneself of having such a life) is accounted for solely by the presence in it of a full amount of the good that happiness consists in. That is what it means to say that *eudaimonia* is "most choiceworthy of all goods . . . not counted as one good among many." (An analogy: What makes it the case that team A beats team B is that A has more points than B. Of course, A needs better players than B, in order to get more points. But having better players is not what constitutes winning. Similarly, if X is what happiness consists in, it might be case that one cannot have X unless one has other goods as well. Even so, being happy consists simply in having X.)

This second reading is the one that best fits the text, for Aristotle's theory of well-being holds that the human good is this and only this: virtuous activity of the rational soul. Happiness consists in just that one type of good, for only one end is at the top of the hierarchy of goods. Lesser goods are to be pursued for the sake of others that are more valuable, and these may in turn be sought because they lead to still others that are better, but the chain of goals must terminate somewhere. That is a fundamental thesis of Book I, Chapters 1 and 2; and that idea culminates (in I.7) in the conclusion that the ultimate end is virtuous activity. That is the good at the top of this pyramid: it is the "dominant" end. It is supremely good in a special way: not only is it better than any other single good, but in addition, "a lifetime of unimpeded virtuous activity plus honor," "a lifetime of unimpeded virtuous activity plus friendship," and so on, do not name a good superior to the one named by "a lifetime of unimpeded virtuous activity."[10]

Of course, Aristotle believes that *human beings* do need honor and friendship in order to achieve *eudaimonia*. But that is because their virtuous activity would be impeded were they to be dishonored and friendless; it is not because honor and friendship are themselves components of the highest good. This, Aristotle believes, is confirmed by the recognition that the living substance that has a better life than anything else in the universe is not a human being but a god who engages in just one activity and who can do so without needing friends, honor, or anything else external to its mind. The rest of the universe depends on a single unmoved mover that unceasingly and forever engages in unimpeded virtuous activity of the best sort, namely the exercise of theoretical wisdom (*NE* X.7–8, *Metaphysics* XII.9, *Politics* VII.1 1323b21–26). It lacks every other good available to human beings, but it is no worse for that, because the one good it does have is the greatest happiness.

There is no passage in which Aristotle says: the good for the sake of which every decision must be made is a composite of virtuous activity, honor, friendship, health, and so on (all of these being things that should be chosen for themselves). Rather, he says: "the human good proves to be activity of the soul in accord with virtue, and indeed with the best and most complete virtue, if there are more virtues than one" (I.7 1098a16–18). Of course, for a human being to live a happy life involves pursuing all of the goals in the hierarchy, the lower ones for the sake of the higher. A happy human life must have many good things in it—not a jumble, but a structure of ends, with one type of end at the top. But when Aristotle says that "the happy person is the one whose activities accord with complete virtue, with an adequate supply of external goods, not for just any time but for a complete life" (I.10 1101a14–16), he is describing the happy human being, not naming the good at the top of the hierarchy of ends.

Because happiness consists not only in *having* the habits, skills, and wisdom of a virtuous person, but the unimpeded *activation* of those qualities of mind on a regular basis over a substantial period of time, it is vulnerable to fortune. Those mental properties cannot be taken from us by others, but the opportunity and wherewithal needed to exercise them can be lost. One cannot exercise the virtues in the political arena if one's city has been destroyed (I.10 1101a8), and one cannot contemplate the basic truths of the world if one lacks the leisure to do so. The Stoics, of course, disagree; they turn away from Aristotle and from common sense and join Socrates in saying that a good man cannot be harmed (*Apology* 41c–d). Aristotle's theory of well-being, by contrast, is an effort to accommodate both the plausible idea that no human being is invulnerable to misfortune and the plausible idea that qualities such as wisdom, justice, and courage do not merely belong on a list of goods, but are in some way on a higher level than others.

Flourishing

Aristotle's deep interest in biology stands behind his conception of well-being. He thinks of the development of our cognitive, affective, and social powers as the analogue in human life to the development of lesser powers in plants and animals. All living things have the potential to live well, each according to its endowment. For plants, a flourishing life is simply a matter of nutrition, growth, and reproduction. For non-human animals, living well also involves locomotion, perception, and (in some cases) a certain kind of sociability. His argument for identifying happiness with virtuous activity in *NE* I.7 rests on the assumption that the human soul gives us the potential to do better than other forms of life. As we might put it, our emotional repertoire and cognitive powers enable us to achieve a life of greater richness and depth than is available to plants and other animals. To exploit these greater possibilities, however, requires a long process of habituation and learning, culminating in the acquisition of practical and theoretical wisdom. Aristotle's best insight, I believe, is that we should think biologically about what is beneficial for living things. Living well—living to one's best advantage—is the flourishing of one's inherent powers.[11]

Notes

1 Unless noted otherwise, the translation used is that of Irwin, T.H. (1999) *Nicomachean Ethics*, 2nd ed., Indianapolis: Hackett.
2 My thinking about this issue has been stimulated by Gavin Lawrence (2006) "Human Good and Human Function," in R. Kraut (ed.), *The Blackwell Guide to Aristotle's Nicomachean Ethics*, Malden, MA: Blackwell, pp. 37–75. He takes success at something to be the central concept that Aristotle exploits in Book I of the *Ethics*. But if succeeding at something is simply doing it well (as success in life is living well), and doing something well is doing it in a way that is good, we must ask: good for whom?
3 This is the interpretation I proposed in *Against Absolute Goodness* (2011), Oxford: OUP, pp. 210–211.
4 To use Scanlon's phrase, this is a "buck-passing" interpretation of the first sentence of the *Ethics*. See Scanlon, T.M. (1998) *What We Owe to Each Other*, Cambridge, MA: Belknap Press, pp. 95–100.
5 Stoic ethics is similarly advantage-centered. According to the synopsis found in Diogenes Laertes, good is "that from which some advantage (*ophelos*) comes." See *Lives of Eminent Philosophers*, vol. 2 (transl. R.D. Hicks) (1925), Cambridge, MA: Harvard University Press, p. VII.94. On my reading, Aristotle works towards this thesis; the Stoics posit it.
6 My translation.
7 For the idea that "happiness" can designate a deep affective condition, see Haybron, D.M. (2008) *The Pursuit of Unhappiness: The Elusive Psychology of Well-Being*, Oxford: Oxford University Press, pp. 128–133 (and elsewhere). He also notes that "what is happiness?" can be understood either as a question about what a certain mental state is, or as one that asks what it is for a life to go well (pp. 29–32). But I doubt that these two senses are, as he suggests (p. 31), as distant from each other as are the two senses of "bank" (for a river bank and a financial institution) (p. 31). For happiness is an elusive state of mind in part because we seek to understand it in a way that explains its great value. (Contrast the ease with which we can keep apart questions about the nature and value of certain other states of mind—anger, for example.)
8 The terms "dominant end" and "inclusive end" were used by Hardie, W.F.R. (1965) "The Final Good in Aristotle's Ethics," *Philosophy* 40. He argues that Aristotle often thinks of happiness as a dominant end, but sometimes as an inclusive end. See too Ackrill, J.L. (1980) "Aristotle on *Eudaimonia*," in A. Rorty (ed.), *Essays on Aristotle's Ethics*, Berkeley, CA: University of California Press, pp. 15–34. He argues that it is only in Book X that a dominant end conception of happiness can be found. For the view that Aristotle consistently conceives of happiness as a plurality of goods, see Irwin, T.H. (2012) "Conceptions of Happiness in the *Nicomachean Ethics*," in C. Shields (ed.) *The Oxford Handbook of Aristotle*, Oxford: Oxford University Press, pp. 495–528.

9 I defend this interpretation more fully in *Aristotle on the Human Good* (1989), Princeton: Princeton University Press, pp. 197–266.
10 I take Aristotle to be assuming, when he says (I.7 1098a16–18) that the human good is virtuous activity of the rational soul, that one cannot be happy if this activity is a rare occurrence in one's life, because one is often impeded by a lack of resources. He spells out this assumption at *NE* VII.13 1153b15–18.
11 I exploit these ideas in my defense of an Aristotelian conception of well-being in *What is Good and Why: The Ethics of Well-Being*, Cambridge, MA: Harvard University Press (2007), pp. 131–204.

Bibliography

Ackrill, J.L. (1980) "Aristotle on *Eudaimonia*" in A. Rorty (ed.), *Essays on Aristotle's Ethics*, Berkeley, CA: University of California Press, pp. 15–34.

Hardie, W.F.R. (1965) "The Final Good in Aristotle's Ethics" *Philosophy* 40: 277–295.

Haybron, D.M. (2008) *The Pursuit of Unhappiness: The Elusive Psychology of Well-Being*, Oxford: Oxford University Press.

Irwin, T.H. (2012) "Conceptions of Happiness in the *Nicomachean Ethics*" in C. Shields (ed.), *The Oxford Handbook of Aristotle*, Oxford: Oxford University Press, pp. 495–528.

Kraut, R. (2007) *What is Good and Why: The Ethics of Well-Being*, Cambridge, MA: Harvard University Press.

Laertes, D. (1925) *Lives of Eminent Philosophers*, Vol. 2 (transl. R.D. Hicks), Cambridge, MA: Harvard University Press.

Lawrence, G. (2006) "Human Good and Human Function" in R. Kraut (ed.), *The Blackwell Guide to Aristotle's Nicomachean Ethics*, Malden, MA: Blackwell, pp. 37–75.

Scanlon, T.M. (1998) *What We Owe to Each Other*, Cambridge, MA: Belknap Press.

3

HEDONISTIC THEORIES OF WELL-BEING IN ANTIQUITY

Tim O'Keefe

Ancient ethics is commonly, and rightly, characterized as "eudaimonistic." At the start of the *Nicomachean Ethics*, Aristotle sets out the overall framework within which most ancient ethicists operate: the highest good is *eudaimonia*, or happiness, which is valuable for its own sake and not for the sake of anything else. Everything else that is valuable is valuable either as an instrumental means to achieving *eudaimonia* or as a constituent of *eudaimonia*. (For Aristotle, wealth would be an example of an instrumental means to *eudaimonia*, whereas interacting with your friends would be one of its constituents.) Aristotle notes that, while everybody agrees that *eudaimonia* is the highest good, this is a "thin" agreement merely on what to *label* the highest good, as people sharply disagree on what the *substance* of *eudaimonia* is (*NE* I 1095a17–22).[1]

The dominant strain of ancient ethics is objectivist and perfectionist: *eudaimonia* is not a state of mind. Instead, it is primarily or entirely constituted by virtue and virtuous activity, that is, by the perfection and exercise of our nature as rational and social animals. Plato, Aristotle, and the Stoics differ on many important ethical questions, but they share a common commitment to the centrality of virtue and acting virtuously to the good life. Virtue is in itself noble and beautiful (*kalon*), and its possession is intrinsically beneficial to the virtuous person.

But there is an important and substantial countermovement within ancient ethics, which characterizes the highest good in subjectivist terms. Democritus, the inspiration for Epicurus' atomistic metaphysics, denied that pleasure was the good, but he did identify the good with a state of mind: *euthumia*, or cheerfulness[2] (*DL* IX 45). Socrates' follower Aristippus was notorious for his willingness to flout conventions of what is proper in his pursuit of pleasure, although our reports conflict on whether he was a full-blown hedonist or not.[3] This chapter will concentrate on the Epicureans and Cyrenaics, who give the two fullest statements of subjectivist theories of well-being in antiquity, both of which explicitly identify pleasure as the highest good. The Epicureans and Cyrenaics fashioned their views against the backdrop of Plato's and Aristotle's extensive discussions of pleasure.[4] Both Plato and Aristotle believe that the best human lives will be pleasant, but they also regard hedonism as mistaken and dangerous. Although our sources do not allow us to assert confidently that the Epicureans and Cyrenaics are reacting to Plato or Aristotle point-by-point in devising their positions, viewing their positions through the lens of Plato's and Aristotle's criticisms of hedonism is useful.

This entry will start with a consideration of how the Epicureans and Cyrenaics try to establish that pleasure is the highest good, before moving on to what each school says about the nature of pleasure. Then we will look at the role virtue plays (or does not play) in the acquisition of pleasure, and the place of epistemic goods such as knowledge of the workings of the world. The entry will close with a brief look at the ethics of the Pyrrhonian skeptics: although not hedonists, their ethics shares surprising affinities to the Epicureans' ethics while breaking from Epicureanism and the rest of the Greek ethical tradition in how to attain the good life.

Hedonism and teleology

The two earliest extant arguments that try to establish pleasure as the highest good are in the writings of Plato and Aristotle. Both start from empirical observations of what is (supposedly) *pursued* for its own sake and derive conclusions about what is *good*. In his consideration of what pleasure is and how it figures into the happy life, Aristotle recounts the hedonistic arguments of Eudoxus, an astronomer, student of Plato, and older compatriot of Aristotle. Eudoxus believes that what is most choiceworthy is what is chosen for its own sake and not for the sake of anything else, and all animals, both rational and non-rational, seek pleasure. And we seek it for its own sake: we never ask somebody for the sake of what they're being pleased, as we assume that the pleasure is choiceworthy in itself (*NE* X 1172b9–28). In *Protagoras* 351c–354e, Socrates gives a similar argument: we pursue pleasure for its own sake and avoid pain for its own sake. We do sometimes embrace pains and avoid pleasures, but that is never because we regard suffering as something in itself good or disdain pleasure as being in itself bad. Instead, we do so precisely because some pains produce more pleasure in the long run, and some pleasures lead to greater pain, and this shows that pleasure is good and pain bad.[5]

These arguments have some ambiguities: as stated, both arguments would seem to establish only that pleasure is *an* intrinsic good, not the *sole* intrinsic good. And in Eudoxus' argument, the relationship between the universal pursuit of pleasure and its goodness is unclear. He says that, just as each species of animal seeks the sort of food that is good for it, all animals seek pleasure. This suggests that perhaps the universal pursuit of pleasure acts as *evidence* for its goodness, rather than being the *reason* for its goodness, just as we may take the characteristic pursuit of some sort of food by a species as evidence that that sort of food is good for those animals, rather than thinking that the food is good for them just because they all pursue it.[6]

The Epicureans and Cyrenaics put forward the same basic argument in favor of hedonism while clearing up these ambiguities. The Cyrenaics say that we are all instinctively attracted to pleasure and we seek for nothing further when we have it, and this is why pleasure is the end (*DL* II 88). The Epicureans assert that the end is what is *sought* for its own sake and not for the sake of anything else, and that the one thing that all animals seek for its own sake and not for the sake of anything else is pleasure. This psychological fact is supposed to be especially evident when we look at the behavior of infants (Cic. *Fin.* I 29–30).

To this behavioral argument, the Cyrenaics and Epicureans add an affective proof of pleasure's goodness and pain's badness. Pleasure is agreeable to all living things, pain repellent, say the Cyrenaics (*DL* II 87), and our affections are the criteria for what is good and bad: our approval of pleasure is what makes it good, our disapproval of pain what makes it bad (Sextus Empiricus, *AM* vii 199–200). Likewise, the Epicureans claim that no long argument is needed to establish the goodness of pleasure and the badness of pain: all that is required is to draw our attention to what each is like in our experience[7] (Cic. *Fin.* I 30). (If somebody doubts that pain is bad, kick them in the shin.)

So the Cyrenaics and Epicureans ground our end in our goal-directed behavior and our pro-attitudes. One could accept this overall approach to determining what our good is while rejecting hedonism by rejecting the supposed psychological facts that support it.[8] Critics of hedonism like Plato, Aristotle, and the Stoics do reject the hedonists' accounts of motivation. But more fundamentally, they reject their approach, because they believe that there are normative standards external to what we happen to pursue and approve of that we should use to evaluate them. Thus, even though the positions needn't have lined up this way, it's probably no coincidence that the dominant strain of Greek ethics, with its objectivist and perfectionist view on *eudaimonia*, is advanced by philosophers with teleological world-views; whereas the subjectivist countermovement consists of philosophers who do not have this sort of world-view. Aristotle believes that our reason has a function it fulfills when it understands and contemplates the truths of cosmology and theology, whereas the Epicureans thinks that organisms and their parts have no inherent purposes or functions, even though they are able to do various things (*DRN* V 772–1090).

For Plato, pleasant things obviously *appear* to be good, and to that limited extent he would agree with Epicurus. But a yummy pastry that seems good might not promote the genuine good of the body, which is health, and a flattering piece of oratory that seems good might not promote the genuine good of the soul, which is for the soul to have its proper order and organization[9] (*Gorgias* 462b–466a, 506c–507c). For Aristotle, not all pleasures are good: the value of a pleasure depends on the value of what it is you are taking pleasure in, and so taking pleasure in an excellent activity is good and beneficial, while taking pleasure in a base activity is bad and harmful[10] (*NE* 1175b24–33).

The nature of pleasure

Although the Epicureans and Cyrenaics agree that pleasure is the good, they sharply disagree on its nature. For the Cyrenaics, both pleasure and pain are psychic "movements," the former a smooth motion we find congenial, the latter a rough motion we find repellant (*DL* II 86–87). We can distinguish between bodily and mental pleasures and pains, e.g., the pleasure of receiving a backrub versus the pleasure of delighting in the prosperity of your country. They held that bodily pleasures are far better than mental ones, and bodily pains much worse than mental ones, and offered as evidence for this that we punish offenders with bodily pains (*DL* II 90). How this argument is supposed to go is not entirely clear, but perhaps it is supposed to show that we abhor bodily pains far more than mental ones, which makes them more effective punishments for both retribution and deterrence. One source identifies the end for the Cyrenaics as bodily pleasure (*DL* II 87), although it would make more sense for the Cyrenaics to include both mental and bodily pleasures in the end, insofar as both are pleasures.

The Epicurean view on pleasure is much more complicated and idiosyncratic. They also accept the distinction between bodily and mental pleasures and pains, but reverse their priority. Bodily pleasures depend just upon the present state of my body, e.g., I am in bodily pain if I am being beaten by a baseball bat. But mental pleasures and pains encompass the past and future too, through memory and anticipation. Even if my bodily state is perfectly fine right now, if I know that several large people are waiting outside my office and will administer to me a sound thrashing with their baseball bats, the anxiety caused by my anticipation of this future bodily pain is itself painful. And when Epicurus was dying painfully, he said that he still felt blessed because counterbalancing the excruciating pain of his kidney stones was the joy he felt at the memory of his past philosophical conversations (*DL* X 22). In fact, the Epicureans recommend training yourself to recall sweet memories as a way to always have pleasure available (Cic. *Fin.* I 57).

The Epicureans also distinguish between "kinetic" and "static" pleasures. Epicurean "kinetic" pleasures are similar to Cyrenaic pleasures *tout court*: they're psychic "movements" that we find congenial. They are also often associated with the process of fulfilling some desire, e.g., the sensation I feel as

I'm eating while hungry. But what of the state I am in *after* I have eaten my fill, when I am satiated and no longer hungry? A key Epicurean innovation is to insist that this sort of state is not merely neutral between pleasure and pain, but is itself a kind of pleasure: a "static" pleasure. *Aponia*, or freedom from bodily distress, is bodily static pleasure: the state of not being hungry, thirsty, cold, itchy, etc. The simple principle that allows us to declare that it is a pleasure and not merely a neutral state is that anything we delight in is a pleasure, just as anything that distresses us is a pain (Cic. *Fin.* I 37). And we delight in being free of pain or need.

In the case of the mind, "joy" is labeled as a mental kinetic pleasure, while tranquility (*ataraxia*) is mental static pleasure: the state of being free from regret, anxiety, and other mental turmoil.

The Cyrenaics deny that merely being free of pain is a kind of pleasure, and they claim that, for Epicurus, the happiest person is a corpse or somebody asleep (Clement, *Strom.* ii 2 130.7–8, *DL* II 88). But this criticism is unfair. Although corpses are free from pain and anxiety, they are not tranquil and do not take delight in being free from fear. While *aponia* and *ataraxia* are defined negatively as freedom from bodily and mental pain, they are still positive mental states that require a person to be aware of them in order to be pleasures.

Not only are static pleasures genuine pleasures, the Epicureans claim that the removal of all pain is the limit of pleasure (*KD* 3), and that once this limit is reached, pleasure cannot be increased but only varied (*KD* 18). The pinnacle of happiness, for the Epicureans, is to achieve both *aponia* and *ataraxia*, with *ataraxia* being far more important. (As Epicurus' own dying example is supposed to show, a person who is able to maintain his cheerfulness and tranquility even in the face of great bodily distress will find his situation, on balance, satisfying and pleasant, even though he would prefer not to suffer the bodily pain.) So even though the Epicureans are hedonists, it turns out that their ethics is chiefly about how to achieve tranquility, as tranquility is the main constituent of the pleasant life.[11]

Hedonism, the virtues, and happiness

The most serious charge leveled against hedonism as a theory of well-being is that it cannot accommodate a proper respect for the virtues: hedonism would justify vicious and shameful actions. Plato depicts the hedonist Callicles as rejecting conventional standards of self-control, respecting others, and taking one's fair share in his unbridled pursuit of pleasure (*Gorgias* 482c–494b). Cicero thinks that hedonism would justify actions such as breaking a promise to a friend on his deathbed when you stand to gain greatly from your betrayal and you know that your betrayal would never be detected (Cic. *Fin.* II 53–60).

This charge is particularly acute for ancient hedonists, as compared to modern thinkers such as Sidgwick who also have hedonistic theories of well-being, because in ancient ethics generally there is no bifurcation between prudential and moral standards of practical reasoning.[12] So the ancient hedonist will not respond that betraying your friend by breaking your promise to him is *prudentially* preferable (because it most effectively promotes your pleasure) but *morally* impermissible (e.g., because it does not maximize overall happiness or because it does not display a proper respect for your friend).

That's not to say that ancient ethicists didn't recognize that prudential and moral evaluations of an action often seem to diverge sharply. The point of the Ring of Gyges thought experiment offered by Glaucon in Plato's *Republic* (*Republic* II 359a–360d) is that standards of justice constrain a person's actions, so that when somebody could be absolutely confident of escaping detection and thus the negative consequences of acting unjustly, acting unjustly in order to get what you want would (apparently) be in your self-interest. And in Plato's dialog the *Gorgias*, Polus says that when a tyrant unjustly inflicts horrific suffering on his enemies, the tyrant's actions are more *shameful* than his victims' suffering, but the suffering is (prudentially) *worse* than engaging in the wrongdoing (*Gorgias* 466a–475d).

Characters like Polus and Glaucon, who think that prudential and moral standards sometimes diverge, do not conclude that moral standards override prudential standards. Instead, Polus thinks that so much the worse for morality: he celebrates the life of the shameful tyrant. And Glaucon, who considers himself a friend of justice and is anxious to defend its value, requests that Socrates show how it is always prudentially better to be a just person than an unjust person, even in cases where the just person suffers terrible consequences because of his justice. When confronted with this request, Socrates tries to show how being a morally upright and just person is in that person's self-interest, rather than rejecting the request as misguided.[13]

Philosophers like Plato, Aristotle, and the Stoics try to reconcile the demands of morality and prudence, not by making morality subservient to prudence, but by incorporating morality into their conceptions of well-being. For example, Aristotle believes that the virtuous person will recognize the fineness of his virtuous friend's character and will seek to promote his friend's welfare for the friend's sake. But in acting in this way, in doing what is noble and praiseworthy, the virtuous person is thereby living well as a human being and fulfilling his *telos*, and he is thus achieving *eudaimonia* (*NE* 1168a28–1169b1). Conversely, the vicious person is both morally reprehensible and living badly as a human being, expressing defects of character and of practical rationality, and thus unhappy.

The Epicureans try to accommodate the virtues in a more straightforward fashion: the virtues are valuable only instrumentally, for the sake of bringing about pleasure, but are nonetheless necessary to achieve *eudaimonia*. An unbridled seeker of pleasure, like Callicles in the *Gorgias*, will end up having a miserable life. While all pleasures are good and all pains bad, not all pleasures are choiceworthy, and not all pains are to be avoided. Many pleasurable activities have bad long-term consequences, and the wise person avoids them, picking and choosing among pleasures and pains in a way that makes her life as a whole pleasant (*Ep. Men.* 129–130).

Epicurus says that prudence is the source of all of the other virtues (*Ep. Men.* 132; *KD* 5). For instance, the prudent person cultivates moderation, because indulging excessive desires for luxurious food and drink damages your bodily health, and possessing these excessive desires that are difficult to satisfy causes anxiety and leads to conflicts with other people. The Epicureans give similar hedonic justifications for the other virtues. While Epicurus is happy to talk about picking and choosing among pleasures and pains, the main emphasis in Epicurean ethics is not on what particular actions to perform, but on cultivating the sort of character that will bring about tranquility. In general, the Epicureans recommend reducing your desires and living simply in order to gain happiness. Vain and empty desires for fame, political power, or great luxury should be eliminated, because they are hard to satisfy and are desires for things we don't really need anyway, whereas desires for food, hydration, and basic shelter are both natural to us as human beings and necessary, either for living at all or at least for living comfortably (*Ep. Men.* 127).

By making the virtues strictly instrumentally valuable, they open themselves up to the charge of unfriendly critics like Cicero that the demands of virtue and prudence will diverge in cases of undetectable betrayals of friends or violations of justice. But the Epicureans stick to their guns and insist that such cases do not arise. The badness of injustice does not consist merely in getting punished if you are caught, but in the anxiety you will experience worrying that you *might* get caught, even if you are not. And we can never be utterly confident that our wrongdoing will escape detection (*KD* 34–35). Besides which, the prudent wise person who has limited her desires has little to gain by engaging in unjust actions. Friendship is by far the greatest means of securing happiness (*KD* 27). It allows us to face the future without fear, knowing that our friends will help us out if we are in need, and we pledge likewise to help them when they are in need. But trust is absolutely essential to having these mutually beneficial relationships. The risks you run in betraying a friend and ruining your reputation, and the anxiety attendant upon running those risks, are never worth any potential gain. In fact, the Epicureans claim that hedonic calculations can justify caring for your friend as much as you care for yourself (Cic. *Fin.* I 65–70), and that the wise person will sometimes die for her friend[14] (*DL* X 121).

Although the Epicureans try to accommodate the virtues, justice, and friendship within a hedonistic ethics, Epicurus sharply rejects Aristotle's account of what motivates the virtuous person. For Aristotle, the truly virtuous person acts for the sake of the *kalon*, the noble or beautiful, i.e., because he recognizes the intrinsic value of virtue, while Epicurus says that he spits upon the *kalon* and on those who vainly admire it, whenever it does not produce pleasure (Athaneus *Deipnosophists* 12, 547a), and that those who burble on about the virtues and wisdom are really referring to nothing other than the means of producing pleasures[15] (Cic. *Tusc.* III 42).

The Cyrenaics are far more cynical (in the modern sense) and iconoclastic than the Epicureans when it comes to the virtues. There is some overlap: they agree that the good person is deterred from acting unjustly by the penalties imposed for wrongdoing and the risk of a bad reputation (*DL* II 92–3), and that we make friends from self-interested motives (*DL* II 91). But they deny that every wise person lives pleasantly and every fool painfully: instead, this is true only for the most part (*DL* II 91). Furthermore, even pleasures resulting from the most shameful conduct are good (*DL* II 88). Epicurus would agree, while insisting that such pleasures are not *choiceworthy*. But characteristically, the Cyrenaics bite bullets that the Epicureans try to dodge. The later Cyrenaic Theodorus asserts that actions like theft and adultery are sometimes allowable. The idea that such actions are by nature base and thus to be avoided is just a prejudice used to keep the foolish masses in line, and the wise person will indulge his passions openly without regard for the circumstances (*DL* II 99). And rather than fitting friendship within a hedonistic ethics, the later Cyrenaic Hegesias denies that friendship exists, because we all act from self-interested motives (*DL* II 93).

The Cyrenaics are dubious that engaging in the sort of prudent picking and choosing among pleasures and pains that Epicurus recommends will result in achieving a happy life. Hegesias taught that it is impossible to achieve happiness, because both the body and soul are full of suffering (*DL* II 93). Death, therefore, takes away great evils, and Hegesias was supposedly banned from giving public lectures because many audience members would kill themselves after he spoke (Cic. *Tusc.* I 83–84).

More generally, the Cyrenaics stand out as the only ancient Greek ethicists to explicitly reject eudaimonism. Epicurus reconciles hedonism and eudaimonism by identifying the happy (*eudaimôn*) life with the pleasant life, and then saying that this life is the highest good. The Cyrenaics instead say that the end is particular pleasure, which is desirable for its own sake. Happiness is the sum of particular pleasures, past, present, and future, and it is not desirable for its own sake, but only for the sake of the particular pleasures that compose it (*DL* II 87–88). This might still seem to justify acting prudently, insofar as we value those particular pleasures for their own sakes and prudence will help us obtain them. But even though they describe prudence as an instrumental good (*DL* II 91), they also think that accumulating the pleasures that produce happiness is most disagreeable, because it involves choosing present pain for the sake of future pleasure (*DL* II 90), and they seem not to advocate it.

The reason for this lack of future concern is not clear: they may believe that carefully planning for the future in order to maximize pleasure is self-defeating, because they are skeptical about our ability to gain knowledge of the external world and because of their belief (*contra* Epicurus) that the memory of past pleasures and anticipation of future pleasures are not themselves pleasant (*DL* II 88). The Annicerean sect of Cyrenaics appear to give a different reason: they deny that life as a whole has any end, instead saying that there is a special end for each action—the pleasure resulting from the action (Clement, *Strom.* ii 2 130.7–8). This suggests that they view what is good for an agent at any time to be a function of the particular pleasures that agent is striving for at that time, with no further overarching end to unify these particular goods.[16]

Hedonism and epistemic goods

Another charge leveled against hedonism as a theory of well-being is that it cannot accommodate epistemic goods in the happy life. In Plato's *Philebus*, Socrates is examining the life of pleasure versus the life of knowledge, to see which is preferable (*Philebus* 20d–21d). He argues that a life with the greatest pleasures but devoid of memory, knowledge, or reason—and thus lacking even the memory that you have enjoyed yourself, the knowledge that you are enjoying yourself, and the ability to figure out how to obtain future pleasures for yourself—would not be a human life, but the life of a mollusk or some other shellfish. Similarly, Aristotle argues that the vulgar and servile masses who think the good is pleasure prefer a bovine life, not a properly human one (*NE* I 1095b15–20).

Just as with the virtues and virtuous activity, both Plato and Aristotle incorporate epistemic good as constituents of *eudaimonia*. For Plato, the rational part of the human *psyche* loves learning and wisdom, and a person who has achieved an understanding of the truth has satisfied the highest and finest part of himself. For Aristotle, the life of theoretical contemplation is the happiest life. The person who has achieved an understanding of the basic principles of theology, ontology, and cosmology, and then spends his time contemplating these truths, has best fulfilled his nature as a rational being (*NE* X 7–8).

And as with the virtues, the Epicureans try to give theoretical knowledge a place in the good life by arguing that it has instrumental value in securing us pleasure. In a few places, Epicureans appear to assert that we can find intellectual activity immediately pleasurable: the Epicurean poet Lucretius describes his awe at beholding the wondrous workings of the universe, as revealed by Epicurus (*DRN* III 28–30), and Epicurus says that the process of learning philosophy is pleasant (*SV* 27) and that the wise person takes more pleasure in contemplation than others do (*DL* X 120). But these passages are exceptional. Instead, theoretical knowledge is typically deemed good because we need it in order to banish fear of the gods and of death and obtain tranquility. We cannot live tranquilly if we are troubled about the gods or other creatures depicted in superstitious myths possibly harming us, and we need natural science to understand the causes of natural phenomena and dispel such fears (*KD* 11–13). The Epicureans believe that death is annihilation, and that if death is annihilation then it is not bad and should not be feared. Your death will not be bad for you, as after your death you will not exist to suffer any misfortune. And since your death will not be bad for you when it arrives, fearing it now is irrational (*Ep. Men.* 125). But we need to have a proper understanding of the nature of the *psyche*, that it is a corporeal organ that dies along with the rest of the body, in order to be secure that death is annihilation, rather than possibly a hazardous transition to an afterlife.

The Cyrenaics do not try to find any role for theoretical knowledge in the good life, for the simple reason that they believe it is impossible for us to gain such knowledge. They believe that we cannot know the nature of the external objects that cause our affections, and they abandon the study of nature because of its uncertainty[17] (*DL* II 92).

The Pyrrhonian skeptics

As represented in the writings of Sextus Empiricus (second century CE), the Pyrrhonian skeptic is an investigator of philosophical and scientific claims. He does not claim to know the truth, unlike dogmatic philosophers such as Aristotle and Epicurus, and he suspends judgment on the metaphysical and ethical questions he is investigating, e.g., on the nature of the gods or on whether cannibalism is by nature bad. But, unlike the Cyrenaics, he also does not claim that it is impossible to apprehend the way things are; on this epistemic question, too, he suspends judgment. So the Pyrrhonian skeptic has no philosophical doctrines, in the sense of positive or negative commitments. But he does have a distinctive skill: a knack for bringing to bear opposing arguments and appearances on the questions he is investigating, so as induce suspension of judgment both in himself and in the people with whom he is interacting (*PH* I 1–11).

Sextus sketches out a subjectivist position on well-being with affinities to the Epicurean position. It is not hedonist, at least by label: Sextus says that, unlike the Cyrenaics, the Pyrrhonians do not believe that pleasure is the *telos*. But Sextus is here contrasting the Pyrrhonian *telos* with Cyrenaic hedonism in particular, according to which pleasure is a "smooth motion." For the Pyrrhonians, the end is tranquility (*ataraxia*), which the Epicureans regard as the limit of mental pleasure and the main constituent of the happy life (*PH* I 215).

Sextus accepts the standard Aristotelian definition of the *telos*, the end or aim. It is that for the sake of which everything else is done, without itself being pursued for the sake of anything else, and it is the final object of desire (*PH* 1 25). But like the Epicureans and others who do not have a teleological world-view, the skeptic looks to what is, as a matter of fact, pursued and desired to discern what the *telos* is. And the skeptic, as a matter of fact, pursues two things for their own sakes: tranquility, and having moderate feelings regarding things that are unavoidable (*PH* I 25). Tranquility is a calmness of the soul and freedom from disturbance (*PH* I 10). Having moderate feelings regarding things that are unavoidable is akin to the Epicurean static bodily pleasure of *aponia,* or freedom from bodily distress, but more modest. Because he is human, the skeptic will inevitably shiver when cold and suffer from other bodily disturbances, and he won't like them, but he aims at not being bothered by such states as much as other people are (*PH* I 29–30).

While the skeptical and Epicurean ends overlap considerably, the skeptic's claims on behalf of his end are much more limited. The skeptic is simply describing what he goes for, without any commitment to its being what all animals pursue for its own sake, unlike the Epicureans. And the Epicureans believe that the goodness of pleasure is obvious in our experience of it, whereas the skeptic, while he cannot deny that tranquility appears good to him, suspends judgment on whether it is good by nature. (That tranquility appears good to the skeptic is good enough to allow him to go after it, without needing to think that this appearance is accurate.)

In fact, suspending judgment on what is good and bad by nature is the main way the skeptic achieves tranquility. Sextus says that those who believe things to be good and bad by nature pursue the purported "natural" good with too much intensity, and when they achieve the "natural" good, they are elated beyond measure, whereas the skeptic is much more relaxed about things (*PH* I 27–28). Suspending judgment on what is good and bad by nature also helps the skeptic achieve moderate feelings regarding what is unavoidable: as he does not regard being chilly or thirsty as bad by nature, they doesn't bother him as much as they do most people, who suffer both from the unpleasant feelings and from the belief that they're undergoing something that is bad by nature (*PH* I 30).

Far from regarding epistemic goods as constituents of happiness or even as instrumental for achieving it, the skeptic is skilled at avoiding epistemic commitments. While Sextus targets ethical beliefs as particularly destructive of tranquility, the skeptic avoids beliefs generally—at least beliefs concerning the unclear subjects that are the targets of scientific and philosophical inquiry[18] (*PH* I 13). At first, says Sextus, the skeptic investigated the vexing anomalies in things in order to resolve them, discover the truth, and thereby achieve tranquility. But being unable to resolve them, and seeing that competing accounts of the phenomena were equally balanced, the skeptic suspended judgment, and then—fortuitously—he thereby achieved peace of mind (*PH* I 28–29). In this way, skeptics are following the example of Pyrrho (c. 365–270), who achieved peace of mind as a result of holding no opinions on the way things are. It is for this reason that the Pyrrhonian skeptics named themselves after him, even though the Pyrrhonian movement was founded centuries after Pyrrho's death[19] (*PH* I 7).

The Pyrrhonian skeptic has fairly little concern with virtue. That's not at all to say that the skeptic will engage in immoral activities whenever he thinks that they will help him achieve what is (prudentially) preferable. The skeptic claims to have a practice which allows him to live correctly, but "correctly" simply in the humdrum sense that he is able to live in conformity with the conventions and laws of his society (*PH* I 17). So, for example, the skeptic is pious toward the gods, in the sense that he follows the laws and customs of his society regarding the gods, and he accepts that piety is good and impiety bad.[20] Going along with the laws and customs allows him to live "well" and virtuously in this modest sense, as well as helping him live an untroubled life. But given the conflicting standards of different societies and philosophers regarding what is fine and base, the skeptic will not affirm that the customary standards he follows are the correct ones or the virtues he cultivates perfections of human nature in Aristotle's sense. This embrace of conventional values sets Sextus against not only Aristotle, but even against fellow subjectivists like the Epicureans, who affirm that we need to use our reason to discover what truly conduces to our happiness, and this would include discerning which social practices are useful and which are pernicious.[21]

Related topics

Aristotle, death, desire-fulfillment theory, epistemic goods, hedonism, Plato, pleasure, Sidgwick on well-being.

Notes

1 Annas (1993) remains the best overall introduction to ancient eudaimonism. Henceforward, references to ancient texts will be made according to the following conventions: Aristotle, *Nicomachean Ethics* = *NE;* Cicero, *De Finibus* (On Goals) = *Fin.*; Cicero, *Tusculan Disputations* = *Tusc;* Clement of Alexandria, *Stromateis* = *Strom.*; Diogenes Laertius, *Lives of the Philosophers* = *DL*; Epicurus, *Kuriai Doxai* (Principle Doctrines) = *KD*; Epicurus, *Sententiae Vaticanae* (Vatican Sayings) = *SV*; Epicurus, Letter to Menoeceus = *Ep. Men.*; Lucretius, *De Rerum Natura* (On the Nature of Things) = *DRN*; Sextus Empiricus, *Against the Learned* = *AM*; Sextus Empiricus, *Outlines of* Pyrrhonism = *PH*.

2 See Warren (2002) for an in-depth treatment of the ethics of Democritus and his successors. Democritus describes *euthumia* as a peaceful and well-settled state of the soul, undisturbed by fear, superstition, or emotion. Although our reports on Democritus' ethics are too sparse to draw any conclusions confidently, *euthumia* appears to differ only verbally from the Epicurean conception of *ataraxia*, or tranquility, the mental pleasure that is the chief constituent of happiness.

3 Tsouna McKirahan (1994) is a balanced and thoughtful consideration of what we can glean from our sources about the historical Aristippus. She concludes that Aristippus himself was not a hedonist, but that many reports attribute to him positions developed by later Cyrenaics. See n. 4.

4 Both Epicurus and Aristippus the Younger, the main developer of the Cyrenaic positions in epistemology and ethics, post-date Aristotle. Unfortunately, the titular founder of the Cyrenaic school is Aristippus the Elder, grandfather of Aristippus the Younger, and disentangling their exact contributions is often difficult.

5 Socrates' defense of hedonism in the *Protagoras* is surprising, given the sharp criticisms of hedonism in many of Plato's other dialogs. If we assume that the *Protagoras* is consistent with other dialogs—perhaps not a safe assumption—the easiest maneuver to maintain consistency is to look at the dramatic context of Socrates' defense and maintain that we should not take him to be advancing these claims *in propria persona*. (Annas 1999: 167–171 convincingly argues this.) However, see Rudebusch (1999) for an attempt to attribute hedonism to Socrates in the *Protagoras* and make it consistent with what he says in other dialogs such as the *Gorgias*.

6 Warren (2009) ably navigates the intricacies of Eudoxus' argument.

7 Sedley (1998) explores the epistemological basis of Epicurean ethics in the feelings.

8 R.B. Perry's naturalistic theory of the good is an excellent example of this. For Perry, goodness consists in being liked and sought for its own sake, and badness in being disliked and being avoided for its own sake. But he is not a hedonist, because hedonism is far too narrow concerning what we do try to obtain and avoid for their own sakes (Perry 1914: 148–149).

9 Moss (2006) is an excellent study of the connection between pleasure and illusion in Plato.

10 Frede (2006) both summarizes Aristotle's doctrine of pleasure well and advocates for it forcefully.

11 Why static pleasures are the greatest pleasures and why, once the state of freedom from pain has been attained, pleasure can be "varied" but not increased, is not entirely clear. The place of kinetic pleasures in the Epicurean theory of the highest good is also unclear: on the one hand, as pleasures, they should be intrinsically good, while on the other hand the Epicurean discussions of freedom from pain as the limit of pleasure seems to exclude them in preference to the static pleasures of *aponia* and *ataraxia*. Some attempts to work through these questions are Gosling and Taylor (1982) Chapters 18–20, Purinton (1993), and Striker (1996).

12 See Sidgwick (1907) for an important example of such bifurcation, and especially the concluding chapter, where he argues that the two cannot be reconciled with one another.

13 Prichard (1912) gives a classic (and influential) argument that it is a mistake to try to show that morality is in your self-interest, as Plato does in the *Republic*.

14 Evans (2004) discusses whether the Epicureans can justify caring for your friend as much as yourself on purely hedonic and instrumentalist grounds.

15 See O'Keefe (2010) for a more detailed exposition of Epicurean ethics.

16 O'Keefe (2002) explores the reasons for the Cyrenaic rejection of eudaimonism and future concern.

17 Tsouna (1998) is the best book on the Cyrenaics' skepticism.

18 Sextus says that, while the skeptic has no beliefs about the way things *are*, e.g., that the honey is really sweet, he is able to live by following the appearances, e.g., that the honey *seems* sweet to him (*PH* I 19–22). How exactly to understand Sextus on this point is not itself clear: does following the appearances involve having some sort of (humdrum everyday) beliefs or not? Burnyeat and Frede (1997) is a collection of classic papers on this subject, and Eichorn (2014) a recent contribution that argues that scholars have made Pyrrhonian psychology and ethics unnecessarily alien and unattractive.

19 How much substantive overlap there is between the Pyrrhonian skeptics and their namesake is a vexed question. The best book on this question and on Pyrrho generally is Bett (2000). He concludes that Pyrrho himself was not a skeptic.

20 Thorsrud (2011) is a useful discussion of skeptical piety.

21 Thorsrud (2003) explores how Pyrrhonian skepticism challenges the near-consensus of Greek ethicists that our reason has a positive role to play in achieving happiness.

References

Annas, J. (1993) *The Morality of Happiness,* Oxford: Oxford University Press.
Annas, J. (1999) *Platonic Ethics, Old and New,* Ithaca: Cornell University Press.

Bett, R. (2000) *Pyrrho, his Antecedents, and his Legacy,* Oxford: Oxford University Press.

Burnyeat, M. and Frede, M. (1997) *The Original Sceptics: A Controversy,* Indianapolis, IN: Hackett.

Evans, M. (2004) "Can Epicureans Be Friends?" *Ancient Philosophy* 24: 407–424.

Eichorn, R. (2014) "How (Not) to Read Sextus Empiricus," *Ancient Philosophy* 34: 121–149.

Frede, D. (2006) "Pleasure and Pain in Aristotle's Ethics," in R. Kraut (ed.), *The Blackwell Guide to Aristotle's Nicomachean Ethics.* Malden: Blackwell, pp. 255–275.

Gosling, J.C.B. and Taylor, C.C.W. (1982) *The Greeks on Pleasure,* Oxford: Oxford University Press.

Moss, J. (2006) "Pleasure and Illusion in Plato," *Philosophy and Phenomenological Research* 72: 503–535.

O'Keefe, T. (2002) "The Cyrenaics on Pleasure, Happiness, and Future-Concern," *Phronesis* 47: 395–416.

O'Keefe, T. (2010) *Epicureanism,* Durham: Acumen.

Perry, R.B. (1914) "The Definition of Value," *Journal of Philosophy, Psychology and Scientific Methods* 11: 141–162.

Prichard, H.A. (1912) "Does Moral Philosophy Rest on a Mistake?" *Mind* 21: 21–37.

Purinton, J. (1993) "Epicurus on the *Telos,*" *Phronesis* 38: 281–320.

Rudebusch, G. (1999) *Socrates, Pleasure, and Value,* Oxford: Oxford University Press.

Sedley, D. (1998) "The Inferential Foundations of Epicurean Ethics," in S. Everson (ed.), *Ethics.* Cambridge: Cambridge University Press, pp. 129–150.

Sidgwick, H.E. (1907) *The Method of Ethics,* London: Macmillan and Company.

Striker, G. (1996) "Epicurean Hedonism," in her *Essays on Hellenistic Epistemology and Ethics,* Cambridge: Cambridge University Press, pp. 77–91.

Thorsrud, H. (2003) "Is the Examined Life Worth Living? A Pyrrhonian Alternative," *Apeiron* 36: 229–249.

Thorsrud, H. (2011) "Sextus Empiricus on Skeptical Piety," in D.E. Machuca (ed.), *New Essays on Ancient Pyrrhonism,* Leiden: Brill, pp. 91–111.

Tsouna, V. (1998) *The Epistemology of the Cyrenaic School,* Cambridge: Cambridge University Press.

Tsouna McKirahan, V. (1994) "The Socratic Origins of the Cynics and Cyrenaics," in P. Vander Waerdt (ed.), *The Socratic Movement,* Ithaca, NY: Cornell University Press, pp. 367–391.

Warren, J. (2002) *Epicurus and Democritean Ethics: An Archaeology of Ataraxia,* Cambridge: Cambridge University Press.

Warren, J. (2009) "Aristotle on Speusippus on Eudoxus on Pleasure," *Oxford Studies in Ancient Philosophy* 36: 249–281.

4

WELL-BEING AND CONFUCIANISM[1]

Richard Kim

Confucianism is an ethical tradition with ancient roots, spanning 2500 years of human civilization. Even today, it remains a *living* tradition, continuing to influence the habits, thoughts, and values of cultures and societies throughout the East. Its origin traces back to the teachings of Confucius or "Master Kong" 孔子 (551–479 BCE), who offered a profound ethical vision of the ideal society characterized by peaceful order and humane relationships.[2] The achievement of such a society, Confucius insisted, rested on following "the Way" (*dao*道)—the correct path of moral transformation—through active participation in rituals (or rites) and the fulfillment of social roles within the context of the family and community.

In this chapter I explore the accounts of well-being offered by two of the most influential Confucian philosophers, Mencius 孟子 (391–308 BCE) and Xunzi 荀子 (310–219 BCE), who understood themselves as extending and refining the ethical vision transmitted by Confucius.[3] Neither of them offered what we would nowadays call *theories* of well-being, and for this reason it is difficult to neatly place their accounts within the contemporary classification system of well-being that has developed over recent years, although, as we will see, they bear interesting connections to certain contemporary accounts.[4] Both thinkers affirmed that virtue, or, more precisely, virtuous activity, is constitutive of well-being. Because these early Confucians saw virtue as inseparable from human flourishing, substantial space will be devoted to discussing their accounts of virtue and moral development.

In addition to taking virtue as a fundamental component of well-being, both philosophers emphasized what we might call *the developmental aspect of the good life*, which takes well-being as consisting in the unfolding of a series of stages that manifests a proper trajectory. They affirmed that a life that goes best would involve a certain unifying narrative structure culminating in the achievement of sagehood, and would be marked by enduring positive emotional states that bear a striking resemblance to contemporary accounts of psychological happiness. The proposal that both virtue and the developmental structure of human lives play a significant role in well-being, and that their realization will be accompanied by a deep and lasting form of psychic fulfillment, are among the most interesting and significant contributions made by these early Chinese thinkers. Fleshing out these ideas will be the central objective of this chapter.

Both Mencius and Xunzi lived in a time and place remarkably different from contemporary Western society. It is thus not surprising that their aims would diverge significantly from the goals that regulate discussions found within the contemporary philosophical literature on well-being, dominated by the posing of theories, offering of counterexamples, and the modification of theories in light of those counterexamples. Instead, they offered discussions of well-being that were less theoretically directed, but rich in practical implications, regularly drawing upon observations of everyday life and the reservoir of common human experience to provide a realizable vision of human flourishing. Their writings reveal a practical orientation, a resolute attitude toward improving the conditions of their society, by providing insights into moral self-cultivation and human fulfillment that could be exemplified within the constraints of human psychology. Because their discussions constantly center on examining fundamental aspects of human experience, they may still offer insights and a fresh perspective that have been either ignored or underappreciated by contemporary philosophers. There is still much to learn from them.

The concept of well-being

If we are to investigate these early Confucians' accounts of well-being, we first need to begin by clarifying what we mean by the term "well-being."[5] This is especially important since "well-being" has been used by philosophers in a variety of ways, and furthermore it is not clear that there is any specific Chinese character or concept that corresponds to this term.[6] A cluster of concepts are sometimes called on to help elucidate the concept of well-being, such as the notions of "happiness," "self-interest," "good for," "good life," and "flourishing." Unfortunately, just how these various concepts, themselves often in need of elucidation, are linked to each other is a difficult issue that requires its own separate treatment. We can perhaps begin by noting that there are broader and narrower senses of well-being that admit of thicker or thinner specifications. The narrower senses of well-being will involve more substantive elements, while the broader senses of well-being will be characterized more thinly, carrying less substantive content. In what follows, I will use "well-being" in a broad sense that closely corresponds to the concept of "the good life," "flourishing," and the ancient Greek concept of *eudaimonia*. The concept of well-being that I seek to discuss is intimately tied to questions such as "what makes a life go well?" and "what kind of life would you want for those you love?"—questions that greatly concerned ancient Chinese philosophers.

One possible concern with construing the notion of well-being broadly might be that the wider concept does not concern *well-being*, but perhaps the most choiceworthy life or life highest in goodness or value.[7] But the early Confucians did not distinguish well-being from the good or most choiceworthy life in a way familiar to contemporary philosophers. Instead, they seemed to have implicitly affirmed that the life of virtue is the life that is best *for* us.[8] This lack of explicit distinction between the good or choiceworthy life and a narrower category of prudential value appears to mirror the beliefs of ancient Greek thinkers who used a single term *eudaimonia* to mark out not only the excellent or choiceworthy life, but also (more contentiously) a life that is good for us.[9] The fact that the concept of "well-being" in the modern sense—specifying an independent, non-moral prudential category of value—carried much less significance for these classical thinkers is an interesting point that merits careful investigation. One possible explanation is that these ancient philosophers had a much wider conception of moral goodness or virtue than contemporary philosophers, being less preoccupied by what we now see as strictly *moral* duties and more concerned with the everyday affairs of practical living. Seeing virtues as a broader range of qualities that are necessary for facing basic challenges confronting ordinary human lives makes it more plausible to think that virtues and basic prudential goods are closely bound together.

For Confucian thinkers, the virtues played a critical role in cultivating proper feelings and attitudes that are necessary for full participation in the life of the family and community, as well as regulating our interpersonal behavior in ways that would strengthen social bonds. And since on the Confucian view no prudentially good life could lack well-ordered, loving relationships or life within a stable community, there may have been less motivation to conceptually distinguish a life of virtue—especially embodying a Confucian, communal orientation—from a life high in prudential value. This point may be rendered more plausible once we appreciate the way in which both thinkers affirmed a deep connection between virtue and psychological happiness. Developing their accounts of well-being, therefore, will require explicating their accounts of moral development and the virtues, as well as the kind of psychic fulfillment that accompanies their conception of the good life.

Mencius: moral sprouts and nature fulfillment

Mencius was, after Confucius, the most historically influential philosopher of the early Confucian tradition. His writings explore a vast range of topics that ultimately aim at clarifying, extending, and refining the ethical teachings handed down from Confucius. To accomplish this, Mencius offers a complex account of human nature, and out of it develops a picture of moral self-cultivation that would lead us toward complete virtue and the achievement of a flourishing life.

Mencius advocates a robust, teleological conception of human nature, and insists that by properly developing certain incipient tendencies we find in our nature, we can achieve a flourishing life. In recent discussions, the view that well-being consists in the development and exercise of fundamental capacities inherent in human nature has been labeled "perfectionism" or "nature-fulfillment theory."[10] Mencius's account shares many important features of Aristotelian perfectionism—the most prominent form of perfectionism within the Western philosophical tradition—but it also diverges from it in significant and interesting ways. For example, while Aristotle sees rationality as the unique capacity that separates humans from other animals, Mencius takes the moral aspects of our nature as what makes us uniquely human; we are, on Mencius's view, best characterized as *moral* animals. I will return to some possible repercussions of Mencius's view of human nature below. Let us first fill in some of the details of Mencius's account of human nature.

Mencius is best known for his claim that "human nature is good," by which he does not naively mean that most humans lead morally good lives, but that all human beings possess certain dispositional traits or "sprouts" (*duan* 端) that are directed toward moral goodness. Here is how he describes it:

> we can see that if one is without the feeling of compassion, one is not human. If one is without the feeling of disdain, one is not human. If one is without the feeling of deference, one is not human. If one is without the feeling of approval and disapproval, one is not human.[11]

These four basic feelings or sensibilities constitute the core of our humanity and can be developed into genuine virtues:

> The feeling of compassion is the sprout of benevolence. The feeling of disdain is the sprout of righteousness. The feeling of deference is the sprout of propriety. The feeling of approval and disapproval is the sprout of wisdom. People having these four sprouts is like their having four limbs. To have these four sprouts, yet to claim that one is incapable [of virtue], is to steal from oneself.[12]

Mencius's claim concerning the goodness of human nature does not imply that all human beings possess completely virtuous characters, but that human beings are endowed with an innate capacity for certain moral feelings that can be cultivated into full-blown virtues. In support of this claim Mencius offered a variety of arguments.[13] The best known is a thought experiment involving a child about to fall into a well:

> Suppose someone suddenly saw a child about to fall into a well: anyone in such a situation would have a feeling of alarm and compassion—not because one sought to get in good with the child's parents, not because one wanted fame among one's neighbors and friends, and not because one would dislike the sound of the child's cries.[14]

By reflecting on this situation, Mencius argues, "we can see that if one is without the feeling of compassion, one is not human" (*Mengzi* 2A6). Although a detailed analysis of each of the four Mencian moral sensibilities and their corresponding virtues is beyond the scope of this chapter, what is important to note for our purposes is that Mencius takes the essence of what it is to be human to consist in those basic moral feelings that he understands as providing us with the fundamental capacity for becoming fully virtuous.[15]

Mencius's claim that human beings by nature possess these four moral sprouts is not meant to be a universally quantifiable statement such that, for every x, if x is a human being, then x has the four moral sprouts. Taking up his limb analogy, statements such as "human beings have two arms and two legs" are not ordinarily meant to apply to every human being, since taken in that sense they would be obviously false. Rather, they are claims that should be understood as picking out characteristic features that are constitutive of the life-form belonging to human beings as such, akin to claims like "owls see in the dark" or "wolves hunt in packs."[16]

Mencius believes that our moral capacities are rooted in our nature as human beings, and that becoming a virtuous agent is a matter of properly expanding those incipient moral tendencies through a process that he calls "extension" (*tui* 推).[17] By both broadening and strengthening these dispositional traits, we can fill them out and develop them into the four virtues of "benevolence" (*ren* 仁), righteousness (*yi* 義), propriety (*li* 裡), and wisdom (*zhi* 智). So, although our nature is directed toward the good, the achievement of moral perfection requires constant attention under suitable conditions that are conducive to moral growth. To illustrate this point Mencius draws upon a number of agricultural metaphors:

> In years of plenty, most young men are gentle; in years of poverty, most young men are violent. It is not that the potential that Heaven confers on them varies like this. They are like this because of what sinks and drowns their hearts. Consider barley. Sow the seeds and cover them. The soil is the same and the time of planting is also the same. They grow rapidly, and by the time of the summer solstice they have all ripened. Although there are some differences, these are due to the richness of the soil and to unevenness in the rain and in human effort.[18]

Even though the seeds contain the full potential of germinating into cultivated barley, the quality of the barley depends upon a range of external factors: richness of the soil, rain, and human effort. Similarly, although human beings carry incipient moral tendencies that can be cultivated into virtues, much depends on the environmental conditions as well as the attention and care put into their development. So, although Mencius accepts that human nature already provides us with the necessary equipment to achieve full virtue, he was quite aware of the significance of social conditions, as well as the critical importance of personal commitment and effort. Over

2000 years later and a world away, John Stuart Mill echoes a strikingly similar message, also with the use of an agricultural metaphor:

> Capacity for the nobler feelings is in most natures a very tender plant, easily killed, not only by hostile influences, but by mere want of sustenance; and in the majority of young persons it speedily dies away if the occupations to which their position in life has devoted them, and the society into which it has thrown them, are not favorable to keeping that higher capacity in existence.[19]

Despite acknowledging the variety of ways that moral development could be thwarted, Mencius and Mill are confident that, under the right social conditions, combined with the necessary time and effort, the development of our moral nature was all within the realm of practical possibility.

Although Mencius emphasizes the importance of the moral sprouts that are inherent in our nature, he affirms that our non-moral desires for pleasure, including our physical appetites for good food, warmth, and sex, are also fundamental aspects of our nature, and that as long as our desires are rightly ordered, the attainment of such pleasures contributes to our flourishing.[20] So for Mencius, the complete flowering of our nature as human beings not only involves the perfection of our moral capacities, but the satisfaction of our non-moral desires as well. Mencius, in other words, is no Stoic; he accepts that pleasure and the satisfaction of our basic appetites have a clear role to play within the economy of our nature.

But, although Mencius does not dismiss the prudential value of the pleasures arising from the satisfaction of our non-moral desires, he believes that a deeper, more fulfilling sort of enjoyment and psychic happiness arise from living virtuously:

> If one delights in them [the virtues] then they grow. If they grow, then how can they be stopped? If they cannot be stopped, then one does not notice one's feet dancing to them, one's hands swaying to them.[21]

> A gentleman regards the benevolence, righteousness, propriety, and wisdom that are based in his heart as his nature. These are clearly manifest in his life and demeanor. They fill his torso and extend through his four limbs. Though he says nothing, his four limbs express them.[22]

The enduring delight that Mencius draws attention to appears to arise from a form of satisfaction generated by the approval of one's own conduct, involving a wide range of possible behaviors, including ordinary acts of benevolence or the successful completion of a ritual.

What is emphasized in these passages is that the particular form of satisfaction and joy accompanying virtuous activities (and one's evaluative judgments about them) would also become manifested in the virtuous person's physical form. We can imagine a deep serenity conveyed in the virtuous person's countenance and bodily posture that is apt to be seen as the mark of an enduringly happy state, free of anxiety, and resting on a kind of composed surety about the direction of one's life: "the gentleman has a concern to the end of his life, but he does not have a morning's anxiety" (*Mengzi* 4B28.7). Although Mencius does not fully articulate the details of the virtuous person's mental state, these comments suggest that he saw joy and positive psychological states (embodied in one's physical form) as necessary concomitants of a good life.

By taking enjoyment as arising from virtuous activities, Mencius again shares the Aristotelian idea that pleasure necessarily follows from, and completes, virtuous activities. One significant difference, however, is that, while Aristotle holds that we come to enjoy virtuous activities for their own sake because of the inculcation of moral habits embedded within our developed second nature (the nature that arises from the influences of education and culture), Mencius takes our untutored first nature (consisting of innate, unacquired characteristic traits) as already partially constituted by moral desires, implying that the pleasures of a virtuous life would also be partly explained by the content of our basic, first nature.[23] By drawing a tight connection between our first nature and our moral sensibilities, Mencius's form of perfectionism may provide further resources for responding to one of the most common criticisms leveled at objectivist accounts of well-being (i.e., accounts that do not take prudential value as necessarily depending on an individual's mental state), which we may call the *alienation problem*.

The alienation problem arises from what many philosophers see as a necessary requirement that any plausible account of well-being must meet, sometimes called the "internalist requirement." As Connie Rosati describes the requirement, "an individual's good must not be something *alien*—it must be 'made for' or 'suited to' her."[24] One way of understanding the core idea is that something can be good for a person only if that person is able to care about it. According to the alienation problem, all objectivist accounts, especially those that take virtue or moral goodness as constituents of well-being, fail to satisfy the internalist requirement as it is always possible that any good or value can become divorced from the particular features of an agent's psychological makeup. But if Mencius is right, because the flourishing life is always connected to the desires of the heart that are partially constituted by moral desires, attaining virtue can never be completely alienated from an agent's psychology.

One likely reply will be that there are clear cases of individuals who are unconcerned about being virtuous and that Mencius's view is therefore simply at odds with our empirical understanding of human psychology. But Mencius could respond by claiming that human beings who lack moral feelings or desires are suffering from a deprivation, much like those who have lost the ability to see or hear. Just as we could still claim that seeing beautiful works of art or listening to sublime music is intrinsically good for human beings, even though some lack the ability to engage in such activities, Mencius could argue that virtuous activity is also intrinsically good for human beings even though some people lack moral desires.[25] This isn't to say that such activities are, as things stand, good for those individuals who are incapable of enjoying them, but that their incapacities are something that we can justifiably regret from a prudential point of view. Such individuals seem to be *missing out* on certain significant human goods.

Moreover, recent work in both evolutionary biology and empirical psychology seem to support Mencius's view that at least some of our moral sensibilities, empathy for example, is hardwired into us. These studies may further support the view that the lack of those moral sensibilities implies a diminished or incapacitated state, similar to being deprived of the capacity for sight or hearing.[26]

Xunzi: virtues and social environment

Like Mencius, Xunzi thought of himself as extending and refining the ethical tradition passed down from Confucius. He too aimed at strengthening the Confucian tradition by refuting alternative schools of thought that had become powerfully influential in early China. But Xunzi is perhaps best known for his disagreement with Mencius about the correct characterization of human nature, with Mencius claiming that "human nature is good" and Xunzi countering that "human nature is bad." In asserting this, Xunzi was denying, *contra* Mencius, that human nature has an inherent tendency toward goodness; our nature does not contain moral impulses that can be organically cultivated into reliable dispositions. According to Xunzi, human nature is a messy unstructured amalgam of generally selfish tendencies that, left on their own, would lead to self-destruction and the kind of society within the state of nature that Hobbes memorably described as "solitary, poor, nasty, brutish, and short."[27]

But despite the disagreement about the makeup of human nature, Xunzi's ethical views converge with those of Mencius in a number of significant ways. They both share, for example, a similar vision of what a well-ordered society would look like. They also agree, in substantial ways, about the content and role of the Confucian virtues and the qualities that a sage would exemplify.

Where their views diverge is in their characterizations of the process of moral self-cultivation, which in turn are rooted in different conceptions of the status and role of human nature. Xunzi believes that because our initial nature consists of disordered, generally self-absorbed tendencies, we should not develop it by drawing out its natural inclinations, but impose upon it, from the outside, those moral impulses that Mencius thought we can discover as internal to our nature. Rather than *build upon* our nature, Xunzi holds, we must *build into it* those moral dispositions and values that are necessary for moral cultivation. Fittingly, Xunzi draws upon craft metaphors to illustrate the processes of obtaining a virtuous character:

> A piece of wood as straight as a plumb line may [with soaking and shaping] be bent into a circle as true as any drawn with a compass, and once the wood has dried it will not straighten out again. The process of bending has made it that way. Thus, if [crooked] wood is placed against a straightening board it can be made straight; if metal is put to the grindstone, it can be sharpened; and if the gentleman studies widely and each day examines himself, his wisdom will become clear and his conduct without fault.[28]

Our moral character is an artefact much like a wheel or a knife and will only develop with conscious reflection and activity (Watson 1963: 169). Just as metal and wood do not carry within them an internal principle of change by which they naturally become knives or wheels, neither does human nature possess an internal moral principle through which it naturally develops moral dispositions.

This conception of human nature leads Xunzi to focus his attention on culture and the role of teachers, rituals, and tradition.[29] For, although by his lights we do not possess the kind of moral nature that Mencius posits, we can undergo a process of reformation to propel us out of the chaos, strife, and disorder that characterize our original, pre-moralized state. This process of reformation, which requires the practice of rituals (*li* 禮) under the guidance of a teacher, is characterized by different stages of moral development, starting from an uncultivated state driven by selfish tendencies, to becoming a "gentleman" (*junzi* 君子), culminating in the attainment of sagehood.[30] As one might expect, transition from a pre-moral state to sagehood requires a long, arduous process of self-cultivation, a process that depends on a number of distinct virtues.[31] Xunzi conceives of the virtues that would move us from the early stages of moral cultivation to the stage of being a gentleman as (borrowing Philippa Foot's terminology) "correctives" that help rectify those desires and tendencies that tend to lead us astray from correct feelings and actions; they presuppose the existence of misdirected passions that need restraint and redirection. Such virtues are especially important for the initial stages of moral development, but also play a significant role even after one becomes a gentleman. For, while the gentleman has developed reliable moral dispositions and has come to appreciate and value virtue for its own sake, he still carries certain wayward impulses that need to be tamed so that they do not draw him away from moral excellence.

These errant tendencies, however, do not apply to those who have reached sagehood; such enlightened individuals no longer need the corrective virtues that are required for the earlier stages of development. Instead, the sage will possess the virtue of "subtlety" (*wei* 微), which allows him to act effortlessly, with no interior discord. Because the sage's desires, emotions, and thoughts always track the good (*dao* 道), corrective virtues are simply unnecessary:

> True subtlety is the quality of the perfect man. What has he to do with strength of will, endurance, and fearfulness? A dull brightness shines about his exterior, and a clear brightness within him. The sage follows his desires, satisfies all his emotions . . . The benevolent man practices the Way through inaction; the sage practices the Way through nonstriving. The thoughts of the benevolent man are reverent; the thoughts of the sage are joyous.[32]

The sage's life and actions are in synch with his values, desires, and emotions. His actions are marked by "nonstriving," a mode of unforced, natural behavior—adorned with emotional fulfillment and joy. Xunzi's conception of the interior life of the sage shares a close affinity to Daniel Haybron's emotional state account of psychological happiness, one of the most powerful theories of happiness developed in recent years.[33] Haybron marks out three dimensions of happiness that correspond to three basic modes of emotional response he calls "endorsement," "engagement," and "attunement":

> At the most basic level will be responses concerning the individual's safety and security: for example, letting one's defenses down, making oneself fully at home in one's life—being in a state of utter *attunement* with one's life, we might say—as opposed to taking up a defensive stance. Next come responses relating to the individual's commitments to or *engagement* with her situation and activities: is it worth investing much effort in them, or would it be wiser to withdraw or disengage from them? Finally, there will be more or less explicit *endorsements* signifying that one's life is not just free of threat and worth pursuing enthusiastically, but positively good, containing things that are to be built upon sustained, repeated, or sought in the future—as, for example, when one has just achieved a goal or received a great benefit.[34]

While acknowledging the need for further discussion, we may for now observe that Xunzi's account of the sage's psychological states appears to capture all three dimensions of Haybron's account of happiness. The sage would surely *endorse* her mode of life since she sees it as following the path prescribed by the Way: "the thoughts of the sage are joyous" (Watson 1963: 137). Also apparent is *engagement* in her life and activities—a mode of active immersion in an activity resembling the process of *flow* described by Mihaly Csikszentmihalyi and a clear feature of the sagely life as captured by the mode of "nonstriving" that Xunzi describes.[35] Finally, the sage's life is marked by a "clear brightness" and a lack of "fearfulness," indicating an emotional state of confidence and inner peace, implying that she is "fully at home" in her life—qualities that Haybron explicitly marks out as fundamental aspects of *attunement*.[36]

We can note two reasons underlying Xunzi's view that the morally perfected life is also the most psychologically fulfilling. First, human desires tend to expand and multiply. Without deliberative effort and training, desires become increasingly unruly, causing not only ruptures in our social relationships, but also steadily increasing personal frustration. Only by transforming our character through the rituals can our desires become controlled so that we not only live according to the Way, but also optimize the satisfaction of our own desires (Watson 1963: 95). Second, Xunzi takes the life of virtue and participation in the rituals as the highest achievable good: "Therefore learning reaches its completion with the rituals, for they may be said to represent the highest point of the Way and its power" (Watson 1963: 20). A life centering on the practice of rituals and virtues can provide us with deeper and more profound sources of satisfaction and joy than alternative ways of living.

A key idea running through much of Xunzi's philosophical system is the adaptability of human beings. Despite the unruliness of our inborn tendencies, through pressure and time our desires and values can become reshaped, fitting us for a civilized life in society. Because Xunzi does not accept the existence of innate moral tendencies posited by Mencius, he stresses the importance of proper external conditions, especially surrounding oneself with the right kind of teachers that can provide correct guidance through the rituals. Xunzi is keenly aware of the impact that societal pressures have on us:

> [I]f a man associates with men who are not good, then he will hear only deceit and lies and will see only conduct that is marked by wantonness, evil, and greed. Then, although he is not aware of it, he himself will soon be in danger of severe punishment, for the environment he is subjected to will cause him to be in danger. An old text says, "If you do not know a man, look at his friends; if you do not know a ruler, look at his attendants." Environment is the important thing! Environment is the important thing![37]

Xunzi's emphasis on the ways in which our peers and our social environment affect our thoughts and behaviors has been reinforced by contemporary research in psychology and sociology, and provides us with reasons for exerting greater effort into investigating what Daniel Haybron has called "human prudential ecology"—the kinds of social environments under which human beings flourish[38] (Haybron 2008: 253–282). This is a topic that has attracted less attention within contemporary philosophy, perhaps because of a pervasive belief in modern liberal societies that Haybron calls *individualism*: "human beings tend to fare best when individuals have the greatest possible freedom to shape their lives according to their own priorities" (Haybron 2008: 255). The opposing view, *contextualism*, claims that we fare better in environments that, to some extent, nudge us toward certain goods and ways of living.

Confucianism unequivocally endorses *contextualism*. On the Confucian view, humans are social beings, susceptible to a variety of social influences; our individual identities are significantly constituted by an interlocking set of relationships formed within the family and society, and therefore, what is beneficial or harmful to us is importantly constituted also by the interests of those that come to inhabit our social domain.[39] Because we are ineradicably social creatures, Confucian thinkers would have been puzzled by an attempt to understand individual well-being that is severed from enquiries into flourishing families and communities. In contrast, contemporary philosophers working on well-being have tended to ignore how the nature of human relationships and our social environments are related to human flourishing, since, at best, they are thought only to provide us with knowledge of the necessary empirical conditions for achieving well-being. But if the human self, as the early Confucians believed, is partially constituted by those relationships we come to establish during the course of our lives, then it may turn out that any satisfying account of well-being must explain the relationships between well-being, family, and the community. Xunzi was especially well attuned to this issue, since many of his writings are directed toward understanding how to organize a society that achieves the common good. Recognizing that the structure and values of one's society play an indispensable role in providing suitable conditions for human flourishing, Xunzi spent considerable time and effort in discussing the kind of society that would best promote a flourishing society, putting special emphasis on the need for hierarchical divisions and clearly demarcated roles relative to each station. A well-functioning, harmonious society, Xunzi believes, requires the fulfillment of rituals and moral obligations attached to one's particular station.

From the perspective of modern liberalism, Xunzi's view will undoubtedly strike many as excessively rigid, perhaps even inherently unjust. But even granting that Xunzi's particular conception of social hierarchy is, to borrow a concept from Bernard Williams, a merely *notional* possibility (Williams 1985: 178–179)—unrealizable for those occupying modern societies— social distinctions continue to pervade modern life, and may simply be an inveterate feature of human societies.[40] Moreover, a case could be made that certain hierarchical values such as respect for the elderly (related to the Confucian value of "filial piety" or *xiao* 孝) are still worth maintaining. Such reflections should at least make us question whether all hierarchical divisions are inherently problematic, and if they are not, which of them may still be worth preserving.

The teleological structure of well-being

I now turn to a key idea that runs through the discussions of both Mencius and Xunzi that connects back to certain features of the good life discussed earlier: the significance of the developmental structure of human life. While a number of philosophers have claimed that the trajectory or the shape of one's life matters for well-being, their discussions have mostly focused on why a life that improves over time is higher in well-being than a life that declines over time.[41] David Velleman and Douglas Portmore have claimed that a life that goes uphill is better than one that goes downhill (all things being equal) just in case, and because, an uphill life involves the redemption of earlier (bad) events in one's life, thereby adding overall meaning to one's life story. I believe that both Mencius and Xunzi would agree with Velleman and Portmore about the significance of redemptive meaning, but I also think that they would emphasize what I will call the *teleological structure of well-being*. This aspect of well-being takes seriously the idea that, in order for our lives to realize the kind of narrative meaning endorsed by Velleman and Portmore, they must be correctly oriented toward ends that have objective value. It is this trajectory toward proper end (or ends) that provides the unifying thread necessary for narrative significance.

As pointed out earlier, both Mencius and Xunzi hold that the best human life culminates in sagehood; becoming a fully virtuous person is the proper end of all our strivings. But despite the fact that they disagree about the process of moral development through which we may attain this end, what they clearly accept is that there is a certain developmental trajectory that must be followed if we are to achieve flourishing lives. On their views, this trajectory takes its particular shape from the psychological, bodily, and environmental conditions that determine the natural rhythms and cycles of human life. Such conditions impose certain constraints on the structure of the process of self-cultivation. One point emphasized by both Mencius and Xunzi is that life unfolds through a series of stages, and that what unifies these stages is the continual progression toward virtue and sagehood; it is the movement toward virtue that provides flourishing lives with their narrative unity. The notion of life-stages is important, and is effectively captured by the different metaphors invoked by our two Confucian thinkers. Recall Mencius' agricultural metaphor for self-cultivation. A good farmer must work with those natural tendencies inherent within the seeds in order to provide them with the necessary care and attention for development. This requires that she understands the surrounding environment, for example, the salinity of the soil and the climate patterns of the region. For Mencius, our moral development also requires a long, slow, and steady process, which takes those natural moral tendencies found in our nature and guides them toward virtue by providing the proper conditions for growth. Just like the maturation and growth of barley seeds, the development of our moral sprouts spans a number of distinct stages, ideally culminating in the achievement of a fully virtuous character. These stages of development are structured by the tendencies of our nature and so it is important to pay attention to the characteristic features of a particular stage of moral development because what is necessary for one stage may not be necessary for another. This point is illustrated by the following parable told by Mencius:

> Do not be like the man from Song. Among the people of the state of Song there was a farmer who, concerned lest his sprouts not grow, pulled on them. Obliviously, he returned home and said to his family, "Today I am worn out. I helped the sprouts to grow." His son rushed out and looked at them. The sprouts were withered.[42]

This brief but insightful parable draws attention to the importance of understanding the natural stages of development and why failing to understand the particular needs relative to each step can have disastrous consequences. Just as the farmer must understand the natural sequence by which his sprouts tend to grow, we must also understand the natural sequence by which we must cultivate our moral sprouts.

Now recall Xunzi's employment of craft metaphors: the molding of clay into vessels, the carving of wood into utensils, and the sharpening of metal into blades. As noted earlier, these metaphors focus on the way in which our moral sensibilities are produced not out of the internal resources of our nature, but by implantation through artifice and design. Nevertheless, even though Xunzi does not believe that there are natural stages of moral growth fixed by the moral sprouts of our nature, he still holds that there are certain steps to moral development that must occur for the achievement of sagehood. Reflect on the process of forging a blade. A blacksmith forging a blade out of metal begins by heating the blade at a high temperature, and then goes on to shape the metal on an anvil with a hammer. This is followed by the process of steady grinding to provide the blade its sharpness, which is then followed by a further heating phase and brought to completion through a final stage of grinding. Xunzi believed that, in a similar way, moral development must occur in a step-by-step process, which begins with the recitation of the *Classics* and introduction into rituals (Watson 1963: 19). Through study and the repeated performances of rituals one's character begins to take on a determinate shape, and as it gradually becomes ordered toward righteous behavior, the agent continues to move forward to subsequent stages of moral development, ending with the achievement of sagehood.

So while Xunzi did not accept, as Mencius did, that our nature carved out the proper developmental path through which we can come to be fully virtuous, he did believe that our initial endowment and the process of cultivation through the correct rituals (a process discovered by the ancient sages) determined the sequence of development that must be traversed to reach the final end of the sagely life.

For both early Confucian philosophers, the correct understanding of well-being could not be separated from the teleological end (i.e., sagehood) that our lives ought to be directed toward; any evaluation of a person's well-being needed to be made in light of how well her life was moving toward her final end. Their focus was not on what some philosophers call *synchronic well-being,* which concerns how well a life is going at any particular moment in time, but rather, *diachronic well-being*, concerning one's life as a whole (or longer stretches of one's life). Moreover, they both accepted the existence of norms that would regulate this developmental process, whether they were grounded in facts about our nature (Mencius) or culture (Xunzi). The weight that was attached to the success of one's life as a whole may explain why the Confucian thinkers did not put much effort into explicating what constitutes a person's good at a time, an issue central to most contemporary philosophical discussions of well-being. On their behalf, we could offer a tentative account of synchronic well-being that takes what constitutes a person's well-being at a time as the realization of those goods that help contribute to (or are constitutive of) the sagely life. But given their focus on the developmental stages of the flourishing life, they may have believed that offering a unified account of what ultimately constitutes a person's well-being at a time may not be possible, as in their views what is good for a person at a time is wholly dependent on the particular life-stage that one occupies. What is good for a developing child, they may have insisted, is significantly different from what is good for a mature, healthy adult, which is also importantly different from what is good for an elderly adult facing the final stages of his life.[43]

Attaching so much weight to a particular substantive end (sagehood), may seem to require an unduly restrictive conception of well-being. Some of this worry may be alleviated by reminding ourselves of the glowing, *attuned* psychological life of those who reach sagehood. Some may want to question this connection between virtue and psychological fulfillment on empirical grounds. But some recent empirical studies suggest that those who engage in charitable activities, and (importantly) *do it for the sake of benefiting others*, enjoy higher levels of psychological happiness.[44] Obviously, such research is far from demonstrating that Mencius and Xunzi were right about the connection between sagehood and psychological fulfillment. But even if one rejects the particular substantive end proposed by both Mencius and Xunzi, their views capture the sense that any attractive account of well-being needs to accommodate the intuitive idea that for a life to go well it must instantiate a meaningful narrative structure that needs to appeal to a notion of a worthwhile end or set of ends that properly organizes one's life.[45]

Conclusion

A number of philosophers, most notably Charles Taylor, have argued that a chronic feature of modern life is a sense of malaise, characterized by "loss of meaning, the fading of horizons" arising from a breakdown of traditional, hierarchical order that "gave meaning to the world and to the activities of social life" (Taylor 1991: 3). What the older system provided us, according to Taylor, is "a horizon of significance"—a background of intelligibility necessary for imbuing our lives and activities with meaning. The Confucian conception of human flourishing, with its strong emphasis on a robust, teleological moral order that can only be achieved within the larger context of one's family and community, perhaps provides a way of avoiding the kind of modern malaise described by Taylor; it offers a way of giving one's life a purpose or direction, a background of horizon that is crucial for attaching a sense of meaning to one's life:

> [R]ites are the highest achievement of the Way of man. Therefore, those who do not follow and find satisfaction in rites may be called people without direction, but those who do follow and find satisfaction in them are called men of direction.[46]

Further reading

B. Schwartz (1985) *The World of Thought of Ancient China* (Cambridge, MA: Harvard University Press) and A.C. Graham (1989) *Disputers of the Tao: Philosophical Argument in Ancient China* (Chicago: Open Court) both provide a comprehensive and stimulating overview of Confucianism and other philosophical traditions in early China. For those interested in virtue ethics in the Confucian tradition, see J. Tiwald (2010) "Confucianism and Virtue Ethics: Still a Fledgling in Chinese and Comparative Philosophy," *Comparative Philosophy* 1(2): 55–63 (a brief, but useful, look at recent developments in Confucian virtue ethics) and S. Angle and M. Slote (eds.) (2013) *Virtue Ethics and Confucianism* (New York: Routledge), a volume that will prove especially useful for contemporary philosophers new to the field of Confucian ethics. The philosophical literature on well-being is already vast and growing, but for two indispensable works see L.W. Sumner (1996) *Welfare, Happiness, and Ethics* (Oxford: Oxford University Press) and D. Haybron (2008) *The Pursuit of Unhappiness: The Elusive Psychology of Well-Being* (Oxford: Oxford University Press).

Notes

1 This work was supported by a grant from the Academy of Korean Studies funded by the Korean Government (MEST) (AKS-2011-AAA-2102). For written comments on this chapter I would like to thank Youngsun Back, Anne Baril, Loy Hui Chieh, Guy Fletcher, Eirik Harris, Philip J. Ivanhoe, Christopher Rice, Justin Tiwald, and Xueying Wang.

2 Here and throughout this chapter I use the term "Confucianism" to refer to an ethical tradition founded on the teachings and writings of Confucius and his followers as represented in the *Analects* and other early Confucian texts such as the *Mengzi*, the *Xunzi*, the *Doctrine of the Mean*, and the *Great Learning*. As this chapter primarily aims to examine substantive philosophical views, I will not attempt to defend this construal of "Confucianism," while acknowledging that some sinologists and historians of thought will contest this usage.

3 I leave aside the *Analects* of Confucius since Mencius and Xunzi provide more systematically developed accounts of human flourishing that extend the core ideas found in the *Analects*.

4 The most widely discussed classification of well-being theories is given by Parfit (1984: 493–502). For more recent taxonomies see Fletcher (2013) and Woodard (2013).

5 Most contemporary philosophers use "well-being" and "welfare" interchangeably. I will stick to "well-being" in this chapter because it seems more apt in capturing the phenomenon of "the good life" or "flourishing" that will be the focus of this discussion. For an analysis of the concept of well-being, see Campbell (2013).

6 One possible candidate might be *li*利, commonly translated as "profit" or "benefit," but because for the early Confucians this term is substantively tied to certain goods such as material wealth or power, it cannot be equivalent to "well-being," which is a more formal concept that leaves open what substantively constitutes a person's interest.

7 See Haybron (2008: Chapter 8), and Heathwood (2010: 653–654). Baril (2014) also takes the concept of *eudaimonia* as referring not to well-being but to the most choiceworthy life.

8 Some may want to argue that they even explicitly believed that the virtuous life is good for us because they argued that "profit" (*li*) would be a corollary of the life of virtue. But as argued above (fn. 6), we should not confuse *li* with the notion of "good for."

9 For an argument that Aristotle understood the *eudaimon* life as the prudentially best life, see Lebar and Russell (2013: 56–58). But for an opposing view, see Lawrence (2008). Baril (2014) argues that the concept of *eudaimonia* is distinct from the concept of well-being.

10 For an articulation and defense of perfectionism about well-being, see Kraut (2007). While Kraut himself eschews this label, and calls his view "developmentalism," it closely fits the description of perfectionism given above. It should also be noted that I'm taking the terms "perfectionism" and "nature-fulfillment theory" as equivalent as this is how they are often used within contemporary philosophy, although it seems plausible that a well-being account that is based on the development and exercise of the virtues that does not rely on human nature could also count as a form of perfectionism.

11 *Mengzi* 2A6. All translations of the *Mengzi* (Mencius) are from Van Norden (2008).

12 *Mengzi* 2A6.

13 Philip J. Ivanhoe classifies these arguments as "indications of childhood," "spontaneous giveaway," "testimonials," and "thought experiments." See Ivanhoe (2002b): 39–40.

14 *Mengzi* 2A6.

15 For more in-depth analyses of Mencius's conception of human nature and the virtues, see Shun (1997), Ivanhoe (2002b), and Van Norden (2007).

16 Those familiar with the works of Philippa Foot and Michael Thompson will recognize these statements as what they call "Aristotelian categoricals" or "natural-historical judgments." See Foot (2001: Chapter 2), and Thompson (2008: Part I).

17 "Extension" (*tui* 推) is a technical concept in Mencius's philosophy that has engendered much controversy. See Shun (1989), Ihara (1991), Van Norden (1991), Ivanhoe (2002a), Wong (2002), and McRae (2011).

18 *Mengzi* 6A7. Philip Ivanhoe has drawn attention to the significance of agricultural metaphors in Mencius's philosophy in a number of papers. For an especially lucid and insightful overview of Mencius's philosophy and the role of agricultural metaphors, see Ivanhoe (2000: 15–23).

19 Mill (1998: Chapter 2).

20 This position is also supported by Graham (2002: 30–32). But it should be emphasized that Mencius did think of our natural desires as hierarchically ordered in terms of their normative significance, and that the moral desires clearly take precedence over the non-moral desires. See *Mencius* 6A14–15.

21 *Mengzi* 4A27.2.

22 *Mengzi* 7A21.4.

23 This point is supported by *Mengzi* 6A7, in which Mencius compares our desire for order and righteousness with our desires for good food, beauty, and music: "Hence, order and righteousness delight our hearts like meat delights our mouths."

24 Rosati (1996: 298). See also Railton (1986). For arguments against internalism about well-being, see Sarch (2011).

25 This line of argument is taken by Lebar and Russell (2013: 59–66). Mencius would also need to provide a more detailed argument to defend the perfectionist account of well-being, for example, by showing why the exercise of those capacities that are essential or fundamental to human nature is good for human beings.

26 The moral psychologist Jonathan Haidt, for example, has argued for an evolutionary psychological foundation for our basic moral values. See Haidt (2012). The primatologist Frans de Waal has also argued for the evolutionary origins of morality, by appealing to the existence of many proto-moral traits shared by primates. See de Waal (2009). The arguments of both Haidt and de Waal help support the idea that our moral capacities have evolutionary roots and are therefore deeply embedded within our nature, a view that in turn may help lend support to Mencius's claims about the moral sprouts.

27 Xunzi does, however, countenance certain other-directed desires such as the affection for one's kin. But even these affections, while not inherently selfish, are not naturally directed toward goodness since without effort and proper guidance they can easily move us to act badly. For more discussion on this aspect of Xunzi's thought, see Hutton (2000: 229–232).

28 Watson (1963: 15). For translations of Xunzi's writings I will use Burton Watson's *Xunzi: Basic Writings* (Columbia: Columbia University, 1963). All references include the page number of Watson's translation.

29 David Nivison speculates that the rituals were slowly developed through trial and error and were applied to society by the sage-kings who sought to eliminate the disorder and violence that gripped the world. See Nivison (2000).

30 Here I use the term "gentleman" to translate *junzi* (君子) as I think it is most faithful to the original meaning of the Chinese character. Of course, this raises the point that Xunzi, as well as Mencius, both held a narrow vision of who could attain sagehood, and accepted certain patriarchal values deeply embedded within the culture of their time. However, I do believe that we can decouple such attitudes from their general moral theory of self-cultivation, in the way that we can decouple Aristotelian ethics from Aristotle's views about the biological basis of women as defective men.

31 See Schofer (2000) for a more detailed discussion of the individual virtues found in Xunzi's writings.

32 Watson (1963: 137).

33 Haybron (2008). Haybron's "emotional state theory" of happiness is much too complex and subtle to be given a full treatment here. Here I only briefly identify some key features of his account that I believe connect with Xunzi's account of the sage's interior life.

34 Haybron (2008: 111–112).

35 The link between *flow* and *engagement* is noted by Haybron (2008: 115). See Csikszentmihalyi (1990) for an account of "flow."

36 Haybron (2008: 115–117).

37 Watson (1963: 174).

38 The situational sensitivity of human behavior has been especially emphasized by Doris (2002) and Harman (2000).

39 These points are also explored in Ivanhoe (2013: 61–62).

40 Haidt (2012) argues that our capacity to value hierarchical divisions has been implanted in us through evolutionary forces, and may, therefore, be an ineradicable feature of human societies.

41 See Glasgow (2013), Portmore (2007), Velleman (2000), and Slote (1983) for accounts of what Glasgow calls the *shape-of-a-life phenomenon*, that a life that goes better over time is better than one that declines,

even if the total amount of enjoyment in both lives are equal. However, Feldman (2004) and Kahneman (2000) deny the existence of the phenomenon altogether.

42 *Mengzi* 2A2.

43 This point is developed in Kauppinen (2009).

44 For a lucid and philosophically informed examination of these studies, see Tiberius (2015: 178–182).

45 In an insightful paper, Antti Kauppinen offers a rich account of well-being that takes seriously the importance of narrative meaning within a teleological structure. In my view both Mencius's and Xunzi's accounts of well-being meet most of Kauppinen's conditions for a life that goes well. See Kauppinen (2012). Alasdair MacIntyre has also stressed the importance of maintaining a narrative unity for one's life in his most famous work, *After Virtue*. See MacIntyre (1981: Chapter 15).

46 Watson (1963: 99).

References

Baril, A. (2014) "Eudaimonia in Contemporary Virtue Ethics," in S.V. Hooft (ed.) *The Handbook of Virtue Ethics*, Durham: Acumen.

Campbell, S. (2013) "An Analysis of Prudential Value," *Utilitas* 25(03): 334–354.

Csikszentmihalyi, M. (1990) *Flow: The Psychology of Optimal Experience*, New York: Harper Perennial.

De Waal, F. (2009) *Primates and Philosophers*, Princeton: Princeton University Press.

Doris, J. (2002) *Lack of Character: Personality and Moral Behavior.* Cambridge: Cambridge University Press.

Feldman, F. (2004), *Pleasure and the Good Life: Concerning the Nature, Varieties, and Plausibility of Hedonism*, Oxford: Oxford University Press.

Fletcher, G. (2013) "A Fresh Start for the Objective-List Theory of Well-Being," *Utilitas* 25(02): 206–220.

Foot, P. (2001) *Natural Goodness,* New York: Oxford University Press.

Glasgow, J. (2013) "The Shape of a Life and the Value of Loss and Gain," *Philosophical Studies* 162(3): 665–682.

Graham, A.C. (2002) "The Background of the Mencian Theory of Human Nature," in X. Liu and P.J. Ivanhoe (eds.) *Essays on the Moral Philosophy of Mengzi,* Indianapolis: Hackett Publishing Company.

Haidt, J. (2012) *The Righteous Mind: Why Good People Are Divided by Politics and Religion,* New York: Pantheon.

Harman, G. (2000) "The Nonexistence of Character Traits," *Proceedings of the Aristotelian Society* 100(1): 223–226.

Haybron, D. (2008) *The Pursuit of Unhappiness,* New York: Oxford University Press.

Heathwood, C. (2010) "Welfare," in J. Skorupski (ed.) *Routledge Companion to Ethics*, London: Routledge.

Hutton, E. (2000) "Does Xunzi Have a Consistent Theory of Human Nature?" in T.C. Kline III and P.J. Ivanhoe (eds.) *Virtue, Nature and Moral Agency in the Xunzi*, Indianapolis: Hackett Publishing Company.

Ihara, C. (1991) "David Wong on Emotions in Mencius," *Philosophy East and West* 41(1): 1–27.

Ivanhoe, P.J. (2000) "Mengzi" in *Confucian Moral Self Cultivation*, Rev. 2nd ed. Indianapolis: Hackett, pp. 15–28.

Ivanhoe, P.J. (2002a) "Confucian Self Cultivation and Mengzi's Notion of Extension," in X. Liu and P.J. Ivanhoe (eds.) *Essays on the Moral Philosophy of Mengzi*, Indianapolis: Hackett Publishing Company.

Ivanhoe, P.J. (2002b) *Ethics in the Confucian Tradition: The Thought of Mencius and Wang Yang-ming*, rev. 2nd ed. Indianapolis: Hackett Publishing Company.

Ivanhoe, P.J. (2013) "Virtue Ethics and the Chinese Tradition," in D. Russell (ed.) *The Cambridge Companion to Virtue Ethics*, Cambridge: Cambridge University Press.

Kahneman, D. (2000) "New Challenges to the Rationality Assumption," in D. Kahneman and T. Tversky (eds.) *Choices, Values, and Frames*, New York: Russel Sage.

Kauppinen, A. (2009) "Working Hard and Kicking Back: The Case for Diachronic Perfectionism," *Journal of Ethics and Social Policy* 1–10.

Kauppinen, A. (2012) "Meaningfulness and Time," *Philosophy and Phenomenological Research* 84(2): 345–377.

Kraut, R. (2007) *What is Good and Why: The Ethics of Well-Being*, Cambridge: Harvard University Press.

Lawrence, G. (2008) "Is Aristotle's Function Argument Fallacious? Part 1, Groundwork," *Philosophical Inquiry* 31(1–2): 191–224.

Lebar, M. and Russell, D. (2013) "Well-Being and Eudaimonia: A Reply to Haybron," in J. Peters (ed.) *Aristotelian Ethics in Contemporary Perspectives*, New York: Routledge.

MacIntyre, A. (1981) *After Virtue*, Notre Dame, IN: University of Notre Dame Press.

McRae, E. (2011) "The Cultivation of Moral Feelings and Mengzi's Method of Extension," *Philosophy East and West* 61(4).

Mill, J.S. (1998) *Utilitarianism*, Oxford: Oxford University Press.

Nivison, D. (2000) "Xunzi and Zhuangzi," in T.C. Kline III and P.J. Ivanhoe (eds.) *Virtue, Nature and Moral Agency in the Xunzi*, Indianapolis: Hackett Publishing Company.

Parfit, D. (1984) *Reasons and Persons,* Oxford: Oxford University Press.

Portmore, D. (2007) "Welfare, Achievement, and Self-Sacrifice," *Journal of Ethics and Social Philosophy,* 2(2): 1–28.

Railton, P. (1986) "Facts and Values," *Philosophical Topics* 14(2): 5–31.

Rosati, C. (1996) "Internalism and the Good for a Person," *Ethics* 106(2): 297–326.

Sarch, A. (2011) "Internalism About a Person's Good: Don't Believe it," *Philosophical Studies* 154(2): 161–184.

Schofer, J. (2000) "Virtues in Xunzi's Thought," in T.C. Kline III and P.J. Ivanhoe (eds.) *Virtue, Nature and Moral Agency in the Xunzi*, Indianapolis: Hackett Publishing Company.

Shun, K. (1989) "Moral Reasons in Confucian Ethics," *Journal of Chinese Philosophy* 16(3–4): 317–343.

Shun, K. (1997) "Mencius on Jen-Hsing." *Philosophy East & West* 47(1): 1–20.

Slote, M. (1983) "Goods and Lives," in M. Slote (ed.) *Goods and Virtues*, Oxford: Clarendon Press.

Taylor, C. (1991) *The Ethics of Authenticity*, Cambridge, MA: Harvard University Press.

Thompson, M. (2008) *Life and Action: Elementary Structures of Practice and Practical Thought*, Cambridge, MA: Harvard University Press.

Tiberius, V. (2015) *Moral Psychology: A Contemporary Introduction*, New York: Routledge.

Van Norden, B.W. (1991) "Kwong-loi Shun on Moral Reasons in Mencius," *Journal of Chinese Philosophy* 18(4): 353–370.

Van Norden, B.W. (2007) *Virtue Ethics and Consequentialism in Early Chinese Philosophy*, Cambridge: Cambridge University Press.

Van Norden, B.W. (2008) (ed.) *Mengzi, With Selections from Traditional Commentaries*, Indianapolis: Hackett Publishing Company.

Velleman, J.D. (2000) "Well-Being and Time," in J.D. Velleman (ed.) *The Possibility of Practical Reason*, Oxford: Clarendon Press.

Watson, B. (1963) *Xunzi: Basic Writings*, Columbia: Columbia University Press.

Williams, B. (1985) *Ethics and the Limits of Philosophy,* London: Fontana.

Wong, D. (2002) "Reasons and Analogical Reasoning in Mengzi," in X. Liu and P.J. Ivanhoe (eds.) *Essays on the Moral Philosophy of Mengzi*, Indianapolis: Hackett Publishing Company.

Woodard, C. (2013) "Classifying Theories of Welfare," *Philosophical Studies* 165(3): 787–803.

5

WELL-BEING AND DAOISM

Justin Tiwald

Daoism is one of the great intellectual and philosophical forces in China, originating in the classical period and attracting millions of adherents for more than two millennia, without pause and with no end in sight.[1] The traditional version of Chinese history holds that its two founding philosophers were Laozi 老子 (fl. sixth century BCE) and Zhuangzi 莊子 (fl. fourth century BCE), the authors of the *Daodejing* 道德經 (also Romanized as *Tao Te Ching*) and the *Zhuangzi* (also Romanized as *Chuang Tzu*), respectively. Its influence has been tremendous, not least because the East Asian form of Buddhism most familiar to the larger world today—Zen, Seon, or Chan Buddhism—is largely a hybrid system that blends Daoist views and concepts with Buddhist metaphysics and soteriology. Historically, much of the appeal of Daoist philosophy lay in its compelling vision of human well-being, which, broadly speaking, has been understood as a life relatively free of attachments and deeply in tune with spontaneous, unselfconscious dispositions and inclinations. As we will see, this is only a general description for diverse views of finer grain that can be found in specific texts and passages, but it is enough to glimpse what is distinctive and philosophically interesting about them.

For many centuries it has been customary to treat the *Daodejing* as a single-authored work. It has also been customary to call both the texts and their purported authors "Daoist," suggesting that they belong to a single school of thought or philosophical lineage. In point of fact, the *Daodejing* (like the *Zhuangzi*) was pulled from multiple, probably like-minded sources, and it is doubtful that the authors of either text self-identified as Daoists, or even saw themselves as belonging to a school or tradition that spanned across both textual traditions.[2] There are some notable differences in the aims of the two texts. Much of the *Daodejing* reads as a call to social and political reform, aiming to reinstate what Philip J. Ivanhoe has described as a "primitive agrarian utopia" (Ivanhoe 2002: xxiv). The core chapters of the *Zhuangzi* show little interest in social and political reform and instead recommend a kind of personal, individual liberation within the social structures and obligations that one has inherited.[3] The *Daodejing* prescribes a life spent in pursuit of basic, naturally achievable goods that require a minimum of training or education. In contrast, the *Zhuangzi* recommends a way of life which, however simple, we can only achieve through a great deal of practice, habituation, and intellectual refinement (Kohn 1992: 57–58).

Still, there are reasons to discuss both texts together here. In terms of their historical influence they have operated as something of a unified force; reflective people who found one attractive have typically found the other attractive as well, and many have aimed to live in ways that they saw as consistent with both. Both propose that a certain kind of unselfcon-sciousness is a major component of well-being, most famously as a form of "nonaction" or *wúwéi* 無為 (also translated as "effortless action" and "nonpurposive action"). And both share a common cause against ways of life they construe as artificial, perhaps in distinctive senses. In what follows I will discuss each of the two Daoist classics in turn, describing their views about well-being and the basis of those views. In the course of doing so, I will discuss some of the implications of their views in terms familiar to contemporary welfare theorists, and describe Daoist treatments of major themes that they address more systematically, including the relationships between well-being and nonaction, desire fulfillment, skepticism, and (for Zhuangzi) death.

Well-being in the *Daodejing*

To describe the text very roughly, the *Daodejing* comprises poetic and often pithy remarks that extol the simple life, propose limits to human knowledge, and point to a cosmic force called "the Way" (or "Dao" 道).[4] It presents at least two forms of life as good for people: the first is the primitive agrarian utopia mentioned in the introduction, meant at minimum for ordinary people and subjects of states; the second is a kind of sagehood that consists in having the right understanding of the Way and its implications, and an ability to influence others accordingly. One could be well off if one successfully adopts either form, but on one plausible reading, being a sage is preferable only in nonideal circumstances, when one hasn't had the benefit of growing up in a society without war, education, and profit seeking. In any case, it is abundantly clear that the simple life of those living in the ideal agrarian society is an exceedingly good life for those who have it. Moreover, this is largely because those who live this way are well off—because it contributes tremendously to their welfare—whereas justifying the life of the sage might require appeals to independent ethical or religious values. For these reasons I will focus on theory of welfare implicit in the *Daodejing*'s primitive agrarian utopia.

According to Ivanhoe, the primitive socio-political order that the *Daodejing* idealizes is "a low-tech, highly dispersed society of independent village communities in which people found and were satisfied with simple pleasures" (Ivanhoe 2002: xxiv). Probably the most vivid and memorable description of this society is in Chapter 80 of the text.

> Reduce the size of the state;
> Lessen the population.
> Make sure that even though there are labor-saving tools, they are
> never used.
> Make sure that the people look on death as a weighty matter and
> never move to distant places.
> Even though they will have armor and weapons, they will have no
> reason to deploy them.
> Make sure that people return to the use of the knotted cord.[5]
> Make their food savory,
> Their clothes fine,
> Their houses comfortable.
> Make them find happiness in their ordinary customs.
> Then even though the neighboring states are within sight of each other,
> Even though they can hear the sounds of each other's dogs and chickens,
> Their people will grow old and die without ever having visited one another.[6]

There are many striking recommendations here. Probably the most astonishing is that the author urges a great degree of ignorance. The people are to be kept illiterate (keeping their records with "knotted cords" rather than writing). They are not to visit other communities, even those within earshot of their homes. Perhaps they have labor-saving tools on hand, but they are not to use them, and one suspects that they are not to invent or seek out new ones. Notably, the chapter countenances some common human desires and not others. People rightly indulge their desires for fine clothes and savory food, but should not avail themselves of tools that could save them time and unnecessary toil. It might also be significant that the text does not account for the well-being of the people solely in terms of a single subjective state like happiness or pleasure. Happiness is just one good among others, alongside comfort and consuming savory food.

There are also some recommendations that would have stood out more prominently for the chapter's original audience. One is an inclination toward pacifism.[7] States in the agrarian utopia lack the expansionist ambitions that invariably lead to wars of conquest. The second is that ordinary citizens give more weight to self-preservation than to achieving wealth or glory. This might suggest that they favor one conception of well-being over another, according to which long life contributes a great deal more to one's welfare than fame or an abundance of material goods (so much that it would rarely be worth risking the former for the sake of the latter). It might also suggest that they put a higher premium on welfare than their nonutopian counterparts, regarding well-being as a greater or more central good than nonwelfarist (ethical?) goods like glory, all things considered.

The Daodejing on desires

Perhaps the most theoretical and generalizable remarks about welfare in the *Daodejing* have to do with what might be called *acquired* desires. We can think of desires as falling on a spectrum between those that arise spontaneously from ourselves (desires that are "natural" or, to use the parlance of the *Daodejing*, "self-so" [*zìrán* 自然]) and desires that come about because of the novel effects of external things, whether those things be material objects or living creatures. Hunger is a good example of the former sort of desire; a craving for some flashy, faddish electronic device is a good example of the latter. The most influential commentator on the text, Wang Bi 王弼 (226–249 CE), suggests a distinction between desires that serve one's own needs and those that "make oneself a servant" (*yìjǐ* 役己) of external things (Wang 1965: ch. 12). Acquired desires are usually to the detriment of the desirer's well-being; satisfying them has little inherent value and pursuing them tends to lead to greater frustration and conflict. Of course, many desires fall somewhere between these extremes. For instance, we have desires whose conditions for gratification more or less map on to those of our natural desires, but whose intentional objects have been narrowed by past experience. Consider a strong preference for arugula—we might prefer to eat arugula rather than another leafy green, such as lettuce, but our natural hunger would be sated whether we eat one or the other, so long as we have enough. The *Daodejing* tends to be suspicious even of the desires like this—that is, desires that are "acquired" in only a partial or weak sense. Consider Chapter 12:

> The five colors blind our eyes.
> The five notes deafen our ears.
> The five flavors deaden our palates.
> The chase and the hunt madden our hearts.
> Precious goods impede our activities.
> This is why sages are for the belly and not for the eye;
> And so they cast off the one and take up the other.[8]

The "five colors," "five notes," and "five flavors" represent the objects desired by people with refined sensibilities, informed by a connoisseur-like appreciation of sensory objects that conventional, civilized people come to understand and distinguish. These are acquired, although they retain some important features of desires that arise from ourselves spontaneously, not unlike the strong preference for arugula. Even so, the *Daodejing* suggests that we have little to gain by pursuing them, either instrumentally or intrinsically. The pursuit of such things tends to drive us mad, and we aren't made much better off by satisfying them, for we become insensitive ("blind," "deadened") to whatever qualities make the desire worth satisfying in the first place. Thus the sage is for the belly and not for the eye.[9]

The Daodejing and current theories of well-being

In late twentieth- and early twenty-first-century anglophone philosophy of well-being, one cluster of theories—desire theories—propose, roughly, that a person is made better or worse off according to how much her desires are fulfilled or frustrated. There is not a lot of hope that an interesting, nontrivial desire theory could account for the *Daodejing*'s views about human welfare. Perhaps most obviously, the text's criticisms of acquired desires suggest that being well off can't consist solely in satisfying whatever desires we happen to have at the moment, which is to say that it's incompatible with so-called *actualist*, *presentist* desire theories. Satisfying some desires—say, for refined music or the latest gadget—contributes little to one's welfare, either inherently or instrumentally. And sometimes it contributes nothing at all.[10]

Most desire theories have ways of coping with this difficulty. *Informed* desire theories say that the desires whose satisfaction contributes to one's welfare are not those that we happen to have at the present moment, but those that we *would* have under more ideal circumstances. Perhaps we could say that the desires that really count are those that are informed by reflection, knowledge of the world, and comparative experiences—for example, comparing the experience of having a flashy new gadget to the experience of eating savory food.

Informed desire theories are also problematic by the lights of the *Daodejing*. One worry is that the very conditions that make someone more informed will also cause that person to develop the wrong desires. In Chapter 80 (the lengthy description of the utopia quoted above) there is an evident preference for ignorance and naiveté: people are not even to read and write, nor travel to other communities, most likely because merely being aware of other possibilities tends to give rise to acquired desires that easily overpower the natural ("self-so") ones. Anyone in a position to make informed choices about life in the agrarian utopia, even moderately informed ones, would no longer be a member of it. There are some obvious solutions to this problem, although most do not strike me as being clean enough for everyday use, requiring that we selectively erase and then restore the memory of the informed subject or engage in other acts of science fiction. Whether this is a problem depends on the use to which the theory is supposed to be put.

In any case, there is a more fundamental difficulty, which is to explain how the informed desire theory could be true to the *Daodejing* in anything more than a trivial way. Let us just stipulate that we could devise a scenario in which the things that people most want are the very things that the *Daodejing* believes make the greatest contributions to human welfare, with or without science fiction. Even if we succeed, the "theory" won't do much theoretical work. One could tailor the circumstances in such a way that the informed subject's desiderata would map on to any of a variety of other theories of well-being. Perhaps it turns out that what people would want, under ideally informed circumstances, is just to maximize their own pleasure, making the theory consistent with hedonism, or to exercise virtues, making it consistent with perfectionism. If the desire theory is to have much explanatory power, it shouldn't just tell us what's good for us; it should also say why it's good for us. It should say that eating savory food is good for us by virtue of the fact that we do (or would) desire it, and not (say) because it is pleasurable or exercises virtues (see Fletcher 2013: 206–209). If we look back at the critique of acquired desires in Chapter 12 (our second quotation), it seems most likely that satisfying a desire would be good by virtue of the experiences it gives rise to. Refined flavors "deaden our palates" and refined music "deafens our ears," suggesting that desires for such things are unhelpful because they don't actually bring about the sensory experiences that make for a better life.[11]

Other familiar welfare theories in the contemporary anglophone literature are hedonism, which holds that someone is well off to the extent that she has a greater balance of pleasure than pain, and the objective list theory, which holds that someone is well off to the extent that she has certain objective goods. It is not clear that these two theories are necessarily in competition with the others: hedonism and the objective list theory are more concerned with enumerating or specifying the particular goods that make one well off, not with explaining or accounting for what makes them good (Fletcher 2013). Still, the *Daodejing's* conception of well-being has significant implications for these theories. Hedonism seems to assume that all goods can be described in terms of two subjective states or aspects of subjective states, pleasure and pain. There is little indication in the *Daodejing* that all contributions to welfare can be measured in terms of pleasure or pain. As noted about Chapter 80, happiness seems to be one good among others, and there is no passage that assumes that people will want to maximize their happiness. In fact, happiness is rarely mentioned as a salutary human motive.[12] None of this rules out the possibility that hedonism could be consistent with the views expressed in the *Daodejing,* but it does suggest that the authors saw little to be gained by reducing all goods to two subjective states or aspects thereof.

The *Daodejing's* views would sit better with some variant of the objective list theory. The text tends to resist the temptation to homogenize different goods, suggesting that we would be better served by a list than by a single value or metric. Moreover, the authors of the *Daodejing* would be little troubled by one of the most popular contemporary objections to the objective list theory: namely, that it imposes a uniform set of goods on everyone, without allowing that the goods can vary fundamentally from one person to the next (Sumner 1996). On my reading, this is a problem that figures prominently in the *Zhuangzi,* but not one that has a major presence—if any presence—in the *Daodejing.*

The *Zhuangzi*

The *Zhuangzi* consists of some essays and a multitude of short, carefully crafted stories and dialogues. Embedded in these are arguments and conceptual devices that enact a kind of philosophical therapy—for example, helping readers embrace certain kinds of skepticism, reconcile themselves to the fact of their own finitude and mortality, find profound meaning in ordinary activities, and see oneself as part of a larger whole. The text exhibits internal tensions and logical inconsistences, some of which are likely intentional and some of which are attributable to the fact that the text has multiple authors. Many modern scholars agree with traditional accounts that regard the first seven chapters of the received version, the so-called "Inner Chapters," as written by the historical Zhuangzi. The remaining work contains some selections that seem largely consistent with Zhuangzi's vision, even if not necessarily authored by Zhuangzi himself, and some passages that seem to have been authored by philosophers and writers of different philosophical orientations. The editor of the received version of the text, Guo Xiang 郭象 (died 312 CE), conducted his work approximately six centuries after Zhuangzi's death, by which time there was a great body of writing that had been attributed to Zhuangzi, probably because of stylistic resemblance and a shared love of radically contrarian ideas. Here I will focus on those passages that offer a relatively unified vision of well-being, based primarily in the Inner Chapters but inclusive of likeminded selections from other parts of the text.

The *Zhuangzi* differs from other major philosophical texts in that it aims not just to present a vision of human well-being, but also to help readers realize that vision for themselves. In this respect it might be compared with Hellenistic philosophers like the Epicureans, Stoics, and Skeptics, who saw proper philosophical instruction and study as doing much of the work of effecting lasting changes of mind and character (Nussbaum 1994). One important difference is that the *Zhuangzi* targets both conscious, deliberate processes and nonconscious, automatic ones. Its goal is not just to change one's explicit beliefs but also to change the wider net of implicit thinking that operates directly (and more consistently) on human activity. For example, one aim of the opening section is to persuade readers to adopt a certain degree of skepticism, raising doubts about the ability of creatures like us, of short lives and limited experience, to draw sound conclusions about the nature of the universe, the fundamental purposes of things, and so on. But it does not simply make the argument that we are poorly positioned to draw such conclusions, it depicts our position with philosophically irresistible allegories and metaphors that tend to linger well after one leaves the study. For example, it invites us to compare the position of those who draw conclusions about their ultimate purpose (etc.) to the position of a morning mushroom trying to draw conclusions about the full sweep of a day (presumably it would know nothing about dawn or dusk). It also describes a mythical tortoise and tree that live tens or hundreds of thousands of years, to whom our epistemic confidence would seem laughable.[13] One of its most effective ways of changing the wider network of our implicit and automatic thinking is to present our own pretensions as comically self-centered or self-important.[14]

A schema for reading the Zhuangzi's *remarks on well-being*

Zhuangzi is not a doctrinal philosopher. That is, his final goal is not to persuade us to adopt certain beliefs by virtue of the fact that they are true, but rather to perform a kind of philosophical therapy, changing enduring features of character and personality.[15] One of the foremost outcomes of these changes is to make us, the text's readers, better off. For this reason among others, the more direct route to Zhuangzi's views on well-being is by looking at the effects that his arguments (and the material that frames or illustrates them) are supposed to have on us. I would like to propose a three-part schema for understanding that effect.

Suppose that there are two mutually opposed perspectives or points of view, characterized not just by what one believes about certain things but also by how they appear to her, and suppose that different philosophical attitudes seem to be warranted by each.[16] The first and most familiar perspective is *human*, and it is characterized by distinctions of value, epistemic confidence, and value absolutism. From this perspective, some ways of life, practices, and states of affairs appear to be clearly and decidedly better than others. We "know" with confidence that it is better, *ceteris paribus*, to be successful than a failure, that being alive is preferable to being dead, that cheating on tests is wrong. Moreover, there are some things that are good for everyone, and good because they are grounded in facts that are true from all perspectives. And these goods are largely found in conventional human society, having to do with things like achievement in one's profession, performing civic duties, and caring for family members.

Following Zhuangzi's metaphor, the second point of view is *heaven's*. To get an intuitive feel for this perspective it helps to think about how things would seem from a broad, perhaps panoramic, view of the universe over the fullness of time, and how human value distinctions, pretenses to knowledge, and absolutism must seem from that perspective. The further we stand back from it all, the more it looks absurd that people care so much about different ways of being and different outcomes of events, and it looks ridiculous when people draw grand conclusions on the basis of extremely limited personal experience and powers of perception.[17] Additionally, from this grander view one will become less attached to one's own values, and therefore more open to the possibility that values are relative to species and cultures.[18]

A couple of caveats about the heavenly point of view. First, my description of the heavenly point of view as "panoramic" is only a heuristic. There are ways of inducing the relevant philosophical attitudes that don't require stepping back from our time and place. For example, we can pick up skepticism by observing that we have no way of confirming whether we are dreaming or awake, or that we can't know something because we can't *know whether we know* it (*Zhuangzi,* ch. 2: 45 and 47–48). Second, if some of these attitudes were understood as philosophical doctrines or positions, they might well be logically inconsistent. For example, it might be that the sort of skepticism Zhuangzi has in mind should also properly cast doubt on things like relativism and value equality. This need not be as troubling as one might think. As we will see shortly, the perspective of heaven is not meant as Zhuangzi's final position, and as mentioned at the outset of this section, Zhuangzi's philosophy is more therapeutic than doctrinal.

To summarize, from the human perspective epistemic confidence, value distinctions, and absolutism seem warranted. From the perspective of heaven, skepticism, value equality, and a certain kind of value relativism seem warranted.[19] The great error that many readers of the *Zhuangzi* make is to recognize the philosophical appeal of the heavenly perspective and assume that it's the end of the matter, that Zhuangzi is just a skeptic, relativist, or value equalitarian.[20] In point of fact, Zhuangzi thinks the two are to be combined in subtle ways, such that our thoughts, feelings and behaviors are moderated by the heavenly point of view even as we appreciate human obligations, purposes, and concerns well enough to pursue them. Zhuangzi illustrates this combination in several different stories, often featuring people who outwardly conform to their inherited social customs but inwardly maintain a cool, dispassionate attitude toward them—the sorts of people who participate in mourning rituals but don't have feelings recognizable as grief or sorrow, or who strive to master some profession but do not truly care whether they succeed or fail (*Zhuangzi,* ch. 3: 52–53; ch. 6: 88–89; ch. 19: 205–206). On my reading of the text, this combination is also, in the final analysis, a way of "seeing" things, one that alters how things seem to us, and not just what to believe by virtue of being true. To mark this fact it would be useful to refer to it as "philosophical double vision." The *Zhuangzi* points to several different ways of justifying philosophical double vision, but the justification that stands out most is simply that it is advantageous for those who adopt it, that it makes them better off. In the next section I will attempt to explain why this is so, in hopes of filling in the text's views about human welfare.[21]

The prudential benefits of philosophical double vision

To get a more well-rounded sense of the advantages of combining the human and heavenly points of view, it might help to imagine someone with human goals but an ability to deploy heaven's point of view strategically, someone who aims to succeed in her career and live a long and healthy life, but sees no reason to think that success, health, and self-preservation really are better than their alternatives. This imparts some obvious and some less obvious advantages. The most conspicuous is peace of mind, because it enables people to face failure and death without the usual feelings of angst and regret. As skepticism is a crucial aid in achieving these goals, scholars have sometimes compared Zhuangzi's use of skepticism with that of the Pyrrhonian Skeptics, who offered systematic and methodological doubt as a means to freedom from anxiety or emotional disturbance (*ataraxia*).[22] But, as Paul Kjellberg has pointed out, of the many uses of skepticism depicted in the *Zhuangzi,* anxiety and emotional disturbance are sometimes the least of the author's concerns, and peace of mind is frequently a means to other ends. Often skepticism is used to treat smugness, lack of creativity, and the sorts of self-conscious, rational thinking that interfere with the effortless and skillful performance of demanding tasks.[23] In what follows I will briefly review theses additional applications of double vision.

One of the more consequential benefits in adopting both the heavenly and human points of view has to do with seeing things as belonging to a unified whole, at the very least in the sense of seeing them as belonging organically to a complete system, and probably also in a more mystical or metaphysical sense. In both of our Daoist texts, perceiving things as "one" or "whole" has a great array of benefits for the perceiver, from providing comfort to undermining the instinct to dig in our heels whenever we come across strong resistance from others (we are more effective when we work with the grain of others' deep-seated dispositions, rather than fight against them). But for a variety of reasons, striving too hard to see the wholeness of things is self-undermining: the more we strive, the more difficult it is to accept that things share a mutual identity, perhaps because it introduces a kind of adversarial, me-versus-world attitude (and perhaps for reasons more profound). Consequently, the only way to succeed at seeing things as whole is not to care about whether one succeeds at doing so, and for those purposes it helps the adopt the value-equalizing stance of heaven, while maintaining aims or goals, as humans do. The *Zhuangzi* illustrates this idea in one of its more memorable allegories.

> [The phrase] "three in the morning" refers to the toiling of the spirit in an effort to illuminate things as one, without understanding that they are the same. What do I mean by "three in the morning"? When the monkey trainer was passing out chestnuts he said, "You get three in the morning and four at night." The monkeys were all angry. "Very well," he said, "you get four in the morning and three at night." The monkeys were all pleased. With no loss in name or substance, he made use of their joy and anger because he went along with them. So the sage uses rights and wrongs to harmonize people and rests them on Heaven's wheel. This is called walking two roads.[24]

As one of the more suggestive and layered passages in the text, it would be difficult to unpack in short order. For our purposes what's most important is that the text urges us to make *strategic* use of the value-equalizing stance. By seeing all outcomes as the same in value—as though they are different but ultimately equal distribution schemes—we become less concerned with our own success or failure, and ironically we become more likely to succeed.

Another major advantage of philosophical double vision is that it meets a necessary condition for optimal performance of skillful activities. One of the most famous and influential ideas in the *Zhuangzi* is that there is a highly desirable way of performing one's tasks called "nonaction" (*wúwéi*). Nonaction is in some respects like the highly skilled performance that people associate with being "in the zone" or what psychologists sometimes call "flow-like activities," characterized by deep concentration and absorption in some challenging activity.[25] It also resonates with a great deal of current research in cognitive science on automatic, "frugal," and usually implicit or nonconscious thinking that does most of the work of guiding us in activities for which we are well trained (Slingerland 2014). But it adds a number of features that aren't as consistently associated with these more familiar phenomena. The most striking is the sense that one is not fully or properly the agent of one's skillful performance, that one is just allowing nature, heaven, or the Way to run its course (Yearley 1996: 154–155, 173). Another characteristic of nonaction is the total absence of certain kinds of self-consciousness, which is expressed as ignoring or "forgetting" about the self-directed reasons or considerations for engaging in the activity in question.[26] Many of the *Zhuangzi's* most vivid and memorable passages are extended descriptions of nonaction, depicting woodcarvers and a famous ceremonial butcher who can describe in moving language how they learned to master their craft.[27] A recurring lesson is that the greatest success in these crafts requires that we *not care* about whether or not we are successful, that we are more likely to perform optimally if we have little emotional investment in doing so.

Nonaction draws on both the heavenly and the human perspectives because it takes up essentially conventional human aims, yet allows us to see those aims as having no stakes worth worrying about. From the purely human point of view, one would typically see some point or purpose in having a job and performing it well, and one would *also* care about or have some emotional investment in doing so. But when the human point of view becomes just one lens in philosophical double vision, the aim or point of doing well seems to be warranted but caring about it does not. Hence, the *Zhuangzi's* exemplars of nonaction accept and, arguably, take some sort of pride in their work, even as they learn not to worry about it.

Another noteworthy advantage of philosophical double vision is that it can elicit more creative thinking about use and usefulness. Many passages refer to cases where someone will encounter something that appears to be useless, such as an oversized gourd or trees too gnarled to use for timber. A sagacious character will then propose a different way of construing usefulness such that the supposedly useless things work to someone's advantage. Oversized gourds, for example, could be turned into boats, and gnarled trees are useful, at minimum, to themselves, for their very uselessness to human beings makes them more likely to survive (*Zhuangzi*, ch. 1: 34–35; ch. 4: 63–67; ch. 20: 209–210). And this important means to (or perhaps constituent of) the human good typically draws on both heavenly and human philosophical attitudes—heavenly because one approaches conventional understanding of usefulness with deep skepticism, and human because something can't be useful unless there is some purpose to which it is put.[28]

In the *Zhuangzi,* our ability to cope with death is often presented as the ultimate test case for philosophical double vision, presenting us with the challenge of seeing some purpose or point in living while remaining indifferent to—or even embracing—the potential loss of one's own life. The text abounds in interesting, strategic uses of heavenly philosophical attitudes to help us overcome fear and anxiety about death. It proposes that the toil and stress that we invariably encounter make living come at a net loss to our own welfare.[29] It suggests that we have no way of proving that we are currently awake and not dreaming, such that we could know that the things we value in life are real (*Zhuangzi,* ch. 2: 47). It proposes that our usual notions of death may be based on too narrow a conception of personal identity, seeing the self as inhering in an individual body and spirit rather than a larger whole or a continuous series (*Zhuangzi,* ch. 6: 88–89; ch. 18: 195–196). Two passages build on the quite plausible premise that we have no intrinsic or inherent claim to our own lives, or at least no claim that we could hold against the natural order of things.[30] One challenging dialogue casts doubt on the very reality of the passage of time (*Zhuangzi,* ch. 22: 245–246). And in the background is the ever-present idea that we have too limited a range of experience and too feeble an understanding to draw sound conclusions about the value of life and death (*Zhuangzi,* ch. 2: 47–48). This recalls Zhuangzi's comparison of our circumstances to that of a morning mushroom making inferences about the character of a complete day, a skeptical treatment that I find even more potent when set alongside the barrage of challenges outlined here.[31]

A conception of well-being for skeptics

What might be most liberating about philosophical double vision is that it frees us from measuring our own lives against fixed standards of the human good, thereby helping us to think more creatively about usefulness and sparing us a gratuitous source of discontent (great hand-wringing about whether one's life is going well adds nothing to a life that is, and too little to the life that isn't). Accordingly, the *Zhuangzi* recommends that we apply skepticism not just to outcomes and ways of being, but also to conceptions of well-being themselves. By extension, it also urges skepticism about many theories of well-being, insofar as they lead us to a fixed conception. But this raises a puzzle: the text assumes that its readers are interested in being well-off; how can they go about pursuing this without knowing what would count as being well-off?

One answer is that Zhuangzi has a certain faith or confidence in our spontaneous, non-rational inclinations to lead us in the right direction. Among the many semantic uses of the Chinese character translated as "heaven" (*tiān* 天), one is to refer to a thing's spontaneous nature. A thing's spontaneous nature is often a more reliable mechanism than deliberate, self-conscious reasoning. One selection makes an example of the millipede, which is far more effective at walking when it relies on nonconscious, instinctual processes than it would be if it pondered every step of every foot (*Zhuangzi,* ch. 17: 183).

But this doesn't exhaust what Zhuangzi might say in defense of his skepticism. In some selections the author's doubts about the knowability of human welfare seem genuine. One of the most compelling selections is a short discourse at the beginning of Chapter 18, "Perfect Happiness." Here the author distinguishes between three possible objects of knowledge: (1) the ultimate or ideal form of well-being; (2) whether the conventional or ordinary conception of well-being is true; and (3) whether the *means* by which people pursue their conceptions of well-being are actually conducive to it. The text suggests that a radical skepticism is warranted for (1). It raises a number of basic questions about ideal conceptions that seem unanswerable—for example, questions about the limits of possibility (how happy could one be? how long might one live?) and about the things that an ideal welfare subject might find enjoyable or hateful (how could we know?). The author also maintains that skepticism of some kind is warranted for (2). In order to know whether ordinary conceptions are true, we would have to be able to know (1). Furthermore, most people take human welfare to be happiness obtained from things like comfort and fine clothes, and the author finds himself too indifferent to such things to determine whether the subjective state of happiness really does attach to them, as ordinary people claim (*Zhuangzi,* ch. 18: 190–191).

But the author adopts a more sanguine attitude about the possibility of knowing (3) whether people adopt the right means to achieve the goods that (they think) should make them happy. He describes the way people run themselves ragged to acquire more things than they can possibly enjoy, how they spend most of their lives in fear of losing those things. On my reading, the author is less skeptical about (3) because it has to pass a different sort of justificatory test: in the other cases, the question was whether we could ever know the true nature or entire substance of human well-being; but in (3), the question is whether ordinary people meet their own standards, whether the means they adopt pass or fail by their own lights: even if we stipulate that their conception of human well-being is correct, it is clear that they are not achieving it. Many of the ground-level goods that people expect to find happiness in are for the sake of one's own body and bodily desires, things like being comfortable, wearing fine clothes, eating rich foods, and simply having the body in a living state. But what people do *in fact* fails to secure these goods, and fails for two reasons. First, and inexplicably, they go to great lengths to acquire goods that they "honor" rather than goods that they enjoy, things like wealth, prestige, great longevity, and moral recognition. Second, they care so much about acquiring these things that they never get to enjoy the bodily sources of happiness, running themselves to exhaustion and being constantly in fear of losing them. What they need is not just to have comfort and rich foods, but to enjoy them as well, and yet their labors and constant apprehension interfere with their enjoyment (*Zhuangzi,* ch. 18: 190). The author then contrasts conventional ways of promoting one's welfare with nonaction, and suggests that at least in the case of nonaction he can be confident that the happiness is genuine (*Zhuangzi,* ch. 18: 191). In short, the way that ordinary people promote their well-being fails by their own standards, while the Daoist way of promoting well-being succeeds by the same standard. This is, of course, only the beginning of an ambitious and stimulating project, but it is enough to see new paths to a different kind of theorizing about human welfare.

The Zhuangzi on theories of well-being

The multi-layered schema that I've described here doesn't lend itself to easy conclusions about the *Zhuangzi's* place in contemporary welfare theory. Consider: if we were to look simply at the sorts of lives that the text presents as good for those who live them, it would be tempting to say that they are most consistent with some variant of perfectionism. The exemplars of nonaction combine certain sophisticated attitudes (great humility and equanimity) with consummate performances of a craft or skill (butchery, woodworking), all of which requires that they perfect certain faculties and aptitudes that seem fundamental to being human. I suspect that the substance of the *Zhuangzi's* picture of human well-being would overlap neatly (but not perfectly) with that of a pluralistic perfectionism, whereby each form of being well would require that the subject refine different core features of the human animal.[32] But when the text begins to justify these ways of life, its justifications aren't always consistent with perfectionism. In many cases they are not even consistent with each other. So in one selection the *Zhuangzi* will recommend nonaction because it's the better way to experience genuine happiness, but elsewhere suggest that it is good by virtue of being a dispassionate expression of the grand Way, which seems not to express itself in terms of happiness. Quite often it proposes that Daoist ways of living are the best guarantee to a long life (*Zhuangzi,* ch. 11: 114), and yet, as we have seen, it also aims to disabuse us of the notion that staying alive is intrinsically or *ceteris paribus* better for someone than dying. Even if we saw a perfectionist argument for living in the Daoist way, we would be well advised not to take it too seriously.

Nevertheless, what appears to be a vice for some theoretical purposes is a great virtue for others. There are very few texts as rich in suggestive, potentially revolutionary arguments and ways of thinking about human well-being, and none so wide-ranging. The text is also distinctive in plunging into the treacherous epistemological waters of devising a conception—and perhaps theory—of well-being that could be justified in spite of the fact that we can't know which particular conceptions are true. And most importantly, at least for those philosophers who love wisdom, it offers arguments about well-being that aim to fundamentally transform the way we see and pursue it.[33]

Notes

1 For my purposes, China's classical period begins in sixth-century BCE and ends in 221 BCE. The founders of most of China's great philosophical traditions lived in this age, and it was also a time of great philosophical pluralism, sometimes called the "Hundred Schools Period" to mark this very fact.

2 Lau (1989: 121–141). The earliest surviving work to characterize them as members of the "Daoist school" is an essay by Sima Tan (165–110 BCE) in the *Records of the Grand Historian,* which was published at least two centuries after the earliest fragments of the *Daodejing* (Sima 1999: 279).

3 *Zhuangzi,* chapter 4: 59–61. Unless otherwise indicated, all page numbers refer to Burton Watson's complete translation of the text (Watson 1968).

4 Any account of the Way is unavoidably controversial, but one prevalent account goes as follows: the Way is a cosmic force that can be seen in different ways depending on the stance that one adopts. When one sees it without desire, it is mysterious, ineffable, yet indivisible and always complete, such that there is nothing in the cosmos that is imperfect or stands in need of improvement. But when seen with desire it can be divided, and words will sometimes be necessary to understand it correctly (1, 37). Furthermore, as seen from the first stance it is like an underlying source or ground that makes the cosmos a unified whole; as seen from the second it is just the sum total of how things behave when they follow their own natural tendencies (25). This reading of the text's comments on the Way resembles A.C. Graham's (1989: 219–223).

5 That is, ensure that the people do not learn to read and write.

6 Translation slightly modified from Ivanhoe (2002).

7 Other chapters that endorse pacifism include 30, 31, 46 and 75.

8 Translation by Ivanhoe (2002).

9 Some chapters in the *Daodejing* recommend being without desires entirely (3, 34, 37, 57). Others suggest that we should limit the desires to a certain set of legitimate or natural ones (12, 19, 80). I suspect that there is some poetic license being used in the former set of chapters, but in any case the recommendation that we be entirely without desires is inconsistent with much of the rest of the book, including its vision of life in the primitive agrarian utopia.

10 There is at least one response available to defenders of the actualist, presentist interpretation: they could say that I have described the objects of the above desires wrongly. What I called a desire for refined music was actually a desire for more primitive music; it's just that it was wrongly interpreted. Meihua thought that she wanted refined music, but in fact she just wanted music that has a direct, raw appeal to her most cherished feelings. So when she hears the refined music her actual desire remains unsatisfied. Much of what I will say about the desire theory in subsequent paragraphs also tells against the revised version of the desire theory implied by this line of defense, but it is also worth noting one worry about it: it threatens to account for the desideratum in a circular manner, saying that listening to primitive music satisfies Meihua by virtue of the fact that she desires it, and that she desires it by virtue of the fact that it satisfies her.

11 A more general but probably surmountable difficulty in attributing a desire theory to the *Daodejing* is the lack of common terms. It would be a mistake to move too quickly from conclusions drawn about desires in the *Daodejing* to theoretical treatments of desires in contemporary anglophone philosophy. Many contemporary debates about desires (but not all) presuppose a different, generally broader sense of "desire" than the equivalent terms in the *Daodejing* ("desire" is often a translation of *yù* 欲). In current and recent discussions of desire theories, there is a worry about desires whose objects of concern are far removed from personal experience, like the desire that a stranger be cured or that the sum of all atoms in the universe is a prime number (for a summary, see Heathwood 2006: 542–543). If these are indeed desires, they aren't the sort that the authors of the *Daodejing* are concerned with. The two envision different sorts of conditions for the satisfaction of a desire. In the former desire would be satisfied so long as "so-and-so is cured of her illness" is true. For the desires under discussion in the *Daodejing,* the conditions for satisfaction have robust experiential dimensions. Perhaps the desire wouldn't be satisfied until the desirer is able to see enough evidence that the stranger's health is restored, or envision the many consequences of her recovery with some confidence that it's not just idle speculation.

12 Other than Chapter 80, the only chapters that mention happiness (*lè* 樂, also translated "joy" and "delight") are 23, 31, and 66. In Chapter 23 it may be understood more metaphorically as describing the attitude of the Way and other abstract entities. In Chapter 31 it describes the motives of those who enjoy killing.

13 *Zhuangzi,* Chapter 1 (Watson 1968: 30). A better translation of this particular passage is in Kjellberg (2001: 209). See also Chapter 17: 175–176.

14 For an excellent summary and analysis of Zhuangzi's uses of humor to alter non-rational cognition, see Carr and Ivanhoe (2010: 132–144).

15 Lisa Raphal's "Skeptical Strategies in the *Zhuangzi* and *Theaetetus*" exemplifies this view, arguing that Zhuangzi's skepticism (like Socrates' in the *Theaetetus*) is not a doctrine so much as a method and a recommendation (Raphals 1996).

16 It is one thing to believe a narrow, wooden suspension bridge is secure. It's another thing for it to *seem* secure. If I believe a bridge is secure without it appearing secure, it's a good bet that I'll feel my heart

in my throat as I cross it. For the present purposes, a "point of view" is about how things seem and not (or not only) what we believe.

17 Sometimes the text describes the Way, not heaven, as having the point of view from which distinctions in value are collapsed (*Zhuangzi*, Chapter 19: 179).

18 There are several senses of the contemporary term "relativism," some more significant than others. A passage in Chapter 2 implies that values would be relative to species and cultures in roughly the same way that the pronouns "this" and "that" are apt only relative to the speaker (what's "this arm" for me is "that arm" for you). See *Zhuangzi*, Chapter 2: 39–40.

19 Chad Hansen has argued that what I'm calling "value equality" would be better described as the absence of any values or evaluation whatsoever (1992: 289–290). I find a good deal of evidence for both ways of framing the heavenly perspective, suggesting that Zhuangzi either did not make Hansen's distinction or saw them as different expressions or proximate characterizations of the same philosophical attitude.

20 Hansen is one of the better-known defenders of the relativist reading of the *Zhuangzi*, which I take to be mistaken (1983, 2003). A useful way of framing his error is to say that he takes heaven's perspective to express Zhuangzi's final position, neglecting the fact that Zhuangzi ultimately recommends a combination of both heavenly and human attitudes (see Ivanhoe 1996: 200–201).

21 It may be that there are still greater or more advantageous ways of seeing the world (for example, see *Zhuangzi*, Chapter 6: 77). Once we move into this area of speculation, however, interpretations will quickly become vexed. Most any plausible interpretation will agree that some sort of double vision is decidedly better for the person who has it than the purely heavenly or purely human points of view. Many will also agree that some form of double vision survives in the better ways of seeing things. So it is both informative and ecumenical to focus on double vision itself.

22 For a list see Kjellberg (1996: 23, n. 10).

23 Kjellberg (1996: 9–15).

24 Watson 1968 (Chapter 2: 41). Translation modified from Kjellberg (2001: 218). See also the translation and notes in Ziporyn (2001: 14).

25 Csikszentmihalyi (1990).

26 *Zhuangzi* (Chapter 19: 126–127). For a richer and more complete account of the nature of Daoist unselfconsciousness, see Ivanhoe (2011).

27 *Zhuangzi* (Chapter 3: 50–51; Chapter 13: 152–153; Chapter 19: 205–206). See also *Zhuangzi* (Chapter 19: 200).

28 Edward Slingerland, using the language of contemporary cognitive scientists, calls this strategy "categorical flexibility" (2014: 139).

29 *Zhuangzi* (Chapter 18: 193–194). A slightly more charitable reading of the human point of view would hold that we mere humans see life as good *ceteris paribus,* or perhaps as having some value that can be outweighed by harms. In this case the "net loss" argument would be consistent with the human point of view, but perhaps it only describes what we *believe* about life and death, not how life and death *seem* to us. No matter what I may believe about it, it often seems terrifying.

30 *Zhuangzi* (Chapter 6: 84–85; Chapter 18: 192–193). This premise is plausible because the natural order, much like a boulder or a table, is not the sort of thing we can rightly make moral demands of. Honoring moral claims and principles of justice is the business of people, not of heaven, earth, or the passage of time.

31 Of the arguments mentioned here, there is an interesting difference between the upshot of those that appear in the Inner Chapters (Chapters 1–7) and those that appear in Chapter 18, "Perfect Happiness." Generally speaking, the former set of arguments lead to the conclusion that we have no reason to prefer either life *or* death, often because we can't know which is better. For most of the arguments that appear in Chapter 18, the natural conclusion is that being dead is actually better than (not just equal in value to) being alive. This difference might be evidence for the view that the Inner Chapters more accurately reflect the historical Zhuangzi's core vision. It is important to bear in mind, however, that the arguments for preferring death in Chapter 18 are meant to be strategic, or useful for some purposes and not others. I tend to read them as floating proposals or possibilities that merely cast doubt on (not refute) the assumption that life is better than death. The point isn't to prove that life comes at a net loss, for example, but merely to raise the possibility or show that it's a plausible interpretation of the evidence. This is more consistent with the skepticism of Zhuangzi's core vision.

32 See Ivanhoe (1996) for a pluralistic reading of Zhuangzi's ethics.

33 My thanks to Richard Kim and Philip J. Ivanhoe for their expert feedback on an earlier draft of this paper.

Bibliography

Carr, K.L. and Ivanhoe, P.J. (2010), *The Sense of Antirationalism: The Religious Thought of Zhuangzi and Kierkegaard,* revised edition, North Charleston, South Carolina: Createspace Independent Publishing.

Csikszentmihalyi, M. (1990) *Flow: The Psychology of Optimal Experience,* New York: Harper and Row.

Fletcher, G. (2013) "A Fresh Start for the Objective-List Theory of Well-Being," *Utilitas,* 25(2), 206–220.

Graham, A.C. (1981) *Chuang Tzŭ: The Inner Chapters,* London: George Allen & Unwin.

Graham, A.C. (1989) *Disputers of the Tao: Philosophical Argument in Ancient China,* Chicago: Open Court.

Hansen, C. (1983) "A Tao of Tao in Chuang-tzu," in V. Mair (ed.), *Experimental Essays on Chuang-tzu,* Honolulu: Center for Asian and Pacific Studies, University of Hawaii, pp. 24–55.

Hansen, C. (1992) *A Daoist Theory of Chinese Thought,* New York: Oxford University Press.

Hansen, C. (2003) "Guru or Skeptic? Relativistic Skepticism in the *Zhuangzi,*" in S. Cook (ed.), *Hiding the World in the World: Uneven Discourses on the* Zhuangzi, Albany: SUNY Press, pp. 128–162.

Heathwood, C. (2006) "Desire Satisfactionism and Hedonism," *Philosophical Studies* 28, 539–563.

Ivanhoe, P.J. (1996) "Was Zhuangzi a Relativist?" in P. Kjellberg and P.J. Ivanhoe (eds.), *Essays on Skepticism, Relativism, and Ethics in the* Zhuangzi, Albany: SUNY Press, pp. 196–214.

Ivanhoe, P.J. (2002) *The Daodejing of Laozi,* Indianapolis: Hackett.

Ivanhoe, P.J. (2011) "The Theme of Unselfconsciousness in the *Liezi*" in R. Littlejohn and J. Dippmann (eds.), *Riding the Wind with* Liezi*: New Essays on the Daoist Classic,* Albany: SUNY Press, pp. 127–150.

Kjellberg, P. (1996) "Sextus Empiricus, Zhuangzi, and Xunzi on 'Why Be Skeptical?,'" in P. Kjellberg and P.J. Ivanhoe (eds.), *Essays on Skepticism, Relativism, and Ethics in the* Zhuangzi, Albany: SUNY Press, pp. 1–25.

Kjellberg, P. (2001) "Zhuangzi," in P.J. Ivanhoe and B.W. Van Norden (eds.), *Readings in Classical Chinese Philosophy,* Indianapolis: Hackett, pp. 207–253.

Kohn, L. (1992) *Early Chinese Mysticism: Philosophy and Soteriology in the Taoist Tradition,* Princeton: Princeton University Press.

Lau, D.C. (1989) *Tao Te Ching,* Hong Kong: Chinese University Press.

Nussbaum, M. (1994) *The Therapy of Desire: Theory and Practice in Hellenistic Ethics,* Princeton: Princeton University Press.

Raphals, L. (1996) "Skeptical Strategies in the *Zhuangzi* and *Theaetetus,*" in P. Kjellberg and P.J. Ivanhoe (eds.), *Essays on Skepticism, Relativism, and Ethics in the* Zhuangzi, Albany: SUNY Press, pp. 26–49.

Sima, T. (1999) "On the Six Lineages of Thought," transl. H. Roth and S. Queen, in W.T. de Bary and I. Bloom (eds.), *Sources of Chinese Tradition,* vol. 1, New York: Columbia University Press, pp. 278–282.

Slingerland, E. (2014) *Trying Not to Try: The Art and Science of Spontaneity,* New York: Random House.

Sumner, L.W. (1996) *Welfare, Happiness, and Ethics,* Oxford: Oxford University Press.

Wang, Bi 王弼 (1965) *Commentary on the True Classic of the Way and Virtue* (*Daode zhenjing zhu* 道德真經注), Taipei: Yi wen yi yin shu guan.

Watson, B. (1968) *The Complete Works of Chuang Tzu,* New York: Columbia University Press.

Yearley, L.H. (1996) "Zhuangzi's Understanding of Skillfulness and the Ultimate Spiritual State," in P. Kjellberg and P.J. Ivanhoe (eds.), *Essays on Skepticism, Relativism, and Ethics in the* Zhuangzi, Albany: SUNY Press, pp. 152–182.

Ziporyn, B. (2001) *Zhuangzi: The Essential Writings,* Indianapolis: Hackett.

6

BUDDHIST UNDERSTANDINGS OF WELL-BEING

Christopher W. Gowans

Introduction

In Buddhist traditions, a good deal was said about well-being, but rather little was said that could be considered a philosophy of well-being. Classical Buddhist thought, in India and elsewhere in Asia, did include philosophical reflection. However, this reflection pertained primarily to topics in metaphysics and epistemology. For the most part, it did not include moral or ethical philosophy similar to that developed by canonical Western philosophers such as Aristotle, Kant, and Mill. Moreover, the main theories of well-being discussed in contemporary Western philosophy were not within the purview of traditional Buddhist thinkers. Nonetheless, it might be hoped that Buddhist thought could be interpreted in terms of these theories or at least that it would be possible to develop a fruitful dialogue about well-being between contemporary philosophers and interpreters or advocates of the Buddhist traditions. In this chapter, I will briefly examine the basis for this hope and assess its prospects for success.

There is tremendous diversity in Buddhist thought and practice from its first expression by the Buddha in India, probably in the fifth century BCE, through the development of Mahāyāna Buddhism around the beginning of the Common Era, to the transmission of Buddhism to China, Tibet, and other parts of Asia in the centuries beyond. In view of this diversity, it is difficult to generalize about Buddhist thought. Nonetheless, it is possible to identify some common themes. In this discussion, we will focus mostly on Buddhist ideas in the Indian (South Asian) traditions from the thought of the Buddha, as represented in the Pali Canon, through the growth of the Mahāyāna approaches.

In contemporary debates about well-being (and related terms), it is usually supposed that well-being pertains to how well or badly a person's life is going for that person. It is commonly thought that a philosophy of well-being is a theory that purports to best explain the central intuitions people have about well-being in their ordinary lives (for example, see the criterion of descriptive adequacy in Sumner 1996: 10–13). A philosophy of well-being so understood was not explicitly articulated and defended in traditional Buddhist thought. In fact, proponents of Buddhist practice were primarily concerned to convince people that a form of well-being is available to them that is superior to any kind of well-being they ordinarily considered. In this regard, they were more interested in changing people's beliefs about well-being than they were in giving an account of the beliefs they already had. I will return to this point at the end of the chapter.

There are three main ways in which well-being is discussed in Buddhist thought. First, according to the doctrines of karma and rebirth, the moral quality of a person's life causally influences the person's future well-being in the present or subsequent lives: virtuous lives bring about greater well-being in the future and vicious lives do the opposite. Second, all lives in the cycle of rebirth are deficient in well-being to some considerable extent because they involve suffering, but it is possible to overcome this suffering by escaping the cycle of rebirth through the attainment of enlightenment. This is the respect in which a form of well-being is put forth as superior to common understandings of well-being. Finally, fundamental Buddhist virtues such as compassion and loving kindness involve a concern to promote the well-being of other people. In this chapter, we will focus primarily on the first two contexts.

There are some serious obstacles to relating these Buddhist perspectives to contemporary discussions of well-being. One of these is the Buddhist "no-self" teaching according to which there is no self in the sense of being a distinct entity with identity through time (and related to this, the Mahāyāna teaching that all things are empty of an inherent nature). Many accounts of well-being in recent debates tacitly suppose that the bearer of well-being is, or involves, such a self. A natural way to circumvent this obstacle is to appeal to the Buddhist distinction between ultimate and conventional truth. This distinction is understood differently in different traditions, but a common understanding allows us to speak of a self at the level of conventional truth, in which we employ the concepts of everyday discourse, even though we cannot speak of it at the level of ultimate truth. In this view, conventional truth is useful in guiding our lives even though it employs concepts with no grounding in ultimate truth. Many Buddhist discussions of well-being appear to be in the language of conventional truth.

Another related obstacle is that the highest stage of enlightenment, sometimes called nirvana or perfect Buddhahood, is often portrayed in terms that do not look like a human life at all. For example, it is said be to a state without consciousness, perception, action, and the like. It is difficult to comprehend how this could be a form of well-being, at least for human beings. However, many accounts, focusing on a lower stage of enlightenment or on enlightenment depicted in the language of conventional truth, portray it in terms that that are more recognizably human. As we will see, by focusing on these it is easier to relate Buddhist thought to the contemporary debates about well-being. In any case, it is best to begin by considering Buddhist accounts of the well-being of persons who are not yet enlightened.

The well-being of unenlightened persons

In the Pali Canon (the earliest Buddhist texts, purporting to represent the teaching of the Buddha) and elsewhere the well-being of persons who are not enlightened is often portrayed in terms of goods such as health, long life, peace of mind, good reputation, wealth, and beauty (for example, see Ñāṇamoli and Bodhi 1995: 1053–1057). We might call these *ordinary goods* in acknowledgment of the fact that they are widely regarded as goods by people in many cultural contexts. It is such goods that, according to karma theory, morally virtuous actions promote. Nonetheless, as long as we are in the cycle of rebirth, no matter how virtuous we are or how many of these goods we obtain, our lives are said to be fundamentally flawed. This is because, as is stated in the First Noble Truth, the lives of all beings in the cycle of rebirth are permeated by suffering or unsatisfactoriness (*dukkha* in Pali).

This is explained in a variety of ways. One common theme is that suffering is closely connected to the fact that all things are impermanent. The connection is easy to see: we suffer because we sometimes lose, and always have reason to fear losing, goods such as those just mentioned. However, although impermanence is often the occasion of suffering, it is not clear that it is the main factor in the Buddhist analysis of suffering. What is more important is our mental response to what happens to us. In an important text, the Buddha said that both an "uninstructed worldling" and an "instructed noble disciple" experience physical pain, but the uninstructed person "sorrows, grieves, and laments" this while the noble instructed person does not (Bodhi 2000: 1263–1265). This suggests that the suffering that is said to permeate our lives is not such things as pain per se, but our aversive mental response to these events. This is in line with the Second Noble Truth and related texts, which state that the immediate cause of suffering is charged desires such as craving, attachment, greed, hatred, and the like. Suffering is the dissatisfaction that comes with strong unfulfilled desires to attain what appears positive and repel what appears negative.

However, the more fundamental source of these desires and their accompanying dissatisfaction is the mistaken belief that we are selves. It may not be obvious why this is. For Mark Siderits, Buddhism is primarily concerned with "existential suffering," the despair that results from believing one's life lacks meaning: the cycle of rebirth may seem pointless, and the realization that there is no self that undergoes unending lives relieves this concern (Siderits 2007a: 19–21). Another view is that it is simply the thought that *this pain is mine* that gives rise to the craving that it go away and the dissatisfaction when it does not. The realization that there is no self undermines this thought and its attendant suffering: ultimately there is no me to think that this pain is mine. At any rate, the main Buddhist teaching about the well-being of unenlightened persons is that it depends on their participation in ordinary goods such as health, good reputation, wealth, beauty, and the like, as governed by karma, but that it is always flawed on account of suffering, a mental state that involves some form of dissatisfaction rooted in delusion. What about the well-being of persons who have attained enlightenment?

The well-being of enlightened persons

The Third Noble Truth and related texts say that it is possible to overcome suffering by eliminating craving and other powerful desires. This is the state of enlightenment.

The primary characterization of enlightened persons is that they have overcome craving and suffering through the deep-rooted realization that they are not selves (or in Mahāyāna Buddhism, that all things are empty of inherent natures). According to one text in the Pali Canon, an enlightened person who is alive "still experiences what is agreeable and disagreeable and feels pleasure and pain." However, this person has extinguished "attachment, hate and delusion" (Ireland 1997: 181). We might say that an enlightened person has many of the same experiences and sensations as everyone else, but is no longer preoccupied with them. In other texts, an enlightened person is said to be free of a variety of turbulent desires and emotions, such as lust, greed, anger, fear, and the like. Hence, a key feature of enlightenment is an overall mental state that might be called contentment. This may be understood in different ways. According to one interpretation, contentment is nothing more than the absence of suffering; what might be called non–dissatisfaction. But some texts depict enlightenment in more positive terms. It is often said that an enlightened person is in a state of peace or tranquility, and it is sometimes said that this person is in a state of bliss (for example, see Ñāṇamoli and Bodhi 1995: 536 and 613). In view of these passages, another interpretation is that contentment involves a positive mental state that might be called joyful tranquility, something that is the opposite of dissatisfaction (not just the absence of it).

In any case, enlightened persons are commonly said to have two other features: wisdom and virtue. Wisdom is the counterpart to the delusion that is a key feature of unenlightened persons: it is centrally the realization of selflessness or emptiness. Virtue is primarily a set of ethical virtues such as compassion, loving kindness, generosity, and patience. It is not obvious how wisdom and virtue relate to well-being. They might be features of enlightened persons that are not aspects of their well-being. In this case, the well-being of enlightened persons would seem to be mainly contentment (either non-dissatisfaction or joyful tranquility). But it is often implied that wisdom, virtue, and contentment are all good states to be in and that they go together: having any one (at least to the greatest extent) implies having the other two. This might be taken to suggest that the well-being of enlightened persons consists of a unified state involving contentment, wisdom, and virtue. On this reading, contentment, wisdom, and virtue are each constitutive features of well-being for enlightened persons.

Can these accounts be unified?

The common element in the accounts of the well-being of unenlightened and enlightened persons is that for both well-being pertains to our mental state: unenlightened persons lack well-being insofar as they are always in some state of dissatisfaction, and enlightened persons possess well-being insofar as they are always in a state of contentment. But the differences in these accounts raise some questions. Participation in ordinary goods such as health, good reputation, wealth, and beauty appears to be an important aspect of the well-being of unenlightened persons in the cycle of rebirth: do these goods play a role in the well-being of enlightened persons as well? Again, on one interpretation, wisdom and virtue are part of the well-being of enlightened persons: do they also play a role in the well-being of unenlightened persons?

It is plausible to think that the answer to the second question is yes: if the presence of wisdom and virtue contributes to the well-being of enlightened persons, then surely the absence of wisdom and virtue detracts from the well-being of unenlightened persons. Moreover, if progress from unenlightenment to enlightenment is gradual (as it is in some, but not all, Buddhist traditions), then it would make sense to suppose that this movement consists in part of a gradual transition from delusion to wisdom and from vice to virtue (as well as from dissatisfaction to contentment). In this respect, there would be a unified understanding of Buddhist well-being that applies to all persons, whether enlightened or not.

The answer to the first question, however, is not so clear. It seems evident that an enlightened person who is still alive might have more or fewer of the ordinary goods referred to in the karma doctrine. For example, such an enlightened person might have better or worse health. In an account of the Buddha's last days he is portrayed as becoming quite ill, being in great physical pain, and then dying (Walshe 1987: 244ff.). Would his life have been better, in the sense of having had greater well-being, if instead he had died a peaceful death without this illness and pain? The question does not seem to have concerned traditional Buddhist thinkers, but we can reflect on the plausibility of possible answers from Buddhist perspectives.

One prominent strand of Buddhist thought and practice is rather ascetic. The Buddha presented the Eightfold Path as a "middle way" between asceticism and a life of sensual pleasure (this is the Fourth and final Noble Truth, explaining the way to attain enlightenment). Yet he advocated a way of life that would look rather ascetic to most people. For example, he seemed to think that enlightenment required celibacy (Ñāṇamoli and Bodhi 1995: 449 and 596–597). The ascetic strand of Buddhism might suggest that the answer to the question in the last paragraph is no, the well-being of an enlightened being such as the Buddha is unaffected by such things as poor or good health. One reason for this might be that the well-being constituted by aspects of enlightenment such as contentment, wisdom, and virtue is so great that other goods such as health make no significant difference to it (just as a couple grains of sand would not make a beach larger). A very different reason might be that such things as health are merely apparent goods, appealed to in karma theory because the belief that they are goods would motivate virtue, even though they are not actually goods at all. A common motif in Buddhism is that Buddhist teaching is an exercise in "skillful means," discourse that is justified on the therapeutic grounds that it promotes enlightenment, not because it is a statement of correct doctrine (there is more about this below). If accounts of karma were interpreted in this light, then they would not be committed to the claim that health and the like are actual goods that contribute to anyone's well-being.

On the ascetic reading—that health and other ordinary goods play no role in the well-being of enlightened persons—it would seem that enlightened persons would be indifferent to the pursuit of these supposed goods except insofar as they were instrumentally important for the exercise of virtues such as compassion and loving kindness (for example, caring for others is facilitated by being in good health). This might seem to strain credibility: how could health not be an inherent part of human well-being? But Buddhist teaching often suggests that the unenlightened cannot fully understand and appreciate Buddhist enlightenment, and perhaps this is the case here.

Another view would be to say that health and other ordinary goods do contribute to the well-being of enlightened persons. This would mean that the Buddha would have been better off in the sense of having more well-being if he had never been ill. In fact, it might be thought that enlightened persons would have such goods to the highest extent possible. This might be regarded as a natural extension of karma theory: if more virtue generates more of these goods, then for enlightened persons being virtuous to the greatest extent would seem to generate the highest level of these goods. However, this claim is very difficult to square with standard Buddhist teaching. After all, the Buddha is portrayed as becoming seriously ill. He is not represented as having health to the highest extent.

So perhaps some enlightened persons are healthier than other enlightened persons and have greater well-being in this respect for this reason (and likewise for other such goods). It might still be allowed that the aspects of enlightenment that are evidently regarded as most important for well-being—contentment and perhaps wisdom and virtue—are much more important for the well-being of enlightened persons than these other goods are. Maybe, in fact, they are incommensurably more important in the sense that no amount of ordinary goods could ever bring about as much well-being as that brought about by contentment and the like. This might explain why virtually no attention was paid to the role of these lesser goods in the well-being of enlightened persons.

Buddhist thought and the contemporary theories

We have now seen some of the main contours of Buddhist understandings of well-being in the Indian traditions. These accounts were presented, not as a philosophy of well-being that best explains everyday intuitions about well-being, but as crucial elements of a soteriological teaching about how to overcome suffering in human life. Nonetheless, it might be hoped that contemporary theories of well-being could be employed to interpret these understandings and that on this basis some dialogue between the two would be possible. Let us now examine this hope by focusing on the well-being of enlightened persons in relationship to four prominent contemporary theories: desire-satisfaction theories, mental state theories, objective list theories and nature-fulfillment (or perfectionist) theories.

According to desire-satisfaction theories, well-being consists of the satisfaction of a person's desires or (in some accounts) the satisfaction of the desires a person would have insofar as he or she was well informed and/or rational. As an interpretation of Buddhist understandings of well-being, this is probably the least plausible of the contemporary theories. Buddhist writers were very much concerned about the ways in which frustrated desires (both not getting what we want and getting what we are trying to avoid) are sources of suffering. But this is not the same as supposing that well-being consists of the satisfaction of desires. In Buddhist teaching, an enlightened person has attained the highest level of well-being, but this person is not depicted as someone who has fulfilled all of his or her desires (much less as having this well-being for this reason). Contentment, a key feature of enlightenment, is better thought of as a state in which a person is unperturbed whether or not his or her desires are satisfied. Likewise, if wisdom and virtue are features of the well-being of enlightened persons, there is no reason to think this is true simply because we desire them.

For mental state theories, well-being consists of the presence of positive mental states and the absence of negative mental states. The best-known mental state theory, hedonism, says that well-being is pleasure and the absence of pain. As we have seen, one important aspect of well-being in Buddhist accounts involves mental states: the suffering that mars unenlightened life consists of dissatisfaction, and a primary reason enlightened persons have greater well-being than unenlightened persons is that dissatisfaction is replaced by contentment, understood either as simple non-dissatisfaction or as something more positive, such as joyful tranquility. If it were argued that this is the whole story about well-being in Buddhism, then Buddhism would appear to be committed to a kind of mental state theory (see Siderits 2007b: 292, for a position close to this).

There are, however, some obstacles to this interpretation. First, it does not seem to be the whole story: at any rate, there are reasons to suppose that wisdom and virtue are part of well-being (and perhaps also participation in ordinary goods), and there is no suggestion in Buddhist thought that they are part of well-being simply because they are positive mental states. Second, contemporary mental state theories are often regarded as plausible because they account for the fact that there is considerable individual variation in what brings about well-being: kayaking may bring one person pleasure and bungee cord jumping may bring another person pleasure, but they are both sources of well-being on a mental state theory such as hedonism because they result in pleasure. For Buddhism, however, there is no aspiration to account for such individual variations in sources of well-being. It is supposed that unenlightened persons as a group are dissatisfied because of craving and delusions about selfhood and that enlightened persons as a group are content because they are free of craving and delusions concerning selfhood. The diverse ways in which different states of affairs bring about positive mental states in people is not a particular concern.

In view of this, it is natural to wonder if Buddhist thought might have more in common with theories that regard well-being as objective in the sense that it does not depend on the particular mental attitudes of different individuals. For objective-list theories, well-being consists of participation in a set of objective goods such as knowledge, friendship, achievement, and the like. Proponents of these theories disagree about which goods belong on the list, but these are common examples. The central contention of objective list theories is that participation in the goods on the list, whatever they may be, directly contributes to the well-being of all human beings—and not because or only if this participation fulfills our desires, brings us pleasure, or any other reason. It has been argued that at least some forms of Buddhism are best interpreted as objective list theories of well-being. Damien Keown has maintained that life, knowledge, and friendship are what he calls "basic goods" in Buddhism (see Keown 2001: 42 ff.), and Charles Goodman has claimed that virtue and worldly happiness are the key goods for Buddhism (Goodman 2009: 61–62 and 80–81). In light of the discussion above, it might also be held that contentment, wisdom, and virtue are objective goods in Buddhism. Since Buddhist thinkers assume that what constitutes well-being and its absence are basically the same for all human beings, there is reason to think that they accepted an objective understanding of well-being in which what brings about well-being for a particular person does not depend on particular states of the person's mind such as what he or she happens to find pleasure in or desire. Moreover, since for many interpreters there appear to be different aspects of Buddhist well-being, an objective list approach is an attractive model for understanding Buddhist discussions of well-being (though the lists just mentioned are somewhat different than one another).

One difficulty with such an interpretation is the common assumption that objective list theories presume that there are several distinct objective goods that are at least largely independent of one another. For example, knowledge and friendship would seem to be rather different goods and it would be quite possible to have a great deal of one and rather little of the other (except in the very specific ways in which friendship might require certain kinds of knowledge, for instance of the needs of one's friend). In some respects, it might be supposed that the elements of well-being in Buddhist discussions are distinct goods. For instance, this might be thought about virtue and worldly happiness, the two items on Goodman's list (although in karma theory virtue brings about happiness in this sense, they still appear to be quite different kinds of goods). In other respects, however, Buddhism might be thought to have a more unified understanding of well-being. For example, wisdom, virtue, and contentment are three aspects of enlightenment that are thought to be closely connected with one another. Although they may be distinguished, it is not possible to fully have any one of these without fully having the other two. Thus, a person with genuine wisdom would have complete virtue, and vice versa. If these three aspects were understood as aspects of the well-being of an enlightened person, then it might be misleading to think of them as a list of distinct goods that contribute to well-being in the way that is common in objective list theories.

Another difficulty concerns the basic rationale of objective list theories in contemporary philosophy. The main argument for these theories is that we have a set of pre-theoretical intuitions that certain kinds of things are human goods and that, contrary to the claims of other theories, there is no adequate explanation as to why these are human goods beyond articulating our intuitions concerning them. As we have already observed, in Buddhist thought there are some understandings of well-being, but there is no theory of well-being that purports to make sense of everyday intuitions about well-being. Hence, even if the Buddhist understandings of well-being could be represented as a list of objective goods, the list would not be an account of what most people would think are goods. In fact, it would probably sharply diverge from this. The well-being of an enlightened person, by Buddhist standards, is arguably a state that many and perhaps most unenlightened persons would not recognize as a form of well-being, much less the highest form. This is both because of the diminished role of ordinary goods and because of what may appear to be an esoteric insistence on the importance of a distinctive conception of contentment (and perhaps of others features of enlightenment such as virtue and wisdom). Whatever may be said in favor of the Buddhist approach, it is not likely to be evident on the basis of commonsense intuitions.

If Buddhism is committed to an objective understanding of well-being, but cannot easily be assimilated to an objective list approach, then the main contemporary theory that it might be thought to resemble is a nature-fulfillment theory (sometimes called a perfectionist theory). According to this approach, well-being consists of the fulfillment or at least development of the most unique, central, or important features of human nature. A proponent of a nature-fulfillment theory might agree with an objective list theorist about which specific aspects of human life contribute to well-being. But the nature-fulfillment theorist would maintain that these aspects contribute to well-being *because* they fulfill significant features of human nature. Hence, a nature-fulfillment theory has a unified explanatory structure that objective list theories lack. Yet it is still an objective theory in that what contributes to a person's well-being depends in an important respect on facts about human nature and not simply on particular mental attitudes such as what that person happens to desire or find pleasurable.

Although nature-fulfillment theories can take different forms, they are commonly associated with Aristotle's eudaimonistic virtue ethics. For Aristotle, well-being—or, at any rate, eudaimonia—consists in significant part in the fulfillment of our nature as rational beings, meaning specifically the development and exercise of a set of practical and theoretical virtues (all of which involve reason). Several commentators on Buddhist thought have suggested that it has significant similarities with Aristotle's ethical theory or with similar theories in the Hellenistic philosophers (for example, see Cooper and James 2005: ch. 4, Flanagan 2011, and Keown 1992: ch. 8; for discussion of such interpretations, see Gowans 2014: chs 5–7). On this interpretation, the well-being of an enlightened person is understood as the fulfillment or completion of the person's nature.

Although this is a common way of interpreting Buddhist thought, it faces an important objection. It has been claimed that nature-fulfillment theories depend on an understanding of human nature that Buddhism rejects, namely, that there is a self or a person with an inherent nature. If, as Buddhism claims, there is no self, or the person is empty of an inherent nature, then it does not make sense to say that our well-being consists in the fulfillment or completion of this self or nature (see Goodman 2009: 70–71 and Siderits 2007b: 292). One response to this objection draws on the aforementioned distinction between conventional and ultimate truth. In this view, although in ultimate truth there is no self or person with an inherent nature, at the level of conventional truth we can speak of such a self or person. Hence, a nature-fulfillment theory interpretation may be plausible as long as it is expressed in the language of conventional truth. Since many discussions of well-being in Buddhism are conducted in the language of conventional truth, this would appear to be a plausible approach. Moreover, a nature-fulfillment interpretation appears to capture a central theme in Buddhist discourse, namely that, though the ordinary condition of human beings makes us prone to suffering, we have the capacity to achieve enlightenment and overcome suffering. Hence, the highest form of well-being in the Buddhist analysis, the well-being of enlightened persons, involves the fulfillment of what is arguably our most important human capacity (or at least an important human capacity).

In Mahāyāna Buddhism our capacity for enlightenment is sometimes described as our Buddha-nature or Tathāgata-garbha, meaning the embryo of the Buddha (for discussion, see Williams 2009: ch. 5). On this view, the three unwholesome roots that (in standard Buddhist teaching) preclude enlightenment—greed, hatred, and delusion—are surface defilements that hide our real nature, namely our Buddha-nature, the fact that there is a sense in which we are always already Buddhas. Enlightenment on this understanding is the realization of what we already are, and this might be expressed in the language of fulfilling or completing our nature. If enlightenment is the highest form of well-being, then well-being in this sense may be thought of as the fulfillment of our Buddha-nature. This might be supposed to have some kinship with Aristotle's contention that *eudaimonia*, interpreted as a life of virtue, is the fulfillment of our nature as rational beings. Of course, it would have to be acknowledged (as it typically is) that there are significant differences in the two understandings of what our nature is or what is most important about it. Buddhist thought does not feature rationality in the way that Aristotle does, and Aristotle does not accept anything that resembles Buddha-nature. Moreover, the ways of life thought to exemplify well-being are very different in Aristotle and Buddhist thought. Nonetheless, it may be said, they are both nature-fulfillment theories, and this is enough to provide a framework for discussing their respective merits.

There is, however, a further obstacle to this interpretation. Although the language of Buddha-nature and Tathāgata-garbha was very common in some forms of Mahāyāna Buddhism, especially in several Chinese traditions of Buddhism, many of the texts employing this language were not primarily philosophical texts. Statements that we all have a Buddha-nature or Tathāgata-garbha were not so much expressions of a metaphysical theory as they were forms of encouragement in promoting spiritual practice. They were ways of saying to followers (or potential followers) of Buddhist practice that, despite evident obstacles on account of the three unwholesome roots, enlightenment is really possible because of our Buddha-nature or Tathāgata-garbha. However, although the overall aim was pragmatic, sometimes the language employed to achieve this aim appeared to be metaphysical assertions. For example, in one text, Tathāgata-garbha was said to possess the "perfections" of "permanence, bliss, self and purity" (King 1991: 12). This may seem rather surprising. In view of the Buddhist emphasis on impermanence and no-self, how could Tathāgata-garbha possess permanence and self?

On account of such language, there have been controversies among Buddhists about discussions of Buddha-nature and Tathāgata-garbha (Hubbard and Swanson 1997). These discussions might seem to presuppose precisely what Buddhism is fundamentally concerned to deny: that there is a self or person with an inherent nature. There are different kinds of response to this objection. Some might appeal to the distinction between conventional and ultimate truth, resolving the conflict by restricting apparently conflicting statements to different kinds of truth. Others might resolve it by developing a more elaborate metaphysics. Still others might reaffirm the point made earlier: these discussions are not really statements of a metaphysical theory, but expressions of encouragement that enlightenment is indeed possible. They are forms of skillful means that are valuable in promoting spiritual practice and are not to be understood as assertions of correct doctrine. According to Sallie B. King, "Buddha-nature thought does not constitute an ontological theory." Rather, it is "a soteriological device" (1997: 188).

This response, however, would seem to substantially undermine the nature-fulfillment interpretation of Buddhist well-being, especially insofar as Aristotle's ethics is considered a paradigmatic example of a nature-fulfillment theory. At least as commonly interpreted, Aristotle assumed a rather robust metaphysical understanding of human nature in claiming that a life of virtue fulfills our nature as rational beings. If Buddhist writers were not assuming a comparable metaphysical understanding, then there is a considerable difference between the two. In order for a nature-fulfillment theory to be plausible as a philosophical theory it must identify some genuine feature(s) of human nature and explain why our well-being consists of the development or fulfillment of that feature. This is a challenge for Aristotelian theories and there would be a similar challenge for Buddhist thinkers if they were committed to a comparable theory, say, that our well-being consists of the fulfillment of our Buddha-nature. However, it is not evident that they were so committed or saw the need to confront this challenge.

There is another objection, not simply to the interpretation, but to the intelligibility of the stance of writers who employed the language of Buddha-nature or Tathāgata-garbha in this way. The objection is that this stance is basically incoherent because this language could encourage the belief that enlightenment is possible only if it was understood to convey a basic truth about the way human beings really are, namely that by nature we all have the capacity for enlightenment. How could we be encouraged unless we understood it in this way? Hence, it might be said, either this discourse was understood as asserting such a truth (in which case it conflicts with Buddhist teaching about no-self and emptiness) or it was not so understood (in which case it is hard to see how it could have its intended result). From this perspective, it might be argued, the metaphysical issues cannot be avoided.

Does Buddhism need a philosophy of well-being?

We now have a brief resumé of the prospects for interpreting Buddhist discussions of well-being in terms of some of the prominent contemporary philosophies of well-being (for a somewhat more detailed account, see Gowans 2014: ch. 5). The prospects are by no means empty, but in any approach there are significant challenges. It was observed at the outset that traditional

Buddhist thought has much to say about well-being, but little that could be considered a philosophy of well-being. By way of conclusion, it is worth pondering why this is.

One answer may be found in a well-known conversation in the Pali Canon, in which Mālunkyāputta asked the Buddha a series of philosophical questions (Ñāṇamoli and Bodhi 1995: 533–536). For example, he asked about whether the world is eternal, whether the body and soul are the same, and whether a Tathāgata (someone who is enlightened) exists after death. Mālunkyāputta said he would follow the Buddha's teaching only if the Buddha first answered these questions. The Buddha responded with a story. A man wounded by a poison arrow would not let the doctor care for him until the doctor answered questions about who shot him, whether he was tall or short, etc. The Buddha said that in order to be healed the man did not need to know the answer to these questions. He simply needed to accept the care of the doctor. Moreover, he might well die if he refused this care until his questions were answered. Similarly, the Buddha said, it was not necessary to know the answer to the aforementioned philosophical questions in order to attain enlightenment and overcome suffering. So the Buddha declined to answer the questions. He said that he taught only what was beneficial for the purpose of achieving enlightenment and eliminating suffering. Hence, rather than answering whatever philosophical questions might be posed to him, he simply taught the Four Noble Truths.

This text may be interpreted in different ways. On most any reading, it suggests that the Buddha's orientation was quite pragmatic in a very specific way: he was interested in teaching only what was necessary to promote the pursuit of enlightenment. This need not preclude answering some philosophical questions, but knowing the answers would need to be important to attaining enlightenment (in terms of the story, it would have been helpful to know what poison the shooter put on the arrow). The Buddha was frequently compared to a physician and his teaching was regarded as analogous to a medical diagnosis (Gowans 2010). This brings out his pragmatic orientation and the limits of his philosophical aspirations.

Of course, some Buddhist schools subsequent to the life of the Buddha did develop rather extensive metaphysical and epistemological theories. Perhaps these were thought to be important in promoting enlightenment. But then we might expect that comparable ethical theories would have been developed for the same reason. Yet there is little in the tradition that looks much like an explicit and systematic ethical theory (for discussion of this, see Gowans 2014: ch. 3). With regard to well-being, there was no interest in developing a philosophical theory that accounts for everyday intuitions about well-being *and* there was no evident concern to develop a philosophical theory of Buddhist understandings of well-being either. Perhaps such theories would have been developed if it had been thought that they were important for pursuing enlightenment. But apparently traditional Buddhist thinkers did not believe this.

In light of this, it might seem that from a Buddhist perspective there is little reason to interpret Buddhist discussions of well-being in terms of any of the contemporary philosophical theories of well-being. However, I would suggest that there might still be a basis for conversation between proponents of traditional Buddhist outlooks and adherents of contemporary philosophical theories of well-being. From the Buddhist side, the primary interest in this conversation would be the commitment to promote enlightenment. Though in the tradition it might have been supposed that there was no need to develop a theory of well-being as a way to encourage enlightenment, it could be that there is such a need in the current context. In recent years Buddhist perspectives have penetrated the Western world in significant ways and to a limited extent Buddhist thought has now reached the attention of some Western philosophers. In this context, Buddhist thinkers might now have reason to engage Western philosophers on topics such as well-being as a way of promoting Buddhist enlightenment to this specific audience. From this point of view, however, Buddhists might well be looking to shift the subject of the debate.

As noted at the beginning, contemporary theories of well-being are primarily concerned to give an adequate account of everyday intuitions about well-being. From a Buddhist perspective, the debate about these theories might be regarded as a distraction from what is really important: realizing first that no matter how well we might think our lives are going, they are probably still marred by suffering, and second, that a superior form of well-being is available to us through Buddhist enlightenment. In this view, what most people think will provide well-being is flawed, and it is important to convince them of this and to bring them to see that there is a better form of well-being that we can attain. The conversation we should be having, then, is one about the most adequate form of well-being available to human beings, not one about how best to account for everyday intuitions about well-being. In fact, the concern about what genuine human well-being would be, where this is not established simply on the basis of commonsense intuitions, is not entirely absent from the contemporary philosophical debate about well-being (for example, it is usually an implicit aspect of nature-fulfillment theories). This might provide an entrée for Buddhists to change the direction of the discussion to a topic they would regard as more worthy of our attention. From a Buddhist standpoint, everyday intuitions about well-being might be a place to begin, but the ultimate aim would be to transform those intuitions.

References

Bodhi, B. (transl.) (2000) *The Connected Discourses of the Buddha: A New Translation of the Saṃyutta Nikāya*, 2 volumes, Boston: Wisdom Publications.

Cooper, D.E. and James, S.P. (2005) *Buddhism, Virtue and Environment*, Burlington, VT: Ashgate.

Flanagan, O. (2011) *The Bodhisattva's Brain: Buddhism Naturalized*, Cambridge, MA: The MIT Press.

Goodman, C. (2009) *Consequences of Compassion: An Interpretation and Defense of Buddhist Ethics*, New York: Oxford University Press.

Gowans, C.W. (2010) "Medical Analogies in Buddhist and Hellenistic Thought: Tranquility and Anger," in C. Carlisle and J. Ganeri (eds.) *Philosophy as Therapeia*, Royal Institute of Philosophy Supplement 66, Cambridge: Cambridge University Press, pp. 11–33.

Gowans, C.W. (2014) *Buddhist Moral Philosophy: An Introduction*, New York: Routledge.

Hubbard, J. and Swanson, P.L. (eds.) (1997) *Pruning the Bodhi Tree: The Storm over Critical Buddhism*, Honolulu: University of Hawai'i Press.

Ireland, J.D. (transl.) (1997) *The Udāna: Inspired Utterances of the Buddha and The Itivuttaka: The Buddha's Sayings*, Kandy, Sri Lanka: Buddhist Publication Society.

Keown, D. (1992) *The Nature of Buddhist Ethics*, New York: St. Martin's Press.

Keown, D. (2001) *Buddhism and Bioethics*, New York: Palgrave.

King, S.B. (1991) *Buddha Nature*, Albany, NY: State University of New York Press.

King, S.B. (1997) "The Doctrine of Buddha—Nature is Impeccably Buddhist," in J. Hubbard and P.L. Swanson (eds.) *Pruning the Bodhi Tree: The Storm over Critical Buddhism*, Honolulu: University of Hawai'i Press, pp. 174–192.

Ñāṇamoli, B. and Bhikkhu, B. (transl. and eds.) (1995) *The Middle Length Discourses of the Buddha: A New Translation of the Majjhima Nikāya*, Boston: Wisdom Publications.

Siderits, M. (2007a) *Buddhism as Philosophy: An Introduction*, Indianapolis: Hackett Publishing Company.

Siderits, M. (2007b) "Buddhist Reductionism and the Structure of Buddhist Ethics," in P. Bilimoria, J. Prabhu and R. Sharma (eds.), *Indian Ethics: Classical Traditions and Contemporary Challenges*, vol. 1, Burlington, VT: Ashgate, pp. 283–295.

Sumner, L.W. (1996) *Welfare, Happiness and Ethics*, Oxford: Clarendon Press.

Walshe, M. (transl.) (1987) *The Long Discourses of the Buddha: A Translation of the Dīgha Nikāya*, Boston: Wisdom Publications.

Williams, P. (2009) *Mahāyāna Buddhism: The Doctrinal Foundations*, 2nd Ed., London: Routledge.

7

WELL-BEING IN THE CHRISTIAN TRADITION

William Lauinger

I will spend the first three sections of this chapter discussing well-being in the thought of Augustine, Aquinas, and Calvin, respectively. Then, in the rest of the chapter, I will focus on some more recent discussions of well-being in the Christian tradition.

Well-being in the thought of Augustine

We know from Book VII of the *Confessions* that Augustine's conversion to Christianity was largely spurred by his reading of some books of the Platonists, probably books written by Plotinus and Porphyry, respectively.[1] With regard to these Platonist books (or, as we would now say, Neo-Platonist books), Augustine says:

> There I read, not of course in these words, but with entirely the same sense and supported by numerous and varied reasons, "In the beginning was the Word and the Word was with God and the Word was God . . . All things were made by him . . . What was made is life in him; and the life was the light of men. And the light shone in the darkness, and the darkness did not comprehend it." Moreover, the soul of man, although it bears witness of the light, is "not that light," but God the Word is himself "the true light which illuminates every man coming into the world."
>
> *(Augustine 1991: 121)*

Thus Augustine saw in these Platonist books a restatement of some of the opening lines of the Gospel of John. Speaking more generally, Augustine saw in these Platonist books a good deal of Christian thought.[2] In providing his account of well-being, Augustine merged Platonic thought and Christian thought in a number of ways. Here consider three sets of points.

First, in both Platonic thought and Augustine's thought there is a strong emphasis on the ascent of the soul, with the bottom levels of the ascent involving the soul's contact with what is physical-sensible, and with the upper levels of the ascent involving the soul's contact with what is immaterial-intelligible. The idea here, of course, is that the soul advances in well-being by rising upward: the higher one ascends, the better off one is. Plato discusses ascents of the soul in the *Symposium* and in the Allegory of the Cave in the *Republic*.[3] And Augustine discusses ascents of his own soul in Books VII and IX of the *Confessions*.[4] In Book VII Augustine describes the ascent of his own soul as follows:

> And so step by step I ascended from bodies to the soul which perceives through the body, and from there to its inward force, to which bodily senses report external sensations, this being as high as the beasts go. From there again I ascended to the power of reasoning to which is to be attributed the power of judging the deliverances of the bodily senses. This power, which in myself I found to be mutable, raised itself to the level of its own intelligence . . . It withdrew itself from the contradictory swarms of imaginative fantasies, so as to discover the light by which it was flooded. At that point it had no hesitation in declaring that the unchangeable is preferable to the changeable, and that on this ground it can know the unchangeable, since, unless it could somehow know this, there would be no certainty in preferring it to the mutable. So in the flash of a trembling glance it attained to that which is. At that moment I saw your "invisible nature understood through the things which are made" (Rom. I:20). But I did not possess the strength to keep my vision fixed. My weakness reasserted itself, and I returned to my customary condition.
>
> *(Augustine 1991: 127)*

Augustine's soul here moved from outward to inward to upward.[5] It first had contact with bodies external to itself; then, through a reflexive turn, it had contact with its own hierarchically ordered faculties, that is, with its own faculty of sense perception and, moving up a level, with its own faculty of reason; and, lastly, it moved upward and had close contact with God. From the end of this quote, we can see that Augustine's peak moment of attaining close contact with God, though joyous, was ephemeral; indeed, he quickly fell back down to the physical-sensible realm.

Second, in both Platonic thought and Augustine's thought there is one thing that stands at the peak of the immaterial-intelligible realm, where this one thing is eternal, immutable, the most real thing there is, and the best thing there is. On Plato's view, this one thing is the Form of the Good; and, on Augustine's view, this one thing is God. Obviously, the Form of the Good is very different from God in that the Form of the Good is impersonal and so cannot love anything, whereas God, according to Augustine, is personal and loves what he creates. And this difference has important implications for well-being, since God, on Augustine's view, loves humans so much that he became a human, died for humans, and showed humans how to live so as to reach heaven, where they can fare as well as possible. Still, the fact remains that the Form of the Good and God, respectively, do (in many ways) play similar roles in thought of Plato and Augustine, respectively. As a further point here, it is worth noting that in both Plato and Augustine there is a strong sense of yearning or longing for the one thing that stands at the peak of the immaterial-intelligible realm. We see this brought out by Plato in the *Symposium*, and, with respect to Augustine, we see this not only in his famous claim that our hearts are restless until they rest in God, but also in his own life-story, that is, in his having wandered restlessly for many years until he finally found the Christian God.[6]

Third, in both Platonic thought and Augustine's thought there is a worry that is present for as long as we are living our earthly lives, namely, the worry that we cannot remain in contact with the best things—that is, the immaterial-intelligible things—in anything like a permanent way. We see this worry expressed by Plato in the *Phaedo*, where Plato says that it is only once we die and thus are rid of our bodies that our souls will be able, in an undistracted and enduring way, to focus on the truth and, more generally, on immaterial-intelligible things.[7] And we see this worry expressed by Augustine at the end of the ascent-of-the-soul quotation from above, where Augustine expresses disappointment at the fact that he was unable to remain at the peak of his ascent (i.e., unable to remain in close contact with God), as, indeed, he quickly fell back down to the physical-sensible realm. Like Plato, Augustine maintains that it is only after we die our earthly-bodily deaths that we can attain an enduring union with immaterial-intelligible things and, most importantly, with God.[8] Here, then, we have Augustine's distinction between the complete and stable sort of well-being that is open to us in heaven and the incomplete and unstable sort of well-being that it is open to us while we are living our earthly lives.

Augustine discusses this distinction at length in Book XIX of *The City of God*. There he mentions a number of goods that we might attain for ourselves during our earthly-mortal lives: bodily health, bodily beauty, a well-functioning intellect, knowledge, the moral virtues (e.g., temperance and courage), friendship, and so on. Augustine is quick to point out that, for as long as we are living here on earth, we cannot possess these goods in anything like a wholly satisfying way. For instance, we are always faced with the possibility that physical-health problems might rob us of bodily goods, and we are always faced with the possibility that a mental impairment such as insanity might rob us of a well-functioning intellect and of knowledge (Augustine 1950: 676–677). With regard to the moral virtues, Augustine asserts that they are in a perpetual war with lust and the other vices that are in us; thus, although the moral virtues are indeed good things, our possession of them is not nearly as satisfying as it would be if we were purged of all vices, as we will be in heaven (Augustine 1950: 677–678).[9] And, in relation to friendship, Augustine notes that we cannot help but always worry that something bad might happen to our friends—that, for example, they might suffer due to famine, or war, or disease, or captivity, or slavery (Augustine 1950: 684). The upshot of these remarks is that, on Augustine's view, there is no way to attain a complete and stable state of well-being while we are living here on earth; the only way to attain a complete and stable state of well-being is in heaven, where we will be united with God in an unmediated and permanent manner, and where our enjoyment of God and other goods will be, as Augustine puts it, "complete and unassailable" (Augustine 1950: 685). It is worth stressing that Augustine's privileging of heavenly well-being over earthly well-being is very strong. He claims that those who hope for heaven "may well be called even now blessed, though not in reality so much as in hope" (Augustine 1950: 698). His view, then, is that earthly well-being has significance or status only inasmuch as it is grounded in the hope for heavenly well-being. With regard to those who lack the hope for heaven, Augustine says that they cannot have anything but a "false" well-being during their earthly lives (Augustine 1950: 698).

Now for a point about translation: most translators do not use "well-being" when they are translating Augustine from Latin to English; rather, most translators use "blessedness," or "the chief good," or "happiness." Further, it is not entirely clear that Augustine's concept of *felicitas* or *beatitudo* can be mapped on to our present-day concept of well-being in a perfectly smooth manner. I am mentioning this translation problem not because I am going to resolve it (I will not), but rather simply so that readers are aware of it. (A similar sort of translation problem arises with respect to both Aquinas and Calvin, and in discussing them I will do what I have been doing in discussing Augustine—that is, I will simply use "well-being.")

One last question here: Should we consider Augustine's view of well-being to be an objectivist view, or a desire-based view, or a hedonistic view, or a hybrid view, or what? In Book XIX of *The City of God*, Augustine references various goods (e.g., unmediated union with God, knowledge, bodily health, and friendship), and he seems to be thinking of many of these goods as being non-instrumental objective goods for humans. With this point in mind, we might conclude that Augustine is a pure objectivist about well-being. However, because Augustine places a strong emphasis on desire (e.g., on our hearts restlessly desiring God), there is some reason to think that Augustine might actually be a hybrid theorist who holds that well-being essentially depends on both objective goods and desire.[10] Moreover, in his book *The Happy Life,* Augustine at one point says to the others (the book is written in the form of a dialogue where Augustine is discussing the nature of well-being with loved ones): "'Do we all now agree that nobody can be happy without possessing what he desires, and that not everyone who has what he wants is happy?' They all expressed their approval" (Augustine 1939: 69). This comment seems to imply that Augustine is a hybrid theorist who holds that one's well-being is a function of (and only of) the fulfillment of one's desires for certain objective goods. That said, this is only one comment, and it was written relatively early in Augustine's life, before his views were fully developed; and, speaking generally, it is not clear to me that Augustine is a hybrid theorist.[11] It seems best, overall, to say this: Augustine is either a hybrid theorist or a pure objectivist about well-being, though it is hard to know exactly which of the two he is.

Well-being in the thought of Aquinas

Like Augustine, Aquinas holds that "perfect" well-being can only be had in heaven and that the best we can do here on earth is to attain an "imperfect" sort of well-being.[12] However, Aquinas seems to take a somewhat more favorable view of earthly well-being than Augustine does. In short, Aquinas seems to hold that earthly well-being, though far from being perfect, nonetheless has some sort of significance or status, taken just in itself. It seems fairly clear, for instance, that Aquinas would reject Augustine's claim that those who lack the hope for heaven cannot have anything but a "false" well-being here on earth. Here consider Aristotle: Though Aristotle did not believe in any form of personal immortality and so did not hope for heavenly well-being of any sort, it is hard to believe that Aquinas would have denied that Aristotle could have attained some measure of genuine (i.e., non-false) earthly well-being for himself.[13]

How, according to Aquinas, can one attain well-being for oneself here on earth? In the *Nicomachean Ethics* Aristotle claims, at least initially, that one's faring well consists primarily in one's having and exercising the moral virtues (e.g., courage and honesty), and secondarily in one's having bodily and external goods (e.g., physical health and friends). I have added the qualifier "at least initially" to the previous sentence because, near the end of the *Nicomachean Ethics*, Aristotle claims that the exercise of the moral virtues is actually only a second-best sort of contributor to well-being; one is best off, Aristotle says, when one is engaged in a god-like sort of intellectual contemplation.[14] Aquinas is convinced that the view of well-being that Aristotle advances in the *Nicomachean Ethics* is, as far as it goes, a correct account of the imperfect sort of well-being that one can attain here on earth.[15] I have added "as far as it goes" here because, whereas Aquinas's view of earthly well-being incorporates an emphasis on religious belief and practice and also on God's grace, the same cannot be said of the view of well-being that Aristotle advances in the *Nicomachean Ethics*.

With respect to Aquinas's view of how grace can impact earthly well-being, two points are in order. First, Aquinas thinks that the natural functioning of every human is to some extent impaired due to original sin and that, with the help of grace, a restorative boost in the functioning of one's natural constitution can occur, where this restorative boost can help one to fare better here on earth than one otherwise would.[16] Second, Aquinas thinks that, as one is living one's earthly life, God can infuse one's soul with supernatural virtues (e.g., faith, hope, and love), thereby significantly enhancing one's earthly well-being.[17]

One more point about the influence of Aristotle on Aquinas: As I have said, Aristotle claims that we are best off when we are engaged in a god-like sort of intellectual contemplation; and, in a way that echoes this claim from Aristotle, Aquinas thinks that in heaven we will be contemplating God's essence directly, and that our doing so will primarily be an intellectual affair.[18] The point here is not that Aquinas leaves all other goods (i.e., all goods besides the good of the unobstructed, intellectual contemplation of God's essence) out of his account of heavenly well-being, for, indeed, Aquinas accepts that other goods will enter into our heavenly well-being (e.g., Aquinas accepts that bodily goods and friendship with other humans will enter into our heavenly well-being).[19] The point here, rather, is simply about what is primary: On Aquinas's view, heavenly well-being is primarily an intellectual-contemplative affair.

Is Aquinas's view of well-being objectivist, or desire-based, or hedonistic, or hybrid, or what? Aquinas is probably most naturally construed as being an objectivist who holds that a human's well-being and the perfection of his or her own human nature are one and the same thing. That said, Aquinas puts much more of an emphasis on desire—or, at any rate, on *natural* desire—than contemporary objectivists about well-being typically do. In particular, Aquinas holds that each of us by nature desires those general objective goods that are perfective of his or her own human nature (i.e., goods such as knowledge and friendship).[20] And, in view of this, it is difficult to rule out the possibility that, if Aquinas were here today (and thus were to have a chance to enter into our contemporary debates about the nature of well-being), then he would be open to the idea of adopting a hybrid theory that entails that well-being is a function of (and only of) both perfectionist value and natural desire (for more on this, see Lauinger 2012: 169–171).

Well-being in the thought of Calvin

As with Augustine and Aquinas, Calvin thinks that heavenly well-being is far superior to earthly well-being. For instance, in Book III, Chapter IX of the *Institutes of the Christian Religion,* Calvin speaks of enjoying the presence of God in heaven "as the summit of happiness" (Calvin 1977: 716), and, with respect to our earthly lives, Calvin says that they are "troubled, turbulent, unhappy in countless ways, and in no respect clearly happy" (Calvin 1977: 713). Moreover, in a way that sounds a great deal like Augustine, Calvin speaks of "how unstable and fleeting are all the goods that are subject to mortality" (Calvin 1977: 713), and he notes that in heaven "a firm condition will be ours which nowhere appears on earth" (Calvin 1977: 717).

Though Calvin claims that we should "accustom ourselves to contempt for the present life" so that we can "be aroused thereby to meditate upon the future life" (Calvin 1977: 712), he soon makes it clear that he does not entirely discount earthly well-being. He says:

> But let believers accustom themselves to a contempt of the present life that engenders no hatred of it or ingratitude against God. Indeed, this life, however crammed with infinite miseries it may be, is still rightly to be counted among those blessings of God which are not to be spurned . . . [B]efore he shows up openly the inheritance of eternal glory, God wills by lesser proofs to show himself to be our Father. These are the benefits that are daily conferred on us by him.
>
> *(Calvin 1977: 714–715)*

It is worth stressing that Calvin does not seem to view the benefits that are daily conferred on us here on earth as being merely instrumental—say, as being benefits that are valuable for us only in the sense that, through them, we are led to God. As Guenther Haas points out, "God has given humans these gifts [i.e., creational goods] not merely for their good, but also for their delight, enjoyment, and comfort. This takes Calvin's understanding of these gifts beyond the bare notion of necessary use, to the sense of loveliness, beauty, and goodness" (Haas 2004: 96).[21]

In view of the foregoing, it seems clear that Calvin holds that Christian believers can attain some measure of earthly well-being for themselves, that is, by attaining various goods that are non-instrumentally beneficial. But what would Calvin say about non-Christians? Can they attain any sort of well-being here on earth? We saw above that, whereas Augustine holds that those who lack the hope for heavenly well-being cannot have anything but a false well-being here on earth, Aquinas holds that some measure of genuine (i.e., non-false) earthly well-being can be attained by those who lack the hope for heaven. Calvin's view of this matter seems to be closer to Augustine than to Aquinas.

Much of the reason for this has to do with the effects of original sin. With reference to the corruption of human nature that is brought about by original sin, Aquinas says: "In the state of corrupt nature he [i.e., man] falls short of what nature makes possible, so that he cannot by his own power fulfill the whole good that pertains to his nature. Human nature is not so entirely corrupted by sin, however, as to be deprived of natural good altogether" (Aquinas 1954: 140–141).[22] And, in another place, Aquinas asserts that, although the damage done by original sin is considerable, it does not reach to the very root of human nature (Aquinas 1954: 127–129).[23] The upshot of Aquinas's view of original sin is that its damaging effects, though considerable, are not so severe as to make it impossible for humans to attain some measure of earthly well-being for themselves without the help of God's grace.[24] On Calvin's view, by contrast, the damaging effects of original sin do reach the very root of the human being, corrupting him or her in an all-pervasive way. As Calvin puts the point, "[T]he whole man is overwhelmed—as by a deluge—from head to foot, so that no part is immune from sin and all that proceeds from him is to be imputed to sin" (Calvin 1977: 253).[25] Thus, on Calvin's view, there is no way for a human being to do anything good or worthwhile at all unless he or she is aided by God's grace.

With respect to earthly well-being, then, I think that Calvin would say that non-Christians who are unaided by God's grace can at best attain only a very shallow sort of earthly well-being (e.g., one where, although they may gain bodily pleasures that are non-instrumentally beneficial, they cannot gain much, if anything, besides that).[26] One point worth noting here, though, is that Calvin holds that some non-Christians receive a restraining grace from God as they are living out their earthly lives. The non-Christians who receive this restraining grace remain corrupt at their very root (i.e., they are not purged from within of original sin in the way that Christian believers are), but this restraining grace bridles them in a way that allows them to act honorably as they are living out their earthly lives (Calvin 1977: 292–293).[27] Perhaps, then, the non-Christians who receive this restraining grace (and who in turn live honorably) can attain more than merely a very shallow sort of earthly well-being. In short, by my reading of Calvin, this possibility should not be ruled out.

Is Calvin's view of well-being objectivist, or desire-based, or hedonistic, or hybrid, or what? Because Calvin references multiple goods, and because he seems to think of many of these goods as being non-instrumentally good for humans, he does not seem to be a hedonist. Moreover, because Calvin holds that original sin so severely damages every faculty that humans have, I cannot see him allowing any human faculty (e.g., the faculty of desire) to play a role in grounding human well-being. He seems, in short, to be an objectivist who holds that a human gains in genuine well-being by, and only by, conforming himself or herself to God's wisdom and will.[28]

Earthly intimations of heavenly well-being

Augustine, Aquinas, and Calvin all assume, as Christians standardly do, that humans are best off in heaven. But what would (or will) heaven be like? This is, to say the least, a difficult question to answer. Nevertheless, many Christians (and also many non-Christians) believe that, during their lives here on earth, they have certain intimations of what heavenly well-being would (or will) be like. Sometimes these intimations arise through the experience of beauty. Jacques Maritain quotes a passage from Baudelaire that expresses this point well:

> it is this immortal instinct for the beautiful which makes us consider the earth and its various spectacles as a sketch of, as a *correspondence* with, heaven. The insatiable thirst for all that is beyond, and which life reveals, is the most living proof of our immortality. It is at once through poetry and *across* poetry, through and *across* music, that the soul glimpses the splendors situated beyond the grave.
>
> *(Maritain 1954: 85–86)*

I think that many Christians (and also many non-Christians) have had (or at least think that they have had) intimations of heaven through the experience of beauty. One witnesses, say, the beauty of the mountains (or the ocean, or the poem, or the music), and one is amazed, stunned, and enthralled. There is a non-instrumental benefit that is present here. But this experience also points beyond itself to another experience, one that will be even more amazing, more stunning, and more enthralling—and that will be so in an enduring way. No doubt the pointing beyond that occurs here is obscure; one's experience here is hard to put into words, since it is "affective and nostalgic" rather than "rational and conceptual" (Maritain 1954: 86). Still, this pointing beyond provides one with (or at least seems to provide one with) an intimation of what heavenly well-being would (or will) be like.

C.S. Lewis suggests that intimations of heavenly well-being can be triggered by one's experiencing a certain sort of disappointment with the wonderful things that are attainable on earth. With reference to heaven, Lewis says:

> Most people, if they had really learned to look into their own hearts, would know that they do want, and want acutely, something that cannot be had in this world. There are all sorts of things in this world that offer to give it to you, but they never quite keep their promise. The longings which arise in us when we first fall in love, or first think of some foreign country, or first take up some subject that excites us, are longings which no marriage, no travel, no learning, can really satisfy. I am not now speaking of what would ordinarily be called unsuccessful marriages, or holidays, or learned careers. I am speaking of the best possible ones. There was something we grasped at, in that first moment of longing, which just fades away in the reality . . . The wife may be a good wife, and the hotels and scenery may have been excellent, and chemistry may be a very interesting job: but something has evaded us.
>
> *(Lewis 1952: 135)*

The idea here is that we (a) experience disappointment at finding out that this wonderful thing (e.g., this marriage, or this trip, or this subject) cannot quite give us all that we want (though perhaps for a time we thought that it could) and then (b) come to the realization that we must want a sort of well-being that does not fall short in the way that the wonderful things that are attainable in this earthly life fall short. This, then, is (or is believed to be) an intimation of what heavenly well-being would (or will) be like: It would (or will) be like this wonderful marriage, or this trip, or this subject, *except that it would (or will) not fall short*.

I should also say something about Christian contemplative practices here. As I noted earlier, Augustine describes two different ascents of his soul to God in the *Confessions*, one in Book VII and another in Book IX. In Book IX Augustine indicates that he and his mother, Monica, shared a contemplative ascent together and that, through this ascent, they gained some insight, however small, into what eternal life in heaven will be like (Augustine 1991: 171–172). Here, in particular, Augustine says that "to exist in the past or in the future is no property of the eternal," and he laments his and Monica's return, after their ascent ended, "to the noise of our human speech where a sentence has both a beginning and an ending" (Augustine 1991: 171). Thus Augustine points us toward the claim that in heaven we will live in a pleasant and peaceful eternal present that somehow transcends all temporal flux and successiveness. Although most Christians who practice contemplation probably do not have the successes that Augustine seems to have had, the fact remains that, for many Christians throughout history and right up to the present day, contemplation has been the main way in which they have gained (or have tried to gain) some insight into the nature of life in heaven.[29]

Before leaving this section, I should stress that everything said here can reasonably be questioned by non-theists. For instance, in response to a Christian who claims to have an intimation of heaven through his or her experience of something beautiful (e.g., a mountain), a non-theist might say: "Your experience of the mountain, wonderful though it may be, does *not* point beyond itself to heaven. Yes, you *believe* that it does. But that is because you are already a theist. If you were working with different background assumptions (e.g., atheistic ones), then you would *not* form the belief that your experience of the mountain points beyond itself to heaven." Or again, in response to the common Christian view (shared by Maritain, Lewis, and Augustine) that life in heaven would (or will) always be pleasant, peaceful, and desirable, a non-theist might (following Bernard Williams) say: "I can see life in heaven being pleasant, peaceful, and desirable for a long stretch of time (say, for hundreds of years). But I cannot see it being pleasant, peaceful, and desirable *forever*. Indeed, at some point along the way, it would surely become intolerably boring or depressing."[30] Though Christians disagree with non-theistic views such as these, nothing said in this section shows that these non-theistic views are mistaken.

Does religion have objective priority over all other welfare goods?

In the last section I focused on heaven, and in this section I want to focus on earth. In particular, I want, if only briefly, to focus on a certain debate that, for the last few decades, has been taking place among Catholic natural law theorists in the Thomistic tradition—though, to be clear, the debate should be of interest to all Christians and, for that matter, to all theists. The debate concerns the role of religion (i.e., religious belief and practice) in one's earthly life. The main participants in the debate are objectivists about well-being, and they all agree that religion is a good that directly contributes to well-being. But, while some parties to the debate think that religion is on a par with other welfare goods such as friendship, knowledge, and aesthetic experience, other parties to the debate think that religion is a superordinate good, which is to say that it has objective priority over all other welfare goods.[31] Here objective priority contrasts with subjective priority. Through one's own subjective choice about how to order welfare goods in one's own life, one might give the good of religion priority over friendship, knowledge, and all other welfare goods. But the question here is about objective priority: It is about whether religion has priority over all other welfare goods in a way that is independent of anyone's subjective choices.

John Finnis is one of the main proponents of the view that religion is on a par with other welfare goods such as friendship, knowledge, and aesthetic experience (Finnis 1980: 81–133 and 403–410). Finnis refers to welfare goods such as religion, friendship, knowledge, and aesthetic experience as "basic goods," and he holds that all of the basic goods are equally fundamental, which is to say that there is no objective hierarchy or ordering among them. Each one of us is, Finnis says, under a requirement of practical reason to find some way of ordering the basic goods in his or her own life, taking into account his or her own preferences, talents, and circumstances (e.g., a scholar might reasonably choose to give priority to knowledge over the other basic goods in his or her own life). But, says Finnis, this ordering of the basic goods in one's own life is subjectively generated, and the fact remains that the basic goods are all objectively equal (Finnis 1980: 103–106). With regard to religion, Finnis says that, if someone claims that religion has objective priority over the other basic goods, then "we must reply by asking whether the glory of God may not be manifested in *any* of the many aspects of human flourishing" (Finnis 1980: 113). Finnis's point here, I think, is that all of the basic goods (not just the basic good of religion) are ultimately grounded in God, and that God's glory is just as much manifested when one engages in friendship, or knowledge, or aesthetic experience, etc., as it is when one engages in religion. Finnis also indicates that "the love of God" can be expressed in many different sorts of "life-plans" (Finnis 1980: 113), with the point being that different lives, ones that exhibit different prioritizations of the basic goods, might all equally express the love of God.

Though Finnis is a Thomistic natural law theorist, his claim that there is no objective hierarchy or ordering among the basic goods seems to cut against Aquinas's view. I say this because Aquinas seems to have accepted something like the following objective ordering of welfare goods: (a) unmediated union with God in heaven is best; (b) close union with God here on earth, which is primarily attained through religious practice (i.e., prayer, worship, and so on), is second best; (c) intellectual contemplation (e.g., of theoretical truths) is third best; (d) the exercise of the moral virtues is fourth best; and (e) bodily and external goods (e.g., physical health and friends) are fifth best.[32] Or, put more simply, Aquinas seems to have accepted that religion is ranked first, knowledge is ranked second, moral virtue is ranked third, and so on. Of course, Aquinas's view could be mistaken, and Finnis's view could be correct. One worry, in particular, about Aquinas's view is that it might be thought to have the implausible implication that, in order to be as well off as possible, each of us should spend all of his or her time praying, worshipping God, and so on. Daniel McInerny, who is among those who defend the view that religion has objective priority over all other welfare goods, addresses this worry. He says:

> But what then of the related, "domination" objection? If contemplation and religious observance are the best goods, why shouldn't I spend all my time with them? To answer this we need to underscore again that higher goods in a hierarchy do not undermine the intrinsic goodness of the goods subordinate to them. My obligation to honor my parents, for instance, binds me to the goods of family life in a way that is constitutive of my happiness. My other obligation to honor God in the practice of the virtue of religion is not a rival to this obligation, even while it remains the more important obligation. The natural law in no way requires that I pursue religious acts to the exclusion of all other obligations. The natural law only demands that the religious obligation is given foremost respect in the tailoring of the hierarchy to my individual circumstances.
>
> *(McInerny 2006: 129)*

An example might help here. Suppose that someone feels called by God to be an artist, and suppose that this person spends more time on artistic pursuits than on anything else, including prayer, worship, and so on. Presumably it would not necessarily follow that this person has put aesthetic experience above religion in his or her own life. After all, it could be that, for this person, religion (and, more generally, his or her relationship with God) is always there in the background, regulating everything (or almost everything) that he or she does; and thus it could be that, for this person, religion does have priority over everything else, including aesthetic experience, even though, as stipulated, this person spends more time on artistic pursuits than on religion. I take it that, if and insofar as this person is indeed allowing religion to regulate all (or almost all) that he or she does, then McInerny would say that this person is properly ordering welfare goods in his or her own life—that is, McInerny would say that this person is living in a way that corresponds to the objective hierarchy that obtains among welfare goods.

Presumably there are responses that Finnis and those who agree with him might offer at this point. But, instead of continuing on with this debate, I will now proceed to the final section of this chapter.

Contemporary Christian philosophers and the nature of well-being

There is no consensus among contemporary Christian philosophers about the nature of well-being. Though it is true that many contemporary Christian philosophers are objectivists about well-being (e.g., see Finnis 1980: 59–99; Murphy 2001: 6–138; and Oderberg 2004: 127–144), it is also true that many are not. For instance, Stewart Goetz is a welfare hedonist, and in partially explaining his view he says:

> It is, then, the pleasure that either accompanies or is produced by instrumental goods such as friendship and knowledge that makes them attractive and the pursuit of them worthwhile, and the fact that pleasure enhances the status of these supposed intrinsic goods in this way undermines their candidacy for being intrinsic goods. Conversely, the status of pleasure as an intrinsic good is not enhanced by the friendship, love, knowledge, beauty, etc. that accompanies or is productive of it.
>
> *(Goetz 2012: 93)*[33]

Like Goetz, Thomas Carson rejects objectivism about well-being, but, unlike Goetz, Carson defends a desire-based theory of well-being. Interestingly, Carson holds that, assuming God exists, we should accept a desire-based theory of well-being that appeals to God's desires rather than to humans' desires, and Carson defends his divine desire theory of well-being against objections similar to those that divine command theories of morality face (Carson 2000: 219–267).[34] Moreover, Robert Adams has proposed that one's well-being consists at least primarily in one's enjoyment of the excellent, where enjoyment is a pro-attitude, and where the excellent is a non-relational, Platonic sort of objective value (Adams 1999: 93–101). Thus Adams accepts (or at least inclines toward) "an enjoyment-of-the-excellent" hybrid view of well-being. Finally, I myself have defended a hybrid theory that entails that well-being essentially depends on both perfectionist value and desire (Lauinger 2012: 3–120).

Is it surprising that there is no consensus among contemporary Christian philosophers about the nature of well-being? I do not think so. Christianity is a diverse religion, full of many different strands, and full of much internal disagreement. Moreover, the claim that we should accept such-and-such a view of the nature of well-being (i.e., an objectivist view, or a hedonistic view, or a divine desire-based view, etc.) is not one of the fundamental claims that all or virtually all Christians accept. Here I have in mind claims such as that God is Triune, that Jesus' death and resurrection is crucial to the salvation of humans, that the Bible is divinely inspired, and that evil and suffering will be overcome, if not here on earth, then at least in heaven.[35] Of course, to this list of fundamental claims we can add the claim that heaven exists and that humans are best off in heaven. And no doubt this claim is accepted by all or virtually all contemporary Christian philosophers. So, if only with respect to this one very important claim concerning well-being, there is a consensus among contemporary Christian philosophers.[36]

Notes

1 Augustine does not say which Platonic books he read; he simply says that he read "some books of the Platonists, translated from Greek into Latin" (Augustine 1991: 121). In commenting on this matter, Henry Chadwick says: "Scholars have disputed whether they [i.e., these Platonic books] were all tracts by Plotinus or all works by his pupil Porphyry. The probability is that Augustine read some by each of them" (Chadwick 1991: xix, n. 2).

2 That said, Augustine does stress that there are large differences between what he read in these Platonic books and what Christianity entails (Augustine 1991: 122). Also, for a discussion of some of the perplexities surrounding Augustine's merging of Platonic thought and Christian thought, see Gilson (1941: 44–62).

3 See 202a–212b in the *Symposium* (Plato 1961: 554–563) and 514a–520e in the *Republic* (Plato 1961: 747–753).

4 The ascent in Book IX is the famous vision at Ostia ascent, which Augustine shares with his mother, Monica (Augustine 1991: 170–172).

5 For a discussion of how Augustine drew on Plotinus in order to learn how to make these ascents, see Chadwick (1991: xxi–xxii). One thing that is essential to the success of the ascent is the inward turn. As Chadwick says, "The method is that of introspection: 'Go into yourself'" (Chadwick 1991: xxi).

6 See 202a–212b in the *Symposium* (Plato 1961: 554–563). For Augustine's claim that our hearts are restless until they rest in God, see the first paragraph of the *Confessions* (Augustine 1991: 3). And, for Augustine's life story, see Books I–IX of the *Confessions* (Augustine 1991: 3–178).

7 See 65a–68b in the *Phaedo* (Plato 1961: 47–51).

8 I should note, though, that the denigration of the body in Augustine is not as strong as it is in the *Phaedo*. This comes out fairly clearly in Augustine's discussion of original sin in Book XIV of *The City of God* (Augustine 1950: 441–477). In particular, see Augustine's comments about why it is wrong to think that all the evils of the soul proceed from the body (Augustine 1950: 443–447).

9 Augustine thinks that, during our earthly lives, there is no hope of our entirely being rid of vice. He says: "For we must not fancy that there is no vice in us, when, as the apostle says, 'The flesh lusteth against the spirit'" (Augustine 1950: 677). In heaven, however, we will be purged of original sin and, in general, all vices. As Augustine says, "There [i.e., in heaven] the virtues shall no longer be struggling against any vice or evil, but shall enjoy the reward of victory, the eternal peace which no adversary shall disturb" (Augustine 1950: 685–686).

10 Germain Grisez, who is a Christian objectivist about well-being, has criticized Augustine for placing too much emphasis on desire and the enjoyment of peace, and not enough emphasis on objective goods such as "life and health, knowledge of the truth, and skill in performance" (Grisez 1983: 127–128).

11 *The Happy Life* was written between the time of Augustine's conversion to Christianity in July of 386 and Augustine's Easter baptism in 387 (for discussion of this point, see Schopp 1939: 28–31). The *Confessions* was written between 397 and 400, and *The City of God* was written between 413 and 426. Needless to say, then, *The Happy Life* was indeed one of Augustine's early works. It is also a work that is light in tone; it is not as sobering as some of Augustine's later works, especially *The City of God* (for discussion of this point, see Schopp 1939: 30–31).

12 Aquinas's distinction between perfect and imperfect happiness (i.e., perfect and imperfect well-being) can be found in various places in *Summa Theologica* I–II, Questions 1–5. For instance, see Question 3, article 2, reply to the fourth objection (Aquinas 1998: 512–513) and Question 3, article 3 (Aquinas 1998: 514).

13 In Book III, Chapter 5 of *On the Soul*, Aristotle says (or at least seems to say) that the agent-intellect is immortal, with the idea presumably being that, when a human dies his or her bodily death, his or her agent-intellect can live on and be absorbed into the divine, eternal mind (Aristotle 1987: 197). But Aristotle makes it clear that this agent-intellect that is (or at least can be) immortal has no memory, and, more generally, the idea seems to be that it has no individual personality at all. Thus it seems that Aristotle does not believe in any personal form of immortality. For a helpful discussion of this matter, see Guthrie 1975: 145–146.

14 For Aristotle's claims regarding the superiority of intellectual contemplation to the exercise of the moral virtues, see Book X, Chapters 7–8 of the *Nicomachean Ethics* (Aristotle 1987: 469–473).

15 See *Summa Theologica* I–II, Question 3, article 5, where Aquinas says: "But imperfect happiness, of the kind that can be had here, consists first and principally in contemplation, but secondarily in the activity of the practical intellect ordering human actions and passions, as is said in *Ethics* 10.7 [i.e., Book X, Chapter 7 of the *Nicomachean Ethics*]" (Aquinas 1998: 518). Also see *Summa Theologica* I–II, Question 4, articles 6, 7, and 8, where Aquinas makes it clear that bodily and external goods (e.g., physical health and friends) contribute to the imperfect sort of well-being that one can attain in this life (Aquinas 1998: 532–536).

16 See, for instance, *Summa Theologica* I–II, Question 109, article 2, where Aquinas speaks of a type of grace that heals the corrupted or impaired natural functioning of humans (Aquinas 1954: 141).

17 For Aquinas on faith, see *Summa Theologica* II–II, Questions 1–7 (Aquinas 1954: 219–292); for Aquinas on hope, see *Summa Theolgica* II–II, Questions 17–21 (Aquinas 1954: 293–341); and, for Aquinas on love (i.e., charity), see *Summa Theologica* II–II, Questions 23 and 27 (Aquinas 1954: 342–368).

18 See *Summa Theologica* I–II, Question 3, articles 4–8 (Aquinas 1998: 515–523).

19 With regard to bodily goods entering into our heavenly well-being, see *Summa Theologica* I–II, Question 4, article 6 (Aquinas 1998: 532–534). And, with regard to friendship with other humans entering into our heavenly well-being, see *Summa Theologica* I–II, Question 4, article 8 (Aquinas 1998: 535–536).

20 On this point, see *Summa Theologica* I–II, Question 3, article 6 (Aquinas 1998: 519–520), particularly where Aquinas says (in the reply to the second objection) that "not only perfect happiness is naturally desired, but also any likeness or participation of it whatsoever," with the implication being that humans by nature desire knowledge and all other general objective goods that are perfective of their own respective human natures.

21 Also see Book III, Chapter X of the *Institutes of the Christian Religion*, where Calvin speaks of God's rendering many things attractive to us, apart from their necessary use (Calvin 1977: 721).

22 This quotation is from *Summa Theologica* I–II, Question 109, article 2.

23 See *Summa Theologica* I–II, Question 85, article 2. What Aquinas seems to be thinking here is this: like all things in the natural order, humans were created by God as good, and they remain good at their very root even after having been corrupted to some extent by the fall.

24 It is worth stressing that "without the help of God's grace" does not here mean "without the help of God." Given that God created the natural order and all things in it, and given that God sustains the natural order and all things in it at every moment, it is not true to say that a human who does something without God's grace does something without the help of God. In short, what God does in providing a human with grace differs from (i.e., goes above and beyond) what God does in creating and (at every moment) sustaining the natural order and all things in it, including humans.

25 This quotation is from Book II, Chapter I of the *Institutes of the Christian Religion*.

26 In Book III, Chapter IX of the *Institutes of the Christian Religion*, Calvin refers to "wicked men flourishing in wealth and honors" and "enjoying deep peace, taking pride in the splendor and luxury of all their possessions, abounding with every delight" (Calvin 1977: 718). But of course, on Calvin's view, this sort of earthly-materialistic flourishing has no substance (i.e., it makes no significant contribution to genuine well-being). In fact, in Book III, Chapter VII of the *Institutes of the Christian Religion*, Calvin goes so far as to say that impious humans who amass great honors and riches "taste not even the least particle of happiness" (Calvin 1977: 699).

27 Calvin's discussion of the restraining grace that is given to some non-Christians can be found in Book II, Chapter III of the *Institutes of the Christian Religion*.

28 As Calvin says in Book III, Chapter VII of the *Institutes of the Christian Religion*: "We are not our own: let not our reason nor our will, therefore, sway our plans and deeds . . . We are God's: let his wisdom and will therefore rule all our actions" (Calvin 1977: 690). One caveat about my claim that Calvin seems to be an objectivist about well-being: Calvin certainly does not think of human well-being as being grounded in human desires or human pro-attitudes of any sort, and, for this reason, it is natural to conclude that Calvin is an objectivist about well-being; however, it is possible (for all I know) that Calvin thinks of human well-being as being grounded in God's desires *vis-à-vis* humans, and, if that is the case, then, instead of referring to Calvin as an objectivist about human well-being, it would be better to refer to him as a divine desire theorist about human well-being. (As I note near the end of this chapter, Thomas Carson is a contemporary Christian who defends a divine desire theory of human well-being—see Carson 2000: 219–267.)

29 For a history of Christian mysticism, see King (2001); and, for an informative present-day book about why Christian contemplation is important, and also about how to do it (e.g., how to work on one's posture, breathing, and mental focus, so as to be able to bring one's mind to stillness), see Laird (2006).

30 For Williams's argument against the desirability of living forever in heaven, see Williams (1973: 82–100); and, for a more recent argument against the desirability of living forever in heaven, see Ribeiro (2011: 46–64). (For a response to Williams and Ribeiro, see Lauinger 2014: 1–28.)

31 This debate involves many participants and has been written about in many places. For instance, see Finnis (1980: 81–133 and 403–410); Hittinger (1987: 93–154); Murphy (2001: 190–198); Oderberg (2004: 147–158); and McInerny (2006: 109–132).

32 See *Summa Theologica* I–II, Questions 1–5 (Aquinas 1998: 482–550).

33 Though Goetz is a hedonist about well-being, he is not a hedonist about value in general. In particular, he explicitly says that he accepts that justice is an intrinsic good (Goetz 2012: 78).

34 To be clear, Carson thinks that, on the assumption that God exists, we should go with a divine desire theory of well-being, and Carson thinks that, on the assumption that God does not exist, we should go with a version of the informed-desire theory of well-being that appeals to humans' desires (Carson 2000: 219–267). Also, though I am speaking of well-being, Carson's book (*Value and the Good Life*) focuses mostly on value in general rather than well-being in particular. Moreover, Carson does at one point express some uncertainty about the defensibility of desire theories of well-being (Carson 2000: 88–92). That said, I think that anyone who reads Carson's book will come to the conclusion that Carson is a desire theorist about well-being.

35 I say that all or virtually all Christians accept these claims, but this may be an overstatement. After all, there seem to be a fair number of "modern" or "liberal" Christians who interpret much of the core of traditional Christianity (e.g., the Trinity and the resurrection of Jesus from the dead) as being false but symbolically important. Thus what I should perhaps say about the claims in question here is that all or virtually all Christians *of the traditional sort* accept them.

36 Thanks to Chris Rice for very helpful comments.

References

Adams, R. (1999) *Finite and Infinite Goods: A Framework for Ethics*, New York: Oxford University Press.

Aquinas (1954) *Nature and Grace: Selections from the Summa Theologica of Thomas Aquinas* (transl. A. Fairweather), Philadelphia: The Westminster Press.

Aquinas (1998) *Thomas Aquinas: Selected Writings* (transl. R. McInerny), New York: Penguin Books.

Aristotle (1987) *A New Aristotle Reader*, edited by J. Ackrill, Princeton: Princeton University Press.

Augustine (1939) *The Happy Life* (transl. L. Schopp), St. Louis: B. Herder Book Co.

Augustine (1950) *The City of God* (transl. M. Dods), New York: The Modern Library.

Augustine (1991) *Confessions* (transl. H. Chadwick), New York: Oxford University Press.

Calvin, J. (1977) *Institutes of the Christian Religion*, edited by J. McNeill, Philadelphia: The Westminster Press.

Carson, T. (2000) *Value and the Good Life*, Notre Dame, IN: University of Notre Dame Press.

Chadwick, H. (1991) "Introduction," in Augustine, *Confessions* (transl. H. Chadwick), New York: Oxford University Press, pp. ix–xxviii.

Finnis, J. (1980) *Natural Law and Natural Rights*, New York: Oxford University Press.

Gilson, E. (1941) *God and Philosophy*, New Haven, CT: Yale University Press.

Goetz, S. (2012) *The Purpose of Life: A Theistic Perspective*, New York: Continuum.

Grisez, G. (1983) *The Way of the Lord Jesus, Volume One: Christian Moral Principles*, Chicago: Franciscan Herald Press.

Guthrie, W. (1975) *The Greek Philosophers*, New York: Harper and Row.

Haas, G. (2004) "Calvin's Ethics," in D. McKim (ed.), *The Cambridge Companion to John Calvin*, New York: Cambridge University Press, pp. 93–105.

Hittinger, R. (1987) *A Critique of the New Natural Law Theory*, Notre Dame, IN: University of Notre Dame Press.

King, U. (2001) *Christian Mystics: Their Lives and Legacies Throughout the Ages*, Mahwah, NJ: Hidden Spring.

Laird, M. (2006) *Into the Silent Land: A Guide to the Christian Practice of Contemplation*, New York: Oxford University Press.

Lauinger, W. (2012) *Well-Being and Theism: Linking Ethics to God*, New York: Continuum.

Lauinger, W. (2014) "Eternity, Boredom, and One's Part-Whole-Reality Conception," *American Catholic Philosophical Quarterly* 88: 1–28.

Lewis, C. (1952) *Mere Christianity*, New York: HarperCollins Publishers.

Maritain, J. (1954) *Approaches to God* (transl. P. O'Reilly), New York: Harper and Brothers Publishers.

McInerny, D. (2006) *The Difficult Good: A Thomistic Approach to Moral Conflict and Human Happiness*, New York: Fordham University Press.

Murphy, M. (2001) *Natural Law and Practical Rationality*, New York: Cambridge University Press.

Oderberg, D. (2004) "The Structure and Content of the Good," in D. Oderberg and T. Chappell (eds.), *Human Values: New Essays on Ethics and Natural Law*, New York: Palgrave MacMillan, pp. 127–165.

Plato (1961) *The Collected Dialogues of Plato*, edited by E. Hamilton and H. Cairns, Princeton: Princeton University Press.

Ribeiro, B. (2011) "The Problem of Heaven," *Ratio* 24: 46–64.

Schopp, L. (1939) "Introduction," in Augustine, *The Happy Life* (transl. L. Schopp), St. Louis: B. Herder Book Co., pp. 3–37.

Williams, B. (1973) "The Makropulos Case: Reflections on the Tedium of Immortality," in B. Williams (ed.), *Problems of the Self*, Cambridge: Cambridge University Press, pp. 82–100.

8

THE LATER BRITISH MORALISTS

Robert Shaver

Sidgwick gives an analysis of "good for me" and argues that only pleasure is good. In the first part of this chapter, I set out Sidgwick's analysis: to say that x is good for me is to say that I ought to desire x when considering myself alone. In the second part, I consider objections. In the third part, I consider his arguments for pleasure as the only ultimate good, highlighting objections by Moore and Broad. In the fourth part, I argue that while Sidgwick does not rely on an account of well-being in the sense current now, he does have this concept. In the last part, I consider how, given his account of pleasure, he can reply to Broad's objection that the order in which pleasures come, and not just the total amount of pleasure, matters. I concentrate on Sidgwick, because he says by far the most about well-being, but I place him in the sequence of philosophers that runs through Moore, Prichard, Ross, Carritt, Broad, and Ewing.[1]

Sidgwick's analysis

Sidgwick considers whether "good for me" means "what I desire for its own sake." He thinks not: I might desire something that is not so good when I get it, a "Dead Sea apple, mere dust and ashes in the eating." I might suppress my desire for something that I believe I cannot do anything to get, such as fine weather, but that does not change its goodness (ME 109–110).[2]

In response, Sidgwick offers a modification to the desire account: "good for me" might be identified

> not with the actually *desired*, but rather with the *desirable*:—meaning by "desirable" not necessarily "what *ought* to be desired" but what would be desired, with strength proportioned to the degree of desirability, if it were judged attainable by voluntary action, supposing the desirer to possess a perfect forecast, emotional as well as intellectual, of the state of attainment or fruition.

Since something might be desired in this sense but not be good for me on the whole, given its consequences and given the alternatives, a more complex account is needed for "good for me on the whole": what one "would now desire and seek on the whole if all the consequences of all the different lines of conduct open to him were accurately foreseen and adequately realised in imagination at the present point of time" (ME 110–112).

Sidgwick comments that this is too elaborate to be "what we commonly *mean*," but the account "supplies an intelligible and admissible interpretation of the terms 'good' (substantive) and 'desirable,' as giving philosophical precision to the vaguer meaning with which they are used in ordinary discourse." A "desire for 'good' conceived somewhat in this way, though more vaguely, is normally produced by intellectual comparison and experience in a reflective mind," and so is not so far from ordinary life. Finally, he comments that the

> notion of "Good" thus attained has an ideal element: it is something that *is* not always actually desired . . . but the ideal element is entirely interpretable in terms of *fact*, actual or hypothetical, and does not introduce any judgment of value, fundamentally distinct from judgments relating to existence;—still less any "dictate of Reason."
>
> *(ME 112)*

Sidgwick then argues for a different account, on which "good for me" should be analyzed as "what I should practically desire if my desires were in harmony with reason, assuming my own existence alone to be considered," or what I ought then to desire.[3] It is

> more in accordance with common sense to recognise—as Butler does—that the calm desire for my "good on the whole" is *authoritative*; and therefore carries with it implicitly a rational dictate to aim at this end, if in any case a conflicting desire urges the will in an opposite direction.
>
> *(ME 112)*[4]

(Similarly, in the second edition, after giving the hypothetical desire view, he writes that acting on these desires is "an ideal which we think [one] 'ought' to try to realise; such an effort therefore is 'prescribed' or 'dictated' by reason" (ME (2) 33).) The point seems to be that identifying what is good for me with what I would desire does not explain why it is a mistake to act on an opposed desire. Say I would, when informed, desire A, but in fact desire B. All that can be said is that I do not pursue what is good for me, or I do not act on a different desire. It does not follow from my desiring B that I have made a mistake. Sidgwick wants to build the rational dictate to pursue what is good for me into the concept of what is good for me.[5]

This makes it unlikely that Sidgwick's worry is that the hypothetical desire account picks out the wrong things as good.[6] The account gives an "intelligible and admissible interpretation." In the third through fifth editions his only objection to it is that it is too complex to be what we mean by "good for me" (ME (3) 108; ME (4) 112; ME (5) 112; also ME (2) 32–33). (Indeed, it is unclear there whether he finally rejects it: after noting that he is "not prepared to deny" the analysis, he makes the complexity point, then simply moves on to endorse taking one's good to be what one ought to desire.) Sidgwick's concern in the final edition seems to be that it does not follow from the account that I ought to pursue what is good for me, rather than that the account makes a mistake about what is good for me.

Although the hypothetical desire account is "admissible," Sidgwick does not appeal, in arguing for ultimate goods, to what I would desire if informed.[7] Judgments about the good are to be settled by "the same . . . procedure that I . . . employ[ed] in considering the absolute and independent validity of common moral precepts," which include an "appeal . . . to . . . intuitive judgment" (ME 400). Similarly, in the first and second editions, after rejecting an analysis of "good" in terms of pleasure, Sidgwick writes that "if the scale in which actions . . . are arranged in respect of goodness . . . is not finally determined by direct intuition, the proper method for determining it has yet to be ascertained" (ME (2) 99; also ME (1) 98).

One advantage of not appealing to informed desires is that Sidgwick avoids the worry that some, when informed, would not, when considering themselves alone, desire only pleasure. He admits that "several cultivated persons do habitually judge that knowledge, art, etc.—not to speak of Virtue—are ends independently of the pleasure derived from them" (ME 401). Sidgwick thinks these people are wrong. It seems more plausible to say that the error concerns what one ought to desire than what one would desire when informed; I seem the best judge of what I would desire when informed.

Before leaving the hypothetical desire account, another possible reason for rejecting it should be considered: perhaps Sidgwick rejects it because of open-question worries. He notes that Spencer thinks that "good (substantive)" means "pleasure." Sidgwick objects that "pleasure is the ultimate good" is now a tautology. He then gives his account of "good" as what one ought to desire and adds that "that is required for a non-tautological principle" (GSM 145). Whether Sidgwick thinks one must go to his ought-to-desire account, or just not define "good" as "pleasure," is not clear. On the one hand, his argument could be generated against a hypothetical desire account: "what I would desire given full information is the ultimate good" would be a tautology if "good" means "what I would desire given full information." On the other hand, after giving the same tautology objection to defining "good" as "pleasure" in the *Methods*, Sidgwick immediately turns to consider desire accounts, and does not offer the tautology objection to them (ME 109).

I do not think that open-question worries should be stressed. Sidgwick admits informative analyses. The hypothetical desire account is too elaborate to be "what we commonly *mean*," but the account "supplies an intelligible and admissible interpretation of the terms 'good' (substantive) and 'desirable,' as giving philosophical precision to the vaguer meaning with which they are used in ordinary discourse" (ME 112). Presumably Sidgwick claims the same for his own account: he does not worry that "the good is what I ought to desire" becomes "what I ought to desire is what I ought to desire." Similarly, "the uninstructed majority of mankind could not define a circle as a figure bounded by a line of which every point is equidistant from the centre: but nevertheless, when the definition is explained to them, they will accept it as expressing the perfect type of that notion of roundness which they have long had in their minds" (ME 353). The real problem with analyzing "good" as "pleasure" is that when the definition is explained, we do not accept it as expressing what we had in mind by "good."[8]

Sidgwick's view is a "fitting attitude" account: "good for me" is analyzed in terms of a fitting desire. He does not, however, give the usual motivations for such an account. Consider the motivations given by Ewing (concerning "good" rather than "good for"): "good" is more puzzling than "ought;" it is a virtue to have one unanalyzable concept rather than two; the analysis removes disagreement between deontologists and ideal utilitarians; the analysis gives a more defensible form of non-naturalism; the analysis explains why claims about goodness cannot be analyzed in non-normative terms; the goodness of a state of affairs plays no role because in justifying a choice we cite only non-normative properties (Ewing 1939; 1947: ch. 5; 1959: ch. 3). Sidgwick says none of this. His motivation seems to be simply that he thinks common sense holds that it follows from A's being good for me that I ought to desire A. Nor does Sidgwick consider some of the standard issues that arise for fitting attitude accounts. Unlike Ewing, he does not consider whether different attitudes might be appropriate for different goods—he always writes of desire, aim, or choice—nor does he consider the now-popular "wrong kind of reasons" objection or the objection that fitting attitude accounts reverse the correct order of explanation (I ought to desire A because A is good for me, rather than vice versa).

Objections to Sidgwick's analysis

I turn to objections.

Synthetic connection

One question is why Sidgwick wants to build the rational dictate into the concept, rather than add it as an independent claim about what I ought to do. Broad notes that one could hold that

> the purely positive, though ideal, definition of "my greatest good on the whole" is adequate; but that it is a *synthetic* and necessary proposition that I *ought* to desire my greatest good on the whole, thus defined . . . It is surely possible that both "good" and "right" are indefinable, as both "shape" and "size" are, and yet there is a synthetic, necessary and mutual relation between them, as there is between shape and size.
> *(Broad 1930: 176, 177)*[9]

Broad is right to think this possible. Sidgwick could give two replies.

First, he could note that his analysis explains why I ought to desire my good.

Second, shape and size do not seem plausibly analyzed in terms of one another. It is at least plausible that "my good" can be analyzed as "what I ought to desire, considering myself alone"—hence the continued popularity of fitting attitude analyses.

Depression and self-loathing

Stephen Darwall objects that I can hold, without conceptual error, that I have no reason to desire what is good for me—say I am depressed, or loathe myself. If so, "A is good for me" cannot be analyzed as "A is what I have reason to desire considering myself alone" (Darwall 2002: 5–6).

Darwall thinks of the depressive and self-loather as making desert claims: the depressive claims that he does not deserve to be better off; the self-loather claims he deserves to be worse off. Presumably both think that if they did deserve some benefit, or if desert were silent, they would have a reason to desire A. This suggests that Sidgwick's analysis could be modified to meet the objection: "A is good for me" can be analyzed as "A is what (given the absence of a defeater such as a desert claim) I have reason to desire when considering myself alone."[10] This allows the depressive or self-loather to say, without conceptual confusion, "A is good for me but I have no reason to desire A" and for Sidgwick to say that both have reason to desire A (since Sidgwick thinks they are wrong in making desert claims).

"Ought" and "can"

Sidgwick thinks "ought" has two senses: the "narrow" or "ethical" sense implies "can"; the "wider" sense does not. The wide sense is needed because we say things like "I ought to feel as a better man would feel" "though I may know that I could not directly produce in myself such . . . feeling by any effort of will." The wide "ought" "merely implies an ideal or pattern which I 'ought'—in the stricter sense—to seek to imitate as far as possible" (ME 33). The objection, raised by Tom Hurka, is a dilemma (Hurka 2003: 604; Hurka 2014: 53). Say the "ought" used to analyze "good for me" implies "can." It follows that if I cannot desire some state of myself, it is not good for me. But that is false. As Sidgwick notes,

since irrational desires cannot always be dismissed at once by voluntary effort . . . we
can not say [that what is good for me is what I ought to desire] in the strictly ethical
sense of "ought." We can only say it in the wider sense, in which it merely connotes
an ideal or standard, divergence from which it is our duty to avoid as far as possible.
(ME (4) 110–111; also ME (3) 107, ME (5) 111)[11]

But now the worry is that the analysis is pointless: there is no difference between saying "that
state of myself is good for me" and "that state of myself is an ideal." Ross notes, against Broad's
example of the wider sense "sorrow ought to have been felt by a certain man at the death of a
certain relation, though it was not in his power to feel sorrow at will," that "all we are entitled
to say is, not that he ought to have felt sorrow now, but that his not feeling it is a bad thing"
(Ross 1939: 45; Broad 1930: 161).[12]

Sidgwick has a reply. Say the "ought" is the wide sense, and that, as he suggests, the wide
sense can be understood in terms of the narrow sense. To say that I ought, in the wide sense,
to desire x, is to say that I ought, in the narrow sense, to desire x "as far as possible." "I ought,
in the narrow sense, to desire x" is made false by my inability to desire x. But "I ought, in the
narrow sense, to desire x as far as possible" is not made false by my inability to desire x. It would
be made false by my inability to desire x as far as possible—but I am *always* able to desire x as far
as I can, since that is to say that I can do what I can do.[13] Put another way: the first horn of the
dilemma depends on thinking that there can be states of myself that I cannot desire (and which
are good). Once the claim becomes "there can be states of myself that I cannot desire as far as
possible (and which are good)," one sees that there can be no such states.

The scope problem

If "good for me" is identified simply with something I ought to desire, many things will be
wrongly included. I ought to desire the pleasure of a deserving stranger, but her getting this
pleasure need not be good for me.[14] Sidgwick avoids this by adding "assuming my own existence alone to be considered" (ME 112). Sidgwick also adds that the issue is "what a man
desires . . . for himself—not benevolently for others" (ME 109) and often associates egoism
with "self-love" (e.g., HUG 31, 33, ME xx–xxi, 89, 93).[15] But both additions face problems.

One might worry, against the first, that if I ought to desire that people get what they non-
comparatively deserve, and I am bad, then "assuming my own existence alone to be considered"
does not exclude the conclusion that my pain is good for me (Kagan 1992: 185).[16]

Perhaps, however, Sidgwick intends "assuming my own existence alone to be considered"
to exclude what he thinks of as "relations" to something beyond my consciousness.[17] Sidgwick
thinks of virtues as states of consciousness that "correspon[d] to an ideal" (ME 400). The ideal
is not part of my consciousness. Similarly, a just distribution of pain is not part of my consciousness. This reading makes sense of Sidgwick's claim that "when any one hypothetically
concentrates his attention on himself, Good is naturally and almost inevitably conceived to be
Pleasure" (ME 405). Concentrating my attention on myself, in the sense of thinking of what
is located in me rather than others, would not exclude thinking of my virtue or knowledge as
good for me—unlike concentrating my attention on myself in the sense of excluding relations
to anything beyond consciousness.

This is not, however, the natural reading of "assuming my own existence to be considered."
Sidgwick contrasts this with having "an equal concern for *all* existence," not with relations to
something outside consciousness (ME 112). And the reading seems to build too much into the
notion of well-being: virtue and knowledge are trivially excluded from contributing to well-being.

There is a variant on this reply.[18] The problem arises because there seem to be goods, located in me, that are not good for me. But Sidgwick, holding that only pleasure is good, would deny this. For him, the only good located in me does benefit me. This reply has the drawback that the acceptability of the analysis depends on controversial arguments about what is good. That, however, may be inevitable, since whether there is a counter-example to the analysis depends on what is good.

The second addition limits the ought-claims to those I make when loving myself, or being (as it were) benevolent to myself. One worry is that, although Sidgwick thinks "the promotion of Happiness is practically the chief part of what Common Sense considers to be prescribed as the external duty of Benevolence," he is unwilling to rule out the promotion of virtue as also prescribed by benevolence (ME 240; also ME 9, 392, Ross 1930: 21).[19] A second worry is that the analysis seems unhelpful, since, as Sidgwick himself notes, "Benevolence . . . manifestly involve[s] this notion of Good" (ME 393).[20] But perhaps here Sidgwick can reply that since his motivation for giving a fitting attitude analysis is to make an analytic connection between "A is good for me" and "I ought to desire A," this does not matter to him.[21] Say that "A is good for me" is analyzed as "A is what I ought to desire when I am benevolent to myself." The circularity makes the analysis unhelpful in one way, since benevolence involves the notion of one's good. But the analysis is helpful in another way: it connects what is good for me and what I ought to desire, something Sidgwick thinks is needed.[22]

Sidgwick's arguments for pleasure as the only ultimate good

Sidgwick gives two arguments for pleasure as the only ultimate good.[23]

The first argument is that

> to me at least it seems clear after reflection that these objective relations of the conscious subject, when distinguished from the consciousness accompanying and resulting from them, are not ultimately and intrinsically desirable; any more than material or other objects are, when considered apart from any relation to conscious existence.
>
> *(ME 400–401)*

This appears terribly inconclusive—Sidgwick is aware that the reflection of others gives a different verdict. But I think he can say *a bit* more.

By "objective relations," Sidgwick means "relations of the conscious mind which are not included in its consciousness" (LE 126n1). For example, when I know that p, I (on most accounts) have a belief, and the belief stands in a certain relation to a state of affairs—it is (at least) true. That the belief is true is not a fact included in consciousness (though my belief that p is true is included in consciousness). Sidgwick is thinking of a case like this: compare two worlds that are alike except that in W_1 my belief that p is true and in W_2 my belief is false. Say this difference makes no difference to me in any way other than making it the case that I know that p in one world and do not know that p in the other. Sidgwick thinks the worlds are equal in goodness.

Sidgwick notes that material objects, such as beautiful objects or mere physical processes, are not ultimate goods. The obvious explanation is that they do not affect consciousness. In the case of physical processes,

> so long as we confine our attention to their corporeal aspect,—regarding them merely as complex movements of certain particles of organised matter—it seems impossible to attribute to these movements . . . either goodness or badness . . . .[I]f a certain quality of human Life is that which is ultimately desirable, it must belong to . . . Consciousness.
>
> *(ME 396)*

But if knowledge is an ultimate good, that explanation cannot be sufficient: in the case above, knowledge does not affect consciousness. The defender of knowledge must say, then, that the explanation for why mere physical processes are not ultimate goods is not just that their existence does not by itself affect consciousness—but that seemed a sufficient explanation.

Moore objects that

> from the fact that no value resides in one part of a whole, considered by itself, we cannot infer that all the value belonging to the whole does reside in the other part, considered by itself . . . Sidgwick's argument here depends upon the neglect of . . . the principle of "organic relations." The argument is calculated to mislead, because it supposes that, if we see a whole state to be valuable, and also see that one element of that state has no value *by itself*, then the other element, *by itself*, must have all the value which belongs to the whole state.
>
> (Moore 1903: 92–93; also Bradley 1877: 25, 27; Seth 1896: 422;
> Hayward 1901: 189, 200–201, 225, 231; Broad 1930: 235–237;
> Irwin 2009: 459–461, 548–549; Hurka 2014: 200)

But it is not clear that Sidgwick makes this argument. When he writes that "these objective relations of the conscious subject, when distinguished from the consciousness accompanying and resulting from them, are not ultimately and intrinsically desirable," he need not be read as *inferring* from (i) knowledge has no value by itself to (ii) knowledge contributes no value to the whole. Rather, the point is that when consciousness is held fixed, there is no difference in value, so knowledge cannot be contributing any value. Sidgwick's case rests on our direct intuition about a case like W_1 and W_2, rather than an argument from the value of parts and wholes.[24]

Sidgwick's second argument for pleasure is that knowledge, beauty, etc. are "not only . . . productive of pleasure . . . but also . . . they seem to obtain the commendation of Common Sense, roughly speaking, in proportion to the degree of this productiveness" (ME 401). Sidgwick's explanation is that they are only instrumentally valuable.

Moore objects that, even granted the proportionality claim, Sidgwick "leave[s] open the alternative that the greatest quantity of pleasure was as a matter of fact, *under actual conditions*, generally accompanied by the greatest quantity of *other goods*, and that it therefore was *not* the sole good" (Moore 1903: 91–92). Broad objects that Sidgwick cannot conclude

> that the hedonic quality of an experience is *sufficient* as well as *necessary* to give intrinsic value. Even if the *variations* in intrinsic value were dependent on variations in hedonic quality and totally independent of variations in any non-hedonic characteristic, it might still be the case that intrinsic value would not be *present at all* unless there were some non-hedonic characteristic in addition to the hedonic quality.
>
> (Broad 1930: 236–237)

Moore and Broad show that Sidgwick's argument, even granting the proportionality claim, is inconclusive. But Sidgwick starts the argument by noting that it "cannot be made completely cogent" (ME 401). Presumably his thought is that his explanation of proportionality is more plausible than the possibilities suggested by Moore and Broad. Moore admits that the explanation that he suggests "might indeed seem to be a strange coincidence" (Moore 1903: 92; also Moore 1965 [1912]: 101).

One might instead attack Sidgwick's argument for the proportionality claim. In *Principia*, Moore does, briefly: he charges that Sidgwick's "detailed illustrations only tend to shew the very different proposition that a thing is not held to be good, unless it gives a balance of pleasure; not that the degree of commendation is in proportion to the quantity of pleasure" (Moore 1903: 92). Moore is right that Sidgwick sometimes claims only that (for example) "it is paradoxical to maintain that . . . any form of social order, would still be commonly regarded as desirable even if we were certain that it had no tendency to promote the general happiness" (ME 401). But Sidgwick also claims, of a "fruitless" branch of science which nonetheless gives "the inquirer the refined and innocent pleasures of curiosity," that "Common Sense is somewhat disposed to complain of the misdirection of valuable effort." He concludes that "the meed of honour commonly paid to Science seems to be graduated, though perhaps unconsciously, by a tolerably exact utilitarian scale" (ME 401–402). The fruitless inquirer, producing a small amount of pleasure, is less commended than a fruitful inquirer. This is a proportionality claim, rather than a claim about pleasure production as a necessary condition for commendation.[25]

Moore and Broad also attack the proportionality claim by giving counter-examples. Moore claims that, in cases like W_1 and W_2 above, we think W_2 is better (especially when there is a great deal more knowledge or virtue or appreciation of beauty in W_2) (Moore 1965 [1912]: 102; see also Ross 1930: 134, 138–139, Ewing 1965 [1953]: 43–44). Broad notes that pleasure in the undeserved pain of another is bad, and "*worse* in proportion as the pleasantness is more intense," even when the malice is "impotent" (Broad 1930: 234; see also Ewing 1965 [1953]: 44–45). This is well-trodden territory, in which Sidgwick makes no special contribution. Like many in the recent empirically informed literature, Sidgwick is more willing to explain away intuitions than his opponents are; but obviously this is inconclusive.

Well-being

One question is whether, when Sidgwick argues for pleasure as the ultimate good, he is arguing for it as what well-being consists in or as what is good.

Sidgwick sometimes suggests that his concern is well-being (Crisp 2011: 27n4). In the chapter on ultimate good, his target is "Good or Well-being" (ME 391, 392), the "Ultimate good for man" (ME 392), "well-being or welfare" (ME 396), "well-being" (ME 397), what is "desirable for the . . . agent" and "good for the . . . agent" (ME 397; 404, also 397). He thinks the debate over ultimate good replays the egoistic Greek debate (ME 392). He takes the Greeks to be concerned with what is "good for himself," "his own true good" (HUG 28, 31). His concern is "the end which a prudent man, as such, has in view" (HUG 29), "one's own good" (HUG 33; also ME 405). Pleasure is offered as one specification of "Well-being or Welfare" (HUG 33).

But there are two reasons for thinking this is misleading.

First, Sidgwick concludes the discussion of ultimate good by noting that he has arrived at utilitarianism (ME 407; also 388). This is false if he has established only that well-being consists in pleasure. If he has established only that, further arguments would be needed to dismiss goods that are not part of well-being.

This is not decisive. For perhaps Sidgwick thinks he has, before the discussion, ruled out goods that are not good for anyone. In that case, by his lights he does arrive at utilitarianism by arguing that only pleasure is good for me. And Sidgwick might be thought to have ruled out goods that are not good for anyone. Against the possibility (endorsed, briefly, by Moore 1903: 83–84) that beautiful objects are good, he argues that "no one would consider it rational to aim at the production of beauty in external nature, apart from any possible contemplation of it by human beings" (ME 114).

However, this is not the best description of what Sidgwick does. Sidgwick assumes that what is good must "exist . . . in minds" or not "exist out of relation to . . . minds" (ME 114). This does not limit him to considering well-being, at least in the sense that makes it plausible to say that knowledge is not part of my well-being. Sidgwick concludes that "beauty, knowledge, and other ideal goods, as well as all external material things, are only reasonably to be sought by men in so far as they conduce either (1) to Happiness or (2) to the Perfection or Excellence of human existence" (ME 114; also 10n5). Existence (at least partly) in a mind is a necessary condition for being good, but the distinction between things that exist and things that do not exist in a mind is not the distinction between well-being and a wider class of good things. Thus later Moore and Ross agree with Sidgwick that existence in a mind is a necessary condition for being good, but not that well-being is the only good (Ross 1930: 140; Moore 1965 [1912]: 70, 103–104, 107 (also 1903: 202, 203)).

Second, Sidgwick's arguments for pleasure do not turn on noting that some feature of well-being favours pleasure and disfavours, say, knowledge or beauty. Here it is useful to contrast current writers. Wayne Sumner writes that what

> distinguishes welfare from all other modes of value is its reference to the proprietor of the life in question: although your life may be going well in many respects, it is prudentially valuable only if it is going well *for you* . . . Since objective theories exclude all reference to the subject's attitudes or concerns . . . the subject-relativity of welfare constitutes a deep problem for any objective theory.
>
> *(Sumner 1996: 42–43; see also 20–25 and ch. 3)*

Fred Feldman writes that

> [s]uppose some pluralist tells me that knowledge and virtue will make my life better. Suppose I dutifully go about gaining knowledge and virtue. After a tedious and exhausting period of training, I become knowledgeable. I behave virtuously. I find the whole thing utterly unsatisfying. The pluralist now tells me that my life is going well for me. I dispute it. I think I might be better off *intellectually* and *morally*, but my welfare is, if anything, going downhill.
>
> *(Feldman 2004: 19; see also 2004: 8–12, 2010: 161–170).*

Similarly, it is popular to defend hedonism from the experience machine objection by explaining the anti-hedonist intuition as resting on the view that, say, achievement is good (but not good for one). This leaves hedonism unscathed as an account of well-being (e.g., Railton 1989: 170; Goldsworthy 1992: 18–20; Sumner 1996: 96; Kawall 1999: 385–386; Silverstein 2000: 290–293; Crisp 2006: 116, 122; Heathwood 2006: 553).

This is not Sidgwick's strategy. He says simply that knowledge and virtue "are not ultimately and intrinsically desirable" or not "ends independently of the pleasure derived from them" (ME 400–401). They are valued in proportion to the pleasure they produce, and the best explanation for this is that they are only instrumentally valuable (ME 401–402). These arguments do not rely on special features of well-being such as "subject-relativity" or on restrictions such as excluding relations or being benevolent to oneself.[26] And if, like Sidgwick, one is arguing for pleasure as the only good, there is no point to the current taxonomic move, which admits other goods.

One might go further. Hurka argues that Sidgwick (and the rest of the school) *lacked* the "present-day concept of welfare" (Hurka 2014: 36; see 34–38 and 2003: 610–612). Sidgwick (and Moore) had the different concept, noted above, of a good located in oneself.

Whether Hurka is right depends on the content of the "present-day concept." What seems crucial is that (a) well-being is a good that, unlike some other putative goods, benefits me;

(b) well-being is a good constituted by other goods, such as pleasure, desire-satisfaction, life-satisfaction, or elements from an "objective list" such as virtue and knowledge. For (a), Sidgwick certainly thinks I can be morally good without that benefiting me. For (b), "good for" is a good that is constituted by other goods—Sidgwick thinks that the concept is "what I ought to desire considering myself alone" and that what I ought to desire considering myself alone is pleasure. In a note on why he translates *eudaimonia* "by the more unfamiliar 'well-being' or 'welfare'" rather than "happiness," Sidgwick argues that "happiness" "signifies a state of feeling" and so is false to Aristotle. "Well-being" is another term for "our being's end and aim," a term that Sidgwick introduces in order to include goods such as virtue (OHE 56n2; also 48). We "may still argue with the Stoics, that virtuous or excellent activities and not pleasures are the elements of which true human Well-being is composed" (ME 92).

Perhaps Hurka thinks "what I ought to desire considering myself alone" is so clearly different from well-being that Sidgwick must have something else in mind. But that seems wrong. (i) Counter-examples to "what I ought to desire considering myself alone" as an analysis of well-being rely on goods such as my getting what I deserve. Sidgwick does not see these as goods, so they are not evidence that Sidgwick must have had something other than well-being in mind. (ii) "Considering myself alone" does seem at least a plausible way to distinguish between goods that benefit me and those that do not. "Good located in me" can be defended as part of an analysis of well-being (Fletcher 2012a). Indeed, it is not clear why the location of a good matters unless one thinks location in me is necessary for me to benefit. (iii) Even if Sidgwick's analysis is unsatisfactory, one might conclude that Sidgwick gave a failed analysis rather than had a different concept in mind. Compare one who, pre-Gettier, analyzed knowledge as justified true belief. We do not think that accepting this analysis, pre-Gettier, shows that the target concept was not what we mean by knowledge.

Order

Sidgwick writes of one's good as a "mathematical whole, of which the integrant parts are realised in different parts or moments of a lifetime," and that "a smaller present good is not to be preferred to a greater future good" (ME 381). He thinks of egoists as aiming at "a total" of pleasure and pain "which we are to seek to make as great as possible" (e.g., ME 123).

Broad notes against Sidgwick that "[m]ost people would be inclined to think that a life which began unhappily and ended happily was to be preferred to one, containing the same balance of happiness, which began happily and ended unhappily." Broad goes on to raise doubts, since "secondary" pleasures and pains of memory and anticipation might alter the totals (Broad 1930: 225–226). But many others are confident that order matters as well as the total amount of pleasure.[27]

Sidgwick's account of pleasure gives him a reply.[28]

For Sidgwick, a pleasure is a "feeling which . . . is at least implicitly apprehended as desirable or—in cases of comparison—preferable," "when considered merely as feeling" (ME 127, 131). Pleasures vary in intensity and duration. Intensity is set by preferability: if, say, I find one minute of feeling x preferable to two minutes of feeling y, and find either x or y preferable to "hedonistic zero," then x is more than twice as intense a pleasure as y.

If so, Broad's case is misdescribed. If I find {x intensity of pain followed by y intensity of pleasure} for a given duration preferable to {x intensity of pleasure followed by y intensity of pain} for the same duration, y must be greater than x just in virtue of my judgment of preferability, and so I find preferable the greater total.[29]

One might object, as Jamie Mayerfeld has, that it seems possible to make a judgment of preferability between the same totals. This is avoided only by keeping judgments of intensity independent of (global) preferability. I think this shows that we have a notion of intensity that is independent of (global) preferability.[30] But Sidgwick can reply that intensity understood in this way—call it "local" intensity—is normatively irrelevant when one makes a global judgment of preferability about the experiences. Say X finds pain first preferable, Y finds pleasure first preferable, and the totals of the local intensities are the same. (Say the pains and pleasures derive their local intensities from one's judgments of preferability at the time of feeling them.) A benevolent person would not be indifferent to which life X and Y get; she would give pain-first to X and pleasure-first to Y. This does not show that local intensity in the presence of a judgment of global preferability is irrelevant—perhaps here it creates a tie broken by the judgment of global preferability. But even if the totals of the local intensities are different, a benevolent person would follow global preferability rather than these totals. She would not, for example, give me pleasure-first, even if it had a higher total of local intensities, if I found pain-first preferable.[31]

***

After Sidgwick, Moore suggests that "good for me" means "the thing I get is good" (Moore 1903: 98; also 99, 170).[32] As Hurka notes, this is close to Sidgwick's analysis, with "good" replacing "ought to be desired" and "I get" replacing "considering myself alone" (Hurka 2003: 611; Hurka 2014: 34–35). Since Moore thinks many things are good other than pleasure, he might seem especially vulnerable to the possibility that a good might be mine without that being good for me in the sense that it benefits me. But Moore is tempted to think that pleasure is a part of any good whole, and so perhaps avoids the objection (Moore 1903: 213, 1965 [1912]: 103–104, 107).

Prichard analyzes "good to me" as what "excites" either "a feeling of satisfaction" or "enjoyment" (a feeling that, unlike satisfaction, does not require a preceding desire) (Prichard 2002 [around 1937]: 174; see Hurka 2014: 35). Prichard does not give this as an analysis of "good," and so avoids the objection that he makes "pleasure is the ultimate good" a tautology. He must think, however, that "pleasure is my ultimate good" is a tautology. In the *Methods* version of the tautology argument, Sidgwick writes that the (objectionable) tautology is "Pleasure . . . of human beings is their Good or Ultimate Good" (ME 109).

Carritt holds that to say that x is good for me is to say that x is "excellently suited to satisfy desire" (Carritt also writes of "advantage," "interest," and "satisfaction") (Carritt 1947: 48; see Carritt 1937: 59, 60, 65, 69–71, 74).

After Sidgwick, hedonism is rejected. Various of the analyses of "my good" that he considers are adopted, without much argument. But then, Sidgwick himself does not argue for his preferred analysis in anything like the depth of accounts now—perhaps because the category of well-being was not so important to him.

Appendix: Changes in Sidgwick's analysis of "good"

In the first and second editions, after rejecting the view that "good" means "pleasure," Sidgwick does not explicitly give any positive view. He writes only that "if the scale in which actions . . . are arranged in respect of goodness . . . is not finally determined by direct intuition, the proper method of determining it has yet to be ascertained" (ME (2) 99; also ME (1) 98).

In the third and fourth editions, he claims that "good," like "right," does not admit "of being analyzed into more elementary notions. We can only make it clearer by determining its relations." As an example of these relations, he notes a relation to desire: "What I recognize as on the whole good . . . for me I either do desire (if absent), or think that I should desire if my impulses were in harmony with my reason,—assuming my own existence alone to be considered." He then gives the hypothetical desire account as an alternative, and, after noting that it is too elaborate to be what we mean, concludes with the "ought to desire" view (ME (4) 110–112; also ME (3) 106–108). "Assuming my own existence alone to be considered" is added in the fourth edition (though it is present earlier elsewhere, e.g., ME (1) 360; ME (3) 402; see Hurka 2014: 35). There is no initial argument given for the "ought to desire" view: it is just asserted as specifying the relation between "good" and "desire." (It is also odd that Sidgwick denies an analysis of "good": one would think "what I ought to desire" just *is* an analysis into more elementary notions. And if the connection between "good" and "what I ought to desire" is not analytic, Sidgwick denies exactly the claim he seems to insist on in the final edition.)

In the fifth edition, after noting that things are not good in proportion to my actual desires—since "we often desire intensely, and even seek to realize, a result that we know to be bad in preference to another that we judge to be good"—Sidgwick writes that "[b]ut I may say that what I regard as on the whole 'good' for me, I regard as 'desirable' if not 'desired': *i.e.* I think that I should desire it if my impulses were in harmony with my reason—assuming my own existence alone to be considered" (ME (5) 110–111). Here "ought to desire" is introduced to avoid a problem for actual desires. Sidgwick goes on to suggest the hypothetical desire account as a different way of avoiding this problem, again notes that it is too elaborate, and again repeats the "ought to desire" view (ME (5) 111–112).[33]

Notes

1 For this sequence as part of a "school," see Hurka (2011, 2014).

2 ME = Sidgwick (1981/1907); ME (1) (the first edition of the *Methods*) = Sidgwick (1874); ME (2) = Sidgwick (1877c); ME (3) = Sidgwick (1884); ME (4) = Sidgwick (1890); ME (5) = Sidgwick (1893); HUG = Sidgwick (1877a); B = Sidgwick (1877b); FC = Sidgwick (1889); OHE = Sidgwick (1902a); GSM = Sidgwick (1902b).

3 Elsewhere he holds that "good" should be defined as "that at which it is reasonable to aim" (ME 92n1), "what one ought to aim at" (ME 381), "what it is reasonable to seek to keep, or aim at getting" (GSM 331), "what all rational beings, as such, ought to aim at realising" (B 411), "the right and proper end of human action" (FC 482), "desirable, choice-worthy, preferable, to be sought" (GSM 145, italics eliminated). He rejects Martineau's (apparent) view of "the judgment of good and ill as non-ethical" (GSM 331).

4 Thus we "do not all look with simple indifference on a man who declines to take the right means to attain his own happiness, on no other ground than that he does not care about happiness. Most men would regard such a refusal as irrational, with a certain disapprobation; they would thus implicitly assent to Butler's statement that 'interest, one's own happiness, is a manifest obligation.' In other words, they would think that a man *ought* to care for his own happiness" (ME 7). This is put in terms of one's own happiness, rather than one's own good, but presumably it is true for one's happiness because happiness is at least part of one's good.

5 For a similar interpretation, see de Lazari-Radek and Singer (2014: 203).

6 Parfit suggests that Sidgwick writes "in harmony with reason" "to exclude the cases where . . . someone's desires are irrational. He assumes that there are some things that we have good reason to desire . . . These might be things which are held to be good . . . for us by Objective List Theories" (Parfit 1984: 500; see also Parfit 2011: 496–497, Darwall 2002: 35–36). I once suggested that Sidgwick's worry is that I might with full information desire A but from weakness of will form a stronger desire for B. If the hypothetical desire account identifies what is good for me with whatever I desire with full information, it would then pick out the wrong thing as good (Shaver 1997). Since Sidgwick's concern does not seem to be about picking out the wrong things, both interpretations are dubious.

7 I owe this point, as well as the reference to ME 400 below, to Tom Hurka; see also Adams (1999: 87n7).

8 For the same take on the open-question argument, see Ross (1930: 92–93) and Broad (1930: 173–174).

9 Broad has in mind "'anything that has shape must have size'" (1930: 236, 266).

10 For a similar suggestion for the goodness of pleasure, see Ross (1930: 137–138).

11 For an example of worrying that an "ought" that implies "can" fails for this reason, see Fletcher (2012b: 86).

12 Ross does think "it would have been right to have felt sorrow" is true here, although "sorrow ought to have been felt" is false (1939: 55). Like Broad and Ewing, Ross thinks there is a sense of "fitting" that does not imply "can" (as does Moore 1922: 319 for "ought") and so can be used in a fitting attitude analysis of "good" (though Ross accepts such an account only for one sense of "good"). It is again not clear, however, how this sense differs from "it would have been good to have felt sorrow."

13 Thus Sidgwick, after noting that "it cannot be a strict duty to feel an emotion, so far as it is not directly within the power of the Will to produce it at any given time," concludes that "it will be a duty to cultivate the affection so far as it is possible to do so" (ME 239).

14 Oddly, Michael Zimmerman seems to give this as an objection to Sidgwick, omitting the "assuming my own existence alone to be considered" qualification (Zimmerman 2009: 430, 434–436). (Zimmerman suggests that Sidgwick should restrict the "ought" to a "prudential" "ought.") For the objection pressed against other fitting-attitude accounts, see (for example) Fletcher (2012b: 79–84). Carritt gives the reverse objection: my escaping prison, or getting wealth, might be good for me but not good (Carritt 1937: 59). But here there is something good—for example, the pleasure that the escape or wealth brings (see Fletcher 2012a: 17–18).

15 In the fourth and fifth editions, Sidgwick writes that what is good for me is what I ought to desire "[p]utting aside the conceivable case of its being my duty to sacrifice my own good, to realise some greater good outside my own existence" (ME (4) 110; ME (5) 111). This is presumably directed at the worry that, although I ought to desire the pleasure of the deserving stranger, her getting the pleasure is not good for me if I must sacrifice my pleasure to produce it. But it does not meet the worry that, even when I need not sacrifice pleasure to produce her pleasure, her getting the pleasure is not good for me. It also includes "my own good" in the analysis of "good for me" (though Sidgwick might not mind—see below).

16 For further objections along these lines, see Sumner (1996: 50–53). For replies different than mine, see Fletcher (2012a). Adams objects that my desire that I be of service to others is a desire for myself but "not a desire for one's own good as such; and in fulfilling it one might be willing to sacrifice one's own good." But he then notes that it "does not seem unreasonable to count it a great blessing to be able really to help other people" (Adams 1999: 88). Sidgwick could reply that, if so, my desire that I help others is a desire for (part of) my good; if acting on this desire is a sacrifice, that is because (in this case) it causes the frustration of other more important desires for myself.

17 I owe this suggestion to Joyce Jenkins; see also Adams (1999: 88–9).

18 I also owe this suggestion to Joyce Jenkins.

19 For use of the similar "sympathy test" against virtue, see Hooker (1996: sec. 5).

20 This is a standard theme in the literature on Darwall (2002) and Rønnow-Rasmussen (2011), who restrict the desires to those "insofar as one cares about the person" or "for the person's sake." It is also raised by Adams (1999: 88–91).

21 For a related reply to the circularity charge, see Darwall (2006: 651–655). In the third and fourth editions, Sidgwick seems to deny giving an analysis (see Appendix).

22 If "A is good for me" is analyzed as "A is what I ought to desire when being benevolent to myself," it no longer follows, from A's being good for me, that I ought to desire A. That follows only if I am (or perhaps ought to be) benevolent to myself (see Darwall 2000: 303–306). The same goes for "A is what I ought to desire when considering myself alone": unless I am (or perhaps ought to be) considering myself alone, it does not follow, from A's being good for me, that I ought to desire A.

23 For a reconstruction of *Methods* III.XIV prior to these arguments, see Shaver (2008). By an "ultimate good," Sidgwick means something good as an end.

24 In *Ethics*, Moore thinks Sidgwick's judgment about a case like W_1 and W_2 is so obviously wrong that he offers the inference as an explanation of why anyone would make that judgment (Moore 1965/1912: 102–106); he does not mention Sidgwick by name.

25 For evidence of a proportionality claim in the case of virtue, see Shaver (2008: 226).

26 In Feldman's terminology, Sidgwick is concerned with the value of "worlds" rather than "lives" (Feldman 2004: 195–198).

27 For a guide to those who make the order objection, see Feldman (2004: 124–126). Since Feldman wrote, Irwin (2009: 510) and Temkin (2012: 109–125) have directed the objection against Sidgwick.

28 For a somewhat different (excellent) reply, see Feldman (2004: Chapter 6). For a very different treatment of Sidgwick on pleasure, see Crisp (2011).

29 Temkin briefly considers measuring intensity in this way. He says that this is not how he measures intensity. He does not explicitly note the bad consequences for his argument if this method of measurement

is adopted (2012: 136n4). Temkin might note, however, that my strategy for defending Sidgwick has a limitation. Sidgwick's claims about mathematical wholes and preferring the greater good are meant to apply to all goods in one's life, not just pleasure (ME 381). If, say, knowledge is part of what is good for me, and I prefer a life in which greater knowledge comes later to a life in which greater knowledge comes earlier, Sidgwick could not argue that my preference makes it the case that there is more total knowledge in the knowledge-later life. The amount of knowledge does not depend on my preferences.

30 Mayerfeld (1999: 68–73). On 77–78, he gives the order example.

31 For a related argument, see Parfit (1984: 496–499).

32 I put aside Moore's other suggestion, that "x is good for me" means "my possessing x is good" (Moore 1903: 98–99).

33 Thanks to Roger Crisp and Joyce Jenkins for written comments, to Joyce and to Tom Hurka for many conversations, and to an audience at Manitoba.

References

Adams, R.M. (1999) *Finite and Infinite Goods*, Oxford: Oxford University Press.

Bradley, F.H. (1877) *Mr. Sidgwick's Hedonism*, London: H.S. King.

Broad, C.D. (1930) *Fives Types of Ethical Theory*, London: Routledge & Kegan Paul.

Carritt, E.F. (1937) "An Ambiguity of the Word 'Good,'" *Proceedings of the British Academy* 23: 51–80.

Carritt, E.F. (1947) *Ethical and Political Thinking*, Oxford: Clarendon.

Crisp, R. (2006) *Reasons and the Good*, Oxford: Clarendon.

Crisp, R. (2011) "Pleasure and Hedonism in Sidgwick," in T. Hurka (ed.), *Underivative Duty*, Oxford: Oxford University Press, pp. 26–44.

Darwall, S. (2000) "Sidgwick, Concern, and the Good," *Utilitas* 12: 291–306.

Darwall, S. (2002) *Welfare and Rational Care*, Princeton: Princeton University Press.

Darwall, S. (2006) "Reply to Feldman, Hurka and Rosati," *Philosophical Studies* 130: 637–658.

De Lazari-Radek, K. and Singer, P. (2014) *The Point of View of the Universe: Sidgwick and Contemporary Ethics*, Oxford: Oxford University Press, 2014.

Ewing, A.C. (1939) "A Suggested Non-Naturalistic Analysis of Good," *Mind* 48: 1–22.

Ewing, A.C. (1947) *The Definition of Good*, London: Routledge & Kegan Paul.

Ewing, A.C. (1959) *Second Thoughts in Moral Philosophy*, London: Routledge & Kegan Paul.

Ewing, A.C. (1965/1953) *Ethics*, New York: Free Press.

Feldman, F. (2004) *Pleasure and the Good Life*, Oxford: Clarendon.

Feldman, F. (2010) *What is This Thing Called Happiness?* Oxford: Clarendon.

Fletcher, G. (2012a) "The Locative Analysis of Good for Formulated and Defended," *Journal of Ethics and Social Philosophy* 6: 1–26.

Fletcher, G. (2012b) "Resisting Buck-Passing Accounts of Prudential Value," *Philosophical Studies* 157: 77–91.

Goldsworthy, J. (1992) "Well-being and Value," *Utilitas* 4: 1–26.

Hayward, F.H. (1901) *The Ethical Philosophy of Sidgwick*, London: Swan Sonnenschein.

Heathwood, C. (2006) "Desire Satisfaction and Hedonism," *Philosophical Studies* 128: 539–563.

Hooker, B. (1996) "Does Moral Virtue Constitute a Benefit to the Agent?" in R. Crisp (ed.), *How Should One Live? Essays on the Virtues*, New York: Clarendon, pp. 141–156.

Hurka, T. (2003) "Moore in the Middle," *Ethics* 113: 599–628.

Hurka, T. (ed.) (2011) *Underivative Duty*, Oxford: Oxford University Press.

Hurka, T. (2014) *British Ethical Theorists from Sidgwick to Ewing*, Oxford: Oxford University Press.

Irwin, T.H. (2009) *The Development of Ethics*, vol. 3, Oxford: Oxford University Press.

Kagan, S. (1992) "The Limits of Well-Being," *Social Philosophy and Policy* 9: 169–189.

Kawall, J. (1999) "The Experience Machine and Mental State Theories of Well-being," *Journal of Value Inquiry* 33: 381–387.

Mayerfeld, J. (1999) *Suffering and Moral Responsibility*, Oxford: Oxford University Press.

Moore, G.E. (1903) *Principia Ethica*, Cambridge: Cambridge University Press.

Moore, G.E. (1922) "The Nature of Moral Philosophy," in G.E. Moore, *Philosophical Studies*, London: Routledge & Kegan Paul, pp. 310–339.

Moore, G.E. (1965/1912) *Ethics*, New York: Oxford University Press.

Parfit, D. (1984) *Reasons and Persons*, Oxford: Oxford University Press.

Parfit, D. (2011) *On What Matters,* vol. 1, Oxford: Oxford University Press.

Prichard, H.A. (2002/around 1937) "Moral Obligation," in J. MacAdam (ed.) *Moral Writings,* Oxford: Oxford University Press.

Railton, P. (1989) "Naturalism and Prescriptivity," *Social Philosophy and Policy* 7: 151–174.

Rønnow-Rasmussen, T. (2011) *Personal Value,* Oxford: Oxford University Press.

Ross, W.D. (1930) *The Right and the Good,* Oxford: Clarendon.

Ross, W.D. (1939) *Foundations of Ethics,* Oxford: Clarendon.

Seth, J. (1896) "Is Pleasure the Summum Bonum?" *International Journal of Ethics* 6: 409–424.

Shaver, R. (1997) "Sidgwick's False Friends," *Ethics* 107: 314–320.

Shaver, R. (2008) "Sidgwick on Virtue," *Etica & Politica* 10: 207–226.

Sidgwick, H. (1874) *The Methods of Ethics,* London: Macmillan.

Sidgwick, H. (1877a) "Hedonism and Ultimate Good," *Mind* 2: 27–38.

Sidgwick, H. (1877b) "Reply to Barratt on 'The Suppression of Egoism,'" *Mind* 2: 411–412.

Sidgwick, H. (1877c) *The Methods of Ethics* (2nd ed.), London: Macmillan.

Sidgwick, H. (1884) *The Methods of Ethics* (3rd ed.), London: Macmillan.

Sidgwick, H. (1889) "Some Fundamental Ethical Controversies," *Mind* 14: 473–487.

Sidgwick, H. (1890) *The Methods of Ethics* (4th ed.), London: Macmillan.

Sidgwick, H. (1893) *The Methods of Ethics* (5th ed.), London: Macmillan.

Sidgwick, H. (1902a) *Outlines of the History of Ethics* (5th ed.), London: Macmillan.

Sidgwick, H. (1902b) *Lectures on the Ethics of T. H. Green, H. Spencer, and J. Martineau,* London: Macmillan.

Sidgwick, H. (1981/1907) *The Methods of Ethics* (7th ed.), London: Macmillan.

Silverstein, M. (2000) "In Defense of Happiness: A Response to the Experience Machine," *Social Theory and Practice* 26: 279–300.

Sumner, L.W. (1996) *Welfare, Happiness, and Ethics,* Oxford: Clarendon.

Temkin, L. (2012) *Rethinking the Good,* Oxford: Oxford University Press.

Zimmerman, M. (2009) "Understanding What's Good for Us," *Ethical Theory and Moral Practice* 12: 429–439.

PART II

Theories of well-being

9

HEDONISM

Alex Gregory

Roughly, hedonism is the view that well-being wholly depends on how you feel. Slightly more precisely, it says that all and only positive experiences are good for you, and that all and only negative experiences are bad for you. Hedonism has seemed like an attractive theory to many people, but crude to others. Without doubt, it is one of the most influential theories of well-being. Historical defenders have included Epicurus, Mill (1863, especially Chapter 2), and Bentham (1789, especially Chapters 1 and 4). In this entry, I shall first briefly survey some arguments for hedonism, and then distinguish some different formulations of it. But the majority of the entry focuses on objections to the view.

Hedonism about well-being should be distinguished from psychological hedonism. Psychological hedonism says that we are motivated to do things only if we expect they will give us positive experiences or allow us to avoid negative experiences. Psychological hedonism aims to describe our actual behavior, whereas hedonism about well-being aims to describe what is good for us. These are different issues, since we might not always do what is good for us. Hedonism about well-being should also be distinguished from hedonism as a theory of value. The hedonic theory of value says that only positive experiences are valuable, and only negative experiences are disvaluable. This view coincides with hedonism about well-being only if we make the additional and controversial assumption that all and only well-being has value. Hereafter, this chapter focuses solely on hedonism about well-being.

A final introductory point: the name "hedonism" may mislead. In everyday English, "hedonists" value the present over the future, and value bodily pleasures over all other pleasures (e.g., intellectual). Hedonism, in our sense, has no such commitments: hedonists might agree that someone who works long miserable hours in order to prepare for an early retirement of peaceful contemplation is efficiently promoting his or her well-being.

Arguments for hedonism

To get a grip on the view, it's helpful to start by looking at what its attractions are supposed to be.[1]

First, it seems to deliver the right results across a wide variety of cases. Torture, depression, and headaches are all bad for us, and a natural explanation of that fact is that they feel bad. Parties, tasty food, and sex are all good for us, and a natural explanation of that fact is that they feel good. To make the point most stark, note that it's very hard to think of a time when your life was going badly but you felt great, or a time when your life was going well but you felt terrible. So hedonism seems to have many plausible implications.

Second, hedonism seems to have plausible implications in a different respect. Whilst people can have levels of well-being, other objects—such as cars, solar systems, and numbers—cannot (cf. Sumner 1996: 14–16). Hedonism is well placed to explain this fact. According to hedonism, only things that have experiences have levels of well-being. This explains why objects such as cars, solar systems, and numbers cannot have levels of well-being: because they do not have experiences. And to the extent that it is debatable whether, say, lobsters, have a level of well-being, according to hedonism that is debatable just because it is debatable whether lobsters are conscious. This all seems plausible.

Third, hedonism might seem attractive because it respects the *experience requirement*: the idea that anything that affects your level of well-being must feature in your experience (Griffin 1986: 7–20). We might think that if your life starts going worse or better, this must be something you notice. Take the following example: imagine that my brother has moved to Australia, and we have no means of contacting one another. Some anti-hedonists might think that how my brother fares affects my level of well-being: because he is part of my family and significant personal relationships contribute to well-being, because I want him to be happy and satisfying desires contributes to well-being, or whatever else. Now imagine that his fortunes change wildly over the day today: he is really enjoying a great party, but then he has an accident and breaks his arm, but then he receives medical attention which numbs the pain, but then the attending doctors notice he has cancer and inform him that he's going to die soon, but then they revise their judgment and tell him they can fix it. What a day he's had! Our anti-hedonist tells us that my brother's ups and downs also affect my level of well-being. But since I'm unaware of everything that's happened to him, this might strike us as incredible. I've been benefited and harmed at various points today, and I didn't even notice? Being tempted by the idea that facts about our own well-being must be accessible to ourselves, we might be tempted to think that they must consist in states of mind. This argument for hedonism has some appeal, though it's not clear whether it merely preaches to the converted. That is, one might think that the experience requirement is so close to hedonism that appealing to the former in support of the later is effectively circular. Still, this is undoubtedly a way in which many people are attracted to hedonism.

We might try and shore up this argument to make it more conclusive. In particular, we might think that alternatives to hedonism are incoherent.[2] According to rivals to hedonism, some things contribute to well-being that do not affect our conscious experience. But something contributes to your well-being only if it is good for you. And how can something be good *for you* unless it affects your conscious experience? But this bolder way of understanding the above argument is suspicious. It's helpful to set it out more formally:

P1 Something contributes to your well-being only if it is good for you.

P2 Something can be good for you only if it is experienced by you as good.

So, C Something contributes to your well-being only if it is experienced by you as good.

The problem is that, although there is a way of understanding the phrase "good for you" that makes P1 definitely true, and a way of understanding the phrase "good for you" that makes P2 potentially attractive, these ways of understanding the phrase "good for you" are distinct. Sometimes, "good for you" means "contributes to your well-being." In that sense, P1 is definitely true, but P2 is so close to hedonism that the argument begs the question. Alternatively "good for you" sometimes means "good from your point of view" (cf. "true for you"). In that sense, P2 *may* be plausible, but P1 makes the highly controversial claim that things can seem good from your point of view only if they make you feel good. Even independently of any doubts about hedonism, that claim is undermined by the fact that we value things other than our own well-being (e.g. the well–being of others). In short, the argument may seem compelling only if we equivocate between different senses of "good for you." So it is not clear that this argument can be understood in a way that makes it soundly provide independent grounds for hedonism.

What is hedonism?

I began by loosely characterizing hedonism as the view that only positive experiences are good for you, and only negative experiences are bad for you. Call this *broad hedonism*:

> *Broad hedonism*: All and only positive experiences are good for you, and all and only negative experiences are bad for you.

Broad hedonism is very vague, since it doesn't specify which experiences are positive and which are negative. But although broad hedonism is vague, it does seem to capture the core of hedonism: what matters for well-being is how you feel, all things considered. It is helpful to think of any more specific formulation of hedonism as a particular member of the hedonism family, and broad hedonism as the umbrella term for the family as a whole. Thinking about hedonism in this manner is helpful since it allows us to distinguish arguments for and against hedonism in general from arguments for and against particular hedonistic theories.

A more standard formulation of hedonism is the following:

> *Classic hedonism*: All and only pleasure is good for you, and all and only pain is bad for you.

There is good reason to think of hedonism as classic hedonism, since the very word "hedonism" comes from the Ancient Greek word for pleasure. But it's best to instead see classic hedonism as merely one version of broad hedonism, combined with further independent assumptions about which experiences are positive and which are negative. Seeing this view in this manner is helpful since it allows us to say some natural things about some objections to classic hedonism.

For example, there is a straightforward —and I think decisive—reason to think that classic hedonism is false. This is that some experiences are unpleasant without being painful, and those unpleasant experiences detract from well-being. For example, consider eating a sand sandwich, having a severe itch that you are unable to scratch, feeling nauseous, or being depressed. These experiences are not painful, as such. So according to classic hedonism they are not bad for you. But these experiences are bad for you. This objection undermines classic hedonism. I doubt that many hedonists will be moved by this problem, and I suggest that this is because their most fundamental sympathies lie with broad hedonism rather than with classic hedonism.

Perhaps classic hedonism should be understood as using the term "pain" in some technical and broader sense. But rather than use words in unusual ways, it is more transparent to formulate hedonism as broad hedonism and see classic hedonism as a more specific, literal, and suboptimal formulation of that broader view. Another better possibility is to adopt the following view:

> *Classic hedonism+*: All and only pleasure is good for you, and all and only displeasure is bad for you.

But there may be further counterexamples to both classic hedonism and classic hedonism+. In particular, if there is a difference between feeling happy and feeling pleasure, we might think that it is feelings of happiness, and not feelings of pleasure, that matter for well-being. Daniel Haybron offers one reason for thinking that there is a difference between feeling happy and feeling pleasure: that insignificant pleasures fail to contribute to happiness. He writes: "I enjoy, get pleasure from, a cheeseburger, yet I am patently not happier thereby" (2001: 505). If this pleasure fails to contribute to happiness, we might think that it also fails to contribute to well-being. In light of this thought, we might abandon classic hedonism+ and instead adopt:

> *Happiness hedonism*: All and only feelings of happiness are good for you, and all and only feelings of unhappiness are bad for you.[3]

Happiness hedonism also avoids the other objection above: feelings that are unpleasant but not painful might presumably detract from happiness at least sometimes, and when they do, it seems plausible that they detract from well-being. So perhaps happiness hedonism is the best formulation of broad hedonism. But even if happiness hedonism should turn out to be false, we might yet continue to endorse broad hedonism.

In short, we should be careful to distinguish different formulations of hedonism. Classic hedonism seems to face decisive objections, and should be abandoned. Classic hedonism+ and happiness hedonism might well be superior theories. But even the falsity of these theories should not by itself convince us that broad hedonism is false.

Objections to hedonism

I shall now examine three popular objections to hedonism, focusing primarily on the first two. Since hedonism has historically often been formulated as classic hedonism, I shall often express the objections as objections to that view. But I shall frequently note how hedonists might respond by moving to another hedonistic view (this is a common theme in Feldman 2004).

Distinctions between pleasures

One major objection to hedonism is the so-called "philosophy of swine" objection. According to hedonism, all that matters for well-being is that you have pleasures, and lack pain. But, so the objection goes, some pleasures are better than others. For example, the pleasures of reading comics contribute less to well-being than the pleasures of reading philosophy. Hedonism wrongly fails to discriminate between different kinds of pleasure, some of which contribute more to well-being than others. (It's not clear if those pressing the objection would also want to discriminate between different kinds of pains, and say that some pains detract from well-being more than others. I assume that everything I say below about pleasure could be extended appropriately.)

We should be careful with the objection here. In one sense, hedonists can definitely accommodate the fact that some pleasures are better than others. In particular, they can definitely allow that one pleasure might be better for you than another because it is more intense, or has a longer duration. The objection then, is that some pleasures are better for you than others, and not merely because they are more intense or have a longer duration. The point is sometimes put by saying that hedonism pays attention only to the *quantity* of pleasure when it should also pay attention to *quality*.

The force of this objection has to be supported by example, and hedonists might well contest those examples. Hedonists might say that some pleasures are better than others for reasons that are entirely compatible with their view, but deny that any pleasures are better than others in ways that are incompatible with their view. Let's examine three examples.

First, there are cases like the one above: we might think that the pleasures of reading comic books contribute less to well-being than the pleasures of reading philosophy. Or, to take a more classic example, we might think that the pleasures of poetry contribute more to well-being than the pleasures of pushpin (an extremely simple game). With respect to such examples, hedonists might follow Bentham's lead and suggest that discriminating in these ways reflects nothing but prejudice (Bentham 1843: Book 3, Chapter 1). Hedonists might insist that they want to hear an explanation of what makes some pleasures better than others, and lacking some such explanation, they might be justified in believing that such discriminations have no basis in fact. Further, in many cases they can offer a debunking explanation of why we are tempted to view some such pleasures as better than others. In particular, there are often good *instrumental* reasons to discriminate between kinds of pleasure. People who read philosophy and poetry might have their minds expanded in ways that contribute to their future pleasure, and the lives of others, in a way that people who read comic books and play pushpin do not. Accepting this is perfectly consistent with hedonism.

A second kind of example to illustrate this objection appeals to immoral pleasures. We might think that a life spent enjoying the suffering of others is not a life well spent, even for the person whose life it is. Again, hedonists might dispute this. They might say that in normal cases, we are inclined to see a life as bad if it involves a lot of immoral activity, but question whether the disvalue of such lives consists in a lack of well-being *for the person who lives it*. After all, we might think that some awful people have had lives that are extremely good for them. Indeed, we might think that it is a familiar feature of life that what's best for ourselves would sometimes involve doing wrong by others.

A third kind of example to illustrate this objection appeals not to differences between pleasures we have, but instead, more starkly, to differences between our pleasures and those of certain animals. The classic example involves comparing the life of Socrates and the life of a pig (Mill 1863: Chapter 2). We might think that the life of Socrates is the better one to live even if these lives involve equal amounts of pleasure, and indeed, even if Socrates' life involves less pleasure than the pig's. Roger Crisp has more recently given a different example involving an extraordinarily long-lived oyster (2006: 630–631). If the oyster's life involves constant mild pleasures—like "floating very drunk in a warm bath"—and survives for long enough, it seems as though its life will contain more pleasure than ours.[4] But do we really want to say that its life is better than ours? Should we be envious of long-lived oysters?

Such examples are unlike the first two in that they involve evaluating not particular pleasures, but instead whole lives. Cases that are similar in this respect (even if very different in many other respects!) involve comparing the lives of humans with severe cognitive disorders with those without such disorders. Do such lives promise equal amounts of well-being? You might think not: you might think that such disorders are bad for those who have them. And we might think that this is true not merely because of their effects on the amount of pleasure such people can experience. As such, these cases might also appear to threaten hedonism.

These examples may be harder for the hedonist to dismiss than the two above. Again, hedonists might argue that there are good *instrumental* reasons to treat our lives as better for us than lives as pigs or oysters would be, and also argue that there are good *instrumental* reasons to prefer to minimize the occurrence of severe mental disorders. Such concessions are consistent with their view. But it's not clear that they are enough to show that hedonism is plausible. When I hope that my child doesn't have a severe mental disorder, I have that hope not merely because of the ways in which the condition might affect how she will feel, nor merely for instrumental reasons given by the impact of her life on others, but also for her sake: such a life itself seems potentially worse in ways that hedonism fails to capture.

If hedonists cannot reject the force of the examples above, they might instead try to reformulate their view to accommodate them. They might take these examples not as undermining hedonism, but instead as placing constraints on how hedonism is best formulated. Mill is an example of one such hedonist who endorsed this general strategy. He endorsed hedonism but nonetheless distinguished between higher and lower pleasures, claiming that higher pleasures are better for us than lower ones (1863: Chapter 2; see also Feldman 2004: 71–78). In what follows, I will use Mill's view to illustrate the points being made, talking about whether hedonists can allow a distinction between higher and lower pleasures. But do bear in mind that this is just for ease: we might want to distinguish between the quality of experiences other than pleasures (e.g., happiness, pain), and we also might want a scale of quality than is more finely grained than a mere two-way distinction between "higher" and "lower."

There is some dispute about whether distinguishing between higher and lower pleasures is consistent with hedonism (Moore 1903: section 47; cf. Feldman 2004: 113–114, 168–187). Since hedonism says that all and only experiences can be good or bad for us, we might think it entails that well-being wholly depends on experience. That is, we might think that hedonism is committed to what we'll call *the supervenience constraint*, which says that there cannot be difference in well-being between A and B unless there is a difference in experience between A and B. If the supervenience constraint were true, then since Millian hedonists claim that higher pleasures contribute more to well-being than lower pleasures, they would also have to claim that the distinction between higher and lower pleasures is a distinction between kinds of experience. That is a significant constraint on how they might formulate their view, since one natural possibility is that the difference between higher and lower pleasures is not a difference between kinds of experience, but instead a difference between the *objects* of those experiences. For example, we might say that one pleasure is of higher quality than another just when it is taken in an object of more value. If we were to draw the distinction between higher and lower pleasures in that manner, then the resulting view would violate the supervenience constraint, since it would permit that well-being is affected by things that are not experiences. For example, imagine that you take pleasure in owning a Ferrari. If we think that your level of well-being depends on whether your pleasures are taken in worthwhile objects, then your level of well-being might depend on the value of Ferraris. That would be contrary to the claim that well-being supervenes on experience alone. So if hedonists are committed to the supervenience constraint, then they cannot distinguish between higher and lower pleasures by appeal to facts about the objects of those pleasures.

Might we accept hedonism but nonetheless deny the supervenience constraint (e.g., Feldman 2004; cf. Fletcher 2008)? Such a view would say that the only things that are good and bad for us are experiences, but also claim that the extent to which those experiences are good and bad for us may depend on other things, such as the value of the objects of those experiences. An analogy may be helpful: The only thing that makes noise in my office is my phone, but just how much noise there is in my office nonetheless depends on other things, since other things can affect how much noise my phone makes (e.g., whether I hand out my office phone number to students). So too, hedonists might say that there is only one source of well-being—conscious experience—but other factors can intensify or attenuate the influence of that source.

Such a view can accommodate the examples we began with, by saying that some pleasures are better than others. And it seems coherent. But we might nonetheless wonder whether the resulting view is consistent with the motivations for adopting hedonism in the first place. After all, the third argument for hedonism appealed to the experience requirement: the fact that our own level of well-being should impinge on our experience. But denying the supervenience constraint may well commit us to the view that our own level of well-being may be opaque to us. Again, imagine that I take pleasure in owning a Ferrari. According to the hedonistic theory at issue, the degree to which this pleasure is good for me depends on the value of Ferraris. But the value of Ferraris might be difficult for me to discern, and in turn it may be difficult for me to tell how well my life is going. That sits unhappily with one of the main original attractions of hedonism. In general, hedonists must tread a fine line between modifying their view so as to make it plausible, but nonetheless retaining enough of the original theory so as to maintain its attractions.

The experience machine

A second popular objection to hedonism—in fact, probably the main objection to hedonism—is Nozick's experience machine (1974: 42–45). Imagine an extremely effective reality simulator, which promises to give you all sorts of pleasures if you plug in (and very little pain—I take this for granted from here onwards). If the machine is effective enough, plugging yourself in will guarantee that you have more pleasure in the machine than you possibly could if you remain outside of the machine. But, we might think, life inside the machine is not necessarily better than life outside: there is something important about living in the real world that hedonism fails to capture. Since hedonism seems to entail that life inside the machine is best for you, hedonism seems to be false.

If this were an isolated example, hedonists might simply dig in their heels and just accept that we should plug in, especially since the machine is such a far-fetched possibility. But on reflection it should be clear that this is just a particularly stark example of a more common phenomenon: we sometimes think that people who feel good, but only because they are ignorant, are living worse lives than they might be. Shelly Kagan adapts Thomas Nagel's example of a businessman who, by the lights of hedonism, is living a great life: he feels great about his job, his family, his children, and so on (Kagan 1994: 311, Nagel 1970: 76). But if he feels this great only because he is ignorant about these matters—his co-workers believe he is incompetent, his wife is cheating on him, his children don't respect him—then it sounds as though his life is not ideal.

How might hedonists respond to such objections? They might claim that deluded lives are no better than informed lives, and argue that the only reason we are inclined to say otherwise is because we get distracted by the irrelevant fact that the actions of the relevant people involved are morally bad: we think that getting into the machine is wrongful since you thereby neglect your obligations to others, and that what is bad in the case of the businessman are the actions of those around him. Moral claims like these are consistent with hedonism, and if they are the only source of our unease about the examples, then the examples do not threaten hedonism. But this response is unconvincing: even when we attend carefully only to facts about well-being and ignore moral questions, it seems clear that life in the experience machine is worse than an equally pleasurable life outside, and clear that the businessman's life is not wholly enviable.

Another response on behalf of hedonism appeals to the claim that in both cases one's pleasures are fragile: they might disappear at any moment if one's ignorance is dispelled. In the long run, pleasure based on knowledge might be thought to be more secure than pleasure based on ignorance, and therefore better for reasons that are consistent with hedonism. So again, hedonists might deny that these examples threaten their view. But again, this alone doesn't seem enough to save hedonism. We might set up these cases so that the relevant ignorance is unlikely to be dispelled. For example, we might imagine that Kagan's businessman is instead an astronaut, who takes pleasure in these thoughts whilst on a one-way mission and already out of contact with the human race. Or we might imagine that the person entering the experience machine will die soon anyway, certainly long before the machine breaks. When we modify the examples in this way, it may still seem that these lives are lacking in ways that hedonism cannot explain.

A third—and better—strategy for hedonists in the face of these objections is to first distinguish two different things that such cases might be thought to show, and then to give different responses to each. In particular, hedonists might distinguish the objection that false pleasures don't contribute to well-being from the objection that some things other than pleasures do contribute to well-being. This seems like a useful distinction to make: one problem is that hedonism values too much, the other that it values too little. With it in hand, hedonists can try to address the two objections separately.

So remember the first possible way of understanding the objection: as attempting to show that false pleasures contribute nothing to well-being. This claim might be disputed. After all, even if your pleasures are false, surely they still count for something: it is better to have false pleasures rather than none at all, and better to have none at all than false pains. Here it can be helpful to redescribe the objection. Above, we described the objection as though what is at stake is whether a fantastically pleasurable life inside the experience machine is better than a moderately pleasurable life outside the experience machine. That issue might be hard to resolve, and one can imagine that some people would agree with hedonism that the life inside the machine is indeed better. But it is helpful to instead attend to a slightly different issue: whether a fantastically pleasurable life outside the machine is better than a fantastically pleasurable life inside the machine. Here, hedonism is committed to the answer that such lives are equally good. But it might seem very plausible that the former life is better, and that as such hedonism must be mistaken. If we press the objection against hedonism in this manner, it is consistent with the possibility that false pleasures count for something. The important claim is that false pleasures contribute less to well-being than true pleasures do, not that false pleasures contribute nothing at all. That more modest claim may be enough to undermine hedonism.

A better strategy for the hedonist is perhaps to concede the force of the objection, but again, to reformulate hedonism in response. Above we explored the possibility of distinguishing higher and lower pleasures, and claiming that higher pleasures contribute more to well-being than lower pleasures. Similarly, we might distinguish true and false pleasures, and claim that true pleasures contribute more to well-being than false pleasures (Feldman 2004: 109–114). Such a view can easily handle the experience machine case, if the upshot of that case is just supposed to be that false pleasures contribute less to well-being than true experiences. Again, such a modification of the view forces us to deny the supervenience constraint according to which levels of well-being supervene on conscious states alone. And so, again, hedonists who wish to respond to the objection in this manner must show that the resulting view retains the merits of hedonism. But this move would at least enable hedonists to respond to the experience machine objection when it is understood in this way.

I distinguished two different upshots that the experience machine objection might be thought to have: either that false pleasures don't contribute to well-being, or that some things other than pleasures do contribute to well-being. Having discussed the first possibility, let us now turn to the second.

To repeat, the second way of interpreting the supposed upshot of the experience machine objection is as showing that some things other than conscious experiences do contribute to well-being. For example, it might be thought to show that achievement, significant personal relationships, or virtue contribute to well-being (cf. Nozick 1974: 43–45). These are things that one can get outside the machine, but cannot get inside (of course, one can get the apparent experience of these things in the machine, but one cannot get the real thing). This time, there is simply no scope for hedonists to fiddle with the details of their view in order to try and accommodate the objection. "Revising" hedonism so as to allow that some things contribute to well-being that are not conscious experiences is not revising hedonism but instead replacing it with another theory of well-being altogether.

If we instead try to find a general argument that only conscious experiences can contribute to well-being, then we ought to return to the third argument above in favor of hedonism: we might think that there is some general reason to believe that anything that affects our well-being must be a state of mind. But sadly, this is just the argument that hedonists must give up if they wish to deny the supervenience constraint, as I suggested they might. So hedonists may instead have to respond to this objection just by taking proposed contributors to well-being one by one, and in each case, formulate arguments that the thing in question makes a difference to well-being only if it makes a difference to our conscious experience. Certainly, they might concede that the relevant item *often* contributes to well-being, but argue that this is so only because it often contributes to giving us positive experiences. Whether this strategy is plausible obviously depends on the thing in question, and here we cannot canvass all possibilities.

Perhaps one of the more difficult cases here is that of achievement. We might think that life in the machine is not so good because it is a life that lacks in achievement. Whilst in the machine it might seem to you as though you are a great athlete, writer, and parent, but whilst in the machine you can't actually succeed in those roles. That might seem to be part of the cost of entering the machine, and a cost that hedonism fails to capture.

Again, less extreme examples of the same phenomenon are available. Freud had cancer in his jaw throughout his life, which caused him great pain. But he supposedly refused to take pain-killers, fearing that they would cloud his thinking and prevent him from doing his work. One natural reading of Freud's decision was that he valued finishing his work over a life of positive experiences. If we think that Freud's decision was prudent, it might seem that we are committed to thinking that achievement sometimes matters independently of the pleasure is brings, and in turn, committed to thinking that hedonism is false. Hedonists might suggest that Freud probably got some pleasure from the knowledge that he could complete his work, and that it is precisely because of those pleasures that we think his choice was reasonable (cf. Crisp 2006: 637). Vice versa, they might add, if Freud didn't get any pleasure as a result of his work, we would indeed think that his choice was foolish. Perhaps such a response is plausible.

Dangers of externalism about pleasure

A final objection to hedonism that we should briefly examine is that it collapses into some version of the desire satisfaction theory of well-being (Kagan 1992: 170–171). Hedonists need some account of the distinction between positive experiences and negative experiences, and one might think that this distinction is best understood as a distinction between states of mind that we want to be in and those that we do not want to be in. But if that is true, then it seems that what really does the work in explaining why certain things are good for us and others are bad are our desires. And if *that* is true, it seems as though we should also think that desires for other things—achievements, friends, etc.—contribute to well-being when satisfied. What is so special about desires for conscious experiences that make their satisfaction affect well-being in a way that the satisfaction of other desires does not? Without an answer to that question, it might seem as though hedonism is just an unduly restrictive version of the desire satisfaction theory of well-being.

One issue here that might turn out to be a red herring is the question of whether pleasure and pain should be analyzed with reference to our desires. If, as I suggested, hedonists should abandon classic hedonism, and instead adopt some other view about which conscious experiences are relevant for well-being, then hedonists may not need to worry about whether pleasure and pain should be analyzed in terms of our desires. But there will still be a worry: hedonists must appeal to *a* distinction between positive and negative experiences when they formulate their view, and hedonism may be on shaky ground if that distinction can be made only by appeal to the desires of the agent in question.

In the face of this objection, hedonists have two responses available to them. First, they might try to draw a distinction between positive and negative experiences that doesn't rely on the role that our desires play. For example, I mentioned happiness hedonism, which claims that the relevant distinction between positive and negative experiences should be understood as a distinction between states of mind that contribute to happiness and those that do not. Since analyses of happiness in terms of desire are rare (the exception being Davis 1981), it might seem that such a view avoids the objection altogether.

The other response available to hedonists is to claim that, although the distinction between positive and negative experiences is best drawn by appeal to our desires, they might argue that this doesn't put hedonists on a slippery slope towards holding a desire satisfaction theory of well-being. They might say that there is something special about desires regarding our own experiences that makes the satisfaction of *those* desires contribute to well-being even though the satisfaction of other desires does not so contribute. Hedonists taking this line would have to explain what it is that makes desires about our own mental lives particularly relevant for well-being. But—perhaps by appeal to some of the original arguments for hedonism that we canvassed above—this might be done.

Conclusion

Hedonism is a highly controversial theory of well-being, one that is popular with some figures but deeply unpopular with others. We addressed three arguments for hedonism, before clarifying the nature of the view, being careful to distinguish hedonism in general from more particular claims about exactly which experiences are good and bad for us. But, in keeping with the literature on the topic, the majority of this chapter focused on objections to hedonism. The first was the objection that some pleasures contribute more to well-being than others. We asked whether hedonists might reject that claim, as well as whether they can reformulate their view to accommodate it. The second objection, and by far the most important, was the experience machine objection. We considered numerous responses to the objection, at least in part because the objection seems so multi-faceted. Here, hedonists will have to get involved in the nitty-gritty details of distinguishing different objections and finding ways to respond to each. Whether they can succeed in that task is an open question. Finally, we briefly examined whether hedonism should be threatened by the possibility that the distinction between positive and negative experiences should be defined in relation to desire. The objection looked serious but, as it stands, indecisive.

Related topics

Hedonistic theories in antiquity, happiness, pleasure, achievements, pain, atomism and holism, the experience requirement.

Notes

1 Two further novel arguments for hedonism can be found in Bradley (2009: 17–40).
2 This argument is not prevalent in the literature, but seems tacit in the kinds of remarks some hedonists make about rival views, and certainly sometimes surfaces in conversation.

3 To be clear, I'm borrowing an argument from Haybron and putting it to use in ways he might well object to. Haybron raises the cheeseburger example in the course of arguing for the broader claim that happiness is constituted by more than feelings alone (2001). That is a claim that hedonists (about well-being) may need to reject.

4 Here, cf. the repugnant conclusion (Parfit 1984: 381–390), which also relies on the claim that a very large number of barely good things need not be that good. If the comparison is apt, another option for hedonists—which I won't explore—might be to deny the aggregative assumption that the value of a life is the sum of the values of its moments (cf. Velleman 1991).

Bibliography

Bentham, J. (1789) *Introduction to the Principles of Morals and Legislation*. Oxford: Clarendon Press.

Bentham, J. (1843) *The Rationale of Reward*. London: John and H.L. Hunt.

Bradley, B. (2009) *Well-being and Death*. Oxford: Oxford University Press.

Crisp, R. (2006) "Hedonism Reconsidered," in *Philosophy and Phenomenological Research* 73(3): 619–645.

Dancy, J. (2004) *Ethics Without Principles*. Oxford: Oxford University Press.

Davis, W. (1981) "A Theory of Happiness," *American Philosophical Quarterly* 18(11): 1–20.

Feldman, F. (2004) *Pleasure and the Good Life*. Oxford: Oxford University Press.

Fletcher, G. (2008) "The Consistency of Qualitative Hedonism and the Value of (at Least Some) Malicious Pleasures," *Utilitas* 20(4): 462–471.

Griffin, J. (1986) *Well-being: Its Meaning, Measurement and Importance*. Oxford: Oxford University Press.

Haybron, D. (2001) "Happiness and Pleasure," *Philosophy and Phenomenological Research* 62(3): 501–528.

Kagan, S. (1992) "The Limits of Wellbeing," *Social Philosophy and Policy* 9(2): 169–189.

Kagan, S. (1994) "Me and My Life," *Proceedings of the Aristotelian Society* 94: 309–324.

Mill, J. (1863) *Utilitarianism*. London: Parker, Son, and Bourne.

Moore, G.E. (1903) *Principia Ethica*. London: Cambridge University Press.

Nagel, T. (1970) "Death," *Nous* 4(1): 73–80.

Nozick, R. (1974) *Anarchy, State and Utopia*. Malden, MA: Basic Books, pp. 42–45.

Parfit, D. (1984) *Reasons and Persons*. Oxford: Oxford University Press.

Sumner, L. (1996) *Welfare, Happiness and Ethics*. Oxford: Oxford University Press.

Velleman, D. (1991) "Well-Being and Time," *Pacific Philosophical Quarterly* 72(1): 48–77.

10

PERFECTIONISM

Gwen Bradford

Perfectionism, broadly speaking, is the view that the development of certain characteristically human capacities is good.

As human beings, we all have certain *capacities* that are deeply characteristic of our nature. Traditionally, perfectionists hold that these capacities include our rationality—both theoretical and practical—and physical capacities, and may include others. The exercise and development of these capacities constitute our good—our *flourishing* as human beings, as some perfectionists put it. Knowledge, achievement, and friendships are good at least in part because they manifest the development of our characteristically human capacities: endeavors such as achievements, learning, and close friendships constitute our flourishing. The more we excel in these domains, the better we fare as human beings.

The view gains motivation in part from the intuitive pull of an objective approach to well-being, but dissatisfaction with objective list theory. According to objective list theory, goods such as knowledge, achievement, and friendship constitute good in a life. The objective list has terrific intuitive appeal—after all, it's a list generated by reflecting on the good life. But as a theory, some find it unsatisfying. What justifies presence on the list? On the traditional conception, it is just a list and not much of a theory at all. Perfectionism captures the intuitive pull of the objective list and provides a unifying justification: the entries on the list share in common a special relationship to human nature (e.g., Brink 2008; cf. Chapter 12, this volume).

The name "perfectionism" is a relatively recent term, but the theory has roots that stretch deep into the history of philosophy. The grandfather of perfectionism is Aristotle, who develops a theory of human good that is based in our nature. Roughly, virtue or excellence (*arete*) is closely tied to our nature, and our flourishing (*eudaimonia*) is a matter of engaging in activities in which we exercise these excellences. Plato also develops a view according to which our doing well is grounded in features of our nature, namely the harmony of the parts of our soul. The Stoics too developed a view that identified our good with virtue. Nietzsche can also be read as holding a perfectionist account (Hurka 2007).

The colloquial sense of "perfectionism," namely, a perpetual dissatisfaction with what is less than perfect, has little in common with perfectionism as a theory of well-being. One might say that the closest thing to a role that perfection has in the theory itself is that our good is constituted by our working toward perfecting ourselves as human beings, but it is certainly not the case that anything that falls short of absolute human perfection has no value—in fact, many proponents of the view pride themselves on holding positions that couldn't be farther from this. One of the appealing points of these contemporary perfectionist accounts is that they capture the value of a wide range of levels of achievement and modes of life and career paths. The emphasis in perfectionism is on the development and exercise of our characteristic capacities that constitute our flourishing, not being perfect. For these reasons, some perfectionists prefer terms such as "developmentalism" or "eudaimonism."

As we are discussing it here, perfectionism is a theory of well-being. But it can alternatively be understood as a theory of goodness *simpliciter*, which is to say final value. When perfectionism is put forward as a theory of value, rather than well-being, the view holds that the exercise and development of the characteristic capacities are intrinsically good. It gives us an account of good that may occur in a life. It is a separate question whether or not this is the *same as* what is *good for* us. Taken as a theory of value, it is also compatible with pluralism about value: there may be other goods in addition to perfectionist goods. Some of these other goods may also be relevant for human life or well-being. Moreover, perfectionism as a theory of final value might even be compatible with a further theory of well-being— perfectionism might give us a theory of what makes for *a good life* or good that one can have in a life, but this could be something quite different than a life that is *good for* the person who lives it (Arneson 2000).

Although these distinctions might sound surprising, Thomas Hurka, one of the central contemporary proponents of the view, explicitly puts his theory as a theory of intrinsic value, and not as a theory of well-being (Hurka 1993). Yet in the philosophical literature, Hurka's theory is appealed to as an example of a perfectionist theory of *well-being*. Since this is a handbook about well-being, this entry is devoted to perfectionism as a theory of well-being.

One can also have a perfectionist *political* theory. Perfectionist political theory is about the role that the state should have with respect to the good of its citizens. It is the view that the state may justifiedly promote certain substantive values. I will take this up below.

Human nature

Because our good is shaped by our nature, perfectionism must provide a descriptive account of the relevant aspects of human nature, and it must specify precisely what our characteristically human capacities are. Such an account needs to be generated in a way that is evaluatively neutral on pain of circularity: an account of which capacities it is good to develop cannot be generated by appealing to the criterion of being a capacity which is good to develop. So the account of human nature and the method of picking out the relevant capacities must be strictly descriptive.

There are a variety of ways of approaching the task of identifying the capacities of human nature that are relevant for our good. What capacities are central to us as human beings? What precisely do we mean by human nature?

One approach is that the relevant capacities are those that are *unique* to human beings. The capacities that are unique to us are those that are possessed by human beings, but not by any other creatures. Rationality has been traditionally thought to be uniquely human—at least the degree and depth of rationality that we enjoy appear to be unique to us—and the same could be said about autonomy.

But even supposing that no other creatures on earth enjoy rational capacities to the extent that we do, for all we know there may be a race of alien beings on a distant planet who do, which would render rational capacities irrelevant for perfection. If we discovered tomorrow that dolphins really do have rational capacities that they exercise and develop in ways that are comparable to our own, then these capacities would no longer be unique to us as humans and therefore no longer be good for us to exercise and develop. Making our good contingent on these points is unappealing (not to mention the resultant issues of epistemic inaccessibility).

More plausibly, our nature might be a matter of the human *essence*. The relevant capacities are essential to humans, which is to say they are the ones that human beings have *necessarily*. All human beings have them and to fail to have these capacities is to fail to be a human being. This approach has more plausibility than the uniqueness approach. One can make an acceptable case that rationality is a necessary feature of humans, and likewise for autonomy. A defense for this view can appeal to the argument that we are not "fully human" without certain baseline capacities for rational thought and autonomous action. Interestingly, whether or not we have physical capacities necessarily depends on other views about our metaphysical nature—a Cartesian dualist about mind and body, for example, will happily relinquish physical capacities from the list of necessary human features; those with different leanings will find it hard to conceive of human beings without physical bodies and certain essential physical capacities.

However, as Hurka points out, certain features that are part of our essence do not seem relevant for our good—the capacity to take up three-dimensional space, for example. Developing this capacity might involve becoming as large as possible, which is an unlikely candidate for being constitutive of our good. Hurka avoids this problem by specifying that the relevant capacities are those that are essential to human beings *conditioned* on being living things (Hurka 1993).

Alternative conceptions identify the relevant capacities as those that are so central to humans that they are omnipresent in human activity. George Sher's view is that the relevant capacities are *fundamental* to human activity (Sher 1997). The capacities that matter are those that are "near-universal and near-inevitable"—it is virtually impossible to engage in activities without making use of these capacities. Sher's view is also teleological: the capacities aim at *goals* that we inevitably pursue in virtue of engaging in human activity, such as forming beliefs from information.

Some perfectionists depart slightly from the position that the description of human nature must be entirely value-neutral. One might hold that an Aristotelian teleological account of proper functioning is *itself* evaluative, and so the assessment of what amounts to a capacity functioning properly is an evaluative judgment. Evaluative assessment is already integral to the component of the view that one might otherwise think is strictly descriptive (Nussbaum 1988).

According to some perfectionists, it is not important that there be a formulaic method for carving out a descriptive account of human nature and picking out the relevant capacities. Instead, another approach straightforwardly appeals to the "categories of common sense," as Richard Kraut does, arguing that "there is nothing sacrosanct about this rough and crude list of human powers"—common sense is subject to change, and we can get at what's relevant in this way (Kraut 2009: 137). This approach avoids unintuitive implications, and is flexible and open to updates and revisions. Although forgoing strict formulaic methodology comes with these appealing gains, it comes at a sacrifice of theoretical structure and substance.

Similarly, in developing a view related to perfectionism, Nussbaum takes a flexible approach to her list, explicitly acknowledging it is open to revision (e.g., Nussbaum 2000: 77). In some of Nussbaum's earlier work she closely aligns her own views with Aristotle's, but in other work where Aristotle exegesis plays a smaller role, she does not explicitly tie the enumeration of the capacities ("capabilities" on her view) to human nature. Instead, her capabilities approach makes use of wide reflective equilibrium that appeals directly to the idea of what capabilities are central for good human functioning, rather than grounding them first in an account of human nature. Although the capabilities approach is not strictly speaking an account of well-being (we return to its relationship to perfectionism below), the methodology concerning central human capacities is a relevant alternative for perfectionist theories of well-being.

So what are the relevant capacities? The list of capacities that are centrally characteristic and relevant for perfectionist value will vary according to how precisely the descriptive component of the view is established. What might we expect to find on the list? Virtually no perfectionist will omit rationality, which is traditionally divided into theoretical rationality and practical rationality. Beyond this, some perfectionists include physical capacities. Many perfectionists also acknowledge that *autonomy* is a capacity that is centrally characteristic of our nature. Beyond these, perfectionists may specify further capacities such as affective, sensory, or social capacities (e.g., Kraut 2009). Rational agency is another element that is central to the perfectionism of T.H. Green (2003 [1883]).

The good

Once a perfectionist has established a methodology for distinguishing the relevant capacities, the next task is to establish the relationship between the good and the capacities. One might think at first that it is simply *having* the capacities themselves that is good, but Aristotle's convincing words about sleepers quickly put this notion to rest (as it were): you can have well-functioning capacities but spend your entire life asleep and this would certainly not constitute a good life, which rather seems to require activity (Aristotle 1999: 162). Moreover, if simply *having* the capacities is good for us, regardless of how well or badly they are exercised, there would be no resources for making distinctions between people who have equal capacities but exercise them in better or worse ways. Josh may be endowed with incredible talents for rationality, autonomy, athleticism, and social relationships, but he squanders his life as a hermitic couch potato. In contrast, Michelle has less impressive rational and social capacities, but strives with inspiring effort to achieve at her job and build meaningful friendships. We would be inclined to say that Michelle flourishes, whereas Josh the couch potato does not flourish, in spite of his more extensive capacities. So faring well isn't simply to *have* the relevant capacities, but to exercise them well.

There is also the further question of the precise locus of good. Is our good constituted by the capacities when exercised, or by the activities that are constituted by this exercised? Is it in the manifestation of the exercise of the capacities, or, further still, in the outputs of the activities that manifest the capacities? This last view would allow us to say that knowledge, art, and so on, are *themselves* valuable (and valuable because of their relationship to human capacities). But the other approaches would say that the *activities* of striving toward achievement, or *learning*, rather than knowledge, are valuable.

Once we have set upon a descriptive account of the relevant characteristic human capacities, the idea is that we fare well when we are exercising or developing these capacities. We might put it this way: our faring well—our *flourishing*—is when we are the best version of a human being that we can be. The better that we excel in our exercise of ourselves, the better we fare.

The locus of our good therefore is in the development and exercise of our capacities, and the activities that make use of them. When we develop and manifest our essential capacities, we are flourishing. This is ultimately how perfectionism captures the motivating intuitions that knowledge, achievement, friendship, and so on are good for us. The objective list items manifest our special capacities—knowledge, achievement, and friendship are constitutive of our good insofar as partaking in them manifests our human capacities.

So we now can see the relationship between the putative goods on the objective list and perfectionism. The objective goods, such as knowledge, achievement, and friendship, all involve exercise and manifestation of certain of our characteristically human capacities. One might establish the connections along the following lines. The excellent exercise of rationality is made manifest in knowledge and learning. Practical rationality and autonomy are made manifest in achievements such as writing a novel, running a marathon, or raising a family. Our capacities for social bonds, emotions, practical rationality, and autonomy are all manifested in our personal relationships.

Some perfectionists also include morally right action or virtue among the goods. T.H. Green, whose views have been crystallized by David O. Brink, develops a view something along the following lines. Green has the view that our rational agency is central to our nature and its development involves rationally deliberating about our desires, and respecting our own rational agency as well as that of others, and hence promoting the common good. In this way, Green generates a theory according to which the good of an individual involves promoting and respecting the good of others (Brink 2003; Green 2003 [1883]). Other perfectionists do not include a capacity for specifically *moral* actions, and so morally right or praiseworthy actions are no more relevant for our good than practical action more generally.

The degree to which someone does well is a further matter. Is doing well a matter of how well you exercise your capacities, measured on some absolute scale, or is the exercise of capacities calibrated relatively, according to your natural abilities? To put this issue another way, does it matter how well you do, or how hard you try? Further, is how well we fare a matter of how extensively we exercise our capacities, or how *well* we exercise them? You can play the piano a lot but not very well, or you can play a little bit, but very well. Which dimension is more significant?

We might also think that *developing* the capacities is relevant for faring well: it's not enough merely to use our rationality, but also to *cultivate* it and improve it. Such an approach would require the assumption that at least some of our capacities can be developed, at least to a certain degree. The question of developing capacities is further complicated by the observation that some capacities require other capacities in order to be developed and improved. Developing rationality, for example, requires a certain amount of willpower, so the limits of the will (if it is a capacity relevant for perfectionist value) will shape the extent to which rationality can be developed. It has also been acknowledged that many of the capacities require external goods in order to be exercised. This latter consideration is the basis for much of the related discussion in social justice in political theory discussed below. For ease of discussion, I simply use the term "exercise" throughout, but bear in mind that different perfectionist theories might specify this notion differently.

Beyond this, perfectionists will also need to take a stand on how value is calibrated in terms of exercise of capacity. Once it is settled whether it is extent of exercise or *quality* of manifestation that matters, or both, perfectionists will need to settle on how to calibrate this scale. Suppose quality matters. Does an exercise of rationality that is double the caliber of another have twice the value, or does value increase at a greater rate than the quality of the capacity?

The answer to this question has very significant implications for the theory. If a perfectionist decides that the quality of the exercise of the capacity matters significantly, the theory may take on a very different shape than if we are more willing to give value to a low-grade exercise of capacity. If *only* a high-quality excellence of exercise of capacities matters, then this may mean that *most people* do not achieve a great deal of value in their lives. Depending where the bar is set, only the Mozarts and Goethes of the world are faring well, whereas most of us with our middling accomplishments and blundering rationality do not fare particularly well. This Nietzschean version of the theory is subject to an objection discussed below: the worry that perfectionism entails elitism. We can see, however, that nothing in the bare elements of the view entails this position. Rather, it is a matter of how we defend the calibration of the value of the exercise of capacities. If a perfectionist is open to the value of low-grade capacities having value, then these problems do not arise in this way.

Another issue that perfectionists need to settle concerns how important each of the capacities is relative to the others. Are all the capacities equally important? Is the exercise of one capacity just as valuable as the exercise of any of the other capacities? Is it as valuable to exercise our rationality as it is to exercise our physical capacities?

The answer one would expect is that they are not on equal ground. Philosophical tradition holds that the exercise of rationality—theoretical rationality—is significant beyond all else. Contemporary perfectionists have challenged the hegemony of theoretical rationality over practical rationality (Hurka 1993). But it is commonly held that physical capacities, while relevant for our good, are not as important as other capacities. The relative value of autonomy is also a subject of great discussion, in particular because of its relevance to political theory, as discussed below.

In sum, perfectionism involves the following elements. The view holds that the excellent exercise of specific human capacities, such as rationality, is good. We fare well, or flourish, when we exercise and fulfill these capacities. Knowledge, achievement, friendship, and so on, are good for us insofar as they are manifestations of the exercise of these elements of ourselves.

One way to understand the various components for perfectionism and how they fit together is captured in Table 10.1. The column on the right lists several different possible conceptions for how the basic components, named in the column to the left, could be developed on any perfectionist account. The table is meant to be a sketch of the terrain and not an exhaustive presentation of all permutations of the view, so there can be further possible conceptions. Some perfectionists may reject certain basic components: what Hurka refers to as "broad" perfectionist accounts do not appeal to human nature at all (Hurka 1993). This alternative approach would then provide an alternative justification for the value of excellence without reference to human nature.[1]

Reflecting on the experience machine (see Chapter 9 for a discussion of the experience machine), perfectionists may say the following. Merely the experience of achieving, or knowing, would not be (one could argue) truly manifesting or exercising the capacity itself. It would merely be the *experience of* manifesting or exercising. Well-being is a matter of actually manifesting our capacities, and this cannot be done in the experience machine. We only have the experience *as if*

Table 10.1 The various components for perfectionism and how they fit together

	Basic component	Possible conceptions
I	Descriptive account of human nature: how the relevant capacities are identified	Unique Essential Fundamental Distinctive
II	Enumeration of capacities: the capacities that are identified by the account of human nature	Rationality Autonomy Physical capacities Emotional capacities
III	Activity of capacities relevant for value	Development Exercise Fulfillment Manifestation
IV	Relationship to good: nature and locus of value	Capacities themselves are valuable Activities that fulfill the capacities are valuable Well-being Intrinsic value
V	How much good: relative value of the capacities and associated goods	Exercise of capacities equally valuable Exercise differs in value for different capacities Value of exercise calibrated absolutely Value of exercise calibrated relative to agent

we were manifesting them. But actually doing so requires some connection with the world beyond us. Or it does in most cases: interestingly, it is possible that some perfectionist capacities in some ways could be manifested in the experience machine. It doesn't seem implausible that one could indeed exercise and manifest the excellent exercise of rationality by playing a game of mental chess, or contemplating the nature and discovery of calculus while in the experience machine. These and other similar activities could take place in the experience machine and would be part and parcel of our good on (at least some) conceptions of perfectionism, or so one could argue.

Objections to perfectionism

Wrong properties

Because of the centrality of a descriptive account of human nature, which is empirical, perfectionism is at a risk for selecting some very counterintuitive features which the view would then entail are good. For example, suppose that the investigation into our nature reveals that central to us is a capacity to grow our fingernails longer than any other species, or to make and wear clothing. Opponents of perfectionism love to point out that we are the only species that hunts and kills for pleasure rather than sustenance, in addition to killing each other, and laying waste to our environment. Surely none of these features are good for us—some of them are even very bad for us. But if the descriptive component of the view indicates that they are central capacities, then perfectionism is bound to claim that they are good.

However, this objection is contingent on the descriptive investigation actually turning up some capacities that have these counterintuitive results. Barring the details of any particular conception of perfectionism, the mere possibility of the objection is not an objection. Further, perfectionist methodology in discerning the features that are relevant for our nature appeals to reflective equilibrium, where refining the theory in light of intuitions is par for the course.

But a deeper worry is that appealing to reflective equilibrium in the face of the wrong properties objection reveals a more serious problem with the view. Dale Dorsey perceptively argues that the perfectionist's willingness to respond to the wrong properties objection by recalibrating the descriptive account of human nature reveals perfectionism lacks independent intuitive compellingness; that is, it is the objective list items and their intuitive pull that drive the theory forward (Dorsey 2010). The appeal to human nature is merely an attempt to frame these goods with a theory, but as a *theory*, the notion of "developing human nature" doesn't have *independent* intuitive pull. If it *did*, then perfectionists would be willing to bite the bullet and accommodate counterintuitive putative goods that follow from the account of human nature. But perfectionists may reply that revising a particular conception of the descriptive account (selecting from the rightmost column in Table 10.1) isn't a threat to the plausibility of the general statement of the view.

Philip Kitcher challenges whether it is even possible to appeal to the notion of "human nature" (Kitcher 1999). Biological categories are far from easy to classify. Listing the features that are necessary or central to any particular species is virtually impossible. But this problem only arises if perfectionism is interested in giving an account of the species *Homo sapiens* rather than a description of humans as falling under a non-biological category, such as *persons*.

Undervaluing pleasure and preference

A significant worry is that perfectionism appears not to capture the relevance of pleasure for well-being (Haybron 2008). Surely the most obvious starting point for any theory of well-being is that if *anything* matters for well-being, pleasure does. But perfectionism appears to have nothing to say about the relevance of pleasure for well-being. As a result, it is subject to making claims about lives that some find implausible, such as the following. Jack lives a life of high achievement, daring endeavors, and mastering important knowledge and skills, but is miserable every day and has absolutely no enjoyment or pleasure. In contrast, James has very slightly less achievement and knowledge, but has a great deal of enjoyment and pleasure and takes the occasional relaxing vacation. Perfectionism appears to tell us that Jack's life has more perfectionist value than James's life and is therefore better. But most of us would surely prefer a life like James's over Jack's.

An obvious reply is to clarify what precisely perfectionism is a theory *of*. If perfectionism is presented as a theory of *good*, rather than a theory of well-being, then there is a sense in which the complaint about pleasure misses the mark. We might be inclined to agree that Jack has a better *life* than James, regardless of how much well-being either enjoys. Perfectionism as a theory of good, but not well-being, captures this, and leaves it open that James may have more well-being. One might say that perfectionism yields an account of *a good life*, but a good life can depart from a life that is good for the person who leads it (Arneson 2000).

But when perfectionism is conceived as a theory of *well-being*, the concern about pleasure has force. Although pluralism is a possible option for a theory of well-being, for perfectionism to acknowledge pluralism about well-being is for it to relinquish one of its main selling points—the unification of the elements relevant for well-being. In other words, if a perfectionist holds that perfectionism gives an account of *some but not all* elements of well-being, and acknowledges that *separately* pleasure and perhaps other elements also constitute well-being, perfectionism no longer offers a comprehensive theory of *all* that is relevant for well-being. But providing a unifying, comprehensive account was the very inspiration for the view at the outset.

A different response for a perfectionist theory of well-being is to hold that there are capacities to enjoy characteristic pleasure. It's a natural thought that a capacity for enjoyment is central to our nature. One could further refine this view by holding that we have a capacity to enjoy certain things in a certain way that is characteristic of us as human beings. Kraut, for example, acknowledges our "affective" and "sensory" powers are among our characteristic capacities (Kraut 2009). Kauppinen (2009) also acknowledges that capacities for relaxation and enjoyment are relevant for perfectionist value.

A problem with this response is that it's not obvious that a capacity for enjoyment can fit the criteria for being a capacity of the relevant sort. Capacities, a perfectionist might plausibly hold, are the sort of thing that must be subject to *development* and cultivation. Surely there are ways of cultivating one's tastes and so on, but this is not the same sense in which we develop our rational capacities or our talents. The ability to enjoy things and take pleasure is too passive to be a capacity; capacities are characterized by *activities* that bring the capacity to fulfillment.

A similar complaint can be raised about preferences. Perfectionism appears to ignore the relevance of our preferences in what's good for us. Perfectionism tells us that a career with high achievements will be a better life for us than a career with only slightly less achievement, but which we strongly prefer (Dorsey 2010). The fact that it is our deepest desire to follow the second career path is, itself, irrelevant for how well our life goes.

Perfectionists who acknowledge autonomy as a relevant capacity can accommodate the worry about preferences, however. Other perfectionists may be inclined to develop an account that captures a capacity to develop and act on reflective preferences, which would be exercised in cases like the one just mentioned. Still other perfectionists will be more inclined to bite the bullet and argue that sometimes we irrationally prefer things that are not as good for us as alternatives, and so preference should be excluded from a theory of well-being.

Disvalue

A related concern is that perfectionism does not naturally yield an account of what is *bad* for us. It does not even seem to entail that pain is bad for us. At most, it appears that a perfectionist may say that the privation of exercise of capacities is a privation of well-being. It is not good for us when we fail to flourish and manifest the excellence of our capacities. But saying this is quite a different claim from saying that something is *bad* for us.

Kraut attempts to capture the bad of pain in perfectionist terms. He claims that painful and uncomfortable physical sensations, including hunger, exhaustion, and nausea, are bad for us simply in virtue of how they feel. It isn't simply that these sensations are instrumental toward a failing in flourishing, but themselves they constitute "unflourishing" in virtue of the fact that they feel bad and for this reason we are justified in disliking them and being averse to them. It's unclear, however, how an explanation like this one really explains *why* these sensations are intrinsically bad for us in perfectionist terms when, in cases of pain, for example, our capacities are functioning very well—i.e., to alert us to pain and injury. It is not clear why the feeling constitutes *unflourishing*—it isn't symmetrical, as we might expect, to flourishing. Flourishing is our positive well-being, which is when our capacities are functioning *well*. If "unflourishing" is to be actually *bad* and not just a privation of good, it should involve something symmetrical at the level of the capacities and their flourishing. But capacities just don't seem to lend themselves to this in a natural way.

An alternative response is very straightforward: pluralism. Pain may be bad for reasons that are *not* explained by perfectionism. But this is no threat to perfectionism if it does not purport to be in the business of explaining why pain is bad.

Yet one might think that it *should* be in the business of explaining why pain is bad. If one accepts that it is a desideratum of any theory of well-being that it gives an account not only of what is good for us but also what is bad for us, then this point may be problematic for perfectionism. Moreover, given the unifying aspirations of perfectionism, we might think this is especially important for this theory.

The threat of elitism

A common concern is that perfectionism entails some kind of elitism, i.e., that perfectionism entails that society should be structured in such a way that favors only the excellent and highest achievers. The worry possibly originates from John Rawls's reason for rejecting perfectionism as it appears in *Theory of Justice* (1999: 285–292). However, it is far from clear that elitist or maximax principles of distribution follow from perfectionism. As Richard Arneson shows, a perfectionist theory of well-being is compatible with egalitarian distributive principles, such as the maximin principle (favored by Rawls himself), according to which resources are given to the worst off first so as to maximize their well-being. When combined with perfectionism about well-being, maximin would have resources given to those at the lowest levels of achievement and other perfectionist value in order that they may engage their perfectionist capacities to achieve more highly (Arneson 2000).

Elitism may be more of a threat if the theory of perfectionism is calibrated in a certain way. A perfectionist theory might hold that mere moderate exercise of capacities is of very little value relative to high-quality exercise of capacities. This would mean that the achievements of average people—graduating from college, raising a family, etc.—are of negligible value relative to the achievements of the extremely talented. Only, say, Parfit's philosophical achievements would be of value in contrast to the piddling accomplishments of most of us. As discussed above, this

Nietzschean perfectionism calibrates value such that only the achievements of the most talented are worthwhile, and the view would be elitist in this sense. Moreover, such a calibration of value would lend itself to elitism of distribution of resources, because only a very few high achievers will be able to utilize resources in a way that will generate significant value. Although such a view is coherent, most contemporary perfectionists defend theories according to which the achievements of average people do indeed have value.

In fact, this is one of the key appeals of contemporary perfectionism—its pluralistic output (Hurka 1993; Brink 2008). Since there are such a wide range of career paths, lifestyles, and activities that make use of the capacities of theoretical and practical rationality and autonomy, perfectionism is able to capture that a wide variety of human endeavors have intrinsic value. In fact, some contemporary perfectionists happily embrace what earlier generations of philosophers would likely have pooh-poohed. Hurka discusses the incredible achievements of professional hockey players as involving a dazzling manifestation of intrinsically valuable capacities of practical rationality. One can even make the argument that the best hockey players may have more perfection than a mediocre philosopher. So contemporary perfectionism has broad-minded appeal.

Justification

Although perfectionism is presented to us as providing a unifying justification for an objective theory of well-being, one can complain that perfectionism in the end does no better than the objective list in explaining or justifying why the objective goods are indeed good. The complaint here is this. Perfectionism offers us a theory of what the goods on the objective list have in common, but it does *not explain why they are good*. It explains why this or that good *is on the list* but it does not explain *why* the list is a list of *what's good*.

Perfectionism and political theory

Political perfectionism extends to the political realm. The political theory with this name is the view that the state may promote certain substantive conceptions of the good (typically perfectionist conceptions). It is usually presented in contrast to *neutrality*, which is the view that the state must remain neutral to any particular conception of the good, and must refrain from promoting any particular conception of good in the lives of its citizens. Although some philosophers treat political perfectionism as involving a perfectionist theory of well-being as the substantive conception of the good (e.g., Sher 1997), political perfectionism may not necessarily incorporate a perfectionist theory of well-being; rather, it may involve simply the rejection of neutrality, holding that the state may justifiedly promote some conception of the good, and that conception of the good need not be a perfectionist theory of well-being (e.g., Raz 1986).

Some of the debate about political perfectionism concerns the relationship between political perfectionism and liberalism, asking about the extent to which individuals should be free to develop their lives in a way of their own choosing. If the state is justified in promoting a perfectionist conception of the good, this means that the state is justified in encouraging certain ways of life and discouraging others. Many people consider such interference by the state an objectionable encroachment on personal liberty. Perfectionists can accommodate the liberal intuition by appealing to autonomy as an element in their perfectionist theory of well-being, but whether or not this is a successful reply, or necessary at all, is a matter of debate.

A further political approach involved in this discussion is the capabilities developed by Nussbaum and Sen (e.g., Nussbaum 1988, 2000; Sen 1992). According to the capabilities approach, state policies should be shaped in such a way as to ensure that citizens attain a sufficient level of capability to function. In other words, the aim is not to promote flourishing directly, but leave citizens free to choose which of their capabilities to fulfill and how. The state's role is to equip the capabilities of its citizens to flourish, and flourish in the manner and to the extent of their choosing. In this respect, the capabilities approach is in direct contrast to political perfectionism. The capabilities approach stresses the significance of liberalism and sees the capability to choose how and whether to exercise one's capabilities is a central freedom. Nevertheless, the common Aristotelian ancestry shared by both the capabilities approach and perfectionism about well-being is evident in the structure of the two theories, both of which hold that there is a set of central human capacities the exercise of which is of great significance for our good.

Note

1 Robert Nozick suggests such an approach is possible (Nozick 1981: 517).

References

Aristotle (1999) *Nicomachean Ethics* (transl. T. Irwin), Indianapolis: Hackett.
Arneson, R. (2000) "Perfectionism and Politics," *Ethics* 111: 37–63.
Brink, D.O. (2003) *Perfectionism and the Common Good: Themes in the Philosophy of T.H. Green*, Oxford: Clarendon Press.
Brink, D.O. (2008) "The Significance of Desire," in R. Shafer-Landau (ed.), *Oxford Studies in Metaethics*, vol. 3, Oxford: Oxford University Press.
Dorsey, D. (2010). "Three Arguments for Perfectionism," *Noûs* 4: 59–79.
Green, T.H. (2003 [1883]) *Prolegomena to Ethics* (ed. D.O. Brink), Oxford: Oxford University Press.
Haybron, D.M. (2008) *The Pursuit of Unhappiness: The Elusive Psychology of Well-Being: The Elusive Psychology of Well-Being*, Oxford: Oxford University Press.
Hurka, T. (1993) *Perfectionism*, Oxford: Oxford University Press.
Hurka, T. (2007) "Nietzsche: Perfectionist," in B. Leiter and N. Sinhababu (eds.) *Nietzsche and Morality*, Oxford: Oxford University Press.
Kauppinen, A. (2009) "Working Hard and Kicking Back: The Case for Diachronic Perfectionism," *Journal of Ethics and Social Philosophy* 1–9.
Kitcher, P. (1999) "Essence and Perfection," *Ethics* 110: 59–83.
Kraut, R. (2009) *What is Good and Why: The Ethics of Well-being*, Cambridge, MA: Harvard University Press.
Nozick, R. (1981) *Philosophical Explanations*, Cambridge, MA: Harvard University Press.
Nussbaum, M.C. (1988) "Nature, Function, and Capability: Aristotle on Political Distribution," *Oxford Studies in Ancient Philosophy* 6: 145–184.
Nussbaum, M.C. (2000) *Women and Human Development: The Capabilities Approach*, Cambridge: Cambridge University Press.
Rawls, J. (1999) *Theory of Justice*, Cambridge, MA: Harvard University Press.
Raz, J. (1986) *The Morality of Freedom*, Oxford: Oxford University Press.
Sen, A. (1992) *Inequality Reexamined*, Oxford: Clarendon Press.
Sher, G. (1997) *Beyond Neutrality: Perfectionism and Politics*, Cambridge: Cambridge University Press.

11

DESIRE-FULFILLMENT THEORY

Chris Heathwood

Introduction and historical background

The desire-fulfillment theory of well-being—also known as desire satisfactionism, preferentism, or simply the desire theory—holds, in its simplest form, that what is good in itself for people and other subjects of welfare is their getting what they want, or the fulfillment of their desires, and what is bad in itself for them is their not getting what they want, or the frustration of their desires. Most or all desire theorists would agree that the stronger the desire, the more beneficial is its satisfaction and the worse its frustration. There is less consensus over whether how long the desire is held is directly relevant to the value of its fulfillment or frustration. On the question of how good an entire life would be for a person, there are two main ways a desire approach might go: it can sum the values of all the instances of desire satisfaction and frustration *within* that life; or it can look to the person's desires *about* that whole life and hold that the best life is the one the person most wants to lead. These views yield different verdicts because a person may prefer to lead a life that contains less preference satisfaction. A desire is fulfilled, according to standard forms of the theory, just if the desired state of affairs occurs; the subject need not know about it or experience any feelings of fulfillment.

The desire-fulfillment theory is a form of subjectivism about well-being in the rough sense that, according to it, getting a good life has to do with one's attitudes towards what one gets in life rather than the nature of those things themselves. There are other forms of subjectivism— e.g., aim-achievement theories, value-realization theories, happiness theories, and some forms of hedonism—but the desire-fulfillment theory is the archetype. Objective theories of well-being—such as perfectionism or the objective-list theory—maintain, by contrast, that at least some things that are intrinsically good or bad for us do not essentially involve our pro- or con-attitudes. Desire fulfillment also plays a central role in some hybrid theories of well-being, which combine subjective and objective elements.

The desire-fulfillment theory is nowadays undoubtedly one of the leading theories of well-being. Some philosophers regard it to be *the* leading theory, "the theory to beat," "[t]he dominant account among economists and philosophers over the last century or so" (Haybron 2008: 3). If it is the dominant theory of the 20th and 21st centuries, it received much less attention before then. Some leading ancient and medieval philosophers brought up the view in order to reject it. In Plato's *Gorgias* (c. 380 BCE), for instance, it is Socrates' foil Callicles who asserts that "he who would truly live ought to allow his desires to wax to the uttermost, and . . . minister to them and to satisfy all his longings" (491e–492a). In *De Trinitate* (c. 416 CE), St. Augustine (416) briefly discusses the idea "that all are blessed, whoever live as they will," claiming that Cicero refuted it (XIII, 5). Augustine goes on to assert, however, that desire (or will) fulfillment is at least necessary for well-being. In *Summa Theologiae* (c. 1274 CE), Thomas Aquinas speaks favorably of "the definition of beatitude that some have posited—viz., that the blessed man is he who has everything that he desires" (I–II.5.8), but he does not in the end endorse a true desire-fulfillment theory.

Some major figures of the early modern period were more sympathetic to the desire-fulfillment theory. Thomas Hobbes is often mentioned as an early adopter due to this passage in *Leviathan* (1651):

> whatsoever is the object of any man's appetite or desire that is it which he for his part calleth *good*; and the object of his hate and aversion, *evil* . . . . For these words of good [and] evil . . . are ever used with relation to the person that useth them, there being nothing simply or absolutely so.
>
> *(ch. 6)*

In his *Ethics* (1677), Baruch Spinoza writes, "in no case do we . . . desire anything, because we deem it to be good, but . . . we deem a thing to be good, because we . . . desire it" (Spinoza 1677: Part III, Prop. IX). It is not clear that Spinoza is talking about well-being as opposed to just plain value, but because Hobbes suggests that he rejects the very notion of value *simpliciter*, there are stronger grounds for interpreting him as talking about well-being.

That is how Henry Sidgwick interprets Hobbes when, in *The Methods of Ethics* (1907), he begins what may be the first in-depth discussion of the desire-fulfillment theory of well-being (I.IX.3).[1] In that discussion, Sidgwick comes to the nowadays orthodox view that the theory is more promising if (simplifying somewhat) we

> identify [a person's good] not with the actually desired, but rather with . . . what would be desired . . . supposing the desirer to possess a perfect forecast, emotional as well as intellectual, of the state of attainment or fruition.
>
> *(110–111)*

Though Sidgwick does not ultimately endorse a view of this sort, the doctrine that he formulates later inspires John Rawls's view in *A Theory of Justice* (1971) that

> A person's good is determined by what is for him the most rational long-term plan of life . . . the plan that would be decided upon as the outcome of careful reflection in which the agent reviewed, in the light of all the relevant facts, what it would be like to carry out these plans and thereby ascertained the course of action that would best realize his more fundamental desires.
>
> *(92–93, 417)*

When the desire-fulfillment theory of welfare finally takes root in the early to mid twentieth century, it does so perhaps most deeply among economists (see Angner, Chapter 40 in this volume). Early welfare economists, such as A.C. Pigou, accept the classical utilitarian doctrine that "the elements of welfare are states of consciousness" (1920: I.5; II.1). But, recognizing the need for something scientifically measurable, Pigou proposes that these welfare states "be brought into relation with a money measure" (II.1). And he saw that this could be done only indirectly: it must be "mediated through desires and aversions." Later welfare economists drop the underlying view that ultimate value lay wholly in the states of mind, and come to understand preference satisfaction itself as constituting rather than merely being a reliable sign of well-being. John Harsanyi, for example, states his adherence to "the important philosophical principle of *preference autonomy*," "the principle that in deciding what is good and what is bad for a given individual, the ultimate criterion can only be his own wants and his own preferences" (1977: 645).

At the same time, philosophers, too, came to endorse preference-based accounts in larger numbers. In *The Varieties of Goodness* (1963), for example, the Finnish philosopher G.H. von Wright explains the notion of "a positive constituent of our good (welfare)" in terms of what "we should rather have than continue to be without" (107). In addition to von Wright and Rawls, other prominent, early advocates among philosophers include the political theorist Brian Barry (1965) and moral philosophers Richard Brandt (1966), Peter Singer (1979), and R.M. Hare (1981).

The desire-fulfillment theory's rise to prominence is also partly attributable to its role in decision theory. Although early statements of the principle of expected utility are neutral as to what things are good for us, utility later comes to be understood simply in terms of desires and aversions. In "Truth and Probability" (1926), for instance, F.P. Ramsey stipulates that he will "call the things a person ultimately desires 'goods'," and "emphasize[s] that in this essay good and bad are . . . to be understood . . . simply as denoting that to which a given person feels desire and aversion" (173–174).

And "[t]oday," some writers believe, "the desire-satisfaction theory is probably the dominant view of welfare among economists, social-scientists, and philosophers, both utilitarian and non-utilitarian" (Shaw 1999: 53).

Arguments for the desire-fulfillment theory

The fundamental principles of value theory might be the most basic normative truths. For that reason we might not expect to find many direct *arguments* for them. Still, there is at least one interesting such argument for the subjectivist approach to well-being, one that provides at least indirect support for the desire-fulfillment theory. The argument appeals to *internalism about well-being*, which Peter Railton (1986: 9) puts as follows:

> what is intrinsically valuable for a person must have a connection with what he would find in some degree compelling or attractive, at least if he were rational and aware.

Since desiring is a paradigm way of finding something compelling or attractive, this principle suggests a link between welfare and desire. Why think the principle is true? I suspect that, to many people, as it does to Railton, it simply seems right: it is hard to believe that we can benefit someone by giving her things with which she is utterly unimpressed and in which she will remain forever uninterested. Other philosophers have offered arguments for internalism.[2]

Another kind of argument for the desire-fulfillment theory is based on the idea that it fits well with a naturalistic metaethic, and hence a naturalistic worldview more generally. This may be related to the theory's popularity among economists. One naturalistic approach in metaethics holds that normative or evaluative properties are to be identified with those natural properties that elicit certain responses, or are the object of certain attitudes, in certain observers. Such an approach might hold that the property of being beneficial for some subject, S, *just is* the property of being an object of a desire of S. This metaethical thesis implies a version of the desire theory of welfare. It is sometimes thought that pluralistic or objective theories of welfare are harder to square with naturalism.[3]

Another way to argue for a desire-fulfillment theory of well-being is from a desire-based, or internalist, theory of reasons for action. The latter asserts, roughly, that the only thing a person has reason to do is satisfy her desires. It may be a datum, something that any theory of reasons must accommodate, that a person always has some reason to do what is in her own interests. The way for a reasons internalist to accommodate this datum is to endorse a desire-fulfillment theory of well-being.[4]

Yet another line of reasoning in support of the desire-fulfillment theory begins with the intuitive idea that getting what you want is at least *a* good thing for us, and then subjects the strengthened, unified hypothesis that it is the *only* good thing to scrutiny, attempting to falsify it; the argument then claims that the unified hypothesis survives the scrutiny, and we are thus justified in accepting it. Hedonism can be argued for on similar grounds. But desire theorists may claim that the desire-fulfillment hypothesis is more plausible than the hedonistic hypothesis in two ways. First, one of the most popular arguments against hedonism—the experience machine objection—does not apply to the desire theory (or at least not as straightforwardly).[5] Second, if we consider someone who is familiar with pleasure and doesn't want it as much as she wants other things, there is some plausibility to the claim that it is better for her to get the other things. This intuition favors the desire theory over hedonism. Hedonistic theories that make use of a desire theory of *pleasure*—the view, roughly, that for an experience to be pleasurable is for the person experiencing it to want to be experiencing it—may avoid this argument, but may also collapse into a desire theory (cf. Heathwood 2006).

The success of this overall line of argument depends on the desire theory's ability to accommodate the goods posited by competing theories. The main competing theories are hedonistic and objective theories. Concerning hedonism, either a desire-based theory of the nature of pleasure is true, or it isn't. If it is true, then the desire theory of well-being can accommodate the data that pleasure is good and pain bad for their subjects.[6] If it isn't, then so much the worse for that alleged data; for if pleasure is instead just a certain distinctive kind of feeling or feeling tone, one a subject may have no interest in, then it's not clear that it is a good thing for such a subject to experience this (to him) neutral feeling (cf. Sobel 2005: 444–446).

When it comes to putative objective goods, such as knowledge or friendship, the desire theorist may note that such goods are desired by virtually everyone. The desire theorist can thus explain why they might seem to be universal, objective goods. And when we imagine a strange person who truly has no interest them, the desire-theoretic commitment that they are of no benefit to that person may be at least as plausible as the objectivist insistence that they are (cf. the doctrine of internalism about well-being, discussed earlier). Desire fulfillment may be the common denominator on the scene in cases of apparent objective and hedonic goods, the factor that indeed explains the value in these cases.

Whether this last overall line of argument for the desire-fulfillment theory can succeed depends on the extent to which the theory has the resources to deflect the many lines of objection that have been advanced against it. To these we now turn.

Arguments against the desire-fulfillment theory

Mere instrumental fulfillments

We begin with a maximally unadorned theory, according to which whenever someone wants something to be the case, and it is or becomes the case, this is a benefit to the person. But suppose the person wants the thing to be the case only as a means to something else. For example, suppose she wants it to snow in the mountains so that the skiing will be good for her upcoming trip there, and only for that reason. Suppose it does snow in the mountains, but that she had to cancel her trip. Intuitively, the fulfillment of her desire that it snow was not in the end of any benefit to her.

The obvious solution is for the desire-fulfillment theorist to restrict the theory to count as intrinsically good for us only the fulfillment of desires for things for their own sakes, or what are sometimes called *intrinsic desires*.[7] This restriction is usually accepted uncritically; however, it isn't obviously unproblematic. Suppose a father wants to see As on his son's report card. The report card arrives and indeed the son has earned straight As. Plausibly, this is a good thing for the father and it is in the spirit of the desire-fulfillment theory to agree. But, for all that, the father's desire might be merely instrumental.

Ill-informed desires

There is a cherry pie before me and I am dying for a slice. Unbeknownst to me, I have recently developed a severe allergy to cherries and so it would in fact not be in my interests to satisfy my desire to eat the slice. This appears to conflict with the unadorned desire-fulfillment theory, according to which *any* desire fulfillment benefits a person. The restriction to intrinsic desires, while it will exclude some ill-informed desires (e.g., those based on false beliefs about what means might bring about a desired end), appears not to help here, since my desire to eat the slice is intrinsic.

About such cases, it might often be true that if the person knew all the facts, he would not have the problematic desire. This inspires the standard solution to the problem of ill-informed desires: idealization. The *informed desire theory* holds, on one of its many varieties, that what is good in itself for us is our getting what we *would* want if we knew and vividly appreciated all of the non-evaluative facts (Sidgwick 1907: §3; Rawls 1971: 417). If I knew how eating the pie would affect me, I probably wouldn't want to eat it.

An alternative response to the objection from ill-informed desires requires no modification to the theory (Heathwood 2005). The objection claims that the unmodified theory implies that it is in my interests to satisfy my desire to eat the allergenic pie. But consider two things we might have in mind when we say that it is in my interests to satisfy some desire. We might mean that it is in my interests overall, or *all things considered*—that is, taking all the effects of satisfying the desire into account. Or we might mean merely that it is good *in itself* for me—intrinsically good for me—to satisfy the desire. The objection assumes, plausibly, that it is not in my interests *all things considered* to satisfy my desire for the pie. But the original unidealized desire theory can accommodate this, for if I satisfy my desire to eat the food, this will cause many of my other desires—desires not to feel sick, desires to go on a hike, etc.—to be frustrated on into the future. The original theory is committed only to the claim that it is *good in itself* for me to satisfy my desire to eat the food. But, ignoring the effects—which is what one does when evaluating a claim of intrinsic value—it intuitively *is* good for me to get to eat this piece of pie I very much want to eat. One advantage of this solution is that it is not hostage to the empirical conjecture that if I were to become idealized, I would lose all desire for the pie. Another advantage is that it avoids the difficult tasks of spelling out the nature and justification of the idealization as well as any new problems that idealization may introduce.

Unwanted fulfillments of ideal desires

Idealizing theories are indeed subject to objections that non-idealizing theories don't face. James Griffin writes,

It is doubtless true that if I fully appreciated the nature of all possible objects of desire, I should change much of what I wanted. But if I do not go through that daunting improvement, yet the objects of my potentially perfected desires are given to me, I might well not be glad to have them; the education, after all, may be necessary for my getting anything out of them. That is true, for instance, of acquired tastes; you would do me no favour by giving me caviar now, unless it is part of some well-conceived training for my palate.

(Griffin 1986: 11)

Suppose we do give Griffin caviar now. The informed desire theory implies that we have indeed done him a favor, since, although he in fact has no interest in caviar, we have satisfied a desire that (we can suppose) he would have had if he were fully and vividly informed about the taste of caviar. Giving caviar to Griffin's *idealized* self might very well benefit *that* person, but theories of welfare are also supposed to tell us what things are good for schleps like you and me. Perhaps the underlying problem here is that an idealized desire theory of the sort under consideration seems to abandon internalism about well-being, a basic intuition that motivates the desire theory in the first place.

The standard response to this problem is not to abandon idealization but to move to the *ideal advisor theory* (Railton 1986: 16; Rosati 1996). One way to understand this proposal is, what is good for a person is not what she would want *for herself* were she idealized, but what, were she idealized, she would want *for her actual, unidealized self*. Although Griffin's ideal self wants caviar *for himself*, perhaps he would not want his roe-averse actual self to get it.

But the ideal advisor version of idealization brings with it new problems. One is that it's at least possible that one's ideal advisor finds one's ignorance, inexperience, and poor taste pathetic, and consequently feels only disdain for one, and wishes one ill. Griffin's ideal advisor might think, "If I'm ever that ignorant and uncultivated, then shoot me," or, less fanatically, " . . . then give me caviar anyway." One might attempt to emend the ideal advisor theory by having it appeal to one's *benevolent* and informed desires. We could stipulate that "The ideal advisor's sole aim is to advance the well-being of the advisee" (Arneson 1999: 127). But such an account appears viciously circular. It seems essentially to be telling us that what is good for a person to get is what someone who wants what is good for this person wants this person to get.[8]

Base desires, malicious desires, pointless desires

Those who think that enjoyment is in general a good thing sometimes doubt that all enjoyment is good, for some instances of it are base and others malicious. But desires can be similarly base or malicious. There are also desires that seem simply unworthy even if not base or malicious, as in Rawls' case of a talented intellect whose aim in life is "to count blades of grass in various geometrically shaped areas such as park squares and well-trimmed lawns" (Rawls 1971: 432).

For desire theorists who have already embraced idealization, it is tempting to call on it whenever problems arise. Thus an ideal desire theorist might hope that no one who was fully and vividly informed about all of their possibilities would want to spend their time breaking crockery while drunk, torturing kittens, or counting blades of grass. But it is hard to see why full and vivid information must in all cases extinguish such desires. Some suspect that ideal-izers who would make such claims are unconsciously assuming that the idealization process includes eliminating desires for things it's simply not good to get. But such an appeal would evidently require there to be desire-independent welfare goods, and thus require abandoning the desire theory.

Another response is simply to "bite the bullet" and insist that the subjects are no worse off for desiring in their unconventional ways. This reply is bolstered when we are reminded that some such desires are still criticizable morally and aesthetically, even if not prudentially. Such a strategy may, however, require its advocates to deny that the fact that some act would benefit someone is always a reason to do it.

Remote desires

"Since my desires can range over spatially and temporally remote states of affairs," L.W. Sumner writes,

> it follows that the satisfaction of many of them will occur at times or places too distant from me to have any discernible effect on me. In such cases it is difficult to see how having my desire satisfied could possibly make my life go better.
>
> *(Sumner 1996: 125)*

A concrete case due to Derek Parfit has become stock in the literature:

> Suppose I meet a stranger who has what is believed to be a fatal disease. My sympathy is aroused, and I strongly want this stranger to be cured. We never meet again. Later, unknown to me, this stranger is cured. On the Unrestricted Desire-Fulfilment Theory, this event is good for me, and makes my life go better. This is not plausible.
>
> *(Parfit 1984: 494)*

A special case of the problem concerns the fact that our desires can be fulfilled after we are dead.

Mark Overvold is a desire theorist who admits that "it is hard to see how anything which happens after one no longer exists can contribute to one's self-interest" (1980: 108), and proceeds to develop a theory that delivers the desired result in the sorts of cases we are considering. On Overvold's proposal, a desire had by some person is relevant to her welfare just in case it is a desire for a state of affairs that can obtain at some time only if she exists at that time (1980: 10n). On this *self-regarding desire theory*, since *the stranger's being cured* can obtain at some time without Parfit existing at that time, the fulfillment of Parfit's desire for it is of no benefit to Parfit. Overvold's theory also rules out posthumous harm and benefit.

Overvold's restriction to self-regarding desires may exclude too much, however. A persuasive example is the desire that the team one roots for wins. It is very important to some people that their team win, and they hope for it as intently as they hope for anything about themselves. It does not seem plausible to claim that the fulfillment of such a desire is of no benefit to the desirer simply because it is not self-regarding. This objection also makes trouble for an alternative solution: that it is the fulfillment of our *aims* rather than our desires that benefits us.

On a third kind of solution, the remoteness that is anathema to welfare is remoteness from what we are aware of, or what we experience (Heathwood 2006: §2). The reason Parfit isn't benefitted when the stranger is cured is that the stranger is cured unbeknownst to Parfit. Note that it does seem more plausible that Parfit receives a benefit in a variant of the case in which Parfit learns that the stranger has been cured. Unlike the previous solutions, this solution allows that the fulfillment of desires that aren't about me, such as my team's winning, can nevertheless benefit me.

This solution does, however, imply that nothing that fails to enter or otherwise affect my awareness or experience can benefit me. If my spouse has an affair—something I am strongly averse to—some thinkers want to say that I am harmed by this even if I never find out about it and it never affects anything else that I have desires about. If I am harmed and, more generally, what you don't know *can* hurt you, then this theory of experienced desire fulfillment fails, and we are left without a solution to the problem of remote desires. Some philosophers bite the bullet up front and insist that things do go better for Parfit when, unknown to him, the stranger is cured (Lukas 2010).

Unwanted desires

"Knowing that you accept a Summative theory"—the kind of desire theory that determines the value of your life by summing the values of the desire fulfillments and frustrations within it—Derek Parfit tells you,

> I am about to make your life go better. I shall inject you with an addictive drug. From now on, you will wake each morning with an extremely strong desire to have another injection of this drug . . . This is no cause for concern, since I shall give you ample supplies of this drug. Every morning, you will be able at once to fulfil this desire.
>
> *(Parfit 1984: 496)*

Parfit believes that few people would take him up on his offer, yet a summative desire-fulfillment theory implies that we would be better off if we did. Although we might often wish that we were not addicted to this drug, the disvalue of these desire frustrations would (we can suppose) be outweighed by the value of the repeated daily fulfillments.

It is sometimes thought that "complication[s] . . . created by the fact that sometimes we have desires—those created by addictions, for example—that we wish we were without . . . can easily be handled in familiar ways by giving special weight to second-order desires" (Kraut 1994: 40). On this proposal, only fulfillments of those desires that one desires to have contribute to one's well-being. This solution may help with the addiction case, assuming that addictive desires are not ones we desire to have, but it would seem to exclude too much. Unreflective people—people who live in the moment and never pause to consider their desires or take up any attitudes towards them—don't all have worthless lives. Likewise for those mentally disabled people and animals who are incapable of higher-order mental states.

Parfit himself believes that his case shows that "global versions" of the desire theory are superior. Since these theories "appeal only to someone's desires about some part of his life, considered as a whole, or about his whole life," they "ignore your particular desires each morning for a fresh injection" (1984: 497). It was a global desire theory that was discussed or endorsed in the earlier passages by Sidgwick and Rawls. But, again, what of those of us who don't have global desires, or can't have them?[9] Another objection to the move to global desires calls into question the presumption that when global and local desires conflict, global desires are always authoritative (de Lazari-Radek and Singer 2014: 221).

There is a familiar distinction among desires, between what a person "truly desires" or finds truly appealing, and what a person wants in the thinner, merely behavioral sense that he is simply disposed to try to get it.[10] This distinction isn't discussed much in the welfare literature, though one exception is Sumner, who, while not a desire theorist, maintains that "[i]t is only in the [former, "true appeal"] sense that preference can be plausibly connected with welfare"

(1996: 120). Perhaps a theory restricted to this narrower sense of desire can answer Parfit's objection, since, as he describes them, the daily desires for the drug seem merely behavioral; taking the drug holds no genuine appeal for the addict.[11]

Idealistic desires, self-sacrificial desires

Robert Adams points out that,

> Altruistic desires might lead you to sacrifice your own good for the good of another. This seems to imply that what you would prefer, on the whole, with full knowledge, is not necessarily what is best, on the whole, for you. . . . Something like [this] problem [also] arises in connection with desires that are not necessarily altruistic but may be called "idealistic." One may clearheadedly do what is worse for oneself out of regard for virtue, or for some other ideal. Love of truthfulness, or of human dignity, may lead a person to tell the truth, or to refuse to abase herself, at great cost to herself and for nobody else's benefit.
>
> *(Adams 1999: 87–88)*

A related case is that of self-sacrificial desires, though the objection here is a little different. According to the argument from self-sacrifice, desire theories fail because they imply, absurdly, that self-sacrifice is impossible (Overvold 1980). For an act to count as an act of self-sacrifice, it would seem that it must be (i) voluntary, (ii) informed, and (iii) not in the agent's best interest. But, the argument claims, if (i) and (ii) are satisfied, (iii) cannot be, given standard desire-fulfillment theories of welfare. For if an act is voluntary, it is the one the agent most wants to do; if it is also informed, then, on either simple desire-fulfillment theories or full-information variants, it is thereby in the agent's best interest, and so condition (iii) cannot be satisfied.

One natural solution to the problems created by idealistic desires is simply to exclude them from the theory by fiat. Mill holds a view along these lines for determining the value of a pleasure, excluding preferences that are based on a "feeling of moral obligation" (1863: 12). In his discussion of the desire theory, Sidgwick sets down that he will consider "only what a man desires . . . for himself—not benevolently for others" (1907: 109).

Such proposals face problems similar to those faced by theories that restrict to self-regarding desires. Plausibly, devoted parents are sometimes benefitted when their intrinsic desires concerning their children's welfare are satisfied; presumably some such desires are altruistic. Conversely, desires based on moral considerations should, intuitively, also sometimes count. People can become quite invested in justice, for example; if the just outcome is their heart's desire, it doesn't seem right to rule out all possibility of benefit.

Perhaps we need not exclude idealistic or self-sacrificial desires to solve the problems they raise. It has been argued that even the simplest, fully unrestricted sort of desire theory can accommodate self-sacrifice, so long as it is of the sort described above as "summative" (Heathwood 2011). Even if an agent brings about the outcome she most prefers, that outcome can still contain within it less desire satisfaction for her than some alternative outcome available to her, making the act not in her best interest, even if voluntary and informed. Another solution, combinable with the one just mentioned, counts only the narrower sense of "desire" mentioned above, the sense of finding the object of the desire truly appealing. These solutions are more flexible than those that simply exclude idealistic desires: they allow us to say that, in cases of grudging obedience to the ideal, no benefit accrues, whereas in cases of enthusiastic embrace of the value, benefit does accrue.

Changing desires

According to Richard Brandt,

> The fundamental difficulty for the desire-satisfaction theory is that desires change over time: Some occurrence I now want to have happen may be something I did not want to have happen in the past, and will wish had not happened, if it does happen, in the future.
>
> *(Brandt 1982: 179)*

Suppose I want, for years, to go skydiving on my 40th birthday. But as the day approaches, my interests change, and I become strongly averse to doing this.

Plausibly, when my 40th birthday comes, it is in my interest to satisfy my present desire *not* to go skydiving at the expense of frustrating my past desires to go skydiving (at least if we assume that I won't later have persistent desires in the future to have done it). And perhaps this remains true no matter how long-held and strong the past desires to go skydiving were. This suggests that to determine what benefits a person, we can ignore her past desires completely.

However, sometimes we do act so as to satisfy the merely past desires of people we care about. For example, we heed the wishes of the dead concerning how to treat their remains. Do we do this for their *benefit*? It's not obvious that we do, but if we do, that implies that we believe that it is in their interests to have this merely past desire satisfied. One kind of theory ignores only those past desires that are "conditional on their own persistence," or that we want satisfied only if we still have the desire when the time comes to satisfy it. Presumably, the desire in the skydiving case is conditional on its own persistence, whereas our desires about how to treat our remains after we die are not.[12] Another possible solution holds that fulfilling a past desire does result in a benefit, but a benefit that occurs retroactively, when the desire was held (Dorsey 2013). Perhaps in the skydiving case we care only about present and future benefit, while in the death case we care about past benefit.

If, however, fulfilling merely past desires is never a benefit at any time, this suggests the view that the desire theory counts only desires for what goes on at the time of the desire. As R.M. Hare, a proponent of this view, puts it, the theory "admits only now-for-now and then-for-then preferences," to the exclusion of any now-for-then or then-for-now preferences (1981: 101–3).[13] But might this exclude too much? Suppose that I do in fact strongly regret, for years, not having gone skydiving on my 40th birthday. If so, perhaps it was in my interests to force myself to go skydiving, despite my strong aversion to it at the time, for the sake of satisfying the "then-for-now" desires I would come to have. If that's right, this suggests a surprising asymmetry: the desire theory of well-being should ignore future-directed desires but count present- and past-directed desires. There is a possible explanation for such an asymmetry. When we have a future-directed desire, we can't now experience its satisfaction. But with present- and past-directed desires, we often are aware that they are satisfied. If the asymmetrical view is most plausible, this may provide an indirect argument for including an awareness requirement into the theory, as discussed earlier.

Conclusion

There are other objections to the desire approach worthy of our attention. When someone can't get what he really wants, he may adapt his preferences to his predicament. If he succeeds in doing this, he is now getting everything he wants. This seems like an unfortunate situation, but the desire theory may be unable to accommodate this intuition.[14]

The theory may even lead to paradox. Suppose that, out of self-loathing, I want only to be badly off. Either I am badly off or I am not. If I am badly off, then my only desire is fulfilled, and so, on the desire theory, I am not badly off. If, on the other hand, I am not badly off, then my only desire is frustrated, and I am badly off. In short, the desire-fulfillment theory appears to imply the contradictory thought that, in some cases, a person is badly off if and only if he is not badly off.[15]

There is a Euthyphro objection: when we are thinking just about ourselves and our interests, don't we want the things we want because they are good for us? But the desire theory suggests the opposite, that these things are good for us because we want them. There is an objection from Buddhism: doesn't Buddhism teach that the way to well-being is the extinction of all desire? There are objections from manipulated or non-autonomous desires: if subliminal advertising brainwashes us into wanting some silly gadget, does it really benefit us to get it?

Despite all of these objections, the desire-fulfillment theory remains a leader. Many thinkers find it difficult to resist the intuition that what is good for a person must be intimately linked with what engages her, or with her pro-attitudes—in a word, with what she wants.

Acknowledgment

I am grateful to Joey Stenberg for research assistance and to Guy Fletcher and Eden Lin for feedback on earlier drafts.

Related topics

Hedonism, objective list theory, monism and pluralism, autonomy and well-being, well-being and the law, well-being and economics.

Further reading

Carson, T. (2000) *Value and the Good Life*, South Bend, IN: University of Notre Dame Press.
Schwartz, T. (1982) "Human Welfare: What It Is Not," in H.B. Miller and W.H. Williams (eds.) *The Limits of Utilitarianism*, Minneapolis, MN: University of Minnesota Press, pp. 195–206.
Tännsjö, T. (1998) *Hedonistic Utilitarianism*, Edinburgh: Edinburgh University Press, ch. 6.

Notes

1 The desire-fulfillment theory also seems to be endorsed by Joseph Butler in his *Fifteen Sermons,* when he writes that "the very idea of an interested pursuit, necessarily presupposes particular passions or appetites; since the very idea of interest, or happiness, consists in this, that an appetite; or affection, enjoys its object" (1726, preface §31).

2 E.g., Rosati (1996) and Velleman (1998). For criticism, see Sarch (2011). For some discussion of how best to formulate internalism, see Heathwood (2014: §2).

3 Although, see Hooker (1991).

4 However, see Lin (2015).

5 The experience machine objection is derived from the thought experiment in Nozick (1974: 42–45).

6 Though see Lin (2014).

7 See, e.g., Sidgwick (1907: 109) and von Wright (1963: 103–104); on a related solution, there simply are no such things as instrumental desires (Murphy 1999).

8 For further problems with idealizing theories, see Sobel (1994) and Rosati (1995).

9 An *idealized* global theory, which asks which whole lives such people would want if they *were* to have global desires, is an option worth considering.

10 See, e.g., Davis (1986) and Schueler (1995: 1).

11 Cf. the view of psychologist Kent Berridge (1999), who argues that "'wanting' can be activated without 'liking'" and that this phenomenon "has special relevance for understanding the causes of addiction." The suggestion in the main text is that the desire theorist counts only those desires that are involved in Berridge's liking, and that Berridge's wanting involves merely behavioral desire.

12 Cf. Parfit (1984: 151) and Bradley and McDaniel (2008: §10).

13 Cf. the "concurrence requirement" in Heathwood (2005).

14 On adaptive preferences, see Nussbaum (2000: ch. 2); Baber (2007); and Bruckner (2009).

15 On the paradox for desire theories of well-being, see Heathwood (2005: §VI); Bradley (2009); and Skow (2009).

References

Adams, R.M. (1999). *Finite and Infinite Goods: A Framework for Ethics,* New York: Oxford University Press.

Aquinas (1274) *Summa Theologiae* (transl. A. J. Freddoso 2014), http://www3.nd.edu/~afreddos/summa-translation/TOC.htm.

Arneson, R. (1999) "Human Flourishing Versus Desire Satisfaction," *Social Philosophy and Policy* 16: 113–142.

Augustine (416) *De Trinitate*, many editions.

Baber, H.E. (2007) "Adaptive Preference," *Social Theory and Practice* 33: 105–126.

Barry, B. (1965) *Political Argument,* London: Routledge & Kegan Paul.

Berridge, K. (1999) "Pleasure, Pain, Desire and Dread: Hidden Core Processes of Emotion," in D. Kahneman, E. Diener and N. Schwartz (eds.) *Well-Being*, New York: Russell Sage Foundation, pp. 525–557.

Bradley B. (2009) "A Paradox for Some Theories of Welfare," *Philosophical Studies* 133: 45–53.

Bradley, B. and McDaniel, K. (2008) "Desires," *Mind* 117: 267–302.

Brandt, R.B. (1966) "The Concept of Welfare," in S.R. Krupp (ed.) *The Structure of Economic Science*, Englewood Cliffs, NJ: Prentice-Hall, pp. 257–276.

Brandt, R.B. (1982) "Two Concepts of Utility," in H.B. Miller and W.H. Williams (eds.) *The Limits of Utilitarianism*, Minneapolis, MN: University of Minnesota Press, pp. 169–185.

Bruckner, D. (2009) "In Defense of Adaptive Preferences," *Philosophical Studies* 142: 307–324.

Butler, J. (1726) *Fifteen Sermons Preached at the Rolls Chapel*, London: J. and J. Knapton.

Davis, W. (1986) "The Two Senses of Desire," in J. Marks (ed.) *The Ways of Desire*, Chicago, IL: Precedent Publishing, pp. 63–82.

de Lazari-Radek, K. and Singer, P. (2014) *The Point of View of the Universe*, Oxford: Oxford University Press.

Dorsey, D. (2013) "Desire-Satisfaction and Welfare as Temporal," *Ethical Theory and Moral Practice* 16: 151–171.

Elster, J. (1982) "Sour Grapes—Utilitarianism and the Genesis of Wants," in A. Sen. and B. Williams (eds.) *Utilitarianism and Beyond*, Cambridge: Cambridge University Press.

Griffin, J. (1986). *Well-Being: Its Meaning, Measurement, and Moral Importance,* Oxford: Clarendon Press.

Hare, R.M. (1981) *Moral Thinking*, Oxford: Clarendon Press.

Harsanyi, J. (1977) "Morality and the Theory of Rational Behavior," *Social Research* 44: 623–656.

Haybron, D. (2008) *The Pursuit of Unhappiness*, Oxford: Oxford University Press.

Heathwood, C. (2005) "The Problem of Defective Desires," *Australasian Journal of Philosophy* 83: 487–504.

Heathwood, C. (2006) "Desire Satisfactionism and Hedonism," *Philosophical Studies* 128: 539–563.

Heathwood, C. (2011) "Preferentism and Self-Sacrifice," *Pacific Philosophical Quarterly* 92: 18–38.

Heathwood, C. (2014) "Subjective Theories of Well-Being," in B. Eggleston and D. Miller (eds.) *The Cambridge Companion to Utilitarianism*, Cambridge: Cambridge University Press, pp. 199–219.

Hobbes, T. (1651) *Leviathan* (transl. E. Curley 1994), Indianapolis, IN: Hackett Publishing.

Hooker, B. (1991) "Theories of Welfare, Theories of Good Reasons for Action, and Ontological Naturalism," *Philosophical Papers* 20: 25–36.

Kraut, R. (1994) "Desire and the Human Good," *Proceedings and Addresses of the American Philosophical Association* 68: 39–54.

Lin, E. (2014) "Pluralism about Well-Being," *Philosophical Perspectives* 28: 127–154.

Lin, E. (2015) "Prudence, Morality, and the Humean Theory of Reasons," *Philosophical Quarterly* 65: 220–240.

Lukas, M. (2010) "Desire Satisfactionism and the Problem of Irrelevant Desires," *Journal of Ethics and Social Philosophy* 5.

Mill, J.S. (1863) *Utilitarianism*, London: Parker, Son, and Bourn.

Murphy, M. (1999) "The Simple Desire-Fulfillment Theory," *Noûs* 33: 247–272.

Nozick, R. (1974) *Anarchy, State, and Utopia*, New York: Basic Books.

Nussbaum, M. (2000) *Women and Human Development*, Cambridge: Cambridge University Press.

Overvold, M.C. (1980) "Self-Interest and the Concept of Self-Sacrifice," *Canadian Journal of Philosophy* 10: 105–118.

Parfit, D. (1984) *Reasons and Persons*, Oxford: Oxford University Press.

Pigou, A. (1920). *The Economics of Welfare*, London: McMillan, 1932.

Plato 380 BCE: *Gorgias* (transl. B. Jowett).

Railton, P. (1986) "Facts and Values," *Philosophical Topics* 14: 5–31.

Ramsey, F.P. (1926) "Truth and Probability," in R.B. Braithwaite (ed.) *Foundations of Mathematics and Other Essays*, London: Kegan, Paul, Trench, Trubner, 1931, pp. 156–198.

Rawls, J. (1971) *A Theory of Justice*, Cambridge, MA: Harvard University Press.

Rosati, C. (1995) "Persons, Perspectives, and Full Information Accounts of the Good," *Ethics* 105: 296–325.

Rosati, C. (1996) "Internalism and the Good for a Person," *Ethics* 106: 297–326.

Sarch, A. (2011) "Internalism About a Person's Good: Don't Believe It," *Philosophical Studies* 154: 161–184.

Schueler, G.F. (1995) *Desire*, Cambridge, MA: The MIT Press.

Shaw, W. (1999). *Contemporary Ethics*, Malden, MA: Blackwell Publishers.

Sidgwick, H. (1907) *The Methods of Ethics*, 7th ed., London: MacMillan.

Singer, P. (1979) *Practical Ethics*, Cambridge: Cambridge University Press.

Skow, B. (2009) "Preferentism and the Paradox of Desire," *Journal of Ethics and Social Philosophy* 3.

Sobel, D. (1994) "Full Information Accounts of Well-Being," *Ethics* 104: 784–810.

Sobel, D. (2005) "Pain for Objectivists: The Case of Matters of Mere Taste," *Ethical Theory and Moral Practice* 8: 437—57.

Spinoza, B. (1677) *Ethics* (transl. R. Elwes).

Sumner, L.W. (1996) *Welfare, Happiness, and Ethics*, Oxford: Oxford University Press.

Velleman, J.D. (1998) "Is Motivation Internal to Value?" in C. Fehige and U. Wessels (eds.) *Preferences*, Berlin: de Gruyter, pp. 88–102.

Von Wright, G.H. (1963) *The Varieties of Goodness*, New York: The Humanities Press.

12

OBJECTIVE LIST THEORIES

Guy Fletcher

Ask people what they want for themselves, for their loved ones, and for their friends and they will likely suggest a few things. Suppose that they answer with the following: health, friendships, romantic relationships, pleasure and enjoyment, happiness, achievement, knowledge. A conception of prudential value which says that well-being is promoted by this collection of items is an instance of an objective list theory.[1] This chapter is divided into three parts. First I outline objective list theories of well-being. I then go on to look at the motivations for holding such a view before turning to objections to these theories of well-being.

Just what are objective list theories?

Unlike the case of hedonism and the desire-fulfillment theory of well-being, it is difficult to characterize objective list theories in general. This is partly because, to a greater extent than is true of hedonism and the desire-fulfillment theory, "objective list theory" names something from within a *very* wide *class* of theories.[2] A natural thought one might have: even if objective list theories are a wide class of theories, we can *still* ask what all such theories necessarily have in common or, to put the point another way, what is *constitutive* of an objective list theory. This brings us to the second and more significant reason why it is difficult to provide a clear and accurate characterization of objective list theories, namely, the label "objective list theory" is used inconsistently in the well-being literature. I will begin by outlining this inconsistency before explaining how I think we should proceed.

It is uncontroversial that *paradigmatic* objective list theories adhere to both of the following claims:

> **Attitude-independence**: it is not the case that G is (non-instrumentally) good for some agent X only if X, or some counterpart of X, has some pro-attitude towards G.

> **Pluralism**: there are a plurality of (non-instrumental) prudential goods.

Note, first, that these theses are both couched in terms of *non-instrumental* goods. Henceforth I'll drop the qualifier "non-instrumental" but this should be read as implied throughout this chapter. Second, as is common in the literature, I express these claims only in terms of basic prudential *goods*. It is natural to assume that a paradigm objective list theory is committed to the corresponding claims about basic prudential *bads*. However, whilst this is a natural combination, an objective list theory need not hold that there are a plurality of bads, just as there are a plurality of goods.[3] Whatever its plausibility, it seems perfectly *coherent* to hold, for example, that there is a plurality of basic goods but only *one* basic prudential bad (pain, for example).

Here are some examples of *paradigmatic* objective list theories, with their lists of basic prudential goods:

Finnis
Life, knowledge, play, aesthetic experience, sociability (friendship), practical reasonableness, "religion."

Fletcher
Achievement, friendship, happiness, pleasure, self-respect, virtue.

Murphy
Life, knowledge, aesthetic experience, excellence in play and work, excellence in agency, inner peace, friendship and community, religion, happiness.

Parfit
Moral goodness, rational activity, development of abilities, having children and being a good parent, knowledge, awareness of true beauty.[4]

These theories are paradigm cases of objective list theories because they are consistent with each of attitude-independence and pluralism. Their consistency with pluralism is obvious—their lists have more than one member—and their consistency with attitude-independence stems from the fact that they do not claim that these items are good for individuals only if they desire them. For example, Finnis makes this feature of his view abundantly clear thus:

> It is obvious that a man who is well informed, etc., simply *is* better-off (other things being equal) than a man who is muddled, deluded, and ignorant, that the state of the one is better than the state of the other, not just in this particular case or that, but in all cases, as such, universally, and *whether I like it or not*.[5]

But why have I said that the theories above are only *paradigmatic* objective list theories? Why not simply define objective list theories as those which accept both attitude-independence and pluralism?

The problem is that, despite the *paradigm* cases of objective list theories embracing both attitude-independence and pluralism, there are two ways in which "objective list theory" is used which falsify this as a view of what is definitive of objective list theories.

First, it has long been standard to divide theories of well-being in a tripartite way thus:

Hedonism	Desire-fulfillment	Objective list

For example, Derek Parfit (1984: 493) writes that "[t]here are three kinds of theory" of self-interest or "what makes someone's life go best" and then proceeds to list "hedonistic theories . . . desire fulfilment theories . . . objective list theories."[6] This gives us a tripartite distinction among theories of well-being. On this categorization, sufficiently common to be accurately regarded as orthodoxy, the category of "objective list theories" thus covers *every* theory that is neither hedonism nor the desire-fulfillment theory. And this makes trouble because not every theory that is distinct from hedonism and desire-fulfillment theory accepts pluralism *and* attitude-independence. Consider, for example, the following theory:

Knowledgism: Knowledge is the only prudential good.

Whatever its ultimate merits or lack thereof, knowledgism is *a* theory of well-being. It should therefore be possible to categorize it. Clearly, knowledgism is neither a form of hedonism nor desire-fulfillment theory. This means, according to the tripartite division stated above, knowledgism is an objective list theory. But knowledgism, though committed to attitude-independence, is inconsistent with pluralism. So knowledgism cannot be an objective list theory *if* objective list theories necessarily embrace both attitude-independence and pluralism. Thus, the way in which the category of "objective list theory" is used to distinguish theories of well-being means that one cannot treat pluralism and attitude-independence as *constitutive* of objective list theories.[7]

The previous reason for not treating attitude-independence and pluralism as constitutive of objective list theories was implicit, stemming as it did from the way in which the category of objective list theories is used. There is however a second, more explicit, reason not to treat commitment to attitude-independence and pluralism as *constitutive of* objective list theories. This is the fact that the literature is flatly, and explicitly, inconsistent on this point. Objective list theories are sometimes explicitly defined as pluralistic:

The objective list theory of well-being holds that a plurality of basic objective goods directly benefit people[8]

even though the idea that pluralism is constitutive of objective list is contradicted by the many times when people allow for the possibility of *monistic* objective list theories. For example, Roger Crisp writes:

But it is worth remembering, for example, that hedonism might be seen as one kind of "list" theory, and all list theories might then be opposed to desire theories as a whole.[9]

And Chris Heathwood:

Also, if one-item lists are allowed, then objective list theories can be monistic. Hedonism is sometimes thought of as such a theory.[10]

Heathwood:

One concern for objective list theories, at least if they are pluralistic[. . .][11]

Shelly Kagan:

On this approach, what the hedonist is endorsing appears to be a version of an objective theory . . . In effect, the hedonist is offering an objective list theory with a very short list. Pleasure is an objective good, and it is the only such good.[12]

Julia Markovits:

> This way of thinking about H[edonism] makes it an Objective List View (OL), with a very short list: pleasure is the only item on it.[13]

Even though some of these come as part of conditional claims, they show that there is no *consensus* that objective list theories are pluralistic in the way that there is a consensus over what hedonism and desire-fulfillment theories claim.[14]

It is for these two reasons that one cannot easily say what is constitutive of objective list theories. The literature sometimes treats pluralism as constitutive of objective list theories, sometimes uses "objective list theory" as a residual category, such that it could not incorporate pluralism, and sometimes explicitly allows monistic objective list theories.

How then should we proceed? Well, notice that the inconsistency in the usage of "objective list theory" concerned only pluralism. There is unanimity that objective list theories are committed to attitude-independence. For this reason, I think that the best way to carve up the logical space of theories of well-being is to say that "objective list theories" are all and only those that specify particular things as non-instrumentally prudentially good (or bad) for people whether or not they have any pro (or con) attitude towards them. More succinctly, the essence of objective list theories is attitude-independence. Some precedent for such a convention stems from the passages cited above, which allow for monistic objective list theories, as well as from characterizations of objective list views such as Parfit's: "On Objective List Theories, certain things are good or bad for us, whether or not we want to have the good things, or to avoid the bad things."[15] This also fits the taxonomy used by Allan Hazlett,[16] which distinguishes Desire-*Dependent* and Desire-*Independent* theories (before then further dividing Desire-Independent theories according to whether they are monistic or pluralistic), and the discussions of how to categorize theories of well-being in Dorsey, Fletcher, and Woodard.[17] One consequence of treating attitude-independence alone as constitutive of objective list theories is that hedonism will then qualify as a particular instance of an objective list theory.[18]

Let me recap what we have seen so far. I have shown that the label "objective list theory" is used inconsistently in the well-being literature, such that one cannot spell out what is constitutive of objective list theories without contradicting at least some of the ways in which the label is commonly used. My suggestion for how to proceed from here was that it would be best to take attitude-independence to be all that is constitutive of objective list theories, and that this would *adequately* fit the way the term is currently used (though for the reasons given above, it could not fit all such uses of the label). However this second point is much less important. After all, better taxonomies of well-being may eschew the label "objective list theory" altogether. The first point, however, is important as it is clear that "objective list theory" is used inconsistently. So one must take care in using the label. In the rest of this entry I will mostly be concerned with pluralistic objective list theories, given that many of the objections to the view, and motivations for it, make most sense in the case of pluralistic views.

One final thing to do in this section is to clear up two potential confusions that one might have about objective list theories.

First, it is *not* constitutive of an objective list theory that it hold that the constituent goods are either good *simpliciter* or *morally* good, aside from being good *for* people. Of course any particular objective list theorist might also hold that the goods are good *simpliciter* etc., but that is an extra, strictly separate, commitment.[19] This means that objective list theories are strictly neutral as to the truth of welfarism (the view that welfare is all that is non-instrumentally valuable or the only thing that generates practical reasons).

Second, the objective list theory gives no fundamental role to people's *beliefs* about what is good for them. Thus we are not free, according to the objective list theories, to "devise our own lists," so to speak. An objective list theorist believes that the items on the list are all and only the things that are good for all humans.[20]

Having explained what "objective list theories" have in common, I move on now to examining the reasons for and against holding such a view. Of course each such argument or objection is the subject of sustained reflection so I only detail the opening moves in the debate about each.

In favor of objective list theories

Pre-theoretical judgements

Objective list theory is, I suggest, analogous to commonsense morality in being a kind of widely held starting point when thinking about well-being. It thus seems to function as the view that one holds before and until one is persuaded to adopt one of the other philosophical theories of well-being.[21] As I noted at the beginning of the chapter, if you ask people what they ultimately want for themselves and their loved ones they will typically give you a list of items—health, pleasure, friendship, knowledge, achievement—without thinking that these can all be reduced to one value and without thinking that the list is determined by what their loved ones in fact desire. Thus one ground that might be offered for holding an objective list theory is that it is supported by our pre-theoretic intuitive judgments about well-being, or the judgments that we make about well-being outside of, or before, philosophical thinking about the nature of well-being. That is to say, one might argue that our pre-theoretical judgments—judgments reflected in the prudential choices we make, the way in which we give prudential advice, and the way in which we care for family and friends—are defeasible *evidence* in favor of objective list theories.

One might dispute this observation, by giving an account of why our everyday prudential judgements are actually better evidence for some *other* theory of well-being. Alternatively, and I think more plausibly, an opponent might concede that the *observation* is correct—that objective list theory is a common starting point and a widely held view among non-philosophers—but dispute its significance, arguing that it is weak or no evidence for objective list theories. One ground for this might be the fact that it is pre-theoretic judgments that are being appealed to, where an opponent of an objective list theory might think that such judgments are naive or unlikely to be accurate. How one thinks progress is to be made on this issue is likely to depend on one's background views of how much trust we should place in pre-theoretic intuitions.

Another kind of argument for objective list theories is that they steer a middle course between hedonism and the desire-fulfillment theory and thus avoid strong objections to these views. These objections I will label "too few prudential goods" and "too many prudential goods."[22]

Too few prudential goods

Hedonism is subject to a "too few prudential goods" objection because it claims that *only* pleasures contribute to well-being. Notice that most objections to hedonism do not dispute that pleasure contributes to well-being. Rather, objections to hedonism tend to target the hedonist thesis that *only* pleasure contributes to well-being.

Take Nozick's experience machine objection.[23] Nozick imagines a machine that one could plug into and enjoy pleasurable experiences. One might, for example, have the pleasurable experience of winning the World Cup, of writing the great American novel, or simply living a very happy life surrounded by loving family and friends. The issue that the example brings out is what to think about lives which are very pleasurable but which are plugged into such a machine. The objection is used to support the following claim: things other than pleasurable and painful experiences determine our level of well-being.

Of course, the experience machine objection does not show, or even purport to show, that the experiential quality of our lives is completely *irrelevant* to well-being. But it does provide strong evidence that there are more things than pleasure that can affect our well-being. This is an instance of the general class of the "too few prudential goods" objection to hedonism. One piece of evidence in favor of objective list theories is their being able to avoid the "too few prudential goods" objection that hedonism is subject to.

Too many prudential goods

Desire-fulfillment theory, at least in its simplest form, is subject to a "too many prudential goods" objection. One particularly well-known form of this objection is the "scope problem."[24] The problem is that if, as desire-fulfillment theory claims,[25] someone's desiring something is sufficient for its being good for that person, then anything that someone desires is good for that person. However, this seems to make many things good for people which plausibly are not.[26]

To take one example, suppose that you desire *that there is sentient life elsewhere in the universe.*[27] According to the desire-fulfillment theory, if there is such life, this satisfaction of your desire is good for you. But it seems implausible that the existence of sentient life elsewhere in the universe is, itself, good for you. And there are limitless other such examples, stemming from the fact that we have desires for a wide range of things that do not seem plausibly good for us. Worries about such cases have typically led desire-fulfillment theorists to seek to restrict the relevant range of desires in some way.[28]

One might similarly think that perfectionist theories of well-being are subject to one, or both, of the too many/too few goods objections and one might therefore hold an objective list theory because one is also unpersuaded by perfectionist theories.[29] Thus one kind of motivation for an objective list theory is its apparent ability to avoid such "too many prudential goods" objections.

The too many/too few prudential goods objections taken together push towards the view that pleasure and a, limited, class of other things are good for people. In light of that, one might think of objective list theories as the natural go-to option for those dissatisfied with alternate theories on the grounds considered above.

Piecemeal arguments for specific goods

Another style of argument for an objective list theory is that of arguing for the prudential value of particular goods on the list. For example, one might argue for an objective list theory by arguing that *knowledge* is prudentially valuable irrespective of whether it is desired or pleasurable, thus contradicting the claims of desire-fulfillment theory and hedonism. One example of this strategy is Finnis, who provides a specific argument to support the claim that knowledge belongs on the objective list, arguing that the contrary position is self-refuting.[30] One can, of course, do the same with any other candidate prudential good that is included on one's objective list. Thus one way of arguing for an objective list theory is to argue piecemeal for its particular constituents.

Arguments from the nature of prudential value

Objective list theories are theories of which things hold prudential value. One might try to argue for an objective list theory answer to this question by, first, defending a particular view of the *nature* of prudential value—*what it is* for something to be prudentially valuable—before then arguing that an objective list theory is a consequence of such a view.

Defensive maneuvers

The final way of motivating objective list theories is that of performing defensive maneuvers on its behalf, by trying to nullify potential objections. In the next section I will cover some standard objections to objective list theories and also explain the best way for the objective list theorist to reply to each of the standard objections, thus demonstrating some such defensive maneuvers on behalf of the objective list theorist.

Problems and objections to objective list theories, and replies

Before starting properly, let me note that many objections to particular objective list theories will depend upon their constituent claims—their list of goods and any further claims they make about the constituents of the list. In discussing problems and objections I will largely abstract from particular objective list theories and consider problems and objections which apply to such theories generally (even if to different extents).

Arbitrariness and explanatory impotence

Ben Bradley gives a succinct spelling-out of a cluster of related objections to objective list theories, objections centered on the idea that theories are problematically arbitrary, nothing but an "unconnected heap," or somehow explanatorily unsatisfying.[31] For example:

> [P]luralism seems objectionably arbitrary. Whatever the composition of the list, we can always ask: why should these things be on the list? What do they have in common? What is the rational principle that yields the results that these things, and no others, are the things that are good?[32]

Although Bradley couches this as an objection to "pluralism," at least part of his objection(s) applies to monistic objective list theories, such as knowledgism or hedonism, equally well and one reply for the objective list theorist to make is to argue that the objective list theory is no more burdened by these challenges than any other theory of well-being. We can ask: "why is pleasure (or knowledge or . . .) alone of prudential value?" or "what is the rational principle that determines that pleasure (or knowledge or . . .) contributes to well-being?"

The same goes for desire-fulfillment theory. Desire-fulfillment theorists spend little or no time providing an *explanation* of *why* desire fulfillment contributes to well-being. And to the extent that the challenge to the objective list theory is a good one, perfectionist theories of well-being owe us an answer to the question: *why* are the exercise and development of our capacities good for us?

There are two good reasons to think that these fundamental questions are, at best, *extremely* difficult to answer. First, the fundamental tenets of a theory of well-being are *necessary* truths and, as such, might be *incapable* of further explanation. Finally, given that the fundamental tenets of a theory of well-being are purported *evaluative* truths, there is a major epistemological challenge to all theories of well-being stemming from the fact that we have no well-worked-out account of how knowledge of evaluative truths is possible. Thus Bradley points out difficulties for the objective list theory but not for the objective list theory in particular.

This reply has some merit. Note, however, that it really shows only that all theories of well-being share the same *kind* of challenge. But this leaves open the possibility that objective list theories (strictly speaking, *pluralist* ones) have an especially difficult instance of the challenge. One reason for thinking this is that it has to provide an account of why *each* constituent good is a fundamental prudential value. Thus, if we are comparing the costs of the theories of well-being, it is a *pro tanto* cost of (pluralistic) objective list theories that they will need to provide a fundamental explanation of, or explanation of our knowledge of, more than one type of good.

A final thread to Bradley's objection is a challenge to the (pluralist) objective list theorist to provide an explanation of the *commonality* between the items on the list. If the idea is that the objective list theorist must provide an explanation of why the items on the list have the common property of enhancing well-being then this collapses into the previous objection. An alternative way of reading it is as a request simply for an explanation of what properties the items on the list have in common. Of course, one answer that the objective list theorist is committed to is that the items on the list have the property *enhancing well-being*. However that is trivial, so we must read the demand, instead, as one of asking what *other* properties the items on the list have in common, aside from contributing to well-being.

At this point objective list theorists have options. They can either question the legitimacy of the demand by asking what reason we have to expect the items on the list will have some property in common, aside from contributing to well-being. Another, more positive, strategy is simply to note that the items on any plausible objective list will have points of commonality.[33] For example, any list with pleasure and happiness on it has the commonality that these two goods enjoy, namely experiential quality, and any list with friendship, virtue, and self-respect on it can point to the traits of character and affective states which are common to these goods. Thus, if such a demand is legitimate, there seems nothing intractable about the demand to provide commonalities between the goods postulated by an objective list theory.

Bradley voices another complaint against objective list theories, thus:

> [P]luralists must tell us, for example, how to compare the effects on well-being of a certain amount of pleasure with the effect of a certain amount of knowledge . . . To the extent that the pluralist refuses to tackle these questions she abandons the philosophical project of understanding well-being; she admits defeat. A theory that tells us that A, B, and C are intrinsically good, but does not tell us why those things are on the list or how to weight them, does not give what we initially wanted out of a theory of well-being. We wanted enlightenment, but we are provided instead with a list and told not to look any deeper. This is not theorizing, but a refusal to theorize.[34]

This passage contains at least two separate objections. One is that discussed above (the "why are *those* things are on the list?" worry) but there is a distinct worry, one echoing the "unconnected heap of duties" criticism of "deontic pluralism" (commonsense morality).[35] This worry is about how much detail the objective list theorist has in the theory. If one were to propose that A, B, and C are the only constituents of well-being and then simply refuse to tackle the issue of how they are to be weighed against each other, then this is certainly a demerit in the theory (or the theorist?). Of course, an objective list theory should either tackle these questions or, alternatively, tackle the issue of why such questions cannot be answered.

However, whilst this shows that a very negative and dogmatic kind of objective list theory is unsatisfying for that reason, this type of objection applies to all theories of well-being. What it highlights is that there is much more work to do than simply specifying what is to go on the list. But equivalent worries apply to hedonism and desire-fulfillment theories.

Take hedonism first. Hedonists need to provide, for example, an account of how to weight: (a) the various elements of a pleasure experience, in calculating the prudential value of a pleasure; (b) the various elements of a pain experience, in calculating the prudential disvalue of a pain; and (c) how to trade-off prudential value and disvalue from pleasure and pain in determining someone's overall level of well-being. To put some meat on these bones, note that it is not obvious how to compare (a) a pain/pleasure which is extremely intense but short-lasting against (b) a pain/pleasure that is mild but long-lasting. Nor is it obvious how one arrives at an overall level of well-being from someone's level of pleasure and pain. Nor is it obvious that there is one homogeneous kind of, e.g., pain (compare, for instance, emotional heartache with the feeling of burning one's hand), and if so one must find a way of comparing different types of pain (or explaining why there is some common, comparable, pain experience that they all have in common).

Move now to desire-fulfillment theory. We might ask of such a theory how it calculates the prudential value of the satisfaction of a pleasure and how it weighs desire satisfactions against non-satisfactions. A very simple form of the theory has an answer, in terms of the intensity of the desire, such that desiring P to degree 10 and it being the case that P has prudential value of +10 (and desiring P to degree 10 and it being the case that not-P has prudential disvalue of −10). But any more sophisticated desire-fulfillment theory, such as one that takes the relevant desires to be those that meet some counterfactual condition or to be those of a relevant counterpart, will have work to do in specifying exactly how much prudential value or disvalue a desire fulfillment or non-fulfillment has.

Overall, then, Bradley is right that it is unsatisfying if an objective list theory says *nothing* about, e.g., relative weightings. But even if that applies to all extant objective list theories, this does not constitute an objection to objective list theories *as such*. It shows that objective list theorists have work to do, and they might have an especially large degree of it, but it is nonetheless work of the same *type* as that which hedonists and desire-fulfillment theorists have to do.

Alienation

A mistaken objection to objective list theories is that they are elitist or paternalistic, where this is the claim that such theories suggest that people should be compelled to have the constituents of the list. The objective list theory, like all theories of well-being, is not a theory of what, if anything, people ought to be compelled to have. One could in principle combine the objective list theory with the most stringent anti-paternalism one could imagine. Thus objective list theories, just as much as hedonism and desire-fulfillment theories, have no necessary connection to paternalism.

A better objection to the objective list theory is the worry that objective list theories might fail to be sufficiently *subject-sensitive* and thereby provide a conception of well-being that is potentially *alienating*.[36] What is the worry? An influential way of putting it is thus:

> It would be an intolerably alienated conception of someone's good to imagine that it might fail in any way to engage him.[37]

One could develop this worry in a number of ways.

One way is as the thought that a conception of well-being is problematic to the extent that it is insensitive to a person's affective states and volitions (tastes, preferences, desires, interests, etc.) such that a person could have a very high level of well-being, according to the theory, even if she was affectively unengaged. This alienation worry certainly applies to some objective list theories. It certainly applies to *knowledgism*, as described above, as one could easily imagine someone who had a lot of knowledge but who just was not *interested in* knowledge, or who did not care about it. In this way *knowledgism* leaves open the possibility of someone having a very high level of well-being despite being completely affectively cold. Thus a conception of well-being that said that only knowledge had prudential value is problematic in giving rise to the possibility of such disconnect between what is good for a person and the person's affective states.

However, whilst some objective list theories clearly provide alienating conceptions of well-being, this does not clearly apply to *all* objective list theories. There is nothing to stop an objective list theorist from taking a *constitutive strategy* on this question and arguing that their theory avoids alienation because the objective list elements are (necessarily) constituted by the agent's affective states and volitions. For example, take an objective list theory with pleasure, happiness, friendship, and achievement on the list. Call this *four goods* for brevity. Each of the four goods is clearly (at least) partly constituted by affective, attitudinal, or volitional states of the person. Thus no one can have these goods without, *ipso facto*, being in these states. For example, a person who experiences pleasure is in the affective states that *constitute* pleasure, the person who achieves something has a volition towards the outcome she has attained, a person who is happy has the affective and/or attitudinal states that are constitutive of happiness, and a person who has friendship has the attitudes of concern and enjoyment that are constitutive of friendship. There is thus, according to *four goods*, no possibility of someone having a high level of well-being whilst being left affectively cold. Thus, an objective list theorist might argue, there is no more problem with alienation for this type of objective list theory than for hedonism or the desire-fulfillment theory.[38]

Someone might think that the reply in the previous paragraph does not fully address the alienation worry because someone could have these four goods (and necessarily therefore be in positive affective states) but lack any *second-order* desires to be in those states (or, have a second-order desire not to be in those states). According to *four goods* such desires for or against the four goods are, in and of themselves, irrelevant to whether these items contribute to well-being. These four goods are the things that contribute to prudential value, whether you desire them or not. Thus in and of themselves whether you desire them is irrelevant.[39] One might then object that the alienation intuition is thereby left unsatisfied because there is this possibility of an agent who does not care about the things which, according to *four goods*, hold prudential value for him. To support this one might argue that the alienation intuition cannot be fully satisfied by the *constitutive strategy* and that alienation can only be avoided some other way.

As this reply brings out, it is no easy matter to work out precisely what the anti-alienation intuition is as the issues involved are very subtle. As a result how plausible one will find the solution exemplified by *four goods*, or the objection to it in the previous paragraph, will depend a lot on one's way of thinking about the alienation worry.

There is a danger here that we might reach a dialectical impasse. The constitutive strategy is certainly one that an objective list theory can take to avoid the alienation worry (construed one way). However some will argue, as in the previous paragraph, that the constitutive strategy is insufficient on the grounds that it still leaves open the possibility of problematic alienation. If this objection rests on the thought that avoiding alienation requires, instead, an *object strategy*—that of making it a necessary condition of some G being good for a person X that X have a pro-attitude towards G—this begs the question against the objective list theory (given its acceptance of attitude-independence) and in favor of something like the desire-fulfillment theory. This is not to claim that the *object strategy* is *not* the truth about avoiding alienation. But there is a danger of reaching a stalemate, with objective list theories like *four goods* claiming that they accommodate the anti-alienation intuition and opponents arguing for a stronger version of the anti-alienation intuition, one that could only be satisfied by an *object strategy*. At this point a lot depends on the relative merits of these two ways of avoiding alienation.

Conclusion

In this entry I first outlined the way in which the label "objective list theory" has been used, pointing out that, whilst paradigmatic objective list theories are pluralist, the literature is inconsistent on this point. It was clear that what *is* essential to objective list theories is a rejection of the idea that something is good for someone only if that person has some pro-attitude towards it.

I then considered some of the reasons that lead people to adopt objective list theories and some of the objections to the view. I argued that the challenges to objective list theories often highlight epistemic or explanation problems faced by all theories of well-being (though not perhaps to equal extents) or the need for further refinement of the views of the sort which can also be demanded of other theories of well-being.

Acknowledgment

For comments and discussion, many thanks to Steve Campbell, Connie Rosati, Debbie Roberts, Allan Hazlett.

Related topics

Monism and pluralism, perfectionism, hybrid theories, hedonism, desire-fulfillment theory.

Notes

1 I use "prudential value" and "well-being" interchangeably.
2 Of course there are differences between different hedonist and desire-fulfillment theories, so each can also be accurately thought of as a range of theories. But it is uncontroversial that one knows *much* more about someone's theory of well-being if one knows that person is a hedonist or a desire-fulfillment theorist than if one knows that the individuals is an objective list theorist.
3 This brings out another terminological difficulty, namely that the literature on prudential value tends to use "well-being" to refer to each of (i) a person's level of prudential value as a whole and (ii) more narrowly, the positive constituents thereof (where this is distinguished from "ill-being"). Note that this ambiguity is also present in talk of "prudential value."
4 Finnis (1980). Note that the scare quotes around "religion" are present in the original text (Parfit 1984: 499; Fletcher 2013; Murphy 2001). This is not necessarily Parfit's view but it is a theory he mentions.
5 Finnis (1980: 72) (italics in original).
6 This might not be the best way to read Parfit as he might be distinguishing extant theories, rather than all possible theories.
7 Woodard (2013), Dorsey (2011).
8 Rice (2013: 196), Lin (Chapter 27, this volume).
9 Crisp (2013).
10 See Heathwood (Chapter 12, this volume).
11 Heathwood (2010: 647).
12 Kagan (1992).
13 Markovits (2009, handout 11).
14 One might try to write these off as deviant uses or errors, but this is implausible.
15 One might point to Parfit's use of the plural as evidence of him presupposing pluralism but that seems strained. Why deal with an essential tenet of this kind of view implicitly in this fashion?
16 Hazlett (2013).
17 Dorsey (2011), Fletcher (2013), Woodard (2013). See also Raibley (2014).

18 Complication: you might think that whether hedonism is an objective list theory depends on the nature of pleasure. If so, feel free to read my claim as "hedonism should then be categorized as one particular instance of an objective list theory, *given* the assumption of a certain kind of theory of pleasure."

19 The denial of such neutrality on the part of the objective list theorist is the best sense I can make of this intriguing passage from Parfit (1984: 499) "[T]here is one important difference between on the one hand Preference-Hedonism and the Success Theory, and on the other hand the Objective List Theory. The first two kinds of theory give an account of self interest that is purely *descriptive*—which does not appeal to facts about *value*. This account appeals only to what that a person does and would prefer, given full knowledge of the purely *non-evaluative facts* about the alternatives. In contrast, the Objective List Theory appeals directly to what it claims to be facts about *value*" (my italics).

20 "Humans" is possibly too specific. One could easily imagine objective list theories being couched as claims about the well-being of *people*.

21 This is admittedly a semi *hunch*, informed by the experience of surveying undergraduates taking courses that include well-being as a topic.

22 To be clear, these objections can be used by those who adopt views other than objective list theory so it's not that they *uniquely* favor objective list theories.

23 Nozick (1974: 42–45).

24 Overvold (1980).

25 I am here only talking about the basic form of the view, for simplicity.

26 Desire-fulfillment theory is also commonly thought to make self-sacrifice impossible. I doubt that this is correct, but it is widely claimed.

27 Note you do not desire to *meet* sentient life and you do not form the desire to *know* that there is sentient life or to be the one that *discovers* it, you simply desire that it be there. Even if unlikely, such a desire is surely possible, which is all that the objection requires.

28 See also Darwall (2002: 27).

29 Hurka (1993), Bradford (Chapter 10, this volume), Dorsey (2010).

30 Finnis (1980: 74). Note: I do not say that the argument is successful. For criticism, see Varelius (2013: 18–20).

31 Bradley (2009: 16) I focus on Bradley's discussion as it provides unusually clear and forthright versions of critical responses to objective list theories which one often hears in discussion but which are not often put into print. Let me note that Bradley's discussion is not part of a sustained discussion of objective list theories so I in no way suggest that he should have considered the possible replies that will be mentioned here. See also Sumner (1996).

32 Bradley (2009: 16).

33 One such strategy is given by Fletcher (2012).

34 Bradley (2009: 16).

35 On this issue see Joseph (1931: 67), McNaughton (1996).

36 For discussion of this worry, see Sumner (1996: 27), Hall and Tiberius (Chapter 14, this volume).

37 Railton (2003: 19). For more detailed discussion of this intuition, see Rosati (1995, 1996). For critical discussion, see Sarch (2011).

38 For elaboration, see Fletcher (2013).

39 It would be relevant if the person who experienced these four things were also filled with regret or anguish, for example, but in and of itself the individuals' desire to have (or not to have) pleasure, happiness, friendship, and achievement does not, itself, make a difference to the prudential value of the four goods.

References

Bradley, B. (2009) *Well-being and Death,* Oxford: OUP.

Crisp, R. (2013) "Well-Being," in E.N. Zalta (ed.), *The Stanford Encyclopedia of Philosophy* (summer 2013 ed.), http://plato.stanford.edu/archives/sum2013/entries/well-being/.

Darwall, S. (2002) *Welfare and Rational Care.* Princeton: Princeton University Press.

Dorsey, D. (2010) "Three Arguments for Perfectionism," *Noûs* 44(1): 59–79.

Dorsey, D. (2011) "The Hedonist's Dilemma," *Journal of Moral Philosophy* 8(2): 173–196.

Finnis, J. (1980) *Natural Law and Natural Rights,* Oxford: Clarendon Press.

Fletcher, G. (2012) "The Locative Analysis of Good For Formulated and Defended," *Journal of Ethics and Social Philosophy (JESP)* 6(1): 1–26.

Fletcher, G. (2013) "A Fresh Start for the Objective List Theory of Well-Being," *Utilitas* 25(2): 206–220.

Hazlett, A. (2013) *A Luxury of the Understanding*, Oxford: OUP.

Heathwood, C. (2010) "Welfare," in J. Skorupski (ed.), *Routledge Companion to Ethics*, Routledge.

Heathwood, C. (in progress) "Monism and Pluralism about Value," in I. Horise and J. Olson (eds.), *The Oxford Handbook of Value Theory*, Oxford: OUP.

Hurka, T. (1993) *Perfectionism*, New York: OUP.

Joseph, H.W.B. (1931) *Some Problems in Ethics*, Oxford: Clarendon Press.

Kagan, S. (1992) "The Limits of Well-Being," *Social Philosophy and Policy* 9(2): 169–189.

Markovits, J. (2009) *24.231 Ethics, Fall 2009*. (MIT OpenCourseWare: Massachusetts Institute of Technology), http://ocw.mit.edu/courses/linguistics-and-philosophy/24-231-ethics-fall-2009. License: Creative Commons BY-NC-SA.

McNaughton, D. (1996) "An Unconnected Heap of Duties?" *Philosophical Quarterly* 46: 433–447.

Murphy, M. (2001) *Natural Law and Practical Rationality*, New York: CUP.

Nozick, R. (1974) *Anarchy, State and Utopia*, Malden, MA: Blackwell.

Overvold, M. (1980) "Self-Interest and the Concept of Self-Sacrifice," *Canadian Journal of Philosophy* 10(1): 105–118.

Parfit, D. (1984) *Reasons and Persons*, Oxford: Clarendon.

Raibley, J. (2014) "Objectivity/Subjectivity of Values," in *Encyclopedia of Quality of Life and Well-Being Research*, Springer, pp. 4438–4443.

Railton, P. (2003) "Facts and Values," in *Facts, Values and Norms*, Cambridge: CUP.

Rice, C. (2013) "Defending the Objective List Theory of Well-Being," *Ratio* 26(2): 196–211.

Rosati, C. (1995) "Persons, Perspectives, and Full Information Accounts of the Good," *Ethics* 105: 296–325.

Rosati, C. (1996) "Internalism and the Good for a Person," *Ethics* 106: 297–326.

Sarch, A. (2011) "Internalism About a Person's Good: Don't Believe it," *Philosophical Studies* 154(2): 161–184.

Sumner, L.W. (1996) *Welfare, Happiness and Ethics*, Oxford: Clarendon Press.

Varelius, J. (2013) "Objective Explanations of Individual Well-Being," in A. Delle Fave (ed.), *The Exploration of Happiness*, Happiness Studies Book Series, 15, Dordrecht: Springer Science + Business Media.

Woodard, C. (2013) "Classifying Theories of Welfare," *Philosophical Studies* 165(3): 787–803.

13

HYBRID THEORIES

Christopher Woodard

In many areas of philosophy we may be tempted to think that some opposing views each capture part of the truth. When this happens, we may try to make progress by combining features of these opposing views in new ways, to create hybrid theories.

Recently this has happened in the philosophy of well-being. Over the past 30 years or so, a number of prominent philosophers have suggested that hybrid theories are amongst the most promising theories of well-being. In most cases, they have suggested that well-being is in part a matter of the objective value of elements of the subject's life, but also in part a matter of her subjective evaluation of those elements. In this way, they have attempted to create a hybrid theory of well-being that combines features of more familiar subjective and objective theories. I will discuss a number of proposals of this kind below.

Proposals like this raise a number of important questions. One central question is whether hybrid theories of well-being form a genuinely distinct class. How, if at all, do they differ from pluralist theories of well-being? Another question is whether hybrid theories must always combine features of subjective and objective theories. Most of the prominent proposals have taken this form, but is there room for some other kind of hybrid? A third question concerns the prospects of hybrid theories. Their advocates hope that they will inherit all and only the admirable features of the parent theories, but of course offspring are not always so lucky. Might hybrid theories face special challenges of their own?

This chapter seeks to answer these questions, and to survey some notable recent proposals in this area. I will claim that hybrid theories are distinguished by a kind of holism; that they do not have to combine features of subjective and objective theories; and that they merit detailed consideration in future discussions of well-being.

Recent subjective–objective hybrid proposals

The most general motivation for a hybrid theory in any domain is that, for each of several alternative theories, one finds at least one of their features attractive. In light of these attractions one is tempted to try to combine those features in new ways. Let us briefly consider how this can happen in the most common kind of hybrid theory of well-being, namely the class of theories that combine features from both "subjective" and "objective" theories.

Subjective theories seek to explain what makes something a constituent of a subject's well-being in terms of that subject's psychological states (Lewis 1989: 113; Dorsey 2012: 407). Desire theories of well-being are subjective in this sense. According to the simplest form of desire theory, the constituents of a subject's well-being are the things that satisfy her desires, and what makes these things constituents of her well-being is the fact that they satisfy her desires (see Chapter 11, this volume). In this way, the desire theory attempts both to *identify* the constituents of the subject's well-being and to *explain* why these things constitute her well-being. The subjective character of the desire theory lies in the nature of the explanation it offers.

One common worry about this simple form of the desire theory is that people can desire the wrong things. This worry needs to be spelled out carefully. First, we are here talking about well-being, so "wrong" in this context must mean that people can have desires whose satisfaction would not contribute to their well-being. We must set aside other ways in which desires might be said to be for the wrong things, including especially the idea that satisfying desires can be morally wrong. Second, even the simplest desire theory can explain one way in which people can have desires whose satisfaction would not contribute to their well-being. If someone has very reckless desires—say, for riding a motorcycle at high speed while drunk—then the simplest desire theory will have to accept that satisfying this desire will be non-instrumentally good for her. But this theory can of course add that satisfying this desire is likely to be instrumentally *very* bad for her, since it is likely to lead to injury that will prevent her from satisfying many other desires. Overall, the satisfaction of this desire may greatly diminish her well-being by the desire theory's lights, even though according to that theory it is a constituent of her well-being (Heathwood 2006: 544–547).

More carefully specified, then, the worry about the desire theory is that people can desire things whose satisfaction would not make *any* contribution to their well-being. Philosophers have shown some ingenuity in constructing examples to illustrate this thought. For example, consider Richard Kraut's *icicle fanatic*:

> [This person] has the project of knocking down as many icicles as he can before they melt. He hires a crew of workers and a fleet of trucks, so that he can reach icicles hanging from tall buildings; and this is how he spends his winters.
>
> *(Kraut 1994: 42)*

To sharpen the example, imagine that the icicle fanatic gains no pleasure from knocking down icicles, even though it satisfies a strong desire of his. In Kraut's view, satisfying this desire does not contribute in any way to this person's well-being (Kraut 1994: 42 and 51 n. 8).

If a desire theorist were inclined to agree with Kraut's judgment about this case, she might try to modify her theory so that it accords with this judgment. Many desire theorists have claimed that what contributes to a subject's well-being is only the satisfaction of her informed desires, or those of her desires that would survive correction of error, or some other "idealized" set of desires (Sidgwick 1907: 109–111; Railton 1986: 54; see Chapter 11, this volume). However, there are several sorts of worry about this move. One is that it might not explain all of the judgments we would want it to explain. For example, it might not explain Kraut's judgment about the icicle fanatic, since as he specified that case it did not appear to involve any error on the part of the subject. Another worry is that idealizing versions of the desire theory involve a kind of closet objectivism. The thought here is that the focus on idealized desires makes sense only if we make the objectivist assumption that some things are more worthy of being desired than others, which would be incompatible with subjectivism (Kagan 2009: 254; Heathwood 2014: 213; but see Sobel 2009 for a reply).

For these or other reasons, we may conclude that in order to explain our conviction that people can desire things whose satisfaction would not make any contribution to their well-being, we have to embrace an objective theory of well-being. According to such theories, the objective value of things enters into the explanation of which things are constituents of a subject's well-being.[1] We may then say that the icicle fanatic goes wrong by desiring something (knocking down icicles) that has no objective value.

Objective theories are really a large and diverse class. For this reason, it is hard to speak in accurate but general terms about them. Much depends on the details of any specific theory, including which thing or things it claims have objective value.[2] However, we can describe some general attractions of objective theories and some general worries about them. Among the chief attractions are that we can tailor an objective theory to match closely our firmest convictions about which things are constituents of well-being. We saw one instance of this a moment ago: in light of our conviction that icicle destruction is not a constituent of well-being, we can construct our objective theory of well-being in such a way that we do not attribute any objective value to this activity. In general, objective theories can be tailored to match any set of convictions about cases that we may have—if necessary, by distinguishing finely between cases in a way that is not constrained by psychological data about what people in fact desire.

Conversely, we may worry about the epistemological and metaphysical commitments of objective theories. Can we make sense of the idea of objective value, metaphysically? If so, can we hope to discover which things have such value, and in particular which things are constituents of well-being?

We must set these important issues aside. Whatever the truth about them, they cannot provide any reason to favor a subjective–objective hybrid over a purely objective theory of well-being. These are worries about the concept of objective value itself, and so they apply to any theory that makes use of that concept, including subjective–objective hybrids.

However, there is a different kind of worry about purely objective theories that may provide some support for a subjective–objective hybrid. According to the *alienation objection*, objective theories wrongly imply that something can be a constituent of a subject's well-being even though she lacks any positive attitude towards it, or even has entirely negative attitudes towards it (Railton 1986: 47).[3]

Now it is certainly the case that some versions of this objection fail with respect to plausible objective theories. For, as Guy Fletcher explains elsewhere in this volume (see Chapter 12), if an objective theory specifies only goods (such as friendship or happiness) that are themselves *constituted* by positive attitudes, the objective theorist can at least say that it is impossible to be well off, by her lights, without having these positive attitudes. So it is too crude to say that objective theories necessarily imply that someone can be very well off even though she is "left cold." However, as Fletcher recognizes, this reply to the objection will not satisfy all. For one thing, some objective theories may specify at least some goods (such as knowledge, in Finnis's theory) that are *not* constituted by positive attitudes. Second, even if all of the goods specified are constituted by positive attitudes, we may still fear some alienation from those goods unless the subject has, in addition, some positive attitudes towards them. She may be happy but not value happiness, for example (see Chapter 12, this volume). In contrast, the desire theory guarantees that the subject has some positive attitude (a desire) towards the things that, it claims, constitute her well-being.[4]

Motivated by the worry about desiring the wrong things, we may see the appeal of an objective theory. But we may then worry about alienation, and see the appeal of the desire theory or of some other subjective theory. Rather than going around in circles, we may look for some alternative.[5] One such alternative is the idea that subjective theories and objective theories each have something right about them. And, in fact, something like this train of thought seems to have inspired several philosophers recently to propose a version of subjective–objective hybrid.[6] These proposals have a common core, but differ in details. The structure that they share in common is expressed in the following claim:

1.   For any subject S and any thing X, X is a constituent of S's well-being if and only if and because (a) S subjectively engages with X and (b) X is objectively good.

According to this claim, there are two conditions for well-being: objective value and subjective engagement of some kind with that value. Each of these conditions is said to be necessary for something's being a constituent of well-being, and together they are said to be sufficient and to explain why the things that constitute a subject's well-being do so. Because the claims about necessity will be particularly important for us, I will refer to this as the *joint necessity model* for hybrid theories.

The joint necessity model enables us to distinguish hybrid views from pluralist views. Pluralism about well-being is the claim that there is more than one kind of constituent of well-being (see Chapter 27, this volume). For example, if we say that *pleasure* and *achievement* are both constituents of well-being, we are committing to pluralism about well-being. In contrast, standard forms of hedonism—recognizing pleasure alone—are monistic theories. How, if at all, do hybrid theories differ from pluralist theories? Are they a distinct class of theory? The joint necessity model gives us answers to these questions. Whereas pluralist theories propose multiple constituents of well-being, joint necessity hybrid theories usually propose multiple necessary conditions for a *single* thing's being a constituent. Thus they are typically special forms of monism.

This is worth emphasis since it will be important later. The crucial point is to distinguish between two issues (Fletcher 2009: 29–30). The first is whether some thing, X, is a constituent of some other thing, Y. We can ask this question about any pair of things. The second question arises only when X is a genuine constituent of Y. We can then ask what explains why X is a constituent of Y. These questions arise in the present context, when we are discussing the constituents of well-being. Pluralism answers the first question, asserting that there are multiple *constituents* of well-being. In contrast, hybrid theories are committed to the view that there are multiple *explaining conditions* of something's being a constituent of well-being. This is an answer to the second question, and it is quite consistent with the (monist) idea that there is only one constituent.

To help keep track of this distinction, let us use terms carefully. When discussing whether something is a constituent of well-being, we will stick to the term "constituent." When discussing whether something contributes to the explanation of whether something is a constituent, we will stick to the term "factor" (short for "explanatory factor"). Thus pluralism is committed to multiple constituents, while hybrid theories are committed to multiple factors. In claim (1) above, for example, the factors are denoted by conditions (a) and (b).[7]

With this clarification in mind, let us briefly review some recent proposals that seem to fit the joint necessity model. Though the overall character of any such proposal will depend, obviously, on what the proposal claims to be objectively good (condition (b)), in practice most philosophers who have made these proposals have spent more time elaborating what is distinctive about their account of subjective engagement (condition (a)), as we will see. Here we will not try to capture all of the complexities of each view, but merely to point out some of their basic features.

First, there are several proposals that we might group together as all being versions of the idea that well-being consists of *enjoying the good*. Robert Adams and Shelly Kagan have made two of the most prominent proposals of this sort.[8] Kagan's specification is as follows: "I am well off if and only if there are objective goods in my life and I take pleasure in them, I enjoy having them" (2009: 255). Adams (1999) specifies a somewhat more complex idea, that well-being consists in "enjoyment of the excellent."

Both note many difficult questions in elaborating the idea fully. For example, must the enjoyment be not only of the good, but caused in the right way by the good? If so, what exactly is the right way (Kagan 2009: 257–260)? To illustrate just one aspect of this issue, consider how much time could elapse between the good thing being possessed or achieved, and the enjoyment of it. On this question, Adams offers the following example: "Suppose [someone] has succeeded in swimming the English Channel. Perhaps the hours she spent in the water were mostly unpleasant, full of weariness, anxiety, and cold. Nonetheless, we may count her swimming the Channel as something that she enjoys in her life, if she savors the achievement" (1999: 96). As this example suggests, it is hard to believe that the enjoyment and the goodness must be simultaneous. Conversely, we might feel uncomfortable with the idea that someone has really enjoyed the good when the enjoyment and the goodness are separated by years or decades. Kagan and Adams each emphasize the necessity and the difficulty of answering questions of this sort in developing the idea of enjoying the good.

Some other authors have proposed a different kind of subjective–objective hybrid, in which the subjective factor is desiring rather than enjoying. According to these theories, well-being consists in the *satisfaction of desires for the good*. Joseph Raz and Richard Kraut both offer versions of this view.[9] Raz's version is that well-being is constituted by success in pursuing worthwhile goals (Raz 1986: Chapter 12).[10] He uses "goals" to refer to "projects, plans, relationships, ambitions, commitments, and the like," noting that he has in mind, roughly, long-term desires or objectives (1986: 291). According to Raz, people pursue their goals because they believe them to be worthwhile or valuable, and this has implications for their well-being. First, their well-being is not augmented just because their goals are achieved, if that was not through their efforts (1986: 298). Second, success in worthless goals does not contribute to well-being (1986: 298–299).[11] Kraut similarly claims that "there are at least three conditions that make a life a good one: one must love something, what one loves must be worth loving, and one must be related in the right way to what one loves" (1994: 44), and by "loving" he seems to mean a range of attitudes that include desiring.[12] Thus according to Kraut, the icicle fanatic does indeed go wrong by desiring something with no value.

It must be emphasized that there is some simplification in presenting these views as being different versions of the same basic idea. In many important details these views differ from each other, and for some purposes these differences dwarf the similarities. But it is true that, in different ways, they each embody the idea that well-being consists in appropriate subjective engagement with objectively valuable things.[13] According to these views, the constituents of well-being are episodes in which these conditions are fulfilled.

Doubts about joint necessity

Joint necessity hybrid theories are subject to the following sort of objection. These theories claim that, in order for something to be a constituent of someone's well-being, it must satisfy at least two conditions—typically, it must be something with which the subject is appropriately engaged (enjoying, desiring, pursuing), and it must be something with objective value. According to the objection, satisfying only one of these conditions is sufficient for something to be a constituent of well-being.

For example, Brad Hooker has made this sort of objection to Raz's claim that well-being consists in successful pursuit of worthwhile goals (Hooker forthcoming). Hooker agrees with

Raz that the *best* lives contain successful pursuit of worthwhile goals. But, contrary to Raz, Hooker claims that mere subjective engagement (with the non-worthwhile), or mere worthwhile achievement (without the subjective engagement involved in pursuit), is itself sufficient for something to be a constituent of well-being. Hooker gives the following example:

> Suppose Ajay has a life with a given amount of successful pursuit of worthwhile goals. (For the purposes of my argument, it doesn't matter whether this amount is high, or low.) Now suppose that Ajay is given an increment of *passive* pleasure, not pleasure from the pursuit of worthwhile goals. Maybe he is introduced to a drink he can savour each night right before bed. Or perhaps he is blessed with particularly pleasurable dreams each night. In either case, hasn't his well-being increased, admittedly only a little, but still increased? I propose that, of any two individuals with equally successful pursuit of equally worthwhile goals, the one whose life contained more pleasure, even if this pleasure is only of a passive kind, has had greater well-being.
>
> *(Hooker forthcoming, italics in the original)*

According to Hooker, the achievement of worthwhile goods can contribute to a person's well-being even if she did not pursue them—and even if she resents or rejects them (Hooker forthcoming). With respect to both the subjective and the objective factors that Raz claims are jointly necessary, then, Hooker claims that each is individually sufficient for something to be a constituent of well-being.

Any hybrid theory that adopts the joint necessity model will be open to a form of this objection. This is the downside of the dialectical situation that, we observed, can often motivate interest in hybrid theories in the first place. Each of the parent views retains its own attractions and provides resources for an attack on the hybrid offspring. Thus, for example, the hybrid proposal that well-being consists in *enjoying the good* is vulnerable to the objection that all enjoyment makes *some* contribution to well-being, even if it is enjoyment of objectively worthless things. To see the appeal of this claim, imagine a life that contains many pleasures taken in worthless things, but nothing else of value, and compare it to a life that is otherwise the same except that it contains no pleasure at all. Don't we want to say that the worthless pleasures make the first life somewhat better? Similarly, this hybrid is open to the objection that possessing or achieving objectively good things makes some contribution, even if it is not enjoyed (Sarch 2012: 444–445). Again, we can compare lives that are alike except in the degree to which they contain unenjoyed objective goods to try to elicit the relevant intuitions. Parallel objections can be made to all hybrids that propose several conditions as jointly necessary.[14]

Faced with objections of this sort, defenders of joint necessity hybrids might try several replies. First, they may reject the intuitive judgments on which the objection rests. For example, they could simply deny that unenjoyed achievements contribute anything to well-being. This may seem flat-footed, but it is worth pointing out that, in one respect, it leaves the proponent of this sort of hybrid in no worse position than a straight hedonist would be, faced with the same example. We do not typically treat the intuition, shared by some, that unenjoyed achievements contribute to well-being, as a knock-down objection to hedonism. On the face of it, then, we should treat the present hybrid theory in the same way. Now it might be said in response that, faced with this example, the hedonist occupies a position that is more stable than the position of the hybrid theorist. For the hybrid theorist is inclined to view achievements as, in the right circumstances (i.e., when enjoyed), constituents of well-being, whereas the hedonist claims that they are never constituents. The hybrid theorist cannot offer the same uniform denial of the claim that achievements are constituents of well-being. However, this may appear to be unstable only if we fail to take seriously the hybrid theorist's claim that both achievement and enjoyment are necessary conditions. So the weight of the objection is ultimately thrown back on the initial appeal to intuitions.

Second, the hybrid theorist may attempt to account for the force of the intuitions concerned without conceding that they tell us about the nature of well-being. One way to try this is to claim that they tell us about some other way in which lives can be valuable. Kagan does just this, in fact, when he claims that "[s]omeone's *life* might be going fairly well, even though *she herself* is not particularly well off. That's the situation we have, I suspect, if someone's life contains objective goods, but the person takes no pleasure in their possession" (Kagan 2009: 257, italics in the original; see also Kagan 1994). This form of reply raises tricky questions about the validity of the distinctions between kinds of value of lives that it employs, and about the transparency of our intuitions. The objector may insist that her intuition is about well-being, not this other sort of value of lives.

Third, the hybrid theorist may claim that, at least with respect to some conditions, the satisfaction of one guarantees (or, makes highly probable) the satisfaction of the other. Adams makes a modest but interesting claim of this sort, when he notes that "[t]here may be relatively little enjoyment that is not enjoyment of excellence. In particular, the enjoyment of physical pleasure as such is normally an enjoyment of healthy life, which I believe is an excellence" (Adams 1999: 100).[15] If that is correct, it will enable defenders of the view that well-being is enjoyment of the good to reconcile their view with the objector's intuition in most, but not all, cases. Moreover, whereas Adams concedes that not all pleasure is enjoyment of the good, Kagan suggests an intriguing way of denying this, at least for sensory pleasures. For, he suggests, sensory pleasure might be thought to be, in *every* case, an instance of enjoying the goodness of one's own body (Kagan 2009: 269–270). If so, one possibility on which we are invited by the objector to train our intuitions—the possibility of a life containing sensory pleasures, but where these are not taken in objectively good things—cannot arise.

However, even if Kagan is correct about sensory pleasures, this will of course not dispose entirely of the sort of objection we are imagining. The objector can point to other kinds of pleasure, such as the pleasure someone may take in counting grains of sand, and claim that, though not taken in anything objectively good, these pleasures are nevertheless constituents of well-being. More generally, hybrid theories that adopt the joint necessity model will always invite the objection that a constituent of well-being can exist even if only one (or at any rate, not all) of the explanatory factors in the model is instantiated. For that reason, hybrid theorists may wish to explore alternatives to the joint necessity model.

Holism

So far we have treated the defining feature of hybrid theories as being that they identify more than one factor, and claim of each that it is necessary in order for something to be a constituent of well-being. This was the "joint necessity" model that we found in several of the proposals that we have examined. Although it succeeds in distinguishing hybrid theories from pluralist theories, it is subject to significant objections, as we have just seen.

But in fact we can distinguish hybrid theories from pluralist theories in terms of a more general idea. We could focus instead on *holism*: the idea that the contribution each factor makes to explaining why something is a constituent of well-being, or a constituent of a particular value, depends on facts about the other factor(s). As it happens, Derek Parfit drew attention to the issue of holism in his influential discussion of the possibility of hybrid theories. He wrote:

Some Hedonists have reached their view as follows. They consider an opposing view, such as that which claims that what is good for someone is to have knowledge, to engage in rational activity, and to be aware of true beauty. These Hedonists ask, "Would these states of mind be good, if they brought no enjoyment, and if the person in these states of mind had not the slightest desire that they continue?" Since they answer No, they conclude that the value of these states of mind must lie in their being liked, and in their arousing a desire that they continue.

This reasoning assumes that the value of a whole is just the sum of the value of its parts. If we remove the part to which the Hedonist appeals, what is left seems to have no value, hence Hedonism is the truth.

(Parfit 1987: 501–502)[16]

As Parfit notes, we might instead believe that the value of a whole depends in a more complex way on the nature of its parts.[17] One version of this idea is expressed in the joint necessity model. For example, we might believe that the awareness of true beauty increases the contribution to well-being of aesthetic pleasures, even though mere awareness, with no accompanying pleasure, has no value. According to the holist, the fact that some feature of a person's life (for example, awareness of beauty) contributes nothing to her well-being when taken by itself, does not entail that it does not contribute anything to her well-being when some other condition (for example, taking pleasure in the awareness) is satisfied.

However, the joint necessity model is just one way, and a particularly strong one, of employing this more general idea. The joint necessity model claims that the contribution of factor X is *zero* whenever factor Y is absent. If we focus on holism rather than joint necessity, a much broader range of possible structures for hybrid theories opens up. In particular, we can explore a large variety of possible structures with the following features:

1. The contribution to the subject's well-being of each amount of factor X depends on facts about at least one other factor Y (holism).

2. The contribution to the subject's well-being of each amount of factor X is not zero when the amount of Y is zero (denial of joint necessity).

To illustrate, consider the following toy theory, which is a possible version of the idea that well-being is enjoying the good. Call the amount of enjoyment that the subject S takes in something, E. Call the amount of goodness of this thing, G. According to this theory, S's well-being, W, is the sum of the contribution made by her enjoyment, E_c, and the contribution made by the goodness she engages with, G_c. So far, this is straightforward and does not involve any form of holism. But according to this theory, E_c depends on G, and G_c depends on E, and in these ways it is holist. These relationships are shown in Figures 13.1 and 13.2.[18]

These figures depict the idea that this theory is holist without conforming to the joint necessity model. According to this theory, enjoyment contributes to the subject's well-being even when the enjoyment is taken in something with zero value; and engagement with goodness contributes to the subject's well-being even when it is not enjoyed at all. So neither enjoyment nor objective value is a necessary condition of something's being a constituent of the subject's well-being. Nevertheless, the contribution of each of these factors increases as the other factor is present to a higher degree.

The purpose of this example is merely to illustrate that holism does not entail joint necessity. The simple relationships between the factors represented in this theory may well not be very plausible, all things considered. But if, as I have suggested, the basic commitment of hybrid

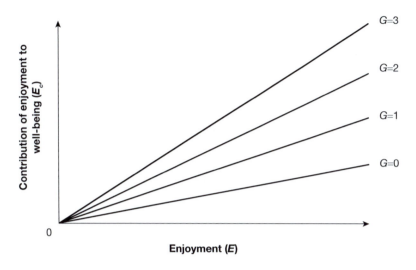

Figure 13.1   Contribution of enjoyment to well-being.

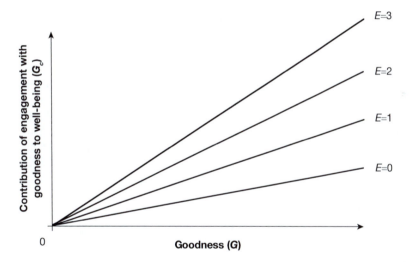

Figure 13.2   Contribution of engagement with goodness to well-being.

theories is to holism and not to the joint necessity model, there is ample scope for exploring other possible theories which posit more complex relationships between the factors (Kagan 2009; Sarch 2012). Hybrid theories of well-being need not accept the joint necessity model.

Subjective–subjective and objective–objective hybrids

So far the theories we have considered have all been subjective–objective hybrids. However, other kinds of hybrid theory are possible.

First, there could be subjective–subjective hybrids. This possibility makes sense if we distinguish between different kinds of subjective evaluation. For example, we may distinguish between a subject's values as expressed in her *desires*, and her values as expressed in her *affective states*. Someone can be doing well in the respect that she is getting what she wants, but nevertheless doing badly in the respect that she is miserable or depressed. If we take seriously the idea that there is more than one kind of subjective evaluation, we might want to explore possible hybrid theories of well-being that combine these kinds. Just as one possible theory of well-being is that it consists of *enjoying the good*, another possible theory is that it consists of *getting what you want and enjoying it*.

Jennifer Hawkins has proposed a subjective–subjective hybrid of this sort with an interesting structure (Hawkins 2010). She appeals to two kinds of subjective evaluation: informed preferences, and affective state. One interesting feature of Hawkins's proposal is the way she suggests that we combine these evaluations. First, we should rank possible lives for a subject according to her affective state in those lives. Next, we should identify a certain threshold, which is defined as being the point below which her affective state is bad enough that the subject's evaluative judgments are distorted (for example, she is sufficiently depressed that she believes that everything in her life is worthless). Hawkins calls this point on the affective spectrum the "*limiting line for affect*" (Hawkins 2010: 66). The theory that she proposes then ranks the subject's possible lives in the following way. Above the limiting line for affect, the subject's informed preferences have priority over her affective states; but below the limiting line, her affective states have priority over her informed preferences. Thus, to put the view in the terms we have been using, the contribution to the subject's well-being made by an improvement in either factor (degree of satisfaction of informed preferences, or affective state) depends on the subject's overall affective state. This is a kind of holism, and one that does not conform to the joint necessity model.[19]

Obviously, other subjective–subjective hybrid theories are possible. These might employ different distinctions between kinds of subjective evaluation than the one Hawkins draws, or make different proposals about the importance of these kinds of evaluation for well-being overall, or both.

Objective–objective hybrids are also possible. One way they could arise is by identifying more than one objective good, and then claiming that the contribution made by at least one of these to well-being depends on facts about another. For example, suppose that we claim that the constituents of well-being are *knowledge* and *virtue*. We might believe that knowledge alone has some value, and that virtue alone has some value, but that together they have enormous value. We might then claim that the contribution to well-being made by an increment of knowledge depends on the subject's degree of virtue (and, let us suppose, vice versa). This would be to introduce the kind of holism about different factors that we earlier identified as the distinctive feature of hybrid theories.

A second kind of objective–objective hybrid is possible. Consider the suggestion made by Brad Hooker, that one of the constituents of well-being is *important knowledge* (Hooker forthcoming).

Important knowledge may itself be a hybrid good. For one thing, important knowledge seems to involve a kind of subjective engagement with (knowledge of) the objectively good; so it involves two factors with a structure that resembles the subjective–objective hybrids we discussed earlier. Second, it is plausible to think that the importance of a piece of knowledge depends both on the value of the object of the knowledge (knowing the structure of the universe matters more than knowing some elementary math, which itself matters more than knowing Audrey Hepburn's favorite color), and on the degree to which it is known (in what degree of detail, with what degree of understanding of underlying principles, and so on). Third, it is plausible to think that the contribution of these two factors to the importance of a piece of knowledge is holist in the way we discussed earlier: the difference made by an increment in the degree to which something is known depends on the importance of that thing, for example.

If we endorse those three claims, then we have a hybrid theory of important knowledge. A theory of well-being that incorporates such a theory of one constituent good would inherit this hybrid component. If it has no other hybrid features, we might say that it would be a *partially* hybrid theory.

Prospects

Hybrid theories of well-being claim that the constitution of well-being depends in some holist way on several factors. As we have seen, these theories form a large and diverse class. The factors they appeal to may be some combination of subjective features, or of objective features, or of both. The precise combination of features identified will of course matter enormously for the character of the resulting theory. Moreover, holism is consistent with very many possible functions from each factor to overall well-being. Furthermore, two theories may agree about the relevant factors *and* about the function from them to well-being, yet disagree about some other important matter, such as what exactly it takes for each factor to be instantiated, or what it takes for them to be instantiated together. Or they may agree in their account of well-being (faring well), but differ in their account of ill-being (faring badly). Or they may agree about all of these things, but disagree in their scope (whether the account applies to children or non-human animals, for example). And so on.

This enormous diversity suggests two things. First, those who are interested in developing or defending hybrid theories of well-being must try to answer many questions. They should not think of their task as limited to identifying the factors they think combine to constitute well-being. As Kagan emphasizes, this is only the beginning: many very difficult questions follow (Kagan 2009). Second, the diversity of hybrid theories suggests that they are not likely to share many characteristics as a class. This should make us very suspicious of claims of the form "all hybrid theories solve this problem" or of the form "all hybrid theories suffer this defect." For example, we noted that one possible motivation for subjective–objective hybrids is the worry that purely objective theories may be alienating. However, consider the following example, due to Chris Heathwood. He writes:

> Imagine a hybrid theory according to which the music of Miles Davis is most worthy of being enjoyed while the music of Madonna is only somewhat worthy. Suppose that we want to reward a friend for some favor, and that our friend would be ecstatic to attend a performance of Madonna's music but would only mildly enjoy attending a performance of Miles Davis's music. We want to do what would give our friend the best evening for her. So long as we describe the case properly, the hybrid theory will imply that we benefit our friend most by sending her to hear Miles Davis's music rather than Madonna's. But that seems wrong, and is not how we conceive of rewarding people and benefiting friends.
>
> *(Heathwood 2010: 652–653)*[20]

Heathwood is right that some hybrids would have this implication; hence they may fail to address the worry about alienation. But others would not have it: in particular, those that give priority to the subject's degree of enjoyment over the quality of the music. Hybridizing—even of a specific sort, such as going for some version of the theory that well-being consists of *enjoying the good*—does not result in a class of theories with uniform characteristics. It neither produces theories that uniformly solve some problem nor produces theories that uniformly suffer some defect.

The upshot is that we should take the trouble to elaborate and evaluate specific hybrid theories in detail. There is no shortcut to doing this. We are only now beginning to explore these possible theories of well-being, and we may yet find that the truth lies somewhere in their midst.[21]

Related topics

Monism and pluralism, atomism and holism.

Notes

1 See Woodard (2013: 798–800). Fletcher (Chapter 12, this volume) defines objective theories in a different way, in terms of attitude-independence. These rival definitions each have their own merits. My definition is narrower, since it picks out one way in which a theory may seek to explain why something is a constituent of well-being without appeal to the subject's attitudes—namely, by appeal to objective values. Fletcher's definition would treat the proposal that biological facts alone explain which things are constituents of well-being as an objective theory, while mine would not. A downside of my definition is that the concept of objective value is not entirely clear.

2 Or, indeed, on whether it is defined in terms of attitude-independence rather than objective values (see note 1). I am grateful to Guy Fletcher for discussion of this point.

3 For a different way of specifying the subject-relativity of well-being, see Tiberius (2007: 375–376).

4 This is true so long as the desire theory takes the "object" form (according to which what is good for the subject is the object desired), not the "combo" form (according to which what is good for the subject is the combination: the object and its being desired). See Bradley (2014: 235).

5 My account of this dialectical situation is indebted to the account given by Kagan (2009: 253–255).

6 See Griffin (1986: Chapters 2–4); Parfit (1987: 501–502); Kagan (2009: 253–255). For a quite different argument for a form of hybridism, see Hurley (1989: Part 1).

7 The fact that a proposed constituent (such as pleasure) may be very closely related to a proposed factor (say, pleasurableness) can make it hard to keep hold of the distinction between constituents and factors. Here I take the basic commitment of hybrid theories to be to multiple factors, but some hybrid theories may in addition claim that well-being has multiple constituents. Some versions of the idea that well-being consists in enjoying the good might, for example, claim that enjoyment and goodness are both constituents. Others might claim that both are parts of a single, complex constituent, enjoying-the-good. Others might claim that there is a single, simple constituent (for example, enjoyment), but that the other factor plays an enabling role (so that, for example, enjoyment is a constituent only when it is correctly related to the good).

8 See also Feldman (2004: 117–122). Parfit (1987: 502) briefly discusses a subjective–objective hybrid, but it is not clear whether it is a version of *enjoying the good*, or of *satisfaction of desires for the good* (see below), or instead a more complex view: *enjoying the satisfaction of desires for the good*.

9 Griffin (1986: Chapters 2–4) also argues for a view about well-being that in some sense incorporates parts of an informed desire theory and parts of an objective list theory. But this is because he challenges the distinction between objective and subjective theories of well-being. He writes: "it would be better if these terms . . . were put into retirement. But if they are not, if the question 'Subjective or objective?' is pressed, then the answer has to be 'Both'" (Griffin 1986: 3).

10 This is a simplification of Raz's view. First, note that he distinguishes between self-interest and well-being, treating self-interest as mainly a matter of a subject's "biological" needs, and well-being as mainly a matter of her goals (1986: 294–299). Second, though, he allows that how someone is faring in terms of biological needs matters to her well-being (1986: 296–297). As a result, Raz claims only that "success and failure in the pursuit of our goals is in itself the *major* determinant of our well-being" (1986: 297, italics added). The remarks in the text are concerned only with the role of success in pursuit of goals in well-being, according to Raz.

11 Raz can be interpreted as offering a deeper explanation of this claim. The explanation is that well-being is a matter of success in practical life, which involves success in practical reasoning; and success in pursuit of worthless goals is a failure of practical reasoning, because it involves failure to recognize the goals as worthless (1986: 299–307). Here I leave that explanation aside, and focus on the hybrid aspect of Raz's claim. I should also note that Raz does not, so far as I am aware, explicitly say that success in worthless goals contributes *nothing* to well-being. He says: "a person's well-being depends on the value of his goals and pursuits . . . To the extent that [the person's] valuation is mistaken it affects the success of their life" (1986: 298–299).

12 In later work, Kraut claims that desire fulfillment "is not even part of the account" of what makes something a constituent of well-being (2007: 146). Note also that in this later work Kraut refers to (and rejects) a "hybrid" form of the desire theory, according to which some things are good for us because we want them, while other things we should want because they are good for us (2007: 118; cf. Griffin 1986: 28–30). This is not the sense of "hybrid" theory with which we are concerned, however; it amounts to holding that the desire theory is true of some goods, while an objective theory is true of others.

13 Darwall's view also fits this schema, though like Raz he claims that it is true only of the "major" constituents of well-being: "a good human life consists of activities that involve the appreciation of worth and merit. I do not claim that appreciating these values is the only source of human good. I only claim, somewhat vaguely, that it is the major source" (1999: 179–180). Wolf's account of meaningfulness in lives is complex, but she says of it "We may summarize my proposal in terms of a slogan: 'Meaning arises when subjective attraction meets objective attractiveness'" (1997: 211).

14 See Sumner (1996: 158–159) for another version of this style of objection, addressed to the claim that well-being consists in veridical happiness. In fact, of course, this kind of objection is just an instance of an even more general objection, to which *all* theories of well-being are subject: namely, that they get the extension of the concept "constituent of well-being" wrong.

15 Similarly, Lauinger (2013) claims that normal subjects desire the basic objective goods, in defense of a desire/objective good hybrid theory.

16 Parfit's subsequent discussion suggests that he thinks that the joint necessity model either is entailed by holism or that it is the most plausible version of it: "Each [side in the debate] put forward as sufficient something that was only necessary" (1987: 502).

17 Strictly, Parfit seems to run together two different assumptions: (a) the value of a whole is the sum of the value of its parts (additivity); (b) the value contributed by each part is independent of facts about the other parts (independence). (Note that we should remember the distinction between constituents and factors in applying these ideas.) Kagan (1988: 14–18) distinguishes the assumptions, though he thinks they go naturally together. For simplicity I will focus on holism, understood as the denial of independence, though we should remember that holism could also arise through the denial of additivity. See also Dancy (2004: Chapters 9–10) and Raibley (Chapter 28, this volume) for discussion of different kinds of holism about value.

18 These graphs are modeled on those used by Kagan (2009: 267–269) and Sarch (2012).

19 Hawkins suggests (2010: 62–66) that this theory reflects appropriate concern with two distinct motivations for subjectivism: wanting to give authority to the subject's evaluative perspective (as is the traditional aim of desire theories), and wanting to give authority to the subject's experience (as is the traditional aim of hedonism).

20 Heathwood frames the example in terms of a concern with paternalism. See also Arneson (2006: 31–32).

21 I am very grateful to Guy Fletcher, Alicia Hall, and Valerie Tiberius for helpful comments on earlier drafts.

References

Adams, R.M. (1999) *Finite and Infinite Goods. A Framework for Ethics,* New York: Oxford University Press.

Arneson, R. (2006) "Desire Formation and Human Good," in S. Olsaretti (ed.) *Preferences and Well-Being,* Royal Institute of Philosophy Supplement 59, Cambridge: Cambridge University Press, pp. 9–32.

Bradley, B. (2014) "Objective Theories of Well-Being," in B. Eggleston and D. Miller (eds.), *The Cambridge Companion to Utilitarianism,* Cambridge: Cambridge University Press, pp. 220–238.

Dancy, J. (2004) *Ethics Without Principles,* Oxford: Clarendon Press.

Darwall, S. (1999) "Valuing Activity," *Social Philosophy and Policy* 16: 176–196.

Dorsey, D. (2012) "Subjectivism without Desire," *Philosophical Review* 121: 407–442.

Feldman, F. (2004) *Pleasure and the Good Life,* Oxford: Clarendon Press.

Fletcher, G. (2009) "Rejecting Well-Being Invariabilism," *Philosophical Papers* 38: 21–34.

Griffin, J. (1986) *Well-being: Its Meaning, Measurement, and Moral Importance,* Oxford: Clarendon Press.

Hawkins, J.S. (2010) "The Subjective Intuition," *Philosophical Studies* 148: 61–68.

Heathwood, C. (2006) "Desire Satisfactionism and Hedonism," *Philosophical Studies* 128: 539–563.

Heathwood, C. (2010) "Welfare," in J. Skorupski (ed.), *The Routledge Companion to Ethics,* Abingdon: Routledge, pp. 645–655.

Heathwood, C. (2014) "Subjective Theories of Well-Being," in B. Eggleston and D. Miller (eds.), *The Cambridge Companion to Utilitarianism,* Cambridge: Cambridge University Press, pp. 199–219.

Hooker, B. (forthcoming) "The Elements of Well-Being," *Journal of Practical Ethics.*

Hurley, S.L. (1989) *Natural Reasons,* New York: Oxford University Press.

Kagan, S. (1988) "The Additive Fallacy," *Ethics* 99: 5–31.

Kagan, S. (1994) "Me and My Life," *Proceedings of the Aristotelian Society,* New Series, 94: 309–324.

Kagan, S. (2009) "Well-Being as Enjoying the Good," *Philosophical Perspectives* 23: 253–272.

Kraut, R. (1994) "Desire and the Human Good," *Proceedings and Addresses of the American Philosophical Association* 68: 39–54.

Kraut, R. (2007) *What is Good and Why. The Ethics of Well-Being*, Cambridge, MA: Harvard University Press.

Lauinger, W. (2013) "The Missing-Desires Objection to Hybrid Theories of Well-Being," *The Southern Journal of Philosophy* 51: 270–295.

Lewis, D. (1989) "Dispositional Theories of Value," *Proceedings of the Aristotelian Society*, Supplementary Volume 63: 113–137.

Parfit, D. (1987) *Reasons and Persons*, Reprint with corrections, Oxford: Clarendon Press.

Railton, P. (1986) "Facts and Values," *Philosophical Topics* 14: 5–31. Reprinted in his book, *Facts, Values, and Norms. Essays Toward a Morality of Consequence*. Cambridge: Cambridge University Press, 2003, pp. 43–68. Page references are to this reprint.

Raz, J. (1986) *The Morality of Freedom*, Oxford: Clarendon Press.

Sarch, A.F. (2012) "Multi-Component Theories of Well-Being and Their Structure," *Pacific Philosophical Quarterly* 93: 439–471.

Sidgwick, H. (1907) *The Methods of Ethics*, 7th ed. London: Macmillan, 1962.

Sobel, D. (2009) "Subjectivism and Idealization," *Ethics* 119: 336–352.

Sumner, L.W. (1996) *Welfare, Happiness, and Ethics*, Oxford: Clarendon Press.

Tiberius, V. (2007) "Substance and Procedure in Theories of Prudential Value," *Australasian Journal of Philosophy* 85: 373–391.

Wolf, S. (1997) "Happiness and Meaning: Two Aspects of the Good Life," *Social Philosophy and Policy* 14: 207–225.

Woodard, C. (2013) "Classifying Theories of Welfare," *Philosophical Studies* 165: 787–803.

14

WELL-BEING AND SUBJECT DEPENDENCE

Alicia Hall and Valerie Tiberius

Introduction

Prudential value is commonly thought to be distinct from other types of value by virtue of its special relationship to individual subjects. Well-being has to do with how people's lives are going *for them*, rather than with how their lives are going from the moral point of view, say. In other words, well-being is, as L.W. Sumner puts it, subject-relative. Sumner argues that this subject-relativity is a central part of our ordinary concept of well-being, which any plausible account of well-being must be able to accommodate. Theories of well-being need to explain why a putative contributor to well-being is good *for* the individual whose well-being it is (Sumner 1996: 20).

Sumner does not say much about the specifics of this relation of subject-relativity; he seems to assume that the exact nature of the relation will be determined by substantive theories of well-being. This may be the right way to think about it, but there are efforts in the meta-ethics of well-being to characterize this feature more precisely. Connie Rosati, for example, proposes a rational fit theory of well-being, according to which the contributors to a person's well-being must be suited to her individual nature. She writes, "We each come into the world with a basic physical and psychological makeup, and the bundle of features we each possess not only creates opportunities for but sets limits for our future development" (Rosati 2006b: 49). Whatever counts toward our good must be something that fits with our own particular "bundle of features." According to Rosati, then, something can provide a prudential benefit for a person only when a relation of "fit" or "suitability" holds between them. To explain further what this means, she analogizes the relation of fit to successful loving relationships. Engagement with activities and goods that fit or suit us will not merely provide shallow feelings of enjoyment or pleasure, but, like excellent friendships or romantic relationships, will help develop and sustain an orientation toward ourselves as individuals with inherent value. Things that fit us will also feature significantly into our self-conception and are self-perpetuating: we are invigorated when engaged with things that fit us and motivated to continue to pursue these goods and activities (Rosati 2006a; Rosati 2013: 45). Since people will find these qualities in different sources, well-being will be relative to the individual differences between subjects.

Another way of characterizing subject-relativity is provided by Stephen Darwall's rational care theory. On Darwall's view, what it is for something to be good for you is for it to be what a person who cares about you ought to want for your sake (Darwall 2002). The attitude of caring for another person for his or her own sake provides a way to understand the sense in which a person's well-being is specially related to him or her.

There are a number of ways of characterizing the relation of subject-relativity, then, and we will not take a stand on which of these is correct. However we characterize this relation, it is widely agreed that some kind of subject-relativity is a feature of the concept or property that substantive theories of well-being should respect and we will turn now to these substantive theories. It might be, as Sumner seems to assume, that we will come to a better understanding of subject-relativity through the process of defending a substantive theory of well-being.[1] Sumner's own view is that the best way to explain the subject-relativity of well-being is to defend a *subjective theory* of well-being, according to which something counts as good for a person only if that person has the right attitude toward it. On this view, subject-relativity is explained by a particular feature of subjects, namely, their psychological attitudes (e.g., desires, or assessments of life satisfaction). (According to this common way of defining subjective and objective theories, objective theories are then those that deny the dependence of well-being on the individual's attitudes. Elsewhere in this volume, Woodard offers a different definition of objective theories (see Chapter 13); we will return to these definitions later.)

Appeal to subjects' attitudes is not the only way to account for subject-relativity, however, since individual people have other features to which we might appeal. For this reason, a broader category than "subjective theories" has been introduced, which Dan Haybron calls *internalist theories*. Internalism about well-being, according to Haybron, "maintains that the constituents of an agent's well-being are ultimately determined wholly by the particulars of the individual's make-up *qua* individual (vs. *qua* group or class member)" (2008: 156–157). We think the acknowledgment of this broader category is important in the well-being literature, but we also bemoan the proliferation of "internalisms" in philosophy. For this reason we are going to take this opportunity to label this broad category *subject-dependent theories*. Subject-dependent theories make what is good for someone dependent on some particular features of the person whose good it is. Alternatively, *subject-transcending theories* (formerly "externalist" theories) are theories that reject subject dependence, as defined here; such theories ground well-being in factors that transcend the particular individual, such as species-level traits or objectively valuable goods.

It is useful to distinguish subject-dependent theories from subjective theories. Non-attitudinal subject-dependent theories typically get classified as objective, which may imply an indifference to variation between welfare subjects. Categorizing these theories as subject-dependent allows us to see that there are ways theories can be sensitive to individual variations without making well-being depend on people's *attitudes*.

With this taxonomy in hand, we can say that subject-relativity is a property of well-being that any theory of well-being (including so-called objective theories) may endeavor to explain. Subjective theories are one type of subject-dependent theory, but there are theories that are subject-dependent without being subjective. Desire satisfactionism is a paradigm example of a subjective (and hence also subject-dependent) theory; since desire satisfactionism is covered elsewhere in this volume (see Chapter 11), however, our chapter focuses on other subject-dependent theories. First, though, we will explore in more detail the advantages of staying within the family of subject-dependent theories.

The advantages of subject dependence

One of the benefits of distinguishing subjective theories from subject-dependent theories is that this allows us to see the benefits of the latter type of theory without being distracted by the myriad problems that have plagued desire satisfactionism (the most prominent subjective theory). The category of subject-dependent theories allows us to consider that there are other promising ways of explaining subject-relativity.

Subject-dependent accounts of well-being explain the subject-relativity of welfare by tying well-being to particular features of the individual. It certainly seems simpler to accommodate and explain subject-relativity if one accepts a subject-dependent theory rather than a subject-transcending theory of well-being. To explain why something is good *for* some individual person, after all, it is natural to turn to features of that person herself. For instance, to determine whether taking up a competitive sport would benefit Sarah, we would normally ask whether Sarah herself is the type of person who would thrive on athletic competition; questions about whether competition fulfills a natural human need, expresses a species-typical human trait, or achieves an objective value seem less significant. Of course, knowledge about species-level trends and traits is useful in making predictions about the likelihood that any given individual will benefit from something, or making general claims about the types of things (such as relationships or accomplishment) that tend to be good for people. However, when it comes to more specific claims of benefit—for instance, whether someone would be better off pursuing accomplishment in one activity or another—it does seem like our normal practice for ascertaining prudential value aims to ascertain distinctive individual predilections and talents.

Subject-dependent theories also provide a way of explaining the motivating power of well-being. Facts about well-being are widely held to be reason giving, at least for the individual well-being subject.[2] As long as someone cares about how her life goes, the fact that something would benefit her should provide at least a *prima facie* reason in favor of pursuing it. This will of course not always be an overriding reason, since we typically care about things other than how our own lives go, but a claim of prudential benefit should generally be motivating to normal people. By connecting a person's well-being to aspects of her own individual makeup, subject-dependent theories make better sense of the fact that we are motivated by considerations that have to do with our own well-being than subject-transcending theories.

These concerns about motivation tie into a related concern about well-being: that a person's well-being, whatever it may turn out to be, should not be something that appears alien to her.[3] In other words, it should not be something she would be indifferent to, that leaves her cold, or seems irrelevant to her life. This does not mean that we must always immediately recognize the value of that which benefits us: subject-dependent theories do not require that well-being be something that is immediately transparent to the well-being subject. People can be held in the sway of misinformation or incapable of thinking clearly about their lives. But if someone is open to correction and advice about how to live well, then she should at some point be capable of seeing how the claims about what would benefit her are relevant and meaningful to her life. Since subject-dependent theories tie well-being to the individuals themselves, the connection between the explanations the theory provides and the things the person can care about are built in. In subject-dependent theories, our well-being is bespoke.

Subject-dependent theories

Subject-dependent theories can be distinguished by which feature of the subject they take to be the central determinant of well-being. The theories we discuss here can be divided into two groups: first are the attitudinal theories that make individual benefit ultimately dependent upon pro-attitudes of some kind. (Notice that such theories are *subjective* theories in Sumner's sense.) In this category are L.W. Sumner's authentic happiness theory of well-being and two value-based accounts of well-being developed by Valerie Tiberius and Jason Raibley. Second, we will turn to more inclusive theories of well-being that make well-being depend on non-attitudinal aspects of the self; here we will discuss theories developed by Dan Haybron and Richard Kraut.

Attitudinal theories

L.W. Sumner develops a subjective theory that takes well-being to consist in authentic happiness. Because Sumner thinks of happiness as a subjective response to one's conditions of life, the theory is a subjective theory, and therefore also subject-dependent—whether some particular good benefits someone in a prudential sense depends on its effects on her attitude of life satisfaction.

Sumner argues that subjective theories can best explain and accommodate the subject-relativity of well-being. He writes,

> Whatever their internal differences, the defining feature of all subjective theories is that they make your well-being depend on your own concerns: the things you care about, attach importance to, regard as mattering, and so on. What is crucial on such an account is that you are the proprietor or manager of a set of attitudes, both positive and negative, toward the conditions of your life. It is these attitudes which constitute the standpoint from which these conditions can be assessed as good or bad *for you*. It follows on this sort of account that a welfare subject in the merely grammatical sense—an individual with a distinct welfare—must also be a subject in a more robust sense—the locus of a reasonably unified and continuous mental life. Prudential value is therefore perspectival because it literally takes the point of view of the subject. Welfare is subject-relative because it is subjective (Sumner 1996: 42–43).

Because Sumner views a person's attitudes as central to well-being, the sense of happiness at work in his theory is attitudinal rather than hedonistic. Happiness, according to Sumner, consists in overall life satisfaction, which has both a cognitive and a conative aspect. The cognitive aspect of happiness involves "a positive evaluation of the conditions of your life, a judgement that, at least on balance, it measures up favourably against your standards and expectations" (Sumner 1996: 145). This cognitive aspect of happiness, then, largely amounts to a judgment or assessment that your life is going well according to whatever values, concerns, or standards you have regarding your life.

There is also an affective aspect to this sense of happiness, and this affective side of happiness involves what Sumner refers to as "a sense of well-being" (Sumner 1996: 146). To be happy in this way, we must not simply judge our lives to be satisfactory; we must also *feel* happy with them. While the evaluative aspect of happiness appears most central to Sumner's theory of well-being, these judgments are only constitutive of happiness when they are accompanied by positive feelings, such as feelings of fulfillment or satisfaction. Being happy in this sense is a matter of both judging and feeling that one's life is going well.

Happiness as life satisfaction is crucial to well-being, but it's not quite all there is to it. According to Sumner, happiness only constitutes well-being when it is *authentic*. Sumner's authenticity requirement is motivated by the same concerns that motivate his favoring subjective theories. Because they make well-being dependent upon people's attitudes of favor and disfavor, subjective theories are responsive to who we are as individuals with our own concerns, priorities, and interests. For various reasons, however—such as adaptation to adverse circumstances—our appraisals of how our lives are going (our satisfaction with life) may not accurately reflect our real concerns. In other words, we may be happy in a way that doesn't represent our real selves. Or, thinking of Rosati's analysis of well-being, we might put the point this way:

we can be happy in a way that doesn't really fit us. To capture fully the subject-relativity of well-being, then, happiness must be fitting to the individual. Sumner cashes this out in terms of an authenticity requirement, which he breaks down into two components: information and autonomy.

First, to count as authentic, a person's endorsement of her life must not be based on mistaken perceptions; it must be an endorsement of her life as it actually is. People therefore need to be informed about the conditions of their lives. However, Sumner does not require that a person have "full" information about her life in order for her assessment of her life to be authoritative. This criterion itself is subjectivized; Sumner writes that a person must not be deceived "in sectors of her life which clearly matter to her" (Sumner 1996: 160), making the individual's own concerns establish the realms in which accurate perception matters. In areas of her life that do not factor into her assessment of how her life is going, accurate information is less important. But when a person's perception of a particular aspect of her life (such as her perception of the quality of her personal relationships or her success at work) is driving her evaluation of her life, it is important that this perception not be dependent on her having faulty information. To the extent that we care about how our lives are *actually* going, our feelings and judgments that our lives are going well are only authoritative signs of our well-being when they derive from an accurate understanding of the relevant facts. The information requirement is therefore a way of aligning well-being with people's actual concerns. (See Sobel 2009 for further discussion of information requirements.)

In addition to being informed, a person's positive evaluation of her life must also be autonomous in order for it to be authentic. Sumner develops the autonomy requirement in response to concerns about adaptive preferences, famously raised by Amartya Sen (1987). Even when someone has a clear, informed understanding of the conditions of her life, we might still worry that her assessment of her life does not reflect who she is as an individual if she was never allowed the chance to develop or act upon her own values and priorities.

The important thing here, for Sumner, is that the values and concerns that inform our assessments of our lives be our own. Since our values are crucial to our own identity and to the way we shape our lives, we should form them autonomously. This requires the ability to engage in critical reflection, which can be hampered by some socialization processes. If we have been subjected to social pressures that deny us our autonomy, then our values may not truly represent who we are. Rather than developing a full account of autonomy, however, Sumner argues that a person's assessment of her life should be considered autonomous unless we have strong reason to believe it is not.

According to this theory, then, a person is living well when she is satisfied with her life, as long as this judgment is not based on non-autonomous values or factual mistakes that would change her assessment if corrected. Sumner holds that this theory of well-being best accommodates the subject-relativity that is central to the concept of well-being by ensuring that it connects well-being to what matters to us as individual well-being subjects.

Some have criticized that the life satisfaction theory for making happiness (and well-being) depends on judgments that are fundamentally dependent on one's perspective. There can be more than one assessment a person could authentically make of her life depending on which standards she brings to bear on this judgment, and it seems largely arbitrary which standard gets emphasized at any time (Haybron 2008). For instance, someone might be satisfied with her miserable life because she is resigned to it and doesn't think she could do any better; in this case, the assessment that her life is satisfying doesn't seem to amount to what we ordinarily think of as either happiness or well-being. Others have tried to solve this problem by defining the perspective from which life satisfaction assessments should be made to count as relevant to well-being (Tiberius and Hall 2010; Tiberius and Plakias 2010).

Sumner's life satisfaction theory ties well-being to what seems particularly important from the individual's own point of view. We might wonder, however, whether these assessments of life satisfaction are important enough in the scheme of a person's life to constitute well-being. Value fulfillment theories aim to avoid the problems related to the potential arbitrariness and transience of life satisfaction judgments by making well-being dependent upon what seems more stably meaningful to a person.

Valerie Tiberius, for example, defines well-being in terms of individuals' *values* (rather than their desires or their satisfaction with life) where achieving or fulfilling our values constitutes a reason-generating ideal (Tiberius 2008). According to her value fulfillment theory of well-being, a person's life goes well to the extent that she pursues and fulfills or realizes a subjectively appropriate system of values together over time.[4] The best life for a person is the one in which she gets the most value fulfillment she can, given her circumstances, and what is good for a person now is to do what contributes to some specification of the best, value-full life. In short, we live well when we realize what matters to us. This includes achieving certain states of affairs (such as career goals) and also maintaining the positive affective orientation that comprises valuing something. If your values include your own enjoyment, relationships with family and friends, accomplishing something in your career, and contributing to certain morally worth-while projects, then your life goes well for you insofar as you realize these values for as long as they continue to be the things you care about.

The notion of a value is central to Tiberius's theory. The sense of "value" that is significant for well-being, according to Tiberius, is one wherein to value something is to care about it in a particular way. Values in this sense are reason giving (at least from the first-person perspective) and serve as the individual's standards for evaluating her life. For example, if you ask someone how her life is going, she may reflect briefly on the important domains in her life (such as family, work, and health) and consider how she is doing in terms of these important ends. In this way, values are different from mere desires; people can have desires that are trivial or even unworthy of satisfaction from their own point of view. This is not to say that the satisfaction of our trivial desires is worthless according to the value fulfillment theory. Value fulfillment theory can say that the satisfaction of even fairly trivial desires (e.g., for a beer this afternoon) is relevant to overall well-being when it contributes to something the person values, such as enjoyment, relaxation, or health. Values, then, are well suited to play a central role in a theory of well-being because they are the very thing that people take to make their lives go well.

A person's values, then, are comprised of patterns of relatively robust attitudes (such as emotions and desires) that we take to generate reasons for action.[5] For example, if you value your job, then you will be disposed to enjoy what you do, to feel proud when you get promoted and disappointed when you don't do your best work. When you reflect on how your life is going you will tend to consider how you're doing in your work, and you'll tend to take your job into account when making plans for the future. Valuing, therefore, has both an affective and a cognitive dimension—it involves our emotions and our judgment. This sense of valuing is broadly inclusive: people can value activities, relationships, broad aims, ideals, principles, particular goals that serve these more general ends, and so on. This characterization thus has features that make it compelling on its own as an account of valuing (as opposed to wanting or desiring). It also comports better with psychological research on values than philosophical theories that identify valuing with either a belief or a desire (Lewis 1989; Smith 1995; Dorsey 2012).

Jason Raibley, drawing on Tiberius's conception of values, also defends a theory that defines well-being in terms of the fulfillment or realization of a person's values: the "agential flourishing theory." According to Raibley, "valuing involves stable identification with one's pro-attitudes"

(Raibley 2010: 606–607). This identification will be "whole-hearted"; values are things we see as central to or representative of who we are. Values that are particularly stable in a person's life Raibley calls one's "ownmost" values: while we expect that some of our concerns will appropriately shift as we move through different stages of life, we see other values as more central to our identities and will be disposed to maintain and protect these values from change (as when we think, "I never want to be the type of person that . . ."). The realization of these "ownmost" values will be most beneficial for a person.

Of course, finding success in the things we value is not simply a matter of luck; a significant part of it, according to Raibley, comes down to possessing certain habits of mind, as well as a body that enables us to pursue a variety of activities. He writes,

> In order to truly *flourish* as an agent, one must do more than successfully realize one's values. One's valuational and motivational systems must be functioning in a particularly robust way, so that one is *stably disposed* to realize one's values to a sufficient degree. In particular, one must be ready to cope with the various forms of adversity that one is likely to encounter in the pursuit of one's values, and one must be poised for further success. In order to count as having these dispositions, it is probable that one must develop certain aptitudes and habits and enjoy a variety of states ordinarily associated with good physical and psychological health. These states constitute the *causal basis* for the disposition to realize one's values. It is therefore directly—as opposed to instrumentally—beneficial to be in these states.
>
> *(Raibley 2012: 1117)*

Raibley focuses on the importance of dispositions in part as a response to one common criticism of subjective theories. It is often claimed that subjective theories cannot adequately explain the widespread intuition that states such as physical and mental health are prudentially beneficial *on their own*, regardless of whether they are explicitly valued or desired. Raibley argues that subjective theories can account for the intrinsic value of these states. Living well is a matter of realizing one's values, and certain states—such as physical and emotional health—make the successful realization of values more likely. Someone who is severely depressed or seriously ill is less likely to flourish because achieving one's values often requires being able to take action, to persevere in the pursuit of one's goals. Good mental and physical health make it easier to take these actions and are therefore directly beneficial. Raibley argues that these states are part of the project of valuing, so while they are themselves non-attitudinal they still fit within an overall subjective framework. According to Raibley, "an adult human person is doing well at a time to the degree that they resemble the paradigm case of the flourishing agent at that time" (Raibley 2012: 1106), and a flourishing agent is one who both successfully achieves her values and has the physical and mental dispositions that enable her to continue to do so.

Value fulfillment theories, like other subjective theories, confront objections that stem from the fact that our actual psychological attitudes (desires, assessments of life satisfaction, or values) can be defective in various ways. As we saw, Sumner solves this problem by adding an authenticity requirement to the subjective state of happiness for it to count as well-being. Tiberius and Raibley aim to solve the problem by appealing to an ideal that can be used to criticize current values. Raibley argues that we should understand the ideal as a paradigm case of someone who successfully and sustainably achieves her values. Tiberius employs the notion of a value-full life and argues that we do not need to specify the precise contours of this ideal in order to apply the value fulfillment theory (Tiberius 2014).

Whole-self theories

The distinction between subject-dependent and subjective theories allows us to see that a theory of well-being can have the benefits of the former without the costs of the latter. The theories we consider in this section are subject-dependent in that they make a person's good depend, at least in part, on her individual features, but they are not subjective theories because they do not take the person's *attitudes* to be the crucial feature for well-being. We are calling these theories "whole-self," because they invoke a more comprehensive or inclusive picture of the self in developing their accounts of well-being, making well-being dependent upon aspects of the self beyond our conative stances.

For instance, Dan Haybron develops a subject-dependent theory of well-being focused upon the idea of self-fulfillment. This account is eudaimonistic but differs from Aristotelian theories in being non-perfectionist and in focusing on individual natures rather than essential human traits.[6] The nature that most individual humans share, according to Haybron, is one in which sentiment and reason have "shared governance" (Haybron 2008: 16) and our powers of reason are quite fallible, particularly in their capacity for achieving well-being. Happiness—an emotional state—plays a crucial part in Haybron's account of well-being and is intrinsically valuable even if the person herself does not judge that it is valuable.

According to Haybron, "to be happy is roughly for one's emotional condition to be broadly positive with only minor negatives, embodying a stance of psychic affirmation" (Haybron 2008: 194). Happiness in this sense does not consist merely of positive affect—it's not simply about *feeling* happy, nor is happiness an assessment of life satisfaction. Rather, it includes, along with positive emotions, longer-term moods as well as emotional dispositions. It is a robust emotional condition that affects a person's response to life, instilling peace of mind, making her more interested and actively engaged in life, and predisposing her to feel more positive emotions. When this happiness is *authentic*—when it reflects who she truly is as a person—then it forms a vital part of her well-being.

Haybron contests the view that subjective accounts of well-being will necessarily be less alienating than non-attitudinal theories like his own. If our emotional natures are important parts of who we are, then focusing only on attitudes to the exclusion of all other parts of our natures presents a picture of the self that is artificially narrow. Haybron writes that, "the objective value of happiness is precisely that it is *not* alien to us: it is deeply bound up with the self" (Haybron 2008: 194). In other words, if someone does not recognize the importance of emotions to her well-being, then perhaps it is her own self, and not the account of well-being, from which she is alienated.

Haybron's self-fulfillment theory is subject-dependent because it defines well-being in terms of a feature of the individual, namely, the person's emotional state. This theory allows that different people, due to differing emotional and physical makeups, will be happy in different circumstances, but it does not make well-being dependent on our attitudes. In Sumner's terms, then, well-being is objective (that is, not dependent on subjective attitudes such as desires). We would be better off, Haybron says, pursuing lives that suit our emotional natures and thereby increase our happiness even if we do not, even *could* not, come to desire it or judge that it is valuable.

The final theory we consider in this subject-dependent category is Richard Kraut's "developmentalism." Like Rosati, Kraut argues that the "good for" relation is one of suitability; for *x* to be good for someone, it must suit her or serve her well. In contrast to the other theories considered in this chapter, Kraut draws on an Aristotelian account of human to nature to inform and fill out his conception of prudential value. According to Kraut, what is good for us is to flourish, and humans (along with all living beings) flourish when they develop and fully utilize the "potentialities, capacities, and faculties, that (under favorable conditions) they naturally have at an early stage of their existence" (Kraut 2007: 131). The capacities the development and exercise of which benefit human beings include our "cognitive, affective, sensory, and social powers" (Kraut 2007: 137) as well as our physical capacities. Because the development of these capacities benefits someone independently of her attitude toward them, this is a whole-self account of well-being.

Although Kraut's conception of human well-being is built upon a species-level account of human development, it is developed in a way that makes it, ultimately, subject-dependent. Kraut allows that there are differences between something's being good for humans and something's being good for a particular individual. According to Kraut,

> there is no saying what is good for some particular individual living being, unless we know a great deal about him or her or it. Some of what we must know pertains to the peculiar circumstances and idiosyncrasies of that particular individual, though other facts we must know pertain to the species to which S belongs.
>
> *(Kraut 2007: 4; see also Kraut 2011 for further discussion of this point)*

In this way, what is good for any given individual will depend on what she, specifically, is like. Although, according to Kraut, all humans could be said to possess certain capacities and potentialities at an early stage of development, these capacities can be developed and exercised through a wide range of activities. Which of these will be beneficial for any given individual will depend upon her specific nature, which may differ in a variety of ways from others of her kind. Unlike other Aristotelian accounts of well-being, according to developmentalism, to say that some good or activity would benefit all humans, it is not enough simply to say that such an activity constitutes the development of species-*typical* capacities. Such capacities must be possessed by all humans from an early age for such a statement to hold, and where there are any variations in specific abilities, prudential value must similarly diverge. It is in focusing on self-fulfillment in this way that Kraut's developmentalism is a subject-dependent account.

Conclusion

Theories of well-being are normally categorized as being either objective or subjective, but the taxonomy we discuss in this chapter may have some advantages over the usual way of dividing up theories. Thinking of theories as either subject-transcending or subject-dependent, and if subject-dependent, whether dependent on attitudes or other features of the subject, can draw our attention to issues sometimes obscured by thinking of theories as either subjective or objective.

First, as noted earlier, definitions of subjectivity and objectivity vary. According to a common definition (the one we employ in this chapter), subjective theories are those in which well-being depends on a person's attitudes, while objective theories are those that reject this attitude-dependence. However, another common definition holds that subjective theories are those in which a person's well-being is determined by her mental states (including, but not limited to, her attitudes), while a separate definition of objective theories (employed by Woodard in this volume: see Chapter 13) holds that they are those in which only objectively valuable goods and states can prudentially benefit a person. Depending on which of these definitions is being used, a theory like hedonism, for example, could be classified as either subjective or objective—objective when using the attitude-dependence criterion (if we say that pleasure benefits someone regardless of her attitudes toward it), subjective according to the mental-state conception of subjectivity, and objective again if pleasure is argued to be objectively valuable.

On one hand, it may not matter how we divide up theories, as long as we are clear about which definition we have in mind. On the other hand, our taxonomy can serve to highlight other salient differences between theories, and it is in this way that thinking of theories as subject-dependent or subject-transcending can be useful.

Consider, for example, the debate in the well-being literature about people's authority over their well-being. Subjective theories are often held to grant the individual some amount of control over, or special knowledge about, what counts as her own good. In response, objective theorists argue that what we want (or care about, or enjoy, etc.) may not be good for us, and what would be good for us we don't always value or appreciate (see, for example, Haybron 2008). This debate is related to the discussion of alienation, mentioned earlier—a commonly raised objection to objective theories of well-being is that, if something can be part of a person's well-being even if she in no way enjoys, desires, or values it, then her well-being will end up being something from which she is alienated. Given the typical subjective/objective framework, this debate often centers on the connection between a person's attitudes and her well-being. Thinking of the various ways in which a theory can be subject-dependent, however, presses this debate further by encouraging us to consider the variety of ways in which a theory can be sensitive to the unique characteristics of individual well-being subjects. Are our attitudes the only or most crucially relevant aspects of ourselves as subjects? Or, as Haybron argues, are other aspects of ourselves at least equally important, in which case any theory that neglects those aspects should also be considered alienating? If, as is often accepted, other aspects of ourselves beyond our attitudes—such as our emotional natures—are important parts of who we are, it may seem odd to call theories that incorporate these aspects into their accounts of well-being objective, and such a label may be unhelpful. Focusing on the differences between subjective and objective theories of well-being seems to encourage a battle of intuitions about particular prudential goods. The focus on the different ways in which a theory can be subject-dependent draws the attention back to the other half of the good-for relationship: the individual subject to whom well-being is thought to be relative. It may be that this shift in focus will also result in a battle of conflicting intuitions, but it seems a strategy worth exploring.

If well-being is, as Sumner and others maintain, subject-relative, then we need to give careful attention to what it is that makes someone a subject. Subject-dependent theories vary in terms of which aspect of the individual they hold to be crucial to well-being. For instance, according to Sumner, what makes human beings *subjects* is consciousness; in particular, we are subjects because, unlike plants or inanimate objects, we have a perspective on the world, and it is that perspective—our attitudes and stances toward the world—that is central to our well-being (Sumner 1996: 27–41). According to Haybron, however, we are emotional as well as rational beings, and as a result our well-being must be responsive to more than simply our cognitive and conative states. Some theories thus make well-being depend solely upon a person's attitudes, while others, such as value fulfillment theories, tend toward inclusivity insofar as the ideals to which values are held go beyond subjective attitudes, and still others cast a wider net in making emotional and physical states or the development of certain capacities important to well-being independently of a person's attitudes toward them. What all of these theories share, however, is a particular way of accounting for the subject-relativity of well-being. According to these theories, something can be good for someone in a prudential sense only when it is in some way responsive to who she is as an individual. Our well-being must fit the quirks and contours of our own lives, whether it is shaped by our attitudes, our values, our physical and emotional natures, or our aptitudes and capacities. While these theories do not offer full-fledged accounts of personal identity, they press us to examine our intuitions about the central or defining aspects of what it is to be a subject.

Furthermore, by drawing more attention to the question of how accounts of well-being can be appropriately subject-relative, thinking about theories in terms of subject dependence also encourages us to consider the meta-ethical question of what exactly the good-for relation consists in. For instance, if Rosati is correct that this relation is one of fit or suitability, then, depending on the correct analysis of fit or suitability combined with a particular conception of subjective agency, this may limit the set of plausible theories of well-being. If, as Haybron (2008) argues, our preferences and judgments of life satisfaction do not always align well with our emotional natures, then conative conceptions of well-being may not be ones that suit us. Other accounts of the good-for relationship could push us back toward conative theories. This is an area that could be explored further in developing subject-dependent theories of well-being.

If well-being is in fact subject-relative, then it may be that we cannot make concrete claims about prudential benefit without attending to the individual welfare subject; and if this is so, then it seems that any plausible theory of well-being must be subject-dependent. In taking seriously the question of which aspects of our selves—our attitudes, values, or emotional or physical natures—are definitive of who we are as persons, subject-dependent accounts strive to ensure that our well-being is subject-relative in a truly meaningful way.

Notes

1 Alternatively, we may find that it is useful to come back to the metaethical characterizations of subject-relativity just canvassed in order to decide between competing theories. We suspect that some back and forth between analyses of subject-relativity and defenses of substantive theories of well-being will be productive and we will come back to some of these analyses later in the chapter.
2 See, for instance, Scanlon (1998), Kraut (2007), Haybron (2008), and Rosati (2009), among others. For an opposing view, see Sarch (2011).
3 See, for instance, Railton (1986) and Rosati (1996). Fletcher and Woodard also discuss alienation in their chapters of this volume (Chapters 12 and 13, respectively).
4 Tiberius actually claims to be defending an account of what it is to live a good life from your own point of view. Since this is a notion closely related to well-being, however, we include it here.
5 For a more detailed version of the account of valuing and values, see Tiberius (2000, 2008). For sympathetic treatments see Anderson (1995), Schmuck and Sheldon (2001), and Raibley (2010).
6 For a discussion of perfectionism, see Bradford (Chapter 10 in this volume).

References

Anderson, E. (1995) *Value in Ethics and Economics*, Cambridge: Harvard University Press.
Darwall, S. (2002) *Welfare and Rational Care*, Princeton, NJ: Princeton University Press.
Dorsey, D. (2012) "Intrinsic Value and the Supervenience Principle," *Philosophical Studies* 157: 267–285.
Haybron, D.M. (2008) *The Pursuit of Unhappiness*, Oxford: Oxford University Press.
Kraut, R. (2007) *What is Good and Why*, Cambridge, MA: Harvard University Press.
Kraut, R. (2011) *Against Absolute Goodness*, Oxford: Oxford University Press.
Lewis, D. (1989) "Dispositional Theories of Value," *Proceedings of the Aristotelian Society* Supplementary 63: 113–137.
Raibley, J.R. (2010) "Well-Being and the Priority of Values," *Social Theory and Practice* 36: 593–620.
Raibley, J.R. (2012) "Happiness is not Well-Being," *Journal of Happiness Studies* 13: 1105–1129.
Railton, P. (1986) "Facts and Values," *Philosophical Topics* 14: 5–31.
Rosati, C.S. (1996) "Internalism and the Good for a Person," *Ethics* 106: 297–326.
Rosati, C.S. (2006a) "Personal Good," in T. Horgan and M. Timmons (eds.) *Metaethics after Moore*, Oxford: Oxford University Press, pp. 107–132.
Rosati, C.S. (2006b) "Preference-Formation and Personal Good," *Royal Institute of Philosophy Supplement* 59: 33–64.
Rosati, C.S. (2009) "Relational Good and the Multiplicity Problem," *Philosophical Issues* 19: 205–234.
Rosati, C.S. (2013) "The Story of a Life," *Social Philosophy and Policy* 30: 21–50.

Sarch, A. (2011) "Internalism About a Person's Good: Don't Believe It," *Philosophical Studies* 154: 161–184.

Scanlon, T.M. (1998) "The Status of Well-Being," in G.B. Peterson (ed.) *Tanner Lectures on Human Values* 19, Salt Lake City: University of Utah Press.

Schmuck, P. and Sheldon, K.M. (eds.) (2001) *Life Goals and Well-Being. Towards a Positive Psychology of Human Striving,* Seattle, WA: Hogrefe & Huber Publishers.

Sen, A. (1987) *On Ethics and Economics,* Oxford: Basil Blackwell.

Smith, M. (1995) "Internal Reasons," *Philosophy and Phenomenological Research* 55: 109–131.

Sobel, D. (2009) "Subjectivism and Idealization," *Ethics* 119: 336–352.

Sumner, L.W. (1996) *Welfare, Happiness, and Ethics,* Oxford: Oxford University Press.

Tiberius, V. (2000) "Humean Heroism: Value Commitments and the Source of Normativity," *Pacific Philosophical Quarterly* 81: 426–446.

Tiberius, V. (2008) *The Reflective Life: Living Wisely with our Limits,* Oxford: Oxford University Press.

Tiberius, V. (2014) "How Theories of Well-Being Can Help Us Help," *Journal of Practical Ethics* 2: 1–19.

Tiberius, V. and Hall, A. (2010) "Normative Theory and Psychological Research: Hedonism, Eudaimonism and Why it Matters," *Journal of Positive Psychology* 5: 212–225.

Tiberius, V. and Plakias, A. (2010) "Well-Being," in J.M. Doris (ed.) *The Moral Psychology Handbook,* Oxford: Oxford University Press, pp. 402–432.

15

EUDAIMONISM

Lorraine Besser-Jones

Eudaimonism holds that the best life is the life well lived, where a life well lived makes optimal use of one's capacities. While it is safe to say that all contemporary forms of eudaimonism owe a substantial debt to Aristotle, what marks out a theory of well-being as eudaimonistic has much more to do with its structure, rather than necessarily with its historic roots. In this chapter I will isolate the structure of eudaimonism, explore the variety of ways in which contemporary theorists (both philosophers and psychologists) fill out this structure, and then consider some of the challenges eudaimonism faces.

The structure of eudaimonism

The Greek word *eudaimonia* is one that notoriously resists easy interpretation. Aristotle uses *eudaimonia* to represent the highest good for human beings, something that he takes to be circumscribed to the function distinctive to human beings. For many years, *eudaimonia* was translated as "happiness." Increasingly, though, philosophers recognize that understanding *eudaimonia* in terms of happiness can be misleading. When we think of happiness, we tend to think first and foremost of positive feelings (of satisfaction, of pleasure). But focusing on these features potentially leads us to overlook the distinctive kind of well-being Aristotle sought to describe, which is something important and valuable in its own right—even independently of the positive feelings associated with it.

To avoid this kind of confusion, many philosophers no longer try to provide an English translation for the word *eudaimonia*, and *eudaimonia* is taken to represent itself a distinctive form of well-being that refers to a state of flourishing, and specifically flourishing *qua* human being. There is much more needed to unpack this concept, but understanding *eudaimonia* in terms of human flourishing gives us a helpful way of anchoring eudaimonism and also delivers some insight into how eudaimonism departs from other contemporary theories of well-being. We can helpfully distinguish eudaimonism from other theories of well-being by highlighting the following characteristics of eudaimonism: First, its effort to characterize an active state of well-being that, while experiential, requires agency and ongoing activity; and, second, its characterization of well-being as objective, dependent upon features of one's life rather than one's attitudes towards one's life. Let's consider each in turn.

Whereas other theories of well-being take well-being to be a largely passive state—something we experience—eudaimonism takes well-being to be an active process of living well, of well functioning. To illustrate this difference in a very simple fashion, consider the contrasting experiences of the young child, learning how to read. Prior to learning how to read, the child experiences books by being read to. This, of course, is an enjoyable experience that is both valuable and meaningful for the child. It is, nonetheless, a different experience than the one the child engages in when she learns how to read for herself. Through the active process of reading, the child experiences the book in a different manner. Reading the book becomes an activity. The book is no longer delivered to her; rather she takes ownership of the experience, through the active exercise of her agency. Eudaimonism is an effort to describe the kind of well-being that arises through this kind of *active exercise of agency*.

LeBar (2013) helpfully describes this contrast as one between seeing oneself as a patient and as an agent.[1] According to LeBar, the patientist approach holds that "what matters is not so much what we do as what happens, and in particular happens to us"; the agentist approach, in contrast, "emphasizes that our lives go well in virtue of what we do, rather than what happens" (2013: 67, 69). A patientist approach to well-being focuses on what happens to us, while an agentist approach focuses on what we do.

This aspect of eudaimonism is also a distinctive aspect of the psychological conception of eudaimonism. Psychologists (e.g. Ryan et al. 2006) describe the contrast between agentist and patientist approaches in terms of the distinction between a process and an outcome. Eudaimonism describes well-being in terms of a specific way of living—a process of living well—rather than in terms of an outcome such as experiencing a particular mental state. This isn't to say that the process of living well isn't associated with positive outcomes, but the hope is that focusing on the process of living well allows us to identify a unique and distinctively human form of well-being, one that highlights our agency and one for which there can be no substitute.

Why might we think the process is itself valuable, independently of the outcome? And why might we think, as many eudaimonists do, that the process is more important than the outcome? While in reality it is difficult to separate the two, reflection on Nozick's arguments regarding the experience machine is helpful (Nozick 1974). The experience machine promises to deliver certain experiences, such as pleasure, to an individual. We might see the experience machine as providing the outcome without the process. Individuals in the experience machine are patients, not agents. Nozick argues that if hedonistic approaches towards understanding well-being are correct, we all ought to and would in fact choose to enter the experience machine. But, of course, we don't. Why? As Nozick writes, "we want to *do* certain things and not just have the experience of doing them" (1974: 613). The point is not limited to hedonism, but extends to any outcome-based, patientist approach to well-being. Readers sympathetic to this line of argument ought to find the eudaimonistic approach to well-being intriguing.

Because eudaimonism describes a process, rather than an outcome, it is often described as presenting an objective theory of well-being, which is the second structural feature of eudaimonism that I will highlight here. While the distinction between "objective" and "subjective" theories of well-being can be somewhat messy, struggling to understand it will help our understanding of the structural features of eudaimonism. Following Sumner (1996), we can take objectivism to describe a form of well-being that is neither defined by nor contingent to an agent's attitudes about how her life is going, while we can take subjectivism to describe a form of well-being whereby these attitudes are a necessary component of well-being.[2] Most conceptions of well-being (objective list theories are a notable exception) take well-being to be comprised almost entirely by these subjective dimensions.[3] A life satisfaction view of well-being, for instance, takes well-being to consist in the having of cognitive and/or affective appraisals of the overall shape one's life takes. But eudaimonism deems such appraisals unnecessary, choosing to focus instead on aspects of flourishing (such as the exercise of practical reason, or the exercise of virtue) that do not depend on one experiencing any particular attitudes regarding how one's life is going. Depending on the variety of eudaimonism, there may be other important attitudes requisite to flourishing, such as concern for others, but positive attitudes regarding how one's life is going are not necessary components.

This form of objectivism follows nicely from the eudaimonist's focus on identifying an active, process-based form of well-being rather than an outcome-based form (of which form subjectivist theories of well-being tend to be). And while outcomes are associated with *eudaimonia*—people who flourish certainly are likely to experience pleasure and life satisfaction—these subjective outcomes are not the goal. The goal is one we can understand in objective terms, by looking at how an individual lives her life, rather than how she feels about the life she lives. Because eudaimonism presents an objective form of well-being that is conceptually independent of these kinds of subjective attitudes, however, some find eudaimonism to be counter-intuitive when presented as a theory of well-being. It seems odd that one could have well-being yet not feel good about how one's life is going, a point we will return to in a discussion of some of the debates surrounding eudaimonism.

Thus far we have identified eudaimonism as describing a form of well-being that consists in the active process of living well, where living well is understood in objective terms of human flourishing. These are the structural features binding together the different versions of eudaimonism, but as these are just structural features, much more needs to be said: What does it mean to live well? What counts as human flourishing? It is in the answers to these questions that different versions of eudaimonism emerge.

Varieties of eudaimonism

Any conception of eudaimonism requires an account of human flourishing, i.e., an account of what it means to live well. Aristotle famously thought that human flourishing had to be explained in terms of the *distinctive* function of human beings. He took this to consist in the "activity of the soul in accordance with reason"(Aristotle, 1962, bk. 1.6). This position—that human flourishing consists in the exercise of practical rationality—informs most contemporary philosophical conceptions of eudaimonism, such as those developed by Julia Annas (2011), Daniel Russell (2012), and Mark LeBar (2013). Annas, for instance, describes eudaimonism as involving a "structured way of thinking of your life" whereby through asking "why" you can come to see that your "actions fit into structured patterns in your life; a snapshot of what you are doing at one time turns out to reveal, when we think about these structures, what your broader aims and goals in life are" (2011: 121–122). LeBar's description of *eudaimonia* is even more explicit in its allegiance to practical rationality:

> The eudaimonistic proposal is that human welfare or well-being consists in living a life of practical wisdom. That is, the nature or content of what a good life is—what such a life amounts to—cannot be specified without recourse to the exercise of practical wisdom.
>
> *(LeBar 2013: 82)*

One nice aspect of this focus on practical rationality is its ability to highlight an individual's agency. Through exercising practical rationality, and developing practical wisdom, the individual can construct and shape her life. She can reflect on her goals and how they fit together, thereby comprising a framework for her to make decisions about which ends to pursue and which course of actions to embrace. Russell describes this as a process of "rational self-construction," writing that, humans are by nature active creatures who live by practical reason. Human action and practical reason are inseparable: humans do not merely *behave*, but rather they *act* because they are capable of reflecting on their impulses and feelings and can—indeed *must*—find reasons for the things they do and the ways they feel.

(Russell 2012: 72)

This aspect of human nature, Russell goes on to argue, ought to define humans' fulfillment:

to be fulfilled as that kind of creature is to be active in accordance with practical wisdom and emotional soundness, since that is how practical rationality functions in a distinctively human way . . . our status as agents with practical rationality is what defines our happiness.

(Russell 2012: 72)

This style of argument is common amongst contemporary eudaimonists and very much echoes Aristotle's position as developed in his function argument. But we might wonder whether or not this emphasis on practical rationality is warranted. While Russell claims that humans "must" find reasons for their actions, as Doris (2002, 2009) argues, psychological research shows it is all too common that we don't find reasons for our actions and that we don't act, as Russell claims, as "active creatures who live by practical reason" (2012: 72). We tend to respond automatically to situational factors of which we are not even aware (Doris 2002) and we are influenced by unconscious biases in largely unpredictable ways (Bargh and Chartrand, 1999). Our behavior rarely reflects our beliefs (Fendrich 1967; Knobe and Leiter 2007), and when we do use reason in moral contexts, it tends to be post hoc, as a means of rationalizing our behavior (Haidt 2001).[4] This research does not eliminate the possibility of using practical reason, but it might make us question whether our capacity for engaging in practical reason is what *defines* us, such that we ought to understand human fulfillment by appeal to practical rationality.[5]

While admittedly eudaimonism is a view about an ideal form of human fulfillment, about the best shape a human life can take, empirical research contesting the very view of agency upon which this idealized form of human fulfillment is predicated might lead us to question this strand of eudaimonism, which has dominated contemporary philosophical discussions of eudaimonism. An alternative approach to eudaimonism, grounded within a psychological understanding of human fulfillment, moves away from this emphasis on practical reason, focusing instead on the satisfaction of needs and the exercise of one's capacities that are essential to this satisfaction.

Psychologists understand eudaimonism, what they call eudaimonic well-being, in this fashion (Ryan et al. 2006; Ryff and Singer 2008).[6] Eudaimonic well-being describes a state of psychological health, of ongoing proper functioning. It shares the structure of philosophical conceptions of eudaimonism, insofar as it seeks to describe the active process of living well, but fills out its account of flourishing by looking at the circumstances in which individuals tend to flourish, and those in which they tend to exhibit pathologies. Analysis of these circumstances enables researchers to posit the existence of innate psychological needs, which are drives individuals have to seek out certain kinds of experiences.[7] According to Deci and Ryan's influential research (2000), we have needs to experience competency over our environments and as such to engage in experiences that allow us to exercise our skills; to experience belongingness with others, to both care for others and be cared for by others; to experience autonomy through selecting and pursuing goals with which we identify. When we engage in these activities in an ongoing fashion, we experience eudaimonic well-being.

So what does eudaimonic well-being look like? Need satisfaction is associated with physical, psychological, and cognitive benefits.[8] It facilitates "optimal functioning of the natural propensities for growth and integration, as well as for constructive social development and personal well-being" (Ryan and Deci 2000b: 68). Ryan and Deci describe individuals experiencing eudaimonic well-being as representing the best of human potential, as "curious, vital, and self-motivated. At their best, they are agentic and inspired, striving to learn; extend themselves; master new skills; and apply their talents responsibly" (2000b: 68). They contrast this state with non-optimal functioning, wherein individuals reject growth and responsibility, and find themselves "apathetic, alienated, and irresponsible" (Ryan and Deci 2000b: 68). Thus living well, according to this form of eudaimonism, consists in continually engaging in the kinds of experiences that satisfy our needs to engage with others, to develop skills, to identify with our goals and pursuits—a way of living explored at length in Besser-Jones (2014).

The psychological conception of eudaimonism clearly de-emphasizes the role of practical reasoning, choosing to highlight needs satisfaction as the distinctive component of living well, rather than the exercise of practical reason. While this is a significant departure from the philosophical conception, it does not eliminate the role of practical reason from living well. Rather, as I argue (Besser-Jones 2014), practical reason ought to be invoked in service of selecting the goals essential to living well and in motivating us to pursue those goals. At the end of the day, we might rightly wonder whether both the philosophical and the psychological conceptions of eudaimonism differ primarily insofar as they assign practical reason a different weight, rather than a different role. As we've seen, the philosophical conception of eudaimonism takes the exercise of practical reason to be primary and justifies the ways of living it leads to by appeal to practical reason, whereas the psychological conception of eudaimonism takes the satisfaction of innate psychological needs to be primary, and justifies the role of practical reason insofar as it plays an important role in needs satisfaction.

The psychological and philosophical conceptions of eudaimonism represent different efforts to give content to the structure of eudaimonism. Both provide helpful springboards for thinking about what is involved in living well, and in what human flourishing consists. Let us now consider some specific dimensions of eudaimonism, making distinctions where necessary between the philosophical conception of eudaimonia and the psychological conception of eudaimonic well-being.

Dimensions of eudaimonism: virtue

Eudaimonism is perhaps most familiar not as an independent theory of well-being, but as a theory of well-being that anchors virtue ethics. This is the context in which Aristotle discusses *eudaimonia* and in which many contemporary eudaimonists explore it (for examples, see Hursthouse 1999; Annas 2011; and Besser-Jones 2014). Annas even defines eudaimonism in terms of involving "an entry point for ethical reflection," which consists in "thinking about how your life is going, thinking that can arise in people who already are, or are becoming, adult, and who are aware that everything in their life is not satisfactory" (2011: 121). Thinking through how to improve one's life involves thinking about how to be a good person; eudaimonism and virtue go hand-in-hand.

The thought is that living well involves being virtuous such that one develops *eudaimonia* or eudaimonic well-being through being virtuous. Consider Hursthouse's definition of the virtues: "A virtue is a character trait a human being needs for *eudaimonia*, to flourish or live well"(1999: 167), which follows straightforwardly from Aristotle: the highest good (eudaimonia) is activity in accordance with virtue (*NE* 1.7, 1098a16–18). This position is standard fare for the philosophical conceptions of eudaimonism, which, as the quote from Hursthouse illustrates, posit a conceptual connection between virtue and eudaimonia. To those working outside the eudaimonistic framework, however, this claim is apt to be met with considerable skepticism.

Consider Haybron, who believes we can find many examples of individuals who lack virtue yet experience well-being, including:

> [T]he successful Southern slaveholder who enjoys the approbation of his community and a comfortable existence with a loving family has obvious moral shortcomings, yet it is hard to see in what sense his life must be "impoverished." Why must he be in any way worse off than he would be were he more enlightened about human equality? Why must he be worse off than a morally better counterpart who enjoys as much wealth, comfort, success, love and reputation, but without ever wronging anyone? (We can assume that both are well-settled in their moral convictions, equally convinced of their righteousness.) This point arises with greater force in the case of a brutal warlord like Genghis Khan, who directed the slaughter of tens of millions. He appears to have done so largely with the blessing of his culture's moral code. It is not hard to imagine that his relatively long life, which appeared to be rather successful on his terms, went very well for him indeed. And while his idea of happiness or well-being is not exactly yours or mine, it is difficult to see the grounds for gainsaying it (as a conception of well-being!). Is humanitarian concern for strangers really necessary for a full or rich, or even a characteristically, human life? History offers little reason for optimism on this count.
>
> *(Haybron 2007: 5–6)*

Haybron's challenge is both a challenge to the idea that there is a conceptual connection between virtue and *eudaimonia* and to eudaimonism, insofar as it emphasizes the perfection of one's capacities (a view he describes as "welfare perfectionism").

What are we to make of this kind of challenge? Hursthouse, anticipating these kinds of challenges, writes that the claim is not that virtue *guarantees eudaimonia*, but only that it is our best bet: "they are the only reliable bet—even though, it is agreed, I might be unlucky and, precisely because of my virtue, wind up dying early or with my life marred or ruined" (1999: 172). Can even this more modified claim hold up, though?

On the psychological conception of eudaimonic well-being, any claims regarding the connection between virtue and eudaimonic well-being are ones that must be borne out by empirical research. Because eudaimonic well-being is defined through reflection on needs satisfaction, rather than through the exercise of practical reason, where virtue is taken to imply the standard set of character traits (being a "good person," let's say), it must be an open question whether or not being virtuous is the only, or even a, reliable bet towards developing eudaimonic well-being. Challenges like Haybron's must be taken seriously.

Do we need virtue to satisfy our innate psychological needs of autonomy, relatedness, and competence and so to experience eudaimonic well-being? The case for thinking comes largely through reflection on the need for relatedness.[9] Reflection on the nature of the need for relatedness suggests that its satisfaction requires relating *well* to others we encounter, and treating them with care and respect. While this may not mean that the development of eudaimonic well-being requires the development of the virtues as they are traditionally construed, it does suggest that being a good person and acting well to others is an important component of needs satisfaction—it is one we are driven to and it appears to be our best means for satisfaction of the need for relatedness. It also is one that allows us to satisfy our needs for autonomy and competence, making it, as I argue elsewhere, our best bet: "acting well—understood to consist in engaging in positive social interaction marked by a mutual level of caring and respect—is the most promising route to the development of eudaimonic well-being" (Besser-Jones 2014: 95). This doesn't mean it is not *possible* for the Southern slaveholder or Genghis Kahn to experience eudaimonic well-being, but it does mean that if we are seriously interested in developing eudaimonic well-being, and in living well, we ought not to gamble on immorality and should instead focus on becoming a good person.

Challenges to eudaimonism

A challenge emerges when eudaimonism is presented, as it is considered here, as an independent theory of well-being to stand up alongside more familiar theories of well-being that involve desire satisfaction, or feelings of pleasure, and so forth. The challenge is to show not that eudaimonism captures a real form of well-being, but to show that eudaimonism captures a compelling form of well-being, and particularly one that we ought to see as normative for us. Theories of well-being, *qua* theory of well-being or prudential value, typically claim a somewhat unique value that carries with it a special sense of normativity in virtue of referring to that which is good for the individual. Unlike other values whose connection to the individual is often indirect and whose normativity often requires lengthy justification, the value and corresponding normativity of well-being are supposed to be direct and transparent. Yet some worry that eudaimonism lacks this kind of value. The problem is that eudaimonism tries to capture a kind of well-being that doesn't just boil down to the having of favorable attitudes towards one's life; for some, this means that eudaimonism lacks the kind of transparency found in other forms of well-being.

Targeting specifically the psychological conception of eudaimonic well-being, Tiberius and colleagues call into question the philosophical salience of the eudaimonic accounts, which they think cannot function as a normative theory of well-being (Tiberius and Hall 2010; Tiberius and Plakias 2010). The worry, in their words, is that the gap between well-being and subjective experience (by which they mean having favorable attitudes):

> gives rise to concerns about the justification of eudaimonistic norms. If the justification of needs based norms ultimately depends on the assumption that satisfying these needs brings us more pleasure, or makes us subjectively happier, then the theory on offer is not really a distinct alternative to hedonism or life satisfaction. Moreover, if this is *not* how needs based norms are justified, it is difficult to see how eudaimonism can have a legitimate claim to be action-guiding in general (and not just for people who already identify with it).
>
> *(Tiberius and Plakias 2010: 410)*

Tiberius and Plakias here, and throughout their discussion of eudaimonic well-being, express skepticism that there is any value inherent in needs satisfaction that is independent of its conduciveness to generating positive attitudes. That is, their discussion suggests that if fulfillment of the needs of competence, relatedness, and autonomy is valuable for the individual, it is valuable only as means towards attaining happiness or life satisfaction.

While Tiberius and colleagues here target the psychological conception of eudaimonic well-being, the challenge is one that arises from the structure of eudaimonism and so applies as well to the philosophical conception of eudaimonia as well. It is based in the objectivity of eudaimonism, a point we touched on earlier. Eudaimonism is objective insofar as it presents a kind of well-being that is independent of the possession of favorable attitudes towards one's life. This means that it is theoretically possible for people to experience the kind of flourishing distinctive to eudaimonism without feeling the positive feelings associated more generally with well-being. While most defenders of eudaimonism defend the view that, in practice, agents who experience *eudaimonia* or eudaimonic well-being also experience pleasure, or some other subjective dimension of well-being, Tiberius and Plakias's challenge remains: if eudaimonism is to stand on its own as a distinct form of well-being, it must make some account of its normativity in a way that shows it to be distinctive.

We find in Philippa Foot one way to justify the normativity of eudaimonism that I'm particularly sympathetic to, and that has been appealed to to justify both the philosophical conception of eudaimonia (e.g., Hursthouse 1999) and the psychological conception of eudaimonic well-being (e.g., Besser-Jones 2014). Foot (2003) argues that *eudaimonia* can be justified by appeal to what she calls "natural necessity"—this refers to those features that are necessary for human development. Reflection on these features gives us a standard of value from which to evaluate the features of human nature. We can then hold up certain features of human nature as valuable in virtue of their role in human development, and from this basis justify norms directing us towards our fulfillment.

Foot uses this method to justify an Aristotelian-inspired focus on our mental capacities and particularly our practical wisdom, such that "rational choice should be seen as an aspect of human goodness" (2003: 81), a move also embraced explicitly in Hursthouse: "in virtue of our rationality—our free will if you like—we are different"(1999: 221). Besser-Jones uses this method to justify focus on innate psychological needs and suggests thinking about eudaimonic well-being in terms of psychological health: given that we have the innate psychological needs that drive us to engage in certain patterns of behavior and lead us to experience pathologies when we don't, "it is good for us to fulfill these needs" (2014: 25).

Appealing to this kind of natural necessity is one way we might establish the normativity of eudaimonism. But skeptics might still worry about whether this meets the challenge. For what this move does, and what eudaimonism going back to Aristotle in general does, is specify norms through reflection on what is "distinctively human" (be it our rational capacities, or our innate psychological needs). The claim is that these features are necessary for our development not as individuals, but as a member of the species. This, in turn, opens up yet another potential gap between eudaimonism and subjective theories of well-being.

Because eudaimonism presents a view of well-being that is specified in terms of our natures *qua* human being, it presents what Haybron (2008) describes as an "external" theory of well-being. [10] Foot's work presents a clear illustration of this aspect of *eudaimonia*. She argues, for instance, that "to determine what is goodness and what defect of character, disposition, and choice, we must consider what human good is and how human beings live: in other words, what kind of a living thing a human being is" (Foot 2003: 51). The relevant contrast here is with internal theories of well-being that specify well-being in terms of facts about the individual, i.e., the actual bearer of well-being. We can quickly see why some might find an internalist approach to well-being compelling. Haybron, for instance, argues that:

> First, what counts toward my well-being must depend on what I am like. My welfare must not be alien to me, a value that floats down from some Platonic realm, and remora-like, affixes itself to me with little regard to the particulars of my constitution. Second, what counts toward my well-being must not depend on what any other individual, or group or class of individuals—actual or hypothetical—is like. It must be possible to specify the ultimate or fundamental conditions of my well-being without making essential reference to other individuals, or to classes or groups of individuals.
>
> *(Haybron 2008: 157)*

The externalist aspect of eudaimonism exacerbates the normativity challenge insofar as we think it possible that what is good for my species may not be good for me.

Is it possible that what eudaimonism holds to be good for me (be it the development of practical wisdom, or the satisfaction of innate psychological needs) is not *actually* good for me in the ways that eudaimonism claims? To deny this possibility, I think, would be to make a blatantly false empirical claim. The fact of the matter is that the kind of flourishing embraced by both philosophical and psychological conceptions of eudaimonism is one based on how human beings *tend* to behave and what kinds of things *tend* to enable them to function well. While this may not satisfy those fully committed to internalism about well-being, defenders of eudaimonism can make recourse here to the fact that, for most of us, following its prescriptions are a good bet towards developing well-being. We saw this move earlier in our discussion of whether virtue or being a good person is necessary for developing *eudaimonia* or eudaimonic well-being. Here, the plausible answers were not that virtue guarantees the development of *eudaimonia* or eudaimonic well-being, but that it provides us with a safe, reliable route—anyone who denies this is taking a risk, and gambling with her own well-being. In a similar vein, we can say the same thing about the individual who thinks that eudaimonism gives a view of well-being that is good for her species, but not good for her. The odds, quite simply, are against this line of reasoning.[11]

Conclusion

Eudaimonism offers a distinctive way of thinking about well-being, marked by its commitment to describing what it means to *live well*—to how it is that we can work our way through life in a way that allows us to flourish. We've seen that while the philosophical and the psychological forms of eudaimonism differ insofar as what they take the distinctive features of human nature to be, they share the structure of eudaimonism by taking well-being to consist in the process of living well, and by seeking to describe an objective form of well-being that is independent of favorable attitudes towards one's life. We've also seen that, especially in virtue of the latter, defenders of eudaimonism face particular challenges justifying the norms it gives rise to. I've suggested that these challenges can be assuaged by thinking of eudaimonism as offering guidance, rather than as offering justifications.

What eudaimonism may not do, then, is provide a quick and easy answer to the question, why be moral (or, even, why embrace eudaimonism?)? It has an answer—because doing so allows one to flourish—but, as we have seen, there are ways for the skeptic to challenge this answer. In a certain sense, though, it is misleading to see eudaimonism in these terms, as a theory of well-being seeking to be a normative theory. Eudaimonism rather is best seen as an effort to describe a life well lived, one that makes use of one's skills and capacities, and as a result that allows individuals to obtain a distinctive kind of well-being. It presents a theory of well-being that does not collapse into other, perhaps more familiar forms of well-being that are subjective, and is instead meant to capture a unique form of life, available only to humans. It should thus perhaps be seen not as just another competitor for the "right way" of thinking about well-being, but as offering a way of living that can be compatible with other, subjective forms of well-being.

Notes

1 See also Russell (2012: Chapter 3).
2 Fletcher (Chapter 12, this volume) describes this in terms of attitude-independence.
3 Woodard (Chapter 13, this volume) explores the plausibility of hybrid theories.
4 I discuss this issue at length in Besser-Jones (2014: Chapter 7).
5 Doris (2009) takes this line of argument even further, arguing that when human beings are defined by appeal to their rational capacities, we will be forced to be skeptical about the very existence of persons.

6 To avoid confusion, I will use "eudaimonia" to refer to the philosophical conception of *eudaimonia* and "eudaimonic well-being" to refer to the psychological conception.

7 My specific focus here will be on the account of innate psychological needs offered within self-determination theory (Ryan and Deci 2000a). There are other ways of carving out and describing the needs in question (e.g., Ryff 1989; Ryff and Singer 2008).

8 See Besser-Jones (2014: Chapter 2) for a detailed overview of these benefits.

9 In Besser-Jones (2014), I argue that acting well and developing virtue are also important means for satisfying the needs for autonomy and competence, albeit, in the case of competence, not the only means.

10 See also Kagan's discussion of the internal/external distinction with respect to well-being (Kagan 1992: 187–189).

11 For an alternative line of response to this challenge, as it is directed against an Aristotelian-inspired conception of *eudaimonia* that highlights the use of practical reason, see Foot (2003: Chapter 4).

References

Annas, J. (2011). *Intelligent Virtue*. New York: Oxford University Press.

Aristotle. (1962). *Nicomachean Ethics* (M. Oswald, Ed.). New York: MacMillan Publishing Company.

Bargh, J.A. and Chartrand, T.L. (1999). The unbearable automaticity of being. *American Psychologist*, 54(7), 462–479.

Besser-Jones, L. (2014). *Eudaimonic Ethics: The Philosophy and Psychology of Living Well*. New York: Routledge Press.

Deci, E.L. and Ryan, R.M. (2000). The "what" and "why" of goal pursuits: human needs and the self-determination of behavior. *Psychological Inquiry*, 11(4), 227–268.

Doris, J.M. (2002). *Lack of Character: Personality and Moral Behavior*. New York: Cambridge University Press.

Doris, J.M. (2009). Skepticism about persons. *Philosophical Issues*, 19(1), 57–91.

Fendrich, J.M. (1967). A study of the association among verbal attitudes, commitment and overt behavior in different experimental situations. *Social Forces*, 45(3), 347–355.

Foot, P. (2003). *Natural Goodness*. New York: Oxford University Press.

Haidt, J. (2001). The emotional dog and its rational tail. *Psychological Review*, 108(4), 814–834.

Haybron, D.M. (2007). Well-being and virtue. *Journal of Ethics and Social Philosophy*, 2(2), 1–26.

Haybron, D.M. (2008). *The Pursuit of Unhappiness*. New York: Oxford University Press.

Hursthouse, R. (1999). *On Virtue Ethics*. New York: Oxford University Press.

Kagan, S. (1992). The limits of well-being. In E. Paul, F. Miller and J. Paul (Eds.), *The Good Life and the Human Good* (pp. 169–189). New York: Cambridge University Press.

Knobe, J. and Leiter, B. (2007). The case for Nietzschean moral psychology. In B. Leiter and N. Sinhababu (Eds.), *Nietzsche and Morality* (pp. 83–109). New York: Oxford University Press.

LeBar, M. (2013). *The Value of Living Well*. Oxford: Oxford University Press.

Nozick, R. (1974). *Anarchy, State, and Utopia*. New York: Basic Books.

Russell, D.C. (2012). *Happiness for Humans*. Oxford: Oxford University Press.

Ryan, R.M. and Deci, E.L. (2000a). The darker and brighter sides of human existence: Basic psychological needs as a unifying concept. *Psychological Inquiry*, 11(4), 319–338.

Ryan, R.M. and Deci, E.L. (2000b). Self-determination theory and the facilitation of intrinsic motivation, social development, and well-being. *American Psychologist*, 55(1), 68–78.

Ryan, R.M., Huta, V. and Deci, E.L. (2006). Living well: a self-determination theory perspective on eudaimonia. *Journal of Happiness Studies*, 9(1), 139–170.

Ryff, C.D. (1989). Happiness is everything, or is it? Explorations on the meaning of psychological well-being. *Journal of Personality and Social Psychology*, 57(6), 1069–1081.

Ryff, C.D. and Singer, B.H. (2008). Know thyself and become what you are: a eudaimonic approach to psychological well-being. *Journal of Happiness Studies*, 9, 13–39.

Sumner, L.W. (1996). *Welfare, Happiness, and Ethics*. New York: Clarendon Press.

Tiberius, V. and Hall, A. (2010). Normative theory and psychological research: Hedonism, eudaimonism, and why it matters. *The Journal of Positive Psychology*, 5(3), 212–225.

Tiberius, V. and Plakias, A. (2010). Well-being. In J. Doris (Ed.), *The Moral Psychology Handbook*. New York: Oxford University Press.

PART III

Particular goods and bads

16

THE ROLE OF PLEASURE IN WELL-BEING

Ben Bramble

Introduction

What is the role of pleasure in determining a person's *lifetime well-being* (i.e., how good his life was for him *considered as a whole*)? I will start by considering the nature of pleasure (i.e., what pleasure is). I will then consider what factors, if any, can affect how much a given pleasure adds to a person's lifetime well-being other than its *degree* of pleasurableness (i.e., how pleasurable it is). Finally, I will consider whether it is plausible that there is any *other* way to add to somebody's lifetime well-being than by giving him some pleasure or helping him to avoid some pain.

The nature of pleasure

Some philosophers distinguish between what they call *sensory* and *attitudinal* pleasure. Fred Feldman, for example, writes:

> Sensory pleasure is a feeling or sensation. You have it when you are experiencing "pleasurable sensations." Attitudinal pleasure is (as the name suggests) a propositional attitude. You have it when you are enjoying, or taking pleasure in, or delighting in, something.
>
> *(Feldman 2004: 2)*

But it sounds odd to me to call a state of being pleased about something a pleasure. Such a state may *result* in pleasure, or be *accompanied* by pleasure, but it does not seem itself to be a pleasure. In any case, in this chapter, I will be considering the role only of what Feldman calls sensory pleasures, pleasures having some phenomenology or feel.

There are two main approaches to the nature of pleasure: *felt-quality theories* and *attitude-based theories*. Felt-quality theories say that what makes a feeling or experience count as a pleasure is just its *phenomenology* (i.e., "what it is like" to be having it, or how it *feels*). Attitude-based theories, by contrast, say that it is someone's having a certain kind of *pro-attitude* (say, one of liking or wanting) toward a bit of phenomenology that makes it count as a pleasure.

The classic felt-quality theory is the *distinctive feeling theory*, on which there is such a thing as "the feeling of pleasure itself," and a bit of phenomenology gets to count as a pleasure just in virtue of having some of this feeling suitably mixed in with it, or else by itself being an instance of this very feeling (Moore 1903; Bramble 2013). But there are other felt-quality theories. According to one, what we might call the *many distinctive feelings theory*, there isn't just one feeling of pleasure, but many such feelings, and it suffices for a bit of phenomenology to count as a pleasure that it have any one of these feelings mixed in with it. It is also open to felt-quality theorists to deny that there is any such thing as the feeling (or feelings) of pleasure itself (or themselves). Some have suggested, for example, that all pleasures are related to each other in the same way that all colored experiences are related to each other. While there is nothing bluish about red, and nothing reddish about blue, there is something that all visual experiences have in common phenomenologically that no non-visual experience (say, an auditory experience) possesses—namely, they are colored (Crisp 2006). Others have suggested that pleasurableness is a single "dimension" along which experiences can vary, like volume when it comes to auditory experiences. What is it for an experience to be pleasurable? It is the same sort of thing as it is for an auditory experience to have a volume (Kagan 1992).

Let us turn now to attitude-based theories. In the classic version of such a theory, it is one's wanting an experience *to continue* that makes it count as a pleasure (Brandt 1979: 38). But there are compelling counterexamples to this theory. As David Perry says,

> I might, on passing a garden by chance, enjoy the scent of flowers without sniffing, lingering, returning, or trying to do these things or having the least inclination to do these things.
>
> *(Perry 1967: 204–205)*

A better attitude-based theory says that experiences are made pleasurable by their subjects wanting, at the time of experience, that they *be occurring*. But this still won't do, for there are many reasons one might want a given experience to be occurring that have no tendency to make it count as a pleasure—for example, that it is interesting.

The most plausible attitude-based theory is Chris Heathwood's, on which a pleasure is an experience whose subject has an *intrinsic* desire at the time of experience that *this particular experience* be occurring (Heathwood 2007).

Let us now consider which of these approaches is best. Here are some problems with attitude-based theories:

No "base" feeling

Attitude-based theories entail that there is always some affectively neutral (i.e., neither pleasurable nor unpleasurable) bit of phenomenology that forms the "base" of every pleasure—i.e., a bit of phenomenology that we take up our pro-attitude to in the first place. But this seems false. Consider, for example, a pleasurable experience of euphoria, or one of "just plain feeling good," or the pleasures of orgasm, and so on. What is the affectively neutral base in these pleasurable experiences supposed to be? What part of their phenomenology could be had without its being a pleasure? I find it hard to imagine. These pleasures seem to be just pure pleasurableness.

The wrong order of explanation

Attitude-based theories seem to get the order of explanation the wrong way around. Intuitively, when one is having an orgasm, it is not the fact that one is liking or wanting what one is feeling that makes it pleasurable. Rather, one likes or wants it *because* it is pleasurable.

Reflective blindness

It seems that one can have pleasures one is entirely unaware of. Consider, for example, certain olfactory pleasures. A patient of Oliver Sacks' writes:

> Sense of smell? I never gave it a thought. You don't normally give it a thought. But when I lost it—it was like being struck blind. Life lost a good deal of its savour—one doesn't realise how much 'savour' is smell. You smell people, you smell books, you smell the city, you smell the spring—maybe not consciously, but as a rich unconscious background to everything else. My whole world was suddenly radically poorer.
>
> *(Rachels 2004: 225)*

If this is right, then it presents a major problem for attitude-based theories (or at least for an attitude-based theory like Heathwood's). This is because one must surely be aware of the *existence* of a particular feeling in order to want *this very feeling* to be occurring.

It may be objected that the relevant sort of awareness, not to mention one's intrinsic desire that the experience in question be occurring, might take place *unconsciously*. While Sacks's patient, for example, was not consciously aware of his olfactory pleasures, he was aware of them *at some level*.

But if we go down this path, we will have to attribute far more than is plausible to the unconscious mind, for it is not just olfactory pleasures that can fly beneath our cognitive radar. At any given time, there are likely hundreds or even thousands of respects in which our experiences are subtly pleasurable. We are getting pleasures from the visual perception of colors, light, depth, the size of things, the shape of things, symmetries and asymmetries in our environment, and so on and so forth. We are getting pleasures also from sounds—the tone of a loved one's voice, the rattle of the trolley car, the rustle of leaves in a nearby tree, the background chatter of people in the bar, the ceasing of the hum of the air conditioner, and so on. Then there are pleasures of having a healthy body in all sorts of ways—of feeling invigorated without realizing it, or having a clear head. There are pleasures of feeling a light breeze on one's cheek, or a patch of warmth from the sun on one's arm as the clouds briefly separate. There are pleasures associated with our unconscious beliefs about the good health of our loved ones, or our continuing success toward our goals, or the coming end to the semester. There are, in addition, many unconscious unpleasurable experiences—subtle aches and pains, vague annoyances, background anxieties, anger or melancholy arising from memories of childhood trauma long repressed or even from the awareness that we are all going to die someday.

At any given time, all these pleasures and pains (and more!) may be going on in one unconsciously. Is it really plausible that unconsciously we have a crystal-clear understanding of all these various feelings we are having—that every one of them is known to us in all its detail or complexity—and that we are holding court unconsciously on the lot of them, simultaneously rendering hundreds of individual judgments concerning whether we want these to be occurring? This just seems like a fantasy. It is highly implausible that we understand the jumble of ways we are feeling at any given time well enough on *any* level to have the sort of fine-grained awareness of it all that is necessary on a theory like Heathwood's to allow us the sort of attitudes that ground pleasurableness.

It may be suggested that an attitude-based theorist could hold an *idealized* attitude-based view, on which the pleasurableness of one's current experiences is determined not by whether one actually wants them to be occurring, but by whether one *would* want them to be occurring *if one were fully aware of them*.

But there are famous problems for accounts that idealize (Sobel 1994). For example, we may wonder whether it is possible for someone to be simultaneously aware of all his currently occurring pleasurable feelings—awareness of some may make impossible awareness of others. Perhaps the idea should be instead that we adjudicate the pleasures individually, one after the other. But even then it seems likely that there are some pleasures whose qualitative character *depends on one's not being clearly or consciously aware of them*—most obviously, the pleasures of *flow* (say, of being immersed in playing tennis, reading a good book, or having sex).

No such desires

It is doubtful whether anyone ever has any intrinsic desires for experiences of theirs to be occurring, even experiences they are fully aware of. There seems some plausibility to the thought that we have desires concerning how our life is going at the present moment (including how we are currently feeling) *only* because we conceive of our life as an extended whole, and are aware that how our life is going right now can make a very big difference (both causally and constitutively) to which whole life is likely to end up being ours. Even my desire to be feeling good right now may depend on my thinking that I am likely to have a certain kind of future, or a future at all. If I came to believe that the present moment was to be my last on this planet, I might easily cease to care what I am feeling during it.

Consider, now, some objections to felt-quality theories.

The heterogeneity worry

Perhaps the most common objection to felt-quality theories—one considered decisive by many—is that they entail that all pleasurable experiences feel alike in some way, but all pleasurable experiences do *not* all feel alike in any way. Feldman, for example, writes:

> Consider the warm, dry, slightly drowsy feeling of pleasure that you get while sunbathing on a quiet beach. By way of contrast, consider the cool, wet, invigorating feeling of pleasure that you get when drinking some cold, refreshing beer on a hot day . . . They do not feel at all alike. After years of careful research on this question, I have come to the conclusion that they have just about nothing in common phenomenologically.
>
> *(Feldman 2004: 79)*

But as many philosophers have recently argued, we can be deeply mistaken about the nature of our own occurrent phenomenology, even after careful reflection. In a series of excellent papers, Eric Schwitzgebel, for example, argues that

> we make gross, enduring mistakes about even the most basic features of our currently ongoing conscious experience (or "phenomenology"), even in favorable circumstances of careful reflection, with distressing regularity . . . The introspection of current conscious experience, far from being secure, nearly infallible, is faulty, untrustworthy, and misleading—not just possibly mistaken, but massively and pervasively.
>
> *(Schwitzgebel 2008: 250)*

If these philosophers are right, it would be naive to assert with any great confidence that there is no feeling of pleasure itself, let alone that all pleasures do not feel alike in *some* way.

Indeed, if there were a feeling of pleasure itself common to all pleasurable experiences, presumably it would not come tacked on to these experiences in any crude sort of way, but rather permeate them. Most instances of it would be, taken by themselves, virtually imperceptible. They would occur in extremely small quantities (or low intensities) and in very abstract or ethereal locations in one's experiential field, locations that are not at all easy to direct one's attention toward or focus upon. What would a pleasurable experience of sunbathing have in common phenomenologically with one of drinking a cool beer on a hot day? Just that it had a whole lot of these tiny, independently virtually imperceptible, feelings scattered throughout it. When you add to this the fact that these feelings may be distributed in quite different patterns, both at a time, and over time, it may be no wonder that Feldman cannot easily identify a felt likeness between these two pleasurable experiences. Indeed, this is roughly what we should expect if the distinctive feeling theory were true (Bramble 2013).

The motivation worry

Some have wondered how, if a felt-quality theory were true, we could explain our reliable attraction to pleasure. J.N. Findlay, for example, writes:

> Were pleasure and unpleasure peculiar qualities of experience, as loud and sweet are peculiar qualities of what comes before us in sense-experience, it would be a gross, empirical accident that we uniformly sought the one and avoided the other, as it is a gross, empirical accident in the case of the loud or the sweet, and this of all suppositions the most incredible and absurd. Plainly it is in some sense trivially necessary that we should want pleasure (or not want unpleasure).
>
> *(Findlay 1961: 177)*

Such critics of felt-quality theories seem to think that if desire were *involved* in pleasure, then we could easily account for our reliable attraction to it.

But there are two problems with this objection to felt-quality theories. First, it is not clear that the best attitude-based theories are better positioned than felt-quality theories to explain our reliable attraction to pleasure. Just as we might wonder why beings are disposed to seek out a particular kind or feature of phenomenology, we might wonder why beings are disposed to seek out experiences that they now believe they would *later* want to be having (or, alternatively, the later state of their having an experience that they would then want to be having). More needs to be said here by these attitude theorists.

Second, felt-quality theorists *can* explain our reliable attraction to pleasures. We are attracted to the relevant phenomenology, they can say, because we see that it is *good* (or, alternatively, good *for* us), and we are attracted to what we think good (or good for us). Irwin Goldstein, for example, writes:

> In the case of pleasure and pain it is the apprehension, or recognition, that pleasure is worth having and pain worth avoiding that leads to the seeking behaviour characteristic of pleasure and the avoidance behaviour characteristic of pain and unpleasantness . . . It strikes one immediately as absurd to say that our preference of pleasure to pain is an arbitrary one; the absurdity lies in the obvious fact that pain does not merit our desire and approval in the way that pleasure does.
>
> *(Goldstein 1980: 354)*

It is a conceptual truth, we might say, that creatures are attracted to, among other things, what they think good (or good for themselves). This seems eminently plausible.

It may be objected that we cannot explain the reliable attraction to pleasure of *babies* and *non-human animals* by appeal to their having an awareness that pleasure is good. Such creatures, after all, do not have evaluative beliefs.

However, it is plausible that we acquire evaluative concepts in the first place *by coming into contact with good and bad things*. If this is so, then it is tempting to think that we acquire these concepts by coming into contact specifically with *pleasure and pain*—after all, these are the things that are *most obviously* good and bad. If this, in turn, is true, then we might ask what reason there could possibly be for thinking that this concept acquisition must happen later, rather than earlier, on in our development. We cannot say "our appreciation of the goodness of pleasure and the badness of pain must wait until we have developed evaluative concepts" if we develop these concepts only by coming into contact with pleasure and its goodness or pain and its badness.

A different objection is that if some felt-quality theory were true, then the relevant kinds or features of phenomenology would not *be* good (or good for us)—divorced from our attitudes, they would be in the same normative boat as all other kinds or features of phenomenology, like, for example, blue visual experiences, the sound of tinkling bells, or the smell of sulfur—and so it could not be our perceiving their goodness that explained our attraction to them. David Sobel, for example, finds it implausible that

> certain flavors of sensation are intrinsically more worthy of pursuit than others independently of one's reaction to those flavors . . . [Anyone] who has the . . . capacities [to feel such sensations], on such a view, would presumably have a reason to experience that flavor of sensation regardless of their response to that flavor. This move is analogous to the thought that everyone has more reason to taste chocolate rather than strawberry ice cream as the former is intrinsically more valuable flavor. This is something most of us say only when joking . . . Most likely pleasure seemed a uniquely plausible recommendation partially because the vast majority of actual people like it. But of course, in other possible worlds, most people do not like that sensation. What could then be said on behalf of the sensation of pleasure?
>
> *(Sobel 2005: 446)*

Sobel's criticism is a version of the so-called "resonance worry" more commonly leveled at *objective list* theories of well-being (on which certain things outside of one's own experiences—for example, friendship, achievement, or nature fulfillment—can be intrinsically good for one whether one likes or wants them or not). The worry is that whatever is intrinsically good for someone must be liked, wanted, or approved of by him in some way (if not actually, then at least if he were suitably idealized)—otherwise, he is objectionably alienated from his own good (Railton 2003: 47). But why accept this idea? It is, of course, true that in general we do not benefit people by giving them things they do not (and would not) like or want. But a natural explanation for this is just that in such cases—cases where someone doesn't like, want, or approve of something (even after having full experience of it)—the odds are high that his getting it would fail to give him any *pleasure*. This is why, presumably, we do not benefit Freddy by giving him violin lessons when he wants only to learn the drums, or benefit Mary by organizing a surprise birthday party for her when she loathes social occasions, or benefit Tom by handing him a chocolate ice cream when he likes only strawberry. If this is the correct explanation, then there seems no reason that a requirement of resonance should apply to pleasurable phenomenology *itself*.

When I think of the most pleasurable experiences I have ever had—experiences of time spent with my lover, of gatherings with family and friends, of listening to *Dark Side of the Moon*, of reading Tolstoy and Eliot, of hiking through the Grand Canyon at dusk, of intellectual and social adventures during my college years, of understanding philosophical problems and thinking about possible solutions to them—these seem so tremendously good for me, I seem so lucky to have had them, not because they provided me with an opportunity to like more stuff, but because of *what they were like*. It's not *all this liking* that I've been so lucky to have, but all this phenomenology itself. Think of your own set of most pleasurable experiences. What are you fond of in recollecting them? Their phenomenology in all its richness, or the fact of your having liked it?

Imagine a being who is constitutionally unable to have experiences of friendship, love, learning, art, etc., but has many blue experiences, the phenomenology of which he likes as much (if you can imagine that) as we like the former sort of experiences. Does this being seem to be made as well off by his many blue experiences? Or does he seem rather deeply unfortunate by comparison with us? Wouldn't he be better off if he were able to have experiences of friendship, love, learning, art, etc., and enjoy *these*?

Return again to the pleasures of orgasm. Just as it does not seem that the feelings involved in these are pleasurable because I like or want them—their pleasurableness, rather, comes prepackaged in them—it does not seem that their *value* for me is dependent on my reactions to them. Their value seems also pre-packaged in the relevant phenomenology. I do not feel lucky to have this phenomenology because I like it. I feel lucky to have it because it is good for me, because it is the sort of phenomenology that enhances lives, and that ought to be liked, wanted, and sought by any beings who are capable of having it.

It is useful also to think about things from the other side. When I wish I could enjoy, say, the taste of cucumber or asparagus, or the music of a particular well-known artist that a lot of my friends like, because I think this would be good for me, that there is value for me in these pleasures, what I want is not simply to have attitudes of liking toward the same phenomenology that these things give me *now*—rather, I want to have *different phenomenology*. I want to have the phenomenology that my friends are getting. I seem to be missing out on the phenomenology that these things provide that is valuable.

Does only degree of pleasurableness count?

Suppose all this is right, and our attitudes make neither our experiences pleasurable, nor our pleasures good for us. Pleasures are just experiences involving a certain kind or feature of phenomenology, and these experiences can be good for us whether we like or want them or not.

Consider, now, a different question: What determines how much a given pleasure adds to a person's lifetime well-being? Is it just its *degree* of pleasurableness (i.e., how pleasurable it is)? Or are other factors at play?

Many philosophers have felt that certain kinds of pleasures—for example, those of friendship, love, learning, and aesthetic appreciation—add more to a person's lifetime well-being than equally pleasurable pleasures of various other kinds—say, pleasures of sex, drugs, or lazing around. Is this idea coherent? Is it plausible?

Feldman suggests that how much a given pleasure adds to a person's well-being depends on whether the object of one's pleasure *deserves* to have pleasure taken in it. Friendship, love, knowledge, and beauty, for example, may all be very worthy of having pleasure taken in them, while bodily sensations may be much less worthy of this (Feldman 2004).

But this assumes that pleasures are propositional attitudes. As I've claimed above, it seems wrong to call a state of being pleased that something is the case a pleasure. Instead, Feldman's view is better thought of as a kind of attitude-based theory of well-being on which how much a given instance of desire satisfaction adds to well-being is affected by the value of the thing desired. This is similar to various *hybrid* theories of well-being, on which well-being arises just where (i) we are subjectively attracted to things that are objectively attractive, and (ii) we can include some of these things in our lives (Raz 1986; Kraut 1994; Adams 1999; Kagan 2009).

There is, however, a view like Feldman's that is available to a hedonist. This is to say that pleasures are just desired *experiences*, but that how much they contribute to lifetime well-being is determined by the objective value of these experiences. On this view, some *experiences* are more worthy of being intrinsically wanted than others. But not only does this view rely on an attitude-based theory of pleasure, it is hard to imagine how affectively neutral experiences might be more or less worthy of being intrinsically wanted.

A different possibility is that pleasurable phenomenology is worth more toward lifetime well-being when it is *caused* by objectively valuable things than when it isn't. It may be the case, for instance, that my experience of listening to *Abbey Road* is as pleasurable as your experience of listening to Beyoncé's album *Beyoncé*, but that the former experience adds more to my lifetime well-being than the latter adds to yours because *Abbey Road* is a more valuable work. But while this view exists in logical space, it is hard to see its attraction.

A final possibility is that certain kinds of pleasurable phenomenology simply add more to lifetime well-being than other equally pleasurable kinds of phenomenology. But while this is a coherent view, in the absence of an explanation of what it is about the phenomenology of the former that is so special, and why it adds more, it is pretty unsatisfying.

There are other reasons to think that how much a given pleasure adds to lifetime well-being is not determined exclusively by how pleasurable it is. For example, it is tempting to think that adding more of a certain kind of pleasure to one's life that one has had many times before adds little or nothing to one's lifetime well-being (even if this pleasure remains equally pleasurable). Consider, for example, the pleasures of enjoying the same silly sitcom over and over again—one may giggle or guffaw as enthusiastically each time one rewatches an episode, but it seems like just a waste of time for one. Or consider Roger Crisp's *oyster*, whose life consists "only of mild sensual pleasure, rather like that experienced by humans when floating very drunk in a warm bath" (Crisp 2006: 630). Adding extra years of more of this same pleasure to the oyster's life seems not to add anything to its lifetime well-being.

Perhaps the explanation for these things is just the obvious one: *purely repeated pleasures*—i.e., pleasures containing nothing qualitatively new in terms of pleasurableness—make little or no intrinsic contribution to a person's lifetime well-being. It may be only pleasures that introduce something qualitatively new in terms of pleasurableness into a person's life that can add anything in and of themselves to his lifetime well-being.

If this is true, it may also help us to explain why the pleasures of friendship, love, learning, aesthetic appreciation, etc., seem to have a good deal more to offer one than bodily pleasures. The former, it seems plausible to think, involve far greater qualitative diversity. What it is like to come to know or love one human being is not just the same as what it is like to come to know or love another. Each person is unique, which makes the pleasures associated with friendships and relationships qualitatively unique for the people involved. Similarly, the pleasures of learning do not consist of just the same kind of pleasure (say, a warm glow or "zing!") over and over again every time one learns a new fact. On the contrary, these pleasures have quite a different phenomenal character depending on what one has learned, the particular way in which one's mind has been opened up, and how one's new knowledge or understanding fits with what one already knows. Likewise, most great works of art, music, and literature offer unique kinds of pleasures. Great novels and films typically transport one to places that no other work does, or involve characters that are so realistic that they are, like real people, unique, or offer insights or explore ideas in ways that no other work does. By contrast, most meals one consumes or beers one drinks, most silly sitcoms one watches, most encounters with different sexual partners are just different *means* to what are qualitatively the same pleasures.

Are there other ways of benefiting?

Some philosophers, *hedonists*, believe that the *only* way of adding to somebody's lifetime well-being is to give him some pleasure, or prevent him from feeling some pain. But most philosophers are not hedonists—they think that there are other ways of benefiting. For example, many believe that the satisfaction of desires concerning aspects of one's own life lying outside of one's experiences (say, that one's projects get completed, that one's children grow up happy, that one's friends and loved ones really do love one in return and are not just acting) can also intrinsically benefit one. Others think that having friendships, achieving things, and being in contact with reality can be good for one even if they are neither wanted by one nor pleasurable for one.

There is a powerful reason, however, to accept the hedonist's view. This is what has come to be known as *the experience requirement*. The experience requirement says that for something to be good or bad *for* someone it must affect his experiences in some way—specifically, it must affect their phenomenology or "what it is like" for him to be having them. If the experience requirement is true, then hedonism is almost certainly true as well—indeed, it would be the reason why the experience requirement is true. There is little plausibility, after all, to the idea that any *non*-hedonic phenomenology (i.e., phenomenology that is neither pleasurable nor painful) is intrinsically relevant to well-being.

But why believe the experience requirement? Hedonists who appeal to it often have nothing or little to say in its defense. However, I want to offer two brief arguments for it. First, it is tempting to think that once a person is dead (i.e., will have no more experiences), his lifetime well-being is settled once and for all—nothing further that happens in this world can be good or bad for him. Now, if something (say, desire satisfaction or achievement) could be good or bad for a person *without* affecting his experiences, then there seems no reason why it shouldn't be able to do so even *after* he is dead. The experience requirement, in other words, is the best explanation of why there can be no posthumous benefits or harms.

The second reason to believe the experience requirement has to do with what a life *is*. It is this:

1. Death is the permanent cessation of a person's experiences.

Therefore,

2. A person's life is the set of all his experiences.

3. Something can be good or bad for a person only if it affects his life in some way.

Therefore,

4. Something can be good or bad for a person only if it affects his experiences in some way.

(1) and (3) are relatively uncontroversial. (2) is the controversial premise. But (2) seems to follow straightforwardly from (1).

These are strong grounds, I believe, for accepting the experience requirement.

Conclusion

In this paper, I have examined the role of pleasure in determining lifetime well-being. In the section on the nature of pleasure, I suggested that we should accept a felt-quality theory of pleasure, rather than an attitude-based one. In the section, "Does only degree of pleasurableness count?," I suggested that it is not only a pleasure's degree of pleasurableness that determines its contribution to lifetime well-being: other factors are relevant as well. Finally, I provided some reasons to think that it is only by adding pleasures to a life (or preventing pains) that one can add to a person's lifetime well-being.

References

Adams, R.M. (1999) *Finite and Infinite Goods. A Framework for Ethics*. New York: Oxford University Press.

Bramble, B. (2013) "The Distinctive Feeling Theory of Pleasure," *Philosophical Studies* 162(2), 201–217.

Brandt, R. (1979) *A Theory of the Good and the Right*. Oxford: Clarendon Press.

Crisp, R. (2006) "Hedonism Reconsidered," *Philosophy and Phenomenological Research*, 73(3), 619–645.

Feldman, F. (2004) *Pleasure and the Good Life*. New York: Oxford University Press.

Findlay, J.N. (1961) *Values and Intentions*. London: Allen & Unwin.

Goldstein, I. (1980) "Why People Prefer Pleasure to Pain," *Philosophy*, 55(213), 349–362.

Heathwood, C. (2007) "The Reduction of Sensory Pleasure to Desire," *Philosophical Studies*, 133(1), 23–44.

Kagan, S. (1992) "The Limits of Wellbeing," in E.F. Paul, F.D. Miller and J. Paul (Eds.), *The Good Life and the Human Good*. Cambridge, UK: Cambridge University Press.

Kagan, S. (2009) "Well-Being as Enjoying the Good," *Philosophical Perspectives* 23(1), 253–272.

Kraut, R. (1994) "Desire and the Human Good," *Proceedings and Addresses of the American Philosophical Association* 68(2), 39–54.

Moore, G.E. (1903) *Principia Ethica*. Cambridge: Cambridge University Press.

Perry, D.L. (1967) *The Concept of Pleasure*. The Hague: Mouton.

Rachels, S. (2004) "Six Theses About Pleasure," *Philosophical Perspectives*, 18(1), 247–267.

Railton, P. (2003) "Facts and Values," in *Facts, Values, and Norms*. Cambridge: Cambridge University Press.

Raz, J. (1986) *The Morality of Freedom*. Oxford: Clarendon Press.

Schwitzgebel, E. (2008) "The Unreliability of Naive Introspection," *Philosophical Review*, 117(2), 245–273.

Sobel, D. (1994) "Full Information Accounts of Well-being," *Ethics*, 104(4), 784–810.

Sobel, D. (2005) "Pain For Objectivists: The Case of Matters of Mere Taste," *Ethical Theory and Moral Practice*, 8(4), 437–457.

17

PAIN, EXPERIENCE, AND WELL-BEING

Guy Kahane

Introduction

We have all felt pain. We enter this world screaming, and we hope to leave it painlessly. In between, our lives are punctuated by moments of pain, often brief and negligible, a mere distraction, but at other times mind-blowingly intense and debilitating, stretching for hours, days, even months and years. Then there are unpleasant experiences such as nausea, an upset stomach, a numb foot or itching scalp, and other kinds of bodily discomfort. Not to mention heartache, bitter disappointment, loss, despair, depression, hopelessness . . .

All lives contain suffering of this kind. This is not a matter of indifference. It barely matters, if it matters at all, how many green afterimages you have experienced in your life. But it matters a great deal how much pain you have had to endure. Pain is bad, and moreover, not bad in some purely impersonal way, as something that just makes the world itself worse, but bad in virtue of being bad *for* the person who has to suffer it. It makes the person's life worse, a little bit worse if the pain is weak and brief, a lot worse if it's awful and long. Long periods of intense pain can really blight a life. And when the pain is intense and unremitting, utterly pervading the end of a life or even an entire life, some would say that the pain makes the life not just bad but not worth living. It reduces well-being to such an extent, it is thought, that even non-existence is better than existence.

It is important to distinguish pain's intrinsic badness—the way it makes a life worse by its very occurrence—from other harms that are often associated with pain, or caused by it. For example, physical pain is normally caused by bodily damage or dysfunction, states which are themselves often harmful. But, considered in itself, pain is just as bad when it is no longer associated with bodily damage—think of pain in a phantom limb, or pain caused by direct brain stimulation.[1]

Strong, continuous pain can also cause further harms: the way it captures our attention can make it hard to think about anything else, and can therefore prevent us from pursuing our goals and projects. And pain can generate such an overwhelming desire to get rid of it that it often disturbs or even distorts our rationality, making us do what we judge to be deeply irrational or wrong—think of how a torturer can make his victim betray those dearest to him.

These effects of intense pain add to its badness: they add further instrumental badness on top of its intrinsic badness. But again they should not be confused with pain's intrinsic badness. We can easily imagine a conscious state that is not aversive at all yet which completely captures our attention and disturbs rational choice. Such a state would have the same bad effects as intense pain yet not be in any way bad in itself. Conversely, someone who is just waiting to die, and no longer has any projects or goals to pursue (except, that is, that of dying with as little pain as possible) may still suffer greatly, and that suffering would be, considered in itself, just as bad for her.

Pain, then, is intrinsically bad for the person who endures it. It gives that person self-interested reasons to try to avoid, prevent, minimize, and end that pain. And it gives others moral reasons to try to alleviate that person's pain, or otherwise feel compassion for her—not to mention stringent moral reasons not to cause others unnecessary suffering

That pain is bad and reduces our well-being is one of the few substantive ethical claims that command near-universal consensus, that is accepted by nearly everyone. As we shall see below, even when pain is presented in a positive light, as something we should approve of or even welcome, at least in some contexts, closer inspection reveals that such claims are best interpreted as perfectly compatible with seeing pain as intrinsically bad.

Whether pain is bad is not the focus of much debate—though I shall touch on this question at the very end. The key philosophical disagreements about pain and its role in well-being lie elsewhere. These debates are not over whether pain *is* bad, but about what *makes* it so, as well as whether it is *always* bad, or even the *only* thing that is bad. But before we can identify what makes pain bad, we need to be clear about what pain is exactly—a surprisingly difficult question.

What is pain? What makes it bad?

To answer this question, you might think we just need to look inside. And when we do so, the answer seems straightforward. Pain is surely a distinctive kind of bodily sensation, a sensation typically caused by bodily damage or dysfunction, and which typically causes certain kinds of behavior, such grimacing or crying out, or a scramble to find a painkiller in the medicine cabi-net, and so forth—behavior that is motivated by our strong desire to get rid of this sensation. But pain itself is neither bodily dysfunction nor a form of motivation or behavior.

On this natural view, pain is a bodily sensation, and what makes it bad isn't that it is associ-ated with bodily dysfunction, dominates attention, or motivates certain forms of behavior. What makes it bad is that it *feels* a certain way—that it feels *bad*. When you stab your finger, this is painful not because of the damage to tissue in your finger, but because of what that feels like. And you want that pain to stop, and take steps to end it, *because* it feels bad in this way. The motivation and behavior aren't just caused by the sensation, but rationalized by it: the way pain feels like gives you reasons to want it to stop, and to take available means to stop it.

Call this the *sensation theory* of pain. This simple view of pain and of what makes it bad has certainly dominated for a long time, and it is also, I suspect, the commonsensical view. Yet for significant stretches of the twentieth century it was widely rejected, even seen as obviously false.[2] In fact, the sensation theory *is* false, strictly speaking. But as we shall see, it is rather close to the truth—far closer than many philosophers have assumed, at least until fairly recently.

The reasons for the eclipse of the sensation theory are multiple. They relate, in part, to larger trends in mid twentieth-century philosophy. One trend was in the philosophy of mind: the rise of skepticism about subjective experience and inner conscious states, and a move towards broadly behaviorist views of the mind. On such views, pain was to be understood from the third person, as a pattern of characteristic behavioral responses to bodily dysfunction, or at least a disposition to such responses. No space was left for thinking that we respond in these ways *because* of some inner experience. But even when behaviorism declined, the accounts of the mind that replaced it often tended to reduce or otherwise discount subjective experience—for example, by understanding pain (and conscious states more generally) in functional terms, as an inner state defined in terms of its typical causal antecedents and consequences.

Naturalist suspicion about the qualitative aspects of experience had its parallel in the twentieth-century metaethical move away from realist or objectivist accounts of value. Value was to be understood in antirealist terms, as grounded in our positive and negative attitudes or desires. On such views, even if pain is a kind of bodily sensation, what makes it bad is not how it feels like, but the fact that we want it to stop. Pain is bad *because* we want it to stop; it's not that we want it to stop because it is bad.

A related trend in ethics was the domination of the desire-satisfaction account of well-being. In its simplest form, this view says that what makes a life go better or worse is the degree to which one's desires are satisfied or frustrated. This view also claims that pain is bad only because it is something we want to end or to avoid. It is again our attitudes that do the real work. How pain feels matters only because (and to the extent that) it is the object of such negative attitudes.[3]

Call this alternative view of pain the *desire theory*. The desire theory does not deny that pain is a bodily sensation, but on that view it does not matter much what pain is exactly, or what (if any) qualitative character it may have. What matters is that we want that state to stop (Brandt 1979; Brink 1997).[4] Such a view is obviously compatible with pretty much any account of pain (or conscious experience more generally), however reductive it may be. The real work is done by our desires, mental states that are not seen as presenting any particular problem for naturalism. Worries about consciousness or objective value can be side-stepped, or even domesticated. The desire theory has another advantage. The sensation theory tells us that pain is bad because of what it feels like. But why *that* is bad must be accepted as a brute fact or, some would say, a mystery. By contrast, the desire theory can easily explain pain's badness by subsuming it under a general account of value and (or) well-being. There is nothing special about pain or its qualitative character—any experience, or for that matter, any thing, would be bad if it were the object of our negative attitudes.[5]

But this advantage of the view is also is greatest weakness. When we look inside, it *does* seem to matter how pain feels like. Think of an awful migraine. Could you really be in the very same qualitative state yet not suffer at all, or even enjoy yourself immensely, simply because it is the object of some positive desire? And it seems equally wrong to think that the experience of an innocent afterimage could become a state of horrific badness just by adding a desire for it to stop or not occur, even if our conscious experience remained exactly the same (Kahane 2009).

Moreover, the three trends I have described had largely tailed off by the end of the last century: behaviorism is now a distant, eccentric episode, and many now accept strongly realist (and even dualist) accounts of qualitative conscious experience. Different forms of realism and objectivism about value are also now widely defended. And desire-satisfaction accounts of well-being have received much criticism, and are no longer as dominant. Conditions might seem ripe for a revival of the sensation theory. But this has not quite happened.[6] The sensation theory remains largely out of favor because of a more specific challenge that many find decisive. The challenge arises from some rather exotic cases from neuroscience. Patients who have undergone frontal lobotomy, or who suffer from a condition called pain asymbolia, report that they still feel the sensation of pain, but that they no longer mind it. We might say: their pain no longer hurts.[7]

To hold on to the sensation theory, we must claim that these patients are somehow confused, or fail to correctly report their own intimate experiences. This however seems implausible. While such a move would preserve the claim that pain's badness resides in the qualitative feel of a certain bodily sensation, it at the same time requires us to deny that this badness is introspectively accessible to these patients. It would force us to hold that such patients, walking around calmly smiling, might in fact be undergoing immense suffering unbeknownst to them. But this possibility doesn't seem to make sense.

These are intriguing cases. They reveal something about pain that would be extremely hard, perhaps impossible, to discover via ordinary introspection or philosophical reflection. No doubt, someone could have proposed such cases as a mere thought experiment. But, if such patients did not exist, would we really accept that these thought experiments describe a genuine possibility?

These cases, I believe, are indeed fatal to the sensation theory. And it might seem that they can be easily accommodated by the desire theory. What these patients have lost, you might think, is the desire for the bodily sensation to go away. And without that desire, pain no longer hurts: it is revealed to be something that, considered in itself, is neither good nor bad.

Some objectivists, such as Derek Parfit, respond to this result by making an important concession. The sensation of pain, they admit, is not bad in itself. We are in a state that is bad only when we dislike our pain, where dislike is understood to be a distinctive kind of negative motivational state. But on this view, it is not the sensation itself that becomes bad, when we dislike it. What is bad is the state of having the sensation and disliking it. It is *this* state that is intrinsically bad, and that we have reasons to try to avoid or alleviate. Call this the *dislike theory* (Parfit 1984).[8]

The dislike theory makes a concession to subjectivism, but it still aims to carve out an account of pain's badness that is not merely an application of subjectivism about value or a desire-satisfaction account of well-being. The dislike theory denies that things become bad for us simply because we have negative attitudes to them. It denies, for example, that if we had a negative attitude towards some sensation in an hour or minute from now, then this would make this sensation bad. It is only the distinctive attitude of disliking one's present sensation that generates badness. And, again, what is bad is not the sensation that we dislike in this way, but the composite state of disliking this sensation. That state, while containing a negative attitude of some sort, is nevertheless meant to be objectively bad. It is meant to be objectively bad in the sense that if we consider the prospect of being in a state of disliking pain at some future point, this would generate reasons for us to try to avoid being in that state, whether or not we now desire to do so.

The sensation theory had little to say to explain why pain is bad. The dislike theory does even worse on this count: it is forced to assert that when you bring together a bodily sensation and a certain motivational state, badness is somehow mysteriously generated. This is also an awkward position for an objectivist to take. Why should a motivational state play such a crucial role in such a central example of (supposedly objective) badness? Some wonder whether the dislike theory is really a stable, or even genuine, objectivist view at all (see Chang 2004; Sobel 2005).

I myself think, however, that the dislike theory is a move in the right direction. Its greatest problem, in my view, is that it endorses the most implausible feature of the desire theory: the implication that the badness of pain ultimately has nothing to do with what it feels like to be in pain, and that it is possible, at least in principle, to be in the very same experiential state we are in when we feel intense, horrific pain, yet for that state not to be bad at all.

This implication seem to me utterly implausible. But, counterintuitive as they may be, don't the puzzling reports of frontal lobotomy patients show them to be correct? No, they don't. What these reports do show is that the bodily sensation of pain is indeed not in itself bad. But it in no way follows from this that the badness of pain does not reside in how it qualitatively feels. That would only follow if the only states that had a qualitative phenomenal character were bodily sensations. But that is plainly false. Conscious thoughts, emotions and, indeed, occurrent desires all have a distinctive phenomenal character. What the frontal lobotomy cases suggest is that the distinctive phenomenal character that makes being in pain a bad state resides, not in the neutral bodily sensation of pain, but in the state that commonly accompanies it but which the exotic neuroscience cases show to be independent, the affective state of finding that sensation aversive (Kahane 2009).

That affective state does seem to have some intrinsic connection to motivation. This is another thing that the neuroscience cases show: that being in a state of intense physical suffering is incompatible either with being completely unaware that one is in that state, or with being completely unmoved by the fact that one is in such a state. Disliking a bodily sensation, finding it aversive, is an affective state that has both a phenomenal dimension and a motivational one. But that is perfectly compatible with retaining the highly intuitive idea that pain's badness resides in how it feels, and that we want pain to stop *because* of how it feels. The motivation pain generates is just an inevitable consequence of our intimate confrontation with the awfulness of its phenomenal character: we might say, of pain, that to know it is to hate it. Call this view the *felt aversion theory* (Kahane 2009).

I have just argued that it is a mistake to interpret the lobotomy cases as showing that pain's badness cannot reside in how it feels like to be in pain. So these cases do not support the desire theory (or otherwise the dislike theory), as is often assumed. But it is anyway odd to think that such cases support the desire theory. One thing that lobotomy cases suggest is that it makes no sense to think that someone could intensely suffer yet remain utterly indifferent. This is certainly in line with the desire theory. But another thing these cases suggest is that it makes no sense to think that someone could intensely suffer yet be completely unaware of that.[9] Yet it seems that the desire theory leaves space for this possibility. According to the desire theory, pain is bad only because we desire it not to occur. But while we normally know what we want, we do not have the kind of strong introspective access to our desires of the kind enjoyed by conscious states. We may sometimes be confused or even self-deceived about what we really want. But this means that in principle the desire theory must allow that we could suffer greatly without being aware of that. If the exotic neuroscience cases highlight the absurdity of that supposition, these cases actually also show the desire theory to be false.

Consider next a further argument supporting my claim that pain's badness resides in what it feels like. Imagine an agent—call her Painless—who has never experienced any kind of pain in her entire life; it does not matter how exactly this was achieved (presumably Painless must have led an extremely sheltered life, and perhaps has powerful painkillers continuously flowing through her veins). Now suppose next that, nevertheless, Painless is an expert in pain science— she knows everything there is to know about the brain mechanisms underlying pain, how pain is typically generated, and what motivational states it gives rise to. It seems to me clear that there is something fundamental that Painless would still fail to know, something she would only come to know when she finally feels pain for the very first time. Only then would she be able to understand why that state—a state she possesses exhaustive knowledge of from the third person—is bad. The desire theory, or any theory that does not locate pain's badness in how it feels, cannot explain why this should be so, since on such views, Painless should already possess all relevant normative knowledge.[10]

The felt aversion theory seems to me superior to the other views we have considered. It entirely preserves the commonsense intuition that pain's badness resides in what it feels like, and that we want pain to stop because it's bad, rather than vice versa. It just makes a minor, if critical, amendment to the sensation theory we started with: the badness does not reside in the bodily sensation of pain itself, but in the aversive experience to which it normally gives rise. This picture of pain and what makes it bad is also nicely consonant with the standard scientific account of pain, where the sensory and affective dimensions of pain are distinguished and seen as independent, and where this primary affective dimension is further distinguished from its secondary affective side—the motivations and evaluations to which it gives rise.[11]

Still, I don't pretend that this is an entirely comfortable resting point. Some would be suspicious of the idea of an experiential state that has both a distinctive phenomenal character and an intrinsic tie to motivation. And the felt aversion theory claims that the most paradigmatic example we have of badness arises from a rather peculiar mental mix, while having nothing to say to explain why badness must arise from that mix. This, however, needn't be seen as a problem. Some things just are bad. Unless one accepts some reductive account of value, explanations of ground-level badness are inevitably going to be rather thin. We can only direct your attention to what it's like to suffer intensely. Pain is bad because it *feels like that*—that's what Painless, in the thought experiment described above, comes to understand. That is all we can say.

Like the sensation theory, the felt aversion theory ties pain's badness to the phenomenal character of conscious experience—essentially tying what is a paradigm case (and on some views, as we shall see below, the only case) of the philosophically puzzling phenomenon of intrinsic badness to the qualitative character of conscious experience, another phenomenon that is deeply puzzling. Now in principle, the felt aversion theory could be combined with any positive account of phenomenal character, however reductive. It seems to me, however, that the intuitions that drive the felt aversion theory also place an important constraint on what *could* be a plausible account of phenomenal character. Such an account needn't offer an explanation of why the experience of pain is intrinsically bad. But it needs to at least leave it intelligible that pain could be intrinsically bad (Kahane 2010). This is something that, I believe, many dominant accounts of phenomenal character fail to do.[12]

The felt aversion theory of pain's badness has several interesting corollaries. First, it forces us to distinguish between two senses of "pain." There is the bodily sensation of pain, a state that, as we have seen, is not bad in itself. Then there is the state of disliking such a sensation or finding it aversive, a state with a distinct phenomenal character (which is missing in frontal lobotomy or pain asymbolia). It is only that latter state that is intrinsically bad. When we talk about pain, we usually fail to distinguish between these two states—states that, indeed, almost always go together. But we should. We can call the first, neutral state *the sensation of pain*. And we can call the second state *unpleasant experience*. But to simplify things, in what follows I will use "pain" only to refer to that second, intrinsically bad state; when I want to refer to the neutral sensation that it often contains, I will explicitly speak of the sensation of pain. As we shall see below, this distinction can help us with some puzzles.

The second corollary builds on the first one. Once this distinction is in place, we can see that the sensation of pain is not only not sufficient for pain in the sense that is bad, but not even necessary for it. For (as hinted at the very beginning) there is a variety of unpleasant experiences that do not, it would seem, involve that specific sensory state. Think of feeling nauseous, or being electrocuted, or drowning. These experiences are all unpleasant, and can involve extreme suffering, yet they are not accurately described as painful. In fact, to the extent that "pain" is taken to refer either to a distinct kind of bodily sensation or even to the state of finding that sensation aversive, it doesn't capture any genuine evaluative kind. The relevant category is that of having unpleasant experiences, with unpleasant painful experiences being just one common instance of these. But to simplify things, I will use "pain" in a broad, loose sense, to encompass all kinds of unpleasant experiences.

In fact, as an evaluative category, I think that "pain" must be understood in an even broader sense. It also needs to cover what is sometimes called "mental pain": negative affective states such as sadness or bitter disappointment, not to mention anxiety and depression. Such emotions may be associated with certain bodily sensations, but they are not caused by (let alone represent) bodily dysfunction. It would be rather hard, I think, for the sensation theory to also encompass such states. Even if one claimed that the bodily sensations associated with these negative emotions are intrinsically bad, this still seems to get things wrong: if we are pained by some loss, it is the loss itself that pains us, not some feeling in the gut.

It is also not obvious how the desire theory could extend to cover mental pain. To be sure, when we suffer some bitter disappointment, that disappointment presumably involves wishing that things had gone differently. But *this* frustrated desire could not underlie the pain of disappointment. It has the wrong object: some state of the world that we wish had been different. But *our* suffering—the anguish that we want to end—is a mental state of ours. The desire theory therefore needs to postulate some second-order desire, a desire *not* to be in such a state of frustrated desire.

In any event, mental pain, just like physical pain, seems bad because of how it feels—a disappointing failure can be a bad thing, but it is also bad because it makes us *feel miserable*. The *experiential dislike theory* is, I believe, best positioned to account for that. The same aversive state that, in physical pain, is directed at a certain kind of bodily sensation can also be directed at losses, setbacks, dangers, and the like. But it is, on this account, the same kind of experience that feels bad, and underlies the badness, in both physical and mental pain.[13]

Is pain always bad? Is it the only thing that is bad?

Few, if any, really question whether pain is bad. The main debate has rather been over whether it is the *only* thing that is bad, or at least the only thing that is bad *for us*, in the sense of being harmful in itself, making our life go worse. Since those who defend such a view nearly always also hold that pleasure is the only thing that is in itself good for us, this is essentially the question of the truth of hedonism as an account of well-being.

Both sides to this debate agree that pain is bad. What is at issue is whether *other* things are also bad in themselves—not bad only because they cause or contain pain. Everyday thinking certainly seems to accept that various things are not only bad, but worse than pain: many hold, for example, that we should be willing to undergo great pain rather than betray our loved ones. It is somewhat less obvious, however, whether everyday thinking also accepts that anything besides suffering can be bad *for* us, as opposed to being *morally* bad. Candidates that have been proposed include the frustration of our desires, the failure of our personal relationships or deepest projects, ignorance about matters of importance, and even moral vice. However, the question of whether these or other things are genuinely bad for us is not a question about pain, and therefore outside the scope of this chapter.

Consider next the question whether pain is always bad, in the sense of being bad for us—whether pain always harms us, making our life worse than it would have otherwise been. One simple argument for this conclusion is as follows. Pain seems to be intrinsically bad. But if pain is intrinsically bad—bad in virtue of its intrinsic properties, of what it feels like—then it seems that whenever we undergo experiences that have this quality, this should be bad for us. So pain is always bad.

There are, however, apparent counterexamples to this conclusion. Some traditions see pain as central to human life, a form of experience that has an important positive function and that, at least in some contexts, is something we should therefore welcome, or at least not wish away. Pain is thought, for example, to play a necessary role in atonement, moral development, or spiritual insight. In some cultures, religious practices often involve the infliction of extreme physical pain. Then there are masochists, people who seem to regard pain as something desirable.

If we are impressed by such examples, we might conclude that pain is bad only when it is not meaningful. But that would be too quick. These are only apparent counterexamples. They are actually compatible with the claim that pain is always bad for us, in the sense spelled out above. On closer inspection, all such apparent counterexample can, I believe, be addressed in one of the following ways:

1. Some of these cases may not even involve pain in the relevant sense. There are, first, those unusual circumstances where what would normally causes intense pain causes no such thing—a famous example is soldiers who fail to notice severe injury on the battlefield. The physiological mechanisms underlying such modulation of pain are now fairly well under-stood (see Wall 2002). Then there are cases where individuals experience only the bodily sensation of pain, without its aversive character. This is one possible way of understanding masochism: in certain sexual contexts, the masochist may still feel the bodily sensation of pain yet, instead of finding it aversive, finds it pleasant; some long-distance runners similarly report finding the pain associated with running rewarding rather than aversive. As we saw, not only is the sensation of pain not always bad, it is *never* bad, considered in itself. But the claim that pain is always bad is not a claim about this sensation.

2. There is also an alternative, more straightforward way of understanding masochism: the masochist does find the sensation of pain aversive, but, when it is given a specific sexual and interpersonal meaning, that experience gives rise to further experiences that are highly pleasurable or otherwise rewarding. Considered in itself, the pain is just as bad. It is just that it causes something whose goodness significantly outweighs (or appears to outweigh) this badness. That bad things can have good effects—let alone, that bad things can be better than even worse alternatives—is hardly mysterious or surprising. That pain is, in this way, sometimes overall a good thing is perfectly compatible with it being always bad, considered in itself.

3. In some cases, the relation between pain and something positive is not merely causal. Pain can also be an essential constituent of something that many would take to be good. Retributivists, for example, often regard the pain associated with the justified punish-ment of wrongdoers as a good thing. Even many non-retributivists are likely to agree that emotions such as grief, remorse, or compassion are, when appropriate, a good (or at least not bad) thing, even though they have an inherently painful dimension. In these cases, however, the goodness in question is moral, not prudential. It is morally good to feel compassion for the suffering of others, but it is far less obvious that this is good *for* you, that it makes your life better in any way. Moreover in most (perhaps all) of these cases, the goodness arises *because*, considered in itself, pain is bad. This is most obvious in the case of retributive punishment, where, if the infliction of pain is morally good, that is so only because it is bad for the wrongdoer (if it was a benefit, could it really be punish-ment?). But something similar might also be at work in compassion or grief: the badness of the loss, for example, is reflected in the badness of our experience of this loss, and in compassion we are pained by others' pain.

4. There may even be cases where pain plays an essential part in generating something that is a benefit for the person who undergoes it—a prudential good, not (or not just) a moral good. To begin with, those who think that moral virtue contributes to our well-being are likely to hold that appropriate compassion and grief are actually good for us. Pain may also be a necessary component of certain forms of achievement and meaning: an achieve-ment may be more valuable, and contribute more well-being to a life, precisely because it involved facing up to, and overcoming, immense suffering. These examples are more controversial, but in any event they do not yet raise an interesting challenge to the claim that pain is always bad for us. Here, again, it actually seems that the supposed overall benefit presupposes the badness, considered in itself, of the experience of pain (it is facing up to this badness that makes some achievement more valuable). And in none of these cases is the experience itself rendered positive—the positive value accrues to some larger whole of which the aversive experience is a part.

Pain sometimes causes good things. It can, in this way, sometimes be an overall benefit even if it remains bad, and a harm, when considered in itself. Pain can similarly play a constitutive part in things that are morally good or even overall prudentially good. But none of this is incompatible with the intrinsic badness of pain itself, and, indeed, pain often plays this positive function precisely because of this intrinsic badness.[14]

A more interesting question is whether, despite its intrinsic badness, pain might nevertheless play a necessary positive role in well-being—that is, whether it is impossible to live a good life without experiencing some, perhaps even much, pain. If this were so, then aiming to abolish all suffering, and wishing that no one felt pain, would be deeply misguided.

Now there is an obvious sense in which pain plays a critical positive role in the actual world. Individuals who are born congenitally insensitive to physical pain tend to have rather short lives because they fail to immediately detect and respond to even severe forms of bodily damage. But this is a contingent fact about our biology, and the kind of world we inhabit. Painless ways of effectively detecting and avoiding bodily dysfunction are surely conceivable. Now, the goodness of attitudes such as grief and compassion may not seem to be contingent in this way. Still, there would be no need for compassion if there were no pain to feel compassion for. And it is not so obvious that compassion (or some alternative fitting response to others' suffering) must itself necessarily involve being pained. Finally, even if pain is necessary for certain benefits, this would not yet mean that it is necessary for a good life. This would only follow if *these* benefits were themselves necessary for a good life.

Skepticism about pain's badness?

There is wide agreement about pain's badness, and as we have seen, some apparent doubts about pain's badness are no such thing. There are, however, some who do appear to genuinely deny that pain, in itself, is bad for us in any way. The Stoics are one famous example. Since much of what the Stoics wrote has been lost, any account of their view of pain must involve some guesswork.[15] Still, the Stoics did claim that virtue and vice are the only things that determined whether one had a good life. This claim implies that the life of a perfectly virtuous person cannot be made worse even by immense suffering, an implication the Stoics explicitly endorsed. And that seems to clearly deny that pain is bad for us. Things are, however, a bit more complicated. The Stoics also held that pain is a "dispreferred indifferent"—something we have reason to avoid even if it is not bad in itself. And presumably, relieving suffering, and not causing pain, are required by virtue. But why should this be so, if pain is not really a harm? Even Hellenistic commentators suspected that the Stoics were merely redefining "bad" to mean morally bad, which would turn their striking denial into something rather unremarkable.

Even if the Stoics did genuinely mean to deny pain's badness, we may still find it hard to accept that such a denial is sincere. Can someone really undergo horrific pain, yet still sincerely believe that *this* experience is in itself completely indifferent, no better or worse than a harmless afterimage? It is as if the experience of pain directly compels us to accept its badness.

There is actually something disturbing about the very idea of denying pain's badness: one would be denying the badness of the immense amount of horrific suffering that surrounds us in every direction. There seems to be something morally repugnant about even entertaining this thought. I nevertheless find that some doubt creeps in when I reflect on the question of why there is such an unusually wide agreement about pain's badness. The natural explanation for this consensus is that when we experience pain, we are directly confronted with its badness. We just can't fail to see it. But there is an alternative naturalist explanation for this consensus: we are compelled to find pain bad simply because we were hardwired to do so by evolution.

Pain plays an obvious evolutionary function: it helps us avoid early death, greatly increasing our reproductive fitness. Our overwhelming conviction that pain is bad also seems to have an obvious evolutionary benefit: it ensures that we give pain sufficient, non-negotiable negative weight in practical deliberation. But from an evolutionary perspective, all that matters is that we strongly *believe* that pain is bad; whether this conviction is in fact true is irrelevant. So it appears that evolution would have ensured that we believe that pain is bad whether or not it really is bad. And this can seem to debunk, or at least cast serious doubt on, our justification for holding on to that conviction (Kahane 2011).

One way to block this worry is to adopt an antirealist account of value, according to which things are bad simply because they are the objects of our negative attitudes (Street 2006). If such a view is correct, and we do in fact desire our pain not to occur, then pain really is bad. No room is left for such skeptical doubts. The problem is that such a view of value leads directly to the desire theory, which we saw to be deeply implausible. But if we can't give up the sense that pain is bad because of how it feels, then our reply to such evolutionary scepticism must be that we can just *see* that pain really is bad. We must hold that the way evolution got us to avoid early death was by associating bodily dysfunction with a state that *really is* bad, and that we can directly see to be bad. When I consider my experience of intense pain, this reply seems persuasive, almost inescapable. It seems hard to believe that the manifest badness of pain is merely an illusion. Yet I find that I cannot entirely dismiss the lingering worry that this is exactly how things *would* seem, if we were simply hardwired to find it non-negotiable that pain is bad, whether or not it really was bad. Seen in such a light, our everyday struggle with pain begins to seem absurd . . . I said that there is something morally repugnant about even entertaining the idea that pain might not be bad. Yet at the same time, to discover that pain really *isn't* bad would be incredibly good news: things would turn out to be so much better than they now seem. This possibility is at once thrilling and utterly preposterous. It is also something neither you nor I could ever come to believe in. And that is almost certainly a good thing.

Further reading

Aydede, M. ed. (2005). *Pain: New Essays on Its Nature and the Methodology of Its Study*. MIT Press; Broome, J. (1996). "More pain or less?," *Analysis* 116–118; Hare, R.M. (1964). "Pain and Evil," reprinted in his *Essays on the Moral Concepts*. London: Macmillan; Mayerfeld, J. (1996). "The moral asymmetry of happiness and suffering," *The Southern Journal of Philosophy* 34.3: 317–338; Mayerfeld, J. (1999). *Suffering and Moral Responsibility*. Oxford University Press; Tabensky, P.A., ed. (2009). *The Positive Function of Evil*, Palrgrave Macmillan.

Notes

1 This point raises a challenge to attempts to explain pain's intrinsic badness by appealing to the badness of bodily damage and dysfunction that pain supposedly represents (e.g., Korsgaard 1996). Such views already face the problem that much of the badness of bodily dysfunction seems to be due to the immediate and long-term pain that it can cause. If bodily dysfunction is bad because often painful, how can it explain the badness of pain? It is even more difficult, however, to explain why a mere representation of something else that is bad should be itself bad—let alone why a *mistaken* representation of bodily damage should be bad at all. But intense pain experienced in a phantom limb is not only bad, but *just* as intrinsically bad as similar pain experienced in a real limb (for attempts—unsuccessful to my mind—to answer this challenge, see Korsgaard 1996; Cutter and Tye 2014). Similar problems arise for attempts to explain pain's badness in terms of its role in the perception of disvalue (see, e.g., Helm 2002).

2 It is worth noting, however, that if we look far enough back—before early modern philosophy and empiricist influences and all the way back to, say, ancient Greek or Hellenistic philosophy—we also find

rather different accounts of pain (though ancient philosophers have tended to say more about pleasure than about pain). I do not have space here to review these views, though I will briefly discuss the Stoic view below.

3 Strictly speaking, subjectivist accounts of value and desire-satisfaction accounts of well-being are logically distinct. Subjectivism about value is a metaethical view, a theory of value in general. The desire-satisfaction account is a substantive view of well-being. These views, however, often go hand in hand.

4 More sophisticated versions of the view spell out the relevant desire more precisely, as an intrinsic desire for this very sensation not to occur (Heathwood 2007).

5 For example, Clark (2005) claims that "there is no phenomenological character specific to painfulness. At best there is a phenomenological character of sensations that are painful."

6 Although for recent attempts, see Goldstein (1989) and Rachels (2000).

7 See Grahek (2007) for a nice survey of the relevant science. Grahek notes that, although philosophers in this area often appeal to the example of frontal lobotomy patients, that case is not as clear or clean as that of pain asymbolia. But for our purposes we can ignore these empirical subtleties.

8 The label "dislike" is somewhat unhelpful, since it would be odd, to put it mildly, to describe someone undergoing horrific suffering as merely disliking the sensation. But we can set the everyday associations of "dislike" aside here, and treat it as a quasi-technical term.

9 Notice that I'm not claiming that we are infallible as to whether we are in pain, or as to whether an experience we are undergoing is intrinsically bad. The claim is only that it seems impossible to be in a state of intense pain, and suffer greatly, without being aware of that. This is compatible with thinking that we might not be aware of some creeping headache or other pains at the periphery of attention. For empirical evidence that people aren't always so good about telling how bad their pain is, see Kahneman et al. (1993).

10 For a full development of this thought experiment, see Kahane (2010). This line of argument is obviously inspired by Frank Jackson's famous knowledge argument (Jackson 1982). For a real-life case of someone congenitally insensitive to pain who came to feel physical pain for the first time, see Danziger and Willer (2005).

11 See Wall (2002). Berridge (1996) offers empirical evidence for distinguishing between the aversive state of liking/disliking and motivational states such as desire.

12 See Note 1 above for some worries about recently popular accounts of pain that try to identify its phenomenal character with the representation of bodily dysfunction. But a similar challenge can be raised for functionalist and higher-order thought accounts of conscious experience.

13 Neuroimaging studies reveal that when people experience so-called mental pain, the brain areas that light up are the same as those implicated in the aversive dimension of physical pain. See Singer et al. (2004).

14 Just as in some circumstances pain plays a constitutive part in larger wholes that are overall good, there may also be circumstances that further augment the intrinsic badness of felt pain, making it an even greater evil. One such case might be torture: the badness of torture has been argued to lie, not merely in the badness of the pain inflicted (horrific as that may be in itself) but in the way in which that badness is used by the torturer to dominate the will of his or her victim (Sussman 2005).

15 Brennan (2005) is an accessible introduction to Stoic ethics.

Bibliography

Berridge, K.C. (1996). "Food Reward: Brain Substrates of Wanting and Liking," *Neuroscience & Biobehavioral Reviews* 20(1): 1–25.

Brandt, R. (1979). *A Theory of the Good and the Right*. Oxford: Clarendon Press.

Brennan, T. (2005). *The Stoic Life: Emotions, Duties, and Fate*. Oxford: Oxford University Press.

Brink, D. (1997). "Rational Egoism and the Separateness of Persons," in J. Dancy (ed.), *Reading Parfit*. Oxford: Blackwell Publishing.

Chang, R. (2004). "Can Desires Provide Reasons for Action?," in J.R. Wallace (ed.) *Reason and Value: Themes from the Moral Philosophy of Joseph Raz*. Oxford: Oxford University Press.

Clark, A. (2005). "Painfulness is not a Quale," in M. Aydede (ed.), *Pain: New Essays on its Nature and the Methodology of its Study*. Boston, MA: MIT Press.

Cutter, B. and Tye, M. (2014). "Pains and Reasons: Why it is Rational to Kill the Messenger," *The Philosophical Quarterly*, pqu025.

Danziger, N. and Willer, J.-C. (2005). "Tension-type Headache as the Unique Pain Experience of a Patient with Congenital Insensitivity to Pain," *Pain*, 117(3): 478–483.

Goldstein, I. (1989). "Pleasure and Pain: Unconditional, Intrinsic Values," *Philosophy and Phenomenological Research* 50: 255–276.

Grahek, N. (2007). *Feeling Pain and Being in Pain*. Boston, MA: MIT Press.

Heathwood, C. (2007). "The Reduction of Sensory Pleasure to Desire," *Philosophical Studies*, 133(1): 23–44.

Helm, B.W. (2002). "Felt Evaluations: A Theory of Pleasure and Pain," *American Philosophical Quarterly* 39(1): 13–30.

Jackson, F. (1982). "Epiphenomenal Qualia," *Philosophical Quarterly* 32(127): 127–136.

Kahane, G. (2009). "Pain, Dislike, and Experience," *Utilitas* 21(3): 327–336.

Kahane, G. (2010). "Feeling Pain for the Very First Time: The Normative Knowledge Argument," *Philosophy and Phenomenological Research* 80(1): 20–49.

Kahane, G. (2011). "Evolutionary Debunking Arguments," *Noûs* 45(1): 103–125.

Kahneman, D., Fredrickson, D.L., Schreiber, C.A. and Redelmeier, D.A. (1993). "When More Pain is Preferred to Less: Adding a Better End," *Psychological Science* 4(6): 401–405.

Korsgaard, C.M. (1996). *The Sources of Normativity*. Cambridge: Cambridge University Press.

Parfit, D. (1984). *Reasons and Persons*. Oxford: Oxford University Press.

Rachels, S. (2000). "Is Unpleasantness Intrinsic to Unpleasant Experiences?" *Philosophical Studies* 99(2): 187–210.

Singer, T. Seymour, B., O'Doherty, J., Kraube, H., Dolan, R.J. and Frith, C.D. (2004). "Empathy for Pain Involves the Affective but not Sensory Components of Pain," *Science* 303(5661): 1157–1162.

Sobel, D. (2005). "Pain for Objectivists: The Case of Matters of Mere Taste," *Ethical Theory and Moral Practice* 8: 437–457.

Street, S. (2006). "A Darwinian Dilemma for Realist Theories of Value," *Philosophical Studies* 127(1): 109–166.

Sussman, D. (2005). "What's Wrong with Torture?" *Philosophy & Public Affairs* 33(1): 1–33.

Wall, P.D. (2002). *Pain: The Science of Suffering*. New York: Columbia University Press.

18

HEALTH, DISABILITY, AND WELL-BEING[1]

S. Andrew Schroeder

The relationship between health and well-being is a vexed one. On the one hand, it seems obvious that the two go hand in hand. Common sense tells us that illnesses, diseases, and injuries are bad for us. We call these instances of *ill* health, and we describe ourselves as *suffering* from them. We worry about having health problems, and we feel sorry for those who do. Parents who fail to prevent sickness or disability in their children are accused of harming them and are labeled negligent. There are, of course, some times we may welcome illness, disease, or injury: the flu may get us out of an exam for which we're unprepared, asthma may excuse us from military service, and a broken leg from an accident may net us a large insurance settlement. But in cases like these, it seems clear that each health problem is itself a bad thing that merely happens to be accompanied by something good enough to outweigh the bad. (We would prefer to get out of the exam without catching the flu, avoid military service without asthma, and get a large sum of money without breaking our leg.) So, there seems to be a strong assumption that health problems reduce well-being—that is, that they are bad for the people who suffer from them—unless perhaps that badness is outweighed by an accompanying good.[2]

Not surprisingly, the academic literature generally endorses this assumption. When philosophers need an example of something that makes a life go worse, they frequently choose a health problem. In discussing the non-identity problem, for example, Kavka uses the example of a handicapped child (1982: 98; *cf.* Parfit 1984: 367–369), and Harman (2004) a deaf child. In contexts where health and well-being are more direct topics of discussion, the same assumption is stated more explicitly:

> To be disabled in any sense is not the same as being differently abled. Being deaf for example is . . . a condition which harms the individual relative to freedom from deafness.
> *(Harris 2001: 383; cf. McMahan 2005: 96)*

Philosophers writing on well-being sometimes include health as a constituent of well-being (Finnis 1980: 85–86; Murphy 2001: 100–105; Kraut 2007: 132–133) and regard it as a serious objection to desire-based theories of well-being that those theories don't give health intrinsic value (Lauinger 2013; Raibley 2013). Most of the epidemiological and health economic literature treats ill health as something of importance primarily because of its impact on well-being (see, e.g., Broome 2002; Neumann 2005: 9). Accordingly, the major economic measures used to evaluate overall health are given names like the Quality of Well-Being Scale, the Health Utility Index, and the EuroQoL (Quality of Life). Finally, many states, such as homosexuality, that were previously thought to be diseases or illnesses became recognized as compatible with health once we learned that they are not bad for their possessor.[3]

All of this, then, points to a strong connection, in both everyday and academic discourse, between ill health and reductions in well-being. Diseases, injuries, and illnesses are bad for us, and that is the primary reason why we should be concerned about them. Set against this, however, is what has been called the disability paradox: many people with what most of us would consider serious disabilities and health problems, such as deafness, paraplegia, and kidney disease, report surprisingly high levels of well-being (Albrecht and Devlieger 1999; Ubel *et al.* 2005; Angner *et al.* 2013)—perhaps as high as the self-reported well-being of people in full health (Riis *et al.* 2005). Some claim they would refuse treatments to restore their health (Hahn and Belt 2004) and go to great expense to conceive children who share their condition (Sanghavi 2006). Even if well-being is lower for those in ill health, some advocates for the disabled argue that that is not because disabilities are themselves bad. Rather, any reduction in well-being is primarily attributable to unjust social factors (Oliver 1996). Disability is in this respect like being a woman, having dark skin, or being gay: these traits are not in any way intrinsically bad or harmful, though in an unjust and discriminatory society like ours, they may in fact tend to reduce well-being.

What, then, should we conclude about the connection between health and well-being? None of the observations in the previous paragraph is sufficient to show that health isn't tightly connected to well-being. (Survey participants might misrepresent their own levels of well-being, people in ill health might refuse treatments out of a concern for something other than personal well-being, etc.) But, taken together, they do give us reason to question the strength of the relationship. In the remainder of this chapter I will investigate the link between health and well-being. I will argue that, for a wide range of health states, the connection is a contingent one.

Further, empirical findings suggest that decrements in health probably have much less impact on well-being than most people suppose. This has important consequences for issues of justice and morality.

Preliminaries

Before we can look at the relationship between health and well-being, a few preliminaries are necessary. First, there are no generally accepted theories of well-being or of health. Ideally, therefore, this chapter would begin by discussing the many alternative theories of well-being and health that have been offered, since what relationship there is between the two may depend on what analysis of those concepts we accept. Fortunately, I think we can make progress without engaging in that arduous task. In this chapter, I won't take a stand on the nature of well-being, except that I will set aside certain theories (mentioned above) which explicitly include health as a component of well-being. (On those theories, the relationship between health and well-being is straightforward.)

When it comes to health, I will assume that it is a matter of proper functioning: healthy eyes are eyes that work the way eyes are supposed to, a healthy immune system is one that works as immune systems are supposed to, and so forth. Decrements in health, which include injury, illness, disease, and disability—or, for short, pathology—occur when part of an organism is functioning improperly in a way that is in some relevant sense inferior. This analysis of health is, I think, our everyday one, and it is standard in medical usage (Wakefield 1999) and economic analysis (Hausman 2010: 281–282). It is also consistent with most philosophical theories of health. (What distinguishes many theories of health is how they cash out the idea of "proper" functioning. Contrast, e.g., Boorse 1997; Wakefield 1992; and Venkatapuram 2013. I won't worry about differences among these views, since in most ordinary cases their judgments of pathology and health coincide.)

This general analysis of health may seem to be controversial. The ears of a deaf person and legs of a paraplegic are, on any plausible account, not functioning properly. Therefore, according to the above analysis, deafness and paraplegia are pathological. Many advocates for the disabled, however, have argued that disability is compatible with health. The US Centers for Disease Control, for example, say, "Having a disability does not mean a person is not healthy or that he or she cannot be healthy" (Centers for Disease Control 2014). This is a complex issue which I cannot fully discuss here, except to say that I believe such claims are often made out of a desire to avoid certain implications that commonly accompany health judgments: for example, that health problems call for medical treatment, or that they are undesirable (Wendell 2001; Bickenbach 2013). Note that neither of those claims follows from the analysis of health I am using. Given that the ears of a deaf person are functioning improperly, it does not follow that the proper response is surgery on the ears. It could be that the appropriate response is to change the environment (to make it more easily navigable for the deaf), or to do nothing at all. Similarly, even if the *ears* of a deaf person function poorly compared to the ears of a hearing person, it does not follow that the *life* of a deaf person is in any respect worse than the life of a hearing person. So, even if my account of health is controversial, I believe it has the potential to address many of the worries that motivate attempts to reject it.

This leads to the second preliminary point. In what follows, much of the literature I cite concerns disability, rather than health. That is because much more has been written about the relationship between disability and well-being than about the relationship between health and well-being. Since standard examples of disability will straightforwardly count as pathologies on the account of health I am working with, we can use the literature on disability to draw conclusions about health. But we should keep in mind that disability is only one type of pathology.[4]

The effects of ill health

Ill health, or pathology, can manifest itself in a number of ways, but two seem most prominent. First, ill health can cause pain or another negative phenomenological state. Some pathologies necessarily involve this. You can't have a headache without experiencing pain, and you can't have an anxiety disorder without experiencing distress. Many other pathologies, like bee stings and late-stage cancer, typically involve pain, but need not. Finally, many pathologies, like blindness, involve no pain at all, and others, such as lactose intolerance, involve pain that can be avoided through medical intervention or behavioral modification.

The second way ill health manifests itself is through limitations on what we can do. This is obvious in the case of musculoskeletal conditions (e.g., a broken hand) and sensory limitations. But it is also true of things like infectious diseases. In addition to the discomfort it causes, the flu affects your respiratory system and causes weakness and fatigue, all of which prevent you from engaging in many activities you otherwise could. At the limit, health conditions that are fatal prevent us from engaging in any activities at all.

So, there are two primary ways that ill health affects us: it can cause pain, and it can restrict our capabilities.[5] The connection between the former and well-being is the clearer of the two. On nearly any account of well-being, pain and distress generally reduce well-being. This is true by definition on a hedonic theory, but other plausible theories of well-being will also make pain a detriment to well-being. We can imagine some situations where pain itself might be good—it might be good to feel distress at the loss of a loved one—but the pain resulting from pathology doesn't seem to be like this. There are also cases where on balance pain can be a good. A friendship might be forged through shared suffering, or a painful experience might spur one to change one's lifestyle for the better. But these seem like the case of the flu excusing one from an exam. The pain here is still bad; it is just accompanied by a good which outweighs it.

A stronger challenge to the claim that pain is bad comes from Wendell: "[L]iving with pain, fatigue, nausea, unpredictable abilities, and/or the imminent threat of death creates different *ways of being* that give valuable perspective on life and the world . . . Some of us would choose to live them even if they were inseparable from the suffering" (2001: 31). If it is true that there are valuable perspectives that one can gain only through pain, then this case may be importantly different than the flu and the exam. The flu and the exam are separable in a way that pain and the associated perspective would not be. At the most, though, Wendell's example could show that pain is sometimes not a bad, not that it is generally good. (Wendell seems to accept this.) So I will set this argument aside, in order to turn to the other primary way ill health affects us: by restricting our capabilities. Its connection to well-being is much less clear.

Restricted capabilities and well-being

Focus, for now, on people living with health problems that prevent them from engaging in certain activities. (We will consider mortality at the end of this section.) What is the effect of that capability loss on a person's well-being? It may initially seem like it must be a bad thing for the person. After all, most of us don't like to have our options taken away. But a little reflection shows that this needn't be so. Mark Twain is reported (erroneously, it seems)[6] to have said, "The man who does not read has no advantage over the man who cannot read." As a point about well-being, this seems right (Silvers 2003: 479). The well-being of a committed vegetarian need not decrease due to a shellfish allergy. So the first point to note is that ill health which restricts a capability that would not have been exercised need not have any effect on well-being.

This point, though, may seem to be of limited importance. Many health problems impact capabilities—movement, sight, cognition—which nearly everyone who is able to exercises in some way. Does the loss of a capability that a person would have exercised lead to a loss of well-being? Again, it is obvious that it need not. If the movie you plan to see is sold out, the effect on your well-being will depend on what you do instead. If your second-choice movie is inferior to your first, then your well-being will decline. But your second-choice movie may instead end up being more entertaining and enlightening than your first choice, increasing your well-being. Or perhaps missing out on the movie leads you to stay home and catch up on housework, increasing your well-being in the long run.

This point may seem obvious and uninteresting. *Of course* being prevented from pursuing an option you would have pursued need not make you worse off. Whether it does will depend on what replaces the foregone option. Nevertheless, when we think about disability, our first thought is usually only of the valuable activities disability can bar us from. The blind person is unable to fully appreciate a brilliant painting. The paraplegic is unable to play soccer. The diabetic may not be able to enjoy an afternoon of wine tasting. Art, athletic competitions, and fine wine are all things that many people enjoy for their own sakes. If disability prevents us from doing these things, that seems like a huge loss. We have, after all, been barred from a legitimately valuable thing. But the above reflections show that that such a conclusion is premature. Before knowing whether losing access to these goods will reduce a person's well-being, we need to know what she will replace them with. If they are replaced with equally valuable substitutes, then the person's well-being will be unaffected. For most of the valuable things that can be taken away by disability, this seems possible. Music and sculpture are no less valuable than painting. Wheelchair basketball can be just as exciting and intense as soccer. And so forth (Moller 2011: 199).[7] While it is true, therefore, that disabilities frequently exclude people from valuable activities and experiences, that exclusion need have no impact on their well-being.

The other main concern people have when thinking about disability is the impact that disability will have on activities people engage in not primarily for their own sake, but for other purposes. Call these things, which for many people include cooking dinner, driving a car, going shopping, or taking a shower, instrumental activities. When we are prevented from engaging in an instrumental activity, our goal usually isn't to find an equally valuable alternative; it is to find an alternative way of accomplishing the same goal that is comparably efficient. Anecdotal evidence suggests that, for many people with disabilities, this is possible if the environment is arranged properly.[8] (In cases where the environment isn't arranged well—e.g. a city with no curb cuts for wheelchairs—it may be plausible to maintain that the resulting reduction in well-being can be attributed primarily to unjust social factors, rather than to the disability itself.[9])

What all of this shows is that the loss of capabilities that accompanies ill health need not reduce well-being. For most lost capabilities, we can imagine equally valuable substitutes for activities engaged in for their own sake, and equally efficient means of carrying out instrumental activities. Of course, in particular circumstances the alternatives may not be available. The clarinetist, forced by arthritis to resign from an orchestral career, may not be able to find a substitute that she finds as fulfilling. And even when equally valuable substitutes are available, there is no guarantee that people will take advantage of them. The extent to which the capability loss that accompanies ill health reduces well-being is therefore a contingent matter. It depends on how often, in fact, people are able to find equally valuable substitutes and equally efficient alternatives.

Since this is, at least in part, an empirical matter, we should turn to the empirical sciences for guidance. The relevant empirical research, though, is difficult to interpret. The social scientists who have studied this, usually called the process of *adaptation* to disability and ill health, often aren't sensitive to alternative theories of well-being. And, more importantly, well-being is difficult to measure.[10] There is no consensus on what well-being is, nor are there any uncontroversial, reliable indicators of it. That said, it seems likely that people unable to find good substitutes and alternatives would tend to report their happiness as being lower than the self-reported happiness of people in full health. The best empirical studies, however, find that once they have had time to adapt to their state, people with a wide range of disabilities report levels of happiness much higher than expected, sometimes as high as the self-reported happiness of people in full health (Riis *et al.* 2005). This continues to hold when researchers attempt to control for factors (such as lowered expectations, self-deception, etc.) that might tend to distort people's self-reports (Ubel *et al.* 2005).[11]

Of course, despite researchers' best efforts, it is still possible that the self-reports are biased in some way. And according to most theories of well-being, well-being is more than felt happiness, so it is possible that the well-being of people in ill health could be low, even if their happiness is high. But these results nevertheless make a strong *prima facie* case that the well-being of people with disabilities is much higher than most people assume. We know that, at least in many cases, equally valuable substitutes for lost activities are available. People with disabilities are telling us that they are happy and satisfied with their lives, suggesting that they believe they have found those valuable substitutes. We should work from the (defeasible) assumption that they have (Goering 2008).

Before moving on to discuss the consequences of this result, we should briefly consider death resulting from ill health. The analysis here is quite simple. We've seen that the loss of capability resulting from ill health need not lower well-being, when good substitutes and alternatives can be found. But, since death involves the loss of all capabilities, we know no such substitutes and alternatives will be available. So, death will reduce well-being for anyone who otherwise would have experienced a life that was on balance good. I will, optimistically and I hope accurately, assume that this is true of most premature deaths.

Health and justice

Most people think that health is an important concern of justice and even a basic human right (Daniels 2007: Chapter 2). Most wealthy countries and many poorer ones provide universal health care to their citizens. People are offended when they see heath inequalities within a population (Anand *et al.,* 2004; Eyal *et al.* 2013). Why does health occupy such a significant place in our thinking about justice? The natural and dominant explanation is that health is so important because it has a large impact on well-being. We need to show a special concern for health because it is a significant determinant of how well people's lives go. Health inequalities are unjust because they mean that some segments of a population are living much better lives than others. We've seen, however, that there is reason to question this. It is true that pain and premature mortality reduce well-being, but long-term capability loss may not have a large effect on well-being. (It often will have some effect, and the process of adaption to a disability involves a temporary loss of well-being. But these losses are relatively small, compared to the well-being losses that most people assume accompany chronic ill health.) Should we, then, say that justice requires only managing pain and extending life, but doesn't require much beyond that when it comes to health? Should public insurance plans stop paying for expensive surgeries to increase mobility or address sensory limitations?

To reject this conclusion—which most find extremely counterintuitive—we need a different justification for making health a concern of justice (Loewenstein and Ubel 2008; Moller 2011; Shakespeare 2013: 100). Two basic alternatives have been proposed. The first looks to preferences. Even if people in ill health are just as happy as people in good health, we know that most people strongly prefer not to be in ill health. If justice involves respecting or catering to people's preferences, then it would require working to prevent and reverse health problems when possible. So far, so good. This approach faces a potential problem, however. Why do people prefer not to become disabled? If the explanation is that they think that disability would make them much less happy, then their preference for health is suspect because it is based on a belief that is probably false. Why should we go to such great lengths to satisfy preferences that are based on false beliefs? Indeed, many desire-based theories of well-being argue that it is the satisfaction of *informed* desires that make one's life go better (Sidgwick 1981: 110–111).

Loewenstein and Ubel (2008) respond to this worry by listing a number of respects in which one can have a rational preference for something that won't increase one's happiness. If we accept Mill's (1863) distinction between higher and lower pleasures, for example, then a cognitive disability that led one to replace poetry with push-pin might leave one's quantity of happiness unaffected, while nevertheless making one worse off. Thus, it would be rational to prefer not having the cognitive disability, while nevertheless recognizing that such a disability would not make one any less happy. In addition to the idea of higher pleasures, Loewenstein and Ubel cite the value of experiencing a range of emotions, participating in meaningful activities, and having a range of options (even if one won't exercise those options).

Each of these points potentially helps to justify a preference-based concern for some aspects of health. But much more argument is needed before this sort of view could ground anything like our current attitudes towards health. The primary problem is that Loewenstein and Ubel's criteria don't apply to most health problems.[12] Someone who is blind or a paraplegic or a diabetic, for example, is just as capable as anyone else of enjoying higher pleasures, experiencing a range of emotions, and engaging in meaningful activities. The only criterion that will be triggered by most health problems is the (possible) value of having a range of options. I will return to this below.

Moller (2011) offers a much narrower version of the preference-based approach. He accepts that many types of ill health will have minimal effect on one's happiness and well-being, but nevertheless thinks that it can be rational to prefer to avoid disability. He offers a comparison with love. I might recognize that I would be equally well off if I were married to someone other than my wife. I would (after a period of adjustment) be just as happy, engage in equally meaningful and fulfilling pursuits, and so forth. But, despite this, loving my wife means valuing my relationship with *her*, and therefore resisting any change to that relationship (Moller 2011: 201). Someone who was prepared to sever a relationship simply because an objectively better partner came along couldn't be said to truly love her original partner. Moller suggests that something like this happens in the case of disability. As we've seen, adapting to disability may involve substituting some valuable activities (e.g., painting) for others (music). Truly valuing something, however, means being attached to it and therefore resisting anything that would require one to give it up. If I am a music lover, I should resist anything that would force me to replace it with a different art form. I can rationally do this while at the same time recognizing that, after making the switch to painting, I would be just as well off as I was before.

Moller's argument seems like it could provide an alternative justification for some of our current beliefs about the importance of health, and it catches a wider range of health problems than Loewenstein and Ubel's suggestions. Unfortunately, though, in its current form it can't justify our commonsense view of the importance of health. Many resources go towards preventing ill health in children, who haven't yet developed the values and attachments upon which Moller's argument depends.

It is worth looking, therefore, to a very different response to the problem, offered by Hausman and Daniels. (In what follows, I will gloss over the important differences in Hausman's and Daniels' views.) According to standard liberal theories of justice, government should remain neutral on the question of what constitutes a good or valuable life. Accordingly, it is not society's job to see to the general well-being of its members; its job is instead to provide them with a space in which to live whatever lives they choose. If this liberal picture of the proper role of government is correct, then a concern for health should not be based on its impact on well-being, since promoting well-being is not the proper aim of public policy. Instead,

> [T]he evaluation of a health state should depend on the extent to which its characteristics and consequences diminish the range of good lives and valuable projects that are available to people. From a public perspective, the significance of bad health lies not in ultimate outcomes, but in the extent to which it diminishes capabilities.
>
> *(Hausman 2010: 287; cf. Daniels 2007: 27)*

We know that ill health, even if it doesn't impact well-being, can nevertheless impact the capabilities people have, so this seems like a compelling justification for regarding health as a matter of justice.

To see what kind of a concern for health this approach would yield, we need to know which "valuable projects" and "range of good lives" it is important for society to make available to people. As Hausman notes,

> The goal of social policy is not, however, to expand the range of activities that are available to individuals without reference to the importance of the activities. Providing individuals with a wider choice of religions is more important than providing them with a wider selection of breakfast cereals.
>
> *(Hausman 2010: 287)*

This leads to a problem. How can we declare one set of projects or range of lives more valuable than another, consistent with liberalism? Aren't these precisely the issues about which the liberal state is supposed to remain neutral?

Depending on the version of liberalism one holds, this need not be the case. *Perfectionistic* versions of liberalism justify liberal neutrality with reference to a substantive account of value. According to Raz (1987), for example, neutrality follows from the importance of allowing people to autonomously choose from a range of valuable options. The state ought to remain neutral among the many different ways of life that are objectively valuable, but needn't be neutral concerning ways of life that are not objectively valuable. If religious observance is an important component of certain objectively valuable lives, but eating breakfast cereals is not, then the state could justifiably give higher priority to health needs that would conflict with religious practice than to health needs that would conflict with eating breakfast cereals.[13]

According to *political* versions of liberalism, the state is not to appeal to a substantive conception of value, so this solution is not available. Nevertheless, a political liberal might still justify a preference for certain ways of life over others, if that preference was agreed on by all reasonable parties—that is, if it was the subject of a Rawlsian overlapping consensus (Rawls 1993: 133–172). Hausman says that the importance of an option will be relative to a given society, and he expresses optimism that within a society there will be broad agreement on such issues (Hausman 2010: 287, *cf.* Daniels 2007: 35–36, 50–52). Perhaps, then, he means to take this route. Regardless, however, the question of how to determine the importance of different options is a difficult one that neither Hausman nor Daniels has fully resolved.

If something like Hausman's or Daniels's proposal is the right way to justify making health a concern of justice, a number of important conclusions follow. Here, I will briefly mention one, emphasized by Hausman (2010, 2015). Cost-effectiveness analyses are used in many parts of the world to determine what treatments are covered by public insurance plans. These analyses typically measure effectiveness in quality-adjusted life-years (QALYs), interpreted as quantifying the well-being associated with various health states. If Daniels or Hausman is correct, these analyses are measuring effectiveness in the wrong way. If we want to continue using cost-effectiveness analyses to guide public policy, we need to modify the QALY so that, instead of measuring the well-being associated with health states, it instead measures the political value of the options or activities that ill health bars us from. Hausman (2015: Chapter 14) has sketched one way in which this might be done, but no system of this sort has yet been developed in detail. Any such system would constitute a major departure from current practices.

Health and ethics

In addition to raising issues of justice, health holds an important place in our thinking about personal morality. Consider, for example, the parent–child relationship. Most of us believe that parents have a special obligation to see to the health of their children. Parents who allow their children to become sick or injured, or who fail to inculcate healthy habits in their children, are seen as negligent. But if blindness, for example, doesn't significantly reduce well-being, why should we condemn a parent who declines to have her newborn treated with erythromycin, an inexpensive eye ointment that can prevent infection leading to blindness (Barnes 2009: 347)? This is not an idle question. Some parents with disabilities like deafness and achondroplasia (dwarfism) seek to conceive children who share their condition. Fertility clinics face difficult questions about whether to aid them in these pursuits (Sanghavi 2006).

This puzzle is, of course, the personal analog of the political question we discussed in the previous section. Unfortunately, we can't simply import either of the earlier solutions wholesale. Preference-based views, like Loewenstein's, Ubel's, and Moller's, will run into trouble because children frequently will have no well-formed preferences about their health. If we instead ask what the child would want if she had a well-formed preference, or if we ask what an advocate for that child would want on her behalf, we run into further problems because disabilities can sometimes be identity-constituting. A child who grows up with a disability or chronic health problem may have experiences so different from those she would have had if healthy, that it is plausible to say that she becomes a different person (Goering 2008: 129; Shakespeare 2013: 99). There is thus no clear perspective from which to ask what the child would want.

Liberal approaches like Daniels' and Hausman's are potentially of more use, but they also can't be directly transposed to this case. We certainly wouldn't want to say that parents have no obligation to promote their child's well-being. But the other aspect of the liberal view does seem relevant. Parents plausibly have a responsibility to prepare their children for a range of possible life plans, rather than narrowly channeling them towards a particular career or lifestyle. Feinberg calls these the "anticipatory autonomy rights" of children—or, more eloquently, the "child's right to an open future" (1992: 77). Since ill health closes off valuable opportunities, this seems a plausible way to ground a parental obligation to promote a child's health.

Of course, as in the political case, there is still the difficulty of specifying which possible life plans a parent should try to keep open. Preparing a child to pursue one possible career often precludes adequately preparing her to pursue another, so we can't ask parents to keep *all* options open. Feinberg sometimes writes as if parents should seek to provide children with as many options as possible (1992: 84), but it is unclear what this means and why we should value quantity over quality (Archard 2011). It therefore appears that we will have to engage in substantive normative reasoning to determine which life plans a parent should try to keep open for her child.[14] This task looks similar to the one facing Hausman and Daniels in the political sphere, but it is important to recognize that it is distinct. The parent–child relationship is not directly analogous to the government–citizen relationship, so there is no reason that the opportunities a parent should preserve for her children must be the same as the opportunities a state has an obligation to provide for its citizens. Also, parents have extensive obligations to look out for their children's welfare, whereas states (on the liberal view) don't have a similar obligation to see to the welfare of their citizens. That suggests that in the parent–child relationship, considerations of welfare will frequently compete with the obligation to maintain an open future. Given both of these factors, it seems likely that if we adopt an opportunity-based view of the importance of health, the health-related obligations of the state may be quite different than the health-related obligations of parents.

Conclusion

Most people think that health is a significant determinant of well-being. If you get sick, injured, or disabled, that is a very bad thing for you. This common view is usually correct when it comes to conditions that involve significant pain or that cause death. But many kinds of ill health primarily or exclusively affect us by restricting our capabilities. When it comes to this sort of health problem, we have good reason to believe that the common view is often wrong. Many conditions of this sort appear to have a relatively small impact on well-being, at least once a person has had time to adapt to her situation. More research needs to be done, especially to determine how well people adapt to specific health states, but the results so far suggest that we need to rethink our stance towards health, at both the individual and societal level. There may be ways to justify the strong interest that we take in preventing and treating non-painful, non-fatal pathologies, but those justifications will have to look very different from the well-being-based justifications that are usually offered, and in any case they have yet to be fully explored.

Related topics

Medicine and well-being, autonomy and well-being, pain, experience, and well-being, well-being and death.

Notes

1   I thank Daniel Groll, Daniel Hausman, Paul Hurley, Adrienne Martin, Nicole James Ross, and Nancy Schroeder for very helpful comments on earlier drafts of this chapter.
2   Throughout this chapter, I will use "X's well-being," "X's welfare," and "good for X" interchangeably.
3   The complete explanation for how homosexuality came to be recognized as non-pathological is a complex and ongoing one. But the American Psychiatric Association's decision, for example, to remove homosexuality from the *Diagnostic and Statistical Manual of Mental Disorders* (DSM-II) was in part motivated by research showing that most people who were gay did not experience distress or social impairments as a result of their sexual orientation (Lamberg 1998).
4   What distinguishes disability from other sorts of pathology? The question is a controversial one, but the common understanding of disability requires at least that disability be long-lasting and perhaps relatively stable over time. So the flu, sunburns, and paper cuts would be examples of pathologies that are not disabilities.
5   The idea that the two salient manifestations of ill health are pain and restrictions on capabilities is a common one, embodied in many health measurement and classification systems. The Health Utilities Index (Mark 3), for example, classifies health states by their impact on two phenomenal dimensions (emotion and pain) and six activity dimensions (vision, hearing, speech, ambulation, dexterity, and cognition).
6   http://quoteinvestigator.com/2012/12/11/cannot-read/.
7   Moller expresses concern that there may be a loss of well-being when the substituted good does not come from the same general class as the lost one. So, he worries that not being able to hear music may reduce well-being. If there is something to Moller's claim, it seems to me he has made the classes too narrow. So long as someone who loses access to music is capable of some form of artistic experience, I see no reason to think there must be a loss of well-being. But this issue warrants further discussion.
8   I am not aware of any studies that attempt to document this from an academic perspective. But a large number of books, articles, and documentaries show people with what most would consider serious disabilities managing instrumental activities with no more difficulty than anyone else. Angner et al. (2013) sometimes appear to claim that disease disrupts daily functioning and, as a result, happiness. But what their study in fact shows is that people who report having their daily activities disrupted by ill health are less likely to be happy. And, surprisingly, their study found that objective measures of ill health were not significantly associated with disruption of daily activities. Thus, their study is consistent with the claim that many people with disabilities have little difficulty with instrumental activities, and accordingly no resultant loss of happiness.
9   There are also a number of respects in which health problems may tend to improve well-being. On certain plausible views of well-being, there is value in overcoming obstacles or accomplishing difficult tasks. By providing such obstacles, ill health could increase well-being. Illness and disability can force us to see the world in a different way, providing us with a valuable perspective inaccessible to those in good health (Wendell 2001; Barnes 2009: 341). Finally, some research suggests that people experience anxiety when faced with a large number of good options (Shenhav and Buckner 2014). By eliminating some valuable options, a disability could therefore reduce anxiety. (Think of the anxiety you might feel when faced with several job offers that all appear to be equally good. If the offers really are equally good, it might have been better for you to have received only one such offer.)

10 See Hausman (2015) for a discussion of some of these difficulties, in the context of health.
11 I know of no studies that attempt to determine which health problems can be most successfully adapted to. See Frederick and Loewenstein (1999), however, for a survey of factors that can make successful adaptation more or less likely. There is also some research suggesting that depression is an exception to the Disability Paradox: people suffering from depression tend to rate depression as worse than the general public does (Pyne *et al.* 2009).
12 In fairness to Loewenstein and Ubel, their suggestions are intended to address problems raised for public policy by adaptation in many areas of life—not just health. The proposals they offer may be more useful in those other contexts.
13 We could imagine a related view according to which health has intrinsic value because it is intrinsically valuable that people have more options available to them. (This view could, but need not, be liberal.) In order to avoid running afoul of some of the arguments offered earlier, such a view would be most plausible if it allowed that increasing options didn't itself increase a person's well-being. In other words, such a view would say that it is good *that* Jane is healthy, although it is not necessarily good *for* Jane that she be healthy. (Sen sometimes sounds like he might hold a view like this. See, e.g., Sen (1999: 189–190).) I thank Paul Hurley for suggesting this possibility to me.
14 Ebels-Duggan (2014) argues for a similar claim, discussing a Feinberg-type view in the context of education. In order to distinguish the issues on which we may appropriately aim to teach our children a particular view (e.g., the theory of gravity, the wrongness of gratuitous murder) from the issues on which we should aim to have them make up their own minds (e.g., the desirability of certain occupations), she argues that we must make substantive normative judgments.

References

Albrecht, G. and Devlieger, P. (1999) "The disability paradox: high quality of life against all odds," *Social Science and Medicine*, 48: 977–988.

Anand, S., Peter F., and Sen, A. (eds) (2004) *Public Health, Ethics, and Equity*, Oxford: Oxford University Press.

Angner, E., Ghandhi, J., Purvis, K.W., Amante, D., and Allison, J. (2013) "Daily Functioning, Health Status, and Happiness in Older Adults," *Journal of Happiness Studies*, 14: 1563–1574.

Archard, D. (2011) "Children's Rights," in E. Zalta (ed) *The Stanford Encyclopedia of Philosophy* (Summer 2011 edition), available at http://plato.stanford.edu/archives/sum2011/entries/rights-children/.

Barnes, E. (2009) "Disability, Minority, and Difference," *Journal of Applied Philosophy*, 26(4): 337–355.

Bickenbach, J. (2013) "Disability, 'Being Unhealthy,' and Rights to Health," *Journal of Law, Medicine, and Ethics*, 41(4): 821–828.

Boorse, C. (1997) "A Rebuttal on Health," in J. Humber and R. Almeder (eds), *What is Disease?* Totowa, NJ: Humana Press, pp. 1–134.

Broome, J. (2002) "Measuring the Burden of Disease by Aggregating Well-being," in C. Murray, J. Salomon, C. Mathers, and A. Lopez (eds) *Summary Measures of Population Health: Concepts, Ethics, Measurement and Applications*, Geneva: World Health Organization, pp. 91–114.

Centers for Disease Control (2014) "Disability and Health: Healthy Living," available at http://www.cdc.gov/ncbddd/disabilityandhealth/healthyliving.html.

Daniels, N. (2007) *Just Health: Meeting Health Needs Fairly*, Cambridge: Cambridge University Press.

Ebels-Duggan, K. (2014) "Educating for Autonomy: An Old-fashioned View," *Social Philosophy and Policy* 31: 257–275.

Eyal, N., Hurst, S., Norheim, O., and Wikler, D. (eds) (2013) *Inequality in Health: Concepts, Measures, and Ethics*, Oxford: Oxford University Press.

Feinberg, J. (1992) "The Child's Right to an Open Future," in *Freedom and Fulfillment: Philosophical Essays*, Princeton: Princeton University Press, pp. 76–97.

Finnis, J. (1980) *Natural Law and Natural Rights*, Oxford: Oxford University Press.

Frederick, S. and Loewenstein, G. (1999) "Hedonic Adaptation," in D. Kahneman, E. Diener, and N. Schwartz (eds), *Scientific Perspectives on Enjoyment, Suffering, and Well-Being*, New York: Russell Sage Foundation, pp. 302–329.

Goering, S. (2008) "'You Say You're Happy, But . . .': Contested Quality of Life Judgments in Bioethics and Disability Studies," *Bioethical Inquiry*, 5: 125–135.

Hahn, H., and Belt, T. (2004) "Disability Identity and Attitudes Toward Cure in a Sample of Disabled Activists," *Journal of Health and Social Behavior*, 45: 453–464.

Harman, E. (2004) "Can We Harm and Benefit in Creating?" *Philosophical Perspectives*, 18(1): 89–113.

Harris, J. (2001) "One Principle and Three Fallacies of Disability Studies," *Journal of Medical Ethics*, 27: 383–387.

Hausman, D. (2010) "Valuing Health: A New Proposal," *Health Economics*, 19(3): 280–296.

Hausman, D. (2015) *Valuing Health: Well-Being, Freedom, and Suffering*, Oxford: Oxford University Press.

Kavka, G. (1982) "The Paradox of Future Individuals," *Philosophy and Public Affairs*, 11(2): 93–112.

Kottke, F.J. (1982) "Philosophic Considerations of Quality of Life for the Disabled," *Archives of Physical Medicine and Rehabilitation*, 63(2): 60–62.

Kraut, R. (2007) *What is Good and Why*, Cambridge, MA: Harvard University Press.

Lamberg, L. (1998) "Gay is Okay With APA—Forum Honors Landmark 1973 Events," *Journal of the American Medical Association,* 280(6): 497–499.

Lauinger, W. (2013) "The Missing-Desires Objection to Hybrid Theories of Well-Being," *The Southern Journal of Philosophy*, 51(2): 270–295.

Loewenstein, G., and Ubel, P. (2008) "Hedonic Adaptation and the Role of Decision and Experience Utility in Public Policy," *Journal of Public Economics*, 92: 1795–1810.

McMahan, J. (2005) "Causing Disabled People to Exist and Causing People to Be Disabled," *Ethics*, 116(1): 77–99.

Mill, J.S. (1863) *Utilitarianism*, London: Parker, Son, and Bourn, West Strand.

Moller, D. (2011) "Wealth, Disability, and Happiness," *Philosophy and Public Affairs*, 39(2): 177–206.

Murphy, M. (2001) *Natural Law and Practical Rationality*, Cambridge: Cambridge University Press.

Neumann, P. (2005) *Using Cost-Effectiveness Analysis to Improve Health Care*, Oxford: Oxford University Press.

Oliver, M. (1996) *Understanding Disability, from Theory to Practice,* London: Macmillan.

Parfit, D. (1984) *Reasons and Persons*, Oxford: Oxford University Press.

Pyne, J.M., Fortney, J.C., Tripathi, S., Feeny, D., Ubel, P., and Brazier, J. (2009) "How Bad Is Depression? Preference Score Estimates from Depressed Patients and the General Population," *Heath Services Research*, 44(4): 1406–1423.

Raibley, J. (2013) "Health and Well-being," *Philosophical Studies*, 165(2): 469–489.

Rawls, J. (1993) *Political Liberalism*, New York: Columbia University Press.

Rawls, J. (1999) *A Theory of Justice (revised edition)*, Cambridge, MA: Harvard University Press.

Raz, J. (1987) "Autonomy, Toleration, and the Harm Principle," in R. Gavison (ed.), *Issues in Contemporary Legal Philosophy*, Oxford: Oxford University Press, pp. 313–333.

Riis, J., Loewenstein, G., Baron, J., Jepson, C., Fagerlin, A., and Ubel, P. (2005) "Ignorance of Hedonic Adaptation to Hemodialysis: A Study Using Ecological Momentary Assessment," *Journal of Experimental Psychology*, 134(1): 3–9.

Sanghavi, D. (2006) "Wanting Babies Like Themselves, Some Parents Choose Genetic Defects," *The New York Times*, 5 December 2006.

Sen, A. (1999) *Development as Freedom*, New York: Anchor Books.

Shakespeare, T. (2013) "Nasty, Brutish, and Short? On the Predicament of Disability and Embodiment," in J. Bickenbach, F. Felder, and B. Schmitz (eds), *Disability and the Good Human Life*, Cambridge: Cambridge University Press, pp. 93–112.

Shenhav, A., and Buckner, R. (2014) "Neural Correlates of Dueling Affective Reactions to Win-win Choices," *Proceedings of the National Academy of Sciences*, 111(30): 10978–10983.

Sidgwick, H. (1981/1907) *The Methods of Ethics* (7th ed.), Indianapolis: Hackett.

Silvers, A. (2003) "On the Possibility and Desirability of Constructing a Neutral Conception of Disability," *Theoretical Medicine*, 24(6): 471–487.

Ubel, P., Loewenstein, G., Schwarz, N., and Smith, D. (2005) "Misimagining the Unimaginable: The Disability Paradox and Health Care Decision Making," *Health Psychology*, 24(4): S57–S62.

Venkatapuram, S. (2013) "Health, Vital Goals, and Central Human Capabilities," *Bioethics*, 27(5): 271–279.

Wakefield, J. (1992) "The Concept of Mental Disorder," *American Psychologist*, 47(3): 373–388.

Wakefield, J. (1999) "Evolutionary Versus Prototype Analyses of the Concept of Disorder," *Journal of Abnormal Psychology* 108(3): 374–399.

Wendell, S. (2001) "Unhealthy Disabled: Treating Chronic Illnesses as Disabilities," *Hypatia*, 16(4): 17–32.

19

FRIENDSHIP AND WELL-BEING

Diane Jeske

I'm out of those chains, those chains that bind you
That is why I'm here to remind you

What do you get when you fall in love?
You only get lies and pain and sorrow
So for at least until tomorrow
I'll never fall in love again

*(I'll Never Fall in Love Again: music by Burt Bacharach, lyrics
by Hal David)*

Introduction

It seems to be so obvious that friends give our lives meaning and value that it almost seems perverse for a philosopher to question the relationship between friendship and well-being. We are far better off with friends than without them, and surely that is the end of the story. Perhaps the philosopher can sensibly analyze just *how* friendship contributes to our well-being, and explore the ways in which various conceptions of well-being accommodate the contributions of friendship. But surely our starting point must be the claim that friendship is a central component of our welfare.

I think, however, that this would be a mistake, a mistake that has been fed by the ways in which, ever since Aristotle, philosophers have approached friendship. Philosophical theorizing on the nature and value of friendship has often lapsed into either idealization or over-intellectualizing (or both). We have a tendency to focus on the best aspects and best examples of friendship and also on the best examples of friends, including the best versions of ourselves as parties to those relationships. Further, in thinking about the role of friendship in the good life, it is natural to compare a life with friends to a life totally devoid of friends. However, such a contrast can obscure the benefits and burdens of *particular* friendships. It can also mislead us in that we may make assumptions about the friendless individual that are the result of prejudice—"Who could possibly be without friends? What must be wrong with such a person?"—thereby making judgments about friendship based on features of the person or of her circumstances that are extrinsic to friendship itself.

The previous two paragraphs are not leading to a defense of a friendless life. Rather, my aim in this paper is to try to distinguish the merely *causal effects* of friendship on the way that our lives

233

are going from the *necessary* contributions of friendship to our well-being. And, in order to do this, we need to consider friendship in its various forms, from the ideal to the not so ideal, and to consider various types of friends, from the virtuous to the just not very nice, from the witty and charming to the dull and tedious, from the happy-go-lucky to the chronically depressed, from the wealthy and generous to the strapped and/or just plain stingy. Are we necessarily better off for having friends, no matter what our nature, our friends' nature, or the particularities of the friendship?

Clearly, the answer to this question depends on both our conception of friendship and on our conception of well-being. In the section on the best of friends I will discuss the Aristotelian conception of friendship[1] in order to substitute for it, for the remainder of the paper, what I regard as a less idealized and thus more plausible conception of friendship.

In the section on pleasure, desire, and friendship I will discuss the connection between friendship and well-being if we adopt some version of a hedonist or desire-satisfaction theory of well-being. On such conceptions of well-being, it will become clear, whether any particular friendship makes one's life better overall depends upon contingent features of the psychology of the individual and the nature of the particular friendship. But this shouldn't be at all surprising, given that, on such conceptions of well-being, the contribution of just about anything will be contingent on human psychology and empirical circumstances. This, of course, is in contrast to an objective goods theory (in the section on friendship as an objective good), according to which certain states of affairs are necessarily valuable, independently of people's contingent attitudes toward those states of affairs. The question is whether the state of affairs of two persons' being friends should be regarded as such an objective good and also how such a good is to be weighed against other objective goods.

Finally, I will address those who claim that the good of our friends is not metaphysically distinct from our good, i.e., that their good is a part of our good in the same way that the good of my future self is part of my own overall good. Such views are attempting to provide philosophical substance to Aristotle's claim that a friend is another self. But even these views, I argue, fail to support the claim that we are necessarily better off for having friends.

The best of friends

As I said in the introduction, I am not interested in interpretation of Aristotle's text, but, rather, in what has come to be known as Aristotle's conception of friendship. Whatever Aristotle really means to be saying in the *Nichomachean Ethics*, there is a well-known reading of the text that is influential and useful as a starting point.[2]

Aristotle distinguishes three types of friendship: friendships for pleasure, friendships for advantage or utility, and friendships between virtuous persons, this last being what he calls "complete friendship." Even if Aristotle thinks that the first two are genuine friendships, i.e., that they fall under the same univocal concept of friendship as does the last, it is clear that he thinks that the last, between two persons of virtue, is the best sort of friendship.[3] Friendships for pleasure and for advantage are distinguished via the attitudes that the parties to the relationship have to each other: friends for pleasure enjoy one another's company, whereas friends for advantage derive some other good—business deals, social status, fashion aid—from their relationship with each other. So friendships for pleasure are specific types of friendship for advantage where the end sought is the pleasure derived from the company of the friend. In these sorts of friendship— both that for advantage and that for pleasure—the friend is viewed purely instrumentally[4]: she is viewed as a means to some benefit for the agent herself, and that benefit is the motivation to enter into and to maintain the friendship. If my friend becomes dull and depressing or ceases to be able to help me to make business connections or to dress fashionably, I then have no motivation to maintain the friendship or to exhibit special concern for my friend.

In friendships between the virtuous, however, the parties to the friendship care about each other for the other's own sake, i.e., they do not view the other purely instrumentally. Given that they love each other for the other's own sake, in order for their love to be justified, each must be virtuous, because virtue is worthy of love —if I am less than virtuous, then my character is not an appropriate object of love. If you have other goals—pleasure, honor, etc.—then you can love me as a means to those ends, but only my virtue makes me lovable for my own sake.[5] Aristotle says that "loving is the virtue of friends. And so friends whose love corresponds to their friends' worth are enduring friends and have an enduring friendship" (1159a35).

In an Aristotelian complete friendship, friends are "other selves" because they mirror each other in virtue. Each party to the relationship can, in admiring and loving the character of the other, thereby contemplate her own character, and can love her friend in the same way that she loves herself, i.e., in response to her virtue. Conversation and time spent together in virtuous activity can support and develop the character of the friends, both in respect of their virtue and in respect of their other capacities (1170a10ff.). These complete friendships will last, because virtue is enduring and virtuous people, in agreeing upon ends, will avoid conflict. They also will not cease to enjoy one another's company, because they will not cease to enjoy the contemplation of the virtue of the other, being virtuous themselves.

What is interesting about Aristotle's account is that he recognizes, at least in some sense, that friendships can vary quite a bit. Also, he makes it the case that for each type of friendship, its endurance is correlated with its contribution to the agent's well-being. Friendships for pleasure and for advantage last as long as the agent continues to derive the relevant advantage from the relationship. Complete friendships last "forever" because the virtue of those involved lasts as long as they live, and "in loving their friend they love what is good for themselves; for when a good person becomes a friend he becomes a good for his friend" (1157b30).

I think that we get closest to the truth about friendship if we start from the idea that friendships vary quite a bit. I think that Aristotle latched on to some important features that friendships often exhibit. Where he went wrong was in thinking that these features are only exhibited by, or only "completely" exhibited by, friendships between virtuous persons. So let's consider these features:

1.   Friends must exhibit mutual concern for each other, and this concern must be for the other's own sake. (See Aristotle 1985: 1155b30ff.)

Aristotle claims that only in complete friendships can the agent care about her friend *for the sake of the friend*—in friendships for advantage or pleasure, the friend is cared about as a means to the procurement of some good for the agent. Even if we agree with Aristotle that friends must exhibit special concern for each other that is not purely instrumental, there is no reason to suppose that such concern only occurs in his complete friendships. Two people can be drawn to each other for any number of reasons—they find each other funny, intelligent, sexy, helpful, etc. Our motivations for initiating a friendship with someone may be our own advantage of some sort, but our interactions with that person can lead us to care about her for her own sake, even if she is not virtuous. Whether such concern or love is justified is another matter entirely—my point here is that, as a matter of psychological fact, it certainly seems that two less-than-virtuous people can care about each other for the other's own sake, even if their own advantage was (and perhaps, continues to be) a major motivation for being in the relationship.

2. Friends must have spent time with one another, or have causally interacted in some other relevant way. (See Aristotle 1985: 1156b25.)

Friendship, as Aristotle points out, cannot happen immediately. Whether or not there is a possibility of love at first sight, it is certainly the case that there is no possibility of friendship at first sight. Friendship does involve certain kinds of emotional attitudes—some sort of concern, liking, love, fondness, etc.—but friendship is not merely the having of those attitudes. Friends have a history with one another, a history of interaction, and this interaction must reveal, in some way, their concern for one another. In most cases, we would expect that friends enjoy at least some of their interactions with one another.

3. Friends must, in some sense, have knowledge of each other. (Again, see Aristotle 1985: 1156b25.)

We seem to know our friends in ways that we do not know other people and in ways in which other people do not know our friends. It is, however, difficult to spell out how exactly this is the case. I have argued elsewhere[6] that we can have many false beliefs about our friends, even false beliefs about central elements of their character and values. For example, in the film *The Third Man*, Holly Martins learns that his old buddy Harry Lime has been involved in very nefarious dealings and is essentially amoral. It seems to me correct to suppose that Holly and Harry really were friends, in spite of Holly's ignorance of Harry's character.

We certainly do not want to understand friends as always knowing *more* about each other than those who stand in no friendship to the persons involved. For example, Paul may tell much more about himself to his psychiatrist than he reveals to his best friend Peter. I don't think that anyone would think that this undermines the claim that Paul and Peter are good friends.

So what is the special way in which friends know one another? I think that this will vary from friendship to friendship. Much of what we know about our friends is experiential in nature— what it is like to be cheered up or consoled by my friend, what it is like to laugh at shared jokes, what it was like when we did such and such, etc. We cannot quantify such knowledge. Often, friends will say that they see a "side" of each other that most others don't see, where what that "side" amounts to may not be explicable merely by stating facts that have been revealed by the friend—it's a way of acting and of interacting that is unique to *us*.

The features that I have listed—mutual special concern, causal interaction, special knowledge— corral together a range of relationships. I think that it is futile to try to give precise necessary and sufficient conditions for a relationship to be a friendship, but I do think that it is clear that we can reject the idea that the parties to the relationship need to be fully or even partially virtuous. As for the rest, perhaps the three conditions above need to be met to some degree, but in what ways and to what degrees will vary from one friendship to another. I suspect that there is probably indeterminacy with respect to whether some relationships are friendships—this can be seen best if we ask about a past friendship, "when did it end?" I doubt that there will be a clear dividing line at some time such that before that time there was a friendship, but not afterwards.

And friendships do end: even very good friendships can end, due to changes in circumstances. So Aristotle's claim that the best friendships must endure seems false to me—a certain friendship may be extremely important and meaningful while I am in my 20s, but play far less of a role or indeed no role at all in my life when I am in my 40s. There is no reason to suppose that I cannot have special concern for a person for her own sake for some limited period of time.

So let's take this more open-ended and inclusive conception of friendship and consider what role it plays in our well-being.

Pleasure, desire, and friendship

In this section, I am going to consider how friends figure into our well-being according to hedonistic and desire-satisfaction theories of well-being. For each of these two types of theory there are many variations, but I am not going to consider all of them. Rather, I am going to try to remain neutral with respect to questions about the nature of pleasure and desire and, thus, talk about hedonism and desire-satisfaction theories in general terms. Hopefully, what I say will apply (with perhaps slight modification) to various versions of these theories.

Hedonists claim that all and only pleasure has intrinsic value. Whatever it is that causes me to experience pleasure—eating pie, playing with my cat, teaching philosophy—has instrumental value in so far as it is a means to intrinsically valuable pleasure. Importantly, it is an entirely contingent matter for a hedonist as to what has instrumental value, because it is an entirely contingent matter as to what causes a person to experience pleasure. Further, what causes pleasure for me—such as eating pie—might not cause pleasure for Ali, who dislikes pie, and what causes pleasure for me at one time—I used to really enjoy running —might not do so at a later time, after my knees have been destroyed by years of pounding the pavement.

So let's suppose that Ali is my friend. Thus, I have special concern for Ali for his own sake. In so far as I am concerned about him, I will take pleasure in his pleasure, so I have a source of pleasure in my friends. In most cases, I will enjoy—at least some of the time—spending time with Ali. Ali will also have special concern for me for my own sake, so he will most likely, when able, put forth effort to see that I am enjoying myself. Thus, friendship, as we know, is often a source of pleasure, and, thus, can contribute to our well-being.

But now we have to look at the flip side of this coin. Just as I will take pleasure in Ali's pleasure, I will be pained in so far as I am aware that he is suffering. The extent to which I enjoy my time with Ali will depend upon our circumstances: if he is ill, either mentally or physically, then my concern will lead me to help him, but if my help is futile, my time spent with him will be difficult and frustrating. And, if Ali is ill, he may not be in a position to promote my pleasure in any way. So friendship can also often be a source of pain.

Hedonists, then, cannot hold any necessary truths about the effects of friendship on our well-being. Whether any particular friendship brings us, on balance, more pleasure than pain will depend upon the nature of the friend and the nature of the circumstances in which both I and my friend find ourselves. The hedonist cannot assert that friendship is essential to well-being.

The same is true of the desire-satisfaction theorist who claims that all and only the satisfaction of intrinsic desires has intrinsic value, where S intrinsically desires X if and only if S desires S as an end (or, for its own sake) and not merely as a means to something other than X. Just as it is a purely contingent matter whether, say, eating pie, gives Ali pleasure, so it is a purely contingent matter whether Ali wants to eat pie or to get the pleasure of eating pie.

If Ali is my friend, we have mutual special concern for each other. Thus, each of us will want to promote the other's well-being: if Ali does well, then I will have my desires satisfied, and if I do well, then he will have his desires satisfied. So friends will often have instrumental value in so far as they are people disposed to promote our welfare. Whether they actually do have instrumental value will depend upon our situation—do they have the resources to actually help us as they want to do? Similarly, the well-being of my friends will satisfy my desires but whether those desires are satisfied is a matter of the extent to which I (and others) am able to help them. For example, if my friend is dying of a painful and debilitating disease, then my desires with respect to him will inevitably be frustrated—he cannot do well and I cannot help to promote his well-being.

It is of course true that in many cases I will share interests with my friends and want to spend time with them. But, again, such desires may or may not be satisfied—perhaps my friend is in the army and has been posted to Afghanistan. In such a case, I may not even have my desire to know that my friend is alive satisfied very often. The bottom line for the desire-satisfaction theorist, as for the hedonist, is that whether any particular friendship makes my life go better is a purely contingent matter dependent upon the circumstances in which my friend and I find ourselves.[7]

Once we abandon the requirement that genuine or true friendship requires virtue in the parties to the friendship, we face further ways in which friendship can actually hinder rather than promote our well-being. As Dean Cocking and Jeanette Kennett (2000) point out in "Friendship and Moral Danger," our friends can get themselves into moral and/or legal trouble and leave us with the difficult choice as to whether to help them "bury the bodies" as it were. Whatever we do, we will experience pain and have severely frustrated desires.

So, if we are hedonists or desire-satisfaction theorists, what is the lesson that we should draw about friendship? I think that the lesson is that friendship is a risk, something of a crap-shoot in fact. Given that we cannot have full knowledge of other people, any particular friendship may, on balance, provide us with more pain than pleasure, more frustration than satisfaction. On either theory, it is possible that some individual S would have been better off having no friends rather than having the friends that S had in the circumstances in which S and her friends found themselves. You may think that a friendless life is unlikely to be a very good life—no shared joys and triumphs, no shoulder to cry on, no private inside jokes, no companionship —but it still, under certain circumstances, may be better than a life with friends.

Some people will take this as an argument against hedonism and desire-satisfaction theories. Surely, they will say, a good life *requires* friends—no one can be well off without friends, and friends always make our lives better rather than worse. To make this the case, we would need a theory according to which something internal to friendship has great value—enough to outweigh the disvalue of any pain or frustration caused by friendship. So let's consider that sort of a theory.

Friendship as an objective good

In *Principia Ethica* (1993), G.E. Moore claimed that we can divide "all the greatest goods we know into the two classes of aesthetic enjoyments, on the one hand, and the pleasures of human intercourse or of personal affection, on the other" (251). Moore's own discussion, in the pages that follow this claim, has a decidedly Aristotelian flavor: he seems to attribute intrinsic value to affection that takes as its object "admirable mental qualities" or to the complex of the affection and the admirable qualities which it takes as its object.[8] But because we have set aside the Aristotelian view, let's consider a modified Moorean view according to which a state of affairs consisting of an attitude of affection and the person who is the object of that affection is intrinsically good.

Using Moore's isolation test, it seems to me that this is a plausible claim. If I imagine two worlds in which I hold everything constant except that in World *A* Richard is indifferent toward Diane and in World *B* Richard regards Diane with personal affection, it seems as though *B* is clearly the better of the two worlds.[9] Given the role of personal affection and/or concern in friendship, we can see that, if the modified Moorean view is right, then friendship will always add something good to the life of the friends: they will be parts of valuable states of affairs both as the subjects and as the objects of personal affection.

But it would be a strange theory of intrinsic value according to which *only* personal affection had intrinsic value. Further, that which has intrinsic value may be instrumentally bad. If Diane develops a painful illness that is gradually killing her, Richard's affection for Diane is an important causal factor in Richard's grief and depression: there is nothing more painful and frustrating than to watch someone about whom we care suffer and not be able to do anything about it.

Richard's grief and depression may interfere with his ability to enjoy his other activities and relationships. So it looks as though Richard's personal affection for Diane (and hers for him) has positive intrinsic value but very negative instrumental value. Thus, his friendship with Diane contributes both to his life going better and to his life going worse.

One might, however, in a Moorean spirit,[10] say that affection is not the only thing that has intrinsic value but that it is a necessary constituent of any whole's having intrinsic value. So a life with lots of pleasure and knowledge, say, but no affection, would have no intrinsic value, a life with affection but no pleasure or knowledge would have intrinsic value, while a life with affection, pleasure, and knowledge would have even more intrinsic value. According to this view, then, friendship would be necessary for a good life if affection always brought friendship along with it. Of course, accepting this view requires accepting some view akin to Moore's view about organic wholes, and also some account of why pleasure, for example, only has intrinsic value if it is experienced by someone who is both the subject and the object of personal affection. We do often speak about how a pleasure shared is always better, but this is clearly not true—think, for example, of gaining solitary sexual pleasure from a fantasy that one wants to make sure that no one else knows about. It seems somewhat implausible and mysterious to me why such a pleasure would only have intrinsic value if the person experiencing it had friends. One could say that the pleasure does have some value, but that the agent's whole life will lack the enormous value that it would have if it contained not only pleasure but also friendship. For our purposes here, what is important is how many controversial claims we would need to adopt in order to render friendship essential to well-being or to any high level of well-being.

Many people want to say that it is always better to have a friend than to not have a friend. What I have argued in the above is that this is—setting aside the organic wholes view just discussed—clearly not true, and that it is difficult to see how it could be. But we have to be careful about what inferences we draw here. Suppose that Ali asks Richard whether, given his, Richard's, grief and depression over Diane's suffering and impending death, Richard wishes that he had never become friends with Diane. Diane will hope that Richard will say, as many good friends would, "Of course not. I just wish that I could do something to alleviate her suffering." Is this a rational response on Richard's part?

What is important is that Richard's reasons have altered from the time before he befriended Diane to the time at which Ali asks his question. His concern for Diane provides him with new reasons, including reasons to avoid, if he, *per impossible*, could alter the past and never become friends with Diane. When we care about someone, what we want is not to not be affected by or to be ignorant of her suffering, but to alleviate her suffering. And if friendship itself generates reasons,[11] then Richard has reason to maintain and act on his special concern for Diane even in situations where the friendship is painful and frustrating. So some of our intuitions about our responses concerning our friends may have to do with our reasons to act rather than with how our friends and friendships are contributing to our own well-being.

Friends as other selves

Aristotle famously said that friends are other selves. This claim could be read as having non-literal meaning, and that is how most of us would understand it: our friends share our triumphs and defeats, they empathize with us, they share our interests, etc. Others, however, have argued that friends are other selves in a more literal sense.

David Brink (1990) has argued that the well-being of our friends is literally a part of our own well-being in the same way that the well-being of our future selves is a part of our overall well-being. He arrives at this conclusion by appealing to a psychological reductionist theory of personal identity. The psychological reductionist claims that me–now is identical with some past person-slice or future person-slice if and only if me–now stands in the relation of psychological continuity with that past or future person-slice.[12] For our purposes here, we can understand two person-slices as psychologically continuous with one another if and only if those two slices are connected via a sequence of psychologically connected slices, and two slices are psychologically connected if there are sufficient memory, personality, character, and other psychological causal connections between them.[13]

According to the psychological reductionist, the connections that hold between me–now and me-at-some-other-time are not in kind different from the connections that hold between me–now and my friend–now.[14] What makes my friend–now distinct from me is not the type of connections between us but, rather, the number and strength of such connections. Thus, Brink argues, if we are to regard the welfare of me-at-some-later-time as part of my own overall welfare, we have the same sort of reason to regard the welfare of my friend as part of my own overall welfare. According to Brink, then, we cannot assess how my life is going without considering how my friend's life is going.

If Brink is right, then, of course, whatever reasons I have to promote my own good I also have to promote the good of my friends. According to this view, there are more sources of good available to me than if the good of my friends was not part of my own good, but there are also more sources of bad available to me. So even if my friends' well-being is literally a part of my own, it will be a purely contingent matter as to whether any particular friendship makes my life go better: if my friend leads a charmed life, my life goes better, but if she gets killed in a death camp, that makes my life go worse, even if I never know about her fate.

So Brink's view does not make friendship essential to well-being. Further, there is a serious issue regarding the plausibility of his view. Even if we accept psychological reductionism, we also have to accept that there is a very real difference between one's own pains and the pains of one's friend: I am directly aware of my own pains but not of the pain of my friends. However the psychological reductionist wants to cash that out—perhaps in terms of a pain state and an awareness directed at the pain state being bundled together—it remains the case that me–now contains no such awareness states directed at Ali's pain or pleasure states. Ali may be experiencing excruciating pain right now and I might never even be aware of that fact. This seems to me to be a serious worry about Brink's view.[15]

Conclusion

Should we be surprised or worried to discover that friendship is not essential to a good life and that any particular friendship could remain a genuine friendship and yet make our lives go worse than if we had never had that friendship? I am inclined to think not. People can matter to us, be important to us, without its being the case that they make our lives go better. Their mattering to us does mean that our well-being is causally tied to their well-being: we will want them to do well and we will experience pleasure when they are doing well. Similarly, we will feel pain when they are faring poorly and we will desire that their suffering cease. Caring about people can bring us joy and make us feel fulfilled, but it can also bring us sorrow and grief, and make us feel empty, abandoned, and impotent. We are not, as a matter of fact, going to stop having friends, so we just need to hope for the best, for their sakes and for our own. As the song says, we may get only pain and sorrow from love and friendship, but we'll be back for more.

Notes

1 Whether what I am calling the Aristotelian conception of friendship is really Aristotle's is a question of exegesis that goes far beyond the scope of this paper. See Note 3 below.

2 All quotations from the *Nichomachean Ethics* are from the translation by Terence Irwin (1985).

3 Aristotle says that "the friendship of good people in so far as they are good is friendship in the primary way, and to the full extent; and the others are friendships by similarity" (*NE* 1157a30). Much more discussion would be needed here to try to figure out precisely in what sense, according to Aristotle, friendship for pleasures or advantage are friendships.

4 This is true at least with respect to the attitudes that distinguish the friendship. One could accept that all persons are such that their good, in and of itself, provides one with a reason to promote that good, independent of how the promotion of their good affects one's own good. The *additional* attitudes that are present due to the friendship involve viewing the friend purely instrumentally. (I have no idea whether Aristotle would regard this as a friendly or as an unwelcome amendment to his theory.)

5 The pleasant and useful are lovable, but if my friends are pleasant or useful, then they are lovable as means to the pleasure and utility.

6 I discuss this in my "False Friends" (unpublished).

7 I have not separately addressed informed desire-satisfaction theories, because it does not seem that the requirement that the agent have sufficient or full information will change my argument here. In fact, if an individual had full information about a potential friend's character and/or future, she might have very good reason to avoid friendship with that person if she can see that such a friendship will bring her, on balance, greater frustration as opposed to satisfaction. Unless full information involved knowledge of the intrinsic value of friendship, my central claims about desire-satisfaction theories hold if we require an informed agent.

8 Moore does say that such a whole will have even greater value if it is "combined with an appreciation of the appropriate *corporeal* expression of the mental qualities in question" (252).

9 I am here assuming that we accept that there is an objective property of intrinsic goodness. Defending such a claim is well beyond the scope of this paper.

10 See Moore's (1993) discussion of organic wholes (79ff.).

11 See my *Rationality and Moral Theory: How Intimacy Generates Reasons*.

12 I am playing fast and loose with the person-slice language here. First, I am leaving it open as to whether the psychological reductionist holds that the person is a temporally extended entity or that the person exists entirely at any single moment, i.e., I am not committing to an endurance view as opposed to a perdurance view or vice versa. And, of course, me-now, considered as a temporal part, is not literally identical to some me-in-the-future temporal part.

13 What counts as sufficient can vary from context to context and may depend on the nature of the connections and their strength. See Parfit (1984), *Reasons and Persons*.

14 Of course, memory is a special case, but it also presents difficulties in the intrapersonal case. See Shoemaker (1959), "Personal Identity and Memory."

15 If the bundle that is me-now did contain a state of awareness directed at Ali's pain state (why that pain state wouldn't then be part of my bundle, I don't know), then it does seem right that Ali's pain state is bad for me in the same way that my pain state is bad for me. But, at least in my experience, it just doesn't work that way.

Bibliography

Aristotle. (1985) *Nichomachean Ethics*, translated by Terence Irwin, Indianapolis: Hackett.

Brink, D. (1990) "Rational Egoism, Self, and Others," in O. Flanagan and A.O. Rorty (eds.) *Identity, Character, and Morality: Essays in Moral Psychology*, Cambridge, MA: The MIT Press, pp. 339–378.

Cocking, D and J. Kennett. (2000) "Friendship and Moral Danger," *The Journal of Philosophy* 97: 278–296.

Jeske, D. (2008) *Rationality and Moral Theory: How Intimacy Generates Reasons*, New York: Routledge.

Jeske, D. "False Friends," unpublished manuscript.

Moore, G.E. (1993) *Principia Ethica*, revised edition edited with an introduction by T. Baldwin, Cambridge, UK: Cambridge University Press.

Parfit, D. (1984) *Reasons and Persons*, Oxford: Clarendon Press.

Shoemaker, S. (1959) "Personal Identity and Memory," *The Journal of Philosophy* 56: 868–881.

20

VIRTUE AND WELL-BEING[1]

Anne Baril

Introduction

Ask a non-philosopher whether it's rational to be moral, and she will likely think the answer is relatively clear: intuitively, what is moral is often at odds with what is rational. For example, although giving a dollar to a needy stranger would be a moral thing to do, the rational thing to do would be to keep it for yourself. Among professional philosophers, by contrast, the answer is not so obvious. Philosophers have subtle views of rationality and morality. Seldom, if ever, do they understand norms of rationality as straightforwardly implying that we single-mindedly pursue our own self-interest, narrowly construed, and seldom, if ever, do they understand norms of morality as straightforwardly implying that we should always help others, regardless of our circumstances.

Among philosophers, then, the proposal that it is rationally permissible, or even required, to be moral, is not dismissed out of hand in light of apparent counterexamples. I propose that philosophers should take the same open-minded attitude to the proposal that virtue is compatible with, or even necessary for, well-being. Philosophers have sometimes denied that virtue is necessary for well-being on much the same grounds that our envisioned person on the street dismissed the possibility that morality may be rationally required: by pointing out apparent counterexamples (Haybron 2007: 5–11; see Chapter 15 by Besser-Jones, this volume). But, just like the question "is it rational to be moral?" the question "is virtue compatible with, or even required for, well-being?" cannot be dismissed so easily, because apparent counterexamples depend on only intuitive, commonsense, pre-theoretical understandings of virtue and well-being.

Any claim about the relationship between virtue and well-being must take the form of a conditional—for example: *if* this account of virtue and this account of well-being are correct, *then* virtue is necessary for (or compatible with, or the best bet for achieving, etc.) well-being.[2] This point sets the structure for this chapter. In this chapter, I will (1) sketch an account of virtue, (2) develop a specific sense in which one might argue that virtue is necessary for well-being, and (3) explore the prospects for the proposal that virtue is necessary for well-being, discussing some of the main accounts of well-being in turn. I will argue that on some (though not all) accounts of well-being, there is reason to think that, when we more fully develop an account of the (fundamental, direct, intrinsic) contributors to well-being, we may discover that virtue is indeed necessary for well-being.

An account of virtue

Among the defenders of most every major ethical theory, there are those who have developed an account of virtue as part of, or as a supplement to, that theory.[3] According to some recent accounts, the virtues are the traits that promote social good (Driver 2001), that are "useful or agreeable to ourselves or others" (Hume 1777/1975: 268; see further Swanton forthcoming), that are possessed by moral exemplars (Zagzebski 2010), that manifest persisting excellence in being positively oriented towards what is (independently) good (Adams 2006; Baehr 2011), or that embody the perfection of agency (Becker 1998), to name just a few.

Some ethical theories are classified as "virtue ethics," paradigmatically the neo-Aristotelian eudaimonist virtue ethics defended by Hursthouse (1999). There is no widely accepted definition of "virtue ethics."[4] For our purposes, it will suffice to say that virtue ethical theories are ethical theories that give the virtues a central, and irreducible, role in their account of how human beings ought to live, all things considered. In this section, I will sketch an account of virtue that (in broad strokes, at least) has been developed by eudaimonist virtue ethicists. Call this account "VE."[5]

According to VE, a virtue is a set of strongly entrenched and systematically interrelated dispositions to act (and to act in a certain manner, for certain reasons), reason, feel, value, choose, perceive, respond (behaviorally, attitudinally, emotionally), and so on. When someone is honest, for example, she has a firm and settled disposition to think, act, reason, feel, etc. in ways that are characteristic of honest people; and, moreover, these dispositions "hang together," mutually supporting one another. Call these sets of strongly entrenched and systematically interrelated dispositions "character traits."[6]

In the most general terms, what makes a character trait a virtue, according to VE, is that it is part of overall virtue: it is part of the collection of character in virtue of which creatures like us—with our psychological dispositions, physical composition, and way of living—are admirable, noble, living excellently and well, rather than badly. The list of virtues, according to VE, includes many traits that also count as virtues on our ordinary, intuitive understanding of virtue, such as honesty, courage, justice, temperance, benevolence, generosity, open-mindedness, and conscientiousness. But these traits may not always match exactly our ordinary intuitive understanding of them.[7] In large part, this is because VE understands each virtue as fitting into a coherent whole: the verdicts of a given virtue do not conflict with the verdicts of practical reason, or the verdicts of any other virtue. I will explain each point in turn.

According to VE, each individual virtue is sensitive to, in keeping with, and generally an expression of, good practical reasoning (Kamtekar 2004; Russell 2009; Hursthouse 2013: section 2). A trait is a virtue only if its verdictive judgments do not conflict with what the agent has sufficient reason to do, all things considered.[8] This contrasts with a commonsense notion of a virtue, according to which the verdictive judgments of a virtue may sometimes conflict with practical reason.

To illustrate: on a popular understanding of honesty, the fully honest person will tell the truth even if there is best overall reason *not* to; on this view, lying is always dishonest, even if it is, all things considered, the best thing to do. Likewise, on a popular understanding of courage, the fully brave person is the one who is consistently willing to risk her own well-being, regardless of whether, upon reflection, that risk is worth taking; on this view, standing down from a challenge or fleeing a fight is always non-courageous, even if, all things considered, it was the best thing to do. This is emphatically *not* the way that VE understands honesty and courage. As VE understands the virtue of honesty, the honest person won't tell the truth when doing so would be stupid or cruel. As VE understands the virtue of courage, the courageous person won't risk her life in service of a worthless cause. Traits that offer verdictive judgments that conflict with practical reason are *not* virtues proper.

Understanding virtue in this way has certain counterintuitive consequences. On this account, it seems, the paradigmatically honest person may even, in certain circumstances, tell a lie![9] But understanding the virtues in this way is necessary if our account is to respect what, according to VE, is the more important intuition about the virtues—the intuition that virtues are *excellences* of character.[10]

The virtues, then, will not conflict with practical reason. Nor will they conflict with one another. This is contrary to a certain popular understanding of the virtues, according to which doing what is honest can be cruel, doing what is kind may be unjust, and so on. VE holds that the fully honest thing to do will never be unjust or cowardly, the fully kind thing to do will never be dishonest or intemperate, and so on.

This proposal is often met with skepticism. Surely, skeptics say, it would be a huge coincidence if the virtues just happened to all "fit together" such that there were never any conflicts among them! But the defender of this view replies that it is not a coincidence at all, but just a natural consequence of understanding the virtues as simply the various parts of overall virtue, and as sensitive to practical reason. The individual virtues are coherent parts of a unified whole, dimensions of overall virtue, which, in turn, is understood as part of human excellence.

A full explanation of VE would involve an in-depth discussion of all of these dimensions of virtue and how they fit together into a synergistic whole. Here, I'll just draw attention to some of the main features of the landscape.[11]

Empathy cluster

A central part of virtue is the cluster of traits connected with the capacity for empathy: kindness, generosity, charity, compassion, and forgiveness, to name a few. The virtuous person is sensitive to the needs and feelings of others. She is able to occupy others' point of view and regard others with empathy and compassion. She is not the type of person who is casually rude to sales clerks and servers. She is patient with children crying on buses and planes. When most of us would find ourselves becoming irritated or frustrated by an obnoxious colleague or passerby, she is sensitive to the factors that might lead the person to act as she does. In social situations, she notices when we are inadvertently making someone uncomfortable, and has the skill to try to remedy the situation. She is kind and thoughtful—she remembers that Susan is dieting and is careful not to flaunt rich foods in front of her; she remembers that John's pet has recently passed away and so doesn't ask about him. This requires sensitivity and skill, and it emanates from a genuine concern for other people.

Honesty–integrity cluster

Another dimension of overall virtue is that cluster of traits including honesty, integrity, uprightness. Hursthouse offers the following as an initial sketch of honest people:

> they do not lie or cheat or plagiarize or casually pocket other people's possessions. You can rely on them to tell you the truth, to give sincere references, to own up to their mistakes, not to pretend to be more knowledgeable than they are; you can buy a used car from them or ask for their opinion with confidence.
>
> *(Hursthouse 1999: 10)*

As illustrated in this passage, a core dimension of the virtuous person's honesty concerns the representation of her self, both to others, and to herself. She does not shy away from confronting her true motives, emotions, abilities, and limitations, and so on.

The honest person is sensitive to when considerations of accuracy are especially important, or at risk of being violated. Hursthouse writes:

> we . . . may notice, if we are fortunate enough to come across someone thoroughly honest, that they are particularly acute about occasions when honesty is at issue. If we are less than thoroughly honest ourselves, they put us to shame, noticing, as we have failed to do, that someone is obviously not to be trusted, or that we are all about to connive at dishonesty, or that we are all allowing someone to be misled.
>
> *(Hursthouse 1999: 12)*

There isn't a simple rule the honest person always follows; honesty involves making sophisticated judgments about what's appropriate in the context. The honest person will be upfront about things with her doctor that she wouldn't be upfront about with casual acquaintances, still less with untrustworthy people whose interest in the information is salacious or malicious. This sensitivity to context is part of the skill of honesty.

Justice–fairness cluster

Another dimension of overall virtue may be characterized as the justice–fairness complex of dispositions. The virtuous person has a clear sense of the moral equality of persons, and her attitudes towards and treatment of others will express respect for persons as moral equals.

As with all virtues, the expression of justice will vary depending on the person's circumstances. She is not the type to take an unfair advantage, by (for example) queue jumping, or taking more than her fair share when she thinks no one will notice. If she is, for example, a manager of a sporting goods store, she may be in a position to determine salaries of employees, distribute the unpleasant duties among the employees, recognize meritorious conduct, and penalize infractions.

An important part of justice is being attuned to decisions or situations that do violence to the moral equality of persons. To continue with the example of the store manager: the fully virtuous person will, for example, notice whether, in group discussions, the women in the room are being undermined in a subtle way, or whether some company policy inadvertently imposes a heavier burden on some than others (for example, whether the policy of expecting employees to have personal experience with the equipment the store sells imposes an unfair burden on poor employees).[12]

The just person does not only *act* justly. She is *fair-minded*—able to consider all sides of an issue, and take a balanced approach. When circumstances warrant it, she is able to abstract away from her own personal circumstances and evaluate positions based on their merits. When she needs to make a judgment about a personal matter—for example, concerning herself or those people or issues close to her heart—she is able to keep her personal feelings from clouding her judgment. (For example, if her children are involved in a dispute with some of the other children at school, and she's trying to work out what happened, she does not see faults in other people's children while being blind to her children's own faults.) Her fair-mindedness extends to her evaluations of more abstract entities, including ideas themselves. She won't show prejudice in her thinking, by, for example, forming beliefs based on what she would like to be true rather than on the evidence.

Open-mindedness

A closely related virtue is the virtue of open-mindedness. Baehr offers the following as an initial characterization of open-mindedness:

> An open-minded person does not cling blindly to her beliefs in the face of challenges or counter-evidence to them. She is not dismissive of beliefs or positions with which she disagrees. Nor does she shy away from rational dialogue or engagement with people who believe differently from her. In these ways, open-mindedness is the *opposite* of traits like narrow-mindedness, closed-mindedness, dogmatism, intellectual dismissiveness, provincialism, and the like.
>
> *(Baehr 2012: 31)*

Open-mindedness has recently been developed as an intellectual virtue[13] (Roberts and Wood 2007: Chapter 7; Baehr 2011, 2012). But, as Nomy Arpaly argues, the truth is often morally salient, and failing to be open-minded—where this is understood as the disposition to be sensitive, not just to truth, but to *morally salient* truth—is not only an intellectual failure, but a moral one. Arpaly gives the example of the colleagues of Ignaz Semmelweis, the doctor who showed that handwashing dramatically reduces fatal childbed fever. Semmelweis's colleagues ignored his results and ridiculed him, even though the evidence was simple and compelling. Perhaps they found it too difficult to admit the truth when doing so would damage their reputations. Perhaps they could not face the thought that they had been inadvertently causing the deaths of the very people they had devoted their lives to helping. Arpaly understands (what she calls) the "moral vice" of closed-mindedness as "exemplified in cases in which someone's mind is closed to the evidence when something morally meaningful is at stake" (Arpaly 2011: 80). Semmelweis's colleagues were closed-minded, in exactly the kind of way that shows how closed-mindedness is not only an intellectual vice, but a moral one: despite the strength of Semmelweis's results, and the fact that children's lives were at stake, they dismissed the results. An open-minded person, by contrast, will be especially willing to look at evidence and reconsider her firmly held beliefs in light of strong evidence that she is wrong when there is something morally significant at stake. (See further Zagzebski 2003, 2004, on the relationship between epistemic and moral value.)

Courage and temperance

Open-mindedness may be understood as (what has been called) an executive virtue: in addition to being an excellence in its own right, it is demonstrably necessary for the acquisition, possession, or exercise of other virtues (Williams 1981: 49). One cannot, for example, make a just decision if one's mind is closed to any evidence that might threaten one's own high opinion of oneself. Likewise for courage and temperance. Roughly, courage is the character trait of responding to threat of harm in accordance with practical reason. The courageous person has the ability "to weigh up correctly the pros and cons of various alternative courses of action when some courses involve danger and the ability to face dangers," and act appropriately (Wallace 1978: 76). Temperance, likewise, is roughly the character trait of seeking and enjoying pleasures in accordance with practical reason. Courage and temperance, like open-mindedness, seem to be not only excellences in themselves, but also crucial for the development, possession, and exercise of other virtues. We all encounter situations in which behaving honestly, or charitably, or justly, or open-mindedly, will have consequences for ourselves—where doing so will risk harming our reputation, our financial stability, or even our life. We won't be able to always act as honesty, justice, etc. require if we are incapacitated by fear of adverse consequences of our actions, or if we can't resist the lure of comfort.

The above gives a brief overview of the character traits that, as part of a synergistic whole, constitutes virtue, according to VE. Each virtue, if it is a virtue proper, is responsive to, and expressive of, practical reason, and compatible with all the other virtues—not by happy accident, but because each virtue, insofar as it *is* a virtue proper, is just part of overall excellence qua human being.[14]

Senses in which virtue might be "necessary for" well-being

I have claimed that investigating whether virtue is necessary for well-being requires us to proceed piecemeal, considering philosophical accounts of virtue and well-being, rather than our own brute intuitions. In the section above, I sketched an account of virtue (one that is, in broad strokes if not in detail, widely defended). In the following section, I will give an overview of some of the main philosophical accounts of well-being, and consider the proposal that virtue is necessary for well-being on the assumption that these accounts of well-being are true. In this section, I will consider what is meant by "necessary." As we shall see, those who defend the claim that virtue is necessary for well-being do not always have strict logical necessity in mind.

It is apparent that a person's acting virtuously can make a *pro tanto* contribution to that person's well-being. Many of us feel good when we act honestly or fairly, and many of us have, among our aims, the aim of being a good person. If experiencing good feelings and achieving our aims are among the intrinsic bearers of well-being, then, other things being equal, having and exercising the virtues will make our lives go better.

But the thesis that virtue is necessary for well-being—call this "VN"—is a far stronger claim, in at least the following ways.

1. VN concerns the *possession,* and perhaps the exercise or expression, of virtue, not merely performing individual virtuous actions.[15]
2. VN concerns the possession of virtue *overall*, not merely some individual virtue (e.g., temperance).
3. VN concerns well-being *overall*, not merely some dimension of well-being (e.g., the pleasant feeling of having done one's duty).

Thus, when considering whether virtue is necessary for well-being, it is not enough to note that some honest, or just, or charitable action makes one feel good, or helps one achieve one of one's many aims. To show that virtue is necessary for well-being, we would at least need to show that the possession of virtue, overall, makes a contribution (a net, not merely gross, contribution[16]) to one's overall well being.

Taking these points for granted, there are still a number of issues to clarify in order to understand VN.

First, what is the scope of VN? Is it to be understood as the proposal that virtue is necessary for well-being for all rational beings? all human beings? all rational human beings? Or even *virtually* all, or even just some, rational, human, or rational human beings?

Second, what *degree* of virtue does the defender of VN hold is necessary for what *degree* of well-being? Is it to be understood as the claim that perfect virtue is required for well-being? Or merely some threshold of virtue? Or perhaps even only aspiring towards virtue? And is it to be understood as the claim that virtue is required for perfect well-being? Or the highest degree of well-being that is available to the person? Or some other threshold of well-being?

Third, what exactly is meant by "necessary"? Philosophers of well-being may be surprised to learn that those to whom VN is frequently attributed don't even always mean strict philosophical necessity. Hursthouse, for example, has argued that virtue is the *only reliable bet* for well-being (more accurately, for flourishing—Hursthouse 1999: 172; see discussion in Chapter 15 by Besser-Jones, this volume). Even those who propose that virtue is, strictly speaking, necessary for well-being may mean merely that virtue is instrumentally necessary, not that it is among the basic contributors to well-being that philosophers of well-being are concerned to identify.

In this chapter, I aim to bring the virtue literature directly into contact with the well-being literature, and so I will not investigate the prospects for VN understood as a claim that virtue is merely instrumentally necessary, or that that virtue is, loosely speaking, necessary (that it is, for example, a "safe or reliable bet"). Rather, as I shall understand VN,

4. VN claims that, for all human beings, some important threshold of virtue is more than merely instrumentally necessary for achieving the highest degree of well-being available to human beings, where "necessary" is understood in the strict, philosophical sense. [17]

In the remainder, I shall understand VN in a way informed by points 1–4.

Virtue and well-being

As has emerged in the last section, the philosophical literature on virtue and the philosophical literature on well-being do not map on to one another perfectly. Philosophers of well-being aim to identify the basic contributors to well-being, understood as what makes a person's life go well *for her*. But many virtue theorists have background assumptions that make it difficult to bring their views about well-being into direct contact with the philosophical literature on well-being. I will note two such background assumptions.

First, some virtue ethicists are critical of the idea that the contemporary well-being literature does indeed identify a distinctive thing, well-being (Brewer 2008). Those in this tradition who talk about virtue as being "good for" a person may not have the same thing in mind as philosophers of well-being. For example, Gavin Lawrence has proposed that the fundamental notion of goodness *vis-à-vis* a human being is the *good of* a human being, and that to the extent that there is a notion of "goodness *for*" a human being, this is derived from the more fundamental notion of the good *of* a human being (Lawrence 2009; see further Toner 2010: 287).

Second, there are some virtue ethicists who appear to understand the connection between virtue and well-being as conceptual, such that virtue is part of the very concept of well-being (Foot 2001: Chapter 6; Toner 2006a). Philosophers of well-being, by contrast—even those who believe that virtue is a basic contributor to well-being—generally do not think virtue is part of the *concept* of well-being (see discussion in Chapter 15 by Besser-Jones, this volume).

My aim in this chapter is to consider whether virtue may be a basic contributor to well-being, as it is understood by philosophers of well-being. Thus, in this chapter, I will proceed on the assumption that: (1) there is some distinctive subject matter about which philosophers of well-being are offering different accounts; and (2) this thing "well-being" does not include virtue as part of its very concept. Granting that there is such a distinctive thing as well-being (in the sense that philosophers of well-being intend), and that virtue is not part of its very concept, I will consider whether, if we assume one or another of the various accounts of well-being on offer, VN (understood in the way I explained in the preceding section) may be true.

I have proposed that any argument for VN must be conditional: *if* some particular account of well-being (and some particular account of virtue) is true, *then* virtue is necessary for well-being. In the remainder, I will assume that the VE account of virtue is true, and consider whether, *if we assume one or another account of well-being*, VN may be true. I will consider a few of the more widely accepted accounts of well-being in turn.

Hedonism

Hedonistic theories of well-being hold that "how good a life is for the person who lives it is equal to the balance of pleasure over pain in the life"; that "the only thing that is fundamentally intrinsically good for us is our own pleasure; the only thing that is fundamentally intrinsically bad for us is our own pain" (Feldman 2004: 25–30; Heathwood 2010: 648; see Chapter 9 by Gregory, this volume). It may seem as though, assuming a hedonistic account of well-being, the connection between well-being and virtue must be merely instrumental: at most, virtue can *bring about* our pleasure, and thus, even if we assume that virtue is necessary for experiencing a sufficiently high degree of pleasure (and a sufficiently low degree of pain) to count as achieving the highest degree of well-being available to human beings, virtue would be merely *instrumentally* necessary for well-being.

Conversely, recall that virtue, according to VE, does not only bring about pleasure; virtue is *constituted*, in part, by the disposition to experience pleasure in certain moments—by, for example, taking pleasure in a just outcome, experiencing joy when one's child does the honest thing, and so on. Such pleasures will be, at the same time, both direct contributors to well-being *and* expressions of virtue.

Still, unless we restrict the pleasures that are eligible to count as direct contributors to well-being, it is implausible that some degree of virtue is non-instrumentally *necessary for* the highest degree of well-being, if well-being is understood in purely hedonistic terms. People—non-virtuous as well as virtuous—take pleasure in all kinds of things. There seems to be no reason to think that without the pleasures of being virtuous one would fail to realize the amount of pleasure in virtue of which one (according to welfare hedonism) achieves the highest degree of well-being of which human beings are capable. That, in any case, is what the defender of VN would need to show, assuming a VE account of virtue and a hedonistic account of well-being (see Chapter 9 by Jeske, this volume).

Informed-desire theory

Informed-desire theories of well-being hold that an individual's well-being is identified with the satisfaction of her informed desires—those desires we would have if we had full information, were rational, sufficiently reflective, and so on (Haybron 2008; Heathwood 2010). What would it take for virtue to directly contribute to well-being, assuming an informed-desire theory?

It would not be enough for virtue to be instrumentally necessary for satisfying desires; somehow the exercise or expression of virtues would have to be *constitutive of* the satisfaction of desires. And it would not be enough for virtue to be constitutively necessary for satisfying the desires of *some* of us, but not others. VN holds that some degree of virtue is necessary for *all* humans to achieve the highest degree of well-being. Thus, for VN to be true (assuming an informed-desire theory of well-being), the exercise or expression of virtues would have to be *constitutive of* (not merely instrumental to) the satisfaction of desires, *for all human beings* (not only for those who happen to desire being virtuous). How could this be?

For VN to be true, assuming an informed-desire theory of well-being, it would have to be the case that:

1. there are some satisfactions of our informed desires that are constitutive of (or exercises of, or expressions of) the virtues—call these "virtuous satisfactions";
2. these virtuous satisfactions can only be had if a person has a certain threshold of virtue; and
3. for any human being, these virtuous satisfactions are necessary if the person is to achieve the highest degree of well-being available to human beings (they can't be "made up for" by other satisfactions).

By "virtuous satisfactions" of informed desires, we might have in mind desires such as the following:

*   the desire to help the needy, satisfied when, for example, one shares one's home with a displaced disaster victim;
*   the desire to distribute goods justly, satisfied when, for example, as part of an ethics review board at a hospital, one determines the just distribution of a scarce vaccine.

One might object that, as evidenced in these cases, the virtue doesn't *guarantee* the satisfaction of the desire. But this is beside the point: we are considering whether virtue is (more than merely instrumentally) *necessary* for well-being, not whether it is sufficient.

Still, virtue does not appear to be a necessary part of the above examples of satisfactions of desires. The desire to help the needy, or distribute goods justly, *may* be an expression of a person's virtue, but on the other hand it may be just a passing whim, or even an expression of vice (if, for example, one's desire to help the needy is rooted in a desire for social approbation). To show that virtue is (more than merely instrumentally) necessary for well-being, assuming an informed-desire account of well-being, we would need to show how virtue could be *part of* the virtuous satisfaction of the desire (and, moreover, that such virtuous satisfactions are necessary for the highest degree of well-being human beings are capable of).

To this end, it might be helpful to introduce a distinction drawn by ancient eudaimonists that is much discussed by virtue theorists: the distinction between *skopos* and *telos*. Both are roughly translated as "aim": *skopos* as "aim" narrowly construed—one's immediate target—and *telos* as "aim" widely construed—one's overall aim.[18] To illustrate: imagine an archer aiming at a target. In a narrow sense, the aim is simply the hitting of the target. This is the *skopos*. But we might also imagine that the archer also has a broader aim—to *shoot well*. This is the *telos*. Thus the archer might achieve the *skopos* of her action while failing to achieve the *telos* (if, for example, she shoots badly but, due to the luck of a gust of wind, hits the target anyway); or, alternatively, she might achieve the *telos* without achieving the *skopos* (if, for example, she shoots well but a corrupt official arranges for the target to be moved at the last second, causing her to miss).

I propose that the prospects for VN, if an informed-desire theory of welfare is true, depend on understanding the desires in the "virtuous satisfactions of desires" as wide, rather than narrow—analogous to *telos* rather than *skopos*. Our examples of virtuous satisfactions, then, will not be satisfactions of desires to in fact help the needy or distribute goods justly, but to *give well* or *distribute well* (in the sense that an archer aims to *shoot well*). And since it is plausible, on the understanding of virtue described above, that giving well or distributing well *just is* acting virtuously, virtue will be (more than merely instrumentally) necessary for the satisfaction of *these* desires.

Still, to show that VN is true, assuming an informed-desire theory of well-being, one would need to also show that these virtuous satisfactions are necessary if the person is to achieve the highest level of well-being of which human beings are capable. Is it really plausible that one can *only* achieve the maximal satisfaction of desires, and thus the highest degree of well-being, through (what I've called) "virtuous satisfactions" of desires? Even assuming the VE picture of virtue, on which virtues are compatible with the verdicts of practical reason, one might be skeptical that without the virtuous satisfactions of desires a person would be unable to achieve the highest degree of well-being. This is the burden that the defender of VN, assuming a VE account of virtue and an informed-desire account of well-being, would need to meet.

Perfectionism

Perhaps the account of well-being in conjunction with which VN seems most promising is a perfectionist theory of well-being. Perfectionism about well-being "identifies the good with the fulfillment of one's nature: the good life for an x is identified by the core facts about what it means to be an x, by the core account of x-hood" (Dorsey 2010: 61; and see Chapter 10 by Bradford, this volume). According to VE, the virtues are individual excellences in virtue of which creatures like us live excellently. If we understand the individual virtues as dimensions of fulfilling our human natures (as many eudaimonist virtue ethicists do) then it seems as though the very traits whose expression realizes virtue are the traits whose exercise constitutes a good life for us.

Objective-list and hybrid theories of well-being

According to objective-list theories of well-being, there are certain goods that are non-instrumentally good for people, independently of their attitudes (see Chapter 12 by Fletcher, this volume). Objective-list theories are usually pluralistic, and standardly include things like meaningful knowledge, accomplishment, friendship, health, happiness, pleasure, self-respect, autonomy, virtue, and aesthetic experience. These goods—called "basic goods"—are *types* of goods, token instances of which are directly good for people.[19]

According to hybrid theories of well-being, well-being is essentially *both* a matter of having basic goods, such as those listed above, *and* having a certain pro-attitude towards these goods—taking pleasure in them, or enjoying them, for example (see Chapter 13 by Woodard, in this volume).[20] For brevity's sake, in the remainder I will focus on objective-list theory, assuming that what I say may easily be extended to hybrid theories as well.

While objective-list theories take each good on the list as a basic good—as contributing non-instrumentally to the agent's well-being—they needn't hold that a person needs to realize *each* good in order to achieve some relevant threshold of well-being, or even the highest level of well-being of which a human is capable. They might, for example, hold that although every token instance of (true) friendship, aesthetic experience, knowledge, etc. contributes non-instrumentally to the agent's well-being, a life can be just as rich if it contains tokens instances of *most* of these types of basic goods as it would if it contains token instances of *all* of these types of basic goods—that one can be maximally well-off if one's life is exceedingly rich in terms of (for example) knowledge and aesthetic experience, even though it is wholly lacking in friendship. For present purposes I will set this possibility aside and assume that achieving the highest level of well-being requires realizing token instances of *each* type of basic good.

Some objective-list theorists have proposed that virtue itself is one of the basic goods (Fletcher 2013). If this is so (and assuming that achieving the highest level of well-being requires realizing token instances of *each* type of basic good), then it is easy to see how VN may be true.

But what if we don't include virtue as one of the basic goods? May VN yet be true, assuming an objective-list theory of well-being?

Determining whether this may be so requires looking more closely at the token instances of the types of basic goods. For brevity's sake, I will focus on one type of basic good: friendship,[21] understood as "a distinctively personal relationship that is grounded in a concern on the part of each friend for the welfare of the other, for the other's sake, and that involves some degree of intimacy" (Helm 2013). (My understanding of friendship in this paragraph draws heavily on Helm's presentation.) So understood, friendships can include not only friendships in the ordinary sense of the word, but romantic relationships, and also certain other intimate relationships (such as certain working relationships—for example, a relationship of longtime collaborators on a creative or research project). Friendships are characterized, in large part, by deep-seated dispositions of the friends. Friends care about each other for their own sakes. They are disposed to consider one another's feelings: to take joy in their successes, share in their disappointments, and so on. Friends are disposed to act on their friends' behalves—to promote their welfare, to support them in their pursuit of their aims, and so on, not for any ulterior motive, but just for the friend's own sake. A friend is committed to reminding her friend "of what's really valuable in life and to foster within her a commitment to these values so as to prevent her from going astray" (Whiting 1991; Helm 2013). Friends trust one another in a way that makes true intimacy possible, sharing thoughts or experiences they wouldn't share with other more casual acquaintances. Friends take each other seriously, in such a way that their values, interests, reasons, and so on provide one another with *pro tanto* reasons to value and think similarly. Moreover, the relationship is *dynamic*—friends mutually influence each other's sense of value in a way that supports intimacy (Friedman 1989; Helm 2013). Friends have a sense of solidarity, premised on the sharing of values and a sense of what is important. They feel empathy towards one another, even to the point of sharing in one another's pride and shame (Taylor 1985; Sherman 1987; Helm 2013). Finally, and perhaps most simply, friends spend time together, not only in the sense that they are in one another's presence, but in the sense that they partake in shared activities in an engaged way.[22]

Assuming an objective-list theory on which some friendships are necessary for the highest degree of well-being, could it be that some threshold of virtue is (more than merely instrumentally) necessary for realizing the good of friendship?[23]

This could be the case if a person cannot realize the good of friendship in her life without expressing virtue—if the expression or exercise of virtue is not merely instrumental to realizing friendship, but is *constitutive of* it. Recall our sketch of the dimensions of virtue in the section on an account of virtue, above. It is plausible that genuinely caring about, and empathizing with, the friend—feeling joy in her successes, disappointment in her failures, even sharing in her pride and shame—depends on—and is indeed an expression of—those traits in the empathy cluster. Sharing thoughts and experiences with friends, in a way that makes true intimacy possible, is an expression of honesty.[24] Doing what is needed to help keep one's friend on course—reminding her of what's really valuable, fostering her commitment to the projects she finds most valuable—is an expression of integrity. The dynamic aspect of friendship—taking one's friend's values seriously, and treating them as *pro tanto* reason providing for me—is an expression of open-mindedness.

The suggestion here is that, among the actions, attitudes, emotional responses, and so on that are partly constitutive of the friendship are those that are, at the same time, expressions of virtue. And, moreover, while it is not the case that every action, attitude, etc. that makes up the token, in a person's life, of the type of friendship, it *is* the case that if a person doesn't have virtue (as understood in the section on an account of virtue, above), she will fail to realize the good of friendship in her life. The suggestion is that such expressions of virtue are constitutively necessary for realizing friendship: constitutive in that they, in part, constitute the friendship, and necessary in the sense that without such expressions the friendship would fail to *be* a friendship.

One might be skeptical that one cannot realize friendship—*any* friendship—without virtue. In this case, I would press a more modest point: that friendships that do not include, as constitutive elements, expressions of virtue are of a poorer quality than friendships that include expressions of virtue, such that even if such friendships directly contribute to a person's well-being, without friendships of the richer kind—the kind that involves expressions of virtue—a person is precluded from having the *highest kind of well-being available to human beings*. It may both be true that low-quality friendships may contribute non-instrumentally to a person's well-being, *and* that without higher-quality friendships such as the one described above (which, I propose, express virtue) a person is not able to achieve the highest level of well-being. VN does not claim that one needs virtue to achieve *any* degree of well-being; it claims only that one needs virtue to achieve the *highest* degree of well-being. If the token instances of friendship without which one cannot achieve the highest level of well-being humans are capable of are constituted in part by expressions of virtue, then some threshold of virtue is constitutively necessary for well-being, and VN is true.

I have assumed an objective-list theory of well-being according to which achieving the highest level of well-being requires realizing token instances of *each* type of basic good. If this is so, then to prove VN, assuming this objective-list theory of well-being, it would be sufficient to show that some threshold of virtue is non-instrumentally necessary for *any one* basic good. If realizing some threshold of virtue is non-instrumentally necessary for realizing token instances of friendship, for example, and tokens of friendship are non-instrumentally necessary for realizing the highest level of well-being, then virtue is non-instrumentally necessary for well-being.

Still, the prospects for VN would be even better if one could show that some threshold of virtue is non-instrumentally necessary for *more than one* basic good. Could the same kind of point be made for any of the other goods objective-list theorists have proposed are basic goods?

Consider token instances of the basic good of aesthetic experience.[25] Imagine, for example, viewing Pablo Picasso's *Guernica*, or reading George Eliot's *Silas Marner*. It is plausible that successful engagement with an aesthetic object is partly constituted by expressions of virtue, as understood above—the ability to occupy others' points of view, the open-minded engagement, the honest assessment, the charitable interpretation. (See further, Goldie 2008.)

Likewise for meaningful knowledge.[26] It is important to restrict the basic good to *meaningful* knowledge, since it doesn't seem that every instance of knowledge is even *pro tanto* good for us.[27] We may wish to broaden that category beyond knowledge to what Zagzebski has called "cognitive contact with reality," since there seem to be valuable epistemic goods, such as understanding and acquaintance, that do not count as knowledge, strictly speaking. Paradigm instances of meaningful cognitive contact with reality include coming to have an understanding of some part of the natural world, grasping something deep about human nature, or deeply occupying the point of view of someone of with very different religious or political beliefs than one's own. Like token instances of successful engagement with an aesthetic object, token instances of meaningful cognitive contact with reality will often be expressions of open-mindedness, fair-mindedness, honesty, charity, and the traits of empathy. (See further, Zagzebski's account of knowledge as beliefs arising from acts of intellectual virtue (1996), and her view of the relationship between moral and epistemic virtue and value (2003, 2004).)

As in the case of friendship, one may argue that individuals can realize token instances of aesthetic experience or meaningful cognitive contact with reality that are not, at the same time, expressions of virtue. In reply, one might make the analogous, more modest, proposal that if we take away the instances of aesthetic experience or cognitive contact with reality that were also expressions of the virtues—"getting something" about the human experience or stepping outside one's comfort zone to grasp a religious or secular truth—then the person is missing out on something deep and important, such that, although the person may be able to achieve *some* level of well-being, by having some limited aesthetic experience or meaningful cognitive contact with reality, she will be unable to achieve the highest level of well-being of which human beings are capable. If this is the case, VN is true: some threshold of virtue *is* (more than merely instrumentally) necessary for the highest degree of well-being of which human beings are capable.

Conclusion

The proposal that virtue is necessary for well-being might mean a number of different things, ranging from the claim that:

> For virtually all people (with rare exceptions), aspiring to realize some degree of virtue is a safe or reliable bet for achieving perfect well-being.

To the far stronger claim that:

> For each and every person, realizing perfect virtue is necessary for even a moderate threshold of well-being; that one cannot achieve well-being to any desirable degree unless one is perfectly virtuous.

The proposal can be evaluated only when we have in mind a certain account of virtue, a certain account of well-being, and a clear sense of exactly how the former is allegedly necessary for the latter. In this chapter, I hope to have shown that the proposal cannot be dismissed out of hand in light of apparent counterexamples, and to have laid a foundation for future investigation.

Notes

1 I am grateful to all those who have given me helpful feedback on this paper, and especially to Lorraine Besser-Jones, Daniel Danner, Guy Fletcher, Allan Hazlett, Connie Rosati, and participants in the works-in-progress workshop at the University of Edinburgh, June 2014.

2 The approach I propose here is foreshadowed by Hooker (1996). Hooker considers whether moral virtue constitutes a benefit to the agent, and does, as I suggest here, consider a number of theoretical accounts of well-being. However, he relies on an intuitive understanding of virtue.

3 For example, Engstrom (1996, 2002) develops the role of virtue in Kant's theory, and Driver (2001) gives a consequentialist account of virtue.

4 For some proposals, see Solomon (1988), Trianosky (1990), Schneewind (1990), Crisp (1996: 5), Oakley (1996), Crisp and Slote (1997: 2–3), Santas (1997), Watson (1997), Russell (2009: ix) and Snow (2010: 1–2).

5 According to the eudaimonist account of virtue, the virtues are traits whose possession or exercise is partly or wholly constitutive of *eudaimonia* (see Besser-Jones, Chapter 15, this volume). Since *eudaimonia* is sometimes translated as "well-being," one might wonder whether it would be possible, on a eudaimonist account, for the virtues *not* to be necessary for well-being. But not all eudaimonists understand *eudaimonia* as equivalent to well-being, as well-being is understood by contemporary philosophers of well-being. For example, Toner proposes that *eudaimonia* may be understood as essentially a matter of standing in "the right relation to 'objects' according to their degrees and kinds of goodness" (Toner 2006b: 613). See also Foot (2001: 97) and Hursthouse (1999: 167–168). See further Baril (2014). In any case, the account of virtue I develop here does not depend on the eudaimonist claim that the virtues are the traits we need for *eudaimonia*, where *eudaimonia* is understood as well-being (as well-being is understood by contemporary philosophers of well-being).

6 Character traits, as they are understood by VE, are, in John Doris's terminology, "global" rather than "local" traits (Doris 1998, 2002; see further Miller 2013: Chapter 1). In contrast with a virtue ethical

view that understands virtues as traits that span only a narrow range of circumstances (for example, classroom-examination-honesty or online-survey-honesty), VE recognizes a virtue of honesty, understood as a single coherent trait that may be expressed in test taking, online surveys, conversations with friends, and in many other contexts.

7 The same will be true of any account of the virtues. No account of the virtues can capture all of our intuitions about the virtues since, as we shall see, some of our intuitions about the virtues are in conflict with others.

8 One might be concerned that, if we allow virtue to be sensitive to reason in this way, we are guaranteeing the truth of the claim that virtue is necessary for well-being. But that would only be the case if practical reason tells us that our sole, ultimate aim should be to maximally promote our well-being—something that virtually no philosophers of well-being believe.

9 That is, if we assume that there are some circumstances in which telling a lie is the best thing to do in the circumstances, all things considered.

10 One might object that it violates intuitions to call a character trait that includes a disposition to lie on occasion "honesty." But there is no philosophical account of an individual virtue that exactly matches our intuitive idea of what the virtue should be. At some point, if the trait that a theorist counts as a virtue looks different enough from our intuitive picture of that trait, then that theorist should give that trait a different name, to avoid confusion. But that decision is a merely terminological one.

11 For some discussions of particular virtues and vices, see: Foot (1978); Wallace (1978); Pears (1980: discussing courage); Williams (1980: discussing justice); O'Connor (1988); Young (1988: discussing temperance); Hursthouse (1999: especially her discussion of honesty, courage, and charity); and Curzer (2012). Most discussions of individual virtues are of Aristotle's virtues, or from a loosely Aristotelian point of view. For a discussion of particular virtues from a non-Aristotelian point of view, see Driver (2001: Chapter 2).

12 The person of developed virtue will be not only sensitive and skillful in her own narrow social sphere; as she develops, she will see how these same qualities commit her to taking steps on behalf of more abstract causes. See further, Becker (1998: 112).

13 Just as there are a number of different accounts of what makes a trait an ethical virtue, so are there different accounts of what makes a trait an intellectual, or epistemic, virtue. James Montmarquet, for example, understands an epistemic virtue as a trait a truth-desiring person would want to have (Montmarquet 1993). See Baehr (2011) and Roberts and Wood (2007) for alternative accounts of intellectual virtues, understood as character traits.

14 This will be important to remember when, in the section on virtue and well-being, I consider whether virtue is necessary for well-being. At various points, I will focus on one dimension of virtue or another, but the reader should keep in mind that what we are asking about is virtue as a whole, not some individual virtue considered independently.

15 I intend "virtuous actions" to be neutral between actions performed from virtue, and the actions the virtuous person would perform. See Audi (1997: 174–189); Swanton (2003: 231–233); Van Hooft (2006: Chapter 5); and Van Zyl (2014).

16 "Net" in the sense that the overall positive contribution of the virtue is not outweighed by the overall negative contribution of the virtue (as, for example, the good feeling one gets from telling the truth might be outweighed by the harm that telling the truth may do to one's reputation).

17 VN, then, as I shall understand it, is not an empirical claim that can be supported or undermined by empirical psychological studies. For an argument on behalf of an empirical connection between virtue and well-being, see Snow (2008).

18 There are a number of ways of drawing this distinction. Here I follow Annas (2003: 24–25). See also Annas (1993: 34).

19 For example, friendship is a type, token instances of which—A's friendship with B, or C—are directly good for A. As Lauinger puts it: "Some (any) state of affairs, X, is a component of the well-being of some (any) human being, A, if, and because, X is, for A, an instance of one of the basic goods" (Lauinger 2013: 272).

20 An objective-list theorist may, however, hold that realizing some token instance of one of these goods in one's life *implies* certain pro-attitudes. On this view, friendship, for example, involves—is in fact partly constituted by—certain pro-attitudes, such as caring about one's friend for her own sake (Fletcher 2013).

21 Objective-list and hybrid theorists who suggest that friendship, or "loving relationships," are a basic good include Finnis (1980), Murphy (2001), Fletcher (2013), Lauinger (2013) and Rice (2013).

22 "He ought therefore at the same time to perceive the being of his friend, and this will come about in their living together and exchanging words and thoughts; this is what living together would seem to mean in the case of people and not, as in the case of cattle, grazing in the same place" (Aristotle 2000: 1170b).

23 Aristotle claimed that true friendships, of the most valuable kind, are only possible between virtuous people (Aristotle 2000, 1156b). I shall set aside the question of whether I can be friends with someone who is not virtuous. The present question is whether I can realize the good of friendship in my life without being virtuous myself.

24 See further, Graham and LaFollette (1986).

25 The view that aesthetic experience or "awareness of true beauty" is a basic good is defended by Finnis (1980) and Murphy (2001), suggested by Lauinger (2013).

26 The view that knowledge, or "meaningful knowledge," is a basic good is defended by Finnis (1980) and Murphy (2001), suggested by Kagan (2009), Lauinger (2013), and Rice (2013).

27 Consider, for example, cases of knowing that there are 32 dust motes on the table, or that the last name of the 16th entry on the 16th page of the Albuquerque phone book is "Alvarado."

Bibliography

Adams, R. (2006) *A Theory of Virtue: Excellence in Being for the Good*, Oxford: Oxford University Press.

Annas, J. (1993) *The Morality of Happiness*, Oxford: Oxford University Press.

Annas, J. (2003) "The Structure of Virtue," in M. DePaul and L. Zagzebski (eds.), *Intellectual Virtue: Perspectives from Ethics and Epistemology*, Oxford: Oxford University Press, pp. 15–33.

Aristotle. (2000) *Nicomachean Ethics*, in R. Crisp (ed.), Cambridge: Cambridge University Press.

Arpaly, N. (2011) "Open-mindedness as a Moral Virtue," *American Philosophical Quarterly* 48(1): 75–85.

Audi, R (1997) *Moral Knowledge and Ethical Character,* Oxford: Oxford University Press.

Baehr, J. (2011) *The Inquiring Mind: On Intellectual Virtues and Virtue Epistemology*, Oxford: Oxford University Press.

Baehr, J. (2012) "Open-mindedness," in M. Austin and R. Geivett (eds.), *Being Good: Christian Virtues for Everyday Life,* Cambridge: Wm. B. Eerdmans Publishing Co., pp. 30–52.

Baril, A. (2014) "Eudaimonia in Contemporary Virtue Ethics," in S. van Hooft (ed.) *The Handbook of Virtue Ethics*, New York: Routledge, pp. 17–27.

Becker, L.C. (1998) *A New Stoicism,* Princeton, NJ: Princeton University Press.

Besser-Jones, L. (2008) "Personal Integrity, Morality and Psychological Well-Being: Justifying the Demands of Morality," *Journal of Moral Philosophy* 5(3): 361–383.

Brewer, T. (2008) "Is Welfare an Independent Good?" *Social Philosophy and Policy* 26(1): 96–125.

Crisp, R. (1996) "Modern Moral Philosophy and the Virtues," in R. Crisp (ed.), *How Should One Live? Essays on the Virtues*, Oxford: Oxford University Press, pp. 1–18.

Crisp, R. and Slote, M. (1997) "Introduction," in R. Crisp and M. Slote (eds.), *Virtue Ethics*, Oxford: Oxford University Press, pp. 1–25.

Curzer, H. (2012) *Aristotle and the Virtues*, Oxford: Oxford University Press.

Doris, J. (1998) "Persons, Situations, and Virtue Ethics." *Nous* 32(4): 504–530.

Doris, J. (2002) *Lack of Character: Personality and Moral Behavior.* Cambridge: Cambridge University Press.

Dorsey, D. (2010) "Three Arguments for Perfectionism." *Noûs* 44(1): 59–79.

Driver, J. (2001) *Uneasy Virtue*, Cambridge: Cambridge University Press.

Engstrom, S. (1996) "Happiness and the Highest Good in Aristotle and Kant," in S. Engstrom and J. Whiting (eds.), *Aristotle, Kant, and the Stoics: Rethinking Happiness and Duty,* Cambridge: Cambridge University Press, pp. 102–138.

Engstrom, S. (2002) "The Inner Freedom of Virtue," in M. Timmons (ed.), *Kant's* Metaphysics of Morals: *Interpretive Essays,* Oxford: Oxford University Press, pp. 289–315.

Feldman, F. (2004) *Pleasure and the Good Life*, Oxford: Oxford University Press.

Finnis, J. (1980) *Natural Law and Natural Rights*, Oxford: Oxford University Press.

Fletcher, G. (2013) "A Fresh Start for the Objective-List Theory of Well-Being," *Utilitas* 25(2): 206–220.

Foot, P. (1978) "Virtues and Vices," in *Virtues and Vices and Other Essays in Moral Philosophy*, Berkeley, CA: University of California Press, pp. 1–18.

Foot, P. (2001) *Natural Goodness*, Oxford: Oxford University Press.

Friedman, M. (1989) "Friendship and Moral Growth," *Journal of Value Inquiry* 23: 3–13.

Goldie, P. (2008) "Virtues of Art and Human Well-Being," *Aristotelian Society Supplementary Volume* 82(1): 179–195.

Graham, G. and LaFollette, H. (1986) "Honesty and Intimacy," *Journal of Social and Personal Relationships* 3: 3–18.

Hales, S. (2013) *This is Philosophy: An Introduction*, Malden: Wiley-Blackwell.

Haybron, D. (2007) "Well-being and Virtue," *Journal of Ethics and Social Philosophy* 2(2): 1–27.

Haybron, D. (2008) *The Pursuit of Unhappiness: The Elusive Psychology of Well-being*, Oxford: Oxford University Press.

Heathwood, C. (2010) "Welfare," in J. Skorupski (ed.), *Routledge Companion to Ethics*, New York: Routledge, pp. 645–655.

Helm, B. (2013) "Friendship," in E. Zalta (ed.) *The Stanford Encyclopedia of Philosophy* (Fall 2013 Edition), http://plato.stanford.edu/entries/friendship/.

Hooker, B. (1996) "Does Moral Virtue Constitute a Benefit to the Agent?" in R. Crisp (ed.) *How Should One Live? Essays on the Virtues,* Oxford: Oxford University Press, pp. 141–155.

Hume, D. (1777/1975) *Enquiries Concerning Human Understanding and Concerning the Principles of Morals*, L. Selby-Bigge (ed.), Oxford: Oxford University Press.

Hurka, T. (2001) *Virtue, Vice, and Value*, Oxford: Oxford University Press.

Hursthouse, R. (1999) *On Virtue Ethics*, Oxford: Oxford University Press.

Hursthouse, R. (2013) "Virtue Ethics," in E. Zalta (ed.) *The Stanford Encyclopedia of Philosophy* (Fall 2013 Edition), http://plato.stanford.edu/archives/fall2013/entries/ethics-virtue/.

Kagan, S. (2009) "Well-Being as Enjoying the Good," *Philosophical Perspectives* 23(1): 253–272.

Kamtekar, R. (2004) "Situationism and Virtue Ethics on the Content of Our Character," *Ethics* 114(3): 458–491.

Lauinger, W. (2013) "The Missing-Desires Objection to Hybrid Theories of Well-Being," *The Southern Journal of Philosophy* 51(2): 270–295.

Lawrence, G. (2009) "Is Aristotle's Function Argument Fallacious? Part 1, Groundwork: Initial Clarification of Objections," *Philosophical Inquiry* XXXI(1–2): 191–224.

Mertz Hsieh, D. (2004) "False Excuses: Honesty, Wrongdoing, and Moral Growth." *The Journal of Value Inquiry* 38(2): 171–185.

Miller, C. (2003) "Social Psychology and Virtue Ethics," *The Journal of Ethics* 7: 365–392.

Miller, C. (2013) *Moral Character: An Empirical Theory*, Oxford: Oxford University Press.

Montmarquet, J. (1993) *Epistemic Virtue and Doxastic Responsibility*, Lanham, MD: Rowman and Littlefield.

Murphy, M. (2001) *Natural Law and Practical Rationality*, Cambridge: Cambridge University Press.

Nussbaum, M. (1999) "Virtue Ethics: A Misleading Category?" *The Journal of Ethics:* 3(3): 163–201.

Oakley, J. (1996) "Varieties of Virtue Ethics," *Ratio* 9(2): 128–152.

O'Connor, D. (1988) "Aristotelian Justice as a Personal Virtue," *Midwest Studies in Philosophy* XIII: 417–427.

Pears, D. (1980) "Courage as a Mean," in A. Rorty (ed.), *Essays on Aristotle's Ethics*, Berkeley, CA: University of California Press, pp. 171–187.

Rice, C. (2013) "Defending the Objective List Theory of Well-Being," *Ratio* 26(2): 196–211.

Roberts, R. and Wood, W. (2007) *Intellectual Virtues: An Essay in Regulative Epistemology,* Oxford: Clarendon Press.

Rosati, C. (2006) "Personal Good," in T. Horgan and M. Timmons (eds.), *Metaethics after Moore*, Oxford: Clarendon Press, pp. 107–132.

Russell, D. (2009) *Practical Intelligence and the Virtues*, Oxford: Oxford University Press.

Santas, G.X. (1997) "Does Aristotle Have a Virtue Ethics?" in *Virtue Ethics*, ed. D. Statman. Edinburgh: Edinburgh University Press, pp. 260–285. Reprinted from *Philosophical Inquiry* 15(3–4): 1-32, 1993.

Schneewind, J.B. (1990) "The Misfortunes of Virtue," *Ethics* 101(1): 42–63.

Snow, N.E. (2010) *Virtue as Social Intelligence*, New York: Routledge.

Sherman, N. (1987) "Aristotle on Friendship and the Shared Life," *Philosophy & Phenomenological Research* 47(4): 589–613.

Snow, N. (2008) "Virtue and Flourishing," *Journal of Social Philosophy* 39(2): 225–245.

Solomon, D. (1988) "Internal Objections to Virtue Ethics," *Midwest Studies in Philosophy* 13(1): 428–441.

Swanton, C. (2003) *Virtue Ethics: A Pluralistic View*, Oxford: Oxford University Press.

Swanton, C. (forthcoming) "Hume and Virtue Ethics," in P. Russell (ed.), *The Oxford Handbook of Hume*, Oxford: Oxford University Press.

Taylor, G. (1985) *Pride, Shame, and Guilt: Emotions of Self-Assessment*, Oxford: Oxford University Press.

Toner, C. (2006a) "Aristotelian Well-Being: A Response to L.W. Sumner's Critique," *Utilitas* 18(3): 218–231.

Toner, C. (2006b) "The Self-Centredness Objection to Virtue Ethics," *Philosophy* 81(4): 595–617.

Toner, C. (2010) "Virtue Ethics and the Nature and Forms of Egoism," *Journal of Philosophical Research* 35: 275–303.

Trianosky, G. (1990) "What is Virtue Ethics all About?" *American Philosophical Quarterly* 27(4): 335–344.

Van Hooft, S. (2006) *Caring About Health,* Burlington VT: Ashgate Publishing Limited.

Van Zyl, L. (2014) "Right Action and the Targets of Virtue," in S. van Hooft (ed.), *The Handbook of Virtue Ethics*, Abingdon, Oxon: Routledge.

Wallace, J. (1978) *Virtues and Vices*, Ithaca: Cornell University Press.

Watson, G. (1997) "On the Primacy of Character," in *Virtue Ethics*, ed. D. Statman. Edinburgh: Edinburgh University Press, pp. 56–81. Reprinted from *Identity, Character, and Morality,* ed. Flanagan and Rorty, 1990.

Whiting, J. (1991) "Impersonal Friends," *Monist* 74(1): 3–29.

Williams, B. (1980) "Justice as a Virtue," in A. Rorty (ed.), *Essays on Aristotle's Ethics*, Berkeley, CA: University of California Press, pp. 189–199.

Williams, B. (1981) "Utilitarianism and Moral Self-Indulgence," *Moral Luck: Philosophical Papers 1973–1980*, Cambridge: Cambridge University Press, pp. 40–53.

Young, C. (1988) "Aristotle on Temperance," *The Philosophical Review* 97(4): 521–542.

Zagzebski, L. (1996) *Virtues of the Mind: An Inquiry into the Nature of Virtue and the Ethical Foundations 2 of Knowledge*, Cambridge: Cambridge University Press.

Zagzebski, L. (2003) "The Search for the Source of Epistemic Good," *Metaphilosophy* 34(1–2): 12–28.

Zagzebski, L. (2004) "Epistemic Value and the Primacy of What We Care About," *Philosophical Papers* 33(3): 353–377.

Zagzebski, L. (2010) "Exemplarist Virtue Theory," *Metaphilosophy* 41(1–2): 41–57.

21

EPISTEMIC GOODS

Allan Hazlett

What of substance can we say about well-being and epistemic goods? The phrase "epistemic goods" is ambiguous.[1] It could be used to refer to the set of things that are both good and (in some sense that would need to be articulated) distinctively "epistemic." Or it could be used to refer to the set of things that are good in some distinctively "epistemic" sense of "good" (that would need to be articulated). We are here interested in well-being, and so we shall adopt the former disambiguation, and understand "good" to mean "good *vis-à-vis* well-being."[2]

This requires us to articulate the notion of the epistemic. The term "epistemic" is ubiquitous in contemporary philosophy, although its intended meaning is sometimes unclear. Here we shall say that something is *epistemic* if and only if it is essentially contained in the *domain of the intellect*, where this comprises the (individual or collective) generation and sharing of information (including the practices and institutions that sustain and regulate these in a society).[3] "Information" is used in its non-factive sense (there can be both true and false information); paradigm epistemic things therefore include: belief formation, inquiry, conversation, hypothesis testing, giving and asking for evidence, heuristics and biases, and education.

Our question will be: what things are epistemic goods, in the sense just articulated? In other words: what things are both epistemic and good *vis-à-vis* well-being?

Terminology and methodology

I assume that *well-being* is what is good for an individual—for this reason, "well-being" seems synonymous with "(good) quality of life," "welfare," and "flourishing," as well as, on at least some readings of these expressions, "living well," "happiness," and "the good life." And I assume that for *x* to be good *vis-à-vis* well-being is for *x* to contribute in some way to well-being—or, as I'll put it sometimes, for *x* to have *eudaimonic value*. Something has *agent-relative* eudaimonic value when it contributes to the well-being of some salient individual. Something has *agent-neutral* eudaimonic value when it contributes to the well-being of individuals in general. I have a broad sense of contribution in mind, such that we can distinguish at least two species of contribution. In one kind of case, one thing contributes to another by being among its causes—this is a *causal contribution*. In another kind of case, one thing contributes to another by being among its parts—this is a *constitutive contribution*. In this kind of case, *x* is valuable in virtue of being part of a valuable whole.[4] When x makes a causal contribution to well-being x has instrumental eudaimonic value[5]; when x makes a constitutive contribution to well-being, we'll say that x has *constitutive* eudaimonic value.[6,7]

Even given these distinctions, the claim that x contributes to y is ambiguous; it could mean any one, or perhaps some combination, of the following:

- that x always contributes to y;
- that x is necessary for y;
- that x normally (or typically, or generally) contributes to y; alternatively, that x is conducive to y;
- that x is more conducive to y than anything else[8];
- that x per se (or as such) contributes to y, i.e. that x contributes to y in virtue of being x;
- that x sometimes, when certain conditions are met, contributes to y.

We must keep the need for disambiguation in mind, in what follows, when we consider the claim that x has eudaimonic value.

So our question is: what things are both epistemic and conducive to well-being (either the well-being of some salient individual or the well-being of individuals in general)? How should we go about attempting to answer this question? You might argue that we must first articulate and defend a theory of well-being, since only once we have settled the question of the nature of well-being will we be able sensibly to determine what things are conducive to well-being. It seems clear that at least some theories of well-being have consequences *vis-à-vis* our question. Assume that knowledge is epistemic, and consider a hedonist who identifies well-being with pleasure; it seems clear that, on her view, it is not the case that knowledge per se contributes to the possessor's well-being, since knowledge is not per se pleasurable for the possessor. Or consider a Platonist who identifies well-being with knowledge; it seems clear that, on her view, knowledge has constitutive agent-relative eudaimonic value. However, we will be best served here by a policy of bracketing the question of the nature of well-being and attempting a theory-neutral survey of candidate epistemic goods. We will of course need to be aware, as we proceed, how the prior selection of a theory of well-being would affect how we answer our question. But we should also consider, to the extent that we can, the pre-theoretical merits of these candidates.

Knowledge

Knowledge is a genus of which there are several species. The most famous is propositional knowledge (e.g., knowledge that the cat is on the mat), but there are others that are equally important, including explanatory understanding (e.g., understanding why the cat is on the mat).[9] Even mere true belief (e.g., that the cat is on the mat) can be understood as a species of knowledge.[10] *Knowledge*, in the present sense, is accurate representation.[11] Representations can be accurate (correct, right, true, veridical) or inaccurate (incorrect, wrong, mistaken, erroneous, false); knowledge is instantiated when a representation is accurate.

For our purposes here we need not worry too much about the boundaries of the concept of accurate representation. Consider the kind of acquaintance that is afforded by perception, the kind of interpersonal knowledge that exists between friends who know each other well, and the kind of practical knowledge that we attribute to those who know (or understand) how to do something. Are these species of accurate representation? We can set this question aside. Later on we'll consider an important species of practical knowledge and an important species of interpersonal knowledge.

Does knowledge have eudaimonic value? Recall the several ambiguities in this question, that I discussed in the previous section. However, two disambiguated claims seem plausible. First, knowledge sometimes causally contributes both to the well-being of the possessor and to the well-being of other individuals.[12] You know that a bus is bearing down on you, so you jump out of the way; you know that a bus is bearing down on someone else, so you pull her to safety. Moreover, you might think that knowledge sometimes causally contributes to well-being in more important ways. Perhaps there are especially useful principles, knowledge of which significantly affects how you think, feel, and act, and thus affects your well-being or the well-being of others.[13] Second, knowledge sometimes makes a constitutive contribution to the well-being of the possessor. Charles Darwin endeavored for many years to understand the origin of species, and as a result of his efforts, he came to understand the origin of species. This understanding was a part of the goodness of his life. You might think, for example, that well-being consists in the incorporation of a plurality of intrinsically valuable things into a harmonious and integrated life.[14] Many philosophers claim that knowledge is intrinsically valuable,[15] and therefore, on the present view, one of those things that might be incorporated into a life of well-being. In any event, knowledge plausibly has both agent-relative and agent-neutral instrumental eudaimonic value, as well as agent-relative constitutive eudaimonic value. This latter view, in particular, is popular among virtue ethicists and virtue epistemologists.[16]

Recall, again, the ambiguity of the claim that *x* contributes to *y*. I just claimed that it is plausible that knowledge *sometimes* contributes to well-being. Can we defend a more ambitious disambiguation of the claim that knowledge contributes to well-being?

Does knowledge *always* contribute to well-being? Imagine that a villain threatens to kill me and everyone I care about unless I remain ignorant of how many jellybeans there are in a jar. (All I need to do, to comply with the villain's threat, is to refrain from counting the jellybeans.) It is easy to imagine that, in this case, knowledge would causally contribute neither to my well-being nor to the well-being of anyone else. This shows us that knowledge does not always causally contribute either to the well-being of the possessor or to the well-being of other individuals—knowledge is not always *useful*. However, the case also illustrates the fact that knowledge does not always make a constitutive contribution to the well-being of the possessor. Even setting aside the villain's threat, knowledge about the number of jellybeans in this jar seems utterly orthogonal to my well-being. Knowledge must be *significant* to (partially) constitute the well-being of the possessor; but there is insignificant knowledge. By contrast with knowledge about the numerosity of these jellybeans, some instances of scientific knowledge, aesthetic knowledge, moral knowledge, and historical knowledge all seem at least relatively significant.[17] Consider what Aristotle calls *sophia* (sometimes translated as "theoretical wisdom")—an understanding of fundamental causes—and which he contrasts with mere propositional knowledge as well as with understanding of non-fundamental causes.[18] It sounds plausible to say that *sophia* has constitutive eudaimonic value. In any event, we can put the present point like this: the constitutive eudaimonic value of knowledge is conditional on its significance.

Significance seems to be a matter of the content of an instance of knowledge[19]—it is natural to say that the significance of an instance of propositional knowledge, for example, is down to the significance of the truth known. You might think that there are additional conditions on the eudaimonic value of knowledge.[20] Recall our example of Darwin's understanding of the origin of species, where we imagined Darwin working for years to acquire this understanding. Compare someone who is indifferent to understanding the origin of species, who just doesn't care about this, and whose deepest values and commitments, what she cares about, her "ground projects" (as Bernard Williams puts it), conflict with understanding the origin of species: to understand the origin of species would interfere with her living a meaningful life; she does not have the time or resources or energy it takes to understand the origin of species, without sacrificing her pursuit of that which she cares about. If you like, we can imagine that she has chosen a different kind of life, a rich and meaningful life, devoted to something other than understanding the origin of species: athletic excellence, raising a family, or a moral crusade. Understanding the origin of species would not be good for such a person. So the eudaimonic value of knowledge seems to be conditional on the sorts of considerations just adduced, such as the values and commitments of the knower and the suitability of such knowledge in the context of her life.

In any event, it seems that knowledge does not always contribute to well-being.[21] Let's now turn to an alternative disambiguation of the claim that knowledge contributes to well-being that is also more ambitious than the claim that knowledge sometimes contributes to well-being: that knowledge is necessary for well-being.

Is knowledge *necessary* for well-being? We should confine our attention to human well-being, for you might think that there are creatures (e.g., plants) for whose well-being knowledge is clearly not necessary. So is knowledge necessary for human well-being? It seems hard to imagine a human being living well without having *some* knowledge. But we must tread carefully here. It might be that it is hard to imagine a completely ignorant human being living well, not because of any non-trivial connection between knowledge and human well-being, but rather because it is hard to imagine a completely ignorant human, full stop. Consider emotion—it is hard to imagine an emotionless human being living well, but it is also hard to imagine an emotionless human being, full stop. (This is why *Star Trek*'s emotionless android Data is interesting.) We would need more than this to defend a non-trivial connection between emotion and human well-being, and so we will need more to defend a non-trivial connection between knowledge and human well-being.

Perhaps the notion of significant knowledge, mentioned above, will help us here. Might we say that significant knowledge is necessary for human well-being? This question is complicated by the appeal of a skeptical tradition, originating with Socrates, that rejects the possibility of significant knowledge while accepting the eudaimonic value of seeking it. Seeking *x* might have eudaimonic value even if acquiring *x* is impossible. Compare: my doctor prescribes that I try to touch my toes, which is good for my health, even though it is impossible for me to touch my toes. (The example also suggests that seeking *x* can have eudaimonic value even when *x* lacks eudaimonic value—touching my toes isn't good for my health; it's only trying to touch them that's good for my health.) So you might think that the necessity of knowledge for human well-being is best articulated as the claim that seeking *or* acquiring significant knowledge is necessary for human well-being.

However, this is not plausible. It is too easy to imagine good human lives that involve no such search, nor any such acquisition. There are too many intuitively valuable things other than knowledge, and too many admirable personal traits other than curiosity, for us to be unable to imagine human well-being without the search for, or the acquisition of, significant knowledge. Athletics, parenting, morality—I mentioned these three above in connection with the case of the person who did not want to understand the origin of species. They serve our present purposes as well: these are projects distinct from the quest for significant knowledge, the pursuit of which inspires our admiration and (in some cases) our allegiance. Moralists tell us that morality is necessary for true happiness; our parents tell us that we ought to have children; sports radio hosts tout the universal importance of athletics . . . and many philosophers say that no one is happy unless she yearns for *sophia*. Better to say that these are all worthwhile projects, but that none is such that pursuit of it is necessary for human well-being (while perhaps conceding that the pursuit of at least some of these is necessary for human well-being).

You might object that the pursuit of athletics, parenting, and morality all require certain items of knowledge—knowledge that is useful *vis-à-vis* these projects. But if this provides the sense in which knowledge is necessary for well-being, then almost anything can be said to be necessary for well-being, so long as some instances of that thing are useful *vis-à-vis* such projects. It seems trivial that knowledge is necessary for well-being, if all this means is that some instances of knowledge are useful *vis-à-vis* the kinds of projects the pursuit of which sometimes constitutes well-being. For this can be said of almost anything.

I conclude that we have failed to find a plausible (non-trivial) articulation of the idea that knowledge is necessary for well-being.

A final point on the eudaimonic value of knowledge. I said, above, that true belief is a species of knowledge. You might think that (in some sense that would need to be articulated) belief aims at truth, and that therefore true belief is valuable, in virtue of being an instance of something that has achieved its aim.[22] But this conclusion, alone, doesn't tell us anything about the eudaimonic value of true belief. We would need to add something like the claim that it is good *for an individual* to have mental states that achieve *their* aim. This doesn't seem true in general. This is why Lieutenant Kaffee (in *A Few Good Men*) can say, "I want the truth," and Colonel Jessup can say, "You can't handle the truth." Jessup doesn't say: "Of course you want the truth, since truth is the aim of belief." We sometimes say that we want the truth, because we don't always want the truth.[23] We sometimes think that true belief will be good for us, and other times think it will be bad for us. So the aim of belief, alone, doesn't tell us anything about the eudaimonic value of true belief.

Intellectual virtues

In this section we'll consider the idea that intellectual virtues contribute to well-being. Like the expression "epistemic goods," the expression "intellectual virtues" is ambiguous. It could be used to refer to the set of things that are both virtues and (in some sense that would need to be articulated) distinctively "intellectual." Call this a *predicative disambiguation* of "intellectual virtue." Or it could be used to refer to the set of things that are virtues in some distinctively "intellectual" sense of "virtue" (that would need to be articulated). Call this an *attributive disambiguation* of "intellectual virtue." Let's consider the present idea—that intellectual virtues contribute to well-being—first on the attributive disambiguation of "intellectual virtue" and then on the predicative disambiguation.

"Intellectual," as this term is used by philosophers, means the same as "epistemic"—so our articulation of the notion of the epistemic (above) will prove useful here.

The attributive disambiguation

Ernest Sosa (1991) articulates a now-familiar attributive disambiguation of "intellectual virtue" when he defines an intellectual virtue as "a quality bound to help maximize one's surplus of truth over error" (225). This understanding of "intellectual virtue" has become standard in contemporary epistemology, where intellectual virtues are understood (more broadly) to be personal qualities conducive to the acquisition of knowledge (as understood above), either by the possessor or by other people.

Do intellectual virtues, so understood, contribute either to the well-being of the possessor or to the well-being of individuals in general? It's natural to think that the answer to this question depends entirely on the answer to the question of whether knowledge contributes either to the well-being of the possessor or to the well-being of other individuals (see above).

The eudaimonic value of personal qualities conductive to the acquisition of *x*, so the thought goes, is entirely derivative on the eudaimonic value of *x*. If this is right, then the eudaimonic value of intellectual virtue flows straightaway from the eudaimonic value of knowledge.[24]

The predicative disambiguation

An intellectual virtue, on the predicative disambiguation, is something that is both intellectual and a virtue. We require articulations both of the notion of a virtue and of the notion of the intellectual.

The notion of a virtue has both a descriptive and a prescriptive aspect, and any account of the nature of virtue must explain both its ontology—i.e., what sort of a thing a virtue is—and its value—i.e., why virtues are admirable or desirable.[25] The following simple account does both of these things: *virtues* are excellences, i.e., character traits consisting of the disposition to Φ at the right time and in the right way. This account is minimal both when it comes to the ontology and the value of virtue. On the side of ontology, you might want to add, for example, that the virtuous person must be responsible for having the virtues that she has, or that the virtuous person must be intelligent in her manifestations of virtue. These issues won't matter here. On the side of value, we must say more about the notion of Fing at the right time and in the right way. We'll return to that issue, below.

What then makes a virtue *intellectual*? There are a few different ways we might answer this question. Aristotle (*Nicomachean Ethics*, IV.1) divides the virtues into those that are excellences of the thinking part of the soul and those that are excellences of the ethical part of the soul; the former are the intellectual virtues. We can call this an *organic* conception of intellectual virtue, since the intellectual virtues are distinguished from the non-intellectual virtues by appeal to the distinctive organ of which they are excellences. Linda Zagzebski (1996: §II.3) characterizes the intellectual virtues by appeal to the distinctive kind of motivation by which they are constituted: intellectual virtues are forms of loving knowledge.[26] We can call this a *teleological* conception of intellectual virtues, since the intellectual virtues are distinguished from the non-intellectual virtues by appeal to the distinctive end towards which they are directed. Alternatively, we can characterize the intellectual virtues by appeal to the distinctive domain to which they essentially belong—the domain of the intellect, as defined above. We can call this an *energetic* conception of intellectual virtue, since the intellectual virtues are distinguished from the non-intellectual virtues by appeal to the distinctive activity—the generation and transfer of information—with which they are concerned. I'll employ this conception here.

Do intellectual virtues, so understood, contribute either to the well-being of the possessor or to the well-being of individuals in general? This seems to depend entirely on how we understand the notion of Φ at the right time and in the right way. We could say that the right time and way to Φ is just whatever time and way to Φ is conducive to the well-being of the virtuous person, in which case it trivially follows that (intellectual) virtue contributes to the well-being of the possessor.[27] Or we could say that the right time and way to Φ is just whatever time and way to Φ is conducive to the well-being of individuals in general, trivially securing the conclusion that (intellectual) virtue contributes to the well-being of individuals in general.[28] Finally, we could say that the right time and way to Φ is just whatever time and way would be good, all things considered.[29] We would then need to argue for a non-trivial connection between well-being and what would be good, all things considered—at a minimum, we would need to argue that well-being is something good.

Let's conclude our discussion of intellectual virtues by considering four candidate intellectual virtues and thinking about the ways in which they might contribute to well-being. First, consider what Aristotle calls *phronesis* (sometimes translated as "practical wisdom"), which consists in some form of perception or judgment about what is to be done, or, in general, about how to live well.[30] *Phronesis*, in this sense, seems thus to yield or to consist in a species of practical knowledge, namely, knowledge about how to live well.[31] It is natural to conclude that such knowledge has agent-relative eudaimonic value: the person who knows how to live well, so the argument goes, is normally going to be better off vis-à-vis living well than the person who does not know how to live well. Or you might think that phronesis itself is a part of well-being; compare the idea that *sophia* is necessary for well-being (see above). In either case, it seems that *phronesis* is conducive to the well-being of the possessor.

Second, consider curiosity, which consists in some form of desire for knowledge. You might connect curiosity and well-being by appeal to an antecedently plausible connection between knowledge and well-being (see above), along with the principle that, if x contributes to well-being, then a desire for x also contributes to well-being. Alternatively, you might argue for connections between curiosity and other things that contribute to well-being. For example, in a series of recent studies, Todd Kashdan and his colleagues (2013) found that curious people were less likely to react aggressively to interpersonal conflict. Assuming the eudaimonic value of being disposed to less aggressive reactions to interpersonal conflict, we can conclude that curiosity is conducive to the well-being of the possessor.

Third, consider optimism, which consists in some form of bias in favor of a positive or hopeful attitude towards the future.[32] Social psychologists have for many years extolled the value of optimism in connection with various intuitive contributors to well-being. For example, in a review of the literature, Charles Carver and his colleagues (2010) argue that optimism is positively correlated with subjective well-being, engagement with other people, physical health, persistence, and success in interpersonal relationships. Assuming that these things have eudaimonic value, we can conclude that optimism is conducive to the well-being of the possessor.

Fourth, consider intellectual independence, which consists in some form of preference for forming opinions on one's own, without the assistance of others.[33] Christian List and Philip Pettit (2004), appealing to Condorcet's Jury Theorem, argue that the success of certain collective decision-making procedures requires individuals to "go their own epistemic way"; otherwise they are "epistemic free riders," whose dependence on other group members undermines the reliability of their procedure. If this is right, and if the reliability of these collective decision-making procedures is conducive to the well-being of the people who employ them, then we can conclude that intellectual independence is conducive to the well-being of the people who employ such procedures.

It is important to note that intellectual virtues, in the present sense, may or may not be intellectual virtues, on the attributive disambiguation of "intellectual virtue." Consider optimism and intellectual independence. You might think that these traits are not at all "bound to maximize your surplus of truth over error"[34]—but this is orthogonal to the question of whether they are intellectual virtues, in the present sense, and, more important, given our general topic, to the eudaimonic value of these traits. The lesson to take away from this is that we need to be open to the possibility of character traits that have eudaimonic value, but which are not intellectual virtues, on the attributive disambiguation of "intellectual virtue."[35]

Being known and being ignored

This section briefly advocates for the idea that being known and being ignored, at least in some cases, contribute to the well-being of the possessor (i.e., the person known or ignored).

This entails that knowing and ignoring said individuals contribute to their well-being, in such cases. Since being known and being ignored, as well as knowing and ignoring other individuals, are epistemic in our sense (see above), these are plausible candidates for being things that are both epistemic and good vis-à-vis well-being.

Both being known and being ignored seem sometimes to have agent-relative instrumental eudaimonic value: the castaway desperately wants to be known; the fugitive desperately wants to remain unknown. But being known and being ignored seem also, in some cases, to have agent-relative constitutive eudaimonic value.

In the case of being known, consider the importance many of us place on being understood by other people, and in particular by people we care about, like our friends, our lovers, and other members of our families. Many of us care deeply about whether these close associates understand us—whether they know "who we really are," whether they "get us."[36] We love it when someone we care about does understand us in some important respect, and we are frustrated when someone we care about persistently misunderstands us in some way. It therefore seems, at least for people of this type, that self-interest prescribes that they try to make themselves known to the people they care about, and that benevolence prescribes that those whom they care about attempt to know them.

However, there can be too much of a good thing. Just as we sometimes struggle to make ourselves understood, we sometimes struggle to avoid the intrusive awareness of other people—both of strangers and of those whom we care about. Most people are familiar with the need to be left alone—which requires other people to direct their attention elsewhere. Being left alone is not a matter of physical but rather of epistemic separation: your partner can leave you alone even when you are reading in bed; one of the best places to be alone is in a crowd of indifferent strangers. What you need, when you need to be left alone, is other people's ignorance of you—of who you are, or of where you are, or of what you are doing, or of what you are thinking. It therefore seems, at least for people of a particular type, that self-interest prescribes that they sometimes evade the knowledge of others, and that benevolence prescribes that other people sometimes ignore them.

So, at least for those of us who care about being known and being ignored, these things contribute to our well-being. This is not a matter of what you know, or even of who you know, but rather of who knows you, and of what they know about you. This interpersonal knowledge, the knowledge we have of one another, deserves our attention, alongside the more familiar epistemic goods, such as *sophia* and *phronesis*.[37]

Conclusion

Our question was: what things are both epistemic and conducive to well-being? We have considered a few candidates: knowledge, intellectual virtue, and being known and being ignored. This has just been a brief survey of a few possible candidate epistemic goods, and was not exhaustive of the possibilities. Recall our definition (above) of "the domain of the intellect." This includes such things as intelligence, sincerity, liberal arts education, freedom of the press, and the scientific method—each of which, you might argue, has (agent-relative or agent-neutral) eudaimonic value.

Can we draw any general conclusion about epistemic goods, understood as things that are both epistemic and good *vis-à-vis* well-being? It is instructive to compare this to the question of whether we can draw any general conclusion about athletic goods, where these are understood as things that are both athletic and good *vis-à-vis* well-being. We might be able to defend a few plausible candidates—it seems like exercise is good for you; athletic excellence seems like a meaningful achievement; being a sports fan is rewarding—but it's unclear what we might say about athletic goods in general. The same, it seems to me, for epistemic goods.[38]

Related topics

On theories of well-being, see Part II (this volume), above; on virtue and well-being, see Chapter 20 (this volume).

Further reading

On the eudaimonic value of knowledge, see M. Lynch, *True to Life: Why Truth Matters* (Cambridge: MIT Press, 2004) and A. Hazlett, *A Luxury of the Understanding: On the Value of True Belief* (Oxford: Oxford University Press, 2013). On theoretical and practical wisdom, see D. Whitcomb, "Wisdom," in D. Pritchard and S. Bernecker (eds.), *The Routledge Companion to Epistemology* (Oxford: Routledge, 2011), pp. 95–105. On intellectual virtues as personal excellences, see L. Zagzebski, *Virtues of the Mind: An Inquiry into the Nature of Virtue and the Ethical Foundations of Knowledge* (Cambridge: Cambridge University Press, 1996) and J. Baehr, *The Inquiring Mind: On Intellectual Virtues and Virtue Epistemology* (Oxford: Oxford University Press, 2011). On the role of the intellect in moral virtue, see J. Annas, *The Morality of Happiness* (Oxford: Oxford University Press, 1993) and J. Driver, *Uneasy Virtue* (Cambridge: Cambridge University Press, 2001).

Notes

1 Cf. Geach (1957), Ridge (2013).
2 This is the right move, even if things that are good in some distinctively epistemic sense of "good" are per se good vis-à-vis wellbeing. The present formulation of our question assumes neither the truth nor the falsity of this view.
3 N.B.: An alternative understanding might be required to articulate the aforementioned epistemic sense of "good" (see Note 11), since the domain of the intellect has no essential connection to knowledge.
4 In a third kind of case, one thing contributes to another by being what it is about—this is an intentional contribution. But we can set this species of contribution aside—it does not sound right to say that well-being per se is about anything.
5 In general, something has instrumental value when it is valuable for the sake of some (wholly distinct) thing; something has final value when it is valuable for its own sake.
6 Suppose that well-being has final value. You might argue that things that have constitutive eudaimonic value also enjoy final (but non-intrinsic) value in virtue of being parts of a finally valuable whole.
7 To say that something has constitutive eudaimonic value is neutral as to whether it also has intrinsic value. You might argue that constitutive eudaimonic value is instantiated only when someone is appropriately related to intrinsically valuable things, or you might countenance the possibility of things that have constitutive eudaimonic value and that would otherwise be worthless.
8 Cf., for example, Rosalind Hursthouse's (1999: Chapter 8) claim that the virtues are the "most reliable bet" vis-à-vis flourishing.
9 See Zagzebski (2001), Grimm (2006).
10 See Sartwell (1991), Goldman (2002: 183–188), Hazlett (2010).
11 Thus a plausible articulation of the distinctively epistemic sense of "good": something is "epistemically good" if and only if it is an instance of knowledge (cf. Zagzebski 1996: 167; Grimm and Ahlstrom-Vij 2013; Hazlett 2013: §9.3).
12 Cf. Kornblith (1993), Zagzebski (2004).
13 Consider also the broadly pragmatist idea that knowledge is essentially useful (James 1907/1975: Lecture VI; Rorty 1989; cf. Papineau 1993: Chapter 3).
14 Cf. Moore (1903/1993: §59), Hurka (2001), Adams (2006).
15 See Ross (1930: 138–139), Finnis (1980: 62), Hurka (2001: 12–13), Zagzebski (2003b: 24–25), Greco (2010: 99).

16 See Finnis (1980: Chapter 3), Sosa (2003: pp. 173–175), Zagzebski (2003a: 140, 2003b, pp. 23–26), Lynch (2004: Chapter 8), Baril (2010), Greco (2010: 97–101). This view is sometimes attributed to Aristotle.

17 See David (2001), Baril (2010), Treanor (2013, 2014).

18 *Metaphysics* A 1–2; see also Zagzebski (1996: 43–51), Baehr (forthcoming), Grimm (2014).

19 Usefulness, by contrast, depends on the situation, and not just the content of the proposition known.

20 Cf. Baril (2010: §4).

21 If we adopt the view that knowledge (at least sometimes) has constitutive agent-relative eudaimonic value, the question of whether knowledge *per se* contributes to well-being is extraordinarily difficult to answer. On the one hand, you might think that it is the nature of well-being, rather than the nature of knowledge, that explains why knowledge contributes to well-being: knowledge contributes to human well-being, so the thought goes, because of the nature of human well-being. However, on the other hand, you might think that the nature of knowledge at least partially explains why knowledge contributes to well-being: it is because knowledge has such-and-such features that it is suitable to serve as a constituent of human well-being. (Compare the ingredients in a recipe, whose presence seems explained both by the nature of the recipe and by their own nature.)

22 Cf. Aristotle, *Nicomachean Ethics* VI.2. See also Williams (1973), Wedgwood (2002), Shah (2003), Steglich-Petersen (2006), Hazlett (2013: Part II).

23 Might we say that we always have some desire for the truth, although this desire is sometimes outweighed by others? This is not plausible in the case of insignificant truths: I just do not care about whether I know the number of jellybeans in the jar, even though this state of knowledge would be one that achieves its aim.

24 We might avoid this conclusion by adopting some version of the view that seeking knowledge, rather than acquiring it, has eudaimonic value.

25 We can arrive at this conclusion via a neo-Humean (cf. *Treatise of Human Nature*, III.iii.1; cf. *Enquiry concerning the Principles of Morals*, §VIII and Appendix I) account of virtue attribution, on which to think that *x* is a virtue is to believe that *x* is a character trait and to have certain non-cognitive pro-attitudes towards *x*. Virtue attribution therefore has both an essential descriptive aspect and an essential prescriptive aspect. Compare the attribution of intellectual virtue, on the attributive disambiguation of "intellectual virtue," which has no essential prescriptive aspect. On this point, cf. Sosa (2007: Chapter 4), Hazlett (2013: §9.2).

26 See also Baehr (2011: Appendix), and compare the attributive disambiguation of "intellectual virtue."

27 In as much as we can translate *eudaimonia* with "well-being," Aristotle suggests something like this (*Nicomachean Ethics* I.4 and I.7; see also 1040a 25–30), and something like it is suggested by other broadly Aristotelian accounts of virtue (e.g., Hursthouse 1999: Chapter 8; Baehr 2011: Chapter 6; cf. Annas 1993: Chapter 1).

28 As suggested by Hume's account of virtues as character traits that are useful or agreeable either to oneself or others (*Enquiry concerning the Principles of Morals*, §IX; cf. *Treatise of Human Nature*, III.iii.1), and by other broadly utilitarian accounts (e.g. Driver 2001: Chapter 4).

29 This has the advantage, over the previous two accounts, of building the value of the (intellectual) virtues into their definition.

30 *Nicomachean Ethics* VI.5; see also Zagzebski (1996: §II.5), Annas (1993: §2.3).

31 Cf. Ryan (1999).

32 Cf. Tiberius (2008: Chapter 6), Hazlett (2013: Chapter 2).

33 Sometimes called "intellectual autonomy" or "intellectual self-reliance"; see Fricker (2006), Zagzebski (2007, 2012: Chapter 1).

34 This complaint is obvious vis-à-vis optimism; on intellectual independence, see Zagzebski (2012: §5.4).

35 Compare Julia Driver's (2000, 2001, Chapter 2, 2003) defense and discussion of "virtues of ignorance."

36 Although we may prefer that our "true self" remain unknown, if and when we are embarrassed by it. Our desire to be known may, in this respect, be conditional on our hope that being known will lead to our being loved or respected. Thanks to Stephen Grimm for this point.

37 Cf. Code (1993), Dalmiya (2001).

38 I presented versions of this material, in 2014, at the University of London's Logic, Epistemology, and Metaphysics Forum and at a workshop on Moral vs. Intellectual Virtue at the University of Edinburgh. For valuable discussions of these matters over the years, I owe thanks to Jason Baehr, Anne Baril, Simon Feldman, John Greco, Stephen Grimm, and Ernest Sosa. Research on this chapter was supported by an Early Career Fellowship from the UK's Arts and Humanities Research Council.

References

Adams, R.M. (2006), *A Theory of Virtue: Excellence in Being for the Good* (Oxford: Oxford University Press).

Annas, J. (1993), *The Morality of Happiness* (Oxford: Oxford University Press).

Baehr, J. (2011), *The Inquiring Mind: On Intellectual Virtues and Virtue Epistemology* (Oxford: Oxford University Press).

Baehr, J. (forthcoming), "Sophia," *Synthese.*

Baril, A. (2010), "A Eudaimonist Approach to the Problem of Significance," *Acta Analytica* 25(2), 215–241.

Carver, C.S., Scheier, M.F., and Segerstrom, S.C. (2010), "Optimism," *Clinical Psychology Review* 30, 879–889.

Code, L. (1993), "Taking Subjectivity into Account," in L. Alcoff and E. Potter (eds.), *Feminist Epistemologies* (Oxford: Routledge), pp. 15–48.

Dalmiya, V. (2001), "Knowing People," in M. Steup (ed.), *Knowledge, Truth, and Duty: Essays on Epistemic Justification, Responsibility, and Virtue* (Oxford: Oxford University Press), pp. 221–233.

David, M. (2001), "Truth as the Epistemic Goal," in M. Steup (ed.), *Knowledge, Truth, and Duty: Essays on Epistemic Justification, Responsibility, and Virtue* (Oxford: Oxford University Press), pp. 151–169.

Driver, J. (2000), "Moral and Epistemic Virtue," in G. Axtell (ed.), *Knowledge, Belief, and Character: Readings in Virtue Epistemology* (Lanham: Rowman and Littlefield), pp. 123–134.

Driver, J. (2001), *Uneasy Virtue* (Cambridge: Cambridge University Press).

Driver, J. (2003), "The Conflation of Moral and Epistemic Virtue," *Metaphilosophy* 34(3), 367–383.

Finnis, J. (1980), *Natural Law and Natural Rights* (Oxford: Oxford University Press).

Fricker, E. (2006), "Testimony and Epistemic Autonomy," in J. Lackey and E. Sosa (eds.), *The Epistemology of Testimony* (Oxford: Oxford University Press), pp. 225–250.

Geach, P.T. (1957), "Good and Evil," *Analysis* 17(2), 33–42.

Goldman, A. (2002), *Pathways to Knowledge: Private and Public* (Oxford: Oxford University Press).

Greco, J. (2010), *Achieving Knowledge: A Virtue-Theoretic Account of Epistemic Normativity* (Oxford: Oxford University Press).

Grimm, S., and Ahlstrom-Vij, K. (2013), "Getting It Right," *Philosophical Studies* 166(2), 329–347.

Grimm, S. (2006), "Is Understanding a Species of Knowledge?" *British Journal for the Philosophy of Science* 57(3), 515–535.

Grimm, S. (2014), "Understanding as Knowledge of Causes," *Synthese* 366, 329–345.

Hazlett, A. (2010), "The Myth of Factive Verbs," *Philosophy and Phenomenological Research*, 80(3): 497–522.

Hazlett, A. (2013), *A Luxury of the Understanding: On the Value of True Belief* (Oxford: Oxford University Press).

Hurka, T. (2001), *Virtue, Vice, and Value* (Oxford: Oxford University Press).

Hursthouse, R. (1999), *On Virtue Ethics* (Oxford: Oxford University Press).

James, W. (1907/1975), *Pragmatism: A New Name for Some Old Ways of Thinking* (Cambridge: Harvard University Press).

Kashdan, T.B., DeWall, C.N., Pond, R.S., Silvia, P.J., Lambert, N.M., Fincham, F.D., and Savostyanova, A.A. (2013), "Curiosity Protects Against Interpersonal Aggression: Cross-Sectional, Daily Process, and Behavioral Evidence," *Journal of Personality* 81(1): 87–102.

Kornblith, H. (1993), "Epistemic Normativity," *Synthese* 94(3): 357–376.

List, C. and Pettit, P. (2004), "An Epistemic Free-Riding Problem?" in P. Catton and G. Macdonald (eds.), *Karl Popper: Critical Appraisals* (Oxford: Routledge), pp. 128–158.

Lynch, M. (2004), *True to Life: Why Truth Matters* (Cambridge: MIT Press).

Moore, G.E. (1903/1993), *Principia Ethica* (Cambridge: Cambridge University Press).

Papineau, D. (1993), *Philosophical Naturalism* (Oxford: Blackwell).

Ridge, M. (2013), "Getting Lost on the Road to Larissa," *Noûs* 47(1): 181–201.

Rorty, R. (1989), "Solidarity or Objectivity?" in M. Krausz (ed.), *Relativism: Interpretation and Confrontation* (South Bend: University of Notre Dame Press), pp. 167–183.

Ross, W.D. (1930), *The Right and the Good* (Oxford: Oxford University Press).

Ryan, S. (1999), "What Is Wisdom?" *Philosophical Studies* 93(2): 119–139.

Sartwell, C. (1991), "Knowledge is Merely True Belief," *American Philosophical Quarterly* 28(2): 157–165.

Shah, N. (2003), "How Truth Governs Belief," *Philosophical Review* 112(4): 447–482.

Sosa, E. (1991), *Knowledge in Perspective: Selected Essays in Epistemology* (Cambridge: Cambridge University Press).

Sosa, E. (2003), "The Place of Truth in Epistemology," in M. DePaul and L. Zagzebski (eds.), *Intellectual Virtue: Perspectives from Ethics and Epistemology* (Oxford: Oxford University Press), pp. 155–179.

Sosa, E. (2007), *A Virtue Epistemology: Apt Belief and Reflective Knowledge, Volume 1* (Oxford: Oxford University Press).

Steglich-Petersen, A. (2006), "No Norm Needed: On the Aim of Belief," *Philosophical Quarterly* 56: 499–516.

Tiberius, V. (2008), *The Reflective Life: Living Wisely with Our Limits* (Oxford: Oxford University Press).

Treanor, N. (2013), "The Measure of Knowledge," *Noûs* 47(3): 577–601.

Treanor, N. (2014), "Trivial Truths and the Aim of Inquiry," *Philosophy and Phenomenological Research* 89(3): 552–559.

Wedgwood, R. (2002), "The Aim of Belief," *Philosophical Perspectives* 16: 267–297.

Williams, B. (1973), "Deciding to Believe," in *Problems of the Self* (Cambridge: Cambridge University Press), pp. 136–151.

Zagzebski, L. (1996), *Virtues of the Mind: An Inquiry into the Nature of Virtue and the Ethical Foundations of Knowledge* (Cambridge: Cambridge University Press).

Zagzebski, L. (2001), "Recovering Understanding," in M. Steup (ed.), *Knowledge, Truth, and Duty: Essays on Epistemic Justification, Responsibility, and Virtue* (Oxford: Oxford University Press), pp. 235–253.

Zagzebski, L. (2003a), "Intellectual Motivation and the Good of Truth," in M. DePaul and L. Zagzebski (eds.), *Intellectual Virtue: Perspectives from Ethics and Epistemology* (Oxford: Oxford University Press), pp. 135–154.

Zagzebski, L. (2003b), "The Search for the Source of Epistemic Good," *Metaphilosophy* 34(1–2): 12–28.

Zagzebski, L. (2004), "Epistemic Value and the Primacy of What We Care About," *Philosophical Papers* 33(3): 353–377.

Zagzebski, L. (2007), "Ethical and Epistemic Egoism and the Ideal of Autonomy," *Episteme* 4(3): 252–263.

Zagzebski, L. (2012), *Epistemic Authority: A Theory of Trust, Authority, and Autonomy in Belief* (Oxford: Oxford University Press).

22

WELL-BEING AND ACHIEVEMENT

Gwen Bradford and Simon Keller

Introduction

Has your life gone well? In seeking to answer this question, you will look back on the good times you have had: good movies you have seen and nice dinners you have shared with friends. But you will also ask what you have done with your life. Have you helped others? What have you done that was worth doing? Have you made the most of your talents and opportunities? Perhaps you have enjoyed a successful marriage, got a degree, or got the best out of yourself in your chosen profession. Perhaps you have written a book or raised happy children. Whether you judge your life to have gone well depends partly on what you think you have achieved. One component of well-being, it appears, is achievement.

The topic of well-being and achievement raises several questions. What is an achievement? How does the value of achievement contribute to the value of well-being, if it does? What might the nature of achievement tell us about the nature of well-being more generally? And is it even possible to understand the value of achievement by thinking about its connection with well-being?

What is an achievement?

Paradigm cases

Begin with some paradigm cases of achievement: things that almost everyone would count as achievements of one kind or another. You might find a cure for cancer, bring up a happy family, or publish a great novel. Paradigmatic achievements like these, as ordinarily imagined, appear to share three characteristics.

First, they all appear to be valuable in their own rights. Writing a great novel is valuable partly because great novels are good to have around. It would be a very good thing to have a cure for cancer, no matter who finds it or how it is found. Happy families are better than unhappy families. In paradigmatic cases, achievement involves doing something that is worth doing, independently of the fact that it is part of an achievement.

Second, in paradigmatic cases, achievement involves effort. Finding cures for diseases is difficult. If it were easy, then it would not be so clear that curing a disease counts as an achievement.

When you imagine someone writing a great novel or bringing up a happy family, you imagine her facing challenges and working hard to meet them. You imagine her attaining her goal through hard work.

Third, in paradigmatic cases, achievement involves purposive activity. Curing cancer is not something you can do just by accident—not as we usually imagine it, anyway. To cure cancer, you need to make plans, cooperate with others, patiently engage in rigorous medical studies, and so on. You need to know what you are doing. You need to set yourself a goal and apply yourself to the task. The same goes for raising a happy family and writing a great novel.

So achievements appear to be characterized by these three features: independent value, effort, and purposiveness. The three features can come apart, and when they do, it can be less clear whether we have cases of genuine achievements. For example, you might set yourself a task, approach it with purpose, and complete it through a good deal of hard work, yet your accomplishment might fail to be independently valuable; perhaps it is pointless or self-destructive. Or it might take a great deal of effort for you to do something that is easy for most people and does not look very valuable in its own right. Or you might do something that is very valuable, but do it easily or without noticing; perhaps you blunder into the solution to a difficult mathematical problem. Whether we count you as securing an achievement in the various cases depends on how we take the three features of paradigmatic achievements, singly or in combination, to deliver a definition of achievement. What precisely do these three features amount to, and what precisely are their respective relationships to achievement? Let us explore each in turn.

Independent value

There is some intuitive plausibility to the thought that for something to be an achievement, it must be in some sense good, or valuable, or worthwhile, independently of the fact that it is an achievement. If you look back at your life and ask what were your greatest achievements, you are likely to choose things that you think were worth doing. If you look back on something you did that involved great effort and purposive activity, but that you now think to have been a waste of time and energy, then you may be reluctant to classify it as one of your achievements.

What could it mean for an achievement to be independently valuable? It could be that it has a valuable product; an achievement could produce happiness, or it could produce something useful or beautiful—something that is good, whether it is the product of an achievement or not. Developing the cure for cancer would be a prime example of an achievement with an independently valuable outcome, likewise producing a great work of art.

Nevertheless some paradigmatic achievements do not result in an independently valuable product. Running a world record for the marathon is an achievement, but it is not clear that the product has value independently of the activity that produces it. Running a world record in the marathon, though, does involve excelling in a difficult endeavor, and to that extent, perhaps, it involves a kind of value that can be specified and recognized independently of the role it plays in an achievement. An achievement like running a marathon might have independent value not due to what it produces, but just because it involves a display of human excellence.

Yet there are some reasons to doubt that it is strictly necessary for something to be independently valuable in order to count as an achievement. We might find some evil deeds very impressive: the perfect murder, perhaps, or an elaborate art heist. Although not good things to do, these are nonetheless formidable accomplishments. If we think that these are genuine achievements, as some philosophers do (Bradford 2013a, 2015), then we should say that achievements need not have positive goals. Still, there may be some respects in which achievements like these involve human excellences—great skill and good planning—even if put to bad ends, and so perhaps they could still be considered to manifest independent values, even if they are not valuable overall.

There are other cases in which it is still harder to identify anything independently valuable about an achievement. It makes some sense to talk of pointless achievements. If you successfully count all the blades of grass on your lawn, then that is arguably an achievement, even if nobody thinks the activity worthwhile. Put it this way: if someone else tries but fails to count the number of blades of grass on the lawn, then you have something that she lacks, even if neither of you does anything that matters for its own sake (Keller 2004).

Further still, a deed that does not look valuable in its own right may come to be recognized as an achievement in light of information about whose deed it is and the circumstances in which it is carried out. Riding a bike might not be an especially impressive activity in its own right, but for someone who needs to overcome great physical and mental obstacles in order to do it, riding a bike might count as a significant achievement. Explaining why these sorts of deeds count as achievements does not seem to be a matter of pointing to the independently valuable things that they produce or otherwise involve.

However that matter stands, there is good reason to think that the nature of achievement is not just a matter of the value of outcomes or activities. It is also a matter of the subjective commitments of the agent. However valuable a deed may be, it is difficult to describe it as an achievement if it does not involve some measure of investment from the person who performs it. If you have absolutely no interest in or knowledge of paleontology, and you happen to stumble upon dinosaur bones for which scientists have been arduously searching, this discovery is not one of your achievements. It may be important and valuable, but it is not an achievement.

That an activity is valuable may conceivably be a necessary condition for its counting as an achievement, but it is not enough to constitute achievement. What needs to be added, at a minimum, is that the agent attains something while in pursuit of a *goal*. Achievement involves achieving a goal, or at least accomplishing something that is a part of or in some other way intimately connected with a goal. Writing a great novel is an achievement if you do it while pursuing the goal of writing a novel, but not if you do it by mistake while intending to make a shopping list.

Effort

There is a good case for thinking that effort is always an integral component of achievements. If you attain something by accident or through no exertion of effort at all, it would sound odd to congratulate you on your achievement. Winning a lottery is not an achievement, and neither is curing cancer, if you do it without having to try. Moreover, appealing to effort can help to order achievements from lesser to greater significance. The greater the effort it takes, we could say, the more significant the achievement.

Since some tasks are more difficult than others, and what is very difficult for one person may not be at all difficult for another, making effort a defining element of achievement can explain why achievement is relative to individuals. Walking a few steps is not very difficult in the ordinary case, but it could take a lot of effort for someone recovering from devastating injury, and so be an achievement for that person.

We might offer the link with effort as a complete definition of achievement, saying that you enjoy an achievement just in case you attain one of your goals through your own efforts. A first possible problem with such a definition, as already indicated, is that it does not discriminate between activities of different values; counting blades of grass or getting away with murder could be as great an achievement as curing cancer.

A further problem is that the condition of effort does not incorporate any constraint on *how* your efforts lead to the attainment of your goal. Suppose that you have the goal of becoming a millionaire by your 25th birthday, and you set out to achieve your goal by pouring enormous amounts of effort into all sorts of misguided schemes for getting rich. Your exertion of effort causes great irritation to your secretly rich grandmother, and finally she can no longer bear to see you working so hard for nothing, so she gives you a million dollars, right before your 25th birthday, just to put your pathetic striving to an end. This looks like a case in which you attain your goal because of your own efforts, but in which you do not *achieve* anything; becoming a millionaire through such a deviant chain of events is not a way of being a high achiever. The case shows that it is not enough that your efforts cause you to attain your goal: they must so do in the right way. Perhaps the way to put it is to say that there is a difference between achieving a goal *through* your own efforts and achieving a goal merely *because* of your own efforts. Then the question is what it takes to get there "through" your own efforts.

Purposiveness

To get the right connection between putting effort towards a goal and attaining it, we can bring in the condition of purposiveness. For something to count as an achievement of yours, we might say, you need to bring it about in the way you intend, or according to a plan, or while knowing what you are doing. Your problem in the case of the accidental millionaire, perhaps, is that in exerting your efforts, you have no idea how they bring you closer to your goal.

Purposiveness could be understood as a matter of achieving your goal through your own efforts and according to your own plan. So construed, imposing a condition of purposiveness would appear to let us cope with cases like the accidental millionaire, in which your efforts are linked with your attainment of your goal, but not in the way you plan. It may be too strong a condition, however. In some cases, you can attain your goal through your own efforts, but not in the way you plan, yet still count as having accrued an achievement. Perhaps you set out to write a novel of one kind, but during the process of writing you divert from your original plan and the novel ends up as something very different, produced according to a very different method, from what you planned. Nevertheless the novel could stand as one of your achievements.

Alternatively, we could understand purposiveness as a matter of knowledge (Bradford 2015). What matters, we might say, is that as you put effort towards achieving your goal, you know what you are doing, and in particular, you know how your effort and the attainment of your goal are connected. The problem in the case of the accidental millionaire, on this diagnosis, is that as you attempt to become a millionaire, you do not know that you are irritating your grandmother in such a way as to make her likely to pay you off. When you count as accruing an achievement though not in the way you planned—as in the case in which you produce a very different novel from the one you set out to produce—that is because, we can say, you know how your efforts lead to the final product, even if your plans are overturned during the process.

Defining achievement?

Independent value, effort, and purposiveness all appear to have something important to do with achievement, but it is not easy to combine them in such a way as to produce a fully satisfactory analysis of achievement. There are at least two major outstanding questions. First, must something be independently valuable or worthwhile in order to count as an achievement? Second, how must the attainment of your goal be connected with your efforts, in order for it to count as an achievement?

There may be no single ultimate analysis of the ordinary notion of achievement. Regardless of the details, achievement appears to play an important role in our lives, quite plausibly as part of our well-being. How might achievement be incorporated within a life that goes well?

Achievement as an aspect of well-being

Constitutive or contingent?

It is plausible to think that achievement is one of the constitutive elements of well-being. Your achievement *itself* makes your life go well for you, apart from or in addition to any further good it does for you or others. Your life goes better for you if you successfully pursue a project such as publishing a novel, finally making par at golf, or pitching a no-hitter. It is reasonable, in addition, to hold that such achievements improve well-being independently of any other contribution they might make to well-being. No doubt achievement often *is* accompanied by feelings of satisfaction or pleasure, but we might be inclined to think that the success *itself* matters for well-being, beyond any feelings it brings. This point is supported by the observation that we often think that achievements are valuable and worth pursuing even if they come at the expense of pleasure. Many paradigmatic achievements involve painful and difficult struggle, yet their successful accomplishment, we often think, makes a life go better.

Some prevailing theories of well-being seek to incorporate this thought, making achievement something that makes an intrinsic contribution to well-being. Others, as we shall see, take the connection between achievement and well-being to be merely contingent.

The objective list theory

The most straightforward way to treat achievement as a constitutive element of well-being is within an *objective list theory* of well-being. According to objective list theories, there is a list of one or more mutually irreducible constituents of well-being. An objective list theory may include achievement among possibly other goods, such as friendship and knowledge. One might even say that the plausible relevance of achievement to well-being is one of the primary motivating features of an objective list theory. The objective list theory offers the simplest and most straightforward way to include goods such as achievement within a theory.

While the objective list theory can honor the intuition that achievement is a self-standing element of well-being, simply placing achievement on a list of objective goods can be theoretically unsatisfying. One might wonder what *explains* the relevance of achievement to well-being. One might also hope that an explanation of why achievement gets on to the list could give some direction towards saying how achievement can be compared in importance with other objective goods. Is there an answer, even in principle, to the question of when it is in your best interests to accrue an achievement, even if doing so will, say, make you unhappy or lose you a friend?

Perfectionism

As a result, philosophers who are attracted to the idea that achievement is a constitutive part of well-being often turn to *perfectionist* theories of well-being. According to perfectionism, the exercise and development of characteristically human capacities are intrinsically good. If some such capacities are exercised in achievements, that could explain the role of achievement in our well-being. Which capacities might be the relevant ones? One thought is that purposiveness and effort engage our *practical rationality*, and practical rationality is one of the perfectionist capacities.

Our capacity for practical rationality is the capacity to set goals and make plans to attain them. The value of achievement, on this approach, is a matter of having complex plans and bringing them to fruition (Hurka 1993).

One might think, however, that not all achievements are characterized by complexity. Some achievements involve quite simple plans, and their impressiveness is more a matter of the sheer effort involved in their accomplishment. Running a marathon is a paradigmatic impressive achievement, but it seems that its impressiveness is not a matter of its complexity. Indeed, it is quite simple—just a matter of putting one foot in front of the other. What is impressive about it is the sheer grit of running for a very long time. As a result, one might think that effort itself matters. This thought can be captured if we think that there is a perfectionist capacity to exert effort—one might think the *will* is precisely this (Bradford 2013b, 2015).

Particular details aside, perfectionist theories capture the relevance of achievement for our well-being because achievement involves setting and following plans: a distinctive and characteristically human activity, and hence a site of human excellence.

Rational life plans

Both perfectionism and the objective list theory acknowledge that there are other aspects of our good beyond achievement. But one might take a different approach and instead think that well-being is a matter of forming and carrying out rational plans—that is, well-being is a matter of attaining our rationally held goals. Our lives go well when we achieve the goals that we have good reason to pursue. If Jane's aim is to get a job, and going to art school will help her get a job, then she has good reason to go to art school and her life goes better when she does (Raz 1986: 301). Achievement, or something very much like it, would then be the central constitutive element of well-being.

The desire-fulfillment theory

Achievement involves the attainment of goals. One might think that to have something as a goal, you must desire it. If so, then our goals form a subset of our desires, and so it is possible that the value of achievement for well-being could be subsumed under a wider value of desire satisfaction. Perhaps the way to explain the significance of achievement for well-being is to take well-being as a matter of desire satisfaction more generally. This brings us to the well-known *desire-fulfillment theory* of well-being.

The desire-fulfillment theory of well-being, in its simplest form, says that something advances your well-being just in case it satisfies one of your desires. The desire theory has a straightforward explanation of why achievement contributes to well-being. If you achieve your goal of curing cancer, then that contributes to your well-being, just because in curing cancer you get what you want.

In this simple form, the desire-fulfillment theory does not discriminate between achievements based on their independent value. All that matters is the strength of the desires involved. If my desire to count the number of blades of grass on my lawn is as strong as your desire to cure cancer, then my counting blades of grass contributes as much to my well-being as your curing cancer contributes to yours. The desire-fulfillment theory also does not discriminate between cases in which you attain your goal through your own efforts and cases in which you attain your goal without trying or through a deviant causal pathway. All that matters is that you get what you want, one way or another.

While the desire-fulfillment theory of well-being incorporates the value of achievement, it does not make achievement, as such, look special. The factors that characterize paradigmatic achievements—independent value, effort, and purposiveness—have no significance under the desire-fulfillment theory. Something's qualifying as an achievement, rather than a mere desire satisfaction, turns out to be incidental. This is true also on more sophisticated forms of the desire theory, including the influential informed desire theory, on which something counts towards your well-being only if you would desire it if you were fully informed and rational. Desire-fulfillment theories can explain why achievement contributes to well-being, but do not find achievement to have significance in its own right.

Hedonism

The desire-fulfillment theory values achievement only insofar as it involves our getting what we want, and we could go a step further and say that achievement is valuable only insofar as it brings us pleasure. The objects of our goals, often, are things that will bring us pleasure. The feeling of achievement itself is often pleasurable. When achievement does not bring pleasure—when your goal was never to make yourself happy, when attaining a goal does not bring the happiness you expect, or when the feeling of achievement is just a feeling of emptiness—we might wonder whether it really contributes to well-being. According to *hedonism*, all that matters for well-being is good subjective experience, and it is not out of the question that hedonism could tell the right story about the value of achievement.

While achievement seems to have something to do with well-being, there are reasons to think that its connection with well-being is contingent. For one thing, there appears to be conceptual space for the claim that a life of achievement is not such a great life for the person who lives it. There is something, at least, to the suggestion that the highest levels of well-being are enjoyed by those who renounce striving and live simply or meditatively, or who just lay around; perhaps a theory of well-being should provide the resources to adjudicate the disagreement over whether achievement is good for us, rather than just announcing that it is. For another thing, we often set goals without thinking that their achievement is in our own interests; often, indeed, that is the point. When you set yourself the goal of curing cancer, your motive may be entirely selfless, even self-sacrificing. Perhaps it is perverse to say that all of your achievements, even of selfless and self-sacrificing goals, automatically contribute to your well-being.

Hedonism offers one way of making it an open question whether any particular achievement, or achievement as a general proposition, is enhancing of well-being. In doing so, however, it reduces achievement merely to one of the many things that may or may not contribute to well-being. It makes the link between well-being and achievement no tighter than the link between well-being and playing tennis, or between well-being and eating chocolate.

Do all achievements contribute to well-being?

Regardless of whether achievement is the only constitutive element of well-being, one among others, or only instrumentally relevant, there is still the question of *which* achievements matter for well-being. According to hedonism, the answer is simple: any achievement matters for well-being insofar as it brings you pleasure. According to the rational plan view discussed earlier, only certain achievements improve your well-being, namely, those with rational goals. But we might think that achieving *any* goal can contribute positively to your well-being (Keller 2004). Indeed, if we reflect on many paradigmatic achievements, we find goals that are not worth pursuing independently from the fact that we set them as goals. Running a marathon, for example, may not be a rational goal insofar as it may conflict with other goals. But successfully running a marathon is a paradigmatic achievement the accomplishment of which improves your life in at least one respect, even if it detracts from other aspects in which it might go well.

One might think that successfully accomplishing even an evil goal makes one's life go better in at least one respect. This seems most plausible when placed alongside the view that there are other goods in addition to achievement that are relevant for well-being. Perhaps someone who accomplishes an evil goal has something going for her that is lacked by someone who tries but fails to accomplish an evil goal, but is evil anyway (Keller 2004). The claim that even evil (and perhaps also pointless and irrational) achievements contribute to well-being might also be made more plausible when conjoined with the view that not all well-being is valuable. Perhaps when an evil person accomplishes an evil goal, her well-being is increased—but perhaps that is not at all a good thing.

Once it is settled which kinds of achievements are relevant for well-being, there is the further issue of *how much* any particular achievement contributes to it, and how much it contributes to well-being in contrast to other goods, if any. Some philosophers hold that the significance of achievements is largely a matter of the comprehensiveness of the plans involved (Hurka 1993; Dorsey 2011) while others think that the amount of effort involved, other things being equal, is a significant factor (Bradford 2015). Another thought is that the amount that achievements contribute to well-being is a matter of how much well-being is initially sacrificed in their undertaking (Portmore 2007).

Achievement and the truth about well-being

Achievement, we have seen, finds different places in the different theories of well-being. A convinced advocate of a particular theory of well-being could appeal to her preferred theory to explain the true nature and value of achievement. The perfectionist may define valuable achievement as a certain manifestation of human excellence, the hedonist may say that the value of a given achievement is a matter of how much pleasure it produces, and so on. To that extent, an investigation of the value of achievement is not especially helpful for selecting between theories of well-being.

Thoughts about the value of achievement may offer more constructive insights for the theory of well-being, however. First, if we judge that achievement advances well-being, or even just that certain specific achievements advance well-being in their own rights, then we can evaluate theories of well-being in light of our judgment. It may be a drawback of hedonism, for example, that it sees many of the things we care about, and for which we are prepared to make demanding commitments and exert great effort, as having nothing to do with our best interests.

Second, achievement is notable for bringing together elements of both "objective" and "subjective" stories about well-being. As mentioned earlier, achievement is naturally taken to have a place in objective list and perfectionist theories of well-being: theories that are classified as "objective" because they say that our well-being is not just a matter of our own attitudes, or of what we happen to care about. Yet, achievement is a matter of achieving goals, and goals are attitudes. When you take on a goal, you commit yourself to trying to achieve it—otherwise it would not really be a *goal*—and so you can be judged as a success or a failure depending upon how close you come to achieving your goal. Whether or not you achieve your goal determines, as we might put it, whether or not you are successful in imposing your will upon the world. A recognition of the importance of achievement for well-being, and of the respect in which achievement is a value naturally seen as both objective (in that it is an element of human perfection) and subjective (in that it involves success according to standards set by an agent's own attitudes) may help to identify a middle road between objectivist and subjectivist approaches to well-being (Keller 2009).

Beyond well-being

For all that, there are reasons to think that the value of achievement has nothing to do with well-being. As much as achievement can contribute to or constitute well-being, let's not forget that achievement can also be a source of pain. In fact, given that effort is a central feature of achievement, we should not be surprised that many achievements are unpleasant to accomplish. In some cases it appears that achievement comes at the expense of well-being—early expeditions to Antarctica, for example. And even if achievements contribute positively to well-being (either instrumentally or constitutively), one might be inclined to think that at least some also have value independently. The invention of the telephone, for example, was an extremely valuable achievement, but its value cannot be fully accounted for by its role in the well-being of Alexander Graham Bell. It may be that the value of achievement is not best explained by way of any connection with well-being.

There are at least two different strategies for explaining the value of achievement beyond its contribution to well-being. First, in many paradigmatic great achievements, the *product* of the achievement has significant intrinsic or instrumental value. The telephone is an extraordinarily valuable contribution to civilization, responsible for improving communication and even playing a crucial role in saving lives. Similarly, we might think that Michelangelo's ceiling of the Sistine Chapel is a great artistic achievement, but its value is hardly a matter of the role it had in Michelangelo's well-being—rather, its value is in the product: one of the most impressive artistic achievements in the world.

Alternatively, however, we might notice that some great achievements do not seem to have a product of any significant intrinsic or instrumental value, nor do they have much of a positive impact on well-being. Consider, for example, Robert Falcon Scott's expedition to the South Pole in 1912. Intuitively, this is a great achievement, but its value cannot be explained by its role (either constitutive or instrumental) in Scott's well-being or that of the explorers, since their expedition was extremely unpleasant and culminated in their deaths. Moreover, it is hard to pinpoint precisely the *product* of the expedition or its value as such. It does not have the value of the telephone or the Sistine Chapel ceiling.

We might think that the value of the achievement is at least in part explained by the sheer grit, perseverance, and frontier spirit of the explorers. Such features, we might think, are valuable in themselves, apart from any role they might play in well-being. This thought can be captured by some versions of perfectionism, when it is construed as a theory of intrinsic value, instead of a theory of well-being. According to this approach, the exercise of perfectionist capacities such as the will and rationality is *intrinsically good*, independently of any considerations of well-being. Because Scott's expedition involved remarkable effort and planning, it scores highly in terms of perfectionist value, independently of its impact (positive or negative) on the explorers' well-being. Alternatively again, we might think that achievement imbues lives with *meaning*. Indeed, achievement is an element in many accounts of *meaningfulness* in life (cf. Metz 2007; Wolf 2010). Meaning can be taken either as an element of well-being or as a kind of value that a life can have, independently of well-being. In Scott's case, taking the meaningfulness of his achievement as an element of well-being may be counterintuitive—it might not seem to have done him much good—but we might think that his achievement made his life valuable insofar as it made his life meaningful, even if not a life high in well-being.

Conclusion

Most of us want to achieve something with our lives. If we can better understand the nature of achievement, then we can make progress in answering the question of what we look for in life and what we take to be a life worth living. Achievement may or may not be valuable for its own sake, and if it is valuable for its own sake, its value may or may not be a matter of its relationship with well-being. The most intriguing aspect of achievement, arguably, is its connection with the will. We express ourselves as willful individuals by setting our own goals and trying to achieve them. A verdict on the value of achievement is a verdict on what place our willful nature takes in a meaningful life, a valuable life, a flourishing life, and a life high in well-being.

Related topics

Desire-fulfillment theory, hedonism, meaningfulness, objective list theories, perfectionism.

References

Bradford, Gwen (2013a). "Evil Achievements and the Principle of Recursion" in Mark Timmons (ed.) *Oxford Studies in Normative Ethics* vol. 3. Oxford: OUP.

Bradford, Gwen (2013b). "The Value of Achievement," *Pacific Philosophical Quarterly* 94(2): 204–224.

Bradford, Gwen (2015). *Achievement*. Oxford: OUP.

Dorsey, Dale (2011). "First Steps in an Axiology of Goals," *International Journal of Wellbeing* 1(1): 167–185.

Hurka, Thomas (1993). *Perfectionism*. Oxford: OUP.

Keller, Simon (2004). "Welfare and the Achievement of Goals," *Philosophical Studies* 121(1): 27–41.

Keller, Simon (2009). "Welfare as Success," *Noûs* 43(4): 656–683.

Metz, Thaddeus (2007). "New Developments in the Meaning of Life," *Philosophy Compass* 2(2): 196–217.

Portmore, Douglas (2007). "Welfare, Achievement, and Self-Sacrifice," *Journal of Ethics and Social Philosophy* 2(2): 1–28.

Raz, Joseph (1986). *The Morality of Freedom*. Oxford: OUP.

Wolf, Susan (2010). *Meaning in Life and Why It Matters*. Princeton: Princeton University Press.

23

MEANINGFULNESS

Antti Kauppinen

Introduction

When he loses his brother, Konstantin Levin, the true hero of Tolstoy's *Anna Karenina*, faces a kind of existential crisis:

> From that moment when, at the sight of his beloved brother dying, Levin had looked at the questions of life and death for the first time through those new [atheist] convictions [. . .] he had been horrified, not so much at death as at life without the slightest knowledge of whence it came, wherefore, why, and what it was . . . . "Without knowing what I am and why I'm here, it is impossible for me to live. And I cannot know that, therefore I cannot live," Levin would say to himself. [. . .] And, happy in his family life, a healthy man, Levin was several times so close to suicide that he hid a rope lest he hang himself with it, and was afraid to go about with a rifle lest he shoot himself.
>
> *(Tolstoy 1877/2001: 528, 530)*

Levin is a respected, wealthy, and hardworking landowner, and a proud father married to a beautiful and insightful woman who loves him deeply. He seems to have it all. Yet he worries that it is all for nothing. It is the *meaningfulness* of his life that is the object of his concern. In idle moments, he asks himself about the point of it all—is there sufficient reason for him to go on living and doing the things he does, or is it all the same if he ceases to exist now rather than a little while later, as he inevitably will?

These are hard questions that many of us with the luxury of reflection must face from time to time. Philosophical theories of meaning in life are attempts to articulate systematically what it would take for our lives to have a point or purpose. Although they are often pursued separately, they seem to be at least closely related to, if not a species of, theories of well-being. Other things being equal, it seems to be in our self-interest to lead a more rather than less meaningful life. Meaningfulness appears to be a central aspect of a life worth living—it seems to be among the things we rationally want for those we care about for their own sake. Indeed, for someone like Tolstoy, life is not worth living without meaning, even if it contains happiness, health, and other putative intrinsic goods.

I will begin this chapter with a brief look at the concept of meaningfulness or meaning in life. Later sections discuss the three leading types of account of what makes life meaningful: supernaturalism, subjectivist naturalism, and objectivist naturalism. It turns out that the main dividing issues concern the role and nature of value. Supernaturalists and objectivist naturalists believe that engagement with objective value is necessary for meaning in life, while subjectivists deny this. Supernaturalists believe, roughly, that God's existence is necessary for the right kind of objective value and the right kind of relation to it, while objectivist naturalists deny these claims. Among objectivist naturalists, the key debates concern the nature and role of subjective engagement with objective value, and the specific kind of objective value needed for meaningfulness.

The section on meaning and well-being addresses their precise relationship, in particular the claim that meaning in life is a distinct kind of value from both well-being and morality. The section on measuring meaning turns briefly to empirical research on meaningfulness, and argues that its proper object is people's finding their lives meaningful. This is an important topic, since sense of meaningfulness is plausibly important for happiness. Meaning itself, however, remains beyond empirical investigation, since it is one thing for someone to find her life meaningful and another for it to *be* meaningful.

What is meaning in life?

Before looking at accounts of what makes life meaningful, it is important to get clear on just what the question is that they're trying to answer—what it is that we say when we say that someone's life is meaningful, or more meaningful than another's. I believe the best way to approach this question is to start with the kind of existential concern that held Levin in its grip. "Meaning," after all, is a word with many senses, some of which have nothing to do with such concerns. Our lives don't have meaning in the way that linguistic items do, for example—they don't have sense or reference. And while words are either meaningful or not, life can be more or less meaningful (Kauppinen 2012: 353–354).

The object of the concern for meaningfulness is evidently something that is desirable or good, indeed, desirable for its own sake. We worry that our lives lack a fundamental feature that is needed to make it worthwhile. Yet, as Tolstoy nicely points out, meaning is distinct from other final goods, such as happiness. It is too broad to say, as Kai Nielsen does, that questions about meaning are questions about "what ends—if any—are worthy of attainment" (Nielsen 1981: 240). In this respect, analyses that maintain meaningfulness is a matter of transcending our own limits and connecting to something larger (Nozick 1981) are superior, since they point to a distinct kind of putative good. But it is unclear just what "transcendence" and "connection" mean here. In any case, Nozick's view may be best understood as an account of what makes a life meaningful, not of what it is for life to be meaningful.

Perhaps it is better, then, to take a different tack. Let us begin with the *valuing attitudes* that we have towards highly meaningful lives. Paradigms of meaning, such as Hannah Arendt or Marie Curie or Mary Robinson, are objects of admiration, esteem, and imitation, and sources of inspiration and elevation. If we're lucky, we also have our own experiences of finding life meaningful. They seem to involve a mix of related first-personal attitudes: a kind of pride in what we've done (call it *agential* pride to distinguish it from, say, pride in one's country), satisfaction with and even excitement about what we're doing, confident hope for the future. Supposing that it is correct that to *find* life meaningful is to have such attitudes, it is plausible that for a life to *be* meaningful is for such attitudes to be *fitting* or *correct* towards it (Metz 2001; Kauppinen 2014b).

Among other things, this analysis of the concept of meaningfulness accounts for the connection between meaninglessness and absurdity. As Thomas Nagel observes, "in ordinary life a situation is absurd when it includes a conspicuous discrepancy between pretension or aspiration and reality" (Nagel 1971: 718). If our lives are bound to be meaningless, a kind of absurdity marks all of our pursuits. On the present analysis, this amounts to the claim that there is a conspicuous discrepancy between our thinking that what we do is worthy of pride and admiration and the reality that nothing is. One kind of worry about meaning, then, is that pride in anything we do is as absurd as a fool's pride in having received a lot of "likes" on social media for building a 7-foot tower out of beer cans.

In short, then, it seems that when we say that someone's life is meaningful or want our own lives to be such, what we say or want is that certain positive attitudes are fitting towards it. Consequently, asking what makes our lives meaningful amounts to asking what makes agential pride, admiration, and elevation fitting. How can we go about answering such a question? The *bottom-up method*, as I like to think of it, is to start with exemplars of meaningfulness—people whose lives it is fitting to admire and be elevated by—and asking what it is that they have to a greater degree than the rest of us. The *top-down method* is to start with the nature of attitudes of pride and admiration and asking what would make them fitting. For example, agential pride seems to involve the thought that we're responsible for something excellent, so it cannot be fitting without some display of excellence. If we're lucky, the two lines of inquiry will converge.

Objectivist accounts of meaning: supernaturalism

For *supernaturalist* views, the source or condition of meaning in life is some entity beyond the natural world (roughly, the world studied by science), such as God or an immortal soul. In this section, I will focus on God-centered views. Conceptions of God differ between and within religions, but the potentially relevant characteristics here include omnipotence, omniscience, omnibenevolence, timelessness, necessity, and being the creator of the world.

According to *divine purpose* accounts, what makes life meaningful is fulfilling God's purpose (for me or for human beings in general). One line of argument for this is that without a cosmos that is "teleologically structured" by God (Cottingham 2011: 305), our lives are random and accidental. As William Lane Craig puts it, without God, our existence has no purpose, because it is the result of "blind interaction of chance and necessity" (Craig 1994: 45). Since what is accidental is not purposeful, a life that's the outcome of blind natural processes will be meaningless. One big problem with this argument is that even if our *existence* has no purpose in this sense, it doesn't follow that our *lives*, comprised of actions and experiences, are meaningless. Indeed, mere existence doesn't seem to be a good candidate for meaningfulness—it's not the sort of thing we're responsible for. Perhaps there is a gap here between meaning *of* life in one traditional sense and meaning *in* life, where the latter has to do with whether our *actions* have a point. The latter, it seems, is not ruled out if life in general and our own existence is accidental in the sense of being a product of natural processes.

Why, then, would fulfilling divine purpose be either necessary or sufficient for meaningful living? When it comes to sufficiency, the idea seems to be that our lives have purpose when they fit into a larger whole, which is itself purposeful, somewhat like a part in a machine has a purpose when it is necessary to make the whole function properly. It is certainly intelligible that pride is sometimes warranted when we have done something that furthers a larger project, such as eradicating a disease. But unless the whole scheme is worthwhile, playing one's part in it is ultimately pointless. In *Anna Karenina*, Levin's crisis begins when he realizes that "for every man and for himself nothing lay ahead but suffering, death and eternal oblivion" (535). All traces of whatever we do for others or for ourselves will eventually disappear—indeed, from a cosmic perspective, they're a mere flash in a pan, and in that sense, at least, entirely futile. This is where divine purpose might be thought to be necessary. God, one may think, has assigned a purpose for the whole universe in creating it, whether we know what it is or not. Religious believers typically think that revelation tells us what our own role is, at least—what we must and must not do to play our part. When we do so, we advance God's plan for the whole cosmos, far beyond the limits of humanity.

One telling objection to the sufficiency of doing God's work is that not just *any* divine purpose would do—the heroism of those who sacrificed themselves for humanity would only be comical if God's plan was to raise us "to provide food for other creatures fond of human flesh" (Nagel 1971: 721). The theistic response is that an omnibenevolent creator would not have such a plan for us. God wants the best for Her creatures, so our role is to do the morally right thing. As Tolstoy's Levin puts it, "In place of each of the Church's beliefs there could be put the belief in serving the good instead of one's needs" (Tolstoy 1877/2001: 537). But this leads directly to a challenge to the necessity thesis: if what gives meaning to our lives is doing the right thing, what does God have to do with it?

At this point, theists like John Cottingham (2003) argue that God is necessary for an objective morality, and objective value in general. The shape of the argument is as follows:

The value argument for divine purpose theory

1. Engaging with objective value is necessary for meaning in life (value connection).
2. The existence of God is necessary for objective value.
3. Hence, the existence of God is necessary for meaning in life.

Suppose that value connection is true. In that case, it is the second premise that is crucial. Here the debate becomes metaethical. And the ground is not favorable for the theist. It is common to believe that objective morality *couldn't* depend on God's will, since such a will would either be unconstrained by independent moral truths (in which case it would be ultimately capricious and unauthoritative) or it would be constrained by independent moral truths, in which case such truths would obviously not require God for their existence. Varieties of this Euthyphro argument (named after the Platonic dialogue, where it was first introduced to the canon) have been influential in convincing most metaethicists that premise 2 is false.

In short, while it is plausible that playing one's part in fulfilling a loving God's purpose for the cosmos would *suffice* to make one's life meaningful, it is hard to see why it would be *necessary* for meaningfulness, if there is some kind of objective value without God.

Subjectivist accounts of meaning

The key argument for divine purpose theory involved value connection, the thesis that objective value is necessary for meaning in life. This assumption is not universally accepted. *Subjectivists* about meaning hold that objective value is not necessary or sufficient for meaning. Instead, our lives are meaningful when we invest them with meaning—when we in some suitable way *subjectively endorse* what we do, whatever it is. As Harry Frankfurt puts it, "Devoting oneself to what one loves suffices to make one's life meaningful, regardless of the inherent or objective character of the objects that are loved" (Frankfurt 2002: 250). On this picture, the image of *meaningless* existence is one in which our heart is not in what we do—we go through the motions, feel alienated from and bored with what we do.

A key motivation for subjectivism is belief in the possibility of meaning combined with skepticism about objective value. Clearly, if there is to be meaning in a world without objective value, it has to come somehow from within. However, defenders of value connection may well be willing to bite the bullet and say that if there is no objective value, our lives are indeed bound to be meaningless and absurd. And they have a strong case to make, for it is easy to come up with examples of activity that remains intuitively meaningless in spite of subjective endorsement: making handwritten copies of *War and Peace* (Wolf 2010: 16), maintaining 3,732 hairs on one's head (Taylor 1992: 36), or lining up balls of torn newspaper in neat rows (Cottingham 2003: 21). Such activities seem no less pointless for being subjectively endorsed—our response isn't to be glad for someone whose life is organized around such activity, but perhaps to feel pity for that person.

Perhaps the most famous example of a meaningless life is found in the Greek legend of Sisyphus, who was condemned by the Gods to repeat eternally the hard toil of rolling a rock up a mountain, until it reaches the crest and rolls down to the valley again, at which point the cycle begins anew. Now, imagine that Sisyphus absolutely *loves* pushing a rock up the hill until it rolls down, and wants to do nothing else. Does this suffice to make his activity meaningful? That is implausible. This conclusion is reinforced if we think about what finding life meaningful actually amounts to. The relevant kind of subjective endorsement is not just wanting to do what you do, but rather, as suggested in the first section, taking pride in what one does or feeling elevated by it. And it is doubtful that everything anyone actually takes pride in is worthy of pride.

In response, a subjectivist may want to distinguish between objective meaningfulness and meaningfulness *for* someone. That is the line that Richard Taylor (1970/2000) takes. Taylor believes that the legend of Sisyphus is an apt image of our lives: none of our achievements is worthwhile beyond our own interest in them or lasts for long—we strive for the sake of more striving, the main difference from Sisyphus being that it is our children and their children who continue the toil into the indefinite future (24–25). But were the gods to mercifully endow Sisyphus with "a compulsive impulse to roll stones," as we are endowed with a desire to do the ephemeral things that comprise our lives, Taylor maintains that "although his life would in no way be changed, it would nevertheless have a meaning for him" (26).

While this sort of response may have some appeal, it amounts to changing the topic. When we ask what it would take to make life meaningful, we're not asking what it is to *find* life meaningful. That's all that life's being meaningful *for* someone amounts to. Instead, we're asking when, if ever, it is *fitting* for someone to find her life meaningful—when it actually *is* meaningful rather than just *appearing* to be such. Since it is a genuine possibility that someone is mistaken on this score—we're not infallible judges of meaningfulness of our lives—there is a gap between reality and appearance here. The kind of subjectivism that Taylor defends thus collapses into skepticism about genuine meaningfulness. While it may be better for us to find our lives meaningful rather than meaningless, that's not because it makes them good in some special way, but just because, other things being equal, it is better for us to feel good rather than feel bad.

Objectivist accounts of meaning: naturalism

In the two previous sections, I've pointed to some problems for supernaturalist and subjectivist accounts of meaningfulness. It is thus unsurprising that the most common kind of view of meaning in life these days is both *objectivist* and *naturalist*. For objectivist naturalists, roughly, our lives are meaningful to the extent we engage with objective value—the true, the good, or the beautiful. What makes the views naturalist is commitment to some metaethical view that endorses the existence of objective value without supernatural entities. But what exactly is engagement with objective value? This section will discuss four forms of objectivist naturalism—meaning consequentialism, the mixed view, the teleological view, and fundamentality theory—and, briefly, issues related to meaningfulness and time.

According to *meaning consequentialism*, all that matters for the meaningfulness of one's life are the effects that one's actions have on the realization of objective value in the world, impersonally considered. Crudely, the more you improve the world, the more meaningful your life is. On utilitarian versions, betterness is understood in terms of welfare, so activities that make life meaningful are those that increase welfare. As Irving Singer puts it, "We attain and feel our significance in the world when we create, and act for, ideals that may originate in self-interest but ultimately benefit others . . . The greater the benefit to the greater number of lives, the greater the significance of our own" (1996: 115, 117). This simple view is at least initially appealing. It seems that many people whose lives we regard as particularly meaningful, such as Martin Luther King or Abraham Lincoln, really did act in ways that had a positive impact on the welfare of many others. Yet it is deeply implausible that meaning is proportional to contributions to *welfare* alone, as the utilitarian variant has it. Scientific or artistic achievement seems to contribute to meaning regardless of its contribution to welfare, nor is morality just about promoting welfare, but plausibly also about justice and respecting rights. This motivates at least moving to a broader consequentialist view that counts the promotion of non-welfare values as well.

The core problem of pure consequentialist views is that it seems to matter for meaning just *how* we promote objective value. First, we may do good *unintentionally*. Susan Wolf observes that it wouldn't contribute to the meaning of Sisyphus's life if his rock rolling, unbeknownst to him, were to scare away vultures that would otherwise terrorize a nearby community (Wolf 2010: 21). (Consider: would we admire or be inspired by Sisyphus in this scenario?) It seems that promotion of value must be suitably connected to our goals for it to contribute to meaning. Second, as Thaddeus Metz (2013) emphasizes, the extent to which we make use of our capacities in promoting the good makes a difference. If there existed what Robert Nozick (1974) called a "result machine" that can be easily programmed to bring about any consequence, anyone with an access to it could bring about world peace in a matter of seconds. This would be a very valuable outcome, no doubt—but it would hardly suffice to make the button pusher's life extremely meaningful. After all, anyone else might easily have done the same. Certainly, bringing about the valuable outcome with the push of a button wouldn't contribute as much to the meaningfulness of her life as bringing it about after years of dedicated effort requiring every last inch of her abilities.

These problems for meaning consequentialism suggest that meaning in life has also a subjective component. According to what I'll call *mixed views*, meaningfulness requires not only contributing to the realization of some objective value, but also finding one's life meaningful. The best-known view of this type is defended by Susan Wolf (1997, 2010). She says that meaning arises from "actively engaging in projects of objective worth" (2010: 26) or when "subjective attraction meets objective attractiveness" (1997: 221). Wolf characterizes subjective attraction as loving, or being gripped or excited or fulfilled by an activity. She regards these as ways of finding what one does meaningful (2010: 22). According to her,

> People who do valuable work but who cannot identify or take pride in what they are doing—the alienated housewife, the conscripted soldier, the assembly line worker, for example—may know that what they are doing is valuable, yet reasonably feel that their lives lack something that might be referred to as meaning.
>
> *(Wolf 2010: 21)*

Consequently, Wolf believes that "If one's involvement brings no such reward [finding one's life fulfilling] [. . .] it is unclear that it contributes to meaning in one's life at all" (2010: 22). On the objective side, Wolf emphasizes the plurality of worthwhile projects, which go beyond morality to maintaining relationships, art, conservation of nature, and developing an excellence, to mention just a few things. What they have in common is just that they have enough value beyond being pleasant or interesting or fulfilling to the agent herself to merit serious investment of time and effort (2010: 37–38). She also observes that it is not enough to *try* to do something objectively valuable, but to actually *succeed* in doing so.

The objections to meaning consequentialism do suggest that some subjective element is necessary, as the mixed view maintains. But does it have to amount to finding one's life meaningful? That is dubious. Suppose that Mahatma Gandhi didn't love what he did—imagine that instead of being excited by the non-violent struggle for independence he was bored by it. As long as he nevertheless aimed to do as he did—it wasn't just an unintended side effect—and exercised his human capacities to a high degree to bring it about, he was sufficiently engaged with the good of peaceful resistance for successful pursuit to contribute to meaning in his life. On this kind of *teleological view*, the fact that someone is not as a matter of fact *fulfilled* by her life doesn't make any difference to whether it is *fitting* for her to be fulfilled by it (Kauppinen 2014b). (Compare: it is no less fitting for me to desire clear drinks when I'm dehydrated if I don't as a matter of fact have the desire.) There is a subjective element to meaningful activity, but it is much thinner than the mixed view allows. Wolf may be right that the lives of the alienated housewife or the reluctant soldier are not as meaningful as they might be, but not because of their lack of fulfillment, but rather their half-hearted and lackluster pursuit of valuable goals.

Objective naturalists agree that meaning arises from engagement with value. But can we say more about the *kind* of objective value that contributes to meaning? Nozick, who maintains that "meaning is a connection with an external value," says that "intrinsic value is degree of organic unity" (1981: 595, 611), where something is organically unified, roughly, when it is a complex whole whose diverse parts are integrated with each other. This is a highly controversial claim in value theory, and neither can, nor need, be settled by an account of meaningfulness. What matters is that Nozick, like many others, seems to be committed to the *value proportionality* thesis that, other things being equal, an activity contributes the more to meaning in life the higher the amount of intrinsic value beyond the self it promotes or realizes. (Plausibly, promoting one's own happiness, though intrinsically valuable, doesn't contribute to meaning.)

In his recent theory, Thaddeus Metz (2013) appears to reject value proportionality. On his *fundamentality theory*, roughly, meaning comes from exercising one's reason so that one positively orients one's rational nature towards fundamental conditions of human existence (2013, 222ff.). Here positive orientation of rational nature is a broad notion comprising things like promoting the realization of, learning about, or creating representations of something. Fundamental conditions of human existence are those "conditions that are largely responsible for many other conditions in a given domain (226)," such as our ability to reason, feel, and relate to each other, or laws of nature that account for what happens to people and their environment. So when we exercise our intelligence in pursuit of social justice or make significant scientific discoveries or create works of art about "facets of human experience responsible for much else about the human experience (230)," we contribute in proportion to the meaningfulness of our life. Thus described, the theory is quite plausible (though vague), and largely coincides with the teleological view. It is questionable, however, whether orientation to fundamental conditions really does the work Metz thinks it does. This is clearest in cases in which the view conflicts with value proportionality. The aesthetic value of a work of art, for example, is unlikely to be a function of the fundamentality of what (if anything) it represents. Nevertheless, painting or composing a piece that is highly aesthetically valuable does seem to contribute to meaningfulness. Likewise, the moral value of an action is unlikely to track positive orientation towards fundamental conditions, for example, when respect for property rights conflicts with an undoubted general good. Again, in such cases it seems that value proportionality holds, and fundamentality theory gives the wrong result.

Naturalist theories of all kinds talk in the first instance about the conditions in which individual activities or projects contribute to meaning in life. But it is very plausible that the degree to which a life is meaningful also depends on how its parts hang together. After all, part of what makes Sisyphus the paradigm of meaninglessness is that his life is so *repetitive*, and even valuable activities can be such. The holistic claim is, however, not that a life of repetitive (or entirely disconnected) individually valuable activities, like repeatedly rescuing drug addicts on the brink, would be without meaning altogether, but that it is not a picture of the *most meaningful* life. It contributes to meaningfulness if one's life moves forward, the later activities building on earlier ones rather than merely amounting to another iteration. There are few explicit accounts of what such direction in life amounts to. Kauppinen (2012) argues that one factor that contributes to the meaningfulness of a life is having a *progressive* shape, which is a matter of earlier activities positively informing later activities with respect to goal setting (the agent's goals are more valuable than they would otherwise be), goal seeking (the agent exercises her capacities more effectively), or goal satisfaction (the agent is more successful) (Kauppinen 2012: 368). When our lives are progressive in this way, individual activities are not only successful within their own bounds but also of (comparably) *lasting* value, since they bear fruit for one's future activities.

To be sure, on any naturalist picture, everything we do will eventually vanish without a trace. Without a divine plan or perhaps an immortal soul, we cannot achieve any kind of permanence. But naturalists strongly object to the necessity of achieving lasting value in that sense. An operation cures a little girl, who returns to joy and excitement—why would the fact that she will eventually perish make it pointless? As Susan Wolf puts it, it's the quality and not the quantity of our contribution to the universe that matters (2010: 29n14). And obviously we can in various ways make a longer-lasting contribution to the life of future generations—what Samuel Scheffler (2013) calls our *afterlife* in a secular sense. Scheffler observes that, were we to discover that the world will end after we die (or that there will be no more children), we would rightly feel demoralized—many of the things we do would lose an important part of their point. This includes not just projects that aim to make a long-term difference, like eradicating a disease, but also activities whose significance hangs in part on their being part of a tradition extending from the past to the future. A natural way to construe this is to say that many of our most important activities have what might be called a *meaning horizon* that extends beyond our own lives (Kauppinen 2014a). But it doesn't follow that the meaning horizon extends into *eternity*. Again, why would it matter to the point of curing cancer if humankind only goes on to exist for 10,000 or 20,000 years afterwards?

Meaning and well-being

Having canvassed the leading theories of meaning in life, we are in a good position to ask about its relation to well-being. There is broad agreement that meaning in life is something *good*; indeed, something that is desirable for its own sake. But is it good *for* someone to lead a meaningful life—is meaning in life a component of well-being or self-interest? There are three main kinds of view on the issue. Some claim it is a distinct kind of value, while others maintain it is either contingently or necessarily prudentially good to lead a meaningful life.

The best-known proponent of the distinct value thesis is Susan Wolf. She argues that meaningfulness is a dimension of value that is distinct both from well-being and the morally good life. (Often, she phrases her claim in terms of meaning being distinct from *happiness*, but this is a much weaker claim, since happiness doesn't exhaust well-being.) Wolf points out that the things that give meaning to our lives are often things we do for love, and they don't seem to fit with ordinary ideas of either prudential or moral value. She observes that when someone stays up all night making her daughter a Halloween costume, she doesn't believe it is good *for her* to "forgo hours of much-wanted sleep to make sure that the wings will stand out at a good angle from the butterfly costume" (2010: 4). Nor is it something done out of sense of moral duty, however. Instead, one acts out of love, as she puts it. If meaning comes from what we do for love rather than from what we do for self-interest or morality, it is a distinct kind of value, she seems to believe.

One response to this line of argument is that our motives (or motivating reasons) for doing something can come apart from the value of doing so (or normative reasons): something can be in our self-interest even if we don't do it out of self-interest. Wolf herself should admit that some of the things that give meaning to our lives *are* done out of a sense of duty rather than love. It doesn't follow that meaningfulness is morally good, however. Similarly, it doesn't follow from the fact that we don't have our self-interest in mind when we do meaningful things, whether out of love or out of sense of duty, that meaning isn't good for us. I may not think about my self-interest when I practice the cello for hours and hours, to use another of Wolf's examples, but just about the aesthetic value of a perfect performance of a difficult composition. Nevertheless, it may be that the (normative) reason for *me* to do so derives from the fact that success in this project contributes to the meaningfulness of my life. It is good for *me* to be an exceptional musician, even if it means sacrificing other opportunities—after all, it makes my life more worthwhile.

Indeed, Wolf herself occasionally states her view more modestly. She says the concept of self-interest is *indeterminate*. The following is suggestive of what she means: "Is the more meaningful life better *for oneself* than the one that is easier, safer, more pleasant? There may be no answer to this question" (2010: 52). One way to read this is as saying that meaning and happiness are *incommensurable* components of our self-interest, but nevertheless each *pro tanto* good for us. On an enlarged conception of self-interest, then, acting for the sake of the good of others may be good for us.

This leaves the issue of whether meaningfulness is contingently or necessarily *pro tanto* good for us. On the former view, meaning in life is good for us only when some condition is met—perhaps it is good for us if we *want* our lives to be meaningful, but not otherwise. On the latter view, meaning is on the objective list of intrinsically good things. In this respect, the status of meaning as a good hangs on a broader picture of well-being.

Measuring meaning?

Insofar as meaning in life is an important component of well-being, it is of considerable interest whether it can be empirically studied. In recent years, psychologists in particular have started to make claims about meaning in life. For example, Samantha Heinzelman and Laura King (2014) conclude their overview of the topic with the claim that "Large scale representative surveys and numerous studies of meaning in life suggest that meaning in life is widespread and relatively high." But what do psychologists really mean when they talk about meaningfulness? To take a few representative examples, Roy Baumeister and co-authors define meaning in life as "a cognitive and an emotional assessment of whether one's life has purpose and value" (Baumeister et al. 2013: 1). And, according to Tatjana Schnell, meaningfulness is "a fundamental sense of meaning, based on an appraisal of one's life as coherent, significant, directed, and belonging" (2009: 487).

Clearly, then, what psychologists are actually attempting to study is to what extent and why people *find* their lives meaningful, not whether they actually *are* such. After all, it's an open possibility that you rate higher on a survey scale of meaningfulness than Nelson Mandela would, but it would hardly follow that your life is more meaningful than his. That's not to say that subjective experience of meaning doesn't matter. It correlates with many good things—for example, people with a sense of purpose live longer (Krause 2009) and are less depressed (Mascaro and Rosen 2005). And of course, feelings that constitute finding your life meaningful are positive ones—who wouldn't like to take pride in her life history and feel excited and fulfilled by what she's doing? Empirical research into factors that contribute to felt meaning can clearly help in designing policies that promote subjective well-being.

Since finding one's life meaningful consists in positive feelings, it is worth asking how it relates to happiness. In the psychological literature, felt meaning and happiness are typically treated as distinct constructs. Indeed, if people are directly asked how meaningful or happy their lives are, their answers correlate with different things—as a recent study summarizes, happiness comes from being a taker, while meaning comes from being a giver (Baumeister et al. 2013). This is plausible if happiness is conceived in hedonistic terms (as respondents seem to do). But think back on Tolstoy's Levin: in the midst of his existential crisis, in spite of being happy with his family, health, and work, is he really happy? Or is he rather quite unhappy in virtue of his doubts about the point of it all? The latter seems more plausible. According to recently popular views of happiness as a broad emotional condition (Haybron 2008), this makes a good deal of sense. Happiness isn't just about being cheerful and taking pleasure in things, but also, more importantly (though less transparently), about being attuned to one's environment and consequently feeling tranquil, unconstrained, and confident, and feeling engaged with what one is doing. So perhaps felt meaning is best thought of as an important part of the emotional condition of happiness rather than something that may conflict with happiness (for full argument, see Kauppinen 2014b).

Conclusion

There are some who maintain, at least in the context of philosophical discussion and reflection, that it is ultimately all the same what we do—nothing really matters. Were such *meaning nihilism* to be true, it would be difficult, if not impossible, for us to have a high level of well-being. The best we could accomplish for ourselves would be a kind of shallow happiness or self-deceptive fulfillment with ultimately pointless activities. And perhaps nothing we do would matter, were we to live inside a computer simulation in an experience machine, boxing shadows. Alas, we don't. What we do can make a genuine difference. As the discussion in this chapter has shown, both supernaturalist and naturalist views of what makes life meaningful say that our lives can have a point if we engage sufficiently with genuine value beyond our own good. Somewhat paradoxically, it may turn out to be better for us to throw ourselves into the challenges of doing right by others or achieving perfection in an artistic or scientific behavior than to strive for our own pleasure and contentment.

References

Baumeister, R.F., Vohs, K.D., Aaker, J.L., and Garbinsky, E.N. (2013). Some Key Differences Between a Happy Life and a Meaningful Life. *Journal of Positive Psychology* 8(6): 505–516.

Cottingham, J. (2003). *On the Meaning of Life*. London: Routledge.

Cottingham, J. (2011). The Meaning of Life and Darwinism. *Environmental Values* 20(3): 299–308.

Craig, W.L. (1994). The Absurdity of Life without God. Reprinted in E.D. Klemke (ed.), *The Meaning of Life,* 2nd edn. New York: Oxford University Press, 2000, pp. 40–56.

Frankfurt, H. (2002). Reply to Susan Wolf. In S. Buss and L. Overton (eds.), *The Contours of Agency: Essays on Themes from Harry Frankfurt*. Cambridge: The MIT Press, pp. 245–252.

Haybron, D. (2008). *The Pursuit of Unhappiness*. Oxford: Oxford University Press.

Heinzelman, S. and King, L.A. (2014). Life is Pretty Meaningful. *American Psychologist* 69(6): 561–574.

Kauppinen, A. (2012). Meaningfulness and Time. *Philosophy and Phenomenological Research* 84(2): 345–377.

Kauppinen, A. (2014a). Flourishing and Finitude. *Journal of Ethics and Social Philosophy*. Available from: http://www.jesp.org/articles/download/flourishing-and-finitude.pdf.

Kauppinen, A. (2014b). Meaning and Happiness. *Philosophical Topics* 41(1): 161–185.

Krause, N. (2009). Meaning in life and mortality. *Journal of Gerontology: Social Science* 64(4): 517–527.

Mascaro, N. and Rosen, D.H. (2005). Existential Meaning's Role in the Enhancement of Hope and Prevention of Depressive Symptoms. *Journal of Personality* 73(4): 985–1014.

Metz, T. (2001). The Concept of a Meaningful Life. *American Philosophical Quarterly* 38(2): 137–153.

Metz, T. (2013). *Meaning in Life. An Analytic Study*. Oxford: Oxford University Press.

Nagel, T. (1971). The Absurd. *Journal of Philosophy* 68(20): 716–727.

Nielsen, K. (1981). Linguistic Philosophy and "The Meaning of Life." Revised edition, reprinted in E.D. Klemke (ed.), *The Meaning of Life*, 2nd edn. New York: Oxford University Press, 2000, pp. 233–256.

Nozick, R. (1974). *Anarchy, State, and Utopia*. New York: Basic Books.

Nozick, R. (1981). *Philosophical Explanations*. Cambridge, MA: Belknap Press.

Scheffler, S. (2013). *Death and the Afterlife*. New York: Oxford University Press.

Schnell, T. (2009). The Sources of Meaning and Meaning in Life Questionnaire (SoMe): Relations to Demographics and Well-being. *Journal of Positive Psychology* 4(6): 483–499.

Singer, I. (1996). *Meaning of Life, Volume 1: The Creation of Value*. Baltimore: Johns Hopkins University Press.

Taylor, C. (1992). *The Ethics of Authenticity*. Cambridge, MA: Harvard University Press.

Taylor, R. (1970/2000). *Good and Evil*. Amherst, NY: Prometheus Books.

Tolstoy, L. (1877/2001). *Anna Karenina*, translated by R. Pevear and L. Volokhonsky. London: Penguin.

Wolf, S. (1997). Happiness and Meaning: Two Aspects of the Good Life. *Social Philosophy and Policy* 14(1): 207–225.

Wolf, S. (2010). *Meaning in Life and Why it Matters*. Princeton: Princeton University Press.

24

NEEDS AND WELL-BEING

Marco Grix and Philip McKibbin

When conceptualizing *human need* and making claims about what it is that human beings need, philosophers have mostly made reference to ends like survival and harm avoidance. The continued existence of a human being is a precondition for living well, as is the avoidance of harm—but neither of these captures the full sense of the word. While human beings need things like very basic nourishment to survive and avoid (serious) harm, they need significantly more than that to actually live *well*.

In this chapter, we argue for a need conceptualization that makes reference to well-being instead of survival and harm avoidance. While it is ends like the latter two that furnish human needs with the considerable normative priority that we ordinarily attribute to them, more advanced degrees of well-being also confer normativity upon the things that are required to secure them—even if that normativity may not approach the priority we attribute to basic needs.

Based on our suggestion that human needs can be grounded in well-being, we proceed to discuss links between need theory and major theories of well-being. We argue that need theory, as we conceive of it, shares considerable common ground with objective list theory and perfectionism, and that proponents of these well-being theories can learn much from need theorists, and *vice versa*.[1]

Needs and human needs

Before we direct our discussion toward well-being, first let us develop a basic understanding of the concepts of *need* and *human need*.

Introducing needs

Historically, the term "need" has been used in many different ways, but only some of those are relevant to a discussion of human needs. It is important to distinguish between needs as inner states and relational/conditional needs, and between instrumental and constitutive needs. It is also important to explain why some needs have normative force while others do not.

Abraham Maslow, the American psychologist whose theory of human motivation is associated with the phrase "hierarchy of needs," uses the term "basic needs" to refer to inner motivating states, especially drives and urges (Maslow 1954). For example, the pangs of hunger that drive Jack to seek food are an expression of his need for nourishment. Maslow's "basic needs" include physiological needs, safety, belongingness and love, esteem, and self-actualization. His needs concept is both descriptive and explanatory. In this chapter, we use the term "needs" to refer to something very different.

Needs as inner states can be contrasted with *relational*, or *conditional*, needs. It is this sense in which we understand and discuss human needs. Relational need statements generally conform to the structure "*P* needs *N* in order to *E*" (e.g., Barry 1965; Braybrooke 1987; Doyal and Gough 1991), where *P* refers to an individual, *E* the end that is to be brought about or secured, and *N* the thing that is required. Whether or not *N* is required by *P* to achieve *E* is a matter of fact: it depends on what the world and the things it contains are like. For example, even if Jack does not want to eat, in order to be able to function properly at work tomorrow morning he needs to eat food containing certain nutrients. This idea can also be expressed as a conditional: if *E* is to be brought about or secured, then *N* is required by *P*. If Jack is to be able to function properly at work tomorrow morning, he needs to eat.

One way of conceptualizing relational/conditional need is *instrumentally*. The statement "*P* needs *N* in order to *E*" may be true because *N* is the means for bringing about the conceptually separate *E*. If this is the case, the obtaining of *E* is a consequence of the separate obtaining of *N*—although *N* alone may not be sufficient for bringing about *E*. For example, Jane needs to pass the final exam in order to pass the course; passing the final exam is a necessary (though possibly not sufficient) condition for the separate, and subsequent, effect of being awarded a passing mark for the course—and so, the need is instrumental.

Another way of conceptualizing relational/conditional needs is *constitutively*. For example, to be a good father, Jack needs to spend time with his daughter Jane regularly. Here, the relationship between *E* (being a good father) and *N* (regularly spending time with Jane) is not one of means–ends, as it is not the case that the obtaining of *N* secures the separate obtaining of *E*. Spending time with one's child is part of what "being a good father" means. *E* is not a consequence of *N*; rather, *N* (partially) constitutes *E*.

The distinction between instrumental needs and constitutive needs is an important one. Both types of need play crucial roles in discussions of human needs, although constitutive needs will be particularly important for us when we consider the substantive claims made by need theories and by theories of well-being, in the subsequent part of this chapter.

Often, whether some *N* represents a particular instrumental or constitutive need tells us nothing, by itself, about its *normative significance*. For example, it may be instrumentally true that Jane needs cold medicine—but if she needs it to make methamphetamine, then she probably ought not to have it; and it may be constitutively true that Jack needs to have a love for his craft to qualify as a good craftsman—but if his craft is bomb making, then he probably ought not to have it.

For a need to have normative weight, the end in question has to have normative significance. This is because needs and ends are inextricably related. If the end in question is worthless, then the things required (instrumentally, or constitutively) to bring about that end will have no normative force. Such needs give us no reasons to act. If, on the other hand, the end is valuable, then whatever is needed can—and, upon meeting other criteria, *will*—have normative force. Thus, the normative force of a need is inseparable from the qualities of the respective end(s).

Before we consider some concrete proposals for human needs, let us clarify two things. First, it is important to note that something may be a need and an end at the same time—in fact, many things are. To return to our earlier example, it may be the case that Jane not only needs to pass the final exam in order to pass the course, but also that she needs to study the textbook in order to pass the final exam. In that case, *passing the final exam* is instrumentally needed for the end *passing the course* to obtain, and *studying the textbook* is instrumentally needed for the (subordinate) end *passing the final exam* to obtain. There is nothing incoherent or contradictory about believing that *passing the final exam* is both a constitutive/instrumental need and an end.

Second, the relationship between ends and instrumental/constitutive needs must be distinguished from the relationship between need types and subtypes (and between need types and tokens). Consider, for example, the human need for nutrients. Such nutrients can be divided into macronutrients and micronutrients, and the latter can be further distinguished—for example, into carbohydrates, fat, and protein as well as minerals, vitamins, and fiber, respectively. It would not be false to use need terminology to refer to the link between nutrient consumption on the one hand and the consumption of macronutrients and micronutrients on the other (because it is true that, necessarily, for nutrient consumption to occur, the consumption of macro- and micronutrients must occur). However, it would be terminologically confusing because it would not express constitutive/instrumental necessity. When specifying what we mean by "nutrients" by making reference to macronutrients and micronutrients (and then further detailing these two in turn), we are—it seems more helpful to say—providing a thicker account of what the consumption of nutrients actually entails. When it comes to the concrete things that a particular person needs (for her human ends to obtain), such entailment will often be affected by environmental and cultural factors, as well as by previous choices. For example, if Jane has chosen to become a nuclear physicist while Jack has decided to become a priest, then Jane will have some concrete educational needs that differ significantly from Jack's.[2]

Human needs

In political philosophy, the term "need" is usually meant to refer to things that are required by any given human being to function as a human being. In this sense, needs are universal. A human being cannot help but have those needs, at least at some stage of her existence.[3] Some theorists refer to such needs as "inescapable" (e.g., Thomson 1987). We will refer to them as "human needs": things that any given human being requires to live, and perhaps even live well, as a human being.

Needs (in the "human needs" sense) are generally considered to have considerable normative force, and thus often normative priority over other (moral) claims. According to Frankfurt, for example, people are "widely disposed to accept the proposition that a need for something preempts a desire for that thing" (1984: 3), which he calls the "Principle of Precedence." Thus, "[w]hen there is a competition between a desire and a need for the same thing, the need starts with a certain moral edge" (Frankfurt 1984: 3). (This priority is partially reflected in the use of terms such as "very basic needs," "basic needs," and "fundamental needs.")

What kinds of things do human beings need, then? The concept of need(s) has a long history in Western philosophy. Almost 2,500 years ago Plato argued that the true creator of the polis is human need, and "the first and chief of our needs is the provision of food for existence and life . . . The second is housing and the third is raiment" (*Republic*, II, 369C–D). Aristotle agrees on the importance of needs: "without the necessaries even life, as well as the good life, is impossible" (*Politics*, I, 1253b).

Human needs have received interest from a number of philosophers since then, although they have not always been recognized as important. Recently, interest in needs revived in the late 1980s and early 1990s with the publication of some important works by Braybrooke (1987), Thomson (1987), and Wiggins (1991).

Braybrooke's influential account (1987) focuses on what he calls "course-of-life needs," needs that every human being can be expected to have, at least at some stage of life. He distinguishes between two categories of needs: physical needs (e.g., for food and water, exercise, and periodic rest/sleep) and social needs (e.g., for companionship, education, social acceptance and recognition, sexual activity, and freedom from harassment).

Doyal and Gough (1991) are concerned with needs as they relate to people's ability to pursue their vision of the good (i.e., goals that are deemed of value by them). They identify two basic human needs: physical health (as optimization of your life expectancy and avoidance of serious physical disease and illness conceptualized in biomedical terms) and personal autonomy (conceptualized in terms of understanding, mental health, and opportunities for new and significant action). These two aggregate needs, in turn, represent intermediate ends on the basis of which intermediate needs are identified (e.g., nutritional food and clean water, protective housing, significant primary relationships, and physical security).

In the context of global justice, Brock (2009) argues for the importance of a set of five central needs which are required to secure human agency: sufficient physical and psychological health, security, understanding, autonomy, and decent social relations.

Max-Neef (1991), focusing on the end of *overcoming poverty*, proposes the following list of human needs that incorporates virtually all of the aforementioned needs (though not necessarily under the same names): subsistence, protection, affection, understanding, participation, idleness, creation, identity, and freedom. Each of these needs has several existential dimensions, including being (physical and mental characteristics of the individual), doing (human actions), and having (e.g., objects, our relationships to objects, and institutions). While this comprehensive account has been influential in the social sciences, especially in metrics concerning measuring needs, it has received surprisingly little attention from philosophers. Given its richness, we will return to it again below for the purpose of illustration.

It is also worth noting that human needs have done a lot of work in practice. For example, as a result of increasing awareness that the existing policy of economic growth and increasing international trade was doing little to improve the well-being of all individuals in developing countries, basic needs emerged on the political agenda in the 1970s and 1980s, both inside and outside of academia.[4] Basic needs fell out of favor with the spread of neo-liberalism in the mid-1980s and the 1990s, but they have retained a following (in human development circles, in particular; e.g., Gasper 2004).

Needs, ends, and well-being

Now that we have developed a basic understanding of concepts like *need* and a feeling for the kinds of things that theorists have proposed as representing human needs, let us consider the role that well-being might play in the context of human needs. Before we do so, however, let us discuss the kinds of ends in relation to which theorists have construed human needs.

Surveying human ends

As we have already explained, need statements can always be put in the form "P needs N in order to E." The key to the connection between needs and well-being, if there is one, would seem to lie in the end, E. The things that human beings universally require in order to bring about what, in Aristotelian terminology, would be called "the ultimate human end"—living a good human life (or, at least, avoiding a bad human life)—are their human needs.

In the philosophical literature on needs, however, the end has rarely been associated with well-being as such. Some thinkers have associated it with survival. For example, for Aristotle "'Necessary' means: That without which, as a concomitant condition, life is impossible; e.g. respiration and food are necessary for an animal, because it cannot exist without them" (*Metaphysics*, V, 1015a20). Relatedly, Braybrooke suggests that "[b]eing essential to living . . . may be taken as a criterion of being a basic need" (1987: 31).

Contemporary philosophers have more commonly focused on harm (or, rather, its avoidance). Human needs (Feinberg 1973), intrinsic needs (Miller 1976), non-volitional and constrained volitional needs (Frankfurt 1984), fundamental needs (Thomson 1987), absolute needs (Wiggins 1991), and basic needs (Doyal and Gough 1991) have been characterized in terms of what is required to avoid harm.

The popularity of understanding the ultimate end as survival or harm avoidance can be explained by the context in which the respective need accounts were developed. Critics had been questioning if needs could have any normative force at all. The need theorists who proposed these anemic ends focused their arguments for normativity on identifying needs which, if they were unsatisfied, would yield a recognizable normative concern—hence the connection to survival and harm. In other words, it was widely thought that the case for needs having normative force would have to rely on the prevention of calamity, like serious harm and death.

Two questions present themselves, here. First, are ends like survival and harm avoidance really the (only) universal, and universally valuable, ends for human beings? Aristotle and his contemporaries did not think so. The common starting point of ancient Greek discussions of ethics was the view that the greatest human good is flourishing. Mere survival and harm avoidance are far too rudimentary concepts to do justice to such a good—which may be the reason why Anscombe conceptualizes the needs of living things by reference to flourishing: to say that an organism needs Z is to say "that it won't flourish unless it has it" (1958: 7).[5] Reader and Brock (2004), too, list "flourishing" as a candidate end for construing what they call "non-contingent needs," but they do not discuss it further.[6] If we accept that something like *flourishing* is the end or purpose of human beings (and their existence), then we can also ask the question, What is needed for such a life?

Second, what exactly do we mean by "harm"? Isn't the concept of *harm* itself best characterized by reference to something like well-being? Some authors have mentioned this link. For example, Wiggins writes that "the suggested elucidation in terms of harm exposes a certain parameter that is always there to be discovered within claims of absolute needing. This is the idea . . . of well-being or flourishing, by reference to which we make judgments of harm" (1991: 11). Thomson also notes that "[t]o say that something harms a person is to say something about the effects of that thing on the person or his life and well-being" (1987: 90–91); "a person is harmed whenever [her] level of well-being is below a certain level or norm" (Thomson 1987: 93).

This connection has not been pursued by many thinkers who have written on needs in the recent past—and when well-being has been addressed, the treatment has been cursory. However, we believe that it is important to explore this link. In the next section we will argue that it is possible to associate degrees of well-being with human needs that have various degrees of normative force. We think that those things that have been referred to as "basic" and "fundamental" needs can be understood as basic or fundamental *degrees* of human need satisfaction—and thus, well-being. This, significantly, leaves open the possibility that other, non-basic needs (or, degrees of human need satisfaction) have normative force as well.

Well-being as ultimate end

It is, we think, uncontroversial that universal human needs like *nourishment* and *understanding* can be satisfied to lesser or greater degrees. It should be equally uncontroversial that different degrees of human well-being condition different degrees of satisfaction of needs like those just mentioned. If we accept both of these points, then we should be able to identify some of these degrees of need satisfaction (and well-being):

S = requirements for sheer survival (as continued existence as a biological life form);

T = requirements for a tolerable existence (as freedom from major calamity, e.g., prolonged and intense pain, depression, hunger, and anxiety);

D = requirements for a dignified existence.

Let us illustrate these degrees of need satisfaction using the example of nourishment. In order to survive, an individual requires a certain amount of food; but biological survival certainly does not require her to exist without extended, even intense, hunger states. A tolerable existence requires considerably more (or better-quality) food; but while such an existence must be free from prolonged intense hunger states, it certainly does not require the individual to be fully nourished. A dignified existence, on the other hand, plausibly requires the absence of (undesired[7]) hunger.[8] The greater the individual's degree of human need satisfaction (including nourishment), the better she lives.

Thus, degrees of well-being correspond to degrees of need satisfaction. The normative priority associated with satisfying the need in question (to the respective degree) will depend on the degree of well-being for which that need satisfaction is a requirement. Not all need satisfaction has the same priority, but assuming that well-being always has at least *some* importance, any given human need satisfaction will have at least *some* normative significance. For example, lifting an individual's degree of human need satisfaction from degree S to T has a greater priority than lifting it from T to D—but the latter has some importance nevertheless.

Well-being, then, seems to be a plausible candidate for the end, E, that conditions certain degrees of need satisfaction. Just as ill-being can be considered to represent the bottom level(s) of well-being, basic needs can be understood as representing what is required in order to bring about a basic degree of human well-being (e.g., a tolerable existence). This suggestion is compatible with the notion that basic needs have overriding normative force. It also allows us to commit to the claim that human beings need certain things to live lives of more than basic qualities, without requiring us to assert that those needs have as much force as basic needs.

An objection to this view might be the following. Given that higher degrees of well-being generally require rather different things for different people (say, the reading of poetry for some, and the climbing of mountains for others), is it not the case that the use of *well-being* as ultimate end renders the respective needs (which we consider human needs) non-universal? If so, then well-being does not seem like a suitable candidate for filling the role of ultimate end, because human needs are supposedly universal.

However, such a view rests, at least partially, on a confusion between degrees of need satisfaction and degrees of thickness of the need characterizations. Just as basic needs (that are construed in relation to basic degrees of well-being, such as avoidance of harm or ill-being) can be considered through both thin and thick characterizations, non-basic or advanced needs (that are construed by reference to higher degrees of well-being) can be considered through both thin and thick characterizations, too. Thus, the question of what *precisely* the satisfaction of advanced needs entails in the case of a particular person in particular circumstances arises as much with regard to basic needs as it arises with regard to non-basic ones. Correspondingly, the kind of idiosyncrasy that is inherent to discussions of what different people concretely need to achieve high degrees of well-being can be avoided in the same way in which it is avoidable when discussing basic needs—namely, by keeping the considerations of need satisfaction descriptively thin.

Substantive human needs: a suggestion

If we accept that well-being (rather than the avoidance of death, harm, or mere ill-being) can legitimately be regarded as the end in relation to which human needs may be conceived, what might human needs substantively look like?

Without making any firm commitments as to its precision and completeness, we use Max-Neef's work to outline and illustrate some central ideas. While Max-Neef does not make reference to an end as we propose it (but rather, to something like *poverty relief*), his matrix of human needs in *Human Scale Development* (1991: 32) is useful for our discussion because it incorporates many of the needs proposed by philosophers. Here is a partial reproduction of that matrix:

Needs		Existentially		
		Being	*Having*	*Doing*
Axiologically	**Subsistence**	Physical health, mental health, equilibrium, sense of humor, adaptability	Food, shelter, work	Feed, procreate, rest, work
	Understanding	Critical conscience, receptiveness, curiosity, astonishment, discipline, intuition, rationality	Literature, teachers, method, educational policies, communication policies	Investigate, study, experiment, educate, analyze, meditate
	. . .	. . .	. . .	. . .

Max-Neef distinguishes human needs along two dimensions: axiological and existential. While the former refers to types of value, the latter would seem to be based on Fromm's (1976) modes of existence.

Axiologically, subsistence and understanding are among the things that are constitutively needed for well-being. Thus, living well (to a certain degree) means that, *inter alia*, one subsists (to a certain degree) and has (a certain degree of) understanding. Although not reproduced above, Max-Neef's complete axiological list also contains *protection, affection, participation, idleness, creation, identity,* and *freedom*.

Existentially, well-being (to use our end instead) requires not just our having things, but also our possessing physical and psychological characteristics ("being") as well as our engaging in action ("doing"). Accordingly, subordinate needs can be grouped along two dimensions. For example, food and shelter are we might call "subsistence-having needs," while physical health and mental health are subsistence-being needs.

Plausibly, not all human needs are equally important with regard to all degrees of well-being (and thus overall degrees of human need satisfaction). For example, while subsistence will play a crucial role with regard to ends like survival and tolerable existence, understanding will be of limited significance for realizing such ends. However, once we are moving from lesser to greater degrees of well-being (say, from a tolerable existence, past a dignified existence, to a good life), greater satisfaction of the *subsistence* need will play an insignificant role, while greater satisfaction of a need like *understanding* will be rather important.

In our view, conceiving of the link between well-being and needs as outlined above helps advance both our understanding of the nature of human well-being and the nature of human needs, because the two are intimately connected.

Human needs and theories of well-being

If human needs can indeed be grounded in *well-being*, then we should discuss the links between need theory and theories of well-being. Ideally, such a discussion will be fruitful for theorists from either of the two areas and suggest avenues for further, collaborative, research.

We do not understand need theory itself as representing a theory of well-being.[9] Rather, we rely on the more modest views that the satisfaction of human needs is at least one of the things that constitute human well-being (understood as that which is good for human beings[10]), and that it is the only such thing that need theory is concerned with.

Well-being has been conceptualized in many different ways. A threefold distinction between theories of well-being has been prominent (e.g., Parfit 1984; Kagan 1998; Crisp 2008): hedonistic theories, desire-fulfillment/preference satisfaction theories, and objective list theories.

Hedonists hold that there is only one value, which is pleasure. Pleasure is most commonly understood as being objectively good (rather than being good because it is seen as good by experiencing subjects).

Desire-fulfillment or preference satisfaction theorists focus on individual attitudes. They hold that well-being consists in the fulfillment of desires, or the satisfaction of preferences. Such accounts are subjective in the sense that a thing is good for an individual only if that individual sees it as good (*qua* desiring or preferring it).

Objective list accounts, by contrast, assume that what well-being consists in is more or less the same for all people. Such accounts typically present a list of goods.

Conceptually, theories of well-being can be distinguished by their substantive and their formal claims.[11] Substantive claims answer the question, What constitutes well-being?—with hedonists, for example, holding that it is the greatest amount of pleasure over pain. Formal claims, on the other hand, answer the question, What makes what the theory considers good things (e.g., pleasure) good, and bad things (e.g., pain) bad?—with hedonists claiming something like "the pleasantness of pleasure," and "the painfulness of pain" (Crisp 2008).

For a full-fledged need theory (with well-being as the ultimate end) to be practically useful, it will have to make substantive claims, too. The list of constitutive needs gives an answer to the question, What constitutes well-being? Namely, things like subsistence and understanding. Thus, our suggested theory (like most others, regardless of whether their end is survival, harm avoidance, or well-being) is substantively pluralist. At the same time, our suggested theory makes a formal claim. What makes things like subsistence and understanding universally good for people is that they are universally needed by human beings to live well. Given that human needs are the only thing constitutive of human well-being that need theory is concerned with, need theories like ours have a very narrow formal scope.

Whether our account is compatible with established theories of well-being will depend on the substantive and formal claims that the latter make.

Formalism

As just noted, need accounts (like ours) are formally narrow. There are, then, three ways in which they may relate to accounts of well-being. First, if a (non-need-based) theory of well-being is formally monist, then we are presented with an incompatibility—unless its formal claims can be (re-)conceptualized in terms of needs. Second, if a theory of well-being is formally pluralist and needs are among the list of things that represent good-for-makers, then we have at least partial compatibility. (Need theory would agree with such an account to the extent that it, too, claims that what makes a thing, Z, good for people is that it is needed by human beings.) Third, if a theory of well-being is silent about formal claims, then it will be entirely compatible with need theory, at least formally.

Substance

Need accounts are substantively pluralist. Again, we need to consider three ways in which our need approach might relate to accounts of well-being. First, if a (non-need) theory of well-being is silent about substantive claims, then here, too, compatibility with need theory is a given. Second, if a theory of well-being is substantively monist, then we are faced with at least partial incompatibility. At most, the theory's sole constituent of well-being will be one member of the list of things that constitute human well-being from a need-theoretical perspective. Third, if a theory of well-being is substantively pluralist, then we are faced with two different pluralist accounts of the things that constitute well-being. In this case, there is, at least, a possibility that these accounts will be very similar, if not identical.

Needs and hedonism

Hedonism is a formally monist theory of well-being: the only good-for-maker of things is pleasantness (Crisp 2008). Need theory (with its contrasting, formally narrow scope that is limited to human need satisfaction as the good-for-maker of things) is incompatible with this claim, because there is no conceptual connection between pleasantness and human need satisfaction.

Although hedonism comes in both pleasure-monist and pleasure-pluralist forms,[12] the theory is substantively monist in the sense that, ultimately, the only thing that is constitutively required for well-being is pleasure (and the only thing that is constitutively required for the avoidance of ill-being is the absence of pain). Thus, the best kind of life is the one with the greatest balance of pleasure over pain. With regard to substance, we have partial compatibility with need theory, because no one can plausibly deny that (at least some) pleasure is needed for a good life, and that the absence of (prolonged and intense) pain is needed for a tolerable human existence.[13] However, for a life to go well, people need things other than pleasure—for example, meaning. Need theorists may agree with hedonists that pleasure is a necessary condition for well-being, but they will not agree that pleasure is a sufficient condition.

Hedonism and need theory, then, have very little compatibility. The only link between them can be found with regard to their substantive claims, and that link is weak at best.

Needs and desire-fulfillment/preference satisfaction theories

Actual desire-fulfillment/preference satisfaction theories (or actual-desire theories) are purely formal theories of well-being. According to these theories, the only good-for-making property is the fulfillment of the desires that an individual, as a matter of fact, has. Given that people can desire anything, anything may be good.

While need theories and actual-desire theories are somewhat similar in that the former are narrow and the latter formally monist, they make incompatible claims about what makes a thing, Z, good. Need theory holds that Z is good for human beings because it is needed by them, while actual-desire theory maintains that it is good because it is desired by them. *Need* and *desire* are distinct concepts. People can, and often do, desire what they do not need (e.g., sugary sweets) and vice versa (e.g., a dose of bitter-tasting medicine). Desires are propositional attitudes; as such they depend on other mental states, like beliefs. It is possible for one and the same thing to be desired by a person under one description (e.g., a woman can be the subject of one's sexual desire), but not under a different one (e.g., if that woman were revealed to be one's long-lost sister). Needs, on the other hand, are not inner states at all. Like desires, they are directed at things, but they are not attitudes of the person who has them. They are independent of one's beliefs. To illustrate, whether or not one understands what essential fatty acids and vitamins are does not change the fact that every human being needs them to live well (or live at all). Given the fundamental differences between desires and needs, actual-desire theories of well-being and need theory are ultimately incompatible.

The same may not be true with regard to informed-desire accounts. Here, an individual's well-being is a function of the fulfillment of "desires that persons would have if they appreciated the true nature of their objects" (Griffin 1986: 11). If, and to the degree that, persons desire what they need (because they fully understand their needs), the informed-desire account would in fact be compatible with need theory—although need theorists would maintain that desire theorists are mistaken in claiming that what makes a thing good is that it satisfies the individual's informed desire. Instead, they would claim that it is the satisfaction of needs (about which people may or may not be properly informed) that makes something what an informed agent would desire. In other words, need theorists may claim that informed-desire theory, so construed, collapses into need theory (or, more precisely, need-based theory of well-being).

As noted above, if a theory of well-being is silent about substantive claims, then it would be compatible with need theory in terms of substance. Desire theories are, in fact, the only popular kind of theory that is (ordinarily) substantively silent. Let us again distinguish between actual- and informed-desire accounts. There is virtually no limit to the particular things that human beings actually desire on an ongoing basis, just as there is no limit to the degree to which actual human desires can be perverted.[14] Neither of those is true with regard to what human beings *need* to flourish. Thus, the overlap between what human beings actually desire and what they need will often be very small—unless the actual desires of human beings are characterized very thinly. Accordingly, while there may be considerable overlap between thinly characterized human needs and thinly characterized actual human desires, such overlap will tend to quickly vanish once we move from greater to lesser abstractness.

With regard to informed-desire accounts, the chances of overlap are considerably greater. In fact, if such an account were construed in terms of "desires that persons would have if they appreciated the true nature of their needs," then we would find perfect overlap. Thus, when it comes to desire-fulfillment/preference satisfaction theories, whether there is compatibility with need theory will depend on the details.

Needs and objective list theories

So far, we have considered need theory (which, to repeat, is formally narrow and substantively pluralist) in relation to well-being theories that are formally monist and either substantively monist or substantively silent. This leaves us with well-being theories that are substantively pluralist and either formally silent or formally pluralist. Formally pluralist theories do not seem to be popular, so the only remaining combination is that of formal silence and substantive pluralism.

A number of objective list theories of well-being fit these combined criteria. As theories that are silent about formal claims, they should be entirely compatible with need theory—at least formally. As theories that are typically substantively pluralist, there is, at least, a possibility that they will be very similar (if not identical) with need theory in terms of substantive claims. Thus, need theorists, it seems, may learn a great deal from objective list theorists, and vice versa. So we will consider objective list theory in detail.

Objective list theories—of which there are many—are, like need theories and unlike desire/preference theories, attitude-independent. What kinds of goods constitute well-being, according to formally silent and substantively pluralist objective list theories? Here are two proposals:

> Finnis (2011): The basic aspects of human well-being are life, knowledge, play, aesthetic experience, sociability (friendship), practical reasonableness, and "religion."[15]

> Fletcher (2013): Well-being is enhanced by achievement, friendship, happiness, pleasure, self-respect, and virtue.

Notice how natural it is for us to refer to each item from these lists as a human need. For example, Finnis's knowledge, play, and sociability fit very well with Max-Neef's axiological needs called "understanding," "idleness," and "affection." Fletcher's happiness and virtue fit perhaps better across most of Max-Neef's axiological needs through the existential dimensions of *being* and *doing*, because happiness is a concomitant of performing well and "virtue" is generally understood in terms of character states, which affect our doings. This adds intuitive force to our earlier suggestion that objective list theory and need theory are highly compatible (and, when it comes to substantive claims, perhaps even similar).

Given that objective list theories and need theory seem to be so congenial, let us consider their mutual implications, how they might support each other, and how well they will fare together when compared to other approaches to human well-being.

The reasons in favor of objective list theories, which Fletcher outlines in Chapter 12 of this volume—e.g., that they accord with pre-theoretical judgments, that, unlike hedonism, they do not propose too few prudential goods, that, unlike desire/preference theories, they do not propose too many prudential goods—apply just as much to need theory (with well-being as its end). Moreover, need theorists may bolster the support for their work by pointing out the great degree of similarity between their lists and the lists generated by objective list theorists. And—of course—objective list theorists can equally refer to need theory.

Do the reasons against (formally silent and substantively pluralist) objective list theories apply to need theories too, then? Yes, but only partially. In fact, it is here that need theory may help objective list theorists. For example, according to the arbitrariness and explanatory impotence objection, objective list theorists find it hard to explain why the items on their lists are, in fact, on their lists, because it is unclear what these elements have in common (see Chapter 12, this volume). Here, need theory has a resource that objective list theory does not have, namely with regard to the formal dimension. While objective list theory is silent about formal claims, need theory is not: it claims that what all items on its list(s) have in common is that they are universally needed by human beings to live well. To the degree that need theorists develop better and better accounts of needs (e.g., conceptually and metaphysically), the detail of what things like *subsistence, protection, affection, understanding,* and *participation* (to use some items from Max-Neef's list) have in common will become richer and richer.[16]

Next, consider the alienation objection that Fletcher (Chapter 12, this volume) mentions: "It would be an intolerably alienated conception of someone's good to imagine that it might fail in any such way to engage him" (Railton 2003: 47). Thus, the objective list theorist's conception of well-being is problematic, some argue, because it allows that people have very high levels of well-being despite failing to be affectively engaged in the things that, allegedly, make their lives go well. In that regard, need theory can help, too. As illustrated above, human needs can be conceptualized along multiple dimensions, namely axiologically and existentially. While the former gives us lists containing items like *subsistence* and *understanding*, the latter distinguishes between *being*, *doing*, and *having*. According to these existential dimensions, all human needs require certain physical and mental characteristics as well as actions. For example, the need called "understanding" requires both curiosity and astonishment (*being*) as well as activities such as studying and investigating (*doing*). Although it may not be obvious as long as we talk about human needs in a highly abstract (i.e., thin) way, all human needs have affective, cognitive, and behavioral dimensions that correspond to the existential being/doing distinction. If this is an effective response that need theorists can make to the alienation objection, then it should work for objective list theorists, too.

Thus, as indicated before, need theorists and objective list theorists would seem to be engaged in conceptually compatible and mutually supportive projects.

Needs and perfectionism

As noted above, some objective list theories of well-being are formally silent. However, others are not, and humanistic perfectionism is an example of such a theory.[17] While humanistic perfectionists, too, propose objective lists of goods, namely lists of human capacities, they try to avoid the criticism that such lists are no more than a disorganized and disconnected heap of goods by providing a unifying justification for their bundle: items on the list share in common a special relationship to human nature.[18] Thus, unlike the objective list theories discussed in the previous subsection, humanistic perfectionism makes a formal claim; and, like need theory, it uses the formal dimension to explain the commonality between the goods on its list(s).

What might a perfectionist list of goods that constitute human well-being look like? Hurka's (1993) theory of Aristotelian perfectionism proposes three fundamental values: physical perfection (or the development of our physical nature), practical rationality, and theoretical rationality.[19] A good life requires the development of these three characteristics to high degrees. Thus, the ideal life is one that combines the bodily development of an athlete like Usain Bolt, the practical rationality of a politician like Cicero, and the theoretical understanding of a scientist like Albert Einstein. As was the case in the previous subsection, it is perfectly natural to say that the things on Hurka's list are needed for a good life (even if we do not agree that all three of them are equally important).

Hurka's list of goods, someone might claim, looks rather different from the one proposed by, say, Max-Neef. But such differences disappear once we realize that goods like understanding, friendship, and creation are simply manifestations of mentioned human capacities. Thus, lists like Hurka's and Max-Neef's can be reconciled.

Some perfectionists limit their list of relevant capacities to those that are unique to (i.e., possessed only by) human beings. Such an approach would overlap only partially with need theory—because, like other animals, human beings clearly need things like physical health. The needs that we share with non-human animals are, in fact, particularly important in the context of survival and basic needs. Thus, it seems that need theorists will find non-unique perfectionism more plausible.

Like the aforementioned objective list theorists, perfectionists can be considered "natural allies" of need theorists, for a number of reasons. First, in contrast to hedonism and actual-desire theory, perfectionism's formal monism is at least *potentially* compatible with need theory's formal claims. In order to specify the characteristically human capacities, perfectionists must provide an account of the relevant aspects of human nature—and such an account may defend something like a human essence. Thus, according to essentialist perfectionists, what makes things like physical perfection, practical rationality, and theoretical rationality good things is that they are essential components of human nature. This view can be (re)stated in need terminology, because essence claims are necessity claims: the relevant capacities are the ones that human beings have necessarily.[20] And although essential necessity and needs (as we have characterized them in the first section) are conceptually different, in practice, essential necessity and constitutive necessity seem to lead to similar results with regard to the question of what it is that human beings substantively need to live well.

Second, as Bradford points out in her chapter on Perfectionism (Chapter 12, this volume), simply *having* the capacities in question cannot be wholly definitive of the human good, because it would (implausibly) imply that the talented individual who squanders her gift lives as well as the equally talented individual who exercises her capacities. Thus, living well must make reference to both having and doing—which is wholly compatible with the existential dimension of needs, as sketched in the previous section.

Third, perfectionists need to consider how important the capacities (and the things that manifest them) are relative to each other. Need theorists must do the same with respect to their human needs—both with regard to well-being as a whole and with regard to different degrees of well-being (e.g., sheer survival, and basic need satisfaction).

Thus, like need theorists and advocates of formally silent and substantively pluralist objective list theories, need theorists and perfectionists can learn from and mutually support each other.

Attending to needs

Why should those who concern themselves with well-being attend to needs—and vice versa? As we have suggested, well-being (rather than survival or harm avoidance) is a plausible candidate for the end, *E*, in reference to which we conceive of human needs. After all, well-being (rather than merely surviving or avoiding ill-being) is the ultimate, and universal, end of human existence. If that is accepted, then needs theorists will have a natural interest in established theories of well-being. As we have demonstrated, both sides can learn much from each other, although that applies to some theories of well-being more than to others. This, at least, is one reason why well-being theorists should attend to needs, and *vice versa*.

As well as having implications for well-being theory, there is enormous potential for needs to positively inform the promotion of well-being. Most of us already associate concepts like *basic needs* with a concern for and the promotion of well-being. We have argued that need theory can inform our thinking not only about lower levels of well-being, but about higher levels as well. Thinking about needs, then, might help us to think about securing well-being at all levels.

We noted that human needs have already done a lot of work—both in theory and in practice. Terms such as "basic needs" still carry an enormous currency, within academic circles and outside of the university. It would be remiss of well-being theorists not to acknowledge that. If they are genuinely interested in realizing well-being, they should think carefully about how they might build on the commitment that needs have already inspired.

Further reading

G. Brock, *Necessary Goods: Our Responsibility to Meet Others' Needs* (Lanham: Rowman & Littlefield, 1998) and S. Reader, *The Philosophy of Need* (Cambridge: Cambridge University Press, 2005) are the most well-known collections on needs. D. Hartley, *Understanding Human Need: Social Issues, Policy and Practice* (Bristol: The Policy Press, 2010) is probably the most comprehensive introductory textbook on needs and human needs.

Notes

1 We would like to thank Gillian Brock and Glen Pettigrove for discussions and comments on drafts of this chapter.
2 Notice that Fraser (1989) and Soper (1993) use "thick" and "thin" terminology in a related sense. While thin needs are abstract, objective and universal, thick needs are particular to, and thus detailed in the context of, the cultural background against which they occur (Drover and Kerans 1993).
3 There may be some exceptions. For example, a (severely) mentally handicapped human being may not have the same need for agency as those who are not handicapped. And we may think that a human being that dies as an infant—to give another example—will never have the need for human agency at all.
4 For instance, the eradication of the worst aspects of human poverty through the satisfaction of basic human needs was proposed as the overriding objective of national and international development policy at the International Labour Organisation's 1976 World Employment Conference (ILO 1976). Subsequently, the basic needs approach was endorsed by governments, workers' organizations, and employers' organizations worldwide and influenced the programs and policies of major development agencies.
5 Notice that Anscombe does not write that the organism "will die or languish unless it has it."
6 Griffin refers to "well-being" terminology as well. For example, he notes that "[w]ell-being . . . is the level to which basic needs are met" (1986: 42). However, in the context of his discussion of needs he has a very narrow understanding of "well-being," so that the end in relation to which he conceptualizes (basic) needs is not unlike the previously mentioned rudimentary ends (like harm avoidance).
7 A person may choose to be hungry (e.g., in the context of religiously or politically motivated fasting).
8 It does not, of course, require the absence of appetite. (We distinguish between appetite as the ordinary and recurring desire for food or drink that accompanies the empty feeling in one's stomach, and hunger as the intense and permanent sensation that accompanies starvation.)
9 The possibility of conceptualizing well-being in terms of (basic) human needs has been indicated in the literature (e.g., Griffin 1986: 327, n8), and we certainly see it as a potential avenue for future research, but we will not argue for it in this chapter.
10 Though not necessarily exhausting the realm of goods.
11 However, not all theories make both sorts of claims.
12 Depending on whether one agrees or disagrees with the view that there is just one basic kind of mental state or property that is pleasure.
13 Remember the different degrees of need satisfaction that we mentioned above.
14 For a discussion of the phenomenon of adaptive preferences, see Elster (1982).
15 By "religion," Finnis means to refer to our relations to the cosmos and the divine.
16 For an attempt to develop our understanding of the ontological dimension of needs, see Lowe (2005).
17 For the distinction between humanistic and non-humanistic perfectionism, see Wall (2008).
18 See Bradford's chapter on perfectionism in this volume (Chapter 10).
19 Notice that Hurka believes that "perfectionism should never be expressed in terms of well-being. It gives an account of the good human life, or of what is good in a human, but not of what is 'good for' a human in the sense tied to well-being" (1993: 17–18). Still, here we shall consider his approach as an example of a perfectionist theory of well-being.
20 Failure to have these capacities is failure to be a human being. See Bradford's chapter on perfectionism in this volume (Chapter 10).

References

Anscombe, G.E.M. (1958). "Modern Moral Philosophy." *Philosophy* 33 (124): 1–19.
Barry, B.M. (1965). *Political Argument, International Library of Philosophy and Scientific Method*. London: Routledge & Kegan Paul.
Braybrooke, D. (1987). *Meeting Needs, Studies in Moral, Political, and Legal Philosophy*. Princeton: Princeton University Press.
Brock, G. (2009). *Global Justice: A Cosmopolitan Account*. Oxford: Oxford University Press.
Crisp, R. (2008). "Well-Being." In *The Stanford Encyclopedia of Philosophy*, edited by Edward N. Zalta. http://plato.stanford.edu/archives/fall2008/entries/well-being/.
Doyal, L, and I. Gough. (1991). *A Theory of Human Needs*. London: Macmillan.

Drover, G, and P. Kerans. (1993). "New Approaches to Welfare Theory: Foundations." In *New Approaches to Welfare Theory: Making and Sorting Claims*, edited by G. Drover and P. Kerans. Aldershot: Edward Elgar Publishing, pp. 3–30.

Elster, J. (1982). "Sour Grapes—Utilitarianism and the Genesis of Wants." In *Utilitarianism and Beyond*, edited by A. Sen and B. Williams. Cambridge: Cambridge University Press, pp. 219–238.

Feinberg, J. (1973). *Social Philosophy, Foundations of Philosophy Series*. Englewood Cliffs: Prentice-Hall.

Finnis, J. (2011). *Natural Law and Natural Rights*. 2nd edn. Oxford: Oxford University Press.

Fletcher, G. (2013). "A Fresh Start for the Objective-List Theory of Well-Being." *Utilitas* 25 (2): 206–220.

Frankfurt, H.G. (1984). "Necessity and Desire." *Philosophy and Phenomenological Research* 45 (1): 1–13.

Fraser, N. (1989). *Unruly Practices: Power, Discourse and Gender in Contemporary Social Theory*. Minneapolis: University of Minnesota Press.

Fromm, E. (1976). *To Have or to Be?* New York: Continuum.

Gasper, D. (2004). *The Ethics of Development: From Economism to Human Development*. Edinburgh: Edinburgh University Press.

Griffin, J. (1986). *Well-Being: Its Meaning, Measurement, and Moral Importance*. Oxford: Clarendon Press.

Hurka, T. (1993). *Perfectionism, Oxford Ethics Series*. New York: Oxford University Press.

ILO. (1976). *Employment, Growth and Basic Needs: A One-World Problem*. New York: Praeger Publishers.

Kagan, S. (1998). *Normative Ethics*. Boulder: Westview Press.

Lowe, J. (2005). "Needs, Facts, Goodness, and Truth." In *The Philosophy of Need*, edited by S. Reader. Cambridge: Cambridge University Press, pp. 161–173.

Maslow, A.H. (1954). *Motivation and Personality*. New York: Harper & Row.

Max-Neef, M.A. (ed.) (1991). *Human Scale Development: Conception, Application and Further Reflections*. New York: The Apex Press.

Miller, D. (1976). *Social Justice*. Oxford: Clarendon Press.

Parfit, D. (1984). *Reasons and Persons*. Oxford: Clarendon Press.

Railton, P. A. (2003). *Facts, Values, and Norms: Essays toward a Morality of Consequence, Cambridge Studies in Philosophy*. Cambridge: Cambridge University Press.

Reader, S., and G. Brock. (2004). "Needs, Moral Demands and Moral Theory." *Utilitas* 16 (3): 251–266.

Soper, K. (1993). "The Thick and Thin of Human Needing." In *New Approaches to Welfare Theory: Making and Sorting Claims*, edited by G. Drover and P. Kerans. Aldershot: Edward Elgar Publishing, pp. 69–81.

Thomson, G. (1987). *Needs*. London: Routledge & Kegan Paul.

Wall, S. (2008). "Perfectionism in Moral and Political Philosophy." In *The Stanford Encyclopedia of Philosophy*, edited by Edward N. Zalta. http://plato.stanford.edu/archives/fall2008/entries/perfectionism-moral/.

Wiggins, D. (1991). *Needs, Values, Truth: Essays in the Philosophy of Value*, 2nd edn. Oxford: Clarendon Press.

25

HAPPINESS

Neera K. Badhwar[1]

To those familiar with discussions of *eudaimonia* in ancient philosophy, but not with contemporary philosophy of happiness and well-being, the difference between happiness and well-being will seem like a difference without a distinction. For a happy life, like a life of well-being, seems to be a life that is good or beneficial for the individual—indeed, the *summum bonum*. The fact that *eudaimonia* is variously translated as happiness or well-being only reinforces the impression that there is no difference between them. To add to the confusion, some contemporary philosophers use "happiness" to mean well-being (Foot 2001; Annas 2011; Russell 2012; Bloomfield 2014), and some psychologists use "subjective well-being" to mean happiness. However, most contemporary philosophers use "happiness" to mean simply a positive psychological state (either dispositional or occurrent), and "well-being" to mean a life that is good for the person living it. To avoid confusion, I will follow this philosophical usage. My focus will be happiness over a lifetime, or some period or domain of a life, rather than happiness at a moment.

The fact that "happiness" and "well-being" are distinct concepts does not, however, mean that they are unrelated. Indeed, according to some philosophers, there is nothing more to a life of well-being than happiness: if your life is happy, you have well-being. On the other extreme, a few philosophers argue that we can have well-being without any happiness at all. Most philosophers, however, occupy the middle ground, arguing that happiness is essential to well-being, but not identical to it.

I will first discuss the main popular and philosophical conceptions of happiness, and then proceed to see what role they play, or don't play, in well-being. I will follow common philosophical practice in using the following criteria for evaluating a conception: (i) coherence: is it internally consistent? (ii) descriptive adequacy: does it sufficiently closely match what we mean by a life of happiness or well-being in everyday (intelligent) discourse and literature? (ii) normative adequacy: does it help explain why we—or nearly all of us— want happiness and well-being for ourselves and others?

Conceptions of happiness

Everyone, or nearly everyone, wants to live a happy life. Great happiness makes us feel as though we are fully alive, and great unhappiness can call into question the point or value of life itself. These facts are enough to make happiness an important topic to consider. But what does a happy life mean to you? If you could have your pick, which of the following lives would you pick as the happiest life for yourself?

(1) A life in which you are wealthy, healthy, popular, and beautiful. Such a life might seem to have all the makings of happiness. After all, what more could anyone want? But surely it is possible for you to be wealthy, healthy, popular, and beautiful and still deeply dissatisfied. Or anxious and depressed. Maybe your popularity is due to your always going along with the crowd, in spite of serious moral reservations, and this has left you feeling like a fraud. Maybe your wealth has made you lazy, preventing you from making the effort you need to make to achieve your career goals. Either way, you feel that your life is sort of lightweight, lacking in meaning and gravitas. Or maybe you are worried because your wealth is attracting people who value you for your money rather than for who you are.

Indeed, not only are these things not sufficient for happiness, they are not even necessary. For it is entirely possible for you to be happy without being wealthy, healthy, popular, or beautiful. Why, then, is it so common for people to think that, if only they had these things, they would be happy? Because these goods are common sources of happiness, and their complete absence often a source of unhappiness. And this points to a further problem for this conception of happiness: instead of shedding light on the nature of happiness, it tells us about its common sources.

(2) A life of unending, varied pleasures for all the senses. Pleasures that leave you feeling wildly alive, as though, in Samuel Taylor Coleridge's words, "on honey-dew" you have fed and "drunk the milk of Paradise" (*Kubla Khan* 1816). What more can a human being want? What can be better than feeling wildly alive in all one's waking moments? Such a life would be the realization of a "vision in a dream," a fantasy that many of us can relate to. But alas, such wild, intense pleasure is not something we are capable of feeling for very long, leave alone over a whole lifetime. It really is only, as Samuel Coleridge calls it, a "vision in a dream."

Nevertheless, even if our capacity for pleasure is limited, perhaps we can still defend a more realistic hedonist theory of happiness.

(3) A (more realistic) hedonist life. According to the hedonist theory, a happy life is one in which pleasure far outweighs pain and displeasure. But what exactly is pleasure? There are at least three philosophical answers to this question: internalist, externalist, and attitudinal. This last, however, is different enough from the other two to merit its own section.

Internalist theories hold that pleasure is a particular sensation or feeling common to all pleasurable experiences. This conception of pleasure goes back in modern times to Jeremy Bentham, who famously declared that the pleasures of poetry and pushpin differ only in quantity, not quality. But this view seems patently false: as John Stuart Mill argued, different pleasurable activities yield distinct kinds of pleasure. The pleasure of a good meal is very different from the pleasure of a good murder mystery. Hence, according to externalist hedonists, pleasure is any kind of positive (satisfying, pleasing, etc.) experience.

Both internalist and externalist hedonist theories of happiness equate happiness with pleasure, and pleasure with a feeling or experience (Bentham 1907: Ch. VII.1; Mill 1969: 210, 234). On the face of it, these theories seem pretty commonsensical. Further examination, however, reveals problems. As the following examples show, it is possible to have lots of pleasurable feelings or experiences in one's life without being happy. Perhaps, having been brought up by puritanical parents, you feel guilty and conflicted about having so much pleasure. Perhaps you are displeased about the course of your life because it isn't really making use of your talents and is altogether too easy—cloyingly easy. Like eating candy all day long. Deep down, you feel bored and restless. If this is happiness, you think, it's overrated. Pleasurable sensations and experiences all by themselves just don't go deep enough for the fulfillment we associate with happiness (Haybron 2008, 2013). Hence, too, they lack the importance we give to happiness.

(4) A life replete with intrinsic attitudinal pleasures. Fred Feldman's attitudinal hedonist theory of happiness avoids the problems with the standard hedonist theories, by arguing that the pleasure that constitutes happiness is not a sensory pleasure, but the propositional attitude of being intrinsically pleased at or with something (2010). To take intrinsic attitudinal pleasure in something is to be pleased with it for its own sake, whereas to take extrinsic attitudinal pleasure in something is to be pleased with it because it has some suitable connection to intrinsic pleasure, such as being a means to it or a sign of it (117–118). Happiness at a moment is identical with intrinsic attitudinal pleasure minus intrinsic displeasure, and the net balance of such pleasures over some period of your life, or entire life, constitutes happiness over that period, or your entire life, respectively (110). Sensory feelings, in which Feldman includes not only physical pains and pleasures, itches, and creepy crawlies, but also cheery and smiley feelings, do not themselves constitute happiness or unhappiness— only our attitudes towards them and other states of affairs do (145).[2] Thus, the new mother is thrilled and happy at becoming a new mother at the very moment of childbirth in spite of the extreme pain (33–34), and the drunk is unhappy that he is drinking his fourth beer in spite of the pleasant taste of the beer.[3]

Feldman's arguments against sensory hedonism are convincing, but his arguments for his own attitudinal hedonistic theory of happiness not quite. One problem is that, although Feldman claims that his concern is with happiness in the ordinary sense of the word, his theory pushes into the background what is ordinarily seen as the essence of occurrent or dispositional happiness: emotion. Think of the joy in running free through an open field. On Feldman's view, you take joy in the fact that you are running free through an open field. But this doesn't quite capture your joy, which is not an attitude towards the running but an emotion inherent in the running, an emotion that is made up of perceptions, images, thoughts, and feelings.[4] Again, infants and animals are capable of happiness, both occurrent and dispositional, whether or not they are capable of propositional attitudes (McKay and Nelson 2014). Happy, well-fed, comfortable infants coo with satisfaction, kick their legs energetically, and smile at their caretaker. Happy dogs wag their tails, enthusiastically play fetch, and leap on their owners to be petted.

Another problem with the attitudinal hedonistic theory of happiness is that it cannot accommodate objectless emotions. Suppose that you have been feeling deeply depressed all week, but have no idea why. Then your depression doesn't count as attitudinal displeasure because attitudinal displeasure at a moment requires awareness of the object of your displeasure (111). Suppose, further, that you are mildly displeased that you don't know why you are seriously depressed. In that case, on Feldman's view, you are mildly unhappy. Commonsensically, however, your deep depression means that you are very unhappy, and your mild unhappiness at not knowing why you are depressed simply adds to your unhappiness.[5] The ordinary notion of (un) happiness can recognize both objectless emotions and emotions with propositional objects as (partly) constitutive of (un)happiness.

A third problem with Feldman's theory is his conception of a happy life as one in which the aggregate of the happy moments outweighs the aggregate of the unhappy moments (122–123). This is a pretty sad view of a happy life. Suppose that you are now 24 years old, and you have spent 12 years plus 1 minute feeling happy, and 12 years minus 1 minute feeling unhappy. Then, according to this view, you have had a happy life so far—even though you were just 1 minute away from a neutral state, and 2 minutes away from an unhappy life! The view that a happy life or happy period of your life is merely a function of happy moments also leaves out something important about happiness as a property of a person or her life. We will return to this under point (7), below.

(5) A life in which all your desires are satisfied. It's hard to see what could be wrong with this. That happiness consists of the satisfaction of your desires seems like a platitude. Yet although

several philosophers have endorsed a desire-satisfaction theory of well-being, hardly anyone has defended a desire-satisfaction theory of happiness. An examination of the argument of one who has shows why. According to Wayne Davis (1981), happiness at a moment consists of the strength of your intrinsic desires—that is, your desires for various things for their own sake—multiplied by the strength of your beliefs that your desires are being satisfied.[6] A happy life is a life in which the aggregate of the happy moments (far) outweighs the aggregate of the unhappy moments over a lifetime.

The problem, however, is that at any given moment we have tons of intrinsic desires that we believe are being satisfied without any effect on our mental state: that the sun rose this morning and is predicted to shine till 8 p.m., that we are not in the middle of an earthquake or other natural disaster, that the people we love are alive and well, or that we are not being eaten by a dinosaur (Feldman 2010), and so on. The frustration of these desires would ruin our lives (or kill us), but their satisfaction has no effect on our happiness because their satisfaction is an ongoing, everyday, only-to-be-expected occurrence. Believing that a desire is being satisfied *can* constitute a positive mental state, but not necessarily so.

(6) A life in which you both feel satisfied with the conditions of your life as you see them, and judge them to be satisfying by your own standards. On this life-satisfaction conception of happiness, defended by L.W. Sumner, you both approve of what you believe to be the conditions of your life (or some aspect or period of your life) in light of your values (or would approve of them were you to reflect on them), and feel emotionally satisfied by them (Sumner 1996: 148–156). Happiness is thus both an affective phenomenon, and a cognitive one.

Daniel Haybron, however, takes issue with the cognitive component of Sumner's conception of happiness (2008, 2013). One reason is that, as some empirical studies have shown (and as Sumner recognizes), our judgments of our lives as satisfying can be notoriously unstable, being affected by trivial situational factors such as the weather or a sleepless night. But do attempts to identify how we feel about our lives overall, or how emotionally fulfilled we are overall, produce results that are any more stable? It would be surprising if they did, because strong emotions about a recent event, or about an important domain of our lives, can overwhelm our basic emotional condition, whether negative or positive. Strong judgments of life satisfaction or dissatisfaction can also have the same effect, since such evaluations don't usually leave us cold. Accordingly, if there is instability in judgments of global life satisfaction, we should also expect some instability in subjects' reports of their global emotional condition. Haybron himself gives several reasons for doubting the many surveys in which between 92% and 94% of Americans report that they are happy in this sense (2013: 47).

Both cognitive and affect measures of happiness would do better—and the former evidently do do better—when the questions asked are narrower. Studies in which subjects are first asked about their satisfaction in domains of their lives that are important to them, and then asked about global life satisfaction, show stability in their judgments of life satisfaction (Tiberius and Plakias 2010: 10). In some of these studies, the correlation between domain and global life satisfaction is 0.70. Moreover, in these studies, there is high retest stability in life satisfaction judgments over time, which shows that people are making their judgments on the basis of what matters to them rather than on the basis of the weather or passing mood. The same should be true of tests of emotional condition if they focus on what is important to subjects.

But Haybron has a second reason for taking issue with the cognitive component of Sumner's view, viz., that people's life satisfaction judgments often diverge from their emotional states. Thus, some people who judge their lives as satisfactory by their own values nevertheless also acknowledge being anxious or sad, and their emotional states have a better claim to being constitutive of happiness or unhappiness than their judgments of life satisfaction or dissatisfaction (Haybron

2008: 84–86). Such a divergence, however, does not seem to be a problem for Sumner, since his theory entails that we are happy iff we are both cognitively and emotionally satisfied. If only one component is positive, we are only partially happy, or not really happy.

(7) A life in which you are emotionally fulfilled. Haybron's "emotional self-fulfillment" theory is the best-worked-out contemporary philosophical theory of happiness (2008, 2013). According to Haybron, happiness is "not merely a state of one's consciousness" but "more like a state of one's being—not just a pleasant experience, or a good mood, but psychic affirmation or, in more pronounced forms, psychic flourishing" (2008: 182). A happy person feels "fully at home" in his life, rather than defensive or alienated (3, 111–112); he is engaged with his life, rather than passive or disengaged; and he endorses his life as "worth pursuing enthusiastically" (2008: 112). Haybron calls these three faces of happiness attunement, engagement, and endorsement, respectively.

Happiness understood thus amounts to a favorable emotional evaluation of our lives (Haybron 2008, 2013: 19). It is worth pointing out the similarity here to Sumner's view that happiness has both a cognitive, evaluative component, and an emotional component. The main difference is that, whereas for Haybron, happiness itself is an emotional evaluation, for Sumner the evaluative component of happiness is cognitive. However, if our emotional states and our judgments of life satisfaction typically influence each other, then the distinction is not as clear-cut as it might seem. And it is even less clear-cut if adult human emotions themselves are partly cognitive. This issue needs further analysis and clarification.

An important feature of Haybron's view is that happiness goes deeper than conscious feelings. For example, someone who has (conscious) episodic feelings of happiness, but also a propensity to be easily irritated, depressed, stressed out, and so on, is not really very happy (2008: 136–138). In this respect, I think happiness is a lot like love. To love someone is to feel at home and engaged with him, to have one's attention drawn by him, to take pleasure in his company, and to be free of an ongoing anger or irritation towards him. It is also, of course, to often feel love for him. But mere episodes of loving feelings, in the absence of the other feelings or the underlying disposition of love, don't amount to love of a person.

A critic might object that happiness doesn't have to be so, well, serious. Feldman complains that, like too many other philosophers, Haybron has a far too intellectual or "deep" conception of happiness, a conception that entails that happy-go-lucky Timmy, who has lots of fun, few worries, and certainly no "dark night of the soul," cannot be happy (Feldman 2010: 147–149).

It is true that some people—especially young people—just are "high on life" without ever thinking about life or happiness or what they want to make of themselves. If infants and dogs can be happy, surely happy-go-lucky Timmy can also be happy. *Contra* Feldman, however, it seems to me that Timmy's happiness does meet Haybron's criteria for happiness. What Timmy derives happiness from may be shallow, but his enjoyment of life seems to be a deep-set disposition that permeates his dreams, and has all three features that Haybron requires: he feels at home rather than alienated, he is deeply engaged with his life, as shown by his enthusiasm over his activities, and he endorses his life as worth living. Timmy's emotional nature is fulfilled.

Let us now see what role happiness plays—or doesn't play—in well-being.

Happiness and well-being

Well-being concerns how well your life is going for you rather than for someone else—or everyone else. Like happiness, well-being is subject-relative or agent-relative. However, this idea is not easy to pinpoint. Can your life be going well for you even if you think and feel that it's going badly? Can it be going badly even if you think and feel that it's going well? Some theories answer both questions in the affirmative. They hold that, so long as you have realized certain values and developed certain capacities, your life is going well for you, regardless of your own judgments or feelings. And if you lack certain values, or certain capacities, such as for friendship, then your life can't be going well for you, regardless of your own judgments or feelings. Hence, the North Pond Hermit, who found a hard-sought contentment only in the forest, where he lived alone for 27 years, lacked well-being.[7]

Some theories, however, while agreeing that certain valuable capacities and activities are necessary for well-being, claim that your life can't be going well for you if you are unhappy or disapproving of your life. Your happiness and positive evaluation of your life are necessary for your well-being. I will call theories that make certain objective values or capacities essential to well-being "objective," and others "subjective." Some philosophers call all theories that make it possible for the individual to be wrong about her well-being "objective" and the others "subjective." But every major subjective theory allows the individual to be wrong about her well-being for one reason or another. Some philosophers call all theories that make positive mental states of one kind or another essential to well-being "subjective" and the others "objective." But every major objective theory makes positive mental states of one kind or another essential to well-being. The one feature that differentiates objective from subjective theories is the value objectivism of the former.

Subjective theories of well-being

(1) Hedonist theories identify well-being with happiness, and happiness with pleasure. Thus they identify well-being with pleasure. We have already seen the problems with identifying happiness with pleasure; identifying well-being with pleasure creates even more problems (Griffin 1986; Sumner 1996). For one thing, the internalist and externalist forms of hedonism ignore the fact that crucial to our well-being is the well-being or success of people and projects that matter to us. In other words, our well-being requires not only positive mental states, but positive mental states in response to certain states of the world, including our own actions. On Robert Nozick's experience machine, you could have a lifetime of pleasant experiences that have no connection at all to what's happening in the world (1974: 42–45; 1989: 104–108). But this is practically no one's idea of well-being.

Like other hedonist theories, Feldman's attitudinal hedonism also identifies pleasure with happiness, and happiness with well-being. As Feldman puts it, "well-being tracks happiness" (2010: 169). Unlike other hedonist theories, however, Feldman's hedonism recognizes the importance of states of the world for happiness, and thus for well-being. The problem lies in the idea of a life of well-being as one in which the totality of happy moments outweighs the totality of unhappy moments. We've already seen why this is implausible as a conception of a happy life; as a conception of well-being, it is even more implausible. Consider, for example, the case of Jamie and Jane (Bradford 2012: 271–272). Jamie is incapable of long-term projects because he has lost his long-term memory, thanks to Korsakov's syndrome. Nevertheless, he has a few more happy moments during his life than Jane, whose memory is intact and who does have meaningful long-term projects. Feldman's view entails that Jamie has greater well-being than Jane (Bradford 2012: 271–272). But it is hard to believe that anyone would want themselves or anyone they love to be Jamie rather than Jane.

(2) Desire-satisfaction theories of well-being identify well-being with the satisfaction of desire. This might seem no different from Wayne Davis's desire theory of happiness, but in fact it is. Whereas Davis thinks of desire satisfaction as an experience or feeling, desire-satisfaction theories of well-being identify desire satisfaction with the occurrence of certain states of affairs.

In doing so, however, they replace the problem with hedonist theories with one of their own. Suppose, for example, that King Midas has only one desire: that everything he touch turn to gold. Then his desire is satisfied when everything he touches does turn to gold. Even though this makes him miserable, the desire-satisfaction theory entails, counterintuitively, that he has well-being.

The informed desire-satisfaction theory of well-being tries to get around this problem by stipulating that desires must be formed through an "appreciation of the nature of the objects of desire" (Griffin 1986: 15).[8] More strongly, desires have to be informed all the way through to count (Angner 2012). Hence, if King Midas desires happiness more strongly than he desires anything else, but doesn't realize that the satisfaction of his desire for a "golden touch" will leave him feeling unhappy, the satisfaction of this uninformed "spoiler" desire does not contribute to his well-being.

But there is a deeper problem for the desire-satisfaction theory that even the informed-desire view cannot overcome. This problem stems from the view, implicit in the theory, that happiness is important for well-being only insofar as the individual whose well-being is in question desires happiness. Making happiness optional in this way entails that someone who cherishes his unhappiness because, let us say, he thinks he deserves it, has well-being. This, however, is a very strange notion of well-being: no one who wishes well to another would ever wish him unhappiness.

(3) L.W. Sumner's life-satisfaction theory, probably the most influential theory of well-being, tries to combine the strengths of the hedonist view with those of the desire-satisfaction view, while avoiding their problems. Well-being, on this theory, is authentic happiness, that is, happiness underwritten by an endorsement that is both autonomous and informed (Sumner 1996: 156–171). Your happiness is authentic iff (i) it is a response to those conditions of your life that you take to be important for your happiness, (ii) you endorse these conditions using values that are truly your own, and (iii) you periodically renew your endorsement. If, for example, your happiness is based on the illusion that your disloyal and deceptive friends love you and are loyal to you, if being disabused of this illusion would destroy your happiness, then your happiness is not a response to the facts of your life. If you endorse the conditions of your life by values that you have been taught to accept but would reject if you were to reflect on them in light of alternatives, your endorsement of your life is not autonomous. Your values are your own only if they survive, or would survive, critical reflection.

Happiness, thus, is essential to well-being, but not sufficient. Only authentic happiness—that is, happiness in your life by your standards—constitutes well-being. By making the individual's informed and autonomous endorsement of her happiness all-important to her well-being, this view explains why well-being is subject-relative, that is, a good for the person who has it (Sumner 1996: 38, 41). However, the claim that your values are your own only if they survive, or would survive, critical reflection in light of alternatives is problematic for a theory that eschews objective values. For in a straightforward sense, internalizing your values, cherishing them, and living by them is enough to make them your own (Badhwar 2014a: 58, 65). The obvious reason for the autonomy requirement is that Sumner thinks that an uncritical acceptance of values we have absorbed from our culture, values that would not survive critical reflection, is not good enough for creatures like us (LeBar 2004: 195–217; Russell 2012: 41–42; Badhwar 2014a: 65). The autonomy requirement is a normative requirement motivated by this implicit realization. In requiring it, however, Sumner implicitly admits that an individual's well-being has to meet certain objective standards, standards appropriate for all human beings capable of authentic happiness. And in so doing, Sumner opens the door to other objective standards.

At the same time, however, Sumner's value subjectivism creates another problem for his theory. Because it imposes no substantive constraints on the values that you may adopt for your life and happiness, the theory becomes vulnerable to the experience machine counterexample. Suppose, for example, that your happiness lies in easy pleasures, the easier the better, and that your highest autonomously endorsed value is having a good time. Then Sumner's theory gives no principled reason why you shouldn't hook yourself to the experience machine for life, with periodic breaks for renewing your endorsement of your life (Badhwar 2014a: 65–67).

(4) Daniel Haybron's individual nature-fulfillment theory of well-being holds that well-being consists of authentic self-fulfillment, that is, the authentic fulfillment of both your emotional nature (happiness) and your rational nature (2008: Chapter 9). This is a eudaimonist view with a modern twist, in that the nature it is concerned with is only individual nature. According to Haybron, well-being has nothing to do with *human* nature fulfillment, because what other human beings are like can have no bearing on what is intrinsically (non-instrumentally) good for you.

Haybron goes further than Sumner in his conception of what authenticity requires, but in doing so, he seems to unwittingly slide into old-fashioned eudaimonism (Badhwar 2014a). Among other things, he argues, authenticity requires "proper functioning," and the "richer, more complex" your way of life, the more authentic is your happiness, because "such ways of living more fully express . . . [your] nature." John Rawls' grass counter's happiness doesn't express "his nature, his individuality," because it lacks "the richness of an ordinary human life" (Haybron 2008: 186).

These claims, however, seem to imply that well-being is, after all, human nature fulfillment. Haybron might answer that his appeal to proper functioning and the richness of an ordinary human life rests on the plausible conjecture that, since most human beings wouldn't be fulfilled by counting blades of grass, neither is Rawls' grass counter. But what if this is false? Someone with highly limited capacities might be able to fully exercise them in counting blades of grass— or pebbles in a jar. So if such a person is happy (and he can be on Haybron's view), there is no reason to think that he can't also have well-being (on Haybron's conception of well-being). It follows, then, that even if he could acquire more of the capacities of a normal human being, he would have no reason relevant to his well-being to do so (Russell and LeBar 2013). By making well-being entirely conditional on a notion of authentic happiness that makes no essential reference to human nature or objective values, Haybron's theory encounters the same problem as Sumner's: it doesn't do justice to the importance of well-being in human life.

(5) The value-based life satisfaction (VBLS) theory of Valerie Tiberius et al. argues that well-being consists of life satisfaction, understood as "a cognitive/affective attitude toward one's life as a whole," an attitude that is grounded in "appropriate values," that is, values that are not based on false beliefs about one's needs, abilities, or circumstances, and that are in accord with one's affective nature (Tiberius and Hall 2010: 218; Tiberius and Plakias 2010: 423). However, VBLS is led by its own internal logic to embrace two counterintuitive conclusions. On the one hand, VBLS allows that if someone values only pleasure, and pleasure suits his nature, then he can have well-being even on Nozick's experience machine (Tiberius and Hall 2010: 221). On the other hand, although happiness is important for most people's well-being (Tiberius and Hall 2010: 218–219; Tiberius and Plakias 2010: 426), in the rare case that someone values unhappiness, and unhappiness suits his nature because, say, he is naturally melancholic, his well-being requires his unhappiness. Indeed, even "serious depression" can be compatible with a person's well-being (Tiberius and Hall 2010: 215–216; Tiberius and Plakias 2010: 426).

The problem, however, is that someone who has well-being must at least *like* living, and it's hard to believe that either someone who opts for a life on the experience machine, or someone who is seriously depressed, likes living. The passive pleasure-monger doesn't like being a choosing, acting agent, and the seriously depressed person is often suicidal. If a life of well-being is the best, the most desirable, life for you from your own point of view, then it can't be something you want to either escape or destroy. Well-being is, in part, a disposition to see life as a blessing, not a burden, to welcome each new day, not dread it, and happiness in the sense of long-term emotional fulfillment is at the core of such a disposition. Claiming that we can have well-being even if we spend our lives hooked to a machine, or in serious depression, seems to rob the concept of the meaning it has in everyday discourse as well as in the long tradition of philosophical accounts of well-being, and makes it hard to see why we should wish it to anyone we care about.

A common objection to subjective theories is that they make well-being compatible not only with highly diminished lives, such as a life counting grass blades or experiencing pleasure on the experience machine, but also with vicious lives. There is nothing in the theories we have just seen that prevents vicious people from having well-being. Objective theories remedy these problems by making certain humanly valuable capacities, activities, traits, or attitudes essential to well-being. There are two main types of objective theories: objective list theories (OLTs), and eudaimonistic theories.

Objective theories

(1) OLTs of well-being equate well-being with a life rich in certain goods, such as knowledge, virtue, family, and friends.[9] These goods are necessary to your well-being, even if you don't desire, or even like, any of them (Finnis 1980). This feature has been called the attitude-independence of OLTs, a feature that, according to many, makes it hard to see how well-being can be the value of the individual's life for her.

It is not clear, however, that attitude-independence is essential to OLTs, since a pro-attitude is part of the very nature of the goods that are often seen as necessary for well-being. Objective list theorists commonly include happiness, pleasure, inner peace, self-respect, friendship, or excellence in work and play (Arneson 1999; Finnis 1980; Fletcher 2015; Griffin 1986, 2000; Murphy 2001). Happiness, pleasure, and inner peace (a state of psychic harmony) are inherently attractive to the person who has them. Self-respect, by definition, consists of a positive evaluation of, and positive feelings about, oneself. Friendship involves liking or loving your friend, and taking pleasure in her company and the fact of your friendship. Hence, even if, *ex ante*, you didn't want these goods in your life, once you have them, you necessarily have a pro-attitude towards them. It's possible, of course, to have a second-order con-attitude towards one's happiness or pleasure, such as guilt, shame, pain, sense of alienation, or disapproval. In such a case, it is open to the OLT to say that, whereas happiness and pleasure are good for you, the second-order negative attitudes are bad for you. Attitude-independence is of the essence of OLTs only in the sense that what is good for you does not depend on your attitudes *before* you acquire this good.

It is true, however, that a pro-attitude is not part of the very nature of all the goods that are sometimes claimed to be necessary for everyone's well-being, such as religion or children. To some people, religion and children are, at best, painful duties, not constituents of well-being. Hence, those who insist that they are necessary for well-being have to tell us what justifies their insistence. If the answer is that they "perfect" or realize human nature, then their defenders must explain what makes them more important "realizers" than the things that are almost universally regarded as central to well-being: happiness and pleasure.

All OLTs, even those that include happiness and pleasure on their list of essential goods, are open to the objection that they fail to give individual differences their due. (Griffin is the only list theorist who acknowledges this problem, and that, he says, is one reason why he calls his account a list account rather than an objective list account: 2000: 282–283.) Whereas everyone's well-being arguably requires happiness and certain personality and character traits, everyone's well-being doesn't require all the same humanly valuable capacities, goals, or activities. For one thing, no one has the time or energy for developing their capacities for every important human good. For another, the absence of a capacity that is central to most people's well-being, such as the capacity for close friendships, sometimes goes hand in hand with the presence of some unusual but valuable capacity. A case in point is Temple Grandin, who understands livestock intimately but human beings not so well (1995, 2006). Another objection to OLTs, this time from eudaimonists, is that when they add virtue to the list of goods necessary for well-being, they actually fail to give virtue its due, because virtue is not just another good like friendship, but a trait that is partly constitutive of goods like friendship or genuine self-respect.

(2) Eudaimonist theories hold that *eudaimonia* or well-being consists of the fulfillment of your nature as a human being and individual. As your highest good, it makes your life "complete" and "lacking in nothing [important]" (Aristotle 1999; see also Annas 1993; Russell 2012: Chapter 3; Badhwar 2014a: Chapter 2).[10] Furthermore, *eudaimonia* is largely in your control and hard to take from you. A eudaimonic life is not only emotionally fulfilling—happy—it is also objectively worthwhile, and happy (largely) because it is objectively worthwhile. But an objectively worthwhile life is, arguably, a virtuous life. Hence, *eudaimonia* consists of happiness in a virtuous life.

Eudaimonist theories thus endorse the idea that virtue is an essential component of well-being, when well-being is conceived of as your highest good. But how exactly is virtue connected with happiness, the emotional-fulfillment component of *eudaimonia*? It is hard to see how it can be if virtue is conceived of as a painful duty of always putting others first, or following rigid rules of behavior, such as never lying, regardless of the circumstances. But virtue in the *eudaimonistic* tradition is an integrated intellectual-emotional trait that embodies an understanding of important aspects of our own individual nature and human nature in general, and that is both self-regarding and other-regarding. By integrating your emotions with your intellect, virtue creates a psychic harmony, and thus is inherently happiness-making. By orienting you to what really matters in life, it frees you from petty anxieties or resentments, and gives you the perspective to enjoy your blessings in fortunate times and overcome many adversities in unfortunate times.

Virtue is also a means to happiness. This is easy to see in the case of self-regarding virtues such as honesty with yourself, or integrity in your work and relationships. If you delude yourself about your needs, interests, or abilities, you open yourself to frustration, and undermine both self-trust and others' trust in you. If you lack integrity in your work or relationships, your work or relationships suffer, as does your self-respect (Bloomfield 2014). But what about other-regarding virtues such as honesty with others and justice? They also serve your happiness by engendering trust, without which you are unlikely to win others' love or cooperation. By putting you in the right relation to yourself, to other people, and to your circumstances, virtue makes your happiness worth pursuing and attaining. And to the extent that you achieve happiness in a virtuous life, you are *eudaimon*.

The eudaimonist case is bolstered by considering the harm done to you by vice. Just as many virtues are both inherently happiness-making and sources of happiness, so many vices are both inherently unhappiness-making and sources of unhappiness. Envy, resentment, insatiable greed, and rage are inherently conflictual and psychologically noxious. This is why both Plato (*Republic,* Bk. IV) and Aristotle (*Nicomachean Ethics* (NE),, IX.4) depict the vicious man as full of conflict and self-hatred, and incapable of friendship and cooperation with others.

Unfortunately, not all vices are inherently noxious. The injustice that is motivated by indifference to the moral status of another spares the unjust individual the emotional cost of injustice that someone motivated by resentment, hatred, and so on must bear. To the extent that he is unjust, his vice still robs his life of worth, but he is unaware of his loss because he is unaware of his vice (*NE*, Book VII.8). He is like a city that faithfully follows its own bad laws (*NE*, VII.10). Of course, this doesn't mean that he gets off scot-free, because even if he derives happiness from his injustice, it is not a happiness worth having. Virtue is not only an essential ingredient of *eudaimonia*, it is the controlling ingredient, incompatibility with which robs happiness of its worth.

However, if *eudaimonism* requires a *eudaimon* individual to be virtuous in every area of her life, it is open to serious objection. Both psychologists (Ross and Nisbett 1991; Bargh and Chartrand 1999) and philosophers (Doris 2002; Merritt et al. 2010) have questioned this Aristotelian ideal on the basis of experimental psychology. But even without the help of experimental psychology, it can be and has been argued that no one has the epistemic or emotional wherewithal to be completely virtuous (Badhwar 1996, 2014a, 2014b; Russell 2009). This, however, does not make virtue and *eudaimonia* impossible: it merely makes *complete* virtue and *eudaimonia* impossible (Badhwar 2014a, 2014b).

These challenges to virtue and practical rationality have not prevented some philosophers from taking the even stronger, Stoic position that a virtuous life is both necessary and sufficient for *eudaimonia* (Annas 1993, 2011; Becker 1999). Sages "can be . . . [*eudaimon*] even on the rack" (Becker 1999: 8). External goods are beyond our control, so a dependence on them for *eudaimonia* makes us vulnerable to loss and, thus, unhappiness. It also makes us vulnerable to wrongdoing. Such dependence is, thus, a double threat to our *eudaimonia*.

But how realistic is this view of *eudaimonia*? One reason for thinking that it isn't is that a eudaimonic life is a life of "embodied" virtuous activity, that is, activity that takes place in our relationships with particular people and particular projects, such that our *eudaimonia* becomes inseparable from these virtuous relationships (Russell 2012: Chapters 9–11). Another reason for thinking that the Stoic view is unrealistic is that it seems psychologically impossible to love virtue and see it as (partly) constitutive of *eudaimonia* without loving the values that the different virtues seek to attain, preserve, or honor, and seeing them as partly constitutive of *eudaimonia* (Badhwar 2014a: 213ff.). For example, it is implausible to think that we can be virtuous parents if our *eudaimonia* is unaffected by our children growing up to be vicious killers.

Conclusion

I have given an overview of most of the important popular and philosophical conceptions of happiness, the place of happiness in the most influential theories of well-being, and the strengths and weaknesses of each of these theories. A satisfactory conception of happiness or of well-being must either accommodate our central intuitions about it, or explain why they are mistaken. It must also explain why happiness and well-being play such an important role in our lives. Of course, there is much more to be said both for and against the theories discussed here, as shown by many of the other chapters in this volume. This chapter is only an introduction.

Notes

1 Many thanks to Daniel Russell for his helpful comments on an earlier draft.
2 Feldman does not explain why he classifies cheery and smiley feelings as sensory feelings instead of emotions, given that they don't involve the senses. What he says suggests that he does this only because they are experiences rather than propositional attitudes.
3 In his earlier book (2004), and "Replies" (2007), 439–450, Feldman denies that there are any sensory pains or pleasures: there are just sensations in which we can take pain or pleasure. His present position (2010) is more plausible.
4 For a discussion of various theories of emotion, see Ronald de Sousa (2014). Feldman tends to reduce the phenomenology of emotions to attitudinal pleasures or displeasures. For example, he states that if

an irritable mood has its own distinctive phenomenology, its unpleasantness for the moody person is identical with "displeasure in the fact that he is feeling moody in the specified way" (142).

5 For similar criticisms, see Zimmerman (2010).
6 See Feldman (2010), 58–69, for a thorough discussion of Davis' theory.
7 http://www.gq.com/news-politics/newsmakers/201409/the-last-true-hermit
8 James Griffin presents his theory as a desire satisfaction theory in (1986), and this is how it has been widely interpreted. But as he makes clear in his "Replies" (2000), it is actually a list theory. See objective list theories below.
9 The moniker, objective list theory, comes from Parfit (1984), although Parfit himself does not support this theory.
10 A note of caution: Feldman calls his own theory of well-being *eudaimonistic* because he takes eudaimonism to hold that well-being tracks happiness (2010: Chapter 8). But neither *eudaimonists* like Plato, Aristotle, and the Stoics, nor their contemporary defenders think that happiness in the psychological sense is all there is to *eudaimonia*. In contrast to Feldman, Besser-Jones (Chapter 15, this volume), takes happiness to be inessential to *eudaimonia*. Finally, although Hursthouse says in one place in her book, *On Virtue Ethics,* that virtue is the best bet for *eudaimonia*, not an essential ingredient of it (1999: 172), she also says in another place that a happiness worth having requires virtue (1999: 9–10, 185).

Bibliography

Angner, E. (2012) "Subjective Well-Being: When, and Why, It Matters," unpublished paper, http://papers.ssrn.com/sol3/papers.cfm?abstract_id=2157140.
Annas, J. (1993) *The Morality of Happiness.* New York: Oxford University Press.
Annas, J. (2011) *Intelligent Virtue.* New York: Oxford University Press.
Aristotle. (1999) *Nicomachean Ethics.* Translated by Terence Irwin, 2nd edn. Indianapolis, IN: Hackett.
Arneson, R. (1999) "Human Flourishing versus Desire Satisfaction." *Social Philosophy and Policy* 16, no. 1, 113–142.
Badhwar, N.K. (1996) "The Limited Unity of Virtue." *Nous* 30, no. 3, 306–329.
Badhwar, N.K. (2014a) *Well-Being: Happiness in a Worthwhile Life.* New York: Oxford University Press.
Badhwar, N.K. (2014b) "Reasoning about Wrong Reasons, No Reasons, and Reasons of Virtue," in N. Snow and F. Trevigno (eds.) *The Philosophy and Psychology of Character and Happiness.* New York: Routledge, pp. 35–43.
Bargh, J.A. and T.L. Chartrand. (1999) "The Unbearable Automaticity of Being." *American Psychologist* 54, no. 7, 462–479.
Becker, L. (1999) *A New Stoicism.* Princeton, NJ: Princeton University Press.
Bentham, J. (1907) *An Introduction to the Principles of Morals and Legislation.* Library of Economics and Liberty. http://www.econlib.org/library/Bentham/bnthPML7.html.
Besser-Jones, L. (2015) "Contemporary Eudaimonism," in Fletcher, G. (ed.) *Handbook of Well-being.* New York: Routledge.
Bloomfield, P. (2014) *The Virtues of Happiness.* New York: Oxford University Press.
Bradford, G. (2012) "Review of Fred Feldman, *What is this Thing Called Happiness?*" *Journal of Value Inquiry* 46, no. 2, 271–272.
de Sousa, R. (Spring 2014) "Emotion," in E. Zalta (ed.), *The Stanford Encyclopedia of Philosophy.* http://plato.stanford.edu/archives/spr2014/entries/emotion/.
Doris, J.M. (2002) *Lack of Character: Personality and Moral Behavior.* Cambridge, UK: Cambridge University Press.
Feldman, F. (2004) *Pleasure and the Good Life: Concerning the Nature, Varieties, and Plausibility of Hedonism.* Oxford: Clarendon.
Feldman, F. (2007) "Replies," *Philosophical Studies* 136, no. 3, 439–450.
Feldman, F. (2010) *What is This Thing Called Happiness?* New York: Oxford University Press.
Finnis, J. (1980) *Natural Law and Natural Rights.* Oxford: Clarendon Press.
Fletcher, G. (2015) "Objective List Theories," in Fletcher, G. (ed.) *Handbook of Well-being.* New York: Routledge.
Foot, P. (2001) *Natural Goodness.* Oxford: Clarendon.
Grandin, T. (2006) *Thinking in Pictures and Other Reports From My Life with Autism.* Expanded edn. New York: Vintage.
Griffin, J. (1986) *Well-Being: Its Meaning, Measurement, and Moral Importance.* Oxford: Clarendon.

Griffin, J. (2000) "Replies," in R. Crisp and B. Hooker (eds.), *Well-Being and Morality: Essays in Honour of James Griffin*. Oxford: Clarendon, pp. 281–314.

Haybron, D.M. (2008) *The Pursuit of Unhappiness: The Elusive Psychology of Well-Being*. New York: Oxford University Press.

Haybron, D.M. (2013) *A Very Short Introduction to Happiness*. New York: Oxford University Press.

Hursthouse, R. (1999) *On Virtue Ethics*. Oxford: Oxford University Press.

LeBar, M. (2004) "Good for You." *Pacific Philosophical Quarterly* 85, no. 2, 195–217.

LeBar, M. (2013) *The Value of Living Well*. New York: Oxford University Press.

McKay, T. and M. Nelson (2014) "Propositional Attitude Reports," in E.N. Zalta (ed.), *The Stanford Encyclopedia of Philosophy* (Spring 2014). http://plato.stanford.edu/archives/spr2014/entries/prop-attitude-reports/.

Merritt, M.W., J. Doris, and G. Harman. (2010) "Character," in J. Doris and the Moral Psychology Research Group, *The Moral Psychology Handbook*. New York: Oxford University Press. Online Sept. 2009.

Mill, J.S. (1969) *Collected Works of John Stuart Mill: X. Essays on Ethics, Religion and Society*. (ed.) J.M. Robson. Toronto: University of Toronto Press.

Murphy, M. (2001) *Natural Law and Practical Rationality*. Cambridge: CUP.

Nozick, R. (1974) *Anarchy, State, and Utopia*. New York: Basic Books.

Nozick, R. (1989) *The Examined Life: Philosophical Meditations*. New York: Simon & Schuster.

Parfit, D. (1984) *Reasons and Persons*. Oxford: Clarendon.

Ross, L. and R.E. Nisbett (1991) *The Person and the Situation*. Philadelphia: Temple University Press.

Russell, D.C. (2009) *Practical Intelligence and the Virtues*. New York: Oxford University Press.

Russell, D.C. (2012) *Happiness for Humans*. New York: Oxford University Press.

Russell, D.C. and M. LeBar. (2013) "Well-Being and Eudaimonia: A Reply to Haybron," in J. Peters (ed.) *Aristotelian Ethics in Contemporary Perspective*. London: Routledge, pp. 52–69.

Sumner, L.W. (1996) *Welfare, Happiness, and Ethics*. Oxford: Clarendon.

Tiberius, V. and A. Hall. (2010) "Normative Theory and Psychological Research: Hedonism, Eudaimonism, and Why it Matters." *Journal of Positive Psychology* 5, no. 3, 212–225.

Tiberius, V. and A. Plakias. (2010). "Well-Being," in J. Doris and the Moral Psychology Research Group (eds.), *The Moral Psychology Handbook*. New York: Oxford University Press, pp. 403–432.

Zimmerman, M.J. (2010) Review of Fred Feldman, *What is This Thing Called Happiness?* https://ndpr.nd.edu/news/24409-what-is-this-thing-called-happiness/.

26

WELL-BEING AND DEATH

Ben Bradley

This is an opinionated survey of some ways in which our thinking about death intersects with our thinking about well-being. Some of the main philosophical questions about death are the following: Is death bad for the one who dies? What *makes* death bad, on those occasions when it is bad? *How bad* is it to die—how great a misfortune is death for its victim—and what determines this? Is there any *time* at which death is bad for its victim? Can someone be harmed *after* she dies—are the dead still subject to benefits and misfortunes? What attitudes and emotions is it rational or fitting to have towards one's death? Our answers to these questions will require us to address questions about the nature of well-being and the place of well-being in the philosophy of death.

In what follows I will assume that there is no afterlife. If there were an afterlife, most of the interesting philosophical puzzles about the badness of death would disappear and be replaced by relatively banal epistemological problems (how can we know what the afterlife is like, will it be good or bad for us, etc.). I will assume furthermore that when one dies, one goes out of existence altogether rather than existing as a corpse—Fred Feldman calls this the "termination thesis" (2000). I make this assumption not because I am convinced it is true, but only because there are at least some cases—cases of annihilation in which no corpse is left behind—in which the deceased goes out of existence altogether; it seems safe to assume that concerning the badness of death, there is no interesting difference between cases where a corpse is left behind and cases of total annihilation.

Death and deprivation of well-being

Let us begin with the most obvious way in which well-being is connected to death. According to the most popular view about what makes death a misfortune, the *deprivation account*, death is bad because it deprives its victim of the good things in life—that is, death is a misfortune because, and when, it results in a net loss of well-being to the victim.[1] This thought is understood counterfactually: death is a misfortune for its victim if and only if the victim *would have been* better off overall if she had not died then. Furthermore, how bad it is to die is determined by how much good the victim is deprived of—that is, how much better her life would have been if she had not died then. If her life would have been worse had she not died then—for example, if she was in excruciating pain with no hope of relief—then her death is not harmful for her,

320

but is beneficial for her. A nice feature of the deprivation account is that it does not require us to take a stand on the controversial question of which is the correct theory of well-being.

Before we proceed, we should note that terminology is sometimes disputed. Here are three questions we might ask about death: (1) Is death *bad* for its victim? (2) Is death a *misfortune* for its victim? (3) Is death *harmful* to its victim? I have so far intentionally treated these synonymously in order to show how natural it is to treat them this way. But some have argued that death can be *comparatively bad*, in the deprivationist sense described in the previous paragraph, without being a misfortune, and without being harmful. Simply failing to get some positive well-being—for instance, by failing to find Aladdin's lamp—is comparatively bad for you, but it may nevertheless not be a misfortune or a harm, as it does not merit any sort of distress (Draper 1999). All parties seem to agree that death is comparatively bad, so let us instead focus on question 2: Is death a misfortune for its victim? And can the misfortune of death be explained by appeal to depriva- tion of well-being? There are several reasons one might think the simple deprivation account of death's misfortune presented here may be lacking. Here are four.

The first problem has to do with the evaluation of the counterfactuals involved in determin- ing the deprivations of death. A victim's death is alleged to be bad if her life would have been better if that death had not occurred. But there are many ways for a death not to occur. For example, consider the following two counterfactual statements about Joan Rivers's (JR's) death:

> If JR had not died (and had never gone for a vocal cord operation before), she would have lived several more happy years.

> If JR had not died (after having had the botched operation), she would have lived a short time longer and not enjoyed her life very much.

Both counterfactuals seem true, but when combined with the deprivation account would give us different answers to the question of whether JR's death was bad for her. This shows that it is difficult and perhaps impossible to *isolate* the badness of death itself and to give a *univocal* answer to how bad death is for someone, even when we know all that can be known about the case. These matters are complicated and important, but do not directly concern the connection between death and *well-being*, so I will not pursue them further.

The second problem is that some deprivations of well-being are fanciful or unrealistic. The case of Aladdin's lamp seems to show that mere deprivation of well-being is not a misfortune. Thus we might think the deprivation account needs to be supplemented in a way that will rule out such cases. Since one cannot reasonably expect to find Aladdin's lamp, we might wish to say that a loss of well-being counts as a misfortune only when the victim could reasonably have expected to receive that well-being.[2] But a young adult who knows she has Huntington's dis- ease cannot expect to receive a long life full of well-being; that expectation is as reasonable as expecting to win the lottery. This does not make us think that her loss of that long life is not a misfortune or that it would be unfitting for her to lament her premature demise. So it is unclear how to adjust the deprivation account in light of these cases.

The third problem involves desires. Some have argued that, in order for death to be a mis- fortune for its victim, in addition to the death's depriving the victim of some well-being the victim must have certain desires.[3] (On a more extreme version of this view, those desires are the only thing relevant to whether death is a misfortune; deprivation of well-being does not enter the picture at all.) Some candidate desires include a desire to live or to have a certain sort of life story. In many cases, desire-based views will have the same implications as the depriva- tion account, because a desire to live and a future with positive well-being tend to go together.

But this is not always the case. So we must examine the cases in which they come apart and see which way we should go.

Sometimes an individual might desire to live even though continued life would not be good for her. In such cases, it still seems very wrong to kill that individual. There are different explanations one might offer for this judgment. One explanation for this would be that death is still harmful to her in some way. If that is so, then the harm of death cannot be fully explained by appeal to the loss of well-being involved. The victim's desire to live offers a possible explanation of this harm. On the other hand, one might just explain the wrongness of killing directly by appeal to the frustration of the victim's desire to live, without the intermediate claim that frustrating that desire constitutes a harm to the victim—thus killing, in this instance, would be a case of harmless wrongdoing.

Some creatures might lack the cognitive sophistication to have desires concerning their own deaths. For such creatures, even though they have good lives, death would fail to be harmful if a desire-based view of death's badness were true. This is sometimes seen as a benefit of desire-based views, as they would provide some support for the thought that it is permissible to kill such animals for food; and in fact this is probably the primary motivation for such views. But it is far from clear that, for example, cows and pigs lack a desire to live; behavioral evidence certainly indicates they want to live. Perhaps their desires insufficiently represent their futures; they desire to eat this now, or they desire to get away from this danger now, but they don't exhibit the kind of long-range planning behavior that would indicate a desire to have a certain kind of long life, nor do they have the abstract representational abilities required to envision their future lives. Even if this is true, though, the problem is that some humans, for example babies, do not exhibit that sort of behavior either. It seems clearly wrong to say that babies are not harmed by dying (DeGrazia 1996: 237).

Someone might falsely believe he will have a bad future, and therefore desire not to continue living. Someone who is severely depressed might lose a desire to live, even though his depression would eventually be cured and he would enjoy life again. In such cases, the deprivation account entails that death is bad for its victim, but desire-based theories do not. This seems to be a point in favor of deprivation accounts, since death does seem to be bad for its victim in these cases. Here the defender of a desire-based theory might wish to appeal to the *ability* or *capacity* to have a desire to live, or to the individual's *past* desire to live, as what is really necessary for death to be harmful.

The fourth problem involves cases where the one who dies is not very connected psychologically to the goods of which death deprives her. Jeff McMahan has developed a time-relative interest account of death's misfortune to account for such cases (2002: 165–174). According to McMahan, we must adjust the misfortune of the deprivation of well-being in light of the degree of psychological connectedness between the victim at the time of death and the victim at the time she would have received the goods of which she was deprived. Desires are one such connection, but not the only one. An extreme example serves to illustrate McMahan's view. Suppose you have a fatal disease that will kill you painlessly in 5 years' time if left untreated, during which time you will still be able to enjoy your life. The cure for the disease will allow you to live for 20 equally happy years, but will also cause deep changes in your psychological profile: you will have different desires, different values, and no memory of your previous life. According to McMahan, it makes sense to refuse the cure. This is because, although refusing the cure will result in you getting far fewer goods than you would get if you took it, the misfortune of missing out on those goods is discounted for the extreme psychological disconnectedness that would obtain between your pre- and post-cure selves.

McMahan thinks this is the right answer to the question of whether to take the cure. But the time-relative interest account is also alleged to do better than the simple deprivation account in other sorts of cases. For example, the deprivation account seems to entail that death is a greater misfortune the younger the victim is, and therefore that the death of a very young fetus is a greater misfortune for it than the death of a young adult is for him. This in turn suggests that it is more seriously wrong to kill a fetus than a young adult, which seems the wrong result. McMahan's view does not have that result because when a fetus dies it is not very strongly connected to the goods it would have received as an adult. There are no shared memories, no continuing desires, and generally no psychological continuity between a fetus and the adult it becomes. Thus the misfortune of losing out on those future goods is sharply discounted in the fetus's case, but not so much in the case of the young adult. The defender of the standard deprivation account cannot claim that death is worse for the young adult, but he can appeal to differences in the moral statuses of fetuses and adults to explain why it is more important to care about the death of the young adult even though the fetus's death is a greater misfortune.

McMahan's view may go wrong in other sorts of cases. In particular, since the relevant psychological connections are between the agent at the time of the harming event and the agent at the time she would have received some goods, McMahan's view seems to entail that it makes a difference *when the harming event occurs*, even if this is unknown to the victim and has no effect on the extent of deprivation (Bradley 2008).[4]

Connections between judgments about death and judgments about well-being

If we think that well-being and the evil of death are connected in the way suggested by the deprivation account, even in one of its modified forms, we may also find ourselves committed to particular views about well-being, depending on what we think about how bad certain deaths are. For example: suppose you must choose whether to save the life of a human or the life of a non-human animal. Knowing nothing else about the situation, you might think that you should save the life of the human. (Let us stipulate that the human is not Hitler or anyone remotely as evil as Hitler.) But suppose the non-human is a young turtle that would live a hundred years if it were saved, while the human is a middle-aged human who would not live even half that long. You might think that doesn't matter; the human is still the one that should be saved. What would make this so?

Perhaps we have special moral obligations to members of our own species: obligations of partiality, such as we might have towards family members. Or perhaps humans have greater inherent moral status than turtles, due to our greater cognitive sophistication, so we have an obligation to save a human rather than a turtle even if we could benefit the turtle more by saving it. I won't here object to either of these views. But there are other possibilities. Perhaps, even though the human would live a shorter life if saved, her death is a greater misfortune than the turtle's. It would be difficult to maintain such a position if, for example, some simple version of hedonism were true. So long as the turtle gets a reasonable amount of pleasure in life, and generally avoids pain, its life would be so much longer that it would accumulate a higher hedonic balance than the human could. This might lead us to reject simple hedonism. We might therefore conclude that there is a difference between higher and lower pleasures, such that higher pleasures of the sort that people get—pleasures of art, music, intellectual activity, and such—are much more valuable than the sorts of lower pleasures a turtle can have. Or maybe there are certain objective goods, such as friendship and virtue, that are inherently beneficial and that can be had by humans but not turtles. It is important that we be careful not to assume too lightly that death is a greater misfortune for a human than for a non-human. After all, we are highly motivated to think that we are more important than non-humans. In any such case we ought to take extra care that we are not merely being self-serving.

Connections also run in the other direction: judgments about well-being can have surprising implications for judgments about the evil of death. For instance, the notion that the "shape" of a life is relevant to well-being has implications for whether death is a misfortune. By the "shape" of a life, I mean such factors as how the well-being in that life is distributed within it (more at the beginning, middle, or end), or how the parts of the life fit together to tell a story (e.g., whether later successes redeem prior failures) (Velleman 1993). According to a study performed by Ed Diener and others, many people are inclined to prefer a life that ends on a very high note to a similar life that reaches the same high note, but continues on for several years with a period of relatively modest positive well-being (Diener et al. 2001). If they accept a deprivation account of death's misfortune, people who prefer the shorter life that ends on the high note are committed to saying that death is beneficial even if it prevents the victim from having several more years of good life, as long as those years are not as good as the peak. It is unclear whether many people would in fact make that judgment about death. If not, then they must reject either the deprivation account or the shape-of-life judgment (Bradley 2009: 157–163).

At what time does death harm?

Epicurus argued that death is not harmful to its "victim." It does not harm you before you die, because you haven't died yet; but at the moment of death you go out of existence, and there is no longer anyone for your death to harm. Since it seems impossible to accept that death is not harmful, philosophers have attempted to find fault with Epicurus's argument. Three strategies have been most popular.

Priorists say that death harms its victim before she dies. How can that be? Wouldn't this require backwards causation, which is impossible? No. There are ways to affect the past without backwards causation. For instance, I can now make it the case, by quitting, that yesterday was my penultimate day at my job. In so doing I *make something the case* yesterday, but not by *causing something to happen* yesterday. In the case of death, it is argued that death harms its victim in virtue of frustrating the plans, goals, and desires the victim had while alive.[5] The harm accrues to the victim at the times when she had those plans, goals, and desires. The advantage of priorism is that it attributes harm to the victim at a time when the victim exists, thereby avoiding potential for unwanted metaphysical commitments.

Priorism requires us to accept a theory of well-being according to which what is good for someone is to have a desire fulfilled, or to achieve a goal. Insofar as we find such theories implausible, we will find this answer to Epicurus unsatisfactory. But even those who accept such a theory might not wish to answer Epicurus in this way. For it seems more natural, when thinking about when one is benefited by having a desire satisfied, to say that one is benefited when the desire is *satisfied*—not when the desire is taking place. A child who wants to become an astronaut, and becomes one as an adult, did not have a better childhood in virtue of later becoming an astronaut (Velleman 1993). If I now want to eat lunch in an hour, I am not better off now in virtue of eating lunch in an hour. And so on.

Subsequentists say that death harms its victim after she dies: in particular, the times after death at which the victim would have been well off, and therefore better off than she is being dead (Feit 2002; Bradley 2004, 2009). The motivation for this view is that it makes the harm of death similar to other harms. If I sleep through a concert I wanted to see, my sleeping is bad for me while the concert is taking place, since it is at those times that I would have been well off but instead have neutral well-being while sleeping. Death is in a way like sleeping through everything, and its harmfulness gets explained in the same way. Unlike priorism, subsequentism does not carry any commitment to a particular theory of well-being.

However, subsequentism does have one implication that may be hard to swallow. It requires us to compare how well off people are at times after they die, and therefore no longer exist, with how well off they would have been at those times if they hadn't died. The subsequentist assumes that, after death, a person has a well-being level of zero; the objection is that a dead person, since she doesn't exist, cannot have a well-being level at all, not even zero. So although the subsequentist is not committed to any particular theory of well-being, he is committed to the claim that it is possible to have a well-being level at a time at which you do not exist, which seems as nonsensical as saying that a non-existent person has a zero level of beauty or health, or that a non-existent object has zero temperature.

It is not clear, however, that well-being is relevantly like beauty or health. The following argument seems sound: for my own sake, I now prefer a future in which I exist and am well off to a future in which I do not exist at all. I am correct to have that preference. Stipulate that a future in which I am well off ranks higher on the X-scale than a future of non-existence. The X-scale is what we are interested in when engaging in prudential evaluation. If the X-scale were not the well-being scale, then well-being would not be what we are interested in when engaging in prudential evaluation. That is absurd; so the X-scale is the well-being scale. So a future of non-existence has a ranking on the well-being scale.[6]

Though this argument seems sound, it remains surprising that someone could have a well-being level after death. Well-being and health do seem like very similar notions, and you can't have a mediocre level of health at a time at which you do not exist. What I am suggesting is that we stop thinking of well-being as being very much like health, and rather think of it as essentially connected to prudential deliberation. We can prudentially deliberate about circumstances in which we do not exist, so we can have well-being levels there too.

Atemporalists object to the assumption that in order for something to be harmful to someone, it must be harmful to them at a time (Nagel 1979; Feldman 1992; Broome 2012; Johansson 2012; Luper 2012). According to atemporalism, there can be *timeless* harms. Death is one of those. It is harmful because it makes the victim's life go worse overall; but there is no time at which the victim is worse off because of death. John Broome gives the following analogy: suppose some words are cut from the end of a book. To determine how many words are cut from the book, you just compare the total number of words it has with the number it would have had; you don't look at which pages would have had more words on them. Likewise, he says, to determine how bad death is, you don't look at how much worse things are for the victim at particular times; you just look at the difference in total well-being between the actual and counterfactual lives. There is no time at which death harms its victim, just as there is no page that is missing words (Broome 2012: 221–222).

Like all analogies, Broome's is imperfect. One relevant difference between the Meinongian judgment that page 1,789 of Parfit's 1,732-page *On What Matters* would have had more words on it, if only the book were a little bit longer, and the judgment that today would have had more well-being for Joan Rivers than it actually does if only her life had been longer, is that page 1,789 doesn't exist, but today does. So Broome's analogy does not support atemporalism over subsequentism, if it was supposed to do so. However, there are many harms that it is difficult to locate in time (e.g., the harm of never getting what one deserves). The question is whether the harm of death can be *fully* accounted for by appeal to timeless harms.

Posthumous harm

So far we have focused on the question of death's harmfulness; but we may also wonder whether events that occur *after* death can harm someone. Sometimes someone cannot quite complete an important project during her lifetime. We may then be faced with a choice about whether to complete that project for her after she died. Often we think we should do that, for the sake of the deceased. Similarly, we think it is important to honor certain wishes of the dead, as expressed in their wills. These attitudes towards the projects and wishes of the dead might be explained by the thought that we benefit the dead by completing their projects or honoring their wishes, and that we harm them by failing to do so.

The hedonist will deny that posthumous harm or benefit is possible, since events occurring after death cannot cause or prevent any pleasure or pain (unlike death itself, which does not cause any pleasures or pains to the victim but does prevent them). Some other theory of well-being must be employed to make sense of such harms and benefits. For example, a desire-fulfillment view is compatible with posthumous harm and benefit, so long as the desire and its object need not obtain at the same time.

Just as in the case of the harm of death, we might ask *when* a posthumous event is harmful or beneficial to its subject. When is the deceased benefited or harmed? We have the same array of possible answers as in the case of the harm of death, but their plausibility might not be the same. For example, we could say that the deceased is harmed or benefited while dead—but this would require not just attributing a well-being level to the deceased, but a *non-zero* well-being level. It seems hard to believe that a dead person could be well off or badly off *while dead*.

More commonly, defenders of posthumous harm endorse a priorist view, and say that posthumous events can affect the subject's welfare level at times while she was alive (Luper 2012). Again, there is no commitment to backwards causation here. The claim is that by, for example, completing the deceased's important project, one makes it the case that the interest she had in completing the project is fulfilled; this benefits the deceased at the times at which she had that interest. And again, this seems like an implausible view given that the fulfillment of a desire does not seem to benefit us at the time of the desire, but at the time of the fulfillment.

Insofar as we think that common attitudes towards the wishes and projects of the dead can be justified, it seems more promising to look for justifications of those attitudes that do not entail that we can affect the welfare of the dead. For instance, we might think that there is a moral duty to honor promises to the dead even though nobody would be benefited by this. Or we might think the universe is a better place when people have certain attitudes towards the dead even though it is not better for anyone.[7]

Well-being and rational attitudes towards death

People have a variety of attitudes towards death, but they tend to be negative. Fear, dread, and horror are common attitudes. Some claim to be more serene, and not to be bothered by death. Which of these attitudes, if any, is rational?[8]

Epicurus thought it was irrational to fear death. This is because, as noted earlier, he thought that death does not harm the one who dies. We might undermine the thought that one should not fear death by showing that death is bad for its victim. But undermining Epicurus's argument is insufficient to show that death should be feared. Even if Epicurus's argument fails to show that death should not be feared, some other argument might do so.

If death is bad for its victim, there is a straightforward argument for the claim that *some* negative attitude towards death is warranted. We merely need a premise that says that, if something is bad, it is fitting to have a negative attitude towards it. If we accept a "fitting attitude" account of value, this would follow straightaway. According to fitting attitude accounts, to say that something is bad is just to say that it is a fitting object of a negative attitude. But we need not accept a fitting attitude account in order to think that negative attitudes are appropriate to have towards bad things.

Consider, though, the way in which death is bad according to the deprivation account: it deprives the victim of positive well-being. This is bad, and warrants some negative attitude—but which attitude? In particular, think of the existential horror many people have when thinking about death. Could such horror be appropriately directed at a mere deprivation of well-being? There are certain attitudes that could be justified by such a deprivation: disappointment, sadness, and frustration seem fitting. But these are not the same as fear, dread, and horror. In cases of deprivation of well-being that do not involve death—missing out on a concert, for example—it would seem very strange if the individual were horrified or terrified to be deprived of these goods.

If attitudes or emotions such as horror are appropriately directed at death, then the explanation for their rationality must come from something other than the loss of well-being that results from death. Perhaps, as Frances Kamm suggests, there is something especially important and terrifying about things being "all over" for us—the "extinction factor"—over and above the loss of well-being that is entailed (Kamm 1993: 49–54). But why would that be? One thought is that the rationality of being terrified at extinction must be explained by appeal to loss of meaning, where meaningfulness in life is understood to be a kind of value that is distinct from well-being. Perhaps permanent death robs life of its meaningfulness in some way; it takes away the point of ever having been alive. Or perhaps we just think it does, and this causes us to have irrational existential angst about our future demise.

Notes

1 See Nagel (1979), Feldman (1992) and Bradley (2009) for just a few examples of deprivation accounts.
2 Draper offers this as a sufficient, but not necessary, condition for death to be harmful (1999: 393). The deprivation theorist can agree that this is sufficient, since there would be a conflict with the deprivation account only if it were necessary.
3 See Cigman (1981), Williams (1993), Belshaw (2009, 2012) for examples of desire-based views.
4 Broome gives an interesting objection to McMahan's account (2004: 251).
5 Feinberg (1993), Pitcher (1993) and Luper (2012) are three examples of this view; Luper also thinks death harms atemporally.
6 This is a brief version of an argument that appears in Bradley (2009: 108–110). See Johansson (2012: 264–266) and Luper (2012: 320–321) for criticism.
7 For further discussion of posthumous harm, see Taylor (2005) and Portmore (2007).
8 See Draper (2012) and Scheffler (2013) for some recent discussions of this question.

Bibliography

Belshaw, C. (2009) *Annihilation*. Montreal: McGill-Queen's University Press.
Belshaw, C. (2012) "Death, Value, and Desire," in B. Bradley, F. Feldman and J. Johansson (eds.), *The Oxford Handbook of Philosophy of Death*. New York: Oxford University Press, pp. 274–296.
Bradley, B. (2004) "When is Death Bad for the One Who Dies?" *Noûs* 38: 1–28.
Bradley, B. (2008) "The Worst Time to Die." *Ethics* 118: 291–314.
Bradley, B. (2009) *Well-Being and Death*. Oxford: Clarendon Press.
Bradley, B., F. Feldman and J. Johansson (eds.) (2012) *The Oxford Handbook of Philosophy of Death*. New York: Oxford University Press.
Broome, J. (2004) *Weighing Lives*. New York: Oxford University Press.
Broome, J. (2012) "The Badness of Death and the Goodness of Life." In B. Bradley, F. Feldman and J. Johansson (eds.), *Oxford Handbook of Philosophy of Death*. New York: Oxford University Press, pp. 218–233.
Cigman, R. (1981) "Death, Misfortune and Species Inequality." *Philosophy and Public Affairs* 10: 47–64.
DeGrazia, D. (1996) *Taking Animals Seriously: Mental Life and Moral Status*. New York: Cambridge University Press.
Diener, E., D. Wirtz and S. Oishi. (2001) "End Effects of Rated Life Quality: The James Dean Effect." *Psychological Science* 12: 124–128.

Draper, K. (1999) "Disappointment, Sadness, and Death." *The Philosophical Review* 108: 387–414.

Draper, K. (2012) "Death and Rational Emotion." In B. Bradley, F. Feldman and J. Johansson (eds.), *Oxford Handbook of Philosophy of Death*. New York: Oxford University Press, pp. 297–316.

Epicurus. "Letter to Menoeceus." Many versions.

Feinberg, J. (1993) "Harm to Others." In J. Fischer (ed.), *The Metaphysics of Death*. Stanford: Stanford University Press, pp. 171–190.

Feit, N. (2002) "The Time of Death's Misfortune." *Nous* 36: 359–383.

Feldman, F. (1992) *Confrontations with the Reaper: A Philosophical Study of the Nature and Value of Death*. New York: Oxford University Press.

Feldman, F. (2000) "The Termination Thesis." In P. French and H. Wettstein (eds.), *Midwest Studies in Philosophy vol. XXIV*. Malden, MA: Blackwell, pp. 98–115.

Fischer, J. (ed.) (1993) *The Metaphysics of Death*. Stanford: Stanford University Press.

Johansson, J. (2012) "The Timing Problem." In B. Bradley, F. Feldman and J. Johansson (eds.), *Oxford Handbook of Philosophy of Death*. New York: Oxford University Press, pp. 255–273.

Kamm, F. (1993) *Morality, Mortality, Vol. 1: Death and Whom to Save from It*. New York: Oxford University Press.

Luper, S. (2012) "Retroactive Harms and Wrongs." In B. Bradley, F. Feldman and J. Johansson (eds.), *Oxford Handbook of Philosophy of Death*. New York: Oxford University Press, pp. 317–335.

McMahan, J. (2002) *The Ethics of Killing: Problems at the Margins of Life*. New York: Oxford University Press.

Nagel, T. (1979) *Mortal Questions*. New York: Cambridge University Press.

Pitcher, G. (1993) "The Misfortunes of the Dead." In J. Fischer (ed.), *The Metaphysics of Death*. Stanford: Stanford University Press, pp. 159–168.

Portmore, D. (2007) "Desire Fulfillment and Posthumous Harm." *American Philosophical Quarterly* 44: 27–38.

Scheffler, S. (2013) *Death and the Afterlife*. Oxford: Oxford University Press.

Taylor, J. (2005) "The Myth of Posthumous Harm." *American Philosophical Quarterly* 42: 311–332.

Velleman, D. (1993) "Well-being and Time." In J. Fischer (ed.), *The Metaphysics of Death*. Stanford: Stanford University Press, pp. 329–357.

Williams, B. (1993) "The Makropulos Case: Reflections on the Tedium of Immortality." In J. Fischer (ed.), *The Metaphysics of Death*. Stanford: Stanford University Press, pp. 73–92.

PART IV

Theoretical issues

27

MONISM AND PLURALISM

Eden Lin

Monism about well-being is the view that there is exactly one basic (prudential) good and exactly one basic (prudential) bad. *Pluralism* about well-being is the view that there is either more than one basic good or more than one basic bad.[1] We can illustrate this distinction by contrasting hedonism and desire satisfactionism, on the one hand, with objective list theories, on the other. Hedonism and desire satisfactionism disagree about *what* the basic goods and bads are, but they agree about the *number*: they both say that there is a single basic good and a single basic bad. By contrast, objective list theories—or at least the paradigmatic ones—posit either a plurality of basic goods or a plurality of basic bads. Parfit, for example, considers an objective list theory on which "moral goodness, rational activity, . . . and the awareness of true beauty" are all basic goods (Parfit 1984: 499).

In the first section of this chapter, I clarify the distinction between monism and pluralism. In the second, I consider some arguments for monism. In the final section, I consider some arguments for pluralism.

Clarifying the distinction

I will begin with some preliminary distinctions. I will then consider a puzzle that clarifies what is at issue between monists and pluralists.

Our topic is monism and pluralism about *well-being* or *prudential value*, not monism and pluralism about other types of value, such as value *simpliciter* (i.e., value "from the point of view of the universe"). Monism and pluralism about well-being concern the number of things that are good *for us*—or perhaps, more generally, good *for welfare subjects*. By contrast, monism and pluralism about value *simpliciter* concern the number of things that are good, period. Depending on how these two types of value turn out to be connected, it might be coherent to endorse both monism about well-being and pluralism about value *simpliciter*: one might hold, for example, that while only pleasure is basically good for us, many things are basically good from the point of view of the universe. It might also turn out to be coherent to endorse both pluralism about well-being and monism about value *simpliciter*.

Monism and pluralism are views about the number of *basic* goods and bads, not the number of *derivative* goods and bads. Some things are merely derivatively good for us: they are good for us solely because they are appropriately related to other things that are good for us—by being

331

means to them, by being composed of them, or perhaps in some other way. Theories of welfare attempt to identify the things that are basically (i.e., not merely derivatively) good or bad for us—or, as some say, *non-instrumentally* or *intrinsically* good or bad for us. A hedonist would agree that many things besides pleasure are derivatively good for us in virtue of being appropriately related to pleasure, but she would say that only pleasure has basic prudential value. It is about the number of *basic* goods and bads that monists and pluralists disagree.

Although most pluralistic theories of welfare are objective list theories, these two categories should not be conflated. Objective list theories are committed to *objectivism*, the view (roughly speaking) that something can be basically good for you even if you lack favorable attitudes toward it and even if it doesn't consist in your having a favorable attitude toward something. But pluralism doesn't entail objectivism. One can be a pluralist while endorsing *subjectivism*, the view (roughly) that nothing is basically good for you unless you have a favorable attitude toward it, or unless it consists in your having a favorable attitude toward something. One could hold, for example, that there are exactly two basic goods: desire satisfaction and the getting of things that you believe to be good for you. Since desire and evaluative belief are both favorable attitudes, this is a subjectivist view. But since desire satisfaction is a different good from the getting of things that you believe to be good for you, this is a pluralistic view.[2] Notice, too, that objectivism doesn't entail pluralism and that monism doesn't entail subjectivism: perfectionism is a monistic, objectivist view.

Monism and pluralism are not views about how many senses there are of the expressions "good for" and "bad for." Obviously, there is more than one sense of those expressions: "good for" means something different in "pleasure is good for people" than it does in "arsenic is good for poisoning." As this example shows, some senses of "good for" are not about welfare: something can be good for poisoning, but the activity of poisoning is not capable of well-being (Rosati 2009). It has been tentatively suggested that there might be more than one *welfare-involving* sense of "good for" and "bad for." For example, there might be a basic sense of these expressions that applies to all welfare subjects (including many non-human animals) and a different sense that applies only to persons (Rosati 2009: 227–228). But monism and pluralism are not views about how many welfare-involving senses of "good for" and "bad for" there are, either. Rather, the debate between these views arises for *each* welfare-involving sense of those expressions. If there is a single welfare-involving sense of "good for" and "bad for," as most believe (and as I shall assume), then the debate between monism and pluralism is about the number of things that are basically good or bad for us *in that sense*. If there is more than one such sense, then for each sense, the question arises: how many things are basically good or bad for us in that sense?

There is a final issue from which our topic should be distinguished. There are a wide variety of welfare subjects, and perhaps the correct theory of welfare for some of them differs from the correct theory for others. For example, maybe hedonism is true of pigs, while an objective list theory is true of humans. But pluralism is not the view that the correct theory for one kind of subject can differ from the correct theory for another kind, and monism is not the denial of this view. The debate between monism and pluralism arises in the search for each correct theory of welfare—however many of these there are. If hedonism is true of pigs while an objective list theory is true of humans, then monism is true of pigs while pluralism is true of humans. I will henceforth assume, as most do, that the same theory is true of all of *us*—i.e., normal human adults. The arguments that I will consider concern whether the correct theory for normal human adults is monistic or pluralistic.

Having identified our topic, we are now in a position to consider a puzzle.[3] I said earlier that hedonism and desire satisfactionism are monistic theories. But there are different kinds of pleasure: gustatory, olfactory, and so on. Since hedonism says that all pleasures are basically good for us, why doesn't it count as a pluralistic view? Similarly, we desire many different things: happiness, pleasure, friendship, and so on. Why doesn't desire satisfactionism count as a pluralistic theory on the grounds that it says that all of these things are basically good for us when we get them? The puzzle also arises in the opposite direction. I said that paradigmatic objective list theories, such as one on which rational activity and knowledge are basic goods, are pluralistic. But why shouldn't we think of such a theory as a monistic theory on which there is a single *disjunctive* basic good?

Without a solution to this puzzle, it would seem that we are mistaken to think that some theories really are monistic while others really are pluralistic. Rather, it would seem equally acceptable to place any theory in either category, and it would therefore appear unimportant whether monism or pluralism is true. I believe, however, that this puzzle can be solved, and that the solution will clarify what is at issue between the two views.

First, notice that monism and pluralism don't concern how many *token* things are basically good or bad. Any monist would acknowledge that, in a typical person's life, a plurality of token things are basically good for her: a hedonist would claim, for example, that all of a person's many pleasures are basically good. Monism and pluralism concern how many *kinds* are basically good or bad. This was implicit in our initial characterization of these views as concerning the number of basic *goods* and *bads*: for a basic good or bad is a *kind* of thing that is basically good or bad. My proposal is that the most plausible account of what makes something a basically good or bad kind will yield the solution to our puzzle.

What conditions must some kind K satisfy to be a basically good kind? It's not enough that *some* members of K are basically good, since that would imply that each basic good generates a plurality of ever-more inclusive basic goods: the basic goodness of *pleasure* would imply the basic goodness of *experiences, events,* and so on. Nor is it enough that *all* members of K are basically good, since that would imply that each basic good generates a plurality of increasingly narrow basic goods: the basic goodness of *pleasure* would imply the basic goodness of *olfactory pleasure, olfactory pleasure due to a rose,* and so on. Rather, K is a basic good just if all of its members are basically good *because they are Ks.* Why does the hedonist think that pleasure is a basic good even though she denies that status to olfactory pleasure? Because she thinks that all pleasures are basically good *because they are pleasures,* but she denies that all olfactory pleasures are basically good because they are olfactory pleasures (rather than simply because they are pleasures). Similarly, a desire satisfactionist thinks that desire satisfaction is the only basic good because she thinks that there is only one explanation of any particular thing's basic goodness for you: it satisfies, or is the satisfaction of, one of your desires.

This account is only approximately correct, though. For consider what a desire satisfactionist might say about a musician who desires admiration and wealth, and who receives a large sum of money and a standing ovation after a performance. Why is it basically good for him to receive the money? Because it's an instance of wealth, the desire satisfactionist might say. Why is it basically good for him to receive the ovation? Because it's an instance of admiration. But these are *two* different explanations. So it seems that, on my view, desire satisfactionism considers *admiration* and *wealth* to be distinct basic goods, and thus counts as a pluralistic view.

To avoid this counterintuitive result, we must make an adjustment. The two explanations offered above are both *partial* explanations. If the musician didn't desire admiration or wealth, the fact that something is an instance of one of those things wouldn't help explain its basic goodness: a complete explanation of either event's basic goodness must include the fact that the event satisfies one of his desires. Furthermore, those two explanations are both *dispensable,* in that their only role is to show that the event in question satisfies one of the musician's desires. A *complete* explanation of the basic goodness of the ovation wouldn't need to mention that it's an instance of admiration: what matters is just that it's something that the musician desires. The desire satisfactionist could offer the same *complete* explanation in both cases: the event satisfies one of the subject's desires. And she would claim that this is the only complete explanation of *any* event's basic goodness for a welfare subject. We should therefore amend the foregoing account of basic goods as follows: kind *K* is a basic good just if (i) all of its tokens are basically good, and (ii) the complete explanation of any of its tokens' basic goodness is that the token is a *K*. This applies, *mutatis mutandis*, to basic bads.

On this view, each basic good or bad corresponds to a potential complete explanation of why a token thing, event, or state of affairs is basically good or bad. In claiming that pleasure is the only basic good, the hedonist is claiming that there is only *one* complete explanation of any particular thing's basic goodness—namely, that it is a pleasure. By contrast, on an objective list theory that deems rational activity and knowledge to be basic goods, there are (at least) *two* potential complete explanations of a particular thing's basic goodness: either it's an instance of rational activity or it's an instance of knowledge. Thus, monism is the view that there is only one complete explanation of a token's basic goodness and only one complete explanation of a token's basic badness. By contrast, pluralism says that there is either more than one potential complete explanation of a token's basic goodness or more than one potential complete explanation of a token's basic badness. We can recast this in terms of *good-making* and *bad-making* properties: monists claim that there is exactly one good-making property and one bad-making property, whereas pluralists claim that there is either more than one good-making property or more than one bad-making property.[4]

It should now be obvious why hedonism and desire satisfactionism really are monistic views: they agree that there is only one complete explanation of any token's basic goodness (badness) for us. We can also see why paradigmatic objective list theories really are pluralistic. To say that a particular token of knowledge is basically good because it is an instance of a disjunctive kind (e.g., rational activity or knowledge) is not to give a *complete* explanation of its basic goodness. For the question remains: in virtue of *which* disjunct does the token instantiate basic goodness? The objective list theory introduced above would say that the complete explanation of the basic goodness of a token of knowledge is that it is a token of knowledge, and that the complete explanation of the basic goodness of a token of rational activity is that it is a token of rational activity. It would therefore be positing a plurality of complete explanations of the basic goodness of particular events.

Thinking of monism and pluralism in terms of explanation clarifies what is at stake between the two views. If monism is true, then any two basically good tokens are basically good for the same reason, and the same is true, *mutatis mutandis*, of basically bad tokens. If pluralism is true, then this isn't so. Thus, whether monism or pluralism is true matters for the same reason that it matters whether there is a single *wrong-making* property or more than one such property. The debate is about the number of complete explanations required to account for all of the phenomena.

Arguments for monism

Assuming that there is at least one basic good and one basic bad, either monism or pluralism must be true, and any argument for one of them is *ipso facto* an argument against the other. Thus, the arguments that I consider in this section are all arguments against pluralism, and the ones that I consider in the next section are all arguments against monism.

There is one obvious way to argue for monism that is beyond the scope of this chapter. If there were a sound argument for a *particular* monistic theory—say, hedonism—then obviously, that would also be a sound argument for monism. But I will restrict my attention to more general arguments—ones that purport to support monism without supporting any particular monistic theory.

According to the *analysis argument*, monism has an advantage over pluralism because the latter entails that basic goodness must be analyzed disjunctively. If F is the sole basic good, the argument goes, then for something to be basically good is just for it to be an F. But if F and G are the only two basic goods, then for something to be basically good is just for it to be either an F or a G.[5] Insofar as it is implausible that basic goodness is to be analyzed disjunctively, pluralism is implausible.

Against this argument, it might be replied that the question "What are the basic goods?" must be distinguished from the question "What is it for something to be basically good?" and that an answer to the former doesn't imply an answer to the latter. After all, Moore famously claimed that goodness is unanalyzable, but he nonetheless named many goods (Moore 1988). Suppose that what it is for something to be good for you is just for it to be such that one should want it for your sake (Darwall 2002: 7). Perhaps there is more than one potential complete explanation of any particular thing's instantiating this *analysans*: maybe we should want some things for your sake because they are your pleasures, while we should want other things for your sake because you desire them. If such a view is coherent, then pluralism is compatible with a non-disjunctive analysis of basic goodness.

The *arbitrariness argument* says that whatever list of basic goods a pluralistic theory provides, it will seem arbitrary that those things, and no others, are the basic goods. As Bradley puts it:

> [P]luralism seems objectionably arbitrary. Whatever the composition of the list, we can always ask: why should these things be on the list? What do they have in common? What is the rational principle that yields the result that these things, and no others, are the things that are good?
>
> *(Bradley 2009: 16)*

Indeed, given the understanding of pluralism that I have argued for, it seems guaranteed that the pluralist can provide no answers to these questions. For if a pluralist claimed that the reason F and G (but no other kinds) are basic goods is that all and only Fs and Gs are members of some other kind H, he would thereby be committing himself to the monistic view that H is the sole basic good: for he would be claiming that the only complete explanation of any particular thing's basic goodness is that it is a member of H. Thus, pluralism appears unavoidably committed to there being no further explanation of why the kinds that are basic goods (and no others) are basic goods.

It might be replied that the charge of arbitrariness is no more of a problem for pluralism than it is for monism. If the monist lists F as the sole basic good, we can ask: What rational principle yields the result that, among all the kinds there are, *this* kind, and no others, is basically good? Indeed, one might argue, the understanding of monism that I have proposed guarantees that if F is the sole basic good, there is no further explanation of why this is so. For if F were the sole basic good because all and only Fs are Gs, then G, not F, would be the sole basic good. Explanations must run out on a monistic view for the same reason that they must run out on a pluralistic one.

The advocate of the arbitrariness argument might reply that a monist who claims that F is the sole basic good *does* have a way of explaining why this is so: she could claim that for something to be basically good for you *just is* for it to be an F.[6] A hedonist, for instance, could claim that the fact that pleasure is the sole basic good is explained by the fact that for something to be basically good for you *just is* for it to be one of your pleasures. By contrast, a pluralist couldn't make the same move without endorsing a disjunctive analysis of basic goodness, which (as we saw earlier) would be implausible. Thus, monistic theories are at least *potentially* less arbitrary than pluralistic ones.

A pluralist might reply that *F*'s being the sole basic good is *incompatible* with the claim that for something to be basically good just is for it to be an *F*. If analyzing one property in terms of another involves *identifying* the former property with the latter, as many philosophers assume, the claim that basic goodness is analyzable in terms of *F*-ness appears to imply that nothing is basically good *because* it is an *F*. After all, since nothing can explain itself, nothing is an *F* because it is an *F*. Thus, if basic goodness is *identical* with *F*-ness, it would seem that nothing is basically good *because* it is an *F*. But if nothing is basically good *because* it is an *F*, then *F* is not a basic good: for a basic good is a kind all of whose members are basically good *because* they belong to that kind. Thus, a pluralist could argue that it can't be claimed both that *F* is a basic good and that being basically good just is being an *F*. If this is right, then a monist can't claim an advantage on the issue of arbitrariness by analyzing basic goodness in terms of the sole basic good that she identifies. Whether this reply on behalf of the pluralist succeeds turns on subtle questions about analysis, however. The monist might reject the assumption that analyses imply property identities, or she might attempt to show that the alleged incompatibility needn't arise (see, e.g., Rosen 2010).

Even if the pluralist's responses to the arbitrariness argument succeed, it might seem that the argument has not fully been answered. Contrast hedonism with a pluralistic theory on which there are, say, exactly 17 basic goods. Even if it is granted that the hedonist cannot explain why pleasure is the only basic good, the pluralistic theory still seems more arbitrary. Perhaps what's doing the work here is just monism's greater *simplicity*, which surely counts in its favor to *some* extent. Pluralists, of course, would claim that the greater simplicity of monistic views is outweighed by the virtues of the correct pluralistic theory.

A third argument for monism starts with the observation that we make judgments not only about *how* well off people are, but about whether or not they are well off. When we judge that someone is well off, we are not merely judging that her level of welfare is above zero: we are judging that it is *high enough* for her to count as well off. Now, certain things appear *indispensable* to your being well off, in the sense that unless you have enough of them, you are not well off—no matter what else you have. Happiness appears to be such a thing: if you are below a certain minimal level of happiness, it seems that you cannot be well off, no matter what else you have. It might be argued that a pluralistic theory on which there is more than one basic good cannot accommodate the indispensability of happiness, even if it grants that happiness is *one* of the basic goods. For if there is at least one basic good distinct from happiness, as any such theory must maintain, it would appear to be possible for you to be well off in virtue of having a sufficient quantity of this other basic good. If happiness and achievement are both basic goods, for example, then it seems that you could be well off even if you were completely unhappy, as long as you had enough achievements. But this implies, contrary to our initial assumption, that happiness is *not* indispensable to your being well off. Thus, pluralistic views appear to have the implausible implication that no basic good is indispensable to your being well off. Call this the *indispensability argument*.

Fred Feldman gives a version of this argument when he writes that a pluralistic theory that counts knowledge and virtue as basic goods would be implausible because "a man might have lots of knowledge and virtue and yet have a life that is not good in itself for him." His thought is that pleasure is indispensable to your being well off, and that no pluralistic theory that includes basic goods besides pleasure can accommodate this (Feldman 2004: 19–20). Shelly Kagan also states a version of this argument when he writes that proponents of objective list theories "seem forced to accept the unappealing claim that I could be extremely well off, provided that I have the right objective goods in my life, even though these things hold no appeal for me, and I am, in fact, utterly miserable" (Kagan 2009: 254). The thought is that objective list theories are implausible because pleasure (or at least not being miserable) is indispensable to your being extremely well off. Kagan uses this objection to motivate the monistic view that the sole basic good is pleasure taken in objective goods: one virtue of this view, he argues, is that it evades this objection (Kagan 2009: 255).

The indispensability argument assumes that the *basic prudential value* of a token of a basic good—i.e., *how* basically good that token is—does not depend on how much of another basic good the subject has. A pluralist could reject this assumption. She could claim that if happiness is indispensable, then if you are below the minimal level of happiness that is required for being well off, each additional token of achievement increases your welfare, but in a way that approaches a limit that is lower than the level of welfare necessary for you to count as well off. In this way, she could maintain both that achievement is a basic good and that happiness is indispensable to your being well off.

A monist might grant the logical possibility of this picture but argue that it is baroque and *ad hoc*. Why would the basic prudential values of the tokens of one basic good depend on how much of another basic good the subject has acquired? Why think that someone could amass an arbitrarily large quantity of a basic good without reaching the level of welfare necessary to count as well off? But pluralists could reply that on the assumption that at least one good is indispensable, any reasons to accept pluralism are also reasons to accept these claims.

A final argument for monism requires some terminological preliminaries. Call a token of a basic good or bad a *welfare atom*. To *ordinally compare* two atoms, X and Y, with respect to basic prudential value is to claim that they stand in some particular basic, two-place comparative relation with respect to their basic prudential values—as when one claims that X is greater in value than Y, or equal in value to it. To *cardinally compare* them with respect to basic prudential value is to measure their basic prudential values on a single cardinal scale—as when one claims that X is m units greater in value than Y, or n times as valuable as Y. The *comparison argument* says that, unlike monistic views, pluralistic views have trouble comparing welfare atoms. Here is Bradley again:

> [P]luralists must tell us, for example, how to compare the effect on well-being of a certain amount of pleasure with the effect of a certain amount of knowledge. This problem has so far proved intractable . . . [I]n the absence of a weighing principle, we do not have a theory with any testable implications at all.
>
> *(Bradley 2009: 16–17)*

The problem isn't that the formal apparatus of pluralism rules out comparisons. After all, nothing prevents a pluralist from stating a weighing principle that cardinally (and thus ordinally) compares all welfare atoms. The thought is that, unlike monistic theories, pluralistic theories imply that we often cannot compare atoms *without going beyond what the intuitive evidence warrants*. If there is only one basic good and only one basic bad, then there is always an intuitively correct verdict about how two atoms compare, and we can build a theory that always delivers this verdict. But if pluralism is true, while there are some comparisons with intuitively correct verdicts (e.g., a faint and fleeting pleasure is less good than knowledge of all of mathematics), there are many pairs of atoms about which there is no intuitively correct verdict about how they compare (e.g., a moderately intense pleasure and a particular piece of geographical knowledge). The pluralist faces a dilemma. If she states a weighing principle that delivers a verdict about the comparative values of every pair of atoms, many of these verdicts will seem arbitrary. But if she doesn't, her theory will have a lot of gaps: she will often be unable to tell us exactly how well off a subject is, or whether the subject would be better or worse off if she had different welfare atoms (e.g., if she had a certain amount of knowledge instead of a certain pleasure).

The monist could go even further: she could argue that if there were two basic goods, many pairs of atoms would be *incommensurable* and *incomparable:* not only would any cardinal or ordinal comparison of them appear intuitively unwarranted, but any such comparison would be *untrue*.[7] If this is right, then the first horn of the pluralist's dilemma is even worse: a weighing principle that compared every pair of atoms would deliver verdicts that are not just arbitrary, but untrue.

The pluralist could reply that even paradigmatic monistic theories cannot compare every pair of atoms without going beyond the intuitive evidence. Consider two pleasures, the second one of which is slightly more intense, but slightly shorter. Does intuition always deliver a verdict about how the two pleasures compare ordinally? Surely not. Thus, any version of hedonism that ordinally ranks the two pleasures will make claims that seem arbitrary. *A fortiori*, so will any version of it that compares all pleasures cardinally (e.g., one on which the basic prudential value of a pleasure is just the product of its intensity and duration). The lesson here, the pluralist might say, is that *inter*-type comparisons are not more problematic in principle than *intra*-type comparisons. In both cases, because the values of the atoms are determined by more than one factor (e.g., intensity and duration, in the case of pleasures), there is no natural way to generate a linear ordering of the atoms from the values of these factors.[8] Indeed, since the monist identifies both a basic good and a basic bad, even she must make *inter*-type comparisons. The task of comparing a token of the sole basic good to a token of the sole basic bad could, in principle, be as challenging as that of comparing tokens of two basic goods: even assuming that pleasures and pains can be measured on the same scale of intensity, it is unclear how the value of a pleasure compares to the disvalue of a pain of equal intensity and duration. Thus, the monist faces the same dilemma as the pluralist.

Pluralists could add that if pluralistic views suggest that some pairs of atoms are incomparable, then so do monistic ones. For the monist's evidence that two heterogeneous atoms (e.g., a particular pleasure and a particular token of knowledge) are incomparable is that there is no intuitively correct verdict about how they compare. The same evidence can be found when we consider certain pairs of homogeneous atoms (e.g., certain pairs of pleasures).

The monist might reply that, if pluralism is true, there are *more* cases in which there is no intuitively correct verdict about how two atoms compare, or in which two atoms are incomparable. Thus, even if the monist and the pluralist face the same dilemma, the dilemma is worse for the pluralist. But if the difference between monism and pluralism on this issue is merely one of degree, perhaps pluralism's disadvantages on this issue are outweighed by its advantages elsewhere.

Arguments for pluralism

A sound argument that two kinds, F and G, are both basic goods or both basic bads would also be a sound argument for pluralism. But as before, I will restrict my attention to general arguments.

Pluralists could give a *comparison argument* for their view, just as monists could. They could claim that the alleged disadvantages of pluralism when it comes to comparing welfare atoms are actually advantages. We often have to choose between two options whose prudential value for us we are at a loss to compare. For example, we might have to decide between a career in business and a career in philosophy, and we might have no idea how to compare the effect that these two careers would have on our well-being. The best explanation of this phenomenon, it might be argued, is that there are many pairs of welfare atoms for which there is no intuitively correct verdict about how their values compare—a claim to which pluralism is committed.

It is unclear how forceful this argument can be, given the pluralists' reply to the *monists'* comparison argument. For, according to that reply, monists are also committed to the existence of many pairs of atoms for which there is no intuitively correct verdict about how they compare. If so, then even if we assume that hard choices of the sort just described are best explained by the existence of such pairs of atoms, the monist could avail herself of this explanation too. Furthermore, it is unclear that this *is* the best explanation of the phenomenon. Even assuming that hedonism is true and that all pleasures and pains are commensurable, we would often be at a loss to compare the prudential values of two options available to us simply because we wouldn't know exactly how much pleasure or pain each option would produce.

The *rational regret argument* begins with the observation that it is often rational to regret having forgone a lesser good in favor of a greater good. Suppose that you must choose between going to a movie and going to a party, and suppose that you know that you would be higher in welfare if you went to the movie. If you go to the movie, it nonetheless seems rational for you to feel some regret about not having gone to the party. For it seems that, although the movie was better for you, there is *something* good about the party that you missed out on—something the loss of which isn't fully *compensated* for by the movie. It might be argued that only a pluralistic theory of welfare can explain this. If pluralism is true, then it could be that there is some basic good that you would have gotten if you had gone to the party that you didn't get from the movie (e.g., social interaction), and this could explain why the movie didn't fully make up for what you lost by forgoing the party. By contrast, if monism is true, then given that each option is good for you in virtue of instantiating the same basic good, it seems that there is nothing you would have gotten from the party that you didn't get in greater quantities from the movie. Monism appears to imply that, since your choice was between a smaller and a greater quantity of the very same good, it makes no sense for you to regret not having gone to the party—just as it would make no sense for you to regret not having picked the smaller of two amounts of money (see Stocker 1990: 271–272).

It is unclear that monists can't explain the rationality of regret in situations like these, however. Suppose that pleasure is the only basic good, and that the reason you would be better off going to the movie is just that you would get more pleasure doing this. The pleasures you would get from the movie are qualitatively very different from those you would get from the party. The monist could argue that there *is* something that you would be forgoing if you went to the movie—namely, the felt quality of the pleasure of convivial conversation—and that this makes it rational for you to feel some regret about not having gone to the party. A pluralist might object that, on this proposal, there are *two* basic goods: the pleasure of convivial conversation and that of watching a movie. But the monist could deny this by insisting that pleasures belonging to these two heterogeneous kinds are nonetheless all basically good for the same reason—namely, that they are pleasures (Hurka 1996).

Another argument for pluralism claims that, no matter what the monist identifies as the sole basic good and bad, we must postulate an additional basic good—namely, having a certain *temporal distribution* of the tokens of that good and bad. For it seems that, whatever that basic good and bad are, your lifetime well-being is fixed not merely by how many tokens of them your life contains and how basically good or bad they are, but also by how they are arranged temporally: it's better, for instance, to have an *uphill life*—one that goes from worse to better—than a *downhill life* (Velleman 1991). This suggests that, whatever the monist's theory of welfare is, it must be supplemented by at least one additional, higher-order basic good (e.g., accruing more basic goodness, and less basic badness, as one's life progresses), and perhaps also by at least one additional, higher-order basic bad. Call this the *shape of a life argument*.

One response would be to deny that the shape of a life necessarily has any effect on its total welfare. A hedonist could argue that your life's having a certain shape makes you better off just if you take pleasure in the fact that it has that shape (Feldman 2004: 131–134). A desire satisfactionist could argue that your life's having a certain shape makes you better off just if you want it to have that shape. On these proposals, your life's having a certain shape is no different from its having any other feature: it benefits you only if it occasions a token of the basic good already postulated by the monistic theory. Alternatively, monists could grant that the shape of a life must have an effect on its total welfare, but deny that this implies the existence of an additional basic good. Perhaps the basic prudential values of your welfare atoms are determined in part by how they are temporally arranged. If so, we can accommodate the claim that lives with certain shapes are necessarily better (other things equal) than lives with other shapes without enlarging our list of basic goods and bads.

The final kind of argument for pluralism that I will consider is more piecemeal: it says that only a pluralistic theory can accommodate all of our intuitions about welfare. One such argument focuses on the *times* at which things can be basically good for you. It seems clear that whenever someone feels a pleasure, he accrues some basic goodness. It also seems that something can be basically good for you even at a time when you are not feeling pleasure. Hedonism can't accommodate both of these intuitions because it can't accommodate the latter: for if pleasures are basically good, they are basically good only when they are felt. Less obviously, desire satisfactionism can't accommodate both intuitions because it can't accommodate the former: even if pleasure is necessarily connected to desire, there is no guarantee that some desire of yours is *satisfied* whenever you feel a pleasure. It might be argued that pluralism is true because only a pluralistic theory can accommodate both of these intuitions (Lin 2014).

But arguments like these are only as convincing as the intuitions that they appeal to. Perhaps it's merely *usually* true that someone accrues basic goodness when he feels a pleasure. Perhaps it's impossible for a pleasureless life to be positive in welfare (Crisp 2006: 122–123), in which case it may also be impossible for anything to be basically good for you during a pleasureless interval. If the monist can undermine the intuitions that the pluralist appeals to, she can undermine his argument.[9]

Further reading

For discussions of monism and pluralism that are not restricted to well-being, see Heathwood (2015), Tucker (unpublished), and R. Chang, "Value Pluralism," in N.J. Smelser and P.B. Baltes (eds.), *The International Encyclopedia of the Social and Behavioral Sciences,* vol. 24 (Oxford: Pergamon, 2012). For a discussion that bears on the shape of a life argument, see D. Dorsey, "The Significance of a Life's Shape," *Ethics* 125: 303–330.

Notes

1 One could instead distinguish monism and pluralism about the *basic goods* from monism and pluralism about the *basic bads*, and say that a theory on which there are a plurality of basic goods but only one basic bad is pluralistic with respect to the basic goods but monistic with respect to the basic bads. In this chapter, I will stick with the coarse-grained definitions that I give above.
2 In Lin (forthcoming), I present a different pluralistic, subjectivist view.
3 Here, I elaborate on a much briefer discussion from Lin (forthcoming).
4 For similar accounts of the monism/pluralism distinction, see Heathwood (2015), Hurka (1996), Lin (2014, forthcoming), and Tucker (unpublished).

5 Richard Arneson appears to assume this when he writes that "the objective-list theory is not merely the provision of a list of putative goods" but is also the view that "what it is to be intrinsically valuable for a person ... is to be an item that belongs on such a list" (Arneson 1999: 119).

6 This does not contravene the earlier claim that the view that *F* is the sole basic good doesn't *entail* an analysis of basic goodness in terms of *F*. Such an analysis can be *compatible* with that view without being entailed by it.

7 For more on incommensurability and incomparability, see Chang (1997; 2015).

8 For a related discussion, see Chang (1997: 16–17).

9 I thank Ruth Chang and Guy Fletcher for their comments on this chapter.

References

Arneson, R. (1999) "Human Flourishing versus Desire Satisfaction," *Social Philosophy & Policy* 16: 113–142.

Bradley, B. (2009) *Well-Being and Death,* Oxford: Clarendon Press.

Chang, R. (1997) "Introduction" in R. Chang (ed.), *Incommensurability, Incomparability, and Practical Reason,* Cambridge, MA: Harvard University Press.

Chang, R. (2015) "Value Incomparability and Incommensurability," in I. Hirose and J. Olson (eds.), *The Oxford Handbook of Value Theory,* New York: Oxford University Press.

Crisp, R. (2006) *Reasons and the Good,* Oxford: Clarendon Press.

Darwall, S. (2002) *Welfare and Rational Care,* Princeton: Princeton University Press.

Feldman, F. (2004) *Pleasure and the Good Life,* Oxford: Clarendon Press.

Heathwood, C. (2015) "Monism and Pluralism about Value," in I. Hirose and J. Olson (eds.), *The Oxford Handbook of Value Theory,* New York: Oxford University Press.

Hurka, T. (1996) "Monism, Pluralism, and Rational Regret," *Ethics* 106: 555–575.

Kagan, S. (2009) "Well-Being as Enjoying the Good," *Philosophical Perspectives* 23: 253–272.

Lin, E. (2014) "Pluralism about Well-Being," *Philosophical Perspectives* 28: 127–154.

Lin, E. (2015) "The Subjective List Theory of Well-Being," *The Australasian Journal of Philosophy* DOI: 10.1080/00048402.2015.1014926.

Moore, G.E. (1988) *Principia Ethica,* Amherst, NY: Prometheus Books.

Parfit, D. (1984). *Reasons and Persons,* Oxford: OUP.

Rosati, C. (2009) "Relational Good and the Multiplicity Problem," *Philosophical Issues* 19: 205–234.

Rosen, G. (2010) "Metaphysical Dependence: Grounding and Reduction," in B. Hale and A. Hoffmann (eds.), *Modality: Metaphysics, Logic, and Epistemology,* Oxford: Oxford University Press.

Stocker, M. (1990) *Plural and Conflicting Values,* Oxford: Clarendon Press.

Tucker, M. (unpublished) "Two Kinds of Value Pluralism."

Velleman, J.D. (1991) "Well-Being and Time," *Pacific Philosophical Quarterly* 72: 48–77.

28

ATOMISM AND HOLISM IN THE THEORY OF PERSONAL WELL-BEING

Jason Raibley

Introduction

Atomism in a particular domain claims that some phenomenon can be wholly understood in terms of its proper parts and the intrinsic properties of these parts. Holism denies this. Instead, holism claims that the thing in question must be understood also in terms of the relations among these parts, or in terms of irreducible properties of the whole.

Prominent ethical theorists including Franz Brentano, the British Hegelians, G.E. Moore, A.C. Ewing, Roderick Chisholm, and Robert Nozick have held that there are important evaluative phenomena that cannot be understood exclusively in terms of the intrinsic properties of their most basic parts. Most famously, Moore formulated the doctrine of organic unities, according to which the intrinsic value of a whole *"bears no regular proportion to the sum of the values of its parts"* (Moore 1993/1903: 79; emphasis in original). Chisholm also sought to defend a view according to which several good parts might combine to form a whole the goodness of which was enhanced (i.e., greater than the goodness of the parts taken individually), partially or wholly defeated (i.e., less than the goodness of the parts taken individually, so that the whole might even be of neutral value), or even transvalued (i.e., made bad on the whole) (Chisholm 1986).

The theorists just mentioned were concerned mainly with worldly intrinsic value, the sort of value that a benevolent God would consider when deciding which possible world to actualize. But the atomism/holism distinction also arises in the context of well-being and prudential value. This is the sort of value that is connected to personal benefit and harm: when a person is benefitted, her well-being is increased; when a person is harmed, her well-being is diminished. Most theories of well-being aim to explain what determines a person's level of well-being at a particular time, what determines a person's level of well-being over intervals of time, and what determines the prudential value of a person's life, i.e., what makes a life go well (or badly) for the person who lives it.

It may not be possible to provide necessary and sufficient conditions for whether a theory is atomistic or holistic. Still, the distinction is a useful one, and it can be generally said that atomistic theories of well-being endorse several related theses about the metaphysics of prudential value and its aggregation. Specifically, atomistic theories endorse (a) *the explanatory priority of momentary well-being*, (b) *momentary well-being internalism*, and (c) *neutrality about the order of episodes when aggregating well-being over time*. Theories are holistic in one respect or another if—and to the extent that—they depart from these theses.

The first of these, (a) *the explanatory priority of momentary well-being,* states that instantaneous, momentary, or synchronic well-being is a more fundamental or basic evaluation than well-being over longer intervals of time, up to and including a whole life. Momentary well-being, on this view, does not derive from diachronic or global features of lives.

The second thesis, (b) *momentary well-being internalism,* holds that well-being at individual times depends exclusively on the intrinsic properties of those times. Or a bit more liberally, an agent's well-being at a time, *t,* is not affected by anything that occurs at any time other than *t.* This thesis appears to follow from a plausible supervenience principle about non-instrumental prudential value. This principle states that, if a condition, situation, outcome, event, or time is non-instrumentally valuable for a person, then its value supervenes entirely on its intrinsic properties.

Momentary well-being internalism has two important corollaries, the first axiological and the second metaphysical. First, the fundamental bearers of prudential value—i.e., the things that are most fundamentally good or bad for one—will be instantaneous or momentary occurrences that are desirable simply for their own sakes, in isolation from other goods.[1] Second, because the value of these fundamentals depends exclusively on features internal to them, they will have their respective values necessarily: if a state of an individual has prudential value *n,* then it's necessary that the prudential value of that state is *n.* This means that atomism involves a commitment to *invariabilism,* the thesis that the fundamental bearers of prudential value make the same contribution to the value of a life at a time, regardless of the context or the combinations in which they occur (cf. Fletcher 2009).

Finally, thesis (c), *neutrality about the order of episodes when aggregating well-being over time,* states that an agent's well-being over intervals of time—up to and including the agent's life—is a simple function from his or her well-being at the smallest well-being-evaluable intervals, whether these turn out to be times, moments, or episodes of longer duration. This function might be summative or averaging, but it pays no attention to the temporal or narrative order of the smallest intervals.

Holists deny some important part of this picture. Some holists deny (a). It might be that *neither* momentary well-being nor well-being-over-time has explanatory priority. One radical possibility is that there is no relation between these phenomena, so that a person could be faring well at each moment of his or her life, but badly overall. Another possibility is that the prudential value of a life has explanatory priority, so that well-being at a time derives from life-time value. A more popular view is that there are temporally extended conditions, situations, or events that are just as important as momentary occurrences when it comes to understanding well-being at a time or well-being over time.

Many holists who deny (a) are also led to deny (b) on the grounds that the values of the fundamental bearers depend also on their extrinsic features. But if, e.g., relational properties make a difference to the values of the fundamentals, various questions arise.

First, there is a question about *how* they make a difference. As Ewing noted, it may be because of "the parts producing an additional value or disvalue in the whole when combined in certain ways while remaining the same in value themselves," or it may be because of "the value of the parts being itself modified by their relation to each other" (1973: 215). In the former case, the inventory of fundamental bearers of prudential value must presumably be expanded to include certain non-instantaneous and relational phenomena. This results in a comparatively weak form of holism: it amounts to saying that there are some fundamental bearers of prudential value that are not momentary phenomena. (A variety of views might be held about how these bearers affect the value of individual times or moments.) But in the latter case, relations among the smallest evaluable episodes *transform* the values of these very episodes. This suggests that the *fundamental* bearers of prudential value are really larger, more complex situations, i.e., that the episodes whose values were transformed were not really fundamental bearers to begin with. Either approach requires that both (a) and (b) be false, though (c) may be trivially true in the latter case.

Another question, of course, is *which* relational phenomena are relevant in this context. Various suggestions have been made here. (Some are discussed in greater detail in the section on holism, below.)

It might be important that the fundamentals occur in certain balanced combinations. This *balancing* view is as old as Plato's *Philebus,* where Socrates suggests that neither a life dedicated exclusively to pleasure, nor a life dedicated exclusively to wisdom, would be ideal. The best life, he holds, would combine both these goods in a particular way (63c–65a). And so episodes of pleasure or knowledge may make a different contribution to synchronic well-being, depending on whether they operate in isolation from other such episodes, or in combination with them (cf. also Hurka 1993).

Another potentially relevant phenomenon is *temporal order,* especially improvement or diminution. Brentano famously held that an "uphill life" is better than a "downhill life" in virtue of the fact that it improves (1973/1897: 196–197). Michael Slote states that "a good may itself be greater for coming late rather than early in life" (1983: 25). On Slote's view, later as opposed to earlier goods have enhanced value. More recently, Joshua Glasgow has affirmed that it is "bad to be worse off than you used to be . . . [W]hen I go from a high level of momentary well-being to a low level of momentary well-being, that *itself* is bad for me" (Glasgow 2013: 668). F.M. Kamm holds a similar view, according to which the *loss* of well-being is non-instrumentally bad (Kamm 2003).

Various other temporal relations might partially determine the values of times or lives. John Broome mentions *evenness*: perhaps it is best for a life "to pass at an even level of well-being, rather than [to] oscillate up and down" (2004: 220). Another possibility, suggested by certain passages from Nietzsche, is the value of having *a high peak.* "At the extreme," Broome writes, "one might think the peak is the only thing that counts; the only point of life is to live very well once" (228). Yet another value that might be missed by momentary analysis is *longevity.* John Harris (1985), for example, argues that lives are marred by not reaching a certain minimum length.

Another popular family of views can be grouped together under the moniker of "*narrativism.*" These views hold that narratable relations among the events of one's life make a difference to its value. Theorists are split on which narrative relations matter and how.

A moderate view held by Dorsey (2015) is that narrative relations that tie the events of one's life into global projects, goals, and achievements help to constitute new, additional fundamental bearers of value: "some contributors to the intrinsic value of a life . . . cannot be locked down to an individual moment, but necessarily involve many moments throughout a life and the relationship between them" (§4). Narrative relations therefore have signatory value—they are signs that one's actions fit into valuable patterns. But it is the achievement of aims or the realization of valued projects that is, strictly speaking, non-instrumentally good for one. Dorsey therefore accommodates narrativist intuitions by adjusting his axiology. But he agrees with atomists about (c), above: the temporal location of good and bad times does not affect their value, and well-being over time can still be aggregatively calculated (§6).

Douglas Portmore endorses a similar view: when an achievement is made possible by past acts of self-sacrifice, the harmfulness of these sacrifices is mitigated—though it cannot be cancelled or erased, because then the acts would no longer be self-sacrificial (to be self-sacrificial, they must lead to lower overall lifetime well-being than available alternatives). Portmore also considers the more radical view that such episodes might affect well-being over time without affecting momentary well-being (Portmore 2007: 26–27).

Antti Kauppinen (2012, 2015) endorses a more robust form of narrativism: he states that there are some narrative relations that might obtain among the events of an agent's life which are themselves fundamental bearers of value. For example, if individual accomplishments add up to success in broader worthwhile projects—or constitute success in a series of coherent and mutually reinforcing projects—this makes a life more meaningful, and meaningfulness is non-instrumentally good (cf. McMahon 2002: 175–185). By contrast, Rosati (2013) holds that it is not the objective existence of narrative relations, but the form of the agent's narrative self-understanding that confers additional value or disvalue on moments and/or longer temporal intervals.

Most of the views just discussed require denying both (b) and (c). However, some theorists *accept* (b) while denying (c). For David Velleman, it is *not* that the narrative relations among one's life events affect the value of those events as they occur. Rather, narrative relations affect the meaning and the value of one's life while leaving the values of moments unchanged. Velleman writes: "[T]he reason why well-being isn't additive is that how a person is faring at a particular moment is a temporally local matter, whereas the welfare-value of a period in his life depends on the global features of that period" (2000: 58). On his view, "an event's place in the story of one's life lends it a meaning that isn't entirely determined by its impact on one's well-being at the time" (63), but "a person's well-being at each moment is defined from the perspective of that moment" (74). For Velleman, well-being over time depends on diachronic features of one's life, but well-being at a time depends only on synchronic features of the person's life.

The remainder of this chapter will investigate various forms of atomism and holism in greater detail by explaining and evaluating some of the main arguments for and against them.

Atomism

Many atomists draw inspiration from G.E. Moore's metaphysics of intrinsic value, perhaps approaching the theory of well-being with the idea that instances of positive human welfare will also be bearers of worldly intrinsic value, and so will need the features appropriate to this role. Moore held that a thing's worldly intrinsic value supervenes exclusively on its intrinsic properties. And if a thing has its intrinsic properties of necessity, then any intrinsic value it has is also had of necessity. Perhaps the thing must also be such that it would continue to have its value, even if it were alone in the universe (though see Lemos 1994 and Zimmerman 2005 for critical discussion of this idea).

Atomists about well-being have sought to defend some analogous claims about non-instrumental prudential value. They begin with the thought that we should look to see whether there are momentary episodes or states that appear to be non-instrumentally good for people, good in virtue of their intrinsic properties, and good irrespective of context. Atomism about well-being can then be thought of as the faith that we can find such episodes and build up from them in a straightforward way to explain all the facts about well-being that there are.

Atomism's best-known defenders, Fred Feldman and Ben Bradley, are *hedonists*: they believe that all and only episodes of pleasure are non-instrumentally good for people. Bradley is explicit that pleasures are non-instrumentally good for people in virtue of their intrinsic properties (2009). They have their intrinsic properties necessarily, and so they are necessarily non-instrumentally prudentially good. Other axiologies are also combinable with atomism. Among monistic theories, non-hedonistic happiness-centered theories fit nicely with atomism. Weaker versions of atomism can be endorsed by desire-satisfactionists and life-satisfactionists. It is even possible to be a pluralistic atomist and hold, for example, that both episodes of pleasure and episodes of knowledge are directly good for one in this way—although goods like knowledge may require weakening (b) moment internalism.

No matter the particular axiology, atomists insist that diachronic or patterned features of lives are not relevant to their value. It might seem that the uphill life is better than a downhill life, even if both lives are equal with respect to pleasure or desire-satisfaction. But this seeming may simply indicate that there are relevant value-laden aspects of the situation that have been overlooked, where these aspects can be recognized from within the confines of atomism. Alternatively, the seeming may be based on a confusion of aesthetic evaluation with prudential evaluation (cf. Feldman 2004: 124–141; Zimmerman 2005).

An atomistic theory of well-being must do several things. It must explain which states are fundamentally and non-derivatively good for people—i.e., it must specify the "atoms" of well-being. It must also say what determines *how* good or bad these states are. Additionally, it must explain how to determine the values of other things, such as times, periods of time, and whole lives (cf. Bradley 2009: 5).

As Feldman notes, previous formulations of atomism have run into serious problems in trying to accomplish these tasks (Feldman 2000: 319–325). Some versions of hedonism, for example, have stated that (a) *only* episodes of pleasure or happiness are non-instrumentally good for a person, while (b) longer temporal intervals (up to and including whole lives) are *also* non-instrumentally good for a person. This appears to be a contradiction. Some versions have also run into problems of "double-counting" when explaining how to estimate the values of life segments, because they imply that the same life segment might contain multiple, overlapping situations or events that are welfare-evaluable.

Feldman outlines a form of atomism that avoids such problems. *Basic intrinsic value states* (or "basics," for short) are central to his approach. Basics will be states whose values do not depend on the values of their parts. They are pure attributions of whichever properties or relations turn out to be of non-instrumentally valuable for a person. They attribute determinate and precise degrees of non-instrumentally valuable properties to subjects at precise instants—e.g., "Jones being happy to degree +12 at noon, March 25, 2000." They attribute valuable properties to subjects through directly referring tags, and not via descriptions or properties. They contain no superfluous information.

An axiology stated in terms of such basics could be adopted by both monists and pluralists about the ultimate sources of well-being. Monists will say that the basics all involve attribution of the same property (or perhaps the same pair of properties, if there are both positive and negative basics). Pluralists will hold that some good basics are pure attributions of one property, while other good basics are pure attributions of others (e.g., "*S* has an insight at *t* that $3 + 3 = 6$," "*T* is pleased that *S* is happy to degree +12 at *t*").[2]

Feldman, of course, is a monist. He suggests that the property that features in attributions of fundamental goodness is *being happy*, where happiness is ultimately analyzed in terms of attitudinal pleasure (Feldman 2000, 2010). The property that features in attributions of fundamental badness is *being unhappy*, analyzed in terms of attitudinal pain. The value of happiness and the disvalue of unhappiness are perfectly commensurable. Happiness and unhappiness both come in intensities; these intensities can be measured on ratio scales. Both are nearly instantaneous occurrences. Feldman assumes that time can be "discretized," or broken up into a sequence of intervals of very tiny duration, such that no two of these intervals overlap, and no period of time falls outside this collection (Feldman 2004: 174).

On this view, the things that are most fundamentally good and bad for people are states of affairs, but times and lives have a derivative form of non-instrumental value. The prudential value of a time for a person is equal to the sum of the non-instrumental values of the positive and negative basics that are about that individual and time. How happy or unhappy a person is over time is a simple additive function of these nearly instantaneous values. The prudential value of an individual's life is the sum of all the basic intrinsic value states that are about that individual and that are true of him or her (Feldman 2000: 324).

This approach appears to address the problems mentioned above. First, the view does not say that happiness or pleasure is the sole bearer of non-instrumental goodness, and that situations and lives are also good. Rather, it says that the non-instrumentally good basics are all pure attributions of pleasure. Second, it does not involve double-counting, because the basic bearers of non-instrumental value are minimal and pure attributions of happiness (pleasure) and unhappiness (pain).

It is part of Feldman's conception of basic intrinsic value states that their values cannot be defeated by their context. He writes: "If we have chosen our basics correctly, then we have chosen our basics in such a way that their value is indefeasible" (2000: 333). Later, he adds: "We have to be sure to choose them in such a way that their values will never be obliterated" (334). By this, he means that, if the basic non-instrumental value for S of a state of affairs is *n*, then any world containing that state of affairs must be *n* units better for S than the world just like it where that state of affairs fails to obtain (334). And so if it turns out that happiness is *not* non-instrumentally beneficial when it is *undeserved*—or when it is *taken in acts of wickedness*—then pure attributions of happiness cannot really be basics. For in this case, the value of an episode of happiness *could* be obliterated by a change in context. Consequently, the real basics would have to be more complex.[3]

Bradley has developed an event-based version of hedonism closely modeled on Feldman's approach. Bradley is more direct about his acceptance of both the supervenience thesis (for him, the idea that when an event is a basic bearer of intrinsic value, its value supervenes entirely on its intrinsic features) and moment internalism.

Bradley thinks that this supervenience claim follows from the idea that the basic bearers of intrinsic value are "instantiations of the fundamental good- or bad-making properties—the properties that are fundamentally and completely responsible for how well a world (or a life) goes," together with the thesis that the non-instrumental value of something depends solely on its intrinsic properties (19). Given these claims, he argues, the denial of the supervenience thesis leads to absurd results. He writes:

> Then there could be two properties, F and G, such that the only intrinsically good states of affairs are those involving the instantiation of F alone, but whose values are determined by whether there are any instantiations of G. But if that were true, then F would fail to be a *fundamentally* good- or bad-making property, for instantiations of F would fail to completely determine what value there is. The fundamental good- or bad-making property would involve both F and G, contrary to our assumption.
>
> *(Bradley 2009: 19)*

Dale Dorsey (2012b) and Jens Johansson (2013) have pointed out a problem with this argument. While Bradley may well be correct that the basic bearers of value must be instantiations of fundamentally good- or bad-making properties, and that the values of these basics must depend on their intrinsic features, this does not mean that basic bearers cannot be complex situations or situations with relational parts. As Kauppinen notes, "Something can be valuable for its own sake or non-instrumentally just because of its relational properties" (2012: 375). For example, a desire-satisfactionist can hold that the situation consisting in *a present ("now-for-then") desire for something at a later time, plus the fulfillment of that desire at that later time*, is a basic bearer of prudential value.

Additionally, Dorsey writes, the more general demand that the non-instrumental value of a situation supervene on its intrinsic properties "would exclude . . . any resonance-respecting theory as a genuine theory of well-being" (284). What does he have in mind? In order for a condition, outcome, or event to be good for a person at a time, Dorsey suggests, this condition, outcome, or event must be positively endorsed by the person at that time. But those theories that respect the supervenience claim above, such as hedonism and concurrentist desire-satisfactionism, violate this constraint. They hold, e.g., that *pleasure* is good for one, whether or not one endorses it, or that *desiring that p while p is true* is good for one, whether or not one actually has any positive attitude towards *p* or this conjunction. Only theories that allow that relational properties such as *being endorsed by S* ground the non-instrumental goodness of a thing for *S* can capture the importance of resonance (280). But Bradley seems committed to the view that such theories entirely miss the concept of well-being.

However we evaluate this criticism, we should note that Bradley holds that the supervenience thesis also applies to times or moments. This commits him to (b) moment internalism. He believes that times and moments are bearers of prudential value, and so when a time is non-instrumentally good for a person, its value supervenes entirely on its intrinsic features. Hedonism is compatible with this idea: "The value of a time for a person is determined by the values of the pleasures and pains experienced by the person at that time" (2009 18). But, Bradley says, so-called "correspondence" theories of well-being (theories of well-being that require a world-to-mind-fit, such as desire-satisfactionism and aim-achievementism) deny this.[4]

However, as already noted, few people believe that times are *fundamental* or *basic* bearers of well-being value. More usual candidates in this context included states of affairs, events, conditions or states of people, or lives. And so, even if we accept the supervenience thesis when it comes to well-being basics, it is questionable whether it applies to times. Additionally, since no event is literally instantaneous, it is not entirely clear that isolated instants or moments—or even the tiny, discretized intervals described by Feldman—are the sorts of things that can have value for people on most axiologies.

The supervenience thesis and moment internalism can be criticized on more specific axiological grounds. Jeff McMahon explicitly rejects the view that a person's well-being is "entirely a matter of the person's intrinsic properties at that time." While it would be a mistake to deny that "the subjective character of a person's mental state" is an important dimension of well-being, well-being is "multidimensional and . . . some of its dimensions are relational" (2002: 180). McMahan argues that the value of a life is enhanced if the elements in it fit together to form a meaningful whole, replete with "intelligible purpose, direction, and overall structure" (175). The next section discusses a number of other axiologies that are in serious tension with the supervenience thesis and moment internalism.

Holism

The leading idea behind well-being holism is that a situation or event that appears to be non-instrumentally good or bad for a person runs the risk of having its value modified by its occurrence in some larger context. While episodes of pleasure appear to be beneficial, perhaps pleasure taken in acts of cruelty is *not* beneficial, or is *less* beneficial. Or perhaps pleasure is of diminishing benefit if it occurs in a life bereft of knowledge, achievement, and virtue. Or perhaps spikes of intense pleasure cannot fully compensate for brief episodes of truly excruciating pain. Or perhaps a high amount of pleasure packed into a very short life would be less good than the same amount of pleasure spread over a long life.

Thoughts such as these suggest that longer temporal intervals may have explanatory priority when it comes to personal well-being. Since some of the contextual features that may alter the value of a particular episode are properties of whole lives, it may be thought that the value of a life has explanatory priority. Such *lifetime well-being holism* amounts to the rejection of both (a) the explanatory priority of momentary well-being and (b) moment internalism. The value of a moment, on this view, derives from the contribution that moment makes to lifetime well-being. This view, favored by Kauppinen (2012: 374–375), among others, does not require the rejection of Feldman's framework of basic intrinsic value states—the basics are just very large.[5] Similarly, it does not require abandoning (c) neutrality about the order of episodes when it comes to aggregation. Once the non-instrumental values of moments are correctly calculated by looking first at their place in the entire life, their values may sum to equal the value of the life.

The idea that the whole has explanatory priority is one way to go. But there are also more moderate forms of holism. On such views, *some* basics are momentary occurrences whose values are entirely internal to them and beyond the threat of alteration or obliteration. The values of conjunctions of these (and only these) states might be perfectly summative. However, there are *other* basics whose values supervene on their relational properties (cf. Dorsey 2015: 325). This form of holism is compatible with (c), so long as we calculate the values of moments or times in full view of their relational properties.[6]

As noted earlier, there is another form of holism, adopted by Velleman, that involves the rejection of (a) and (c), but not of (b). On this view, which we can call *organic well-being holism*, when it comes to calculating the value of a whole life, features that have no bearing on the value of its moments become important. This form of holism closely resembles Moore's organic unity doctrine: the parts (here, the *moments*) of a life have specific, determinant values, but there is no simple function that takes one from the values of these parts to the value of the whole. This view has some important considerations in its favor. It does not imply, as versions of lifetime well-being holism and moderate well-being holism may, that we cannot specify the value for a person of a moment or an interval of time without waiting to see how her whole life turns out. Additionally, it avoids the strange idea that future events can affect one's current momentary well-being. Still, it is somewhat mysterious why well-being at a time and well-being over time would be as disconnected as Velleman proposes.

Ought we to accept one of these forms of holism? Here, axiological considerations are decisive. We must ask: does the true account of well-being require us to recognize value-conferring or value-transforming relations that would mandate some such approach? The remainder of this chapter presents and discusses several such relations that have been mentioned by holists. It does not discuss every possible variant of holism, and space constraints prohibit the thorough evaluation of any particular proposal.

Temporal order

Brentano was an early advocate of the importance of temporal order and his principle of *bonum progressionis* states that processes that go from bad to good are better than processes that go from good to good, which are themselves better than those that go from good to bad (1973/1897: 196–197). As mentioned above, Joshua Glasgow and F.M. Kamm also hold that going from high to low levels of momentary well-being is non-instrumentally bad, and that going from low to high levels of momentary well-being is non-instrumentally good. Relatedly, it was noted that Michael Slote holds that later-occurring goods have enhanced value, so that their value is greater than goods occurring earlier in life.

Dorsey has raised some difficult questions for these views (2015). Against Slote, if we consider a smaller timeframe—e.g., a single weekend—it does not seem reasonable to hold that later goods have enhanced value. So why, Dorsey asks, should later goods have enhanced value when it comes to an entire life? With respect to the more traditional view shared by Brentano, Glasgow, and Kamm, Dorsey points out that it seems to matter how the high levels of well-being are generated: if a life contains no bads, and the only goods it contains are sensory pleasures generated by an experience machine, it is not clear that diminution is any worse than improvement (cf. Kauppinen 2012). This suggests that the *bonum progressionis* principle is too broad. Additionally, Dorsey says, suppose we restrict our attention to two lives that are overall quite good for those who live them. Suppose that momentary well-being rarely dips low in either of these lives. Suppose, though, that the first life features modest improvement in momentary well-being, while the second features modest decline. If the view endorsed by Brentano, Glasgow, and Kamm were true, there would be reason to prefer the first over the second from the prudential point of view. It is not clear, however, that there is such reason. If this is correct, the general principle needs to be weakened or adjusted.

Other temporal patterns

Additional questions arise concerning other temporal patterns. These questions can be illustrated using a hedonistic axiology, but they arise for many other axiologies, too.

First, it does not seem prudentially irrational to prefer a life that steadily delivers medium-grade pleasures over a life of wild oscillations (i.e., a series of intense pleasures and intense pains), even if this second life features a greater sum-total of pleasure. Indeed, it does not seem irrational to seek to avoid pain, altogether. Suppose one life involves 1,000 "hedons" and 0 "dolors," while a second life includes 1,011 "hedons" and 10 "dolors." Is it not rational to prefer the first, and for entirely self-interested reasons? If so, then (a) must be qualified, and either (b) or (c) must be false.

Or consider two lives, the first of which generates 10,000 "hedons" overall, and the second of which generates 10,010 "hedons." Suppose, however, that the first lasts for 75 years and culminates with a peak experience of high-intensity pleasure, while the second lasts for 100 years and includes no such peak, but rather an even amount of pleasure. If it is rational to prefer the first of these lives over the second, then perhaps a life with a higher peak amount of positive value at a time is preferable. Or perhaps we should aggregate well-being over time by applying an analogue of Daniel Kahneman's "peak-end rule," which does seem to fit how people evaluate certain experiences. In either case, again (a) must be qualified, and either (b) or (c) must be rejected.

Yet another possibility is that longevity provides diminishing benefits beyond a certain point. This idea fits naturally with the view that there is an ideal *length* of a human life, perhaps around 85 years (cf. Harris 1985). This view could be worked out in a number of ways. We might say that, if one dies before 85, the value of one's life is diminished in proportion to the earliness of one's death. Simultaneously, we might hold that, though it is not positively disvaluable to live past this ideal stopping point, the value of positive experiences that occur after this point ought to be discounted. A main problem with this and similar views is the apparent arbitrariness involved in specifying an ideal length. Still, it does capture the idea that there is something especially tragic about early deaths, no matter how much pleasure, satisfaction, and achievement they contain.

On the other hand, there is the "James Dean effect" (Diener et al. 2001: 157). Many people judge that a triumphal life can actually be made *worse* by the addition of years of positive but mediocre value. The early years of James Dean's life, for example, were full of early achievement, aesthetic excellence, and enjoyment. Some people judge that his early death was *better for him* than, e.g., a normal-length life where he made B-movies and performed in Las Vegas nightclubs would have been. If this is true, it again suggests that either (b) or (c) is false.

However, Bradley points out that this assessment of Dean's life is inconsistent with the "difference-making principle," which states that the value of an event for a person is equal to the difference between the value of the person's life had the event occurred, and the value of the person's life had the event *not* occurred (i.e., the value of the person's life in the nearest—and most relevant—possible world where the event does not occur) (Bradley 2009: 159–160). Bradley suggests that those who believe in the James Dean effect are misled by their aesthetic intuitions: "Dean's actual life makes for a better story than the imagined longer life, but this clearly has nothing to do with whether it is a better life *for him*" (160).

Balancing

Balancing holism requires a pluralistic account of the basic bearers of intrinsic value. Brentano affirms a simple version of this view. His principle of *bonum variationis* states that it is better to combine two dissimilar goods than to combine two similar goods—so that (assuming perfect comparability of goods) it is better for one's life to contain *n* units of pleasure, *n* units of knowledge, and *n* units of achievement, than for it to contain 3*n* units of pleasure, alone. Thomas Hurka's perfectionism, if interpreted as a theory of well-being, is also a form of balancing holism. Hurka writes (1993): "Even if our individual accomplishments are not great, their proportion can mirror that of Renaissance lives, and for many of us this proportion is, other things equal, a good" (88). A life characterized by over-specialization or narrowness (in knowledge or activity) is less good, Hurka holds, than a life of otherwise equal achievement that is better rounded (cf. Kauppinen 2012). It seems natural for pluralists about the basic bearers of prudential value to incorporate balancing holism into their axiology; many of the same thoughts that motivate pluralism also motivate balancing.

Narrative relations

Alasdair MacIntyre was one of the first to affirm the importance of narrative relations: "What is better or worse for X depends upon the character of that intelligible narrative which provides X's life with its unity" (1981: 209). However, there are several importantly different ways of fleshing out MacIntyre's insight.

One idea is that the more one invests in a goal, the more its achievement contributes to one's well-being. According to Portmore, the cost of goals enhances the value of their achievement and the disvalue of their failure (2007). As he puts it: "The redemption of one's self-sacrifices in itself contributes to one's well-being—the closer that one's self-sacrifices come to being fully redeemed, the greater the contribution their redemption makes to one's well-being" (13).

Kauppinen develops another approach (2012, 2015). One determinant of the prudential value of a life, according to Kauppinen, is *meaningfulness*, which has to do with a life's degree of purpose, direction, and depth (2012: 352). A life is meaningful in virtue of the fact that (and to the degree that) it objectively warrants pride, joy, self-esteem, fulfillment, and elevation on the part of the agent, and admiration and inspiration on the part of others (353). But the degree to which a life objectively warrants these feelings is determined not only by the objective value of its projects and the degree to which the agent is suited to them and engaged by them, but also by the degree to which these projects add up to a balanced and coherent whole (2012: 346). For this reason, it is directly valuable when certain narratable relations obtain among the events that constitute one's life (2015: §2).[7]

It is important to note that, for Kauppinen, "coherence . . . is not based on any kind of story, true or fabricated, that the individual herself tells of her life, but on the strictly factual connection between earlier and later activities" (2012: 369). By contrast, for Rosati, the sense-making stories that we actually tell about our lives make a difference to our lives' value. This value, for Rosati, overlaps with the benefit of our actually achieving valuable ends, which makes story telling possible, as well as "the benefit that comes of being the controlling authority over ourselves and our lives, of being able to . . . represent them to ourselves as a product, ultimately, of our own autonomous efforts" (2013: 37). But for Rosati, making sense of our lives through story telling is also *non-instrumentally* beneficial, apart from the good things that make story telling possible and the good effects story telling sometimes has.

Consistency, coherence, and practical rationality

Some who accept conative theories of well-being such as desire-satisfactionism, aim-achievementism, or the values-realization theory believe that relations among an agent's desires, aims, or values are important when it comes to estimating well-being. Jason Raibley (2012) argues that it is bad for a person to have inconsistent aims or values, either at a time or over time. At least, the realization of several values that are at odds with one another does not make the same contribution to a person's well-being at a time (or over time) that the realization of the same individual values would if such conflict were absent. On his view, this is explained by the fact that well-being of an adult human person is largely determined by the degree to which he or she is functioning as a rational agent. Robust agential functioning requires synchronically and diachronically consistent values.

Kauppinen defends a similar view: the value of a series of achievements is enhanced when these achievements complement and build on one another (especially when later activities are "positively informed" by earlier ones), while the value of a series of achievements should be discounted if they are radically disconnected from one another, so that they have nothing at all to do with one another (Kauppinen 2012: 366–368).

These theorists also argue that the epistemic processes that determine how desires, aims, or values are selected, modified, pursued, and sometimes rejected ought to exhibit certain features. Raibley argues that it is best for a person when modifications of conative states are governed by epistemically reliable processes, so that the modifications are appropriate, given the actual features of the world, the agent's own abilities, and the agent's affective nature. Kauppinen similarly emphasizes the importance of "intelligent revision of original plans in response to negative feedback" (2012: 361). Valerie Tiberius details various dimensions of practical wisdom or intelligence that are arguably non-instrumentally beneficial when exemplified (Tiberius 2008).

Atomistic conative theorists will of course insist that the "output" is all that matters: if an agent has inconsistent or disconnected desires, aims, or values, this will likely result in less satisfaction or achievement, overall. Similarly, if the agent is practically irrational or unwise, this will likely diminish their lifetime sum of desire-fulfillment or value-realization. Holists insist, though, that lives characterized by internal conflicts, disconnection, or by practical irrationality are less good simply in virtue of these facts, even in those rare cases where these features do *not* diminish sum-total satisfaction or achievement.

Notes

1 It is widely assumed that the fundamental building blocks of well-being will be episodes that are desirable for their own sakes. However, Bishop's recent network theory of well-being questions this (Bishop 2015). For this reason, it can be seen as yet another challenge to atomism.

2 However, if one embraces pluralism, the requirement that only situations with *determinate* non-instrumental value bear upon the values of the wholes in which they figure may need to be relaxed (Lemos 2006). It is very difficult to assign precise and commensurable prudential values to episodes of pleasure, knowledge, achievement, virtue, and friendship.

3 Feldman himself sometimes seems to prefer a theory that would take into account whether the objects of a person's happiness deserve to have happiness taken in them (2004: 172–182; 2010: 210–215).

4 More broadly, Bradley argues that correspondence theories have difficulty explaining when benefits occur. This is because, on such theories, it is not clear whether benefits accrue at the time a desire or aim is *formed*, at the time at which it is fulfilled, or during the time at which it is both desired or aimed at and fulfilled or achieved (21–30). However, it seems natural to say that what benefits people is for them to get what they want while they still want it (or for them to achieve an end while they still value it, aim for it, or intend it) (Heathwood 2005). And so a natural answer to Bradley is that the benefit represented by a desire satisfaction or achievement occurs *during* the time that the pro-attitude and its object coincide.

5 Kauppinen defines the value of a moment or time for a person as how non-instrumentally valuable the moment would be for that person *if it were considered in isolation from the rest of her life* (347). It seems better to say that this is the *virtual* non-instrumental value of the moment or time for the person, while its *actual* non-instrumental value derives from the contribution that it makes to the whole (i.e., is equal to its *contributory value*, as Kauppinen defines this term) (cf. Zimmerman 2005).

6 Another form of moderate holism might accept (b) but qualify (a), saying that there are *some* basics that are non-momentary phenomena; these basics do not have an impact on momentary well-being, but *do* have an impact on the values of longer stretches of time, up to and including whole lives. This form of holism could be compatible with (c), provided that, when aggregating, we included all the temporal intervals necessary to capture the extant basics within a given time-frame.

7 Kauppinen writes that the value of events "is a multiple of three factors: their positive or negative causal contribution to the agent's present or future goals, the value of those goals, and the degree to which success in achieving a goal is deserved in virtue of exercising agential capacities" (2015).

Bibliography

Bishop, Michael. (2015). *The Good Life: Unifying the Philosophy and Psychology of Well-being.* New York: Oxford University Press.

Bradley, Ben. (2006). Two Concepts of Intrinsic Value. *Ethical Theory and Moral Practice* 9(2): 111–130.

Bradley, Ben. (2009). *Well-being and Death.* Oxford: Clarendon Press.

Brentano, Franz. (1973/1897). *The Foundation and Construction of Ethics.* Trans. Elizabeth Schneewind. London: Routledge.

Broome, John. (2004). *Weighing Lives.* New York: Oxford University Press.

Chisholm, Roderick M. (1986). *Brentano and Intrinsic Value.* New York: Cambridge University Press.

Diener, Ed, Derrick Wirtz and Shigehiro Oishi. (2001). End Effects of Rated Life Quality: The James Dean Effect. *Psychological Science* 12(2): 124–128.

Dorsey, Dale. (2012a). Can Instrumental Value Be Intrinsic? *Philosophical Quarterly* 93(2): 137–157.

Dorsey, Dale. (2012b). Intrinsic Value and the Supervenience Principle. *Philosophical Studies* 157(2): 267–285.

Dorsey, Dale. (2015). The Significance of a Life's Shape. *Ethics* 125(2): 303–330.

Ewing, A. C. (1973). *Value and Reality: The Philosophical Case for Theism.* New York: Humanities Press.

Feldman, Fred. (2000). Basic Intrinsic Value. *Philosophical Studies* 99(3): 319–346.

Feldman, Fred. (2004). *Pleasure and the Good Life: Concerning the Nature, Varieties, and Plausibility of Hedonism.* New York: Oxford University Press.

Feldman, Fred. (2010). *What is This Thing Called Happiness?* New York: Oxford University Press.

Fletcher, Guy. (2009). Rejecting Well-Being Invariabilism. *Philosophical Papers* 38(1): 21–34.

Glasgow, Joshua. (2013). The Shape of a Life and the Value of Loss and Gain. *Philosophical Studies* 162(3): 667–669.

Harris, John. (1985). *The Value of Life.* London: Routledge.

Heathwood, Chris. (2005). The Problem of Defective Desires. *Australasian Journal of Philosophy* 83(4): 487–504.

Heathwood, Chris. (2011). Preferentism and Self-Sacrifice. *Pacific Philosophical Quarterly* 92(1): 18–38.

Hurka, Thomas. (1993). *Perfectionism*. New York: Oxford University Press.

Hurka, Thomas. (1998). Two Kinds of Organic Unities. *The Journal of Ethics* 2: 283–304. Reprinted in *Drawing Morals: Essays in Moral Theory*, 2011. New York: Oxford University Press.

Johansson, Jens. (2013). The Timing Problem. In Ben Bradley, Fred Feldman, and Jens Johansson (eds.), *The Oxford Handbook of the Philosophy of Death*. New York: Oxford University Press.

Kahneman, Daniel. (1999). Objective Happiness. In D. Kahneman, E. Diener, and N. Schwarz (eds.), *Well-Being: Foundations of Hedonic Psychology*. New York: Russell Sage Foundation, pp. 3–25.

Kamm, F.M. (2003). Rescuing Ivan Illyich: How We Live and How We Die. *Ethics* 113(2): 202–233.

Kauppinen, Antti. (2012). Meaningfulness and Time. *Philosophy and Phenomenological Research* 84(2): 345–377.

Kauppinen, Antti. (2015). The Narrative Calculus. *Oxford Studies in Normative Ethics* 5.

Lemos, Noah. (1994). *Intrinsic Value: Concept and Warrant*. New York: Cambridge University Press.

Lemos, Noah. (2006). Indeterminate Value, Basic Value, and Summation. In Kris McDaniel, Jason R. Raibley and Richard Feldman (eds.), *The Good, The Right, Life, and Death*. Aldershot: Ashgate.

MacIntyre, Alasdair. (1981). *After Virtue: Revised Edition*. South Bend, IN: Notre Dame University Press.

McMahon, Jeff. (2002). *The Ethics of Killing*. New York: Oxford University Press.

Nozick, Robert. (1981). *Philosophical Explanations*. Cambridge, MA: Harvard/Belknap Press.

Plato. *Philebus*. Trans. Dorothea Frede. In John M. Cooper (ed.), *The Complete Works of Plato*, 1997. Indianapolis, IN: Hackett Publishing.

Portmore, Douglas. (2007). Welfare, Achievement, and Self-Sacrifice. *Journal of Ethics and Social Philosophy* 2(2): 1–28.

Raibley, Jason. (2012). Welfare Over Time and the Case for Holism. *Philosophical Papers* 41(2): 239–265.

Rosati, Connie. (2013). The Story of a Life. *Social Philosophy and Policy* 30(1–2): 21–50.

Sarch, Alexander. (2012). Multi-Component Theories of Well-Being and Their Structure. *Pacific Philosophical Quarterly* 93(4): 439–471.

Slote, Michael. (1983). Goods and Lives. In *Goods and Virtues*. New York: Oxford University Press.

Tiberius, Valerie. (2008). *The Reflective Life*. New York: Oxford University Press.

Velleman, David. (2000). Well-Being and Time. In *The Possibility of Practical Reason*. Cambridge: Cambridge University Press

Zimmerman, Michael J. (2005). Virtual Intrinsic Value and the Principle of Organic Unities. In Toni Rønnow-Rasmussen and Michael J. Zimmerman (eds.), *Recent Work on Intrinsic Value*. Dordrecht, Netherlands: Springer, pp. 401–413.

29

THE EXPERIENCE MACHINE AND THE EXPERIENCE REQUIREMENT

Jennifer Hawkins

One particular thought experiment—Robert Nozick's experience machine (Nozick 1974: 42–45; Nozick 1989: 104–108)—has had a huge impact on the way philosophers think about well-being.[1] Indeed, many assume it completely refutes hedonism once and for all, and not merely hedonism, but any theory that focuses exclusively on mental states. However, as we shall see, Nozick's example and its implications are more complex than people typically realize. The original example goes like this:

> Suppose there were an experience machine that would give you any experience you desired. Superduper neuropsychologists could stimulate your brain so that you would think and feel you were writing a great novel, or making a friend, or reading an interesting book. All the time you would be floating in a tank, with electrodes attached to your brain. Should you plug into this machine for life, preprogramming your life experiences?
>
> *(Nozick 1974: 42)*

In essence, Nozick asks us to imagine the possibility of a machine capable of giving someone *any* experience she might want. In more contemporary terms, we could think of it as the most powerful virtual reality machine ever conceived. The machine stimulates all of the brain's sensory input channels, providing experiences as phenomenologically rich as any in real life. For example, it could give someone the experience of skiing down a snowy mountain complete with vision of mountains, snow, and trees, the feel of wind on her face, and the bodily sensations of gliding smoothly and swiftly downward. Indeed, we are to imagine that the machine is so good that, from within, it is *impossible* to tell the difference between real experiences and machine-produced ones. It is also important to note that, once someone enters the machine, the machine ensures that she forgets where she is and how her experiences are being crafted. She believes her experience is real, even though it is not.

Nozick expresses confidence that most people would not want to plug in. However, *if* the quality of experience is all that matters in a life, then it seems that one ought to want to plug in, since the machine is, by hypothesis, the best way to ensure large quantities of high-quality experience. Interestingly, this is true no matter how you define "good" experience. I shall use the label "experientialism" for any theory that defines well-being purely in terms of mental states, i.e., any theory that says only experiential states can be bearers of intrinsic welfare value. Hedonism is simply one form—albeit the most familiar—of experientialism. Although Nozick's original target was hedonism, the thought experiment, *if* it works, works equally well against any form of experientialism. Many philosophers take the example to show both that ordinary people do not think about welfare in (exclusively) experientialist terms, and that the correct theory of well-being—whatever else it is—is not experientialist.

Despite the apparent simplicity of this thought experiment, the issues it raises are complex and relatively underexplored. The aim of this chapter is to rectify that. I begin by considering how the experience machine differs from other common objections to hedonism. I take a closer look at the structure of the argument it is supposed to provide against experientialism. In particular, I highlight some of the confusions and problems that arise from the specific way Nozick sets up his thought experiment. I then consider whether it is possible to reformulate the example in a way that avoids these problems. I next consider the question: what would follow if we *did* reject experientialism? As we shall see, there would still be much to decide about which non-experientialist theory of well-being to accept. Finally, I consider the relationship between rejecting experientialism (as Nozick hopes we will do) and rejecting what has come to be known as "the experience requirement," explaining why these are not precisely the same thing.[2]

A distinctive kind of objection

The original target of Nozick's thought experiment is hedonism, a view about well-being according to which the only thing intrinsically valuable (from the prudential point of view) is pleasure and the only thing intrinsically bad (from the prudential point of view) is pain. Hedonism aims to tell us something quite general about what makes lives better or worse.

One prominent, traditional strategy of critics of hedonism is to find fault with hedonism's account of valuable mental states. The basic aim of such an objector is to establish that there are more types of valuable consciousness than simply pleasure (and more types of bad consciousness than simply pain). How successful any such objection is depends partly on one's views about what is valuable in conscious experience and partly on how elastic one is willing to be in one's definition of terms such as "pleasure" and "pain." A few examples may make this clearer. John Stuart Mill famously defined "happiness" in terms of pleasure and the absence of pain (2005/1861: 7). But various people, over time, have objected to his simple equation of happiness with pleasure. Even assuming that "happiness" is the name for a psychological state, many have claimed it is the name for a distinct psychological state—one that is both more complex and more valuable than mere pleasure.[3] If one were to adopt such a view of happiness and combine it with the claim that well-being consists of happiness, one would be defending a version of experientialism. It would not, however, deserve the label "hedonism" because of the explicit rejection of the idea that pleasure is the major welfare value.

Some objectors in this category go even further and argue that among the valuable types of consciousness are some painful or unpleasant states. For example, if we sometimes care more about the *process* of thinking or about the *contents* of our thoughts than about how we feel, we might sometimes reasonably prefer sensory pain over sensory pleasure despite the fact that hedonism views such a preference as prudentially irrational. James Griffin offers the example of Sigmund Freud, who during his final illness preferred to think in torment without pain medications given that the medications dulled his thoughts (Griffin 1986: 8). If we think Freud's choice makes prudential sense, then this suggests we do not accept the hedonist characterization of valuable consciousness. However, in itself, it does not challenge the basic idea that internal mental experience is what matters. After all, according to the story, Freud tolerated pain for the sake of *thinking*.

Nozick's thought experiment has gained so much attention precisely because it departs radically from this familiar type of criticism and instead offers a critique of experientialism in all its forms. Whereas traditional objectors focused on the idea that there are more types of valuable consciousness than just pleasure, Nozick's example is meant to establish that there is more to well-being than valuable consciousness *however* one chooses to define "valuable consciousness."

It is worth noting that, although the experience machine is the example used most often to attack experientialism, there are a number of other, closely related examples in the literature on well-being that are intended to make a similar point. These typically don't involve a machine, but simply posit deception or ignorance such as might arise in the ordinary course of living. And the person in the example is not lacking all or even most knowledge of her life, but simply knowledge of one or more key aspects. For example, L.W. Sumner describes a case in which someone is happily involved in a relationship, but doesn't know that her partner is unfaithful (1996: 157). T.M. Scanlon uses the example of someone who is secretly despised by those he falsely thinks of as friends (1998: 112). And still other theorists appeal to examples in which someone happily believes she has accomplished something when she hasn't really (Kagan 1998: 36; Shafer-Landau 2012: 53). The differences are less important than the similarities, however. For as with Nozick's example, the point is to elicit the intuition that something in these lives is not good, or at least not as good as it could or should be, and this despite the fact that the agents in question are happy in their delusions: a conclusion a hedonist cannot accept.

Problems with the argument

Despite its fame, the experience machine example can be confusing. Because it is a thought experiment, we are supposed to draw conclusions on the basis of our own intuitive reactions to the case. Nozick thinks most people will *not* want to sign up for life in the machine. But is he right? And what really follows if he is?

Insofar as there is an argument, it seems to be *roughly* this:

1. If some form of experientialism is true, most people will, upon encountering the thought experiment, want to sign up for the machine.

2. In fact, most people who encounter the example want *not* to sign up for the machine.

3. Therefore, no form of experientialism is true.

Let me begin with some remarks about premise (2). Nozick writes as if he is confident that no one (or almost no one) would want to sign up for a life in the machine. However, we don't really know whether that is correct. Philosophers sometimes write and talk as if it is a well-known fact that most people do not want to sign up. But that is an empirical question that (to my knowledge) has never been rigorously tested. Of course, there is lots of anecdotal evidence from philosophers who have taught the example over the years. But the anecdotal evidence is mixed, and all sorts of factors may contribute to the replies students give. Classrooms are hardly controlled environments. So we just don't know how most people would respond (although see the discussion below of DeBrigard 2010).

Nonetheless, it is natural to wonder: *if* he were right, and most people did not want to sign up, would that demonstrate that experientialism is false? Not necessarily. In fairness, there is an important core truth in the way the example is set up. But other features of Nozick's presentation make it difficult to draw any clear conclusions.

The core truth, which is worth stating, is just this: *if* hedonism or some other version of experientialism were true, then assuming the machine really is as powerful as claimed, it would make most sense (from a purely prudential point of view) to sign up. This is because the machine would be able to give a person *the best life possible*. No other option would be as good. Some people claim that real life—at least in theory—could compete with the machine. For example, if we assume that pleasure is what matters, then the claim would be that it is at least possible for a real life to contain as much pleasure as a machine life. If that were the case, then an extremely pleasurable life might be tied with machine life for best. But although this isn't logically ruled out, it is extremely unlikely. Moreover, since even in that scenario no life is *better* than the machine life, and since machine life is so much more dependable than real life, the machine would clearly be the better prudential choice for any given individual.

However, the argument requires people to recognize this fact and *then* make a decision about whether to sign up *based purely on considerations about their own welfare*. Now given that not every motive a person has for doing something is a motive related to her own welfare, this immediately raises the question of how to distinguish reasons of self-interest from other types of reasons. This is important because it is plausible to think that various welfare-irrelevant reasons may influence the choice people make, either consciously or unconsciously. But if other motives are at work then premise (1)—which states that: "If some form of experientialism is true, most people will want to sign up for the machine"— might be false. Experientialism might be true even though most people do *not* wish to sign up. Unless we can confidently rule out the influence of such reasons, which requires that we first be able to reliably identify them, we can't interpret lack of willingness to sign up as indicative of the truth or falsity of experientialism.

In the literature one can find many different expressions of the same basic concern, namely that people may refuse to sign up for reasons other than having rejected the thesis that it is prudentially good to do so. Many people have found it difficult to really grasp and take seriously a possibility so remote from real life. Even though technology is more sophisticated now than when Nozick wrote the example, it is still a long, long way from being able to substitute plausibly for all of our five senses, much less for any length of time. Thus, it can be hard to give credence to the idea that a machine might really be that powerful, and this might make us reluctant to sign up. In a similar vein, it can be hard to put aside worries that the machine might malfunction, or might fail to deliver the best possible experiences. As part of the thought experiment we are supposed to assume it won't malfunction, but how could we ever know that about any real machine (Sumner 1996: 95)? As we shall see in the next section there are also credible worries about personal commitments (Kawall 1999) and unconscious motives such as status quo bias (DeBrigard 2010).

Many of the problems arise from the fact that Nozick presents the example as a *choice* for the reader. We are asked whether we—who are, by hypothesis, not now living in a machine— would agree to sign up for life. This puts us in a very funny position. It is stipulated that in the machine we will have great experiences of whatever type we value. Moreover, we will not— once in the machine—know that our experiences aren't real. But of course, as we contemplate whether to sign up, we know that future experiences in the machine will not be real. And because this invites all sorts of welfare-irrelevant reasons to come into play, it creates problems.

People can desire things other than their own welfare, and sometimes these desires are strong enough to lead them to act in ways that are not welfare maximizing. Experientialism in itself doesn't rule this out. It is just a theory about what is good for us, and it could be a true theory about our good even if we do not always choose what is good for us (Kawall 1999; Silverstein 2000; Hewitt 2010). For example, people can have purely altruistic desires, desires for the good of another person. If that is possible, then a person might not want to sign up because by doing so she would make it the case that she could no longer help others. After all, once in the machine she would no longer really be interacting with other people, just computer simulations of people. Anticipating this particular kind of worry, Nozick stipulated that part of the thought experiment should include imagining that others are well off and not in need of our help (1974: 43; 1989: 105). But while that might handle purely altruistic desires, these are not the only potentially problematic desires.

Consider the fact that many people have a strong, brute desire to know things, a desire that is not obviously welfare-related. Although we talk about curiosity killing the cat, we invented that expression to talk about *ourselves*. It points to the idea that there is a stubborn quality to this particular human desire, that people often desire to know things even when it is not good for them to know. Precisely because entering the machine requires us to give up all knowledge, it is plausible to think that people might balk at the idea regardless of whether it would be good for them to enter. In my own case, at least, I know I would be unwilling to enter the machine, because it would entail not knowing what happens to those I love. Indeed, I would go as far as to claim that part of what it is to love someone is to want to know what happens to them. Of course, the primary desire of one who loves is the desire for the welfare of the loved one. But one also wants to see the other's life unfold, to track the loved one's progress through the world. It would be small comfort simply to be assured that my loved ones will be okay if I enter the machine. I would still understand that a choice to enter is a choice to forgo any further knowledge of these people. The issue, of course, is about what such reluctance *means*. I admit that my own sympathies are not experientialist, so I tend to assume that (in most cases at least) knowledge of the sort that matters to me is also good for me. But in fairness to experientialists, I am also pretty sure that my desire to know has no grounding in, and is not limited by, facts about my welfare: that I would still want to know *whether or not it was good for me*. It seems plausible that many people have similarly strong, welfare-independent strands of curiosity. Suppose now that it turns out that many people do not want to sign up for the experience machine, and they cite as their reason a desire to know how things really are in the world. Unless we can rule out the possibility that these desires are welfare-irrelevant desires, we cannot draw any conclusions about experientialism from the fact of their reluctance.

In short, the example as formulated is unable to escape from a certain kind of dilemma. On the one hand, if we had some reliable way of stipulating ahead of time which desires are self-interested, we might be able to show that people were rejecting the machine for self-interested reasons, which is what the argument against experientialism needs. However, we can only have such a distinction if we already have a theory of well-being. It simply begs the question against the experientialist to begin with such a stipulation. On the other hand, without it, it will in many cases be unclear what to conclude even if, as predicted, many people don't want to sign up.

Just how bad is machine life?

Another problem with Nozick's example is that it invites a certain kind of misreading, or (if not literally a misreading) at least a conflation of issues. Many people assume that the point of the example is to persuade us that we should *never for any reason* sign up for the machine. Certainly some of what Nozick says in his original presentation suggests that interpretation. But it is not necessary to accept this strong claim in order to reject experientialism. A non-experientialist can consistently grant that it *sometimes* makes sense to sign up for the machine. The example thus conflates the project of rejecting experientialism and the project of defending a strong view about the intrinsic value of connection with reality.

To see the problem more clearly, it can help to think of theories of well-being as giving us rankings of possible lives. Obviously a theory of *well*-being aims to tell us what makes *good* lives *good*. But ideally it should also tell us what makes bad lives bad, and which possible lives are in the middle and why. It should give us insight into those features of lives that make them better or worse, and so enable us—at least in theory—to rank possible lives from best to worst.

Hedonists rank lives according to a total score, reached by adding up pleasure, adding up pain, and subtracting the pain from the pleasure. A positive net score (more pleasure than pain) is good, but the best life is a life of maximal pleasure and no pain, and the worst would be a life of maximal pain and no pleasure. Different experientialist theories will, of course, produce different rankings, but the approach to ranking will be similar. As we saw in the last section, the important truth about the experience machine is that *if* some version of experientialism is true and *if* we grant that the machine really is as powerful as it is claimed to be, then life in the machine represents the best possible life, or at least the best possible life choice.

To reject experientialism is to reject the idea that machine life is *best*. But notice that this is still a far cry from claiming that machine life is bad or even worst. Among those who reject the idea that machine life is the best life, there could still be lots of disagreement about where precisely in the ranking of possible lives machine life falls. Only the extreme claim that machine life is the *worst* possible life would support the claim that it never, no matter the alternatives, makes sense to sign up. Indeed, many theorists who are not hedonists allow that happiness is a significant, intrinsic prudential good. But if that is true, then machine life will most likely be better than some of the alternative lives very low in happiness.

In his second, later discussion of the experience machine, Nozick is clear that the proper question is whether machine life is *best*. He writes, "The question is not whether plugging in is preferable to extremely dire alternatives—lives of torture, for instance—but whether plugging in would constitute the very best life, or tie for being best" (1989: 105). However, even though he makes the point, he undermines its strength by offering only one possible example of a life worse than machine life: a life of torture! So it is not surprising that this point is often lost. Many discussions of the experience machine still assume that the point of the example is to establish that machine life is very bad.

This matters because it speaks to a frequent reaction people have to Nozick's example. As we have seen, people interpret him as holding that it is always better to be outside the machine. Many students initially respond by insisting that whether it makes sense to sign up must depend on the alternatives. Perhaps for a homeless orphan living in a slum in one of the poorer countries of the world—someone with little hope of improving her situation—the experience machine would be a good option. As far as it goes, the point is reasonable. Even if Nozick would disagree (and given the quote above, it is not clear he would), many other non-experientialist philosophers would agree. However, the important point is just that this *is not a defense of experientialism*. Even if Nozick ranks machine life low, the experience machine example undermines experientialism (if it does) by suggesting that machine life is not best.

In an interesting set of empirical studies, DeBrigard (2010) presented students with scenarios in which they were asked to imagine discovering that they are living in an experience machine. The memories they have of their lives are, they now discover, simply memories that were produced by the machine. However, though they do not remember it, they once had a life outside of the machine, and they could return to it. They are given the option of staying in the machine or returning to real life. DeBrigard developed different versions of the scenario. In one version no information is given to suggest anything about what the real life would be like. In the other two versions information about real life is given (in one case suggesting it is not good, in the other case suggesting it is good). The results were quite divided, but were definitely sensitive to the information about how good or bad the "real" life was.

DeBrigard takes it as a starting point that most people presented with Nozick's case do *not* want to sign up. He then sees himself as looking for an explanation of the *dual* fact that when people contemplate signing up they are reluctant to do so, but when people are asked to contemplate getting out, they are also reluctant to do so. He offers an interesting hypothesis in terms of status quo bias, the idea, well established in psychology, that people are exceedingly cautious about giving up what they have. People have a tendency to overvalue what they already possess or what they already know. Given this tendency, an alternative must be viewed as considerably better than the status quo in order to motivate people to make a change.

There are two points I wish to make. First, *even if* we could draw a straightforward conclusion from DeBrigard's results, the conclusion, though interesting, would not tell us anything useful about *experientialism*. By straightforward conclusion, I mean the conclusion that would be suggested if we could be sure that nothing other than welfare-relevant considerations were contributing to choice. DeBrigard's examples are intended to test the view that machine life is one of the worst possible lives. If it were true that most people believed this, then one would expect people who are told that they are in an experience machine to want to come out. Since they did not all want to leave the machine, this suggests that people do not all see machine life as the worst possible life, or even as particularly bad. It all depends on the alternatives. However, even if DeBrigard's results could be read as showing this (and I don't think even he thinks they clearly can, because of probable status quo bias), it would not tell us about the truth or falsity of *experientialism*. This is because, although showing that machine life is not the worst life might be interesting, it doesn't speak to the issue of whether machine life is best.

One might counter that if machine life is best, no one should have wanted to leave. But in DeBrigard's example, unlike Nozick's, machine life was not characterized to make it clearly best, for in DeBrigard's example, machine life is simply the life the person has lived up until now, which, like most lives, has both good and bad elements.

Second, and more importantly, if his hypothesis about status quo bias is correct, then it is hard to know what to conclude. I refer interested readers to the details of DeBrigard's article. But in general, I think that the combined lesson of the last two sections is that setting up machine examples in terms of personal choice allows too many irrelevant factors to enter in. I want now to consider whether it is possible to reformulate the example to isolate intuitions about *experientialism*.

A reformulation

Is there a way to reformulate the example, so that it does a better job of isolating the relevant intuitions: intuitions that would distinguish experientialists from non-experientialists? Whether or not it solves all the problems, the following—from Roger Crisp (2006: 117–119)—strikes me as a significant improvement. In what follows I have developed the example with my own details, but in a way faithful to Crisp's presentation.

Consider twin girls, Molly and Polly. Imagine that Molly is born and has a great life in the real world. Readers can fill in the details of the life in whatever way is likely to make it seem attractive. This way we ensure that her life is qualitatively good. And let us imagine that she lives to a ripe old age of 100, ensuring her life is quantitatively good as well. Polly, her identical twin, is born a few minutes later, but Polly is immediately whisked away by the same superduper neuropsychologists Nozick describes, who hook her up to an experience machine. Inside the machine Polly lives a life that is qualitatively *identical* moment for moment to Molly's life. Whatever Molly really does, Polly has a virtual experience that is—from the inside—indistinguishable. Like Molly, Polly also lives for 100 years and then dies content, never knowing that her life was unreal. What we then ask ourselves is this: do we think that their lives are equal in prudential value or do we think that one of them had a better life than the other? An experientialist should say the lives are equally good. But a non-experientialist will think that Molly's life is a better life, even if neither Molly nor Polly is positioned to make this assessment.

Framed this way, the example escapes many of the earlier concerns. For one thing, worries about how to imagine such a powerful machine have less traction, since we don't worry about the future. We are simply told what the life was like and that it has already occurred, which somehow seems easier to believe or grasp, precisely because it is more determinate. Similarly, worries about machine malfunction seem to evaporate from this perspective, since we are no longer peering into an uncertain future for ourselves, but contemplating a completed life where it is just stipulated that the machine did not malfunction. We are simply told (and we fairly easily accept) that the machine gave Polly a life qualitatively identical to the one lived by Molly.

Most importantly, since no one is asked whether she wants to sign up, there is no room for welfare-independent desires (ours or Polly's) to distract us from the primary question. Polly never makes a choice and neither do we. Because of this, we can more easily focus on our intuitions about the goodness of her life. We do not have to face all the problems that come from thinking about what it would mean to give up the life we have already begun, the life we are already invested in. Though we may be prone to status quo bias when making choices for ourselves, this should not be triggered here. Nor will other welfare-irrelevant desires get in the way.

Instead, we have to decide whether Polly's life is lacking something important that Molly's has. Finally, because the reformulation stipulates that both lives are enviably good from the inside, no distracting issues about ranking arise. Even if one thinks that Polly's life is worse than Molly's, one might also think that Polly's life is better than the real life of someone who is desperately poor, ill, and alone. In short, this version doesn't invite the conclusion (as Nozick's discussion seems to) that machine life is *never* choiceworthy. It forces us to focus on the narrower question of whether a good real life is better than an experientially good machine life.

States of affairs versus knowledge

Suppose we think Polly's life is worse than Molly's. What does this show? There are (at least) two ways of explaining the difference in value, and the literature on these issues does not typically make this clear (Hawkins 2015).

First, someone might think that what matters in life are the facts about what really happens. More precisely, we might think it matters which states of affairs come about. If we take this approach, we need some way of identifying which states of affairs matter: which states of affairs are relevant to the value of this person's life. Desire theory uses (some of) an individual's desires to pick out the relevant states. According to desire theory, if I desire to accomplish some goal G, then what has value for me is the coming to be of the state of affairs in which I actually accomplish G. Usually, of course, when such states of affairs come about, I know this. But on the first view, knowledge is not *required* in order for a state of affairs to have positive (or negative) prudential value. A person's life could thus be better than she thinks or worse than she thinks. I shall call theories like this—that accord value directly to states of affairs—SA theories, for *prudential value of states of affairs*. It is important to remember that desire theory is only one, albeit the most famous, example of an SA theory.

A very different, alternative conclusion one might reach emphasizes the prudential value of knowledge or some other positive epistemic relation such as true belief or justified true belief. For simplicity, I'll just discuss knowledge. On this view, knowledge about the facts of my life has positive prudential value for me. Again, of course, a theorist drawn to this idea will need a way of saying which things it is good to know. Presumably not all knowledge has value. For example, there is probably no prudential value in knowing the number of ants living in my backyard! Precisely because knowledge is a *relation* between mind and world, it is the kind of thing that Molly might have and Polly lack, even though their lives are experientially identical. I shall call theories like this—that accord value to epistemic relations—ER theories, for the *prudential value of epistemic relations*.

SA and ER are very different, and offer competing explanations of why Polly's life is worse than Molly's. Inside the experience machine Polly lacks knowledge. Most of her beliefs are false, even though she doesn't know this. And so an ER theory would see less value in her life than in Molly's. But notice as well that most of the significant facts of her life are not as she wants them to be either. Using the desire theory as an example of an SA theory, suppose that Polly (like Molly) at one point wishes to visit Japan. Whereas Molly actually visits Japan, Polly merely has virtual experiences that are Japan-like. Though she doesn't realize it, her desire is frustrated, not satisfied. Indeed, presumably most of Polly's significant life desires are frustrated, making her life quite bad from the standpoint of a desire theory. If we think that Polly's life is worse than Molly's the interesting question is—*why?* Is it because Polly is so ignorant of the truth about her life? Or is it because the facts are not as she wants them to be? Or is it both?

To illustrate vividly the difference between SA and ER, consider the following four possible lives. Again, let a desire theory serve as our example of an SA theory. Suppose that these four different scenarios occur in lives that are otherwise identical in every way, so that any difference in the value of these lives must be traceable to differences in these cases.

> Life 1: Polly has a desire to G, her desire is frustrated, and she knows this.
>
> Life 2: Polly has a desire to G, her desire is satisfied, and she knows this.
>
> Life 3: Polly has a desire to G, her desire is frustrated, though she never knows this.
>
> Life 4: Polly has a desire to G, her desire is satisfied, though she never knows this.

A desire theorist will rank these lives as follows: lives 2 and 4 are equal in value and both are better than either 1 or 3 (which are also equal in value). Someone who accepts an ER theory that accords no direct value to states of affairs will instead say that lives 1 and 2 are equal in value and both are better than either lives 3 or 4 (which are also equal in value). Of course, many plausible non-experientialist theories of well-being may allow that *both* states of affairs and epistemic relations are important. One does not have to accept one and reject the other. The point of doing so here is just to illustrate, as dramatically as possible, that they really are different theses. It is also true that many plausible non-experientialist theories of well-being will accord intrinsic value to things *other than* states of affairs and epistemic relations. For example, many theories will accord happiness some, though not exclusive, weight. If that's correct, then rankings will be complicated in more ways than illustrated here.

Still, it is worth emphasizing the difference between SA and ER, if only because, historically, philosophers have tended to overlook ER and other alternatives to a pure SA theory. According to one familiar story about the development of theories of well-being, the obvious solution to the problem posed by the experience machine is to adopt a desire theory. But while it is true that desire theory, which is a pure SA theory, is an alternative to experientialism, it is not the only one. Nor is tacit acceptance of desire theory the only explanation of the intuition that Polly's life is worse than Molly's. That intuition by itself only tells us to reject experientialism. But once you do, there are various alternative views to choose from.

Experientialism and the experience requirement

James Griffin coined the phrase "experience requirement" in the course of talking about the move from experientialism to desire theory (1986: 13). Whereas experientialism embraces, desire theory rejects "the experience requirement." But what precisely is the experience requirement?

Following Griffin, people discussing the rejection of the experience requirement typically have in mind a theory that goes beyond the mental in a very strong sense. They typically have in mind a theory that gives no central role to mental states—a theory like a desire theory that assigns intrinsic value only to states of affairs, and only indirectly and contingently to mental states if these happen to be constituents of desired states of affairs. For example, a person can desire the state of affairs in which she is happy or the state of affairs in which she knows things. When that occurs, mental states figure indirectly in the account of welfare. But there is no requirement that prudential goods or bads be experienced by the person who is thus made better or worse off.

Having said this, it is important to note that there is disagreement in the literature about what it means to reject or, alternatively, incorporate an experience requirement. Some people assume that if a theory makes good experience necessary for welfare, it incorporates an experience requirement. Alternatively, and more in keeping with Griffin's usage, an experience requirement could be understood as the requirement that anything that affects welfare (positively or negatively) must enter experience. These two can come apart.

L.W. Sumner's theory is a case in point (1996). According to Sumner, welfare is authentic happiness, where this phrase requires explanation. First, happiness is understood as a complex psychological state. It involves judging one's life to be good *and* feeling good. As such, happiness for Sumner has both cognitive and affective dimensions. However, the theory is a hybrid theory in the sense that it also has non-mental requirements. Although happiness is necessary for welfare, it is not sufficient. In addition, Sumner imposes an authenticity condition, which has two parts. I will not go into great detail about these, but they entail that a person who is psychologically happy can nonetheless be worse off than she thinks if either (a) her happiness depends upon false information, or if (b) her happiness is based on values that are not authentically hers.

The interesting feature of Sumner's view is its asymmetry: a person can be worse off than she thinks she is, but she cannot be better off than she thinks she is. Happiness is necessary for a good life. Since you know you are happy if you are happy, you are either doing as well as you think, or (if your happiness fails the external conditions) doing worse than you think. This theory clearly assigns a central role to experiential states. If we assume that an experience requirement simply means making certain kinds of experience necessary for a good life, then Sumner's theory has an experience requirement. This appears to be Sumner's own understanding of the idea, since he describes himself as building the experience requirement back in (1996: 175).

However, if we consider Sumner's view in light of the second definition of experience requirement, we can see that it doesn't build in an experience requirement. Sumner doesn't insist that anything that affects welfare must be experienced. Certain kinds of negative facts, which if known would undermine happiness, can, without actually undermining happiness, make a person's life worse than she thinks it is. In short, states of affairs outside awareness can nonetheless have an impact on welfare. So in the second sense Sumner's view does not incorporate an experience requirement.

As is often true in philosophy, the really important point is not which definition we adopt, but that we see the difference and track it in our theorizing. However, since I think more people understand the experience requirement as the idea that something must be experienced if it is to have an impact on welfare, I suggest to the profession that in future we adopt this definition.

We must then simply keep in mind that it is possible for a theory to give great intrinsic weight to experience without incorporating an experience requirement.

What then of the relationship between experientialism and the experience requirement? To reject experientialism one must think that at least some of the bearers of intrinsic welfare value are non-mental. But it is possible to reject experientialism and still assign a big role in one's theory to experience (as Sumner does). And it is even possible to reject experientialism without rejecting the experience requirement at all. For it is possible to hold a view like the one I have elsewhere called the conditional value thesis, which maintains that the intrinsic bearers of welfare value are states of affairs, but insists that these have value for a person only if they are known (Hawkins 2015). Assessing whether or not such a view has plausibility is beyond the scope of this chapter, and although I have described it elsewhere I do not defend it there. I mention it simply to underscore the point that the rejection of experientialism and the rejection of an experience requirement are not the same thing.

Related topics

See in particular Chapter 9 of this volume, "Hedonism," by Alex Gregory.

Notes

1 I treat "well-being" and "welfare" as synonyms. I assume that theories of well-being (or of welfare) are about a special kind of value, the kind under discussion when we discuss what is good *for* a particular person. I also sometimes refer to this kind of value as "prudential value" and occasionally use the adjective "prudential" to signal a focus on reasons relevant to a particular person's good.
2 The phrase "experience requirement" originates with James Griffin (1986: 13).
3 Two prominent examples of theorists who reject the equation of happiness with pleasure in favor of more psychologically complex accounts of happiness are L.W. Sumner (1996), and Daniel M. Haybron (2008). Though both authors are deeply interested in the nature of happiness, their respective accounts are quite different. Importantly, neither is an experientialist, since neither accepts a simple equation of happiness with well-being.

References

Crisp, R. (2006) *Reasons and the Good*, Oxford: Oxford University Press.
DeBrigard, F. (2010) "If You Like It, Does It Matter If It's Real?" *Philosophical Psychology* 23 (1): 43–57.
Griffin, J. (1986) *Well-Being: Its Meaning, Measurement and Moral Importance*, Oxford: Oxford University Press.
Hawkins, J. (2015) "Well-Being: What Matters Beyond the Mental?" in M. Timmons (ed.) *Oxford Studies in Normative Ethics*, Vol. 4. Oxford: Oxford University Press.
Haybron, D. (2008) *The Pursuit of Unhappiness: The Elusive Psychology of Well-Being*, Oxford: Oxford University Press.
Hewitt, S. (2010) "What Do Our Intuitions About the Experience Machine Really Tell Us About Hedonism?" *Philosophical Studies* 151 (3): 331–349.
Kagan, S. (1998) *Normative Ethics*, Boulder, CO: Westview Press.
Kawall, J. (1999) "The Experience Machine and Mental State Theories of Well-Being," *Journal of Value Inquiry* 33 (3): 381–387.
Mill, J.S. (2005/1861) *Utilitarianism*, New York: Barnes and Noble.
Nozick, R. (1974) *Anarchy, State and Utopia*, New York: Basic Books.
Nozick, R. (1989) *The Examined Life*, New York: Simon and Schuster.
Scanlon, T. (1998). *What We Owe To Each Other*, Cambridge, MA: Harvard University Press.
Shafer-Landau, R. (2012) *The Fundamentals of Ethics*, 2nd edn., New York: Oxford University Press.
Silverstein, M. (2000) "In Defense of Happiness: A Response to the Experience Machine," *Social Theory and Practice* 26 (2): 279–300.
Sumner, L. (1996) *Welfare, Happiness, and Ethics*, Oxford: Oxford University Press.

30

CHILDREN'S WELL-BEING

A philosophical analysis

Anthony Skelton

In *A Theory of Justice*, John Rawls writes that

> we can think of a person as being happy when he is in the way of a successful execution (more or less) of a rational plan of life drawn up under (more or less) favorable conditions, and he is reasonably confident that his plan can be carried through.
>
> *(Rawls 1971: 409)*

In "Facts and Values," Peter Railton writes that:

> an individual's good consists in what he would want himself to want, or to pursue, were he to contemplate his present situation from a standpoint fully and vividly informed about himself and his circumstances, and entirely free of cognitive error and lapses of instrumental rationality.
>
> *(Railton 1986: 16)*

These are prominently offered up as theories of well-being.[1] A theory of well-being provides an account of what is non-instrumentally good or bad for an individual. Such theories track or explicate the prudential value of a life or part of a life, or how well it is going from the point of view of the individual living it.

It may not be obvious that Rawls is offering us a theory of prudential value. He speaks of happiness rather than well-being. It is important to notice that there are two senses of happiness, a psychological sense and an evaluative sense (Haybron 2008: 29–30).

In the first sense, happiness is a descriptive notion: one is happy when one possesses or is in a certain mental state. To provide an account of this variety of happiness one develops a psychological theory about it. In the second sense, happiness is an evaluative notion: one is happy when one is faring well. To call an individual happy in this sense is to evaluate that individual's life or part of her life. To provide an account of evaluative happiness one develops a theory of the nature of well-being, that is, a theory of prudential value.

Rawls is clearly interested in the second kind of happiness or with well-being. His is a theory telling us what is non-instrumentally good or bad for an individual. He is not in the business of providing a descriptive or psychological view. Rawls's theory is distinct from both a theory of descriptive happiness and a theory of the ingredients of well-being.

With this background in place, ask yourself the following questions. What makes an individual's life go well? What is non-instrumentally good or bad for an individual? In answering it, think of someone just like you. The frameworks described above seem like suitable, if not plausible, answers to these questions.

Now, ask yourself another question. What makes a young child's life go well? What is non-instrumentally good or bad for a young child? It is unclear that these views provide suitable answers to such questions. These questions are the focus of this chapter. It considers only young children, leaving older children and adolescents aside for the time being.[2] The focus is on locating a theory of well-being that fits with the abilities and capacities that young children typically possess.

Philosophers have spent surprisingly little time theorizing children's well-being; consequently, there is no meaningful body of philosophical literature devoted directly to it.[3] This is remarkable.[4] The nature of children's well-being is of great relevance to a host of moral, political, and practical questions relating to the treatment of children.

This chapter has three main sections. The first argues that the above views fail to provide accounts of young children's well-being. The second discusses and evaluates some existing views of well-being that are applicable to young children. The third articulates and evaluates three highly attractive accounts of children's well-being.

Philosophers' views fail to provide accounts of young children's well-being

Rawls's view fails to provide an account of what makes a young child's life go well because young children are incapable of framing a rational plan of life, that is, "[a] plan . . . made up of subplans suitably arranged in a hierarchy, the broad features of the plan allowing for the more permanent aims and interests that complement one another" (Rawls 1971: 411). It may be that a child's life must, in some sense, go according to a plan for it to go well. But any suitable plan will depend on, rather than provide, a view of well-being. In thinking about which plan to direct a child towards we think at least in part about what will make her life go well for her.

Railton's view makes sense when thinking about an individual with a mature perspective, e.g., an adult, where difficulties in determining that individual's well-being are plausibly thought to be removable through the imposition of exclusively formal standards correcting for various cognitive and motivational limitations. There is in this case something to Railton's claim to have captured the "range of assessment" involved in judgments about what makes one's life go well (Railton 1986: 11). But does his view capture the "range of assessment" involved in judgments about what makes a young child's life go well? When thinking about what makes a young child non-instrumentally better or worse off from her perspective, it is less obvious that we think only about what might or might not be endorsed by her in the presence of full information and in the absence of mistakes in instrumental reasoning.[5] It is more common to rely, at least in part, on substantive views of what is good for a child in thinking about her well-being. This is due somewhat to the fact that, unlike in the case of adults, a young child is not thought to have a mature or fully developed point of view or perspective that under suitable conditions might credibly fix her well-being. Indeed, the child is thought to have an immature or undeveloped point of view that cannot, it is credible to think, alone fix what is good for a young child. A substantive standard seems part of what fixes what is prudentially good for a young child.

One might reply on behalf of these views that young children's well-being consists in whatever is necessary to putting children in the position to fare well according to them. Faring well as a child might involve doing whatever conduces to having rational plans or informed preferences. Children do like to get an inkling that they are developing and maturing, and there is a sense in which we think things go less well for a child when she fails to progress toward a typical adult existence. The idea, then, might be that a child is faring well to the extent that she is developing toward meeting the conditions set out by these views.

This suggestion faces a formidable criticism. It does not explain why what matters to a child's well-being is exclusively a function of what conduces to making an adult's life go well. The views just considered claim that in the case of an adult one's well-being depends crucially on one's own chosen plans or on one's own informed desires, that is, on facts about the well-being subject him- or herself. Why, then, shouldn't accounts of children's well-being similarly depend on facts about them and their perspective? The suggestion here is not that there are radical differences between young children's well-being and adult's well-being. Indeed, it would be worrisome if views about each of these were in tension with each other. The claim is rather that the development of a theory of well-being for a set of well-being subjects is done best with the nature of those subjects clearly in view.

That the above views do not extend to young children may be fatal to them. Wayne Sumner argues that, to be adequate, a theory of well-being must be general in two senses (Sumner 1996: 13–15). In the first sense, a theory must be able to explain the range of our well-being judgments, positive, negative, at a time, and across time. In the second sense, a theory of well-being must apply to all core subjects of well-being assessments, including young children, adults, and non-human animals. One might argue on the basis of the second sense of generality that, because the views outlined above fail to extend to young children, they are insufficiently general, and thus should be rejected.

This is, however, too quick. There is another option: deny that theories of the nature of well-being need be general in the second sense. We can hold that some theories have a restricted domain. They apply only to some core well-being subjects. Why think, after all, that one theory fits every well-being subject? Why not think instead that there are distinct views of well-being for different well-being subjects and that the applicable view will depend on facts about the sort of being in question? *A fortiori* one might argue that to make sense of the range of individuals to which the concept of well-being applies we must reject the idea that a theory of it must be general in this sense.

Rejecting generality may, indeed, be desirable.[6] It leaves us free to select from a broader range of views, such as the ones discussed, for the case of adults. We do not have to reject a view for the case of adults simply because it does not fit children. We are, in this case, more likely to locate accounts of well-being for children and for adults that fit with our considered intuitions about what faring well involves in each case.

One might complain that we cannot have different conceptions of well-being for young children and adults because it is "arbitrary" to hold a view that limits itself to what is good for, say, an adult human being (Kraut 2007: 106, 109). But there is no reason to think that a view that is limited to adults or to children is arbitrary if there is reason to treat the two classes somewhat differently. If it is true that young children and adults are somewhat distinct from each other in terms of their various capacities, there is nothing arbitrary about thinking they fare well in distinct ways.

One might worry that this reply involves treating young children as separate beings like non-human animals. This is not true. Treating young children and adults differently is merely a reflection of the fact that childhood, especially in its early stages, is distinct in many ways from the other stages in life. It may even be that facts about children make possible certain experiences that are closed to adults. There are different ethical rules for how to treat young children. Why not think that there are different views of what is prudentially good for children?

Existing views of well-being that are applicable to young children

Some existing theories of well-being do fit young children, including hedonism and objective-list views. It is typical that in discussions of them adult well-being subjects are the focus (Skelton 2014). This need not persuade us that they fail to provide accounts of faring well as a young child. Even if we reject them as accounts of well-being for adults, they may remain promising accounts of well-being for young children.

Before evaluating these accounts of well-being, it is worth discussing two other views of well-being that also fit young children but that seem especially unpromising, the "normal functioning" view and the actual-desire satisfaction view.

David Archard advances an account of children's well-being according to which it consists in "the normal functioning of the entity in question" which, in the case of a child, comprises normal physical and emotional development (Archard 1993: 150). He relies on this to explain the harm of child abuse, which he believes must be understood in terms of a "detriment to well-being" (Archard 1993: 150).

This account of well-being may suit Archard's purposes. It captures and explains our attitude that emotional and physical abuse of children is harmful and therefore wrong, for such abuse does in typical cases impede, at the very least, emotional development. All the same, Archard's account is not the only or the most persuasive account of well-being to do so. The main problem is that he provides no account of what "normal" development involves. What counts as "normal" in this context? Archard has in mind good physical and emotional development. This surely has some role in faring well as a young child.[7] However, it is far from clear that this is the whole story about faring well as a young child, which surely involves, among other things, friendship and happiness, the prudential value of which is not exhausted by their contribution to "normal" development.

Indeed, the proper account of what counts as "normal" physical and emotional development seems in part to be established by a view of well-being. In this case, the appeal to what is normal exploits rather than provides an account of what well-being consists in. In most cases in which we lament the lack of emotional and physical development or growth we do so on account of the fact that this lack interferes with well-being by, for example, interfering with happiness or with the pursuit and maintenance of valuable relationships that are satisfying to their participants or with enjoyable intellectual activity.

The actual-desire satisfaction view of well-being states that what is non-instrumentally good for a child is the satisfaction of her desires and that what is non-instrumentally bad for a child is the frustration of her desires. A child's life is going well, according to this position, insofar as she has on balance more desire satisfaction than frustration. The very best life for a child has the greatest sum total of desire satisfaction.

This view faces a serious objection. Many of the desires that young children have are poorly formed or unreasoned. My children, for example, have at various points in their lives wanted to touch the animals in the zoo, to jump into deep water without being able to swim, and to cross a busy road without looking. It is not obvious that the satisfaction of these desires makes them better off. True, many of the desires that adults have are based on poor information, poor reasoning, and on mistakes in logic. This is why it is common for those who defend the desire-satisfaction approach to well-being to adopt the account according to which well-being consists in the satisfaction of desires that one's fully informed self would want one to want in one's actual circumstances (Railton 1986: 11). This view, we noted, is not suitable for young children. We cannot rely on it to defend the desire-satisfaction approach to children's well-being.

Is there another way to save the actual-desire satisfaction view? Perhaps. One might argue that the reason that the satisfaction of a child's desire to touch the animals in the zoo does not appear to make him better off is not due to the fact that it fails to be non-instrumentally good for him; on the contrary, the reply continues, the satisfaction of the desire does make the child non-instrumentally better off to some extent. The reason that it is not good for the child to satisfy the desire is that it is non-instrumentally bad for him to satisfy it all things considered. Its satisfaction conflicts with the satisfaction of the other and stronger desires that he has, namely, the desires not to be mauled by a wild animal, not to suffer, and to carry on seeing the rest of the animals in the zoo. One can save the actual-desire satisfaction theory from the objection that many of our desires are poorly formed not by moving to a fully informed desire satisfaction view but by, as Sumner puts it, bringing "into play the full structure of . . . [a child's] preferences, including . . . [her] priorities among them" (Sumner 1996: 131). That is, to defend the desire view all one need do is bring into view a child's "full hierarchy of preferences" (Sumner 1996: 159).[8]

This defense of the actual-desire satisfaction theory may work when thinking about well-being for adults. It will not do in the case of young children, for two reasons. The first is that this reply presupposes that there is a hierarchy of desires that is reasonably stable and reasonably authoritative. The initial objection could not be deflected without this presupposition. This assumption may ring true in the case of adults. It does not do so in the case of young children. One fact about most young children is that they do not typically have stable preferences or preferences arranged into authoritative hierarchies. We cannot assume, as we might in the case of an adult, that the full structure of her desires reflects the entirety of what is non-instrumentally good for her.

Furthermore, for this reply to work we must assume that the pool of desires at issue ranges over all the matters that, intuitively speaking, make a difference to how one is faring. In short, we must assume that the preference set is robust. Is this assumption plausible in the case of young children? My child does seem to have the desires that are appealed to in the case of desiring to touch the zoo animals. But what about the case in which my child does not want to develop his intellectual abilities? What about the case in which my child does not want to seek out certain valuable relationships? It is not clear that we can appeal only to his desires to show that it would not be good all things considered for him to expand his mind or to seek valuable relationships. That young children lack the desires that might be appealed to in the above cases explains why we encourage them to develop those having to do with the development of their intellectual, physical, and social abilities.

The views just discussed are not suitable accounts of well-being for young children. A more promising option is hedonism. When philosophers do deign to discuss children's well-being they often suggest that it consists exclusively in pleasure or enjoyment or cognate state of mind. R.B. Brandt, for instance, maintains that well-being consists in happiness, which consists in surplus enjoyment, and that "[o]bviously in the case of children, animals, and mental defectives we want to make them happy and avoid distress" (Brandt 1979: 147).

Hedonism is the view that well-being consists in surplus pleasure, and that ill-being consists in surplus pain. Pleasure is non-instrumentally good for a child and pain is non-instrumentally bad for a child. One's life is going well when it has, on balance, more pleasure than pain, and one's life is going poorly when one has, on balance, more pain than pleasure. The very best life is the one with the greatest sum total of surplus pleasure.

Hedonism is compelling: there does seem to be a strong connection between faring well as a child and experiencing pleasure. That this is true explains the emphasis on the importance of having fun and on the importance of innocence in childhood.

Rawls accuses hedonism of being "unbalanced and inhuman." He thinks that the pursuit of all and only the sensation or feeling of pleasure when thinking about one's own good is like an "overriding desire to maximize one's power over others or one's material wealth" (Rawls 1971: 557). It has, in short, little merit.

Rawls's criticism is aimed at Sidgwick. Sidgwick defines pleasure as:

> feeling which the sentient individual at the time of feeling it implicitly or explicitly apprehends to be desirable;—desirable, that is, when considered merely as feeling, and not in respect of its objective conditions or consequences, or of any facts that come directly within the cognizance and judgment of others besides the sentient individual.
>
> *(Sidgwick 1907: 131; also 127, 398)*

He might deflect Rawls's complaint by noting that he denies that there is "common quality" among the states of mind called pleasure (Sidgwick 1907: 127) and that his definition includes "every species of 'delight,' 'enjoyment,' or 'satisfaction'" (Sidgwick 1907: 93).

Indeed, he might adopt Sumner's view of young children's well-being, according to which it consists in affective happiness: "what we commonly call a sense of well-being: finding your life enriching or rewarding, or feeling satisfied or fulfilled by it" (Sumner 1996: 146, 147). On this view, what is non-instrumentally good for a young child is feeling satisfied with her life. What is non-instrumentally bad for a young child is feeling dissatisfied with her life. A child is faring well when her life is on balance satisfying to her. The very best life contains the greatest sum total of satisfaction. This retains hedonism's animating idea, that only one's own mental states are relevant to one's well-being, while capturing all of the affective conditions that seem relevant to it, and (seemingly) all of the intuitions about well-being that hedonism captures.

It is not clear that this view is "unbalanced and inhuman." A proponent of this view might further deflect this criticism by noting that one does not best acquire happiness by pursuing it directly; instead, it is obtained best by aiming at things other than happiness, including, in the case of young children, play, valuable relationships, and intellectual activity. One might recommend this in part because these things are reliable indicators of what will make a child happy and in part because there is a paradox of happiness: the more one attempts intentionally to obtain happiness directly the more unlikely it is that one will get it.[9] This view seems less susceptible to Rawls's charge; it encourages pursuing a broad range of goods and affective states and motivations.

This kind of view faces one serious criticism due to Robert Nozick (1974: 42–45). It is aimed at hedonism, but Sumner's view is susceptible to it, too. Nozick asks us to imagine that scientists have invented an experience machine. It is capable of providing those who plug into it with any range of affective experiences that they might choose. While in the machine they think that the things from which they derive satisfaction are real when in fact they are not. Suppose that we could plug a child into this machine and that it would provide her with more satisfaction on balance than she could acquire in the real world. Would this imply that life in the machine would be best for her?

Nozick believes that it would not imply this. Many agree, thinking that there is more to faring well than surplus happiness. The best life would not be determined simply by summing the magnitude of the mental states that one experiences. But not everyone is convinced. Some think it possible to undermine our intuitive reactions to Nozick's thought experiment and to vindicate the mental state view.[10] Establishing the acceptability of these replies would require a detailed analysis of them. Fortunately, it is not necessary to address them. The better tack is simply to ask why one would persist in defending a mental state view in the face of this objection. For it is possible to capture many of the main claims of mental state views by arguing that happiness, as Sumner understands it, is a necessary rather than a necessary and sufficient condition of well-being.

The main reason that philosophers want to defend mental state views is, it appears, to avoid claiming that possessing certain kinds of things, e.g., knowledge, is good for an individual in the absence of some positive mental state (Sidgwick 1907: 398, 401; Crisp 2006: 122). They accept the strong intuition that nothing can make our lives go well in the absence of positive affect.[11] But one does not have to reject this intuition when one rejects the claim that well-being consists in positive experiences alone. The claim that happiness is a necessary condition is effective in capturing the intuition.

It is, after all, difficult to see what is gained by showing that children's well-being consists in happiness alone. Sidgwick argued for the view in part on the grounds that it was, of those he considered, the only one fit to supply a systematic and "coherent account of Ultimate Good" (Sidgwick: 1907: 406). But this reason for accepting the view is no less controversial than the view itself. It is not clear that this is a compelling enough reason to accept the happiness view.

There may be some peculiarities associated with the view that happiness is a necessary condition of faring well. One may wonder why, e.g., a valuable relationship contributes to a child's well-being when she experiences happiness in it, but not when she fails to experience happiness in it. In reply, one might argue that insisting that happiness is a necessary condition of young children's well-being is crucial to capturing many of our common-sense beliefs about children's well-being and that it is a way to ensure that a child's perspective is registered in thinking about children's well-being. In addition, the view registers the fact that happiness is not all that matters to children's well-being because of the relative immaturity of their perspective and that therefore other factors play a role in determining what is prudentially good for them.

It is not clear, then, that only states of mind such as happiness make a young child's life go well. There appears to be more to children's well-being than happiness. One plausible account is that a child's life goes well when she possesses in addition to happiness certain things in which it is good for her to be happy, e.g., intellectual activity, valuable relationships, and play (Skelton 2014).

It is useful to pause here to discuss the objective-list view. The most common versions of the view are articulated with adults in mind.[12] But it is possible to defend a version of the view that is suitable for young children. One of the attractions of the view is that it can accommodate differences between children and adults in terms of the kind of prudential goods it recommends. Such an objective-list view might state that what is non-instrumentally good for a child is to possess the goods just mentioned. What is non-instrumentally bad for a child is to lack these goods or to have dissatisfaction, disvaluable relationships, intellectual passivity, and so on. A child's life goes well when she has a surplus of objective goods, and it goes poorly when she has a surplus of objective evils. The very best life is the one with the greatest sum of objective goods.

The objective-list view provides a compelling view of young children's well-being.[13] We encourage children toward certain goods, e.g., friendships, physical activity, artistic creation, on grounds that these are fundamentally good for children. We do not face the (perceived) problem that we face in the case of adults, namely, that of dictating to other people what is or is not good for them. That a theory of well-being allows for paternalism about prudential ends in the case of children is a mark in its favor. *A fortiori* we tend to think that not every experience that a child wants is equally good for a child. We seem to have a decided preference for some over others.

A standard worry for the objective-list view is that it seems unable to explain why the things that it says are good for us are in fact good for us when we take no satisfaction in or care nothing for them. This worry is starkest in cases where it says that, e.g., intellectual activity is good for us even though we derive no happiness from it (Fletcher 2013). That we have this worry explains our reservations about Tiger Mothers and Gradgrindian educations.

Objective-list theorists have replies. One is to argue that it just seems correct that the possession of certain goods in the absence of happiness or positive affect is good for you. Richard Arneson argues that, if you think otherwise, you have to concede that a life rich in objective goods, whatever they are, is one that contains, implausibly, no well-being when one takes no satisfaction in them. Surely these goods contribute something to well-being in the absence of a positive attitude or happiness (Arneson 1999: 141).

A second reply involves arguing that only goods that have positive attitudes built into them are good for you. On this view, only goods involving certain positive attitudes—desire, endorsement, and so on—matter to one's well-being, e.g., friendship, achievement, and virtue. This allows the objective-list theorist to say that the things that are good for one are not so independently of one's pro-attitudes (Fletcher 2013: 216).

These are reasonable replies. It is just not clear why one would bother with them. What is gained in showing that the objective-list view is a complete picture of well-being? The proponent of the objective-list view is typically worried about views that entail that something is good for one even though one is engaging in something that appears on the face of it to be shallow, bizarre, or perverse.[14] One can deflect this worry by holding that the possession of goods is a necessary condition of well-being. This allows one to retain the animating idea of objective-list theories, that more than the magnitude of mental states matters to well-being, without having to deal with or accept the claim that one can fare well even when one is unhappy or unsatisfied with the goods one's life instantiates.

This is a more plausible route for the objective-list theorist to take than offering either one of the above replies. The first reply seems anyway to secure only a weak intuition about an unusual case in which our intuitions are unlikely to be firm. The second reply is open to being undermined by a different version of the original objection. For it is not clear that, even if the goods do contain a pro-attitude, it is the right attitude for the purposes of avoiding the problem of being alienated from the putative constituents of one's well-being. One might, for instance, claim that intellectual activities contain a desire but that this is not enough to show that a child's pursuit of it alone would be good for her, since such a good, even with the positive attitude, in the absence of happiness (the right valuing attitude) would not be good for a young child.

Three accounts of children's well-being

Both happiness and the pursuit of things in which it is good for her to be happy seem like important elements of faring well as a young child. Neither of these things alone appears to tell the whole story about faring well as a young child. Perhaps, then, the right position is that happiness and the possession of things that it is good for a child to be satisfied with are individually necessary and jointly sufficient. Well-being, on this view, is a hybrid.[15] In the case of young children, it seems that one's life goes well when one is both satisfied/happy and when one's satisfaction/happiness is experienced in things in which it is good for one to experience satisfaction or happiness, e.g., play, valuable relationships, intellectual and physical activities.[16]

It is not clear, one might object, that this view captures all of our common-sense judgments about what is non-instrumentally good for a young child.

One worry is that it cannot explain why it is beneficial for a child not to suffer because the view holds that, just as well-being involves both happiness and things in which it is good for a child to experience happiness, ill-being involves both unhappiness and things in which it is bad for a child to experience unhappiness. This is a mistake. This worry supposes that well-being and ill-being are symmetrical. However, it is not obvious that an individual who holds the view of well-being above must hold the corresponding view of ill-being. These two notions might not possess the same structure. It might be that for ill-being it is sufficient that one suffer, in which case a proponent of the hybrid view of well-being can hold that it is bad for a child to suffer. To suffer is to fare poorly. To be relieved of suffering is therefore a non-instrumentally beneficial improvement in a child's well-being.

A second worry is that, on this view, if a child has some positive but simple experience which is not taken in something in which it is good to experience satisfaction, e.g., enjoyment in cloud watching on a warm summer day, she is not in any way prudentially benefitted. Yet, it does seem that this experience makes a child, to some extent, prudentially better off. It contributes directly to her well-being.

One reply is to stand firm and argue that such pleasures are not directly good for a child. Joseph Raz, for example, takes this approach to such experiences, which he describes as "passive pleasures" (Raz 1994: 7).[17] He thinks that such pleasures might contribute to one's well-being provided that one takes an interest in them, that is, provided "they fit in with one's active concerns and plans" (Raz 1994: 7). Otherwise, they make no non-instrumental contribution to one's well-being.

One might reasonably balk at the suggestion that it is only in virtue of fitting into an individual's "active concerns and plans" that something makes one non-instrumentally better off. Why think that this is the relevant criterion for determining whether something makes (especially) a young child directly better off?

This is a reasonable response. Nonetheless, Raz is, it seems, on to something. If passive pleasures are not ones in which a child takes satisfaction, it is compelling to think that they make no direct contribution to her well-being.

It is unclear that this provides a complete defense of the hybrid view. It implies that something like satisfaction or happiness alone makes a young child non-instrumentally better off. But this is compelling. After all, what do we say about a world in which there are no opportunities for pursuing things in which it is good for a child to experience happiness, one in which there are no opportunities for play or valuable relationships or for meaningful intellectual and physical activities? It is not unreasonable to say that in this world, although it would not be one in which a young child is faring terribly well, it would be prudentially better for a child to be happy in so-called passive pleasures than to be sad. If so, then happiness is sufficient for well-being.

Accepting that happiness is sufficient for faring well (to some extent) as a young child suggests a different view. According to it, the hybrid provides an account of young children's full well-being or full fare, but that in some cases happiness by itself is sufficient for well-being, though this well-being is low well-being or low fare (Skelton 2014).

This view has its own troubles. One worry is this. Is happiness alone always inferior to happiness experienced in things in which it is good to experience happiness? Suppose a child is choosing between a day full of lots of happiness in experiencing Raz's "passive" pleasures, and a day full of only a small amount of the hybrid, say, some (surplus) happiness in drawing and playing Junior Monopoly. Is the latter clearly prudentially better for the child? This may be hard to accept. If the amount of surplus happiness is great, it is not implausible to think that it is better for the child to experience the day full of happiness in the passive pleasures.

The proponent of this second view could concede that it is better for the child to experience the happiness alone. This is a small concession, for cases in which a child experiences (simple) happiness alone are going to be quite rare on account of the entanglements between happiness and things in which it is good for a child to experience happiness and on account of the fact that we seem to hold (in our reactions to the experience machine objection) that provided we have enough of the hybrid no amount of simple happiness is sufficient to outweigh it. After all, our objection to the experience machine is not that it is not on full blast.

A second worry about this view is that it allows that happiness alone is capable of making a young child better off while (apparently) denying that the possession of things in which it is good for a child to experience satisfaction in the absence of happiness makes a child better off. But, one might think, the possession of valuable relationships and intellectual activity, even in the absence of happiness, makes a young child better off at least to some extent, however small.[18] It is not entirely implausible to hold that intellectual development is good for a child despite her experiencing no satisfaction in it.

A third view captures this intuition. It holds that the hybrid is full fare, but that both happiness alone and things in which it is good for a child to experience happiness alone make a young child prudentially better off, though these are cases of low well-being.

Raz provides a counter to the view that something in which it is good to experience satisfaction makes one better off in the absence of happiness (Raz 1994: 6). He suggests that, while one does not have to reflectively endorse or have a second-order desire for such a good in order for it to contribute directly to one's well-being, one does have to pursue it "with the spirit suitable to the activity" (Raz 1994: 6). By this he means that for something to contribute directly to one's well-being one must pursue it in the absence of "resentment, pathological self-doubt, lack of self-esteem, self-hate, etc" (Raz 1994: 6). Again, Raz is on to something, though it is more compelling to say in the case of children that for something to contribute to well-being it must be in the very least satisfying, for this is what these other, negative attitudes tend to interfere with. This view is attractive in the case of a young child.

Of course, this entails accepting that in a world in which a child cannot experience happiness, but in which she can experience the things in which is it good to experience happiness, she cannot fare well. It may not be entirely unpersuasive to say that this is a world in which a young child cannot fare well and that this is one reason to lament this world. And a child may in this world have elements of the good life, since this might include things beyond what makes a young child non-instrumentally better off.

Conclusion

What is non-instrumentally good (bad) for a young child? This question has been the focus of the foregoing discussion. It began by outlining some views of well-being that are incapable of serving as accounts of well-being for young children. This was designed to highlight that children's well-being has been ignored in the philosophical literature on well-being. The second section of the chapter discussed some views of well-being that do serve as accounts of young children's well-being. It was argued that these are not acceptable views of children's well-being and that perhaps the most appropriate account of children's well-being is a hybrid. The third section of the paper discussed objections to this view. In this context, two other, similar views of well-being were discussed. Both accepted that the hybrid is an account of full well-being for young children. One version of this view allowed for the possibility that in some cases happiness by itself is sufficient for well-being, but that this counts as low well-being or low fare. Another version of this view allowed for the possibility that in some cases the possession of certain goods in the absence of satisfaction was sufficient for well-being, but that this counts as low fare. Each of the views faced some challenges. It is not yet clear which of them is true.[19]

Further reading

R. Kraut, "Desire and the Human Good," *Proceedings and Addresses of the American Philosophical Association* 68 (1994): 39–54, evaluates the desire-fulfillment theory of well-being with special reference to children's well-being. A useful set of papers focusing on the nature of children's well-being and its role in practical deliberations is A. Bagattini and C. Macleod (eds.), *The Nature of Children's Well-being: Theory and Practice* (New York: Springer, 2014). David Wendler, *The Ethics of Pediatric Research* (Oxford: Oxford University Press, 2010) and "A New Justification for Pediatric Care without the Potential for Clinical Benefit," *The American Journal of Bioethics* 12 (2012): 23–31, outline and defend a conception of children's well-being with a view to justifying some non-therapeutic pediatric research.

Notes

1 On Railton's view, only a sub-set of these desires matter to one's well-being.
2 For older children, especially adolescents, a separate treatment seems appropriate.
3 Although Kraut (2007) devotes considerable attention to the nature of children's well-being.
4 For speculation about why philosophers have ignored children's well-being, see Skelton (forthcoming).
5 Rosati (2009: 208–209) agrees, though for different reasons, that Railton's view does not fit young children. I owe this reference to Eden Lin.
6 This is not to deny that generality is a desirable feature of a theory. The point is that it is not a constraint at the outset.
7 For discussion, see Kraut (2007) and Brighouse and Swift (2014).
8 For a similar view, see Heathwood (2005). Note that Sumner is offering this as a defense of the actual-desire satisfaction view as applied to adults.
9 That is, one might defend Sumner by relying on Sidgwick's tools for defending hedonism. See Sidgwick (1907: 401ff).
10 See, for example, Silverstein (2000), Crisp (2006), and Hewitt (2010).
11 For example, pleasure, enjoyment, and satisfaction. In what follows, the focus will be on satisfaction.
12 For discussion, see Skelton (2014).
13 For an objective-list view of children's well-being, see Brighouse and Swift (2014: 52, 62–65).
14 Parfit (1984: 500–501); cf. Fletcher (2013: 216–217).
15 A similar view is defended in Kraut (2007). The view of children's well-being discussed here differs from Kraut's in that it relies on happiness rather than pleasure and it disregards the appeal to human nature and to healthy development. For discussion of Kraut's view, see Skelton (forthcoming).
16 For a detailed discussion of these goods, see Skelton (2014).
17 Raz does not consider children's well-being.
18 This criticism could be directed at the first, hybrid view of well-being.
19 I wish to thank Brian Ball, Guy Fletcher, Stephen Campbell, Anne Skelton, Carolyn Macleod, Eden Lin, and audiences at St Anne's College, Oxford University, at the Carnegie-Uehiro-Oxford Conference in Practical Ethics, and at the Institute of Applied Ethics, University of Hull for helpful feedback on previous versions of this chapter.

References

Archard, D. (1993) *Children: Rights and Childhood*, London: Routledge.
Arneson, R. (1999) "Human Flourishing versus Desire Satisfaction," *Social Philosophy and Policy* 16: 113–142.
Brandt, R. B. (1979) *A Theory of the Good and the Right*, Oxford: Oxford University Press.
Brighouse, H. and Swift, A. (2014) *Family Values: The Ethics of Parent–Child Relationships*, Princeton: Princeton University Press.
Crisp, R. (2006) *Reasons and the Good*, Oxford: Oxford University Press.
Fletcher, G. (2013) "A Fresh Start for the Objective-List Theory of Well-being," *Utilitas* 25: 206–220.

Haybron, D. (2008) *The Pursuit of Unhappiness: The Elusive Psychology of Well-being*, Oxford: Oxford University Press.

Heathwood, C. (2005) "The Problem of Defective Desires," *Australasian Journal of Philosophy* 83: 487–504.

Hewitt, S. (2010) "What Do our Intuitions About the Experience Machine Really Tell us About Hedonism?," *Philosophical Studies* 151: 331–349.

Kraut, R. (2007) *What is Good and Why: The Ethics of Well-being*, Cambridge, MA: Harvard University Press.

Nozick, R. (1974) *Anarchy, State, and Utopia*, New York: Basic Books.

Parfit, D. (1984) *Reasons and Persons*, Oxford: Oxford University Press.

Railton, P. (1986) "Facts and Values," *Philosophical Topics* 14: 5–31.

Rawls, J. (1971) *A Theory of Justice*, Cambridge, MA: Harvard University Press.

Raz, J. (1994) "Duties of Well-Being," in *Ethics in the Public Domain: Essays in the Morality of Law and Politics*, Oxford: Oxford University Press.

Rosati, C. (2009) "Relational Good and the Multiplicity Problem," *Philosophical Issues* 19: 205–234.

Sidgwick, H. (1907) *The Methods of Ethics*, 7th edn, London: Macmillan.

Silverstein, M. (2000) "In Defense of Happiness: A Response to the Experience Machine," *Social Theory and Practice* 26: 279–300.

Skelton, A. (2014) "Utilitarianism, Welfare, Children," in A. Bagattini and C. Macleod (eds.) *The Nature of Children's Well-being*, New York: Springer.

Skelton, A. (forthcoming) "Two Conceptions of Children's Welfare," *Journal of Practical Ethics*.

Sumner, L.W. (1996) *Welfare, Happiness, and Ethics*, Oxford: Oxford University Press.

31

WELL-BEING AND ANIMALS

Christopher M. Rice

Animal well-being has received significant attention over the past several decades as philosophers and the wider public have begun to question the way that non-human animals (henceforth "animals") are treated in contemporary society. Much of this debate has centered on the moral status of animals and on how much weight should be given to their interests in moral decision making. These questions, in turn, relate to debates about practices such as factory farming, animal experiments, zoos and aquariums, and the pet trade. In this chapter, I will not directly address the morality of these practices or the question of how much weight should be given to animal interests. Rather, I will focus on the related question of what these interests are—on what makes life go well for animals. To do this, I will examine several theories of animal well-being.

Most basically, animal well-being concerns what is good for an animal—what is in its interests, benefits it, and makes life go well for it. The term "animal welfare" is often used to refer to this as well. Almost everyone would agree that things such as adequate food, shelter, and socialization are generally good for animals, but different people might explain the value of these things in different ways. This suggests the need for a general theory of animal well-being that identifies what is ultimately (or non-derivatively) good for animals. The search for such a theory raises interesting philosophical issues, but is also of practical importance since there are cases where people want to promote an animal's interests but disagree on what these are. For example, some debates about the proper care of pets and zoo animals hinge on this question.

Theories of animal well-being can be classified as subjective or objective. Subjective theories hold that states of affairs benefit animals because of some positive subjective attitude or attitudes that animals hold toward them (or might hold toward them under certain conditions). In contrast, objective theories hold that states of affairs benefit animals for reasons that are independent of the subjective attitudes that animals hold toward them (or might hold toward them under certain conditions). There can also be hybrid theories that combine both subjective and objective elements. In the next two sections, I will examine some subjective and objective theories of animal well-being.[1] Then, I will discuss some strategies for resolving—or at least understanding—the disagreement between proponents of these two approaches.

Subjective theories

Some of the most prominent thinkers in recent animal ethics have appealed to some set of animals' feelings or desires in explaining their well-being. In this section, I will first consider hedonism. Then, I will consider the preference-based theories of animal well-being that have been defended by Peter Singer and Tom Regan, as well as some related issues that are raised by their views.

Hedonism is perhaps the most straightforward theory of animal well-being. This view, which identifies well-being with the balance of pleasure over pain an individual experiences, was famously defended by the classical utilitarians as an account of both human and animal well-being (Bentham 1988: 310–311, n. 1; Mill 2001: 12). Contemporary hedonists about human well-being, such as Roger Crisp (2006: 98–125), would presumably extend their accounts to the case of animals as well.[2] Many people are first moved to show concern for animals because animals can feel pleasure and pain. Hedonism captures the thought that these feelings are important to animal well-being and so gains support from this kind of sensitivity. Significantly, though, hedonism holds that an animal's well-being is determined entirely by the quality of its mental states. This means that an animal's activities and the external circumstances of its life can affect its well-being only to the extent that they affect its pleasure or pain.

Hedonism is sometimes assessed by considering cases where individuals lead lives that are pleasant but lack other things that are often associated with well-being. For example, Robert Nozick describes the case of the experience machine in which people can plug into a device that produces a series of pleasant illusions for them while they remain passive and unconnected to reality (Nozick 1974: 42–45). This presents a challenge to hedonism since the machine yields a life that is high in pleasure but that many people would not want for themselves. But, should we want this kind of life for animals? We can imagine plugging an animal such as a dog into the experience machine. As in the human case, people are likely to have mixed reactions about this. It may seem less troubling to deprive a dog than a human of active engagement with reality, and even less troubling to plug a frog or a fish into the experience machine. Still, while these animals would experience a continuous input of pleasure in this scenario, it is unclear whether this would be the best possible life for them.

Peter Singer rejects hedonism and instead favors a preference theory of well-being (see Singer 2011: 13). Accordingly, he connects an animal's well-being to the satisfaction of its desires or preferences, which in some cases extend beyond its immediate pleasure and pain. Still, there is a significant overlap between this view and hedonism in the case of many animals. Singer, like the classical utilitarians, identifies the capacity for enjoyment and suffering as what first marks off individuals as having well-being and thus deserving moral consideration (Singer 2011: 50). Further, Singer describes the well-being of many cognitively simple animals in terms of pleasure and pain, presumably because they do not desire much, if anything, beyond this (Singer 2011: 85–87, 111–112).[3]

Still, Singer does stress that some animals have preferences that extend beyond their own immediate experiences. He argues that some non-human animals should be considered persons, mentioning the great apes as good candidates for this status, as well as elephants, dolphins, dogs, cats, pigs, and certain other animals as possible persons (Singer 2011: 100–103). Singer defines a person as a rational, self-conscious being and argues that persons can form desires concerning their futures that provide especially strong reasons against killing them (Singer 2011: 73–85). If the animals just mentioned can form desires for their futures, then they can presumably also form desires for other things that extend beyond their own immediate pleasure and pain, such as the desire to eat certain foods, move and play in certain ways, and interact with other members of their social group. This would expand the scope of their well-being such that it consists in the satisfaction of their specific preferences for the present and future, not just in pleasant feelings of any kind.

Of course, it is hard to determine which, if any, animals can form the kind of complex desires just described. For that matter, there are gray areas about exactly which simple animals can feel pleasure and pain. In these cases, subjective theorists need to rely on empirical data from biology and other sciences to determine which animals have the kinds of feelings or desires that figure in their theories, as well as what different animals enjoy or prefer and how to compare the relative strength of these attitudes.

Beyond this, one challenge for preference theories of well-being is that both humans and animals sometimes desire things that do not seem to be in their best interests or fail to desire things that do seem to be good for them. This can happen when desires are formed in light of bad information, oppressive living conditions, or limited thought for the future. In response to these cases, theorists of well-being have often qualified preference theories in some way. Singer, for example, suggests that a preference theorist might identify a person's well-being with those preferences "that we would have if we were fully informed, in a calm frame of mind and thinking clearly" (Singer 2011: 14). Similar theories identifying well-being with the satisfaction of rational and informed desires have been defended by other thinkers as accounts of human well-being. This raises the question, though, of how to apply these conditions to the case of animals. This is a tough issue since, even if some animals are rational and self-conscious, they are presumably less capable than many humans of reasoning about facts that pertain to their long-term well-being.

Gary Varner has highlighted this issue by describing the case of a cat that desires to go outside but is not able to understand the risks that are present there, such as fleas and the feline leukemia virus (Varner 1998: 59–60). Here, it is not just that the cat is uninformed about these risks, but that it is completely unable to understand them given its limited cognitive abilities. For this reason, it does not really make sense to ask what the cat would want if it were fully informed.

One way to respond to this case would be to insist that an animal's well-being consists in the satisfaction of its actual preferences, or in the satisfaction of those preferences it would have if it were presented with any facts that it is capable of understanding. However, this would lead to counterintuitive results in cases like the one Varner describes. Of course, another option would be to reject preference theories in favor of hedonism or some other account of well-being, such as an objective view.

Yet another possibility is described by Nicholas Agar in his discussion of Varner's case (Agar 2001: 75–77). Agar suggests that this case might be addressed by linking an animal's well-being to not just its present desires, but also to the desires it is likely to form in the future under different scenarios.[4] If, for example, Varner's cat is allowed to go outside and gets a viral infection, it is likely to have many frustrated desires in the future as a result of this. If these are also used in determining the cat's well-being, then going outside may not advance its overall well-being, even if it has no current desire to avoid the outdoors. On this view, it is worth noting that the satisfaction of poorly informed desires would still count toward an animal's well-being in some way. It is just that this value could be outweighed by the frustration of other desires that would arise in the future as a result of this (Agar 2001: 76–77).

Tom Regan presents another account of well-being that is capable of responding to the concerns raised by Varner's example. Regan holds that animals enjoy well-being to the extent that three conditions are satisfied: "(1) they pursue and obtain what they prefer, (2) they take satisfaction in pursuing and getting what they prefer, and (3) what they pursue and obtain is in their interests" (Regan 2004: 93).[5] The first two clauses here connect both pleasure and desire to well-being. In particular, Regan holds that the pursuit and attainment of goals must be both pleasant and desired in order for it to contribute to an animal's well-being.

Beyond this, Regan includes a third clause in his account to further restrict the set of desired states that contribute to animals' well-being, stating that these states must be "in an animal's interests." By this, he seems to mean that they must enable, or at least not compromise, future opportunities for satisfaction.[6] Regan notes that animals have biological, psychological, and social needs which they must satisfy as a way to access key opportunities for satisfaction (Regan 2004: 88–90). Further, Regan stresses that it is important that an animal's various desires be satisfied in a harmonious way over time, stating that:

> The notion of harmonious satisfaction is crucial. It is not enough for an animal to have all the water she wants but no food, or all the food she wants but no water. Neither is it enough to satisfy all her desires on rare occasions. To live well, relative to one's capacities, is to have one's several desires satisfied in a harmonious, integrated fashion, not occasionally but regularly, and thus not just today but generally, throughout the time one retains one's psychophysical identity.
>
> *(Regan 2004: 89)*

Forms of satisfaction that conflict with this kind of harmonious satisfaction are not in an animal's interests, and so fail to satisfy Regan's third condition for well-being (Regan 2004: 91). If, for example, going outside would not be in the long-term interests of a cat, then this would not form part of its well-being. Like Agar's proposal, this restriction helps with many cases in which animals desire things that do not seem to be good for them. One difference is that Regan does not seem to count the satisfaction of these desires toward an animal's well-being at all, since they do not satisfy his third condition for well-being, while the view Agar describes would give their satisfaction some weight while stressing that this might be outweighed by the frustration of their other desires.

David DeGrazia observes that it is not entirely clear whether Regan's theory is subjective, objective, or some of each (DeGrazia 1996: 231, n. 41). On Regan's view, the only thing that directly contributes to an animal's well-being is the pleasant satisfaction of its desires. This gives his view a strong subjective cast. At the same time, though, the requirement that an animal's interests be secured in a harmonious way always operates in the background, limiting the specific desires that can count toward well-being and requiring some attention to an animal's overall biological, psychological, and social good. This requirement helps Regan avoid some counterintuitive implications, but also places limits on the kind of preferences that can be satisfied as part of well-being—limits that are not set by an animal's desires themselves, but by the standard of integrated, harmonious satisfaction that Regan presents.

Objective theories

Despite the influence of subjective theories in recent animal ethics, many thinkers have defended objective accounts of animal well-being. These views typically connect an animal's well-being to its flourishing as a member of its kind, often described in terms of its natural functioning. In this section, I will focus in particular on the views of Rosalind Hursthouse and Martha Nussbaum.

Hursthouse presents an especially detailed account of what it means for an animal to flourish as a member of its kind. As part of her account, she holds that many animals can be evaluated in terms of four aspects, their "(i) parts, (ii) operations/reactions, (iii) actions, and (iv) emotions/desires" (Hursthouse 1999: 200). These aspects, in turn, can be evaluated with respect to how well they serve a number of natural ends, namely, "(i) individual survival, (ii) the continuation of the species, and (iii) characteristic pleasure or enjoyment/characteristic freedom from pain," as well as, in the case of social animals, "(iv) the good functioning of the social group" (Hursthouse 1999: 200–201). Hursthouse's view, which extends the related work of Philippa Foot, is that an animal flourishes as a member of its species to the extent that it achieves its natural ends in the ways characteristic of that species (Hursthouse 1999: 197–205; see also Foot 2001: 25–37).

Hursthouse's account of flourishing draws on the Aristotelian view that things are good as members of their kind to the extent that they exercise certain defining functions of their nature (Aristotle 1999: 8–9). Hursthouse explains that judgments about animal flourishing do not depend on people's desires or values, but on facts about the species in question which form part of certain natural sciences, such as zoology and ethology (Hursthouse 1999: 202–203).

Significantly, Hursthouse does not present her account of animal flourishing as a theory of animal well-being or welfare.[7] Still, her account fits well with many people's views about what is good for animals. For example, people are often concerned when a pet or zoo animal is not acting in a natural way, even if it is otherwise happy and content. Further, several thinkers have employed the idea of natural flourishing in their accounts of animal well-being or closely related concepts (see, for example, Nussbaum 2006: 325–407; Rollin 2006: 94–142; Walker 2007; Taylor 2011: 60–71).

One important feature of Hursthouse's view is how closely it connects an animal's flourishing as a member of its kind to what is characteristic of its species. Hursthouse holds that only "characteristic" pleasure and freedom from pain form part of an animal's flourishing as a member of its kind and that this flourishing involves the pursuit of each of an animal's natural ends in ways that are typical of its species (Hursthouse 1999: 197–205).[8] She notes, for example, that what counts as contributing to the good functioning of a social group will vary among different social animals. Flourishing wolves typically hunt in a pack and defer to a leader, while members of other species might bond with each other by grooming or playing in ways that are typical of their kind (Hursthouse 1999: 201). Her view is that the flourishing of these animals as members of their species is tied to the particular activities that characterize these kinds.

In fact, Hursthouse stresses that an animal's flourishing as a member of its species is tied to the pursuit of its natural ends in ways that are characteristic of its species even when this conflicts with the pursuit of certain of these ends, such as survival (Hursthouse 1999: 204). For example, Hursthouse describes the way in which birds of some species typically put themselves at risk to distract predators from the nests where their young are developing. Hursthouse explains that a member of one of these species that did not distract predators in this way would be deficient with respect to its flourishing as a member of its kind, even if this enhanced its own survival and freedom from pain (Hursthouse 1999: 204). This is because avoiding pain and danger in this way is not characteristic of the species in question, while promoting the continuation of the species by distracting predators is typical of these kinds of birds.

This case presents a challenge for thinkers who wish to use Hursthouse's account as not just a theory of animal flourishing, but also an account of animal well-being. It may make sense to say that the bird that does not distract predators is not a good specimen of its kind, but it is harder to say that this defect is bad for the bird in the sense relevant to well-being. This is especially true if, as Hursthouse seems to assume, the bird in question is not frustrated by its disinclination to distract predators and will not mourn the loss of its young if they are killed. This is an area where intuitions are mixed. If a captive bird is prevented from flying, nesting, or spending time with its young, many people would say that the bird is worse off at least in part because it is prevented from engaging in these characteristic behaviors. Yet, if the captive bird is prevented from defending its young in a way that puts its life in danger, that would be less troubling—and possibly not a loss of well-being at all.

Martha Nussbaum defends a connection between animal well-being and flourishing, but would not analyze the case just described in the same way as Hursthouse. As part of her view, Nussbaum identifies a list of basic capabilities that typically benefit animals when they are exercised. These capabilities—which parallel her well-known list of basic human capabilities—are (i) life, (ii) bodily health, (iii) bodily integrity, (iv) senses, imagination, and thought, (v) emotions, (vi) practical reason, (vii) affiliation, (viii) relation to other species, (ix) play, and (x) control over one's environment (Nussbaum 2006: 393–401). Nussbaum explains that these are objective values and contrasts her account with subjective views that define an animal's well-being in terms of pleasure or desire-satisfaction (Nussbaum 2006: 338–346). While she affirms that certain kinds of pleasure and freedom from pain form part of the capability of "senses, imagination, and thought" and certain other capabilities (Nussbaum 2006: 393–401, especially 396), she also holds that the appropriate exercise of capabilities can benefit animals even when this is not experienced as pleasant or would not be missed in its absence (Nussbaum 2006: 345, 393–401).

Nussbaum explains that the ways in which different animals should be supported in exercising their capabilities are "species-specific and based upon their characteristic forms of life and flourishing" (Nussbaum 2006: 392; see 365). Still, Nussbaum does not hold that everything that is characteristic of an individual's species and relates to a basic capability will form part of its well-being. Rather, she refines her account by appealing to people's judgments about what is good and worth having for animals.

Nussbaum notes that her account of well-being is not purely descriptive, but draws on people's normative judgments. As she explains:

> In the human case, the capabilities view refuses to extract norms directly from some facts about human nature. We should know what we can about the innate capacities of human beings, and this information is valuable in telling us what our opportunities are and what our dangers might be. But we must begin by evaluating the innate powers of human beings, asking which ones are the good ones, and the ones that are central to the notion of a decently flourishing human life, a life with human dignity . . . The conception of flourishing is thoroughly evaluative and ethical; it holds that the frustration of certain tendencies is not only compatible with flourishing, but actually required by it.
>
> *(Nussbaum 2006: 366)*

Nussbaum continues by stating that, in regard to animal well-being, "[t]here is a danger in any theory that alludes to the characteristic flourishing and form of life of a species" (Nussbaum 2006: 366–367). The danger is that humans will "worship" or "romanticize" nature and be unwilling to criticize those aspects of an animal's characteristic behavior that are detrimental to its good or to the good of others (Nussbaum 2006: 366–367). Nussbaum concedes that it is often difficult, if not impossible, to ethically evaluate an animal's life and that it is often best to let animals live the lives they choose for themselves, especially in the wild (Nussbaum 2006: 367, 371–372). Still, her appeal to people's normative judgments gives her theory some latitude in determining what counts as an animal's well-being.

For example, Nussbaum explains that lions have genuine predatory instincts but that these can be satisfied in ways that do not involve hunting gazelles, as would be typical of lions in the wild. In place of this, Nussbaum states that lions kept in captivity can flourish by playing with balls that approximate the size and resistance of gazelles (Nussbaum 2006: 370–371). Given this flexibility, she might also judge the bird described above could enjoy well-being even if had no opportunity to distract predators from its nest. Nussbaum holds that "altruistic sacrifice for kin" can form part of an animal's good (Nussbaum 2006: 345), so she would find some value in the bird's protective behavior when it occurs as part of a rich social relationship in the wild. But, she would presumably judge that a bird is faring better when it can express social affiliation in less dangerous ways, as might occur in zoos or in areas where the bird's natural predators are no longer a threat.

I do not want to overstate the contrast between Hursthouse and Nussbaum here. Although Hursthouse suggests that animal flourishing should be defined by appealing to sciences such as zoology and ethology (Hursthouse 1999: 202–203), these disciplines themselves embody certain kinds of evaluation. This is especially true if, as Hursthouse suggests, experts in these fields typically endorse the four natural ends on her list and evaluate animals by reference to them. The difference between Hursthouse's and Nussbaum's views seems to be that Hursthouse only allows evaluative judgments at this level (when identifying natural ends) and then ties an animal's flourishing as a member of its species to the pursuit of these ends in whatever way is typical of its kind.[9] In contrast, Nussbaum allows evaluative judgments to enter into the process at two points: first in identifying the list of basic capabilities, and second in determining which ways of pursuing these are consistent with broader ethical concerns and what she calls "the well-being and dignity of the individual creature" (Nussbaum 2006: 357).

Still, as noted above, Nussbaum does appeal to a species' characteristic form of life in some way within her theory. It does not, as just indicated, define an exact way in which animals must behave in order to enjoy a life of flourishing according to her view, but it does play a role in determining which general ways of expressing capabilities have significance from the perspective of justice. In this regard, Nussbaum holds that what justice requires of human agents is that each sentient animal be supported in reaching or maintaining a level of capability that is typical of its species (Nussbaum 2006: 365)[10]. Accordingly, she concludes that it is appropriate to provide an injured dog with a special wheelchair if its back legs are injured, but that justice does not require teaching language to chimpanzees (Nussbaum 2006: 363–366). Nussbaum notes that it may not be practical to secure even a species-specific level of flourishing for every animal—especially those in the wild (Nussbaum 2006: 372–380)—but that, when animals' good is being considered, the species norm should determine what is due to them as a matter of justice. In this way, it can serve as an objective standard that governs human interaction with animals. Whereas subjective theories might focus exclusively on pleasure or desire-satisfaction in determining how animals should be treated, Nussbaum favors connecting concern to support for animals' basic capabilities.

Comparing approaches

As is true in the case of human well-being, subjective and objective theories of animal well-being often overlap in practice. Both, for example, would conclude that many animals raised on factory farms have a low level of well-being since they experience significant pain and desire-frustration and fall short of the characteristic flourishing of their species. Still, there are important differences between objective and subjective views at the level of theory and there are presumably some real cases in which subjective and objective theories come apart. For example, there may be some animals that can be kept in small cages with relatively few frustrated desires but which are still prevented from exercising certain basic capabilities of their nature. These animals might score high in well-being according to some subjective theories but low according to objective views.

In practice, animal welfare legislation and those involved in animal industries often adopt a mixed approach to animal well-being. This is exemplified in the five freedoms proposed by the Farm Animal Welfare Council of the United Kingdom, which include both subjective and objective criteria for well-being. These five freedoms are:

1. **Freedom from Hunger and Thirst**—by ready access to fresh water and a diet to maintain full health and vigour.

2. **Freedom from Discomfort**—by providing an appropriate environment including shelter and a comfortable resting area.

3. **Freedom from Pain, Injury or Disease**—by prevention or rapid diagnosis and treatment.

4. **Freedom to Express Normal Behaviour**—by providing sufficient space, proper facilities and company of the animal's own kind.

5. **Freedom from Fear and Distress**—by ensuring conditions and treatment which avoid mental suffering.

(Farm Animal Welfare Council 2009)

These freedoms are not meant to provide a philosophical theory of animal well-being and do not include an account of how to balance concern among the five freedoms listed to determine an animal's overall well-being. Still, it is noteworthy that they include subjective and objective criteria side by side. This illustrates the extent to which both subjective and objective judgments about animal well-being operate in contemporary discussions of animal welfare.

When presented with this set of judgments, and with the subjective and objective theories I have described above, proponents of either approach might try to argue that the most important concerns of the opposing side are captured within their view. For example, subjectivists can suggest that the best way to promote an animal's pleasure and preference-satisfaction is usually to allow it to live in a way that is characteristic of its kind. This would give concern for natural flourishing an important derivative role in their theories and might explain our intuitive wariness of cases where animals are prevented from living in a natural way. Similarly, objectivists can point out that a favorable balance of pleasure over pain and the satisfaction of an animal's most central desires are fairly reliable indicators of natural flourishing and so could play an important derivative role within objective views. The most controversial cases are those in which animals enjoy pleasure or desire-satisfaction apart from their natural flourishing and those in which animals flourish in ways that do not bring them significant desire-satisfaction or enjoyment. As in analogous cases concerning human well-being, a lot depends on how these cases are evaluated.

David DeGrazia discusses another context in which subjective and objective theories of animal well-being function differently and that can accentuate the differences between these two approaches. This concerns the comparison of well-being across species. DeGrazia focuses, in particular, on comparing the harm that premature death causes to typical members of different species—say, a human and a dog, or a dog and a mouse (DeGrazia 1996: 231–257). Here, DeGrazia understands harm as the loss of future well-being so this closely corresponds to the question of which kinds of animals typically enjoy the greatest well-being as they live their lives. In what follows, I will focus on the question in this positive form and so set aside further issues related to the ethics of killing and letting die. Many people agree that humans typically enjoy greater well-being than other animals and that, beyond this, cognitively sophisticated animals typically enjoy greater well-being than cognitively simpler ones (DeGrazia 1996: 232, 237).

In fact, as DeGrazia notes, even thinkers who defend strong duties to animals have often been willing to affirm this general view (DeGrazia 1996: 232–234, 237; see also, for example, Regan 2004: 324). But, as DeGrazia explains, subjectivists and objectivists about well-being will have to support this claim in different ways.

Subjectivists will want to connect their arguments to the kinds of subjective goods that figure in their theories. With respect to the comparison of humans and other animals, they will most likely want to argue that typical humans experience quantitatively more pleasure, desire-satisfaction, or whatever other subjective goods count toward well-being than typical non-human animals (DeGrazia 1996: 237–240, 252–253). In particular, they will presumably want to argue that typical humans enjoy, on balance, stronger or more satisfying subjective fulfillments than typical members of other species (DeGrazia 1996: 238–239). Significantly, though, this analysis will need to take into consideration not only the special highs that are open to humans on account of their distinctive abilities, but also the lows of human life that are not typically experienced by other animals (DeGrazia 1996: 239–240, 252–253).[11]

Objective theorists, in contrast, can choose to focus on qualitative differences between how the objective goods they affirm are realized in human and animal lives (DeGrazia 1996: 243–247, 253–254). For example, these thinkers might argue that humans typically attain objectively more valuable forms of reasoning, social affiliation, and other goods than non-human animals and that this explains their differing levels of well-being (DeGrazia 1996: 243–244). Here, it is not a quantitative difference in how much of something is realized in different lives, but a qualitative difference in the value of certain objective goods.

As DeGrazia notes, there are also other ways in which thinkers have tried to address the issues he raises. One way is to insist that it is impossible to compare well-being across species, or at least decline to do so (DeGrazia 1996: 247–248). Another possibility is to use hypothetical choice situations in which people are asked to imagine lives from different species and choose which they would want for themselves—a method suggested in some way by both John Stuart Mill and Peter Singer (DeGrazia 1996: 240–243). Returning to the subjective and objective strategies described above, both have some intuitive appeal but also face challenges in working out the precise details of how to compare well-being across species. These concerns can prompt defenders of both views to further specify how they define well-being and how they would use their theories in interspecific contexts.

DeGrazia's concerns also raise a more fundamental question about the extent to which theories of animal well-being should be integrated with theories of human well-being, such as those considered in the other chapters of this volume. Some thinkers have argued that it is important for the best theory of animal well-being to share a common structure with a theory of human well-being, such that the two form a single theory and explain human and animal well-being in similar ways (see, for example, Sumner 1996: 14–15; Kraut 2007: 3–8). The alternative possibility would be that human and animal well-being are so different that they do not share a similar structure, even at the level of theory. While it is not entirely clear how much weight should be given to the concern for a unified theory, some degree of unification between theories of human and animal well-being does seem desirable.

If this concern is given significant weight, then it is not necessary to consider animal well-being in isolation from human well-being but would be best to consider both together. This would allow insights from the debate about human well-being to inform our assessment of various theories of animal well-being and allow examples and arguments concerning animals to inform our views about human well-being. Here, animals would represent a special case that could help test and refine our more general thoughts about well-being. Many animals are less capable of rational thought than humans, but also possess special skills and inclinations that are not shared by our species. These factors make animal well-being an important area of inquiry in its own right, but also allow discussions of animal well-being to contribute in a unique way to the debate about human well-being.[12]

Notes

1 While hedonism is variously classified as a subjective or an objective theory, I will group it with the subjective theories in this chapter.
2 Fred Feldman defends a somewhat unorthodox form of hedonism (Feldman 2004), which he believes applies to animals as well as humans (Feldman 2002: 607).
3 In *Animal Liberation* (Singer 2009), Singer also describes animal well-being in terms of pleasure and pain, but this may be part of his desire to remain open to competing moral theories in that work (Singer 1999: 292).
4 This is a dialectical point Agar makes in considering the case Varner describes. Agar's own detailed theory of value is presented throughout Agar (2001).
5 Although some of his points may hold true more broadly, Regan typically uses the word "animal" to refer to "mentally normal mammals of a year or more" in age (Regan 2004: 78).
6 In the text, Regan connects the idea of "welfare-interests" to that of "benefits," which he describes as instrumental goods that "make possible, or increase opportunities for, individuals attaining the good life within their capacities" (Regan 2004: 87–88; see also Regan 2004: 92).
7 One indication that Hursthouse would not directly equate an animal's well-being with its flourishing is her remark that some animals are "individually benefitted" by things that detract from their flourishing as members of their species (Hursthouse 1999: 205).
8 In some cases, she would also consider an animal's subspecies, sex, or social role within a species in assessing its characteristic flourishing (Hursthouse 1999: 205).
9 Hursthouse draws on further evaluative judgments in her assessment of humans and their ways of pursuing the natural ends (Hursthouse 1999: 192–193, 222–224, 228–229), but I confine my remarks here to her account of animal flourishing.
10 While non-sentient animals may have a good of some kind, Nussbaum restricts her account of justice to sentient animals or (were they to exist) non-sentient animals that have other higher capabilities on her list, such as reason or emotion (Nussbaum 2006: 361–362).
11 Rather than merely aggregating all of an individual's subjective benefits, DeGrazia notes that a theorist might give special weight to the highest highs in calculating overall well-being. While this strategy might help to vindicate the greater value of human over animal well-being, DeGrazia worries that it is ad hoc and not well motivated (DeGrazia 1996: 240).
12 I would like to thank Matt Ferkany, Christopher Gowans, Richard Kim, and William Lauinger for helpful comments on an earlier draft of this paper.

References

Agar, N. (2001) *Life's Intrinsic Value: Science, Ethics, and Nature*, New York: Columbia University Press.
Aristotle. (1999) *Nicomachean Ethics*, trans. T. Irwin, 2nd edn., Indianapolis, IN: Hackett Publishing Company.
Bentham, J. (1988) *The Principles of Morals and Legislation*, Amherst, NY: Prometheus Books.
Crisp, R. (2006) *Reasons and the Good*, Oxford: Oxford University Press.
DeGrazia, D. (1996) *Taking Animals Seriously: Mental Life and Moral Status*, Cambridge: Cambridge University Press.
Farm Animal Welfare Council. (2009) "Five Freedoms." Available from http://www.fawc.org.uk/freedoms.htm (accessed 25 September 2014).
Feldman, F. (2002) "The Good Life: A Defense of Attitudinal Hedonism," *Philosophy and Phenomenological Research* 65, no. 3 (November 2002): 604–628.
Feldman, F. (2004) *Pleasure and the Good Life*, Oxford: Clarendon Press.
Foot, P. (2001) *Natural Goodness*, Oxford: Oxford University Press.
Hursthouse, R. (1999) *On Virtue Ethics*, Oxford: Oxford University Press.
Kraut, R. (2007) *What Is Good and Why: The Ethics of Well-Being*, Cambridge, MA: Harvard University Press.
Mill, J.S. (2001) *Utilitarianism*, 2nd edn., Indianapolis, IN: Hackett Publishing Company.

Nozick, R. (1974) *Anarchy, State, and Utopia*, New York: Basic Books.

Nussbaum, M.C. (2006) *Frontiers of Justice: Disability, Nationality, Species Membership*, Cambridge, MA: Belknap Press of Harvard University.

Regan, T. (2004) *The Case for Animal Rights*, 2nd edn., Berkeley, CA: University of California Press.

Rollin, B.E. (2006) *Animal Rights and Human Morality*, 3rd edn., Amherst, NY: Prometheus Books.

Singer, P. (1999) "A Response," in D. Jamieson (ed.) *Singer and His Critics*, Malden, MA: Blackwell Publishers, pp. 269–335.

Singer, P. (2009) *Animal Liberation: The Definitive Classic of the Animal Movement*, revised edn., New York: HarperCollins Publishers.

Singer, P. (2011) *Practical Ethics*, 3rd edn., Cambridge: Cambridge University Press.

Sumner, L.W. (1996) *Welfare, Happiness, and Ethics*, Oxford: Oxford University Press.

Taylor, P.W. (2011) *Respect for Nature: A Theory of Environmental Ethics*, 25th Anniversary edn., Princeton, NJ: Princeton University Press.

Varner, G.E. (1998) *In Nature's Interests? Interests, Animal Rights, and Environmental Ethics*, Oxford: Oxford University Press.

Walker, R.L. (2007) "The Good Life for Non-Human Animals: What Virtue Requires of Humans," in R.L. Walker and P.J. Ivanhoe (eds.) *Working Virtue: Virtue Ethics and Contemporary Moral Problems*, Oxford: Clarendon Press, pp. 173–189.

32

THE SCIENCE OF
WELL-BEING[1]

Anna Alexandrova

Nowadays the social and medical sciences are increasingly focused on well-being. To some extent this is not a novelty. The social scientists, from the eighteenth century onwards, have charged the disciplines of political economy, sociology, and psychology with the task of finding the laws of improvement of the human condition. Still, today is special. Well-being is no longer just a background motivation, but a direct object of study at an unprecedented scale.

Throughout this chapter I will use the "science of well-being" as an umbrella term for all the research efforts that have as its goal, explicitly or implicitly, the study of well-being. I mean this term to encompass fields known as happiness studies, hedonic psychology, prudential psychology, studies of subjective well-being, life satisfaction, flourishing, quality of life, and the like. The science of well-being is practiced as part of psychology, economics, sociology, development studies, and health sciences. Erik Angner's chapter in this volume covers economics in depth (see Chapter 40). While much of this chapter also applies to the case of economics, I will concentrate on other social and medical sciences.

It is no surprise that this whole enterprise is shot through with epistemic, metaphysical and normative assumptions, making it fit for consumption in a handbook on the philosophy of well-being. Sometimes these assumptions are familiar from theories of well-being in philosophy, but at other times, scientific research independently raises new issues. The successes and failures of this science should thus be judged in part on philosophical grounds. But similarly, the philosophy of well-being can be judged on how well it equips the science in its goals. With this in mind, the goal of this chapter is to highlight those aspects of the science of well-being that philosophers should attend to.

I start with a general characterization of the field by identifying five methodological commitments that make the science of well-being what it is today. They are (1) measurability of well-being, (2) the possibility of generalizations, (3) value-ladenness, (4) policy relevance, and (5) construct pluralism. These features raise various foundational questions about this enterprise. For some these questions are fatal criticisms of the science, while for others they are opportunities to reform philosophy in the face of science.

What sort of science is the science of well-being?

At this point, the science of well-being is mature in the sociological sense. There are professional societies, specialized journals, a wealth of publications in prime venues, policymakers' attention and other standard accouterments of a discipline. It is also mature in the intellectual sense in that there are many sophisticated measures of well-being, causal models at many different levels of analysis, and a wealth of knowledge about how to test and apply these models. Thomas Kuhn's notion of "normal science" naturally suggests itself. For Kuhn normal science started when fundamental philosophical disagreements ended and paradigm-based puzzle solving began. Some features of the new status quo in the science of well-being make it look positively "normal." Below I enumerate these basic commitments.

Well-being is measurable

Well-being was not always thought to be measurable, but the science of well-being bets that it is. At least in the relevant circles, the very idea of measuring well-being is no longer thought to be controversial (Kahneman and Krueger 2006; Angner 2013). At this point the debate has moved on to the virtues and vices of specific measures. Some of these measures use objective indicators (such as health or income), others subjective ones (happiness, life satisfaction) and yet others are a mixture between the two. Exactly which indicators are used remains up for grabs in this young field unburdened with rigid common standards. Angner shows that two traditions of theoretical justification of measurement currently coexist—axiomatic and psychometric—corresponding, respectively, to economic and psychological approaches to the measurement of well-being (Angner 2009). In economics the key to the measurement of well-being is a representation relation between preferences and behavior, while in psychology and the clinical sciences the key is a valid questionnaire. Neither approach is uncontroversial. Still, studying the absolute and relative levels of well-being thus measured is a quantitative project at heart and this basic commitment is now rarely challenged.

Yet a third measurement tradition—the experience sampling method—aims at detecting and recording the lived experience as it happens. Going through their day, subjects get prompted by a beeper to rate themselves on a variety of positive and negative emotions, their quality, and intensity. Out of these ratings there emerges a picture of how individuals felt as time went on and their circumstances and activities changed. Using this method social scientists have studied the daily experience of Texas women who famously found taking care of children to be not so pleasant (Kahneman et al. 2004b).

In addition to these newer methods, the old and trusted qualitative tools of anthropology and sociology are alive and used heavily. Its users may resist thinking of themselves as *measuring* well-being, but that just depends on what we mean by measurement. Ethnographies, open questionnaires, and structured interviews aim at detecting how subjects are doing. Recent examples of explicitly ethnographic research on well-being include studies of refugees (Kopinak 1999), families on welfare (Chase-Lansdale et al. 2003), intensive care nurses (Einarsdóttir 2012), and many more. With the rise of cross-cultural studies of well-being, these methods have become all the more prominent and important (Diener and Suh 2000; Camfield et al. 2009).

Notably, even in thoroughly quantitative approaches in economics—for example, measurement of preferences through choices—the latest methods have abandoned the classic economic skepticism about tapping human experience. There is widespread recognition that only *some* preferences and only *some* choices can reveal what really matters to people and that to detect those requires a host of psychological and cultural knowledge, and perhaps even talking to people (Benjamin et al. 2012).

Well-being claims are generalizable

The second sign of normalcy is the development of more or less general causal models of well-being incorporating various determinants and risk factors at biological, psychological, and social levels (see Diener 2012 for references). Well-being is no longer thought of as an idiosyncratic personal phenomenon that does not admit of population-level analysis. Instead, the science of well-being operates on the assumption that the social world has causal laws or at least generalizations that could play the role of laws. These laws needn't apply to all humans at all times and places. They may hold only at the level of community or individuals in specific circumstances (such as caretakers of the chronically ill, or poor single mothers in the UK). The generalizations in question usually relate well-being to a socioeconomic or psychological variable such as unemployment or a personality trait, or an activity, such as volunteering or commuting. These generalizations are discovered empirically following qualitative or quantitative methods. Their causal status is established if not experimentally, then by randomized controlled trials or the instrumental variables approach. One recent randomized controlled trial examined the effect of job training and supplemented income on a group of poor single mothers in the UK. The findings are clear and unexpected: their subjective well-being was lowered by greater professional expectations and greater earning power (Oswald and Dorsett 2013).

Another example is the study of *stability*, or lack thereof, of well-being. Which changes in our environment most affect our well-being and which ones don't? Two purported effects have occupied well-being researchers and captured the public imagination. The first is the alleged human ability to adapt, i.e., to regain previous levels of well-being (judged by life satisfaction or happiness reports), to what seem huge changes in their circumstances, such as winning the lottery, or becoming disabled. The second is the apparent fickleness of judgments of well-being: finding a coin, or seeing a person in a wheelchair, or being reminded of the weather, seems to drastically change one's evaluation of well-being. To explain these effects scientists postulated the *set point theory*—genes and early environment give us a range of happiness to which we invariably return after perturbations.

An example of progress in testing generalizations is the recent updating, or even debunking, of these early claims. Quite apart from the problems with relying on heritability scores of happiness, it turns out that adaptation has a fairly restricted domain and a variable pattern across people. Divorce, serious disability, and unemployment are very hard to get over, while adaptation to the death of a spouse is long but doable (Lucas 2007). And judgments of life satisfaction are far more robust than claimed, so much so that the weather/coin/wheelchair effects that so excited scholars and the public just a few years ago cannot be replicated (Lucas 2013).

Science of well-being at this point is mostly a field science, although some projects in economics and psychology are model-based and/or laboratory-based.

Well-being is valuable

The third commitment of the science of well-being is its value-ladenness: well-being is a normative category, unlike, say, an electron. So the decision to identify a given state as an instance of well- or ill-being is a decision based on a view about what is good for us in a prudential sense.

Ernest Nagel, reflecting a traditional view that science is descriptive, counseled against the admission of this latter type of value-ladenness (Nagel 1961). For "thick" concepts such as efficiency, health, and well-being,[2] he recommended that we separate the "appraising" element from the "characterizing" one and keep our science focused only on the latter, not the former (pp. 490–491). A social scientist appraises when she takes a stance on what well-being is and then uses it to judge whether a person or a community is doing well. On the contrary, she estimates, when, using a theory of well-being, she judges how much a person or a community exhibit the features this theory deems as well-being-constitutive. In the first case, there is a genuine value judgment, while in the second a mere use of a normative criterion to make an empirical claim.

Although a Nagelian value freedom still finds adherents, by and large the science of well-being does not follow his advice. Well-being researchers readily engage in normative discussions, i.e., in appraising. True, some research can proceed relatively value-free—take a range of those emotions that people call positive and find their causes, correlates, and consequences in the environment. Often, however, scientists are more ambitious than this. They have views on whether national well-being should take into account happiness and inequality, as we shall see shortly. They also wish to know whether and which positive emotions are *good for us*: how they enable better functioning both at individual and community levels (Fredrickson 2001), but also whether they harm us sometimes (Gruber et al. 2011). In referring to "better functioning" and "harm," these researchers presuppose a notion of well-being and this is where the substantive normative assumptions enter. Psychologist Jane Gruber documents the negative effects of positive emotions on problem solving, social bonds, and mental health. The title of her article—"A Dark Side of Happiness? How, When, and Why Happiness Is Not Always Good"—reads very much as an appraisal claim.

In the section on three foundational questions, below, I will return to this kind of value-ladenness to ask whether it threatens the objectivity of this science. But for now I merely note that normative claims, albeit not always explicit and satisfying to philosophers, are part and parcel of the science of well-being.

Well-being can be a policy goal

Out of the search for generalizations and the value of well-being arises the fourth commitment of the science of well-being—its policy aspirations and, to some extent, its social activism. This science is often undertaken and recruited to tell us what is wrong with the way twenty-first-century Westerners live and with what they value: from isolation, to consumerism, to the medicalization of grief and sadness. Its founders have positioned this field explicitly as an exercise in policy evaluation and recommendation (Kahneman et al. 2004b; Diener et al. 2008, and others). The science of well-being is, in large part, supposed to show which policies, therapies, interventions, and community arrangements relieve suffering and improve the well-being of all concerned. Some practitioners have been very successful at putting themselves in the policy arena at high levels in Canada, the UK, France, the USA and, increasingly, elsewhere. The movement for evidence-based policy has been a convenient bandwagon to jump on, as evidence about well-being is increasingly sought out and advertised. The proliferation of positive psychology, including Buddhism-based approaches such as mindfulness-based stress reduction, used in armies, schools, prisons, workplaces, and hospitals, is a typical example of the science's therapeutic aspirations.[3]

There are many constructs of well-being

The fifth feature of the science of well-being is that no single conception of well-being persists across disciplines and projects; rather many different ones coexist at once. I call this phenomenon *construct pluralism* and summarize it in Table 32.1.

The three columns in Table 32.1 describe *theories*, *constructs*, and *measures* of well-being. Very roughly, theories are the preoccupation of philosophers, while constructs and measures are the preoccupation of scientists. A theory of well-being is a study of well-being's essential properties. The term "construct" is just another name for an attribute or a phenomenon, in our case the state of well-being in the subjects of a scientific study. Constructs are so called because they are usually unobservable, but have various observable manifestations. Out of these manifestations measures are usually developed.

Table 32.1 Theories, constructs, and measures

	Philosophical theory of well-being	Scientific construct of well-being	Measures of well-being
Psychological sciences	Hedonism	Average affect	Experience-sampling methods, happiness questionnaires
Psychological sciences	Subjectivism	Subjective satisfaction	Satisfaction With Life Scale, World Values Survey, Gallup World Poll
Psychological sciences	Eudaimonism	Flourishing	Seligman's PERMA, Psychological Well-being Index, Huppert's Flourishing
Economics	Subjectivism	Satisfaction of ("clean") preferences	Economic indicators
Development economics	Objective-list theory	Quality of life	Literacy + Mortality + Consumption, Human Development Index
Health sciences	?	Quality of life under various social and medical conditions	Nottingham Health Profile, Sickness Impact Profile, World Health Organization Quality of Life, Health-Related Quality of Life, QUALEFFO
Child well-being	?	Adequate satisfaction of children's physical and mental needs	UNICEF's index, US Department of Health and Human Services, Children's Bureau Child Well-being Measure (three domains of assessment—family, education, mental health and physical needs)
National well-being	?	A consensus on the many values of a nation	UK's Office of National Statistics Measure of National Well-being, Legatum Prosperity Index

PERMA, positive emotion, engagement, positive relationships, meaning, accomplishment/achievement; QUALEFFO, Quality of Life Questionnaire of the European Foundation for Osteoporosis; UNICEF, United Nations Children's Fund.

Since this handbook provides ample information of the theories of well-being listed in the first column, I shall move on straight to the second and third columns.

Psychology

This field sports three traditions corresponding to the first three rows in our table. The first tradition takes well-being to be "hedonic balance," that is, the ratio of positive to negative emotions in a person over time. Nobel-prize winner Daniel Kahneman is famous for, among other things, reviving classical hedonism and adapting tools of modern psychology for measuring the day-to-day experience of life (Kahneman et al. 2004b). This can be done either by experience sampling or by having subjects keep a diary. But, most importantly, it should not be done by asking subjects to summarize their experience with a single judgment about their lives of the kind "How happy are you overall?" People, modern hedonists maintain, inevitably distort their experience, introducing all sort of biases routed in their immediate surroundings.

The second tradition embraces these biases as a feature, not a bug. For them well-being is life satisfaction, i.e., an endorsement of the balance of the many values and priorities in life. We care about lots of things and life satisfaction reflects how we are doing taking them all into account

(Diener et al. 1985). If experience is only one of our priorities, it is no wonder life satisfaction judgments diverge from hedonic balance. The Satisfaction With Life Scale (SWLS), developed by the psychologist Ed Diener, consists of five questions that all invite people to make such a summary judgment. Note that, though I put life satisfaction in the same row as desire fulfillment, the two are not identical. Desire-fulfillment theorists normally define fulfillment as *actual*, not just felt, realization of the person's wishes. The SWLS, on the other hand, can, of course, only pick out individuals' own sense of how they are faring.

The union of hedonic balance and life satisfaction is often referred to as subjective well-being. This combination construct has gained much prominence in academia and policy circles.

Finally, the third tradition identifies well-being with flourishing, taking inspiration from perfectionism and/or eudaimonism. Again, it is not quite the flourishing that Aristotle talked about, but rather *a sense* of flourishing, a subjective version of the theory. But notably, unlike the other two traditions, eudaimonists in psychology understand flourishing not as a unified phenomenon but as encompassing several components: a sense of autonomy, mastery, purpose, and connectedness to people (Ryff 1989). Unlike in philosophical eudaimonism, these distinct components of well-being are derived not from a theory of human nature, but rather from psychometric tests.

As we can see, all of these constructs are subjective, but all in different senses. Hedonic balance requires favorable emotional balance, life satisfaction—a favorable judgment of one's life, and flourishing—a sense of meaning and accomplishment.

Economics

This field has its own two constructs: the orthodox preference-based one used in welfare economics and the capabilities approach in development economics (see Chapter 40, by Angner, for an in-depth look at these). For us the main point is that on the first approach well-being is the satisfaction of preference as revealed by economic indicators such as gross domestic product, while development economists conceive of well-being as access to basic goods or capabilities depending on the precise version.

A non-capabilities but nevertheless objective approach to well-being is put forward by a Cambridge economist, Partha Dasgupta, who proposes the notion of *aggregate quality of life* (Dasgupta 2001). It is aggregate in two senses: first, it represents the state of many people and, second, their quality of life is constituted by several elements. Dasgupta writes: "a minimal set of indices for spanning a reasonable conception of current well-being in a poor country includes private consumption per head, life expectancy at birth, literacy, and civil and political liberties" (Dasgupta 2001: 54). Private consumption is food, shelter, clothing, and basic legal aid. Life expectancy at birth is the best indicator of health, while literacy is the best indicator of of basic primary education. Civil and political rights allow people to function independently of the state and their communities. Each of these is necessary. They cannot be reduced to some one item or replaced by a monetary value, for they may be undervalued by people themselves and hence by the market.

However, current quality of life is not the only thing we mean when we ask "How well is a country doing?" Sometimes we also mean to inquire about what Dasgupta calls a country's *social well-being*. This concept encompasses, along with the current quality of life, the *sustainability* of this current lifestyle—how well does a country balance the needs of its current population with the needs of its future generations? The concept of social well-being is necessary for evaluating policy because planning is a forward-looking exercise and future generations are sometimes included in the calculation of a nation's well-being. A high quality of life at a time may conceal the fact that a community is consuming its resources without making adequate provision for the future, so Dasgupta defines social well-being as a pattern of consumption that strikes the best balance between current and future quality of life. Measuring social well-being, Dasgupta claims, requires a concept of a country's *wealth*. He defines wealth in broad terms, which include the nation's capital: human, intellectual, natural, and manufactured. Importantly, the value of this capital needs to be judged not by the market prices but by its social value. Clearly this is a departure from both the preferentist approach of classical economics and from the overwelmingly subjective approach of psychology.

Health sciences

The health sciences focus on living with disability, chronic illness, or just old age. Here the terms "quality of life" and "well-being" are used apparently interchangeably and their meaning has little in common with the eponymous constructs in economics or even psychology. Rather, well-being here is a combination of subjective satisfaction and objective functioning, where the latter is understood as the ability to go through one's day reasonably autonomously and the standard of functioning is adjusted specifically by age and the specific health condition.

Some studies identify quality of life as general healthy functioning. Measurement instruments such as the World Health Organization Quality of Life questionnaire, Nottingham Health Profile, and Sickness Impact Profile provide a general picture of the subject's health, both subjective and objective, including pain and environmental stressors.

Because these instruments gauge health as a whole they are known as generic. Non-generic measures are developed for people with a specific illness. For example, the Quality of Life Questionnaire of the European Foundation for Osteoporosis (QUALEFFO) is a questionnaire specially developed for people with vertebral fractures and osteoporosis. This questionnaire consists of 48 questions falling in five areas: pain, physical function (activities of daily living, i.e., sleep, bath and toilet, dressing, jobs around the house, mobility), social function, general health perception, and mental function.

Non-generic measures abound. Many aging people care for their spouses with serious chronic illnesses. This is frequently a time of great hardship in the life of caregivers; they are at an increased risk of depression and complications with their own health. Researchers invented the notion of caregiver strain to mark this hardship: sleep disturbance due to the illness of the care recipient, loneliness, lack of control over personal and social plans, family adjustments and arguments, upsetting behavior of the care recipient, his or her loss of the former self, worry, fatigue, and financial strain (Gerritsen and Van Der Ende 1994). Freedom from this strain is then combined with life satisfaction to make a special measure of well-being for caregivers.

Child well-being

The second half of the twentieth century saw a rise in international and national efforts to measure and study the well-being of children. In the social indicators tradition pioneered by the United Nations Children's Fund's first *State of the World's Children* report in 1979 and later adopted by other major non-governmental organizations, child well-being is summarized by a list of indicators that include under-five mortality, morbidity, access to schooling, and other basic conditions of children's functioning. More recent efforts, such as the Child Health Indicators of Life and Development project, conducted as part of a European health monitoring program, identified 38 national indicators grouped within four domains—demographic and socioeconomic, child health status and well-being, health determinants with risk and protective factors, and child health system and policy (Rigby et al. 2003).

In the welfare services tradition, child well-being is understood as the individual child's mental and physical health, education, and permanence in family arrangements (United States Department of Health and Human Services 2006). There are also distinct conceptualizations of child well-being in the fields of developmental psychology, psychiatry, demography, and criminology (see Raghavan and Alexandrova 2015 for references).

Whatever the approach, objective indicators dominate the study of child well-being, with subjective indicators used only for older children and even then only selectively. Although it is hard to find an explicit commitment to a theory of child well-being, all these pursuits betray a host of theoretical presuppositions to the effect that childhood is a special time of crucial development, requiring protection and nurturing.

National well-being

In an oft-cited speech in his 1968 address at the University of Kansas, Lawrence, Bobby Kennedy argued that traditional measures such as gross national product count many of the wrong things and leave out many of the right things that make a country great, concluding that "it measures everything, in short, except that which makes life worthwhile." His concerns are increasingly being taken on board. In 2012 the UK Office for National Statistics conducted a country-wide inquiry called "What matters to you?," soliciting views and recommendations from the public, experts, and communities all across the UK (Self et al. 2012). The outcome of this exercise is a measure of UK well-being that contains both subjective well-being and objective indicators, such as life expectancy and educational achievements. In 2009 three major economists, Joseph Stiglitz, Amartya Sen, and Jean Paul Fitoussi, produced a report commissioned by the then French President Nicolas Sarkozy outlining a multidimensional measure of national well-being that also includes subjective indicators (Stiglitz et al. 2010). Questions remain over which of the three constructs in psychology to use in nationwide measures.

Daniel Kahneman and Richard Layard, along with other eminent economists and psychologists, are pushing for a purely hedonic measure of national well-being—a nation is doing well to the extent that its populace has on average a favorable balance of positive over negative emotions (Kahneman et al. 2004a; Layard 2005). Life satisfaction, which is easy to use and supposedly respects personal priorities better, still has plenty of adherents too (Diener et al. 2008).

A great deal rides on the choice of construct. One recent study has shown that income and economic indicators correlate much better with life satisfaction than with hedonic balance (Kahneman and Deaton 2010). So depending on which measure of well-being we pick, pursuit of economic growth, rather than job protection, becomes a national priority. The UK, avoiding controversy, settled on measuring all three using one question on life satisfaction, one on flourishing, and two on positive and negative emotions.

Two requirements seem to be crucial to a notion of national well-being. First of all, such a measure needs to capture the values and priorities of the people whose well-being it is supposed to represent. Dan Haybron and Valerie Tiberius coin the term *pragmatic subjectivism* precisely for this purpose (Haybron and Tiberius 2012). They argue that, even if one adopts an objectivist theory of well-being, when it comes to well-being policy as a political project one should adopt a kind of subjectivism. Not an actual preference satisfaction view, but a more sophisticated subjectivism: one that differentiates between stated or revealed preference and deeply held values and prioritizes the latter. Because policy contexts present special dangers of paternalism and oppression, governments should defer on the nature of well-being to the individuals they represent. (None of this implies that governments should stay out of promoting citizen well-being.) Second, a measure of national well-being needs to represent a certain level of consensus, not a mere sum of individual well-beings. Together these two requirements explain why in this context, more than in any others, it is particularly important to consult people on their prudential values and to use these views as the most important basis for a measure. (This is presumably what the UK's Office for National Statistics tried to do in their consultation)

On this basis other candidates for inclusion into a measure of national well-being are sustainability, which we have already encountered in the discussion of Dasgupta's social well-being, and also social capital. As argued famously by Robert Putnam (2001) in his book *Bowling Alone*, social capital, a measure of cohesiveness of a community, has been decreasing steadily in the West since World War II: we spend less time around each other, volunteer less, join organizations and societies less, trust strangers less, and so on. Social capital is likely connected to subjective well-being, but even independently of this link we might want to ask "what sort of community are we if we don't trust or relate to each other?," and on this ground alone include social capital into our understanding of national well-being.

Three foundational questions

Let us take stock. The science of well-being is characterized by commitments to measurement, empirical generalizations, value-ladenness and policy relevance of its findings. It also exhibits construct pluralism. Now we can wade into the more controversial waters and pose critical questions about the whole enterprise. I choose to raise three. I don't think of these questions as genuine objections to the science of well-being, though no doubt some philosophers will take them as such. As often happens in the history of science, the practice of science proceeds in willful ignorance of, and without a solution to, the underlying philosophical puzzles. But paying attention to these puzzles is nevertheless a good idea. Thinking of them will enrich philosophy and might even have an effect on the course of the science.

What is measurement if well-being is measurable?

Plenty of worries have been raised about the existing methods of measuring well-being. Life satisfaction judgments require an unrealistic aggregation of a great many factors such as satisfaction with various domains of life, plus the norms of gratefulness, non-complacency, and possibly more (Haybron 2008). Experience-sampling methods ask subjects to put a number to a feeling and then compare these numbers across subjects. Who knows how individual idiosyncrasies about the number–feeling association add up in practice? Are errors washed away or multiplied (Wilkinson 2007; Gilbert 2009)? Neither the life satisfaction nor the happiness-based approaches engage subjects in a real open conversation that allows them to set the agenda about their own well-being (McClimans 2010). Finally, the very idea of psychological and social measurement, as a procedure for assigning numbers to states, can be challenged (Michell 1999).

To answer these and other such worries we need an account of measurement that deals explicitly with the sort of controversies that arise when thick concepts with uncertain boundaries, such as health, well-being, and freedom, enter into the realm of science. The orthodox accounts are the representational theory of measurement in economics and the psychometric tradition in psychology and medicine. Serious worries have been raised about their ability to answer the objections in question (Borsboom 2005). Alternatives are still in their infancy (Cartwright and Bradburn 2011). However they turn out, worries will remain about whether this is truly measurement as legitimate as measurement of time or temperature, for example.

Can the science of well-being be objective?

The science of well-being is value-laden in a special way: to characterize a phenomenon under study is to take a normative stance on the nature of well-being. Value-ladenness of this sort raises difficult problems: can a science whose central category is normative still retain its objectivity? Can it avoid becoming merely a political tool? Can it retain the primacy of empirical evidence? Making progress on these issues requires a theory of objectivity. Recently philosophers of science in the feminist and social epistemology traditions have formulated accounts of objectivity friendly to values. It is now thought that political, moral, and social ideals have a place in the choice of research agenda, choice of methodology, choice of the required levels of confirmation, let alone the traditional requirements that scientific research does not hurt, abuse, or deceive its subjects (Anderson 2004; Douglas 2009; Kitcher 2011). When science is practiced in a pluralistic community with the right venues and attitude to criticism, values do not threaten objectivity, so long as scientists avoid distorting evidence to suit their values (Longino 1990; Kourany 2003; Lacey 2005).

However, it is not clear that these principles of objectivity are sufficient for securing objectivity of the science of well-being. Indeed, it is not clear what an objectivity of an enterprise in which values are an essential and central part would amount to.

One option is to follow Nagel and insist that these normative discussions should be kept out of the science of well-being. They are part of ethics and politics, while the science should study only *what people call* "well-being," much like anthropologists might study what people call "morality." Such a proposal is too restrictive in my view: the very acts of measuring well-being and validating these measures, let alone applying the results of these measures for policy, require value-based decisions. The science of well-being does not even get off the ground without them. There are lots of things people might call well-being, too many to study them all, and the decision as to which ones of them to concentrate on must be a value-based decision. The value-free ideal also requires an artificial and impractical separation of pure and applied science, as it forces, say, a developmental psychologist to study only what people call child well-being but not what is actually good for children. Doesn't a developmental psychologist know a lot about what's good for children in virtue of her expertise?

A better option in my view is to embrace the values, but develop principles to ensure that the science does not impose objectionable conceptions of well-being on the concerned subjects and policymakers. Objectivity about prudential values would have to be part of scientific objectivity. But this story is yet to be told.

Is construct pluralism a mistake?

Taken at face value, construct pluralism appears to show that the science of well-being operates with several different notions of well-being and no single theory to direct when to use each. Sometimes there just simply isn't a well-worked-out theory behind the constructs, as the question marks in the first column of Table 32.1 indicate. At other times, constructs are loosely inspired by philosophical theories such as hedonism, subjectivism, eudaimonism, and Rawlsian primary goods. But these theories do not function as philosophers would normally expect. Rather than specifying the essential constituents of well-being, in the current set-up they are used as toolboxes, selectively and opportunistically. A psychiatrist wants to develop a flourishing measure, so she turns to Aristotle, and so on.

This setup is a challenge to the status quo in philosophy. For the most part, philosophers do not think of themselves as engaging in mere conceptual exploration of different notions of well-being; rather they argue about what well-being is, ultimately and all things considered. They disagree about what it is and this disagreement is supposed to be resolvable. If so, either construct pluralism stays or the status quo in philosophy stays, but not both. Those of us with naturalistic intuitions take the peaceful coexistence of distinct notions of well-being in the sciences as a cause to abandon the philosophers' grand dream of the single correct theory of well-being.

Or perhaps there is a way of reconciling the philosophical and the scientific project. Perhaps there is a single theory, unrepresented in my table, that regulates which constructs are chosen for which contexts and for what reasons. Right now the literature is silent on what this theory might be. The viability of this option depends on the philosophers' willingness to start engaging with scientific practice in a serious way.

Notes

1 This chapter features some material previously published in Alexandrova (2012, 2014, 2015).
2 Nagel did not use this example, nor did he use the expression "thick concepts" later popularized by Bernard Williams. Thick concepts (shame, guilt, wisdom), unlike thin ones (good, right), are known for the entanglement of normative and descriptive content. For more on their role in the science of well-being, see Tiberius (2013). The notion of thick concepts is now fairly mainstream in philosophy, but their characterization is far from uncontroversial (Kirchin 2013).
3 For examples see the work by Martin Seligman and Felicia Huppert, among others.

Bibliography

Alexandrova, A. (2012) "Well-being as an Object of Science," *Philosophy of Science* 79(5): 678–689.
Alexandrova, A. (2014) "Well-being," in Cartwright, N. and Montuschi, E. (eds.) *Philosophy of Social Science: A New Introduction*, Oxford: OUP, pp. 9–30.
Alexandrova, A. (2015) "Well-being and Philosophy of Science," *Philosophy Compass* 10(3): 219–231.
Anderson, E. (2004) "Uses of Value Judgments in Science: A General Argument, with Lessons from a Case Study of Feminist Research on Divorce," *Hypatia* 19(1): 1–24.
Angner, E. (2009) "Subjective Measures of Well-being: Philosophical Perspectives," in H. Kincaid and D. Ross (eds.), *The Oxford Handbook of Philosophy of Economics*, Oxford: Oxford University Press. pp. 560–579.
Angner, E. (2013) "Is it Possible to Measure Happiness?" *European Journal for Philosophy of Science* 3(2): 221–240.
Benjamin, D.J., Heffetz, O., Kimball, M.S. and Szembrot, N. (2012) "Beyond Happiness and Satisfaction: Toward Well-Being Indices Based on Stated Preference." *NBER Working Paper* No. 18374.
Borsboom, D. (2005) *Measuring the Mind: Conceptual Issues in Contemporary Psychometrics*, Cambridge: Cambridge University Press.
Camfield, L., Crivello, G. and Woodhead, M. (2009) "Wellbeing Research in Developing Countries: Reviewing the Role of Qualitative Methods," *Social Indicators Research* 90(1): 5–31.
Cartwright, N.D. and Bradburn, N. (2011) "A Theory of Measurement," *The Importance of Common Metrics for Advancing Social Science Theory and Research: Proceedings of the National Research Council Committee on Common Metrics*, pp. 53–70.
Chase-Lansdale, P.L., Moffitt, R.A., Lohman, B.J., Cherlin, A.J., Levine Coley, R., Pittman, L.D., Roff, J. and Votruba-Drzal, E. (2003) "Mothers' Transitions from Welfare to Work and the Well-being of Preschoolers and Adolescents," *Science* 299(5612): 1548–1552.
Dasgupta, P. (2001) *Human Well-Being and the Natural Environment*, Oxford: Oxford University Press.
Diener, E. (2012) "New Findings and Future Directions for Subjective Well-being Research," *American Psychologist* 67(8): 590.
Diener, E.D., Emmons, R.A., Larsen, R.J., and Griffin, S. (1985) "The Satisfaction with Life Scale," *Journal of Personality Assessment* 49(1): 71–75.
Diener, E. and Suh E.M. (eds.) (2000) *Culture and Subjective Well-being*, Boston, MA: MIT Press.
Diener, E., Lucas, R., Schimmack, U. and Helliwell, J. (2008) *Well-being for Public Policy*, New York: Oxford University Press.

Douglas, H. (2009) *Science, Policy and the Value Free Ideal*, Pittsburgh, PA: Pittsburgh University Press.

Einarsdóttir, J. (2012) "Happiness in the Neonatal Intensive Care Unit: Merits of Ethnographic Fieldwork," *International Journal of Qualitative Studies on Health and Well-being* 7: 1–9.

Fredrickson, B.L. (2001) "The Role of Positive Emotions in Positive Psychology: The Broaden-and-build Theory of Positive Emotions," *American Psychologist*, 56(3): 218.

Gerritsen, P. and Van Der Ende, P. (1994) "The Development of a Care-giving Burden Scale," *Age and Ageing* 23(6): 483–491.

Gilbert, D. (2009) *Stumbling on Happiness*, New York: Random House.

Gruber, J., Mauss, I.B. and Tamir, M. (2011) "A Dark Side of Happiness? How, When, and Why Happiness is Not Always Good," *Perspectives on Psychological Science*, 6(3): 222–233.

Haybron, D.M. (2008) *The Pursuit of Unhappiness: The Elusive Psychology of Well-Being*, New York: Oxford University Press.

Haybron D. and Tiberius, V. (2012) "The Normative Foundations of Well-being Policy," The Papers on Economics and Evolution, 1202, Evolutionary Economics Group. Jena: Max Planck Institute. https://papers.econ.mpg.de/evo/discussionpapers/2012-02.pdf.

Kahneman, D. and Deaton, A. (2010) "High Income Improves Evaluation of Life but not Emotional Well-being," *PNAS* 107(38): 16489–16493.

Kahneman, D. and Krueger, A.B. (2006) "Developments in the Measurement of Subjective Well-being," *The Journal of Economic Perspectives* 20(1): 3–24.

Kahneman, D., Krueger, A., Schkade, D., Schwartz, N. and Stone, A. (2004a) "Toward National Well-Being Accounts," *American Economic Review* 94: 429–434.

Kahneman, D., Krueger, A.B., Schkade, D.A., Schwarz, N. and Stone, A.A. (2004b) "A Survey Method for Characterizing Daily Life Experience: The Day Reconstruction Method," *Science* 306(5702): 1776–1780.

Kincaid, H., Dupre, J. and Wylie, A. (eds) (2007) *Value-Free Science? Ideals and Illusions*, Oxford: Oxford University Press.

Kirchin, S. (ed.) (2013) *Thick Concepts*, Oxford: OUP.

Kitcher, P. (2011). *Science in a Democratic Society*, Amherst, NY: Prometheus Books.

Kopinak, J.K. (1999) "The Use of Triangulation in a Study of Refugee Well-being," *Quality and Quantity* 33(2): 169–183.

Kourany, J.A. (2003) "A Philosophy of Science for the Twenty-First Century," *Philosophy of Science* 70(1): 1–14.

Lacey, H. (2005) *Values and Objectivity in Science: The Current Controversy About Transgenic Crops*, Lanham, MD: Lexington Books.

Layard, R. (2005) *Happiness: Lessons from a New Science*, London: Penguin.

Longino, H.E. (1990) *Science as Social Knowledge: Values and Objectivity in Scientific Inquiry*, Princeton: Princeton University Press.

Lucas, R.E. (2007) "Adaptation and the Set-Point Model of Subjective Well-Being Does Happiness Change After Major Life Events?" *Current Directions in Psychological Science* 16(2): 75–79.

Lucas, R.E. (2013) "Does Life Seem Better on a Sunny Day? Examining the Association Between Daily Weather Conditions and Life Satisfaction Judgments," *Journal of Personality and Social Psychology* 104(5): 872–884.

McClimans, L. (2010) "A Theoretical Framework for Patient-reported Outcome Measures," *Theoretical Medicine and Bioethics* 31(3): 225–240.

Michell, J. (1999) *Measurement in Psychology*, Cambridge: Cambridge University Press.

Nagel, E. (1961) *The Structure of Science: Problems in the Logic of Scientific Explanation*, New York: Harcourt, Brace & World.

Nussbaum, M. and Sen, A. (1993) *The Quality of Life*, Oxford: Oxford University Press.

Oswald, A. and Dorsett, R. (2013) "In-Work Benefits and Human Happiness: A Large Randomized Experiment," presented at Well-being and Preferences Workshop, Collège d'Etudes Mondiales, Paris, France.

Putnam, R. D. (2001) *Bowling Alone: The Collapse and Revival of American Community*, New York: Simon and Schuster.

Raghavan, R. and Alexandrova, A. (2015) "Towards a Theory of Child Well-being," *Social Indicators Research* 121(3): 887–902.

Rigby, M.J., Köhler, L.I., Blair, M.E. and Metchler, R. (2003) "Child Health Indicators for Europe: A Priority for a Caring Society," *The European Journal of Public Health* 13(3): 38–46.

Ryff, C. (1989) "Happiness is Everything, or is it? Explorations on the Meaning of Psychological Wellbeing," *Journal of Personality and Social Psychology* 57(6): 1069–1081.

Self, A., Thomas, J. and Randall, C. (2012) *Measuring National Well-being: Life in the UK, 2012,* London: Office of National Statistics.

Stiglitz, J.E., Sen, A. and Fitoussi, J.P. (2010) *Report by the Commission on the Measurement of Economic Performance and Social Progress*, Paris: Commission on the Measurement of Economic Performance and Social Progress.

Tiberius, V. (2013) "Thick Theorizing: on the Division of Labor between Moral Philosophy and Positive Psychology." In Kirchin, S. (ed.) (2013) *Thick Concepts*, Oxford: OUP, p. 217.

UNICEF (1979) *The State of the World's Children,* New York, NY, UNICEF.

United States Department of Health and Human Services (2006) Administration for Children and Families, Children's Bureau. *Children and Family Services Reviews: Procedures Manual,* Washington, DC: United States Department of Health and Human Services.

Wilkinson, W. (2007) "In Pursuit of Happiness Research: Is it Reliable? What Does it Imply for Policy?" Cato Institute Policy Analysis No. 590, Washington, DC: Cato Institute.

33

THE CONCEPT OF WELL-BEING

Stephen M. Campbell

When contemporary philosophers write about well-being, they are typically preoccupied with the search for the best *substantive theory of well-being*. Substantive theories of well-being purport to tell us what ultimately makes something good or bad for an individual and, more broadly, what makes a life go well or poorly for the one who is living it. Hedonists tell us that it all comes down to pleasure and pain. Desire-fulfillment theorists say it is the fulfillment of our actual or idealized desires. Objective-list theorists claim that it is a plurality of things, some of which need not resonate with the person who receives them. Perfectionists maintain that it is a matter of developing and exercising one's natural capacities. And, of course, a range of other theories have been proposed and discussed.

To properly engage with this debate, one needs to have some grasp of what these philosophers take themselves to be offering theories of. What do philosophers have in mind when they talk about "well-being"? Being clear on the *concept of well-being* is important for at least two reasons. First, it is crucial for comprehending the very content of well-being theories. To understand what the hedonist is claiming about well-being, it is not enough to know how pleasure and pain are being understood. One must also have some understanding of what well-being itself is supposed to be. If we have no pre-theoretical understanding of this, we will lack any clear sense of what distinguishes hedonism about well-being from various other hedonisms (e.g., hedonistic theories of value, of happiness, and of motivation), perfectionism about well-being from other forms of perfectionism, and so on. Second, clarifying the concept of well-being is important because it will provide insight into the most effective methods for adjudicating between competing theories of well-being.

This chapter concerns the concept at the heart of contemporary philosophical discussions of well-being. I begin by reviewing what philosophers standardly say to clarify the topic of well-being. This provides a rough picture of what they take well-being to be. The next section distinguishes two ways of proceeding. The first is to begin the search for the best substantive theory of well-being; the second is to seek an analysis that will provide us with a sharper picture of well-being. In the following section, I examine four analyses. I then discuss two challenges to the assumption that there is a single, coherent topic under discussion in the philosophical literature on well-being. The chapter closes with some reflections on the implications of those challenges.

The standard picture of well-being

Most philosophical essays and books on well-being proceed in two stages. At the first stage, the author provides some clarifications about well-being so that readers will have a clear enough sense of the subject matter. At the second stage, the author moves into a discussion of substantive theories of well-being with the ultimate goal of making some progress toward identifying the best theory. Let us review what philosophers most commonly say at the first stage.

The most popular method for clarifying the topic of well-being is to highlight a range of associated terms and phrases. Well-being is often discussed under the heading of *welfare, self-interest, one's interests, one's advantage, one's good, prudential value, quality of life, flourishing,* or *the good life.* Things that make a positive contribution to your level of well-being are things that are *good for you, benefit* you, have *prudential value* for you, and make you *better off.* Things that have a negative impact on your well-being are *bad for you, harm* you, have *prudential disvalue* for you, and make you *worse off.* Your well-being is a matter of *how well you are doing, how well things are going for you,* or *how well your life is going for you.* It is what you attend to when asking yourself "What's in it for *me?*"

What is *good for you* should be distinguished from what is *good* in an unqualified way (i.e., good *simpliciter,* impersonally good, good absolutely). To say that something is good *simpliciter* is to say that it makes the world a better place and, perhaps also, is desirable in the sense of being fittingly or appropriately desired. Saying that *x* is good does not bring to light a special relationship between *x* and any individual in particular, nor does it imply that any particular person will be benefited by *x.* In contrast, to say that *x* is good for Sam implies that Sam stands in a special relationship to *x:* it is something that benefits *him* and improves *his* well-being. The concept of well-being thus involves a kind of "subject-relativity" that is lacking in the concept of good *simpliciter.*[1]

Just as we must take care to distinguish the concepts of good for and good, so too must we distinguish the concept of a *prudentially good life*—a life high in well-being, a life that goes well for the one who lives it—from a range of other concepts.[2] Consider some other types of "good lives":

- an *impersonally good life*: a life that directly or indirectly contributes much good *simpliciter* to the world;
- a *morally good life*: a life that exemplifies moral virtue and behavior;
- a *spiritually good life*: a life in accordance with a religious ideal or in which one achieves deep connection with a spiritual reality;
- an *aesthetically good life*: a life of artistic achievement or aesthetic appreciation;
- a *perfectionistically good life*: a life in which one successfully develops or perfects one's nature;
- an *admirable life*: a life in which one merits admiration;
- a *choiceworthy life*: a life that is worth choosing or aiming to have.

Philosophers of well-being generally agree that these seven concepts are all distinct from the concept of a prudentially good life. This does not close off the possibility that some of these concepts pick out the same type of life. For instance, suppose that developing and perfecting our nature is the only thing that is good for human beings. This would mean that, given any set of possible lives, the prudentially best lives are the perfectionistically best lives. This is just what perfectionists about well-being claim. Even so, there are two independent concepts in play. That is why the perfectionist's assertion is an interesting and controversial substantive claim rather than a conceptual truth that everyone should accept.

The concept of well-being is widely agreed to be related to various concepts, attitudes, and emotions.[3] Well-being is what an *egoist* or purely *selfish* person always tries to promote for herself, and what the *altruist* tries to promote for others. It is what one knowingly fails to promote for oneself when engaging in *self-sacrifice*. It is what one tries to promote for another against her wishes when acting *paternalistically*. It is what is affected, for better or for worse, when one has *good or bad luck*. It is something that we seek to affect when we *reward* and *punish*. *Caring* or *having concern* for someone involves wanting what is good for that person. Having *ill-will* and *malice* toward others involves desiring what is bad for them. *Pity* is an emotion that is responsive to the perception that someone is doing poorly in some respect. *Envy* is a response to the perception that another is doing better than oneself.

It is generally assumed that, whatever well-being turns out to be, it will be something with great personal and moral significance.[4] It is something that is worth promoting for ourselves, for our loved ones, and even for strangers. Most moral and political theories take well-being into consideration in some form or other. Utilitarianism and other "welfarist" theories hold that well-being is the only thing that matters. Most other theories take well-being to be one very important value among others. Since well-being and harm are conceptually related, well-being plays a role in deontological views that place restrictions on harming others or imposing risk of harm to others.

These are the most common ways in which philosophers try to clarify the topic of well-being. These clarifications comprise what I will henceforth call *the standard picture of well-being*.

Two ways forward

The standard picture is fuzzy in certain respects. Although it clarifies some aspects of well-being, other important aspects remain obscure. Consider two examples:

1. *Scope*. What sorts of beings have a well-being? It is not uncommon to hear talk of what is good or bad for plants, cultures, corporations, nations, the economy, and the environment. Are these entities capable of being benefited and harmed, or should we instead interpret welfarist language applied to some or all of these things as merely metaphorical?[5]
2. *Normativity*. What, if anything, is the normative upshot of well-being? If the occurrence of some event *e* would be very bad for me, what normative implications does this have? Do I thereby have a special "prudential" or "self-interested" reason, possessed by no one else, to desire that *e* not occur? Or do facts about well-being only generate reasons that apply more broadly?[6]

The standard clarifications about well-being do not shed much light on these and many other questions about well-being. Thus, from what has been said so far, there is still some mystery surrounding our topic. If our ultimate goal is to gain insight into the nature of well-being and to identify the best substantive theory of well-being, how should we proceed?

One approach is to move directly from the standard picture into the search for the best theory. Call this the *substantive theory strategy*. Most philosophers of well-being have opted for this strategy. Armed with our rough sense of what well-being is, they have presented arguments for and against hedonism, desire-fulfillment theory, perfectionism, objective-list theory, and various other theories of well-being. There is room for debate as to whether this is the most promising strategy. On the one hand, it might seem counterproductive to throw ourselves into the project of answering the question "What is the best theory of well-being?" at this stage. Lacking a clear understanding of what is being asked, there is the risk that our attempts to defend and articulate theories of well-being will ultimately prove to be wasted effort. On the other hand, sometimes the best way to gain clarity on a question is to start trying to answer it.[7] Even if we are not crystal clear on what well-being is at the outset, it is likely that an ongoing investigation into different theories will eventually yield insights about our topic.

An alternative approach is to postpone the search for the best substantive theory until we arrive at a sharper picture of well-being and prudential value. We may call this the *analysis strategy*, since it has most often taken the form of defending some analysis of prudential value. There are different types of analysis. A traditional *conceptual analysis* will seek to provide conditions that are both necessary and sufficient for the application of our concept of prudential value. This might be a worthwhile approach if there is more to our concept of well-being than is revealed by the standard picture. However, if the philosophical concept of well-being is as fuzzy and indeterminate as it appears to be, a straightforward conceptual analysis may do little to illuminate the nature of well-being. A *revisionist conceptual analysis*, on the other hand, seeks to modify or replace our current concept of prudential value. Presumably, this revision will be motivated by the fact that the revised concept is more precise, sufficiently close to our original concept, and well (if not better) suited to play some or all of the roles associated with that concept. A *property analysis* seeks to provide insight into the property to which our concept refers. Like revisionist conceptual analyses, property analyses of well-being tend to move beyond the limits of our current concept of prudential value. However, they also move beyond the focus on our concept of well-being and make claims about well-being itself.

Four analyses of prudential value

What would a plausible analysis of well-being look like? Various proposals have been made in recent years.[8] In this section, I discuss four analyses, with special attention to their implications for the scope and normativity of well-being.[9]

The rational care analysis

The most widely discussed proposal in the well-being literature is Stephen Darwall's rational care analysis.[10] This analysis centers around the insight that caring for someone, whether ourselves or another, involves wanting that individual to fare well. Insofar as I care about you, I will tend to desire things that are good for you and hope that you are not subjected to harm. However, it would be a mistake to analyze well-being in terms of what people *actually* desire for themselves or others out of concern. Such desires are often misguided due to faulty reasoning or misinformation. Plus, there may be some unfortunate people or animals who are not loved or cared for by anyone, and we do not want to claim that nothing is good or bad for such individuals. Darwall's ingenious move is to introduce two normative concepts into the analysis of prudential value. What is good for you, he suggests, is what people have *reason* to want for you provided that you are *worthy* of care. More formally, we may state his proposal as follows:

The rational care analysis

p is good for S = if S is worthy of care, then there is reason to desire p out of care for S.

p is bad for S = if S is worthy of care, then there is reason to want not-p out of care for S.[11]

This analysis has the ring of truth to it, and it seems to yield a sharper understanding of the scope and normativity of well-being. What sorts of beings have a well-being? Any type of being for which we might desire things out of concern for them. On the face of it, this seems to allow that plants, animals, and people have a well-being. Perhaps the circle of inclusion can be drawn even wider than this, depending on what the attitude of care allows. What is the normative upshot of prudential value on this view? The rational care analysis yields a fairly clear and explicit answer. Facts about what is good for an individual provide reasons for desire that apply to anyone, on the condition that the individual in question is worthy of care. This means that the normativity of well-being is "subject-neutral" in the sense that it has the same normative implications for everyone.

The locative analysis

G.E. Moore once claimed that the phrase "good *for me*" must be understood in terms of what is "*good absolutely*" (Moore 1993/1903: 150). Following Moore's lead, some philosophers have thought that prudential value, or the closest intelligible thing to it, should be analyzed in terms of the presence of good and bad things in a life.[12]

The locative analysis

p is good for *S* = *p* is good *simpliciter* and is located in *S*'s life.

p is bad for *S* = *p* is bad *simpliciter* and is located in *S*'s life.

This analysis brings together two ideas. The first is the idea of goodness and badness *simpliciter*. Imagine a world that is much like ours except that it contains much more knowledge and beauty and far less misery and injustice. All else being equal, this imagined world seems better and more desirable than our world precisely because it contains more knowledge and beauty and less misery and injustice. To think that knowledge and beauty are things that make the world a better and more desirable place just is to think that they are good things. In contrast, misery or injustice are bad things insofar as they make the world worse and detract from its desirability.

The second idea is location within a life. Many of the things that we consider to be good or bad *simpliciter* are things that occur within people's lives. Consider the four examples above. Misery and knowledge are always the misery and knowledge of this or that individual. Injustice is often perpetrated by one individual or group of individuals and befalls another. Beauty is something that can be exemplified, created, promoted, and appreciated by us. To assess an individual's level of well-being on the locative interpretation, then, we must examine the extent to which her life contains or is appropriately related to good and bad things.

What does the locative analysis tell us about the scope and normativity of well-being? It implies, first, that the kinds of beings that have a well-being are those with lives that can contain good or bad things. Presumably, this rules out non-living entities on the grounds that they lack lives. Whether it allows that all living entities have a well-being is less clear. Does a beautiful orchid have high well-being in virtue of the fact that beauty—arguably, something of impersonal value—is located within its life? The answer to this question will depend on precisely how we interpret the idea of a life and of location within a life. Turning to the issue of normativity, facts about goodness and badness *simpliciter* are generally thought to have normative implications for everyone. If some event would make the world a better and more desirable place, then it makes sense for anyone to desire that this event take place. This means that, given a choice between increasing or decreasing anyone's well-being, it is fitting for us to prefer the former option, all else being equal. That is because it is fitting to desire things that will make the world a better place.[13]

The positional analysis

We as individuals inhabit different positions or circumstances in the world. Our positions are distinguished in countless ways—our physical appearance, health, mental capacities, wealth, opportunities, experiences, relationships to other people and things in the world. Taking such differences into account, it is evident that some positions are more desirable to occupy than others. All else being equal, it seems far more desirable to be in the position of one who is happy, healthy, and safe from danger than one who is miserable, malnourished, and afraid for her safety. These are things that impact the degree to which a position is desirable to occupy. In contrast to the locative analysis, which assesses lives by their relation to the desirability of the world, the positional analysis concerns the desirability of occupying positions in the world.[14]

The positional analysis

p is good for S = p contributes to the desirability of being in S's position.

p is bad for S = p detracts from the desirability of being in S's position.

The first thing to clarify about this analysis is the idea of a position. A position is associated with some set of properties or features, and to occupy or be in a position is to have those associated properties. We may understand *one's position at a time* to be associated with all of the individual's properties at that time. In contrast, *one's overall position* is defined by the complete set of properties had by that individual at any time. Interpreting the term "life" in a broad way, it may be said that occupying one's overall position just is to have that individual's life. So, the positional analysis also pertains to the desirability or undesirability of having one's life.

The next thing to clarify is the notion of desire. "Desire" should not be understood as referring to a bare motivational urge to pursue something, irrespective of whether one has any positive feeling toward the thing. (Philosophers often use the term in that broad way.) Instead, on the relevant notion of desire, it is essential to my desiring some state of affairs that I like or take some pleasure in the prospect of it. It must be something that *appeals* to me. There is a corresponding negative attitude that essentially involves an attitudinal element of disliking a thing and not merely a motivational tendency to avoid it.

On the positional analysis, the scope of well-being is restricted to beings whose positions and lives can be more or less desirable to occupy. This applies most naturally to beings with a conscious perspective on the world, and it seems to exclude non-living entities like economies and rivers. What is less clear is whether it makes sense to think of non-conscious living beings (e.g., flowers, individuals in a permanent vegetative state) as occupying a position in the world. This will depend on our interpretation of the idea of a position. As for normativity, to say that someone has a high level of well-being is to say that it is fitting or appropriate to desire to be in that person's position. On a common interpretation, this claim is subject-neutral: if a certain position is desirable to occupy, it makes sense for *any of us* to desire to occupy it. Thus, on the positional analysis, the concept of well-being has normative implications for what we as individuals have reason to desire for ourselves. Whether we should value or promote the well-being of others is an open normative question.

The suitability analysis

We talk quite comfortably about things being good or bad for a wide range of entities, both living and non-living. Getting water and sunlight is good for most plants. Failing to change the oil in an automobile is bad for the engine. The rampant burning of fossil fuels is harmful to the environment. What is evident from these examples is that whether some x is good or bad for some y depends crucially, not only on the nature of x, but also on the nature of y and on whether there exists a certain *fit* or *match* between the two. x must be *well suited* to y. Drawing on this line of thought, Richard Kraut has proposed the following analysis of prudential value:[15]

The suitability analysis

p is good for S = p is suitable for S in that it serves S well.

p is bad for S = p is unsuitable for S in that it serves S poorly.

The suitability analysis provides a striking contrast with the previous three analyses in terms of its implications about the scope and normativity of well-being. What sorts of things fall within the scope of well-being? Anything for which it is true that there is something else that is well suited to it and serves it well. According to Kraut, this includes plants (growing is good for plants), artifacts (dry air is bad for pianos), activities (watches are good for telling time), and individuals *qua* professionals (thinking fast is good for corporate lawyers) (Kraut 2007: 3, 9, 87). So, on this view, the scope of well-being is quite broad.

Does this broad scope imply that we have reason to promote or protect the interests of artifacts, activities, and professional roles? It seems not. While there is clearly an evaluative element in the suitability analysis (pertaining to the quality of fit between two things and to one thing's being served well by the other), it does not appear to have normative implications for action or attitudes in the way that the rational care, locative, and positional analyses do. As Kraut puts it, "When we say that something is good for someone, that statement leaves entirely open the question . . . whether anyone has reason to do or want anything" (Kraut 2007: 75; see also pp. 63–64, 81). Thus, on a natural interpretation of the suitability analysis, assertions about what is good or bad for an individual thing or person (even oneself) do not entail anything about what we have reason to do or feel. Whether we have any such reasons is a matter for normative debate.

This brief survey of four analyses of prudential value leaves a great many questions unanswered. What kind of analysis is being offered? Is the analysis non-circular and informative? Does it allow us to draw important distinctions (e.g., between intrinsic and instrumental prudential value, between "momentary well-being" and "lifetime well-being")? How well does the analysis fit with the various elements of standard picture of well-being? Does it rule out any seemingly intelligible substantive theories of well-being? Addressing such issues is crucial for assessing the plausibility of an analysis of prudential value.

Concepts of well-being?

There is an assumption that seems to underlie both the substantive theory strategy and the analytic strategy—namely, that a single, coherent topic lies at the heart of philosophical discussions of well-being. Hedonists, desire-fulfillment theorists, perfectionists, and objective-list theorists generally take themselves to be in genuine disagreement with each other over a common subject matter that is both coherent and significant. Likewise, analyses of well-being are often presented as casting new light on *the* concept or property of well-being. But is there more than one topic in play in the well-being literature? Should we recognize multiple concepts of well-being? Let us consider two possibilities that would undermine the assumption of a single topic of well-being.

Talking past

A first possibility is that, in some cases, philosophers of well-being have been "talking past" one another—that is, talking about different topics while wrongly believing that they are talking about the same topic. It is not difficult to see how such miscommunication could occur. As noted earlier, the dominant approach in the well-being literature has been the substantive theory strategy. Philosophers of well-being usually gesture toward the standard picture—or, more commonly, a limited portion of that picture—and then move directly into discussion of substantive theories of well-being. This practice leaves us in the dark about what precisely (or imprecisely, as the case may be) different well-being theorists take well-being to be. Do they have the full standard picture in mind or only some parts of it? Are they giving more emphasis or weight to certain elements? Do they have some particular analysis in mind?

To the extent that philosophers of well-being have different concepts in mind, their disagreements might be merely apparent. To illustrate this, imagine two philosophers, A and B, who are debating about the best theory of "well-being." A favors hedonism. B is a die-hard objective list theorist. Yet, A is drawn to the positional analysis and assumes that B is as well; B is drawn to the locative analysis and assumes that A is as well. These philosophers need not have any real disagreement between them. A favors hedonism as a theory of (let us call it) *positional well-being*, whereas B favors an objective list theory of *locative well-being*. These two views might both be true. It might be true that pleasure and pain are the only things that make a position more or less desirable to occupy *and* that there is a plurality of things that have impersonal value and can be located in a person's life. With better communication, A and B both might come to endorse the other's favored theory without abandoning their own. This is not to deny that these philosophers might still have a genuine disagreement about what constitutes the best way of sharpening the standard picture of well-being or about which concepts are worth talking about. But, at the level of substantive theories, there does not seem to be any genuine disagreement.

The popularity of the substantive theory strategy has created an environment in which it is often unclear what a given well-being theorist means when talking of "well-being." It would not be at all surprising if there has been some talking past. This represents one way in which there might be multiple topics under discussion in the well-being literature.

Conflation

Even where philosophers of well-being are not talking past each other, they might be conflating two or more distinct topics. This is a possibility explored by Shelly Kagan in his essay "Me and My Life" (1994).[16] On the standard picture of well-being, "how well you are doing" and "how well your life is going for you" are two ways of getting at the same idea. According to Kagan, this runs together two distinct concepts: how well a person is doing (which he calls "well-being") and how well one's life is going ("the goodness of one's life"). Imagine a businessman who dies in a happy state, ignorant of the fact that his wife was unfaithful to him, his children didn't respect him, and his business will soon go bankrupt (Kagan 1994: 311). Kagan sees this as a case where well-being and the goodness of one's life come apart. Arguably, the *life* of the radically deceived businessman did not go well for him, but *he* was doing perfectly fine during his life since the various things about which he was deceived had no negative impact on his mental or physical state. If Kagan's hypothesis is on the right track, philosophers have been mistakenly treating two separate topics as if they were one, and we will want to distinguish two concepts of well-being. Of course, even if Kagan's particular conflation hypothesis is not on the right track, there may be other conflations at work in the well-being literature.

Let me now propose the outlines of a new conflation hypothesis, which draws upon different elements of the standard picture. Recall, first, that well-being is standardly thought to be the thing we are tracking when we judge a person pitiable, enviable, lucky, or unlucky.[17] Two features of these judgments are worth highlighting. First, there is a very broad range of things that can lead us to make judgments about pitiability, enviability, and luckiness. I might believe that my neighbor is enviable and lucky because she is the great-great-granddaughter of Tolstoy. If I later find out that she just made that up to impress people, I would probably think her pitiable on the grounds that she feels compelled to lie to win people's favor. The fact that these judgments are intelligible suggests that it is also intelligible to think that such properties—being descended from Tolstoy, being disposed to tell lies to impress others—can impact one's well-being. The second feature to highlight is that judgments of pitiability, enviability, and luckiness need not depend upon the subject's own attitudes toward these things. I can intelligibly think someone who is descended from one of the world's great novelists is enviable and lucky in that regard even if she herself is completely unmoved by this fact about her genealogy. I can believe that my neighbor is pitiable for lying to others even if she has no reservations or regrets about it, and even takes great pride in her skills of deception. This suggests that the concept of well-being must be quite broad and must allow for the possibility that something's being good or bad for a person bears no essential connection to his or her favorable or unfavorable attitudes.

Similar lessons can be drawn from well-being's putative relation to the attitude of care or concern. Well-being, it is said, is something that we desire for a person insofar as we care for that individual.[18] There is a wide range of things that people can be led to want out of concern for a person, and these things need not meet with his or her approval or positive feelings. Indeed, it seems that anything that might render someone pitiable is something that we will not want for that person out of concern. Likewise, caring for someone involves wanting that person to enjoy good luck and not suffer bad luck. So, some aspects of the standard picture of well-being—in particular, well-being's putative relation to pitiability, enviability, luck, and care—call for a concept of well-being that is characterized by a certain breadth and attitude-independence.

Yet, other components of the standard picture seem to imply that well-being is intimately connected to subjects' attitudes. Take self-sacrifice. Well-being is standardly thought to be the thing that is knowingly sacrificed when a person engages in self-sacrifice.[19] Ordinarily, we think that a self-sacrifice must be *felt* or *experienced* as a sacrifice by the one making it. A "sacrifice" that one does not mind making is no sacrifice at all. To illustrate this point, imagine a student who is deliberating about whether to pursue a career in art or in medicine. She believes that, on balance, life as an artist would be best for her—because she would enjoy the work, and it would result in many valuable achievements. Yet, she feels alienated by the idea of making such artistic achievements; that aspect of the artistic life does not really resonate with her, though she does think it would help to make her life go better for her. Conversely, she is quite excited about pursuing a career as a doctor, primarily because she is eager to improve people's lives in a robust way, but also because she thinks it would be the life with greatest overall life-satisfaction for her. Even if she judges that the life in medicine would not be the prudentially best or most enviable life of the two options before her, it is nonetheless the one that she desires the most and that resonates with her most strongly. If she opts for the medical career, we would not normally say that she has engaged in self-sacrifice. This suggests that the notion of well-being that figures in our ordinary concept of self-sacrifice must bear some intimate connection with the attitudes of the person making the sacrifice.

Next, consider reward and punishment. The standard picture suggests that well-being is what we seek to influence in rewarding and punishing.[20] In many contexts, the point of rewarding and punishing is, at least in part, to repay someone for past deeds or to influence future behavior.

Either way, reward and punishment can lose their point if they are not appropriately connected to the affective and motivational states of those who receive it. Similarly, our practices of giving gifts and doing favors are quite often driven by the desire to please. We typically want our gifts and favors to be such that, on balance, they meet with the approval of the recipients, just as we want acts of retaliation and revenge to meet with the recipients' disapproval. A concept of well-being that does not bear any essential connection to the attitudes of the person will be ill suited to characterize the sort of "benefits" and "costs" that we seek to bestow on others when we reward, give gifts, do favors, punish, and take revenge.

Still other aspects of the standard picture suggest a more restrictive concept of well-being—in particular, one that screens off the possibility that acting morally, in and of itself, is good for us. The egoist is standardly defined as one whose sole ultimate aim is the promotion of his or her own well-being.[21] Yet, many philosophers have seen the egoist as a natural critic of morality and someone who must be convinced that being moral can, by some indirect route, serve his or her own best interests. They do not seriously entertain the possibility that the egoist might view being moral as an important component of the good life. What may underlie this tendency is an assumption that well-being is *morality-excluding* in the following sense: it is either impossible or deeply implausible that being moral is intrinsically good for us.

Another element of the standard picture that seems to call for a narrow concept is the idea that well-being has an important role to play in moral theory. If well-being is not morality-excluding, it threatens to introduce a regress into moral theories. For suppose that morality requires us to promote the well-being of other people, and suppose that being moral is a component of well-being. The result would be that morality requires, among other things, that we strive to promote moral traits and action in others, which will partly involve those individuals striving to promote moral traits and action in others, which will partly involve those individuals striving to promote moral traits and action in others, which will partly involve . . . There seems to be a kind of emptiness to this dimension of our moral obligations. To avoid this result, we need a narrower concept of well-being that is morality-excluding.

All of this appears to indicate that the standard picture of well-being is a conflation of two or more concepts. A single concept could not possibly satisfy all of these demands. It cannot be the concept of something that is both independent from *and* dependent upon the attitudes of the subject. It cannot both include *and* exclude being moral as a possible component of well-being. This brings to light a second way in which, contrary to initial appearances, there may be multiple topics at work in the well-being literature.

Conclusion

Perhaps it is time for us to rethink our approach to the topic of well-being. For the past three decades, the philosophical literature on well-being has been dominated by the substantive theory strategy. Most philosophers working in this area have invoked the standard picture of well-being and then moved directly into the debate over the best theory. Some have pursued the analytic strategy, attempting to arrive at a sharper picture of well-being. Yet, both of these approaches are typically pursued with the assumption that we are dealing with a unified subject matter. The considerations discussed in the previous section cast doubt on that very assumption. They give us reason to suspect that there is more than one topic in play in the philosophical literature on well-being. If there has been talking past, the obvious remedy is better communication. Philosophers of well-being need to be more explicit about precisely what they take well-being to be. If there has been some conflation, this raises several challenging questions. What led philosophers to this conflation? What exactly are the conflated topics? What light might this conflation shed on disagreements between well-being theorists over the past several years? And, most pressingly, which concept or concepts *should* be our focus as we move forward? Needless to say, these are issues that must be addressed before we can hope to make serious progress in the philosophy of well-being.[22]

Notes

1 An influential discussion of the subject-relativity of well-being appears in Sumner (1996: 20–44).
2 Sumner (1996: 20–25); Scanlon (1998: 111–113); Feldman (2004: 8–9); Campbell (2013: 335–336).
3 For a similar catalogue of relations, see Sumner (1996: 10–20); Darwall (2002: Chapters 1–2); Feldman (2010: 160–170); Heathwood (2010: 646); Heathwood (2014: 199–201); and Campbell (2013: 336–339).
4 Sumner (1996: 1–4); Scanlon (1998: Chapter 3); Tiberius and Plakias (2010: 402).
5 On the issue of welfare's scope, see Sumner (1996: 14–16); Kraut (2007); and Rosati (2009a).
6 As commonly understood, a normative reason for some attitude or action is "a consideration that counts in favor of it" Scanlon (1998: 17). For an influential discussion of well-being's normativity, see Darwall (2002: Chapter 1).
7 I owe this point to Dale Dorsey and Gwen Bradford.
8 See, for instance, Darwall (2002: Chapters 1–3); Rosati (2006); Kraut (2007: 81–88); Zimmerman (2009); Tenenbaum (2010); Skorupski (2010: 267–269); Fletcher (2012a); and Campbell (2013).
9 For present purposes, I will remain neutral on whether each analysis is best interpreted as a traditional conceptual analysis, revisionist conceptual analysis, or property analysis.
10 This analysis is defended in Darwall (2002: Chapters 1–3). For critical responses, see the symposia in *Philosophical Studies* 130 (2006) and *Utilitas* 18 (2006); Skorupski (2010: 284–85) and Fletcher (2012b: 86–90).
11 This formulation is adapted from Darwall (2006: 642), where he clarifies his analysis in response to Fred Feldman (2006).
12 See, e.g., Regan (2004); Brewer (2009: Chapter 6); Fletcher (2012a); McDaniel (2014); and Hurka (forthcoming: Chapter 1).
13 One objection to the locative analysis is that it fails to capture the special relationship that people seem to have to their own well-being. Ordinarily, we think that people have more reason to care about their own well-being than that of strangers. Yet, as Sergio Tenenbaum observes, "there is no reason why, on this view, it should matter more to the agent that a good occurs in his life than that it occurs in the southwest corner of San Antonio" (Tenenbaum 2010: 215). For a more complex locative analysis that handles this worry, see Fletcher (2012a).
14 For a more detailed introduction and defense of this analysis, see Campbell (2013).
15 See Kraut (2007: 85–87, 94–96). My formulation of the suitability analysis is drawn from Rosati (2009a: 212), who critiques Kraut's analysis and challenges the idea of a single good for relation.
16 He reports a modification in his view in Kagan (2009: 257).
17 Philosophers routinely defend substantive claims about well-being by appealing to claims about envy and pity. See, e.g., Sumner (1996: 12); Adams (1999: 84, 97); Darwall (2002: 3); Heathwood (2010: 646); and Tenenbaum (2010: 206–7, 222). Brad Hooker (1996: 149–155) and Daniel Haybron (2008: 32) both introduce tests that depend on the well-being/pity relation. On the relation between luck and well-being, see Rescher (1990: 7) and Lippert-Rasmussen (2014).
18 See, for instance, Adams (1999: 91–93, 97–98, 101); Darwall (2002); Feldman (2004: 9–10); Toner (2006: 225–226); Kraut (2007: 51–52, 125, 192); and Haybron (2008: 159–160).
19 Overvold (1980); Darwall (2002: 53); Rosati (2009b).
20 See Crisp (2006: 639); Heathwood (2010: 646, 653); Heathwood (2014: 201); and Bradley (2014: 229). The association between well-being and reward is also evident in such questions as "Is virtue its own reward?"—the title of a 1998 essay by L. W. Sumner on the relationship between virtue and well-being.
21 See, e.g., Shaver (2010).
22 Many thanks to those who provided feedback on this chapter—including Anne Baril, Anne Barnhill, Gwen Bradford, Brad Cokelet, Dale Dorsey, Billy Dunaway, Guy Fletcher, Chris Heathwood, Richard Kim, William Lauinger, Eden Lin, Sven Nyholm, Jason Raibley, Connie Rosati, Alex Sarch, Wayne Sumner, and David Wasserman. I also benefited from conversations with the participants at the 2014 Kansas Well-Being Workshop.

References

Adams, R. (1999) *Finite and Infinite Goods: A Framework for Ethics*, Oxford: Oxford University Press.

Bradley, B. (2014) "Objective Theories of Well-Being," In B. Eggleston and D. Miller (eds.) *The Cambridge Companion to Utilitarianism*, Cambridge: Cambridge University Press, pp. 220–238.

Brewer, T. (2009) *The Retrieval of Ethics*, Oxford: Oxford University Press.

Campbell, S.M. (2013) "An Analysis of Prudential Value," *Utilitas* 25: 334–354.

Crisp, R. (2006) "Hedonism Reconsidered," *Philosophy and Phenomenological Research* 73: 619–645.

Darwall, S. (2002) *Welfare and Rational Care*, Princeton: Princeton University Press.

Darwall, S. (2006) "Reply to Feldman, Hurka, and Rosati," *Philosophical Studies* 130: 637–658.

Feldman, F. (2004) *Pleasure and the Good Life*, Oxford: Oxford University Press.

Feldman, F. (2006) "What is the Rational Care Theory of Welfare?" *Philosophical Studies* 130: 585–601.

Feldman, F. (2010) *What is This Thing Called Happiness?*, Oxford: Oxford University Press.

Fletcher, G. (2012a) "The Locative Analysis of *Good For* Formulated and Defended," *Journal of Ethics & Social Philosophy* 6: 1–26.

Fletcher, G. (2012b) "Resisting Buck-Passing Accounts of Prudential Value," *Philosophical Studies* 157: 77–91.

Haybron, D. (2008) *The Pursuit of Unhappiness*, Oxford: Oxford University Press.

Heathwood, C. (2010). "Welfare," in J. Skorupski (ed.) *The Routledge Companion to Ethics*, London: Routledge, pp. 645–55.

Heathwood, C. (2014) "Subjective Theories of Well-Being," in B. Eggleston and D. Miller (eds.) *The Cambridge Companion to Utilitarianism*, Cambridge: Cambridge University Press, pp. 199–219.

Hooker, B. (1996) "Does Moral Virtue Constitute a Benefit to the Agent?" in R. Crisp (ed.) *How Should One Live?*, Oxford: Oxford University Press, pp. 141–55.

Hurka, T. (forthcoming) *British Ethical Theorists from Sidgwick to Ewing*, Oxford: Oxford University Press.

Kagan, S. (1994) "Me and My Life," *Proceedings of the Aristotelian Society* 94: 309–324.

Kagan, S. (2009) "Well-Being As Enjoying the Good," *Philosophical Perspectives* 23: 253–272.

Kraut, R. (2007) *What is Good and Why: The Ethics of Well-Being*, Cambridge, MA: Harvard University Press.

Lippert-Rasmussen, K. (2014) "Justice and Bad Luck," in E. Zalta (ed.) *The Stanford Encyclopedia of Philosophy* (Summer 2014 Edition), http://plato.stanford.edu/archives/win2010/entries/egoism/.

McDaniel, K. (2014) "A Moorean View of the Value of Lives," *Pacific Philosophical Quarterly* 95: 23–46.

Moore, G.E. (1993/1903) *Principia Ethica*, revised edition. T. Baldwin (ed.) Cambridge: Cambridge University Press.

Overvold, M. (1980) "Self-Interest and the Concept of Self-Sacrifice," *Canadian Journal of Philosophy* 10: 105–118.

Regan, D. (2004) "Why Am I My Brother's Keeper?" in R.J. Wallace, P. Pettit, S. Scheffler and M. Smith. (eds.) *Reason and Value: Themes from the Moral Philosophy of Joseph Raz*, Oxford: Clarendon Press, pp. 202–230.

Rescher, N. (1990) "Luck," *Proceedings and Addresses of the American Philosophical Association* 64: 5–19.

Rosati, C. (2006) "Personal Good," in T. Horgan and M. Timmons (eds.) *Metaethics After Moore*, Oxford: Oxford University Press, pp. 107–132.

Rosati, C. (2009a) "Relational Good and the Multiplicity Problem," *Philosophical Issues* 19: 205–234.

Rosati, C. (2009b) "Self-Interest and Self-Sacrifice," *Proceedings of the Aristotelian Society* 109: 311–325.

Scanlon, T. M. (1998) *What We Owe to Each Other*, Cambridge, MA: Harvard University Press.

Shaver, R. (2010) "Egoism," in E. Zalta (ed.) *The Stanford Encyclopedia of Philosophy* (Winter 2010 Edition), http://plato.stanford.edu/archives/win2010/entries/egoism/.

Skorupski, J. (2010) *The Domain of Reasons*, Oxford: Oxford University Press.

Sumner, L.W. (1996) *Welfare, Happiness, and Ethics*, Oxford: Clarendon Press.

Sumner, L.W. (1998) "Is Virtue Its Own Reward?," *Social Policy & Philosophy* 15: 18–36.

Tenenbaum, S. (2010) "Good and Good For," in S. Tenenbaum (ed.) *Desire, Practical Reason, and the Good*, Oxford: Oxford University Press, pp. 202–233.

Tiberius, V. and A. Plakias (2010) "Well-Being," in J. Doris & the Moral Psychology Research Group (eds.) *The Moral Psychology Handbook*, Oxford: Oxford University Press, pp. 402–432.

Toner, C. (2006) "Aristotelian Well-Being: A Response to L.W. Sumner's Critique," *Utilitas* 18: 218–231.

Zimmerman, M. (2009) "Understanding What's Good for Us," *Ethical Theory and Moral Practice* 12: 429–439.

PART V

Well-being in moral and political philosophy

34

WELFARISM

Dale Dorsey

"Welfare" is an *evaluative* term: it is the index by which we measure the goodness of lives for the people who live them. Someone with a better life just *is* someone with a higher degree of welfare.

Welfar*ism*—at least in the sense I'm interested in discussing—refers to the suggestion that this evaluative concept—welfare—is the only thing that makes a *normative* difference. Utilitarianism, for instance, accepts this claim: utilitarianism is a *welfarist* theory. Kantianism (at least as understood by Kant) is not.[1] But welfarism isn't just about morality. One can be a welfarist about many different normative domains: about morality, about political justice, about etiquette or aesthetics, and so on. Welfarist theories of different domains will obviously maintain different degrees of plausibility, and welfarism isn't all or nothing: one needn't be a welfarist about aesthetics, for instance, to be a welfarist about political justice. In this chapter, I focus on morality. I'm interested in doing two things here. First, I'd like to say a little more about what welfarism *is* (at least when it comes to welfarism about morality), and to spend some time assessing its prospects. Though I won't be able to settle the ages-old dispute of whether we should accept welfarism, I hope (at least) to point to considerations that can be said to count in favor of this doctrine, and those objections to which welfarism (about morality) *is*, and *is not*, vulnerable.

What is welfarism?

As I use the term, welfarism is a pretty broad doctrine. Of course, in defining a term like welfarism, there isn't much philosophical ground to fight over: any account of what "welfarism" really refers to is surely stipulative. But it would help in narrowing it down by discussing a few accounts of welfarism, some of which don't seem to get to the heart of the view as commonly understood.

Some statements of welfarism are too broad. Take the suggestion, made by many, that welfarism is the view according to which "welfare is the only value."[2] The belief that welfare is the only value is of course common among welfarists. But it is far from exclusive to them. One could, for instance, believe that welfare is the only value but divorce moral obligation from value of any kind. One could instead accept that the right is independent of the good, and hold that moral obligation has little to do with welfare, despite the fact that it is "the only value."

Other accounts are too narrow. Start with a prime critic of welfarism, Amartya Sen. According to Sen, welfarism is "the principle that the goodness of a state of affairs depends ultimately on the set of individual utilities in that state, and—more demandingly—can be seen as an increasing function of that set."[3] According to L.W. Sumner, welfarists accept five crucial tenets. First, "[w]elfarists believe that there are right answers to questions in ethics, answers which can, at least in principle, be discovered and defended by means of evidence and argument." Second, welfarists hold that "the project of theory-building in ethics is not futile or misguided." Third, "[w]elfarists believe that the structure of the best moral theory will assign priority to just one" general moral concept "by using it to derive and justify all of the others." Fourth, "[w]elfarists affirm the priority of the good," according to which deontic concepts like *rightness* and *wrongness* are derived from concepts like *goodness* and *badness*. Fifth, "[w]elfarists believe that the foundational values in ethical theory are agent-neutral" in the sense that "everyone has a reason to promote it, or at least to want it to come about."[4]

To see how narrow these statements of welfarism are, take, first, Sen's account. I see no reason to limit the term "welfarism" to those views according to which moral value (or, for that matter, the goodness of states of affairs) is an increasing function of "individual utilities." Imagine, for instance, an *egalitarian* view, according to which the equality of welfare in a state of affairs counts in favor of that state of affairs, morally speaking.[5] According to this view, the moral value of individual actions is very clearly not an increasing function of individual utilities. In fact, given the possibility that equal welfare levels will be achieved only by "leveling down" the better off, it may be that in certain circumstances, moral value and aggregate welfare are inversely related. But there's no reason, so far as I can tell, to refuse to call such a view "welfarist." After all, it *cares about well-being*, not about primary goods, capabilities, autonomy, respect, or anything else of that sort. It simply holds that the morally best distribution of well-being is an *equal* one.

My disagreements with Sumner run somewhat deeper. Welfarists need not commit to any particular account of the epistemic or metaphyiscal status of moral claims. Welfarism as I understand it is a normative position: it is a position about the factors that influence the moral obligations we have. It needn't be a position about the metaethical *status* of such factors or obligations.[6] In addition, welfarists could in fact believe that theory building in ethics is futile. It could be, for instance, that welfarism is a *constraint* on proper moral theorizing; it just happens that no acceptable theory can be articulated compatible with that constraint and/or other constraints on moral theorizing. It's also not clear to me that welfarists should accept that the welfarist concept will settle all moral issues. Though, of course, welfare is an important moral concept for welfarists, as noted above, it's possible for welfarists to disagree about a number of other issues that require further inquiry that is not simply given by the welfarist foundation (equality versus maximization, for instance). Fourth, and perhaps most importantly, there is no requirement for welfarists to affirm the "priority of the good." For instance, I could hold that morality requires that individuals improve the well-being of the most possible people, but be agnostic about whether doing so would be good; indeed, I could even hold some bizarre view about the nature of value according to which doing so would be neutral, or even of negative value. But that would certainly not prevent me from being a welfarist about morality or moral obligation. Finally, imagine a form of ethical *egoism*, according to which one is morally required to promote one's own well-being. According to this view, the "foundational values in ethical theory" are not agent-neutral, as compared to agent-relative. But, nevertheless, moral egoism is as welfarist as any other moral doctrine.

So what is welfarism? On my view, one can be a utilitarian or egalitarian welfarist, a welfarist rights-theorist, a welfarist virtue ethicist, a welfarist deontologist. Welfarism, as I understand it, is a view about what, for any particular domain, fundamentally explains that domain's evaluations.

For instance, one is a moral welfarist if moral evaluation is ultimately determined *by facts about well-being*. If one is a moral egalitarian, one can be a welfarist if the extent to which a state is more equal than another is determined by facts about well-being—that the "equality of what?" question is answered by: "welfare." If one is a consequentialist, one is a welfarist to the extent that the goodness of consequences is determined by facts about *welfare*. One is a welfarist about moral rights if rights are given in terms of welfare, and so on. Put more generally, then:

> *Welfarism*: a theory θ of domain *d* is welfarist if and only if the *d*-evaluation of evaluative targets (acts, in the case of morality; social institutions, in the case of political justice, and so forth) according to θ are determined by facts about welfare.

Question: what does it mean for a fact to be "about" welfare? In my view, this phrase should be interpreted broadly. Facts about welfare can go *way* beyond the actual *distribution* of welfare in a given state of affairs, i.e., who achieves welfare and to what extent. Take an example: though I don't actually shoot anyone when I randomly fire my pistol out of my window in the dead of night, one might say that I act in a morally condemned way in so doing. But this proposal is compatible with welfarism as stated, insofar as *risk* of welfare loss is certainly a fact about welfare. Although it is broad, this account of welfarism seems to capture the beating heart of the claim so often referred to obliquely: well-being is the currency of moral evaluation; moral concern for a particular person *x* is concern for *x*'s well-being.

Some arguments against welfarism—indeed, some of the most powerful—will apply only to those theories that fit a more narrowly drawn understanding of welfarism. Sen, for instance, asks us to consider two choice scenarios. The first concerns whether to implement a scheme of redistributive taxation. The no-tax option would yield a welfare distribution of well-being among two people like this: {*r*: 10; *p*: 4}. Taxation, on the other hand, would yield a distribution like this: {*r*: 8; *p*: 7}. Now consider the second choice, stated as follows: "let *r* be a romantic dreamer and *p* a miserable policeman. In *b* the policeman tortures the dreamer; in *a* he does not. The dreamer has a happy disposition ('the future is ours') and also happens to be rich, in good health, and resilient, while the policeman is morose, poor, ill, and frustrated, getting his simple pleasures out of torturing."[7] In this scenario, the no-torture option would produce the following distribution: {*r*: 10; *p*: 4}. The torture option, on the other hand: {*r*: 8; *p*: 7}. Sen writes:

> Welfarism leaves us free to rank [no torture] over [torture] *or* the other way round (or as indifferent), just as it leaves us free to rank [no taxation] vis-à-vis [taxation] in either way, when we consider these rankings separately. However, it requires that [torture] and [no torture] be ranked *in exactly the same way* as [tax] and [no tax], respectively. That is, welfarism would insist that the state of affairs with redistributive taxation . . . is better than that without taxation . . . *if and only if* the state of affairs with the torture . . . is better than without torture . . . Many people would, however, hold that the case involving redistributive taxation is better . . . but the case involving torture is not. One is free to hold such a view only by rejecting welfarism.[8]

But must a welfarist of the sort I've indicated here accept this view? No. This is because welfarism so defined is *not* equivalent to the claim that two choices with identical welfare outcomes are morally identical. One could hold, for instance, that individuals have a right not to be tortured, even a morally decisive right, but that this right is formulated *in welfarist terms*: one has a right not to be harmed in the manner typically imposed by torturing. This right does not apply to the right not to be taxed, because taxation typically involves a less significant harm than torture. (One might think of this as a right against torture given torture's much higher risk of welfare loss, say, for the average person.) Thus the moral wrongness of being tortured, for the person in question, is explained by facts about welfare associated with torture. Whether this view is ultimately plausible or not, it's a version of welfarism. (Of course, this is not to say that Sen doesn't make philosophical progress here; it's just to say that his argument, if it works, works only against a much narrower account of welfarism and not welfarism more generally.)

Why be welfarist?

Welfarism is a popular doctrine, but it's strikingly difficult to come up with any direct argument for it, at least when it comes to morality. However, this does not entail that there are not at least *some* attempts. Though I'll refrain from commenting on their plausibility here, among others one might consider the following:

> *Contract argument*: Morality is the result of a contract/hypothetical contract for the mutual advantage of diverse parties. These parties care only about their welfare, and hence any resulting set of principles or rules will guide action solely on the basis of the welfare of those affected.[9]

Qua argument for welfarism, this is pretty weak. In particular, it relies on two controversial premises, each of which could be cogently (even plausibly) denied. First, a metaethical premise, viz., that the content of moral demands is the result of a contract or a hypothetical contract between divergent parties for their mutual interests. Second, on the interests of parties to such a contract. According to this proposal, the parties care only for their own well-being, and hence the terms of any contract between such parties will be welfarist in form; evaluations on the basis of the resulting contract will be guided only by that which the parties to the contract care about, viz., their own welfare. The assumptions required to make the contract argument work seem plausibly to be an *outcome* of a commitment to welfarism, rather than a method by which to justify such a commitment.

Consider a second argument, viz., the:

> *Beneficence argument*: Morality is a product of our natural attitude of beneficence, expanded, perhaps universally. But because beneficence toward others is concerned with those others' well-being, any set of principles or rules generated by expanding the range of natural beneficence will guide action solely on the basis of the welfare of those affected.[10]

Of course, beneficence is welfarist: when I care about someone, or take a beneficent attitude toward them, my interest is in improving their welfare, in protecting them from harm, and so forth. But the metaethical presumption at work in the above argument is totally question begging. That morality is an outcome of our beneficent attitudes, rather than some other sort of attitude, requires a presumption of welfarism about morality, and hence (like the contract argument) cannot establish it.

For my money, the most powerful appeal in favor of welfarism makes reference to what might be called the *welfarist's intuition*:

> *Welfarist's intuition*: the moral domain cares exclusively about the quality of people's lives.

One might think I'm a bit off my rocker in calling the welfarist's intuition the most powerful appeal in favor of welfarism. After all, as must be strikingly obvious, the welfarist's intuition is just a vague account of welfarism itself, viz., that moral evaluations are explained by facts about welfare. To argue in favor of welfarism by reference to the welfarist's intuition is, at best, to simply pound the table. Of course, this doesn't mean that no argumentative ground is gained by reference to the welfarist's intuition. Indeed, the welfarist's intuition (as far as I'm concerned) is itself *very intuitive*, and creates at least a strong presumption in favor of welfarism as a doctrine. As Simon Keller writes:

> A moral theory that concerns itself only with distributions of resources or opportunities, for example, will sometimes instruct us to give someone extra resources or opportunities even when we know that doing so will make his life worse, in the fundamental sense, and even when we know that the alternative is to make somebody else's life better. When a moral theory has this consequence, does it not seem to have lost sight of what really matters?[11]

In addition, this intuition is confined to the moral first order, and doesn't rely on any controversial claims about the source of moral claims or their metaethical status. It is simply a very basic claim about what the moral point of view cares about: it cares about how well people's lives go.[12]

Objection: the welfarist's intuition, despite being quite plausible, masks the fact that there are really two principles at work. The first holds that morality *cares about the quality of people's lives*. Surely this is correct. Any moral theory according to which there is so much as a reason against harming others accepts this claim. However, there is a second claim at work in the welfarist's intuition: morality cares about *nothing else*. And while the first claim is as intuitive as all get out, the second can be sensibly questioned. Indeed, it is upon this crucial presumption of welfarism that most objections to this doctrine focus. To these I now turn.

Why not be welfarist?

There are a lot of objections to welfarism, of which I will be able only to scratch the surface. However, I'll try to hit the highest points, beginning with the general claim that welfarism cannot account for the importance of individual autonomy, the claim that welfarism succumbs to problematic cases of adaptation, and the proposal that moral consideration focuses not on a person's welfare, but instead on her *preferences* more broadly construed.

Autonomy

A classic response to welfarism is that moral/political obligation cannot simply be explained by facts about well-being. There are other values or important concepts that play a role. Consider, for instance, *autonomy*. One way to see the significance of autonomy for moral theory is to consider the plausible moral presumption against paternalism. Though some have defended anti-paternalism on welfarist grounds,[13] it is much more plausible to say that the general moral reason against acting in paternalistic ways toward people is not that doing so risks their welfare. Instead, the moral reason seems to be explained by a concern to maintain people's capacity to make autonomous choices for their own lives, even if this results in a loss of their own welfare.

Something like this objection is at work in Martha Nussbaum's objection to welfarism in the political domain (though much of her reasoning translates straightforwardly to the moral domain). For Nussbaum, political justice should focus on the *capability* to achieve states of well-being (or "functioning"), not welfare itself:

> [I]f we were to take [welfare] itself as a goal of public policy, pushing citizens into functioning in a single determinate manner, the liberal pluralist would rightly judge that we were precluding many choices that citizens may make in accordance with their own conceptions of the good, and perhaps violating their rights. A deeply religious person may prefer not to be well nourished, but to engage in strenuous fasting. Whether for religious or for other reasons, a person may prefer a celibate life to one containing sexual expression. A person may prefer to work with intense dedication that precludes recreation and play . . . Where adult citizens are concerned, *capability, not functioning is the appropriate political goal.*[14]

Nussbaum is certainly on to something. After all, if welfare is constituted by (or if the necessary conditions for welfare include), e.g., healthy sexual expression, being well nourished, recreation, and play, then it would seem quite implausible to hold that a just society would force individuals to engage in those activities if they didn't wish to do so or if they didn't value such activities. In the case of many states that contribute to welfare, forcing people into them would appear to generate a society that exists only in one's worst nightmares. Individuals, it may be claimed, have the power of autonomy—the state should not force them into choosing things that would be good for them.

Can a welfarist respond to a critique like this? Possibly. Note that objections to welfarism on grounds of autonomy are more plausible when the nature of welfare is construed *objectively* rather than *subjectively*; in other words, when it is the case that a particular state ϕ can improve the welfare of some person p without p valuing ϕ. If, for instance, sexual functioning is itself a good regardless of whether the person in question values it, surely it's the case that morality cares about more than well-being. But you should ask yourself: is the person who is forced into sexual functioning, rather than remaining celibate as he would prefer, living a better life than he would be had he not been so forced? Surely not! Having such results in mind, welfare theorists are tempted to accept the following constraint on purported prudential values:

> *The subjectivist's constraint* (SC): a necessary condition of any event, object, or state ϕ to be intrinsically good for p is for p to take a valuing attitude toward ϕ.

SC requires that all welfare goods are valued by those for whom they are good. If we accept SC, however, the welfarist has the power to respond to Nussbaum's rejection of welfarism. Welfarism will never urge people to dragoon others into states that, while they may constitute flourishing, are not valued by the person whose goods they are.

In addition, accepting the subjectivist's constraint can go some distance toward solving worries about paternalism. Notice that it is much more plausible to insist on a moral reason not to promote states in others that they do not value. But it is hard to see why morality would care, specifically, about my capacity to avoid states that I *myself* value or endorse. Put this another way: if I value a particular state ϕ *and* to promote ϕ would be to improve my life, what moral reason could there be not to help me achieve it, or to promote it for me in some other way? Surely morality cares about my capacity to live my life according to my own values. But surely morality couldn't care less about my capacity to choose *against* those values.

The failure of the argument from autonomy (at least in its current guise) illustrates a general challenge for those seeking to argue against welfarism. Welfarism holds that facts about welfare determine the evaluation of welfarist normative domains. But this leaves open exactly *what* the nature of well-being is. To offer counterexamples to welfarism then requires the critic to come up with cases in which someone's welfare is *actually* affected in a certain way (positive or negative) but in which there are non-welfarist considerations that oppose the welfarist consideration. To put the matter somewhat more bluntly, it's easy to argue against welfarism if one's background assumption is a very implausible theory of welfare—the argument from autonomy plausibly falls into this trap.

Adaptation

Another classic argument against welfarism is more promising. Pressed by Sen and Nussbaum, among many others, this argument proceeds by noting that a person's subjective mental states, such as her capacity to take pleasure in states of affairs, her desires or other pro-attitudes, and so on—many of which are relevant in determining the content of her intrinsic good—are *malleable*. This malleability or *adaptation* seems to render concern for an individual's well-being an incomplete account of *moral* concern for this person. According to Sen:

> The hopeless beggar, the precarious landless labourer, the dominated housewife, the hardened unemployed or the over-exhausted coolie may all take pleasures in small mercies, and manage to suppress intense suffering for the necessity of continuing survival, but it would be ethically deeply mistaken to attach a correspondingly small value to the loss of their well-being because of this survival strategy.[15]

Notably, Nussbaum offers an additional defense of her non-welfarist approach by explicitly linking "subjective welfarism" to the problem of adaptation:

> The normative approach based on human functioning and capability . . . rejected utilitarian preference-based approaches as a basis for fundamental political principles precisely because they were unable to conduct a critical scrutiny of preference and desire that would reveal the many ways in which habit, fear, low expectations, and unjust background conditions deform people's choices and even their wishes for their own lives.[16]

Typically, according to Nussbaum, "an individual's preferences are shaped to accord with the (frequently narrow) set of opportunities she actually has."[17] In light of the fact of adaptation, it may seem quite wrong to hold that morality looks *solely* at the well-being of particular individuals in evaluating acts that affect them. It may be that the decision to end slavery for a particular person doesn't do much for her achievement of preferences, her states of happiness, given this person's adaptation to her awful condition. But it may very well be the *right* thing to do, in a way that cannot be fully explained by this act's impact on her well-being.

Objections to welfarism on the basis of adaptation are notable in that they do not rely *specifically* on any particular theory of well-being, nor do they violate the subjectivist's constraint. Quite the opposite. My endorsement of particular states, what I value, what I take pleasure in, and so forth, all appear to be malleable in ways that have the potential to yield problematic forms of adaptation. And hence any theory of well-being that grants significant importance to, e.g., pleasure (such as hedonism) or pro-attitude (such as desire-satisfaction accounts or indeed any account that accepts the subjectivist's constraint) will yield a welfarism that succumbs to the problem of adaptation.

This problem has been exhaustively discussed. And at the risk of treating this issue with far too blunt an instrument, it seems right to say that there are really only two potential responses on behalf of the welfarist. The first is to hold that the phenomenon of adaptation doesn't merely cause problems for the moral preferability of the adaptively preferred states, or, say, the adaptive states of pleasure, but also causes problems for the *welfare* value of adaptive states. For instance, if my preferences are adapted to my own poor circumstances, this entails (so it might be claimed) that these preferences are not authoritative as concerns my good (or the adaptive states of pleasure don't qualify as intrinsically valuable for those who feel them, say). Indeed, this proposal has immediate plausibility. Imagine, for instance, that I am a landless laborer of the sort Sen describes; would we say that my life is particularly high in welfare, despite the fact that my own subjective attitudes are adapted to my conditions? I think a very plausible answer here is "no."

Of course, this requires the welfarist to offer an account of welfare that would rule out the so-adapted preferences.[18] But this is a challenge. The most obvious such explanation would be to hold that well-being can be independent of the mental states that are prone to problematic forms of adaptation. Instead, one might introduce a set of objective welfare values: perhaps *not being a landless laborer* is a welfare value that is independent of one's pro-attitudes or states of pleasure.

However, introducing the possibility of objective values is not a successful strategy. We can see this clearly if we consider versions of an objectivist theory of welfare. Consider, first:

> *Objectivism full stop* (OFS): a necessary and sufficient condition of any event, object, or state ϕ to be intrinsically good for p is for ϕ to be valuable independently of any pro-attitude taken by p toward ϕ.

This proposal avoids worries of adaptation: welfare is entirely determined independently of one's adaptation-prone mental states. However, though OFS clearly jettisons adaptive preferences when coming to an understanding of human welfare, it runs smack-dab into the problem of autonomy, introduced in the previous section. Welfarism in conjunction with an objective theory of value seemed to entail that we have moral reasons to cajole, force, or dragoon people into the achievement of states they don't value (even if to do so would be to increase their well-being). Responding to the problem of autonomy required the partisan of objective welfare values to accept the subjectivist's constraint—purported welfare goods, to be good for a person, must be valued by that person. The objectivist could accept SC together with the possibility of objective values if she accepts, instead:

> *The objectivist's constraint* (OC): a necessary condition of any event, object, or state ϕ to be intrinsically good for p is for ϕ to be valuable independently of any pro-attitude taken by p toward ϕ

OC and SC are both necessary conditions, and are hence compatible. But merely accepting OC, along with SC, rules out the possibility that objective welfare values could help solve the problem of adaptation. One important form of adaptation is the *refusal* to value particular states, i.e., the state of not being a landless laborer (for instance).

A second possibility (at least in the case of adaptive preferences or pro-attitudes in particular) is to hold that there is something specifically defective about *adaptive*, rather than non-adaptive, preferences, just in the way that traditional desire-satisfaction theories of well-being hold that there is something defective about *ill-informed* preferences or pro-attitudes.[19] A proper theory of well-being, or so it is said, will entail that these pro-attitudes lack welfare-determining authority. However, this response is limited in its force. It seems right, as a general claim, to say that the plausibility of welfarism itself should not be a limiting condition on proper theories of well-being.

It would be illegitimate, in other words, to argue for a particular theory of welfare on grounds that it renders welfarism more plausible (that is, unless there is some other independent argument for such a theory). To do so would objectionably render welfarism a trivial or uninteresting doctrine. But the current proposal flirts with this result: it may seem quite implausible to come up with an *independent* reason to rule out the problematic adaptive preferences while ruling *in* preferences that seem to develop in more humdrum, less problematic ways (including, for instance, one's preference for the success of a particular baseball team).

I've argued elsewhere[20] that the way to justify ruling out adaptive preferences (while keeping the welfare relevance of non-adaptive preferences) from within a theory of well-being is to hold that *some* adaptive preferences do not adequately reflect the *values* of an individual agent. If, for instance, I adapt to my shoddy circumstances merely as a result of a coping mechanism or survival strategy, it would be a mistake to say that I *value* these circumstances, or that the preferences I maintain show that I do not value an improvement in my circumstances. However, while this proposal can rule out the welfare relevance of *some* adaptive preferences, it cannot rule out all of them. This is because valuing, like any pro-attitude, can also be adaptive. I may, as a result of my shoddy circumstances, come to prefer my circumstances not simply as a coping mechanism, but as a genuine aspect of my evaluative perspective. If so, the current rationale has no grounds for ruling out such preferences in a an account of the good for a person.[21]

Thus I think that the best the welfarist can do is to rule out only *some* adaptive preferences as counting in an account of a person's welfare (those that fail to represent a person's genuine values). But at this point, the welfarist should fight back. Under the most problematic cases for welfarism, it is true that the dominated housewife, for instance, *will not live a better life* were it the case that her state of domination were alleviated. This will be either because being a dominated housewife contributes positively to her welfare, given that she genuinely values this state, or because, though this state is objectively valueless and hence worthless (as per OC), it is not possible to make her better off insofar as she fails to value states that are objectively valuable (as per SC). Either way, to alleviate her state, at best, does nothing to improve her life's quality. But if this is so, if such alleviation will not make her better off to any degree, why believe there is moral pressure to alleviate this state? If we accept the objectivist's constraint on welfare states, we might very well *regret* the fact that this person's well-being is tied so closely to being dominated, and perhaps we would morally blame those (if any) who are responsible, when there could have been options open for her to value more objectively valuable states. If we reject this constraint, and hold that her evaluated states actually make it the case that being a dominated housewife makes her *better off*, gives her a *better life* than alternatives, it seems objectionable to insist on a moral reason that she live a *worse life*. If we reject the objectivist's constraint, though we may react negatively to her life, our reactions do not track the facts about what is good for her. Perhaps this is a problem, not with welfarism, but with our reactions.

Welfare versus preferences

Finally, and in conclusion, I discuss the objection to welfarism that I find most important. The objection begins by noting that virtually no one is *only* concerned with their own well-being. Indeed, I may value, have preferences for, be extremely concerned about, states that go beyond my welfare, do not contribute at all to the quality of my life. I value, for instance, the health of my daughter. Indeed, I value it so highly that I'd gladly be willing to give up substantial elements of my own well-being to protect her health. I may prefer my life go worse were I to contribute in some way to a good to which I am committed; say, the preservation of some wildlife area, or the rebuilding of New Orleans, or the relief of suffering for the billions currently in poverty worldwide, or the preservation of the works of an important but unknown artist.

But here's the question. I have a number of preferences among states: some of those states will improve my well-being, others won't. But why, then, should proper moral consideration of me focus strictly on my *well-being* in comparison to the other states I care about, when I may very well prefer the latter to the former? Consider:

> *Fire rescue*: My baby daughter and I are trapped in a high floor of an apartment building during a blazing inferno. A firefighter has appeared, but can save only one of us. I demand that he save my daughter.

Here it would appear that the morally correct thing to do in this case would obviously be for the firefighter to save my daughter. But why? The welfarist must explain this in terms of well-being: it may be that my daughter's well-being is in some sense more morally important than mine; perhaps there's more overall welfare to be achieved in saving her in comparison to saving me. But these explanations seem artificial and not to reflect what's going on in the case. Rather, surely at least *a* very strong moral reason for the firefighter to save my daughter rather than me has to do with a proper moral attitude toward *me*: a respect for that which I value or prefer, rather than my own well-being. On this point, David Sobel writes:

> Consider . . . the thesis that the appropriate object of moral concern must be endorsed by the agent as such given knowledge of how those preferences will be conjoined with others' preferences in moral aggregation. The fundamental idea behind [this] principle is that we should take people into account morally in a way that they rationally endorse. It is an odd sense of acting for my sake which can lead to acting contrary to what I rationally want. Welfarists can console themselves that they are taking a person into account in the sense of taking that person's interests into account, but it remains obscure why this counts as adequately taking that person into account. A non-welfarist version of consequentialism which respected [this] principle would have less difficulty explaining why giving weight to what they do constitutes taking the agent into account morally.[22]

According to Sobel's principle, an adequate account of what it means to take me into consideration in a moral way must be endorsed *by me*. But, given my preference structure, it is obvious that in some cases I will not endorse a method of taking me into moral consideration that strictly concerns my well-being. I will demand, of the firefighter, to rescue my daughter "on my behalf," "out of respect for me," and so forth. Though my daughter's interests here are obviously morally significant, *part* of what justifies (even requires) the firefighter's decision to save my daughter is the fact that I prefer, or value more highly, his doing so.

As a card-carrying welfarist, I regard this as an extremely difficult challenge; perhaps the most significant of all. No theory of welfare could plausibly insist that, e.g., the preference that my daughter be rescued is relevant to *my own well-being*.[23] Indeed, even for preference-based or desire-based theories of welfare, there is broad consensus that such other-regarding preferences must be expunged before coming to a genuine account of what makes a person better off.[24] Some have claimed that an inability to do so is a dispositive reason to reject views according to which welfare is a function of preference satisfaction.[25] And hence it appears to be a mere data point that the satisfaction of such other-regarding desires does not count when it comes to determining how well off someone is. Thus it would appear that welfarists cannot accommodate the intuition on offer in *fire rescue*: it is a fact not about my well-being, but instead about my preferences or values, that yields a moral reason to rescue my daughter (though, certainly, not the only moral reason).

I'm inclined to believe that, difficult though the problem is, *fire rescue* does not present an insuperable challenge for welfarism. Consider the following case:

> *The Queen*: The Queen's subjects genuinely love her, and believe that her own well-being is more significant than their own. Given the choice, each of them prefer to advance the welfare of the Queen in comparison to their own interests.

If we accept that moral concern for a particular individual should focus on their preferences rather than on their own well-being, it would appear that, for every person, advancing that which is morally considerable in their case requires one to advance the welfare of the Queen. However, this strikes me as a *desperately* wrong result, at least from a moral point of view: it is a state of affairs that does not accord each person sufficient moral consideration. This is feudalism, not morality! But this result is incompatible with Sobel's view: if to consider a person morally is to take seriously their preferences, rather than their welfare, there could be no problem of moral consideration in simply advancing the welfare of the Queen in contrast to the welfare of others.

By way of a first stab in providing a rationale for welfarism in light of this case, note that one of the advantages of Sobel's proposal, or so it would have seemed, is that in indexing moral consideration to a person's preferences rather than their well-being, folks can choose to render their own interests less important than those of others; morality must respect this choice. But in *The Queen*, we see that doing so is *not* morally unproblematic. Perhaps, morally speaking, you can choose to advance the interests of others rather than yourself—but you cannot choose to have your own well-being a less significant object of moral consideration. What, then, to say about *fire rescue*? Ultimately, it seems that the welfarist must simply bite this bullet. Morality, or so it should be said, rejects individuals' preferences to render their own welfare less important than other worthy goals. I may be required, say, *as a father* to prefer my daughter's welfare to my own. But the evaluation of my acts *qua* father—or so the welfarist should say—differs from *moral* evaluation of my acts in which it is my welfare that matters, no matter my preferences to the contrary. If we are to evaluate the firefighter's decision to rescue my daughter *strictly* in moral terms, my other-regarding preferences should be left out.

Ultimately, I'm not sure that this response is convincing or even cogent. However, I do want to underscore how particularly important this challenge is to welfarism. Welfarists ignore it at their peril.

Conclusion

Welfarism is a broad and important doctrine with a fine historical pedigree. Many classic challenges to welfarism can be shown to be mistaken given a sophisticated understanding of the nature of human welfare. But not all such objections can be so easily expunged. In this chapter, I have tried to indicate which objections are best left to the side and which, to my mind, anyway, should keep the welfarist up at night.

Notes

1 See, most significantly, Kant's *Groundwork of the Metaphysics of Morals*, Ak. 4:395.
2 Simon Keller, "Welfarism," in *Philosophy Compass* 4 (2009), 86. Keller offers an alternative critique of this account of welfarism (86–87).
3 Amartya Sen, "Utilitarianism and Welfarism," in *Journal of Philosophy* 76 (1979), 464.
4 L.W. Sumner, *Welfare, Happiness, and Ethics* (Oxford: Oxford University Press, 1996), 184–185.
5 For views of this kind, see Larry Temkin, *Inequality* (Oxford: Oxford University Press, 1993).

6 For instance, one could be a normative welfarist but also a metaethical *fictionalist*: claims about ethics are not truth-apt, or at least are not truth-apt in the standard way, despite its being the case that our moral obligations are welfarist in nature.

7 Sen, "Utilitarianism and Welfarism," 473.

8 Sen, 473–474.

9 John Harsanyi, "Morality and the Theory of Rational Behavior," in *Social Research* 44 (1977). For contract-based opposition to this view, see John Rawls, *A Theory of Justice* (Cambridge, MA: Harvard University Press, 1971) and T.M. Scanlon, *What We Owe to Each Other* (Cambridge, MA: Harvard University Press, 1998), 214–216.

10 For a classic statement of the beneficence argument, see Francis Hutcheson, *An Inquiry into the Original of our Ideas of Beauty and Virtue*, ed. W. Leidhold (Indianapolis, IN: Liberty Fund, 2004), 126–130. See also H. Sidgwick, *The Methods of Ethics* (Indianapolis, IN: Hackett Publishing Company, 7th ed., 1981 [1907]), 430–439.

11 Keller, 91.

12 Indeed, some hold that welfarism (at least about morality) is not simply highly intuitive but *conceptually true*. Philippa Foot, Bernard Williams, and G.J. Warnock all hold that the distinguishing marks of moral inquiry, as opposed to inquiry in other domains (such as etiquette) are morality's welfarist character. P. Foot, *Virtues and Vices* (Oxford: Oxford University Press, 1978), 106–107; B. Williams, *Morality* (Cambridge: Cambridge University Press, 1972), 73–80; G.J. Warnock, *Contemporary Moral Philosophy* (London: Macmillan, 1967), 56.

13 See, especially, John Stuart Mill, *On Liberty* (Indianapolis, IN: Hackett Publishing Company, 1978).

14 M. Nussbaum, *Women and Human Development* (Cambridge: Cambridge University Press, 2000), 87. Nussbaum uses the word "functioning" rather than "welfare," but this makes no never mind here. For Nussbaum, "welfare" simply refers to the achievement of those things that constitute human flourishing or well-being.

15 Sen (1987), 45–46, my emphasis.

16 Nussbaum (2000), 114.

17 Nussbaum, "American Women: Preferences, Feminism, Democracy" in Nussbaum (1999), 151.

18 Consider, for instance, M. Rickard, "Sour Grapes, Rational Desires and Objective Consequentialism," in *Philosophical Studies* 80 (1995).

19 This possibility is explored by D. Dorsey, "Preferences, Welfare, and the Status-Quo Bias" in *Australasian Journal of Philosophy* 88 (2010); Jon Elster, "Utilitarianism and the Genesis of Wants" in *Utilitarianism and Beyond*, ed. A. Sen and B. Williams (Cambridge: Cambridge University Press, 1981); Sumner, op. cit., Ch. 6; and others.

20 D. Dorsey, *The Basic Minimum: A Welfarist Approach* (Cambridge: Cambridge University Press, 2012), ch. 3; "Adaptation, Autonomy and Authority" in *Adaptation and Autonomy: Adaptive Preferences in Enhancing and Ending Life*, ed. J. Raikka and J. Varelius (Berlin: Springer, 2013); "Idealization and the Heart of Subjectivism," MS.

21 Donald Bruckner, "In Defense of Adaptive Preferences," in *Philosophical Studies,* 148 (2009).

22 D. Sobel, "Well-Being as the Object of Moral Consideration" in *Economics and Philosophy,* 14 (1998), 280.

23 For an alternative view, see M. Lukas, "Desire Satisfactionism and the Problem of Irrelevant Desires" in *Journal of Ethics and Social Philosophy,* 4 (2010).

24 Cf. D. Parfit, *Reasons and Persons* (Oxford: Oxford University Press, 1984), 494; M. Overvold, "Self Interest and Getting What You Want," in *The Limits of Utilitarianism*, ed. H.B. Miller and W.H. Williams (Minneapolis, MN: University of Minnesota Press, 1982), Sobel, op. cit., and many others.

25 Most importantly, see Richard Arneson, "Human Flourishing versus Desire Satisfaction" in *Social Philosophy and Policy* 16 (1999).

35

WELL-BEING AND THE NON-IDENTITY PROBLEM

Molly Gardner

Introduction

What has come to be known as the *non-identity problem*[1] raises some puzzling questions about the relationship between the well-being of others and our reasons for action. The non-identity problem arises in what I will call a *non-identity case*: a case in which an action that is the condition of an individual's worthwhile existence also imposes certain constraints on the individual's prospects for well-being.[2] For example, consider a case in which some prospective parents use *in vitro* fertilization and select an embryo for implantation on the basis of a gene that will result in a particular disease. If the resultant child has a life worth living, then she is made no worse off in any respect by her parents' action of selecting for disease than she would have been, had they not performed that action. After all, if they had not selected for disease, the embryo with the gene for the disease would have been discarded, and the resultant child would not have existed: she is *non-identical* to anyone who would have existed, had her parents not acted as they did. Nevertheless, many people have the intuition that there is a moral reason against the kind of action that the parents performed. A solution to the non-identity problem must either justify the intuition that there is a moral reason against the very action that brings someone into existence in a non-identity case or explain that intuition away.

This chapter will consider two different strategies for trying to justify the intuition that there is a moral reason against the action in a non-identity case. One strategy attempts to show that, when an action results in constraints upon an individual's prospects for well-being, it harms her, *even if* it fails to make her worse off than she would otherwise have been. Call this strategy the *harm-based approach* to the non-identity problem. The other strategy attempts to show that, although the resultant individual is not harmed by the action, the reason against the action is at least partly grounded in the value of her well-being from an impersonal perspective. Call this strategy the *impersonal value approach*. Since both approaches appeal to either the personal or the impersonal value of an individual's well-being, I will call these approaches the *well-being approaches* to the non-identity problem. Well-being approaches can be contrasted with a number of other proposed solutions to the problem, such as those that attempt to show that the action violates the individual's rights even though it does not harm him or her (Woodward 1986; Smolkin 1994), those that focus on the defective attitudes or motives of the agent (Heyd 1992; Kumar 2005), those that locate the wrongness in a form of exploitation (Liberto 2014), and those that reject the intuition that the action is in any way morally objectionable (Schwartz 1978; Boonin 2008, 2015).

The main advantages of the well-being approaches are that they affirm the intuitions that (1) there is a wrong-making feature of the action in a non-identity case and (2) such a feature is fundamentally connected to the value of the individual's well-being. Nevertheless, both of the well-being approaches face some serious challenges. In what follows, I will discuss the harm-based approach and the impersonal value approach in more detail, and I will outline some of what I take to be the main challenges for each approach.

The harm-based approach

Recall the non-identity case that I mentioned at the outset. In that case, a set of prospective parents select an embryo on the basis of a gene for a disease, and the embryo then grows into a child who has the disease. One of the intuitions that gives rise to the non-identity problem is that the child has not been harmed by her parents' action because it does not make her worse off in any respect then she otherwise would have been. Let us formulate this intuition as a general principle about harming:

> The *counterfactually worse-off condition on harming:* An action harms an individual only if it makes her worse off in some respect than she would have been, had the action not been performed.

This necessary condition on harming has a great deal of intuitive support. In paradigmatic cases of harming, an individual *is* made worse off in at least some respect: Smith pushes Jones off the balcony, and now Jones has a broken arm. More importantly, the counterfactually worse-off condition on harming seems to be the best explanation for the intuition that harming is morally objectionable: if harming necessarily makes someone worse off, then we have a straightforward explanation for the claim that there is a moral reason against it.

Nevertheless, the counterfactually worse-off condition on harming does not seem to get the right results in every case. Take, for example, a standard preemption case:

> *Preempted shooting:* Andy is attempting to collect a debt for his boss, Stanley. As Stanley watches, Andy shoots Vincent in the knees. If Andy had not shot Vincent in the knees, Stanley would have, and Vincent would have suffered exactly the same injury.[3]

In this case, Andy's action does not make Vincent any worse off than he would otherwise have been, for if Andy had *not* shot Vincent in the knees, then Stanley would have. Nevertheless, it is intuitively clear that Andy has harmed Vincent.

Non-identity cases are a second class of cases in which the counterfactually worse-off condition is not satisfied. After the prospective parents select for the disease, the resultant child is not any worse off than she would otherwise have been, but many people still have the intuition that by causing her to suffer from the symptoms of the disease, her parents have harmed her.

If we take preemption cases and non-identity cases to be counterexamples to the counterfactually worse-off condition on harming, then we will need to find an alternative. One such alternative appeals to a *non-comparative account* of harm, according to which harm is a state of affairs that is bad for an individual, such that the badness of the state does not derive from its being worse for the individual than some other state that the individual was or would have been in (Shiffrin 1999; Harman 2004, 2009; Woollard 2012). We can conjoin the non-comparative account of harm to a *causal account of harming*, according to which harming an individual is causing that individual to suffer a harm (Harman 2004, 2009; Thomson 2011). The combination of these two accounts yields the following:

> (H) Harming an individual is causing a state of affairs that is non-comparatively bad for that individual.

H seems to justify the claim that, in *preempted shooting*, Andy harms Vincent. After all, Andy causes the state of affairs in which Vincent has injured knees, and having injured knees seems to be a good candidate for a non-comparatively bad state of affairs for Vincent. H also seems to justify people's intuitions about harm in non-identity cases. For example, by selecting the embryo with the genetic disease, the prospective parents cause their child not only to exist, but also to suffer from all the effects of the disease. Suffering from the effects of a disease also seems to be a paradigmatic example of a non-comparatively bad state of affairs. If so, then H implies that the parents harm their child.

Despite the promise that it holds as a harm-based solution to the non-identity problem, H faces a number of challenges. First, there appear to be cases in which an action or event causes an individual to be in a state that is bad for her without harming her. Second, there appear to be cases in which an action or event harms an individual without causing her to be in a state that is bad for her. Third, it is difficult to determine just what it is that makes a state of affairs non-comparatively bad *for some individual,* especially in cases where a similar state of affairs would not be bad for another individual.

The first problem is motivated by cases like the following:

> *Dim vision.* Jones has been blind for many years as a result of retinal damage. Recently, Dr. Smith has developed a surgical operation that can repair some, but not all, of the damage. Dr. Smith operates on Jones and improves his vision from a state of blindness to a state in which Jones can see, but not very well: Jones now has what we will call *dim vision.*[4]

It seems that Jones's having dim vision is a state of affairs that is bad for Jones. Dr. Smith causes that state of affairs. Thus, it would seem that if H is true, then Dr. Smith harms Jones by performing the operation. However, it is intuitively clear that Dr. Smith does not harm Jones.[5]

The second problem for H is illustrated by the following:

> *Death.* Sam, a healthy and happy 25-year-old, is attempting to cross the train tracks when his foot gets stuck. A train hits him and he dies instantly.[6]

The event that consists of the train's hitting Sam does not appear to cause a state of affairs that is bad for Sam. That is because the state of affairs that the accident brings about is one in which Sam no longer exists, and it is difficult to see how a state of affairs can be bad for an individual who no longer exists. However, it is intuitively clear that the train accident harms Sam.

One might think that if we had a more precise account of what it is for a state to be non-comparatively bad for someone, we could explain away the apparent counterexamples and somehow rescue H. However, a dilemma arises when we attempt to make the account of non-comparative badness more precise. Non-comparative badness for an individual must either be absolute or relative. But the most plausible account of badness as an *absolute* notion still renders H susceptible to apparent counterexamples, and the most plausible accounts of badness as a *relative* notion either undercut the original motivation for H, or else, like the absolute account, they render H susceptible to apparent counterexamples.

The most plausible account of non-comparative badness as an *absolute* notion holds that a state of affairs is non-comparatively bad for an individual if and only if it would be bad for *anyone*. What it is to be *bad for anyone* is defined extensionally: states that involve pain, suffering, disease, disability, and so on are bad for anyone. The problem with this account is that there appear to be cases in which an event harms someone by causing him to be in a state that would *not* be bad for just anyone. Consider the following:

> *Loss of fortune.* Jeeves was once a world-renowned physicist with extraordinary intellectual abilities. He then had a stroke and suffered brain damage. The brain damage left him with average intellectual abilities.[7]

It seems that having average intellectual abilities would not be a bad state for just anyone. Nevertheless, the stroke *harmed Jeeves*.

An alternative way to explain what it is for a state to be non-comparatively bad for an individual is to relativize the badness to something about the individual. However, it is difficult to determine what it is about the individual that the badness should be relativized to. Although Elizabeth Harman (2009) suggests that badness should be relativized to the norm for the individual's species, *loss of fortune* illustrates the problem with that approach. Jeeves is a member of the human species, and it does not *seem* to be bad for a human to have average intellectual abilities, even though coming to have average intellectual abilities is a harm for Jeeves.[8]

Could non-comparative badness be relativized to the individual's will or desires?[9] Neither choice is promising. A dog with cancer has neither the will nor the desire to be cancer-free, for she does not have the concept of cancer that is a necessary condition for having such a will or a desire. Nevertheless, when she gets cancer, she is harmed.

How about interests?[10] If we hold that a state is non-comparatively bad for someone if and only if it is contrary to one of her interests, we are only pushing the problem back a step. For we must now decide whether to take an absolute or relativistic approach to deciding *which* interests an individual has. If we attribute the same interests to all sentient individuals, then we face the kind of problem that arose for making the concept of non-comparative badness absolute: the set of universal interests will inevitably be too broad or too narrow. Either we will say that blindness is contrary to the interests of a bat, and thus, that a bat's mother harms him when she conceives him (and thereby causes him to exist in a state of blindness), or we will say that having average intellectual abilities is *not* contrary to Jeeves's interests, so the stroke that causes Jeeves to have average intellectual abilities does *not* harm him.

On the other hand, if we relativize interests, we must decide what to relativize them to. If we relativize interests to species membership, desires, or will, we will again have trouble explaining why Jeeves or the dog with cancer is harmed. Suppose we relativize interests to the level of well-being that individuals *previously* had, or to the level of well-being that individuals *would have had* if some event had not occurred: we say that Jeeves has an interest in having extraordinary intellectual abilities because having such abilities would restore his well-being to pre-stroke levels, or because having such abilities would boost his well-being to the level at which it *would* have been if he had not had the stroke. If we take this option, we undermine one of our original motives for accepting H, which was to vindicate the notion that individuals in non-identity cases can be harmed by actions that restrict their lifetime prospects of well-being even if such individuals *never had* or *would not have had* unrestricted prospects.

Jeff McMahan suggests that whether an individual is "unfortunate" can be relativized to her "native potential" for having a certain level of well-being, where native potential has something to do with "the physical constitution of the individual" (1996: 22). Let us attempt to formulate this idea as an account of a non-comparatively bad state:

> *The native potential account of non-comparative badness:* A state of affairs is non-comparatively bad for someone when it is worse for her than some other state of affairs that could have obtained, given her native potential.

This suggestion is again at odds with the motivation for H. In the selecting for disease case, the child's disease is a consequence of her physical constitution; she is genetically predisposed to develop it. Since she does not have the potential *not* to have the disease, the native potential account implies that her having the disease is not bad for her.

H is in trouble. H says that harming an individual is causing a state of affairs that is non-comparatively bad for that individual. But it seems that, however we define what it is for a state to be *non-comparatively bad for* someone, either we undercut the original motivation for H, or else we invite apparent counterexamples. And if H is in trouble, then so is the harm-based response to the non-identity problem, for without something like H, the harm-based response lacks a solid theoretical grounding.

The impersonal value approach

As an alternative to the harm-based approach, some philosophers have taken the *impersonal value approach,* which attempts to ground the moral reason against the action in non-identity cases in *impersonal value,* or value from an impersonal perspective. Those who take this approach typically hold that, in addition to having value *for* the individual whose life it is, an individual's well-being also has impersonal value. Bringing an individual with a life worth living into existence is a way of increasing impersonal value, and the better the individual's quality of life, the greater the increase in impersonal value.

In order to use this approach to explain why actions in non-identity cases are morally objectionable, philosophers need to formulate a specific principle that relates impersonal value to reasons against actions. Here is a first pass at such a principle:

> *Maximize value* (MV): There is always a reason against failing to maximize impersonal value.

Upon first consideration, MV might seem to solve the non-identity problem. When the prospective parents select for disease, they are bringing into existence someone who, we might expect, would *not* enjoy maximum well-being. Thus, MV explains why there is a reason against their action.

Nevertheless, MV runs into the following problem. Suppose that our only options are to either (a) improve the welfare of existing people or (b) bring into existence a large number of individuals whose lives are only barely worth living. Suppose that, although the lives of the individuals who would exist if we chose (b) are only barely worth living, the sheer number of those individuals makes it true that taking option (b) will maximize impersonal value. Then MV implies that there is a reason against our choosing (a), when it seems intuitively clear that there is no such reason. Let us call the implication that we have reason against choosing (a) the *more people implication*.[11]

To avoid difficulties like the more people implication, some philosophers restrict the scope of impersonal value principles to *same-number choices,* or choices in which the same number of individuals will exist no matter which alternative is chosen. This is already a problem for the impersonal value approach, since not all non-identity cases are same-number choices. Suppose, for example, that in the selecting for disease case, the parents were deciding between selecting for disease or having *no child at all.* In that case, theirs was a different-number choice, so an impersonal value principle restricted to same-number choices cannot explain why there was a reason against their action.

Even if we construe all non-identity cases as same-number choices, impersonal value principles that are restricted to such choices face additional problems. One example of a restricted principle is the following:

> *Same number quality principle* (QP): In a same-number choice, there is some ethical reason not to act so that those who live will be worse off, or have a lower quality of life, than those who would have lived.[12]

On first consideration, QP also holds promise for explaining why the action might be wrong in same-number non-identity cases. Suppose that some prospective parents face a choice between selecting for disease or selecting a non-diseased embryo. Selecting for disease makes it true that the resultant child is worse off than the child who would have lived, had the parents not selected for disease. Thus, QP straightforwardly implies that, in that case, there is a reason against the parents' action.

Nevertheless, QP does not imply that this reason against the action is very strong. To see this, consider what QP says about another case:

> *Goat.* A couple can either raise a child or a goat, but they can't raise both. The couple know that whichever individual they raise will have a life worth living, and they also know that neither the child nor the goat will exist unless they agree to raise it. Ultimately, the couple choose to raise the goat.[13]

Goat is also a same-number choice, and it seems plausible that the goat will be worse off, or have a lower quality of life, than the child. After all, we would expect the child to develop sophisticated cognitive abilities, to form deep and meaningful relationships, to appreciate music and art, and so on, but we would not expect the goat's life to have any of these features. Since these features would presumably contribute to the child's having a higher quality of life than the goat, QP implies that there is a reason against raising the goat instead of the child.

Greene and Augello (2011) argue that the goat case is a counterexample to QP. In their view, there is no moral reason against raising the goat instead of the child. Since QP implies that there *is* such a reason, QP is false.

However, it may be that reasons come more cheaply than this. Some philosophers might say that there *is* a reason against raising the goat: in doing so, the couple give up their chance to raise a child who will have a better quality of life. Nevertheless, this does not solve the problem for QP. Even if there is a reason to refrain from raising the goat, such a reason is weak, in the sense that it could be easily overridden by countervailing considerations. For example, the consideration that you would impress your friends might be sufficient to render goat raising permissible. Conversely, the reason against the action that brings an individual into existence in non-identity cases is stronger. The consideration that you would get lots of sympathy from your friends if you had to raise a sick child would not be sufficient to render selecting for genetic disease permissible. Thus, Greene and Augello are right that the goat case raises a problem for QP even if they are wrong about the nature of the problem. Whether or not there is a reason against raising the goat, QP fails to explain why the reason against the action in a non-identity case is *stronger* than the reason (if there is any) against raising the goat.

Recall that this objection to QP relies upon the claim that the goat is worse off than the child. Such a claim could be challenged. After all, there is a sense in which the goat is *not* worse off than the child. If the goat is born healthy, it can be expected to fare perfectly well *for a goat,* just as a child who is born healthy can be expected to fare perfectly well *for a human.* Indeed, the goat and the child may in some sense be *equally* well off. In support of this idea, McMahan argues that "we distinguish between an individual's level of well-being, on the one hand, and whether [an] individual is well off or badly off, or flourishing or unfortunate, on the other" (1996: 9). He uses the term "fortune" as a technical term to "express a relation between an individual's level of well-being and a standard against which well-being is assessed" (1996, p. 9). I take it that *fortune,* as McMahan understands it, is well-being that is *relativized.*

An advocate of the impersonal value approach can use McMahan's concept of fortune to formulate a principle that would distinguish the choice between a typical human and a disabled human, on the one hand, from the choice between a typical human and a typical goat, on the other. Here is a schematic for such a principle:

> *Same-number quality principle relativized (QPR):* In a same-number choice, there is some ethical reason not to act so that those who live will be worse off, relative to X, than those who would have lived, relative to Y.

Suppose that we fill in various species norms for X and Y. This version of QPR—call it QPRS—implies that there is reason against bringing into existence one individual who will fare badly relative to the norm for her species rather than another individual who will *not* fare badly relative to the norm for his species.

QPRS seems to get the right results, both for same-number non-identity cases and for *goat.* In the same-number version of the selecting for disease case, the actual child's well-being is lower than that of a typical human, whereas the well-being of the possible child who the parents would raise, were they not to select for disease, would not be. QPRS thus implies that there is a reason against selecting for disease. In *goat,* the child will be just as well off relative to a typical human being as the goat will be relative to a typical goat. Therefore, QPRS does not imply that there is a reason against raising the goat.

However, there is a problem for QPRS. Species membership is a notion that does not admit of degree: one cannot be a goat to a greater or lesser extent. Conversely, similarities between organisms stretch along a continuum: a human can be more or less goat-like. Imagine, then, an individual who is roughly in the middle of the continuum between humans and goats; perhaps she is a genetically engineered organism whose DNA is half-human, half-goat. There is either an answer to the question of what species she belongs to or there is not. If there is no answer, then QPRS cannot tell us whether there is a reason against bringing such an individual into existence, and is therefore incomplete. If there is an answer, then there must be a distinct cut-off line that distinguishes humans with goat-like qualities from goats with human-like qualities. There will also be two possible individuals, one on either side of the line, who will be almost qualitatively identical in terms of their phenotype and their lifetime level of well-being. One will be badly off for a human, but the other will be well off for a goat. QPRS implies that there is a reason against bringing the former individual into existence (instead of a typical individual of any species) but no reason against bringing the latter into existence (instead of a typical individual of any species). This implication is objectionably arbitrary.[14]

One might try to rescue QPR by assigning to X and Y values other than species membership. But what other values would it make sense to relativize well-being to? As I noted in the previous section, McMahan suggests that fortune may be relative to an individual's "native potential," where native potential has something to do with the "physical constitution of the individual." Once again, however, the appeal to native potential will not vindicate the judgment that there is a reason against selecting for disease. That is because a genetic disease does not prevent a child from reaching her potential; it helps determine her potential.

Like the personal welfare approach, the impersonal value approach is in trouble. The advocate of the impersonal value approach must find a principle that explains why there is a strong reason against selecting for disease but merely a weak reason (if there is any reason at all) against raising a typical goat instead of a typical child. Neither MV, nor QP, nor QPR and its variants seem to be up to the task.

Conclusion

In this chapter, I have explained the non-identity problem and discussed two strategies for solving it: the harm-based approach and the impersonal value approach. Both approaches appeal to the value of an individual's well-being to explain why there is a reason against the action that brings him or her into existence. The harm-based approach focuses on the value of the individual's well-being to the individual, whereas the impersonal value approach focuses on the value of the individual's well-being from an impersonal perspective.

Both approaches face a number of challenges. Since proponents of the harm-based approach deny the counterfactually worse-off condition on harming, their main challenge is to find an alternative principle that determines whether an individual has been harmed. The most plausible candidate—a principle that associates harming with causing non-comparatively bad states—has trouble getting all the cases right, especially when it comes to explaining why certain states are bad for some individuals but not for others. On the other hand, proponents of the impersonal value approach face the task of explaining why not all failures to maximize utility are equally objectionable.

Notes

1 The term "non-identity problem" was coined by Derek Parfit (1984), but the fundamental tensions that constitute the problem were identified, somewhat independently, by Parfit (1976), Robert Adams (1972), and Thomas Schwartz (1978).
2 There is some disagreement about how, exactly, to define a non-identity case. Some philosophers classify as non-identity cases only those cases in which it appears to be all-things-considered wrong to bring one individual into existence instead of some other individual (see, for example, Harman 2009). However, I think the debate proceeds more fruitfully if we (1) include cases where *no other* individual would have come into existence if the action had not been performed and (2) ask whether there is a *reason* against the action (and not merely whether the action is all-things-considered wrong).
3 This kind of case is discussed by Hanser (2008), Bradley (2012), and Woollard (2012).
4 This example is an adaptation of cases that appear in Hanser (2009), Harman (2009), and Thomson (2011).
5 Harman (2009) responds to this objection by distinguishing between a "particular bad state" and a "general bad state." She claims that causing an individual to be in a *general* bad state is a sufficient condition for harming him or her. If dim vision is a *particular* bad state, it does not follow from Harman's principle and claim that Dr. Smith caused Jones to be in dim vision that Dr. Smith harmed Jones.

Nevertheless, this response raises some questions about how we are to distinguish between general and particular bad states.

6 This case is inspired by Hanser's (2008) argument that, in general, state-based accounts of harm cannot successfully explain why death is a harm. A state-based account of harm is one according to which a harm is a state of affairs; the non-comparative account of harm is one such account. As an alternative to state-based accounts, Hanser favors an event-based account of harm. I do not critique his account here, but see Thomson (2011) for some objections to Hanser's view.

7 This case is modeled upon the Bertrand Russell case in Jeff McMahan (1996) and the case of the Nobel Prize winner in Hanser (2008).

8 This objection to H does not apply to Harman's (2009) view. That is because Harman argues that causing someone "to be in pain, to be in mental discomfort, to be in physical discomfort, to have a disease, to be deformed, to be disabled, or to die" is a *sufficient condition* for harming, not a necessary condition (p. 149). However, Harman's view has the problem that it does not offer a complete analysis of harm, and so cannot explain *why* causing someone to be in pain, discomfort, and so on is sufficient for causing harm.

9 Seana Shiffrin holds that harms are "conditions that generate a significant chasm or conflict between one's will and one's experience, one's life more broadly understood, or one's circumstances" (1999: 123). Similarly, George Pitcher writes, "An event or state of affairs is a misfortune for someone (or harms someone) when it is contrary to one or more of his more important desires or interests" (1984: 184).

10 Joel Feinberg (1984) defends a highly influential account of harm that relativizes harm to an individual's interests. However, he endorses a comparative account of harm.

11 The more people implication is similar to what Derek Parfit (1984) refers to as the "Repugnant Conclusion."

12 This is a principle that Mark Greene and Steven Augello (2011) formulate and then reject. Their formulation is an adaptation of a principle that Derek Parfit calls, "The Same Number Quality Claim, or Q" (1984: 360).

13 This case is an adaptation of "The Good Life" in Greene and Augello (2011).

14 I have adapted this objection from an argument that Greene and Augello (2011) employ against objections to selecting for disability.

References

Adams, R. (1972) "Must God Create the Best?" *The Philosophical Review* 81(3): 317–332.

Boonin, D. (2008) "How to Solve the Non-Identity Problem," *Public Affairs Quarterly* 22(2): 127–157.

Boonin, D. (2015) *The Non-Identity Problem and the Ethics of Future People,* Oxford: Oxford University Press.

Bradley, B. (2012) "Doing Away with Harm," *Philosophy and Phenomenological Research* 85(2): 390–412.

Feinberg, J. (1984) *Harm to Others,* Oxford: Oxford University Press.

Greene, M. and S. Augello (2011) "Everworse: What's Wrong with Selecting for Disability?" *Public Affairs Quarterly* 25(2): 31–139.

Hanser, M. (2008) "The Metaphysics of Harm," *Philosophy and Phenomenological Research* 77(2): 421–450.

Hanser, M. (2009) "Harming and Procreating," in ed. M. Roberts and D. Wasserman (eds.), *Harming Future Persons: Ethics, Genetics and the Nonidentity Problem,* Dordrecht: Springer.

Harman, E. (2004) "Can We Harm and Benefit in Creating?" *Philosophical Perspectives* 18(1): 89–113.

Harman, E. (2009) "Harming as Causing Harm," in M. Roberts and D. Wasserman (eds.) *Harming Future Persons: Ethics, Genetics and the Nonidentity Problem,* Dordrecht: Springer.

Heyd, D. (1992) *Genethics: Moral Issues in the Creation of People,* Berkeley: University of California Press.

Kumar, R. (2005) "Who Can Be Wronged?" *Philosophy and Public Affairs* 31(2): 99–118.

Liberto, H. (2014) "The Exploitation Solution to the Non-Identity Problem," *Philosophical Studies* 167(1): 73–88.

McMahan, J. (1996) "Cognitive Disability, Misfortune, and Justice," *Philosophy & Public Affairs* 25(1): 3–35.

Parfit, D. (1976) "On Doing the Best for Our Children," in M. Bayles (ed.) *Ethics and Population,* Cambridge, MA: Schenkman.

Parfit, D. (1984) *Reasons and Persons,* Oxford: Oxford University Press.

Pitcher, G. (1984) "The Misfortunes of the Dead," *American Philosophical Quarterly* 21(2): 183–188.

Schwartz, T. (1978) "Obligations to Posterity," in R. Sikora and B. Barry (eds.) *Obligations to Future Generations*, Philadelphia: Temple University Press.

Shiffrin, S. (1999) "Wrongful Life, Procreative Responsibility, and the Significance of Harm," *Legal Theory* 5(2): 117–148.

Smolkin, D. (1994) "The Non-Identity Problem and the Appeal to Future People's Rights," *The Southern Journal of Philosophy* 32(3): 315–329.

Thomson, J. (2011) "More on the Metaphysics of Harm," *Philosophy and Phenomenological Research* 82(2): 436–458.

Woodward, J. (1986) "The Non-Identity Problem," *Ethics* 96(4): 804–831.

Woollard, F. (2012) "Have We Solved the Non-Identity Problem?" *Ethical Theory and Moral Practice* 15(5): 677–690.

36

AUTONOMY AND WELL-BEING[1]

Sarah Conly

Many people believe that for us to flourish we need to be in charge of certain significant aspects of our own lives: we need, as it is put, to have our autonomy respected. This is a popular view in the political world: Tea Partiers in the USA object to the requirement to buy health insurance as the end of humanity as we know it, but even rational people worry about the increasing numbers of regulations to which we must comply and about the breakdown between public and private. Philosophers and political theorists, too, have argued that interference in personal decisions by social or state action is a danger to the individual, and that even if such interference succeeds in making people happier, it will have made a desert and called it peace: those who are happier will not really be persons. Philosophers with outlooks as distinct as Immanuel Kant (1785) and John Stuart Mill (1859, 1861) have agreed that subjective contentment is not sufficient for well-being, at least when it comes to humans: the main objection to being controlled by others is not just that they don't do that to our advantage, but that they do it at all.

This objection to outside interference in our choices rests on two claims, both of which, I will argue, are wrong. The first is that choice is uniquely constitutive of the individual. The second is that insofar as choices do help constitute us, interference by others will undercut these constitutive choices in a way that diminishes our ability to reach real personhood.

The first issue is what makes us the persons we are. Even if we concede that there is no metaphysical freedom of the will of the type Kant appears to have believed essential to agency (Kant 1785), there is nonetheless (it is argued) a need for both freedom of choice and a sense of integrity: "in the relevant sense there is no *you* prior to your choices and actions, because your identity is in a quite literal way *constituted* by your choices and actions." And our choices constitute us not just as individual entities but as persons, because, unlike animals, "[w]hen you deliberately decide what sorts of effects you will bring about in the world, you are also deliberately deciding what sort of a cause you will be. And that means you are deciding who you are" (Korsgaard 2009: 19). Or, in a somewhat more qualified description, "[A]utonomy is a capacity that is (partly) constitutive of what it is to be an agent. It is a capacity that we have a responsibility to exercise and that grounds our notion of having a character" (Dworkin 1988: 32).

This may well be true, on some interpretation. It is hard to imagine being a person who never reflects on what she wants to do, or why. And it is equally true that what we do has an effect on us, and thus that it at least helps to constitute us.

However, the political conclusion that other people, and particularly the state, should refrain from interfering with a certain kind of choice rests on the second claim: that this kind of constitutive choice will be undercut or entirely destroyed by certain sorts of interference. Thus, others shouldn't deprive us of certain sorts of options, and should refrain from trying to influence us too much to choose one thing over another, or generally, in our values. Such proscriptions on others' action are typically seen as reflecting our rights as agents:

> Human rights can then be seen as protections of our human standing, or, as I shall put it, our personhood. And one can break down the notion of personhood into clearer components by breaking down the notion of agency. To be agent, in the fullest sense of which we are capable, one must first choose one's own path through life—that is, not to be dominated or controlled by someone or something else (call it "autonomy"). And (second) one's choice must be real; one must have at least a certain minimum education and information. And having chosen, one must then be able to act; that is, one must have at least the minimum provision of resources and capabilities that it takes (call all of this "minimum provision"). And none of this is any good if someone then blocks one; so (third) others must also not forcibly stop one from pursuing what one sees as a worthwhile life (call this "liberty"). Because we attach such high value to our individual personhood, we see its domain of exercise as privileged and protected.
>
> *(Griffin 2008: 33)*

So, personhood itself depends on the ability to make choices, or at least, a certain kind of choice, where "choice" includes two things: making a decision and the ability to act on that decision. And, in turn, autonomous choices make such persons' own well-being possible: "The autonomous person is part author of his life . . . An autonomous person's well-being consists in the successful pursuits of self-chosen goals and relationships . . . Autonomy is opposed to a life of coerced choices" (Raz 1986: 370–371).

These are somewhat different claims, but they have in common the connection between a kind of freedom of choice and the possibility of a robust human existence. To some extent, I will concede, these claims are correct. Certainly, a life in which we could literally never act in accordance with our decisions would be a bad one. I don't know if we would fail to be persons, but that's in part because I can't quite imagine what such a life would be like. I do imagine it would be unhappy, and I can see that it would be very hard to think of oneself as an agent if none of one's desires could be made effective in the world. Nor, indeed, would there be much point to thinking how you ought to act or who you want to be if no choice whatsoever is open to you.

That has very little to do with the permissibility of outside interference in choices, though, since it is very hard to imagine a state that would have the power to do this, or indeed that would have the desire to deprive its citizens of all choices. The practical question is what realistic state interference per se is likely to do to our psychology, and there I think the answer is for the most part, nothing significant. Well, it may affect our lives very deeply, but nothing significant in terms of depriving us of personhood, integrity, or meaning. It is true that we have a prima facie desire that our desires be fulfilled, since that is entailed by the nature of desire. While we naturally want our desires to be fulfilled, there is nothing peculiarly destructive about government intervention, even into the valued sphere commonly thought of as the realm of privacy.

The intrusion of others into our decision making can be felt as disturbing, and can have detrimental effects on our development into fulfilled persons, to be sure. This is not so much a function of the fact of intrusion as what sort of intrusion it is, and why it is taking place. Intrusions that harm us—for example, that cause us fruitless pain, or that make it difficult or impossible to engage in worthwhile, fulfilling pursuits—are indeed bad. It is also detrimental to our self-esteem and to our ability to feel engaged in life if we see the intrusion as indicative of an egregious inequality, one that makes us feel that we are seen as part of an inferior class. For most humans, status is an extremely important aspect of satisfaction, and things that diminish our status are likely to be destructive. None of this suggests that depriving us of options, and taking away even significant choices, is by itself destructive.

The importance of choice

Do we need to satisfy all of our desires, to have selves, or to be persons, or however we describe this desirable state of the psyche? Obviously not, or none of us would be persons. The argument seems to be that some particularly significant choices should be free. The question is what these are, and why they are seen as so significant.

Critically affirmed desires:

A number of people have argued that not all desires play the same role in constituting person-hood. We desire to ram right into the car that clearly sees our turn signal but still won't let us into its lane, even when the driver can see our own lane is ending and we will soon be forced into a cement wall. We also desire to live in civic harmony and rise above the irritations caused by the peccadillos of Boston drivers. And so forth. So, one argument is that the more significant desires in terms of integrity are those we endorse, that we approve of: yes for rising above irritations caused by unenlightened fellow citizens, no for ramming the selfish driver, etc.

Harry Frankfurt famously argued that, when it comes to personhood, not all desires are equal. Our desires may themselves be the object of desires, in that I may desire to have a desire I have (participating in civic harmony) or I may desire not to have a desire (car ramming). These are desires of the second order, as he put it, and the fact that we can have a particular sort of desire about our own desires—a desire that a given desire become my will—is, for him, "essential to being a person" (Frankfurt 1971: 10). Merely having desires for certain things doesn't supply the unity we need to become an integrated being. We know, after all, that some desires are mere passing fancies, whose satisfaction seems unimportant to who we are, and some desires, even if strongly felt, may conflict with others, so that acting on all of them will not be expressive of, nor constitutive of, a unified self. Indeed, even where a desire is long-lasting, strongly felt, and doesn't conflict with another desire, action on it isn't constitutive of you as a *person*, for Frankfurt—many animals, he noted, have desires "of the first order." Only persons, though, have "the capacity for reflective self-evaluation that is manifested in the formation of second-order desires" (Frankfurt 1971: 7).

Whether it is put as the relationship between first- and second-order desires, or whether people speak more generally of endorsing desires, or perhaps even more generally of having values, it is certainly widely believed that there are some desires that play a larger role in our identity than do others—they may provide more general guidance in our lives, or may be felt more strongly, or be more stable across time, or may simply be thought by ourselves to be more important than our other desires.

Does this, however, imply that we should refrain from interfering in actions that reflect second-order volitions? Is it destructive to put regulations in place that are contrary to the considered goals we have constructed for our lives?

First, as something of an aside, I suggest that we shouldn't exaggerate the extent to which these reflective self-evaluative desires actually do constitute us as individuals. It's possible that this ability differentiates us from other *species* in a significant way, although even this is debatable—it may be that what matters is not the specific capacity to form second-order desires but the intelligence and self-consciousness required to do that. In any case, even if such a capacity determines our species as persons, it shouldn't be taken to mean that it is only action on desires endorsed by a second reflective desire that is constitutive of our identity as *individuals*. Much of what makes us distinctive from one another, what gives our lives the particular flavor they have, will be quite unrelated to the choices made upon endorsement of first-order desires. How often do we actually engage in rational reflection in order to differentiate the desires we want to endorse from those we don't? I must admit that I, at least, haven't gone through a reflective process when it comes to the choices that are most significant in my life—whom to marry, whether or not to have children, what kind of work to do. I fell in love. I always wanted to have children. As an undergraduate I took a philosophy course and I liked it so I decided to major in philosophy—and so forth. The most formative aspects of my life have been those I didn't really deliberate about. I honestly remember doing more conscious reflection on where to go for vacation than on whether to have children. I have pondered this quite a lot, whereas I always knew since my own childhood that I wanted to have children and never wavered in that. I don't think, though, that choosing a particular vacation destination actually helped me create myself more than my unreflective choice to have children. Not surprisingly, my being a mother has had much more profound effects on my life than did the Mexican Caribbean. So did my job, the person I married, etc.

A follower of Frankfurt might say that, insofar as I could have deplored (that is, emphatically not endorsed) having children, and didn't, I was implicitly endorsing it. A process of reflection and evaluation was going on beneath the surface, so far beneath that even I didn't notice it. That's possible—it's so hard to say what might have been happening unconsciously. It seems at least as likely, though, that it is a desire on which I could have reflected, in other circumstances (say, had I been aware of the dangers of overpopulation) but upon which, in the actual circumstances, I didn't. We don't want to beg the question by assuming that if a choice is significant to my life then in some sense I must have engaged in reflective self-evaluation about it.

Of course, it's quite possible that I'm just not really a person, or not a full person—who am I to say? Or, it might be that I have the capacity to be a person but don't engage it. To the extent that the more significant aspects of my life, the ones that seem most to have shaped me, are unreflecting predilections, a promoter of autonomy can say I'm something to which things have happened, as opposed to a person who has constituted herself by reflective choice.[2] I find, though, that the more I'm told I'm not really a person, the less I'm persuaded that personhood is really valuable.

However, for purposes of argument let us say that to be persons we need to have these second-order desires, to exercise the capacity to endorse some of our desires and not others. Does that require in turn that we should be able to act, without state interference, on those endorsed desires?

What happens if we cannot act upon our endorsed desire? In the short run, of course, we are likely to be unhappy, but that does not make us less a person (although of course there other reasons to avoid unhappiness!). The problem for those who promote freedom of action may be that, in point of fact, if it is established that something is impossible, we are likely to stop wanting to do that thing. We will change our values. We are not likely to want, or to value, something we can't possibly get. In the face of impossibility, we may even disvalue something that, were it within our reach, we would want very much. For one thing, we simply have limited imaginations—we are not likely to formulate a desire for something that is so unavailable that we haven't even heard of it. Cave men did not construct life plans around being a CEO—they probably did not calculate success in life in terms of "career advancement." Beyond that, though, even when we meet with the impossibility of attaining a goal we do recognize, we often come to stop wanting to want that thing. We don't like frustration, so if we can avoid it by not valuing the thing we can't get, we often do that. We can and do change both our first- and our second-order desires according to circumstances.

Insofar as government interference makes certain options impossible, that may well affect the structure of our desires and of our values. This would be bad if it meant we didn't want anything, if our capacity for desire, or for evaluation, atrophied. But why would it? Government interference is not likely to mean the removal of all options from people, and if it did, that would be a very bad government. A good government will remove only some options (and, of course, will also create other and better options). But there is nothing in that that will undercut either the formation of values, or the relationship between values and desires. What we will get is different values, and different desires.

Where, after all, do second-order desires come from? It has been pointed out that there is no particular reason to think that our second-order desires are any better founded than our first-order desires (Watson 1987). Even if we reflect, in the sense that we consciously consider what we want to want, these reflective desires may be as arbitrary as any others. They are a product of circumstance. Jan Elster has discussed at length the existence of adaptive preferences, where one adapts one's first order-desires, one's second-order desires, and for that matter, one's beliefs, according to the availability of success (Elster 1983). Just as the fox, in the fable of the sour grapes, comes to believe that the grapes he wanted but can't reach are really sour, we can come to believe that things we can't do aren't really desirable, and can come to value what we are able to do. Removing an option may mean we stop wanting it, but not that we live a life of anomie, stripped of enlivening desires; we can want something else in its stead.

After all, government interference aside, we know that what we come to value is always in large part a function of things beyond our control. We are raised in a certain way, and that affects our values. Our culture promotes one thing over another, and that affects our values. And, certain options are not open to us, and that affects our values. Even where options exist in a general sense, so that I have the concept of them the way the caveman mentioned above does not have the concept of corporate success, we tend not to care about constructing a certain kind of life if that isn't possible for us. I have never aspired to be an NBA player, and presumably that is largely a function of the fact that I'm no good at basketball. I suffer no sense of frustration at not being able to play in the big leagues because it never crossed my mind that it would be possible. I have, on the other hand, come to value some of the things I can succeed at, because it is much more fulfilling to value what I can do than what I can't. Government is part of that world that shapes what we want: "Whether people have a preference for a commodity, a right, or anything else is in part a function of whether the government has allocated it to them in the first instance" (Sunstein 1991: 8).

Integrity, the wholeness of a life lived in accordance with one's values, can come either from the freedom to act in accordance with one's existing values or from a change of values to reflect the actions we are free to take.

This does mean that our values are subject to change, and not always as a result of thoughtful reflection. As an option, previously open, becomes closed, we will, if we are to avoid frustration and a sense that our lives are no longer our own, come to value some of those things that remain open to us. Change, though, is compatible with being a full-fledged person, with having an integrated self. Indeed, we think it is rather peculiar if people's values don't change as their circumstances change. If someone does indeed have a shot at the NBA, he may value making it very much, but if it turns out he doesn't make the cut, we naturally hope that he will change his goals and aspirations. If he doesn't, it will seem obsessive, rather than a sign of admirable integrity of character. This will be true for many of our youthful—and indeed, middle-aged—aspirations: you get over it when certain hopes don't turn out, and if you don't, we think you have a problem with how to constitute the self, rather than that you are really good at it.

Personal choices

Others, though, who object to government interference claim it is not the status of a desire—first- or second-order, endorsed or unendorsed—that matters, but what that desire pertains to. Many have claimed that there are areas of personal decision that need to be protected precisely because they are personal (Mill 1861; Brandeis and Warren 1890; Fried 1968; Rachels 1975, Cohen 2012). Generally, we think of the realms of the private as something deserving special protection. Some might say that this is trivially true, that the private is by definition the realm into which state action does not interfere, but that is not the point being made here. Rather, the argument is normative—that there are certain sorts of things that ought to remain off limits to outside scrutiny, and to outside intervention. The focus is typically on what we think of as domestic life—who one lives with, the organization of one's family, and one's own activities in the home. The idea is that failing to respect these limits will damage our ability to live as whole persons, because freedom of faction in these areas is peculiarly important to our self-conception.

There is some force to the argument that the decisions we make, the relationships we share, and the activities we partake in outside the public eye are uniquely important for most of us. These relationships are especially important to me, and play a major role in who I am. I have other relationships—those I have as a citizen, for example, where I am bound by duties to the community, and generally receive reciprocal advantages. But those, for most of us, just don't have the same significance as my personal friendships, or the relationships I have within my family, however we may define family. How we live, whether we marry and whom we marry, whether to have children, what sort of activities we engage in—these are seen by many people as central to the lived experience of a life. And, for that reason, it is argued, they must be protected:

> Practically speaking, the strength or very possibility of intimate relationships varies inversely with the degree of social intrusion into such relationships generally tolerated.
> *(Shoeman 1980: 14)*

The more important the relationship or activity, the more we think interference is at the least morally suspect, and often absolutely impermissible.

This is a standard picture. It is, however, odd. How much control do we have over these things, after all? Consider my control over my activities: the activities I most enjoy depend on leisure, which I'll define for present purposes as time off from working. Leisure is important to me, and like most people, I don't relish the idea of the state or anyone else coming into my home and forcing, or even cajoling, me into leisure activities they believe to be more valuable than those I actually want to engage in. Still, can it be said that I ever control my leisure? First and foremost, I obviously don't control how much leisure I have. A lot of that arises from laws that mandate we get a certain amount of time off, or from contracts that labor unions worked for. None of that was determined by me. And almost none of us have a choice about whether we want to work in the first place, something that entirely changes the shape of our lives. We just need the money, so we work. Still, we don't find ourselves rising up against the need to work as an unconscionable intrusion into our freedom. We may not want to work, but we certainly don't think that insofar as we do we aren't persons, or don't have selves. My total lack of control here has left my claims to personhood untarnished.

And this is generally true of these important, constitutive choices: take our right to control whom we marry. I have control over whom I marry in that I can decline any marriage I don't want, but honestly, in my case that choice doesn't come up much. I clearly don't have the freedom to marry Benedict Cumberbatch, much as I would like that. I don't even have the power to *meet* Benedict Cumberbatch, and then there is the fact that Mr. Cumberbatch himself would have to be willing. The constitution of our domestic lives is always tremendously constrained, by where we happen to live, whom we happen to meet, and (among others) who happens to want to marry *us*. Personhood is not dependent on freedom vis-à-vis any particular choice, or on the possibility of acting on some particularly significant desire.

Of course, what you do in your life makes a difference to who you are. But only part of that is ever chosen, and when it is chosen, it is always chosen from a relatively narrow set of options: options constrained by knowledge, by talent, by physical capacities, by geographical location, by the years in which you live. And, by state actions. Constraint on choice is ubiquitous. Furthermore, the unchosen things that happen to you in your life can make just as big a difference to the quality of your life as can the things you choose—or, at times a bigger difference. For some this is tragic—there was nothing they could do about the car that crashed into their child and killed him. For others, it can be wonderful—they were born into a family both rich and benevolent, they luck out with the child who is healthy and sanguine, etc. Of course, one may say we can choose how to react to these things, but again, that, too, is always within a severely constrained set of options.

The source of interference

None of this is a secret. Proponents of autonomy as necessary to identity do realize that our values are affected by our situation:

> We all know that persons have a history. They develop socially and psychologically in a given environment with a given set of biological endowments. They mature slowly and are heavily influenced by their parents, siblings, peers, and culture. What sense does it make to speak of their convictions, motivations, and principles, and so forth as "self-selected"? . . . We can no more choose *ab initio* than we can jump out of our skins. To insist upon this as a condition is to make autonomy impossible.
>
> *(Dworkin 1976: 24)*

And,

> The fact that our self-interest, and more generally, what counts towards our well-being, is to a considerable extent determined by our own actions, does not presuppose free or deliberate choice of options. To be sure our well-being is not served by projects we are coerced into unless we come willingly to embrace them. But not everything we willingly embrace is something we have freely or deliberately chosen from among various alternatives open to us.
>
> *(Raz 1986: 369)*

So, reasonable proponents of autonomy accept that we are never fully in charge of our values, endorsements, and so forth. But people still see a huge problem when the interference in our lives comes from other people. More specifically, they find it objectionable when interference in our lives comes from other people who are interfering *intentionally*.

Consider, for example, state interference in how many children we have. The Chinese one-child policy has received great condemnation as an invasion of privacy. Granted, the Chinese situation is made much worse by the fact that the Chinese sometimes invade the body through forced abortions or sterilizations, but even without that most people (at least, outside of China) seem to believe that the very idea of government coercion, even through the customary Chinese sanction of fines, is an impermissible interference into one of the most significant private relationships we can have. Conversely, the fact that we may feel compelled to limit how many children we have because we can't *afford* to have more seems to arouse no general indignation. The costs of fines that keep people from having children may be proportionately much less than the cost of college tuition that also keeps people from having more than a certain number of children, but the first, not the second, is seen as grounds for outrage, even though the fact that in the USA our universities cost as much as they do (sometimes upwards of $250,000 per child) is clearly a function of human activity, and the aggregation of human choices—it's not some natural fact that must be taken as a given. Not surprisingly, prudent parents, especially those who intend to send their children to private colleges, find themselves refraining from having large families.

Yet, the fact that these costs intrude into our lives in ways that affect these very personal preferences arouses nothing like the general indignation the Chinese laws do. Similarly, the fact that so many Americans haven't been able to afford even basic health care is a function of choices the society has made, yet, while it is often perceived as unfortunate that some sick people can't see a doctor, most people don't see it as an impermissible infringement on liberty. The idea that the federal government would require that people get health insurance so that everyone can afford a doctor's visit, though, calls for protest against those who are taking away our rights to privacy. When we regard abject poverty as an unfortunate accident, we don't resent it as much as we do an intentionally tyrannous government, even though, as Amartya Sen has pointed out, poverty can be at least as destructive (Sen 2000).

So, while we regret impersonal circumstances that stop us from doing what we want to do, we don't see them as significant obstacles to the constitution of the self—we don't see them as interventions that rob of us of personhood. The significant difference in our reaction is a function of whether or not we see the obstacle as intentional. What is it about intentional interference that makes it so dangerous? Even Elster, who stressed the heterogeneous origin of preferences, wrote that interference from others is at least prima facie incompatible with liberty in a way that other interferences aren't:

> My view is that unless the obstacles have been created for the purpose of preventing one from doing x, one has the formal freedom to do x. Moreover, I believe that this formal freedom is a valuable thing, even if it does not go together with full ability. This is so for at least two reasons: it is a good thing in itself not to be subject to another person's will; and when one is not so subject, the chances are better that one may be able to achieve something substantially equivalent. If I cannot afford to buy a book, I can borrow it from the library; if the government forbids its sale, it will also forbid its being available in the library.
>
> *(Elster 1983:126 fn55)*

The example Elster gives, though, does not illustrate his claim. It's false to say that we are either subject to another's will when the government bans a book, or free when we have to get it from the library due to a lack of money. If I cannot afford to buy a book, whether or not I can get it at the library is *entirely* a function of others' will. They have to will to fund libraries, and someone at the library has to will the acquisition of this book for lending purposes. And, of course, someone had to will to write it. This is merely a footnote in Elster's work, but it is significant in that it suggests a kind of belief that is common—that if institutions, like libraries, have been in place a while, we don't think of them as arising through acts of will, but as somehow naturally occurring and fixed. This, of course, is not true. Institutions arise from acts of will. Not all existing institutions arise from acts of will intending their creation (the first person to invent monetary scrip may not have thought "I am now making capitalism possible") but they are still a function of willed actions, and some institutions that we accept, like libraries, do arise from specifically intended acts of will, and in particular acts of will arising from government officials. Living without being affected by any willed social institution at all is possible, but would require solitude most people can't imagine—even anchorites had someone who willed to bring them food.

So again, why is the particular species of willed act that involves interfering in my options so upsetting? We can easily agree that a sense of frustration is disagreeable, but we know that desires can be frustrated in various ways, and that, as above, a systematic interference is likely to result in us retooling our preferences. Why would a law forbidding me from marrying Benedict Cumberbatch be so much worse than Benedict Cumberbatch's complete indifference—which, were we to meet, would no doubt evolve into a positive distaste for marrying me? If the answer is that in the absence of a law, I might hope Benedict Cumberbatch would change his mind, that is true—I might *hope* that, but it wouldn't make that hope correct. It would be better to give up all hope and develop a preference for someone who is not an international television and film star, which is what most of us do. And for that matter, laws can be changed—much more easily than Benedict Cumberbatch's affections.

Bad government

The answer is that there are particular dangers to one's sense of integrity, identity, and personhood that may arise from government action, and we are particularly alert to these. These dangers may arise from people outside government, too, but those that are enacted into law tend to be particularly opprobrious and particularly hard to fight. Consider a state that systematically enforces laws that people will be treated unequally, and in particular interferes in personal life in ways that are oppressive to a particular group. Some interference limits our options in ways we can't adjust to—not all desires are malleable. Those interferences merely make us unhappy, and resentful, and bitter, and angry, with no corresponding advantages to compensate for what we have lost.

In some cases inequality is like this—something we just can't get used to. We long to be free of the state's yoke, and feel ourselves diminished, incapacitated, and fractured when we cannot free ourselves and act on our desires. Or, in other situations, unequal treatment may limit our options in ways to which we do indeed adjust, through adaptive preferences, but this can still cause injury. If adjusting to inequality means people accept beliefs about their own inferiority in order to cope with the system that treats them unequally, this conflicts with other, deeper preferences: the need for self-respect, for example, and the confidence needed to pursue one's projects successfully.

It is entirely true, then, that some government interventions in freedom are bad. A law forbidding me in particular from marrying Benedict Cumberbatch would come with the recognition that people in power think I am inferior and unworthy. A law forbidding anyone from marrying him might, presumably, make him feel the same way—unless, in either case, there is some reason for the law that doesn't depend on a an assessment of us as generally unworthy. (A genetic study has been done, and our children would introduce a new and fatal strain of . . . And so forth.) Sometimes the pain and oppression that accompany a bad law may be intentional, and in other cases it may not, but either way the effect is to diminish people's lives. This doesn't show that government interference has to be bad. Clearly, regulations should treat us equally where we are equal. More generally, regulations shouldn't interfere in ways that lead to greater dissatisfaction. The fact that we disapprove of regulations that make us unhappy, or regulations that promote oppressive adaptive preferences, doesn't show that we should disapprove either of regulations in general or adaptive preferences in general. Regulations should be geared to making us better off, and if they do this, we will flourish.

It is true, to be sure, that new regulations tend to arouse resentment, even when they are beneficial. We feel coerced when an option we are used to having is taken away, because we grew up in a certain landscape of options and our desires were shaped by them, and because we often can't believe that a regulation that wasn't around before could possibly be necessary now (unless we ourselves perhaps have vividly understood the changing circumstances that have made it necessary). We see a change in the opportunities we are used to as if it were a right that is being revoked—the way we feel resentment when someone takes "our" seat in a classroom.

This, though, just isn't a good indication of the actual moral worth of the regulation, nor a good prognostication as to what it will do to our development to have to abide by it. We get used to things. There are many intrusive regulations we now accept as not only permissible but absolutely obligatory: regulations against domestic violence, for example, which obviously do intrude into the realm of the family, but which we now all applaud. Government regulations as to child welfare—requirements that children be educated, maintained with some specified level of shelter and nutrition, etc.—are now seen as necessary in a decent society. Even paternalistic regulations are accepted once they've been around long enough—like requiring prescriptions for medicine.

Again, this is not to say that we are infinitely malleable creatures. We have some needs that remain constant, and failing to meet these can in fact infringe upon our ability to live fulfilled human lives. Some of these are biological in origin: food, warmth, shelter. Some are psychological: we need social interaction, self-expression through communication, education, some range of options in which we can exercise choice, and I think, to be treated as equal in some significant realm. These are needed, but their value is not a function of our having chosen them.

Conclusion

Intrusions into personal choice are inevitable. Sometimes it's a function of the impersonal universe. Sometimes it's a function of a society unaware of its effects on individuals. Sometimes it's the intentional action of those in the government. Not only is government interference not the worst of these, it can be the best. It is something that can be controlled far more easily than the workings of the impersonal universe or the indirect effects of society on the individual: it is malleable, and it is conscious, and chosen, and therefore a suitable subject for deliberation. And, of course, state intervention can expand options, liberating people from some choices to pursue more meaningful ones. If I'm not allowed to smoke, I'm then allowed to spend more healthy years in pursuit of gratifying activities, activities I can indeed choose and allow to define me. Interference can allow us to constitute better selves than they could otherwise. Can government make bad or even evil choices? Obviously. But we don't want to let justified caution turn into mere laziness, an unwillingness to do the work of considering what government measures are actually desirable. As we don't want to accept each and every government measure as beneficial, neither should we reject the idea of interference as destructive. What matters is if people have better or worse lives. If interventions promote happiness and self-development, they are not a problem.

Notes

1 I would like to thank those present at conferences at Umeå University and the University of Chicago for their comments on this paper.
2 Cf. Korsgaard "Movements that result from forces working *on* me or *in* me constitute things that happen to me ... For a movement to be my action, for it to be expressive of *myself* in the way that an action must be, it must result from my entire nature working as an integrated whole" (2009: 18–19). But—my *entire nature*? Really? How often does this happen?

References

Brandeis, L. and Warren, S. (1890) "The Right to Privacy," *Harvard Law Review* 4(5): 190–220.
Cohen, J. (2012) "What Privacy is For," *Harvard Law Review* 126(7): 1904–1933.
Dworkin, G. (1976) "Autonomy and Behavior Control," *Hastings Center Report* 6(1): 23–28.
Dworkin, G. (1988) *The Theory and Practice of Autonomy*, Cambridge: Cambridge University Press.
Elster, J. (1983) *Sour Grapes: Studies in the Subversion of Rationality*, Cambridge: Cambridge University Press.
Frankfurt, H.G. (1971) "Freedom of Will and the Concept of a Person," *Journal of Philosophy* 68(1): 5–20.
Fried, C. (1968) "Privacy," *Yale Law Journal* 77(3): 475–493.
Griffin, J. (2008) *On Human Rights*, Oxford: Oxford University Press.
Kant, I. (1785) *Groundwork of the Metaphysics of Morals*. Reprinted as Hill, T.E. Jr. and Zweig, A. (eds.) (2002) *Groundwork for the Metaphysics of Morals*, tr. A. Zweig, Oxford: Oxford University Press.
Korsgaard, C. (2009) *Self-Constitution: Agency, Identity, and Integrity*, Oxford: Oxford University Press
Mill, J.S. (1859) *On Liberty*. Reprinted as Warnock, M. (ed.) (2003) *Utilitarianism and On Liberty*, Oxford: Blackwell Publishing.
Mill, J.S. (1861) *Considerations on Representative Government*. Reprinted (2008) Oxford: Oxford University Press.
Rachels, J. (1975) "Why Privacy is Important," *Philosophy and Public Affairs*, 4(4): 323–333.
Raz, J. (1986) *The Morality of Freedom*, Oxford: Clarendon Press.
Sen, A. (2000) *Development as Freedom*, New York: Knopf.
Shoeman, F. (1980) "Rights of Children, Rights of Parents, and the Moral Basis of the Family," *Ethics* 91(1): 6–19.
Sunstein, C. (1991) "Preferences and Politics," *Philosophy and Public Affairs* 20(1): 3–34.
Watson, G. (1987) "Free Action and Free Will," *Mind* 96(382): 145–172.

37

WELL-BEING AND DISADVANTAGE

Jonathan Wolff and Douglas Reeve

Yalding in Kent, UK, is no stranger to winter floods. This small village at the confluence of the rivers Tiese, Beult, and Medway experienced the Christmas flood of 1927, the multiple floods of 2000, and their latest inundation on Christmas Eve, 2013. Residents of the unfortunately named Little Venice Country Park in Yalding suffered evacuation and loss of property. A serious problem no doubt, but not as severe as those suffered by many others elsewhere. Lives were not lost. Prime Minister David Cameron, on a televised visit to the area, seemed genuinely taken aback when a local resident scolded him for lack of action in preventing or responding to the latest torrent engulfing the village. Imagine his further discomfort when just one week later the Environment Agency announced it was cutting jobs in flood protection in England as part of a major restructuring of the organization, albeit that this decision had been taken several months earlier. On the face of it, some investment to protect the well-being of Kentish villagers would seem justified. However, a protective barrier for Yalding would cost around £20 million, and raising that sum has not proved easy in times of budget cuts and austerity. The challenge for government policy makers is not just how best to allocate the Environment Agency's funds but also how to distribute scarce funds across multiple diverse areas, including the environment, health care, pensions, education. It is a complex challenge and probably a thankless task, in that even an optimal allocation of resources will leave many problems unresolved.

How should local and central government politicians respond to such situations, and what, if anything, can philosophers offer to guide their efforts? Most politicians would accept that they are in their roles to protect and promote the well-being of their constituents. Political philosophers have debated at length what constitutes well-being and how governments should act. Egalitarian theorists have invested enormous efforts exploring what exactly should be equalized without reaching a broadly held consensus. But whilst many such theorists differ on the details, it appears that most agree on one common factor: *to identify the least advantaged and prioritize actions to reduce their disadvantage.* Of course there will be differences of opinion amongst egalitarian philosophers about how strongly one should prioritize such actions but the nature of the proposals that follow does not require that the priority be absolute. Indeed, the general aim is left sufficiently vague to enable the inclusion of non-egalitarian theorists. It is assumed that the proportion of philosophers and policy makers who would deny any priority to the least advantaged would be small. This limited convergence is sufficient to get the investigation started and our aim is to suggest practical measures for policy makers based on the theories and research of human well-being in political philosophy and other academic disciplines. (The background and research for much of this chapter are detailed in Wolff and de-Shalit 2007.)

If policy makers are to prioritize actions to reduce disadvantage amongst the least advantaged it follows that, first of all, they need an understanding of what it is to be disadvantaged. It is perhaps natural at first glance to link disadvantage with poverty, and poverty with low income. However, it is now widely accepted that disadvantage can take many forms, that might not be directly connected to low income, including poor health, loneliness, or addiction. Indeed, some of these forms of disadvantage may not be adequately offset by increases in income. Recognizing that the many determinants of well-being may not be reducible to a common currency such as income leads to the view that advantage and disadvantage are best understood in a pluralist form. Unfortunately, this insight on its own is not enough to enable policy makers to achieve their task.

One response to the multi-faceted nature of well-being is to identify and address "separate spheres" of disadvantage, arguing that, because they are incommensurable, they are best subjected to local justice, in the sense of treating each area in isolation from others. Arguably, this is what often happens in practice, with separate government departments focused on distinct issues, such as education, transport, and health. However, this response leaves the problem of how to allocate budgets across the separate spheres. It also leaves the concern that the least advantaged overall may not have been identified and prioritized.

A second response, that we advocate in the main body of this chapter, builds on a modified version of the Capability Approach developed by Amartya Sen and Martha Nussbaum, and originally proposed in Wolff and de-Shalit (2007). The final part of this piece furthers this approach by incorporating research on Self-Determination Theory (SDT), pioneered by the social psychologists Richard Ryan and Edward Deci, to extend the practical guidance offered to policy makers.

Extending the Capability Approach

The well-established Capability Approach, extensively debated over the last 20 years, seeks to understand someone's well-being by attending to what she can do or be, known as her "capability to function." Although Sen has withheld from defining a list of such functionings or capabilities, Nussbaum has published and refined a working list of central capabilities that have become a starting point for many interested in this field.[1] An abbreviated form of Nussbaum's list is as follows:

1. Life: Being able to live to the end of a human life of normal length.
2. Bodily health: Being able to have good health, including reproductive health; to be adequately nourished, to have adequate shelter.
3. Bodily integrity: Being able to move freely from place to place; being able to be secure against assault, including sexual assault, child sexual abuse, and domestic violence; having opportunities for sexual satisfaction and for choice in matters of reproduction.
4. Sense, imagination, and thought: Being able to imagine, think, and reason—and to do these things in a way informed and cultivated by an adequate education. Freedom of expression, speech, and religion.
5. Emotions: Being able to have attachments to things and people outside ourselves; to love those who love and care for us.
6. Practical reason: Being able to engage in critical reflection about the planning of one's life.

7. Affiliation: Being able to live with and toward others, to recognize and show concern for other human beings, to engage in various forms of social interaction. Having the social bases of self-respect and non-humiliation. Not being discriminated against on the basis of gender, religion, race, ethnicity, and the like.

8. Other species: Being able to live with concern for and in relation to animals, plants, and the world of nature.

9. Play: Being able to laugh, to play, to enjoy recreational activities.

10. Control over one's environment: Being able to participate effectively in political choices that govern one's life. Being able to have real opportunity to hold property. Having the right to seek employment on an equal basis with others.

In looking to identify the least advantaged and develop practical guidance for policy makers, Nussbaum's list prompts several questions. Firstly, is it complete: have all the central capabilities been identified? Secondly, are all ten capabilities of equal importance, and if not how should they be weighted? A quick inspection suggests they cannot be of equal importance since *life* is more fundamental than *play*, and with that realization comes the specter of even greater complexity facing would-be policy makers when trying to identify the least advantaged. However, through a combination of intuition and empirical research, supported by practical results from the field of epidemiology, the apparent complexity of the Capability Approach might be restricted and some enhancements made possible. *Disadvantage* examined how Nussbaum's list of ten capabilities was tested for completeness and relative importance (Wolff and de-Shalit 2007).

Dynamic public reflective equilibrium

The process adopted was a form of "reflective equilibrium." In general, this refers to the testing of various parts of our moral outlook, or a new theory, by checking for coherence with the remainder of our moral and non-moral beliefs. Beliefs that do not cohere in one way or another raise an alarm. It could be that the theory under consideration itself is unsound and should be modified, or, it could indicate that some other element of our overall belief system is doubtful and in need of further examination.

John Rawls famously introduced the technique in his *A Theory of Justice*, although he drew similarities to earlier techniques of justification described by Nelson Goodman (Rawls 1971: 20). Rawls describes a thought process that might perhaps better be labeled as "private reflective equilibrium," in which the thinker tests her provisional moral theories for coherence with her broader set of beliefs. In such a case both the theory under examination and the broader set of beliefs are specific to the experimenter and may be at odds with the population at large.

A second approach that might be termed "contextual reflective equilibrium" emerges from the work of Michael Walzer (1993, 1994). His views seem to imply that theories of political philosophy should be assessed against the moral beliefs of the particular communities to which they are applied. In this model, the philosopher observes the actions and expressed views of a given society and develops theories to represent their morality. However, although the behavior observed may accurately reflect the views of the community, the theory remains solely that of the philosopher.

Taking this line of development one stage further leads to a model of "dynamic public reflective equilibrium," by which the theories considered are those of the society at large, as well as the philosopher, and where the philosopher engages the public in the process of finding a reflective equilibrium. In this way, the philosophers' theories are revised and modified according to the theories and intuitions of the selected participants. This model asserts that people's intuitions, beliefs, and theories should be a primary input for a political philosophy that seeks to influence practical policies. The voices of the disadvantaged are specifically included.

Applying this approach to Nussbaum's list of central capabilities involved four initial steps:

1. General exploratory discussions about how well the categories of capability (functionings) covered the positions of those most would consider disadvantaged in some way or other.
2. Identification of additional categories of functionings that might be considered central.
3. Testing of the combined list of functionings with initially 38, and later another 60, interviewees from Israel and England selected for their special knowledge of disadvantage—either as workers with disadvantaged individuals or groups, or their clients.
4. Further revision of the list of functionings based on the interviewees' input.

What emerged from this process was that Nussbaum's list appears admirably comprehensive but with room for the inclusion of possibly four further functionings.

The first of these increments is a response to the idea that the original ten functionings may place too much emphasis on the person as receiver; a focus on what one is entitled to and how one benefits from the process of distribution. With a nod to republican thinking, it was suggested that what matters on the topic of well-being is not just what one is entitled to, but also what one is able to contribute to society. Caring for others is seemingly an important part of one's well-being. The potential new functioning might be captured as:

*   Doing good to others. Being able to care for others as part of expressing your humanity. Being able to show gratitude (Wolff and de-Shalit 2007: 45–61).

The remaining three incremental functionings that surfaced during the process were:

*   Living in a law-abiding fashion. The possibility of being able to live within the law; not being forced to break the law, cheat, or to deceive other people or institutions.
*   Understanding the law. Having a general comprehension of the law, its demands, and the opportunities it offers to individuals. Not standing perplexed facing the legal system.
*   Being able to communicate, including being able to speak the local language, or being verbally independent.

Some might argue that these additional categories overlap with, or replicate, other capabilities that are already on the list. It perhaps depends upon how one understands the terminology, but the aim here is to avoid any important omissions.

Having addressed the question of possible completeness we are able to turn to the question of relative importance.

Interviewees were asked to identify the most important categories of functioning, and the resulting analysis suggested a broad consensus for the following:

*   life;
*   bodily health;
*   bodily integrity;
*   affiliation (more often described as "belonging");
*   control over one's environment;
*   sense, imagination, and thought (including education).

This step of reducing from 14 to the six most central or core functioning categories might seem like progress but it does not remove the weighting problem, to which we return later.

Functioning security

To this point we have not focused on the distinction between *functioning*, such as being well nourished, and the *capability* or freedom to achieve full nourishment. The former is more easily measurable while the latter emphasizes the important freedom to choose, and hence in accounts such as Nussbaum's what matters is whether people have the capability to achieve functionings, whether or not they choose to do so. In some cases the appeal of this view is clear: it is important, for example, that people have the capability to pursue their preferred religion if they choose to do so, but it would be quite wrong for the state to force, or even encourage, individuals to pursue religious goals. However it is unclear how far this example generalizes. Sen points out that a wealthy person may choose to go without food and thus lack the functioning of being nourished, while all along having the capability to be nourished. Such a person has no claim on the government for food. But in practical terms the force of the example is less clear. We can make sense of a wealthy person who for religious or political reasons chooses to starve, yet such a person would not in any case seek food from the state. In other cases where someone deliberately chooses to be undernourished we typically regard her behavior as exhibiting an eating disorder, needing medical attention, rather than an exercise of freedom on the model of religious freedom.

From these reflections it is far from clear that it is right to assume that only capabilities and not functionings are the legitimate concern of governments. Furthermore, the relationship between choice and well-being is complex. In the case of nourishment, for example, what seems important may not be whether one chooses to be nourished or not, but rather that one is able to choose how to obtain nourishment: i.e., to be able to exercise freedom in choosing the foods and meal times that one prefers or feels most appropriate. We will return to this important issue in the final section.

To recap, Sen and Nussbaum emphasize the notion of capabilities, yet whether or not people achieve functionings can also be a legitimate concern of governments. From this it be might thought possible to identify disadvantage with regard to one aspect of bodily health simply by observing whether an individual is, or is not, adequately nourished. However, this overlooks an important element that is missing in the standard Capability Approach, the element of future risk. The comfortably positioned individual with a good income and stable surroundings will not only be well nourished today but can expect to be so next week, next month, and next year. Another equally well-nourished individual may, however, be down to her last few items of food with no income or obvious means to provide for her own or her family's nourishment in the near or distant future. Current levels of functioning can in this way mask a major disadvantage in future functioning. Risk to central capabilities may induce choices and behaviors that compound the problem. The father with an empty cupboard may be forced to consider high-risk employment or breaking the law in order to feed his children, thus spreading the risk associated with one functioning to another. Furthermore, the impending loss of a central functioning is not only a disadvantage in itself but the anxiety created by functionings at risk is an additional disadvantage with probable further impacts on health and well-being. It follows that functioning security is a vital part of one's well-being and its absence is a major contributor to disadvantage.

Policy makers might reasonably respond to this state of affairs by providing opportunities for individuals to secure their functionings. For example, they may offer employment opportunities to enable single mothers to provide shelter, clothing, and food for their families. They may consider their obligations fulfilled with the provision of this opportunity regardless of whether or not it is taken up. Such opportunities may, however, carry cross-functional risks for the beneficiaries. The well-being of the children may be jeopardized while the mother is at work, as might also be her capability to care for them and her feeling of self-esteem. What seems important is that opportunities presented by policy makers are reasonable for the recipients to take up, all things considered, and not simply theoretical or formal.

Incorporating these factors (interconnectivity of functionings, realistic nature of opportunities, and the risk to functioning security) is arguably the main revision to the capabilities approach presented in *Disadvantage* (Wolff and de-Shalit 2007): what matters for individuals is not only their level of functionings at any particular time, but also their genuine prospects for sustaining that level. On this reading, disadvantage is defined as the lack of genuine opportunities for secure functionings.

While the inclusion of risk to functionings in the Capability Approach increases its completeness, it also adds to its complexity, raising a further challenge to its effective application. Identifying the least advantaged seems even more difficult when functioning risk has to be included.

Clustering of disadvantage

How are we to compare the lack of genuine opportunity for one particular secure functioning with that of another? After a review of much empirical data the conclusion was reached that precise weightings may not matter because the most extreme disadvantage typically occurs when several disadvantages cluster together. One need only consider the homeless, with no employment prospects, little money, no family support network, and failing health to see how the least advantaged might be relatively deprived in several functionings. It matters less which is the most severe deprivation than that their cumulative impact be recognized and addressed. It follows that government policies might be considered successful if they reduce the clustering of disadvantages.

Amongst several studies that suggest that clustering of disadvantage is commonplace, the research of Michael Marmot, Richard Wilkinson and associates, on the social determinants of health, is particularly informative. This shows a clustering of several of the above-mentioned core functionings, specifically, life, health, affiliation, sense, imagination and thought, and control over one's environment. The research also stresses the importance of one's position in the social hierarchy in a relative rather than absolute sense. Marmot suggests that the functionings of affiliation and control over one's environment explain why hierarchies impact on health.

> The lower in the hierarchy you are, the less likely it is that you will have full control over your life and opportunities for full social participation. Autonomy and social participation are so important for health that their lack leads to deterioration in health.
>
> *(Marmot 2004: 248)*

Wilkinson and Marmot also suggest that unemployment (a component of "control over one's environment") clusters with other disadvantages, particularly the increased risk of premature death. They emphasize that this risk increases not only when people actually become unemployed but also when they sense the risk that they may lose their employment. This observation ties in closely with the earlier point about functioning security.

Accepting that clustering occurs, one might still question why disadvantages in separate functionings link together and persist or accumulate over time. The sequence of events in which a person becomes unemployed, then homeless, and then friendless, and finally becomes ill, suggests a causal dynamic. However, it would be wrong to conclude from this that the clustering of disadvantage always starts with unemployment. What is reasonable to conclude is that clustering is dynamic and one functioning deficiency may well lead to another. Marmot and Wilkinson's research identifies some of those dynamic linkages, i.e., the social determinants of health, but one might conceive of alternative starting points for a cluster of disadvantage, including poor education or social discrimination. It seems likely that the dynamics of clustering may vary from one social group to another, and from one time to another, and that there is no fixed causal relation between one disadvantage and another. If this is the case, then the challenge for policy makers includes researching the prevailing clustering dynamics in their target population.

Declustering of disadvantage

If we accept that a key role of government policy makers is to identify the least advantaged and prioritize actions to reduce their disadvantage, then the evidence of clustering is doubly important. Not only does it suggest short cuts for identifying the least advantaged but it also raises possibilities for tackling the problem. By addressing one low functioning we might, through the interconnectivity of clustered functionings, positively impact further disadvantages. For example, policy makers could focus on "corrosive disadvantages," the presence of which triggers further disadvantages, and "fertile functionings," the securing of which can enhance further functionings. Indeed, one appeal of the latter is that an investment in fertile functionings is most efficiently rewarded with positive returns across a range of functionings.

Corrosive disadvantages and fertile functionings

Some might consider these two categories as two sides of the same coin, but the situation is not quite so simple. Take, for instance, the functioning of bodily integrity. Someone living in fear of bodily attack is open to a range of negative effects, including stress-related illness, and an unwillingness to go out to work or play. In this way the risk to bodily integrity can be classified as a corrosive disadvantage. However, the absence of that risk is not necessarily fertile. Similarly, if someone falls into drug addiction following the loss of employment, the provision of a new job may not be sufficient to end that addiction. Or, to use a well-known example, if someone is run over by a steam roller, the cure is not to reverse the engine back over him or her. In other words, finding a corrosive disadvantage is not the same as finding a fertile functioning jackpot. Nevertheless, identifying corrosive disadvantages and fertile functionings within a particular context is an important step, we would argue, on the path to reducing disadvantage. Corrosive disadvantages provide guidance for preventive action. If, for example, addiction to drugs or alcohol is a corrosive disadvantage, governments have good reason to identify and implement policies that make addiction less likely. By contrast, government should seek policies that encourage the development of fertile functionings.

In searching for catalytic functionings we should not limit ourselves to those six most central functionings identified earlier. Rather, we are looking for variables that impact on those core functionings. These may be what otherwise might be considered minor functionings, or components of functionings, or even preconditions for functionings. Investigations in this field are far from complete but existing research has suggested three promising candidates: affiliation, education, and poverty.

Affiliation

It is unclear to some whether poverty (low income) causes lack of affiliation or vice versa, or if indeed both causal paths are equally strong. However, in the interviews conducted for *Disadvantage,* the participants identified *affiliation* as amongst the most fertile of functionings. They reported that those who experience a high degree of affiliation are better equipped to cope with threats and risks to their other functionings. One reason offered to support this view is that those with strong affiliations enjoy higher self-esteem and feel more self-assured in their dealings with authorities. Indeed, some claimed that "affiliation was the best means to achieve empowerment." There is also evidence to suggest that lack of affiliation can be corrosive. Typical of such feedback was the example of one interviewee who told of his growing up in the close-knit slums of post-war London. Although deprived of indoor bathrooms and the like, his family benefited from strong community bonds. Unfortunately when they were moved to "improved" housing in newly built tower blocks, that sense of community and mutual dependence was lost, partly as a result of less communal space, and his family eventually became unemployed and homeless. In another interview within the same research a social worker claimed that the most important functioning for elderly people was a sense of affiliation because it could help them cope with everything else. Such cases give support to the view that affiliation can be both a corrosive disadvantage and a fertile functioning. If that view is correct, then measures that encourage affiliation could also be very helpful in addressing other forms of disadvantage. Such steps could include building clubs for the targeted people to meet and improving town planning to ensure adequate local facilities such as shops, community centers, and sports facilities.

Education

Many would probably accept that providing better education, part of *sense, imagination, and thought,* would be key to addressing other functionings and therefore an important fertile functioning. For those, the evidence regarding education can be surprising. For example, the European Social Survey suggests the correlation between education and how satisfied people are with their lives is not statistically significant. However, life satisfaction may not be the most appropriate factor for our analysis, and other indications, such as the reported correlation between education and health, suggest education is after all an important fertile functioning. While this fertility may be difficult to prove in all contexts, there is strong evidence that lacking education is frequently a corrosive disadvantage, often through its impact on employment. Research suggests that, typically, the lower one's education, the lower one's chance of finding employment, particularly a well-rewarded and interesting position.

In this sense, education is not limited to the standard academic subjects or even the three Rs, but extends to include what are often called the soft skills. These include communication skills (essential for any interview or job application), social skills (essential for negotiating), and parenting skills. Shortcomings in any of these areas can negatively influence one's sense of autonomy and control over one's environment. Indeed, it is easy to visualize how underdeveloped soft skills might be a corrosive disadvantage. Whether it is also a fertile functioning might depend upon the context and the skill levels of others.

Poverty

It is still commonplace for many people to associate disadvantage with poverty in the sense of low income. They hold that if the incomes of the poor were increased then they would be able to afford to buy many of the things they need. They don't necessarily believe that the increased money would "compensate" for other disadvantages but merely that it would help cope with those disadvantages. However, there are arguments against a focus of raising incomes. Robert E. Lane (2000) has provided evidence that, once one is beyond the poverty level, a larger income contributes almost nothing to happiness. But again, happiness and adequate functioning may be quite different matters. Furthermore, the risk of being inadequately funded may be a serious problem for "control over one's environment," even for those well above whatever poverty line one applies. This in turn can lead to people taking risks with other functionings. Insecurity of income can thus be a corrosive disadvantage, even though being affluent may not necessarily be a fertile functioning.

One might think that the corrosive nature of income poverty would be enough to justify an increase in income for all parties below some recognized threshold, but research by Susan Mayer (1998) indicates that some caution is required. She has expressed the view that increasing the incomes of the long-term poor is likely to lead to increased spending on consumer goods rather than, for example, the types of cultural activities that could lead to improved educational outcomes for their children. Supporting this view, one interviewee suggested that people invest for the long term when they have a positive experience of progress over time (Wolff and de-Shalit 2007: 149). However, the poor have not had such an experience. In fact their experience is more likely to have been that they stand to lose in future whatever they currently have. On this view it is better to consume quickly on holidays and celebrations before the good luck goes away. Whether this explanation is correct is open to debate but it remains a worry that lack of a secure income is a corrosive disadvantage, and that the simple solution of providing more money may not be as fertile as first assumed.

Nevertheless, income poverty can join education and affiliation as key areas for focus whenever policy makers explore their communities for the key levers to decluster disadvantage.

Policies for declustering disadvantage

One might imagine from this that the solution to disadvantage would simply be the provision by government of resources, structures, and opportunities to identify and create fertile functionings and remove corrosive disadvantages. But such a conclusion overlooks a vital component: the importance of the active involvement of the recipients in their emergence from disadvantage. The motivation levels of such individuals will have a major bearing on that involvement and on the efficacy of targeted resources, structures, and opportunities. Consequently, any approach to policy making should place considerable emphasis on factors affecting the motivation of intended beneficiaries.

The psychologists Edward L. Deci and Richard M. Ryan, and their numerous collaborators, have conducted extensive empirical research into human motivation and well-being. Their SDT holds that motivation is dependent upon the satisfaction of basic psychological needs to develop skills and capacities, to act on one's own accord, and to connect to others and the environment. Ryan and Deci refer to these needs as competence, autonomy, and relatedness. Research has shown that people become amotivated when their needs for competence, autonomy, and relatedness are thwarted (Boggiano 1998). SDT also predicts that fluctuations in the satisfaction of the three needs will directly predict fluctuations in psychological well-being. Furthermore, it predicts that each of the three needs is necessary for optimal human development so that none can be neglected without negative consequences. "Psychological health requires satisfaction of all three needs, one or two are not enough" (Deci and Ryan 2000: 228).

Unlike bodily needs, such as hunger, that persist over time, the neglect of psychological needs can lead to the accommodation of substitute fulfillments with significant psychological costs. For example, if the need for relatedness is thwarted when an individual is young, that person might compensate by attempting to improve her sense of worth by accumulating money or possessions. However, this replacement goal can interfere with the attainment of her real need for relatedness, triggering further psychological costs (Deci and Ryan 2000: 248). Unfortunately, this implies that the least advantaged may have suffered damage that is not easily repaired by the correction of the original component disadvantages.

It is interesting to note the similarity between Deci and Ryan's work and Marmot's epidemiology, mentioned earlier. Marmot's work suggests that poor social networks (relatedness in SDT terms), low control over one's life (autonomy in SDT terms), and poor education (part of competence in SDT terms) will lead to poor outcomes in terms of the secure functionings of health and life. By comparison, Deci and Ryan specify that their three needs are essential for psychological growth, integrity, and well-being.

It is also possible to map the SDT needs to the central functionings on Nussbaum's list:

Relatedness:	5 Emotions
	7 Affiliation
	8 Other species, and possibly
	9 Play
Competence:	4 Sense, imagination, and thought (including education)
Autonomy:	6 Practical reason
	10 Control over one's environment

Finally, if we refer to the six most central functionings identified from the interview process discussed earlier, and set aside the three somatic functionings, life, bodily health, and bodily integrity, we are left with:

Affiliation

Control over one's environment

Sense, imagination, and thought

The first two of these seem very close to the SDT needs of relatedness and autonomy, and the third bears a reasonable resemblance to competence. Leaving aside the accepted differences between the terminology of functionings and needs, the apparent congruence is interesting and informative. For example, SDT suggests that the non-somatic functionings (numbers 4–10 on Nussbaum's list) may be important not only for their direct contribution to well-being but also for their impact on psychological growth and motivation. This raises the possibility that the fertility or otherwise of a particular functioning in a given context may be influenced by its contribution to an individual's motivation. Indeed, motivation may be a key to fertile functionings.

The purpose of introducing SDT at this point is not simply to draw support for the philosophical view of disadvantage presented here but also because of its extensive practical application in the field of policy making. Ryan and Deci, working with numerous colleagues, have researched the application of SDT in various fields, including:

- education;
- environmental sustainability;
- health care;
- organizational behavior;
- sports, exercise and physical education.[2]

A common thread running through much of this research is the positive role of autonomy support. For example, it has been reported that long-term medication adherence is substantially a function of patient autonomy, which is promoted by prescriber autonomy support.[3] Similar linkages to autonomy support have been found in the fields of weight-loss treatment and substance abuse management. A general conclusion drawn from these and other studies is that, "When patients have their psychological needs for autonomy, competence, and relatedness supported in the process of their health care, they experience more volitional engagement in treatment and maintain outcomes better over time" (Ryan et al. 2008).

This, of course, prompts the question of how these psychological needs are to be supported. Regarding autonomy support, Ryan and Deci place emphasis on three elements: real choice for the recipient, clear rationales for the options, and full engagement with the recipients' feelings and perspective. Key to this support is that the choices on offer allow values and interests to be engaged and expressed without any pressure and without excessive options. It is less clear, perhaps, to see how real choice can be incorporated into policies designed to reduce disadvantage. However, awareness of the consequences of being overly prescriptive may help in the design of such initiatives. This observation clearly resonates with the earlier observation that, in some cases, what matters for well-being is not whether people have the choice to achieve, or not achieve, a functioning, but rather having choices that allow them to achieve a functioning in their own particular way.

Turning to relatedness (affiliation) support, and competence (sense imagination and thought) support, it is possible to see how the SDT view might reinforce our philosophical introspections. If we step back and consider what determines an individual's genuine opportunities for secure functionings, we find three key dimensions: internal resources, external resources, and the social and material structure. The structure determines the rules of the game and the resources represent the tools for playing the game. Internal resources include natural abilities and aptitudes but also education and skills training, including soft skills. External resources in this context include available funds and access to facilities and equipment. The social structure includes the laws and customs of the society, formal power relations, and cultural and other social norms. Consequently there are many entry points for possible actions that a policy maker might consider. Amongst these, perhaps the most obvious is the provision of financial benefits to compensate or help offset a particular disadvantage. Nevertheless, leaving aside cases where financial compensation is completely inappropriate, the provision of such benefits can bring unwanted problems. For example, if the benefit is designed to target specific groups of people, then being part of such a group may stigmatize the intended beneficiaries. The process of claiming one's entitlement may bring shame to the individual or cause a social division between the claimers and the providers. SDT provides a framework for better understanding why selective financial benefits may be counterproductive: they undermine one's relations with the rest of society (relatedness), and they undermine one's sense of control over the environment (autonomy). The alternative of providing universal benefits, such as child benefits paid to all mothers, gets around these difficulties by avoiding the socially divisive selection process. However, the high cost of universal benefits makes them an inefficient tool for many problems and would draw resistance from those who seek to minimize redistribution.

If we conclude from this that cash compensation is not the best way to increase an individual's opportunities for secure functioning, we need to look elsewhere within the spectrum of internal resources, external resources, and social and material structure. One such approach, identified in *Disadvantage*, seeks to strengthen social connections rather than divide them. The thought is that governments should develop opportunities for people to meet and establish social connections. This could include rethinking the use of public spaces, improving public transport, and providing subsidies for evening classes and clubs. Not only would this be a benefit to those needing to increase their circle of contacts, or at risk of needing such support, but it would also strengthen society as a whole. Governments would not always need to shoulder the whole cost of setting up and maintaining such facilities but merely provide the seeds for local social groups to nurture. Increasing opportunities in this way might be termed a status enhancement, a beneficial change to the social and material structure with the potential for individuals to increase their internal resources—both hard and soft skills. Through the SDT lens such a proposal appears sound in that it supports the need for relatedness, in providing increased opportunities to meet and work with new contacts, it supports the need for competence, in that it allows people to pursue or develop their skills and interests, and it supports the need for autonomy, in providing a choice for individuals but with no pressure to participate. In this way the targeted groups might be motivated to engage with others in their efforts to emerge from disadvantage.

As the months passed following the 2013 flooding in Yalding and the rest of the UK, a number of government policies emerged. Some new barrages were proposed, further dredging in certain areas, even talk of council tax rebates to fund improved home defenses. For people affected by recent floods or at risk from future floods all such measures may seem helpful. However, many of these individuals would not fall into our category of the disadvantaged. Despite the tremendous inconvenience, financial cost, and emotional upset that a flood can bring, many of the victims are sufficiently resilient to recover from the setback. However, there will be some unfortunate individuals for whom a flood or risk of flood is a sufficient knock to their *bodily health* functioning (including adequate shelter) to tip them into the category of least advantaged. Their cluster of disadvantages may have become so significant that they require the attention and support of government agencies. For such people the best solution may not be a new barrage somewhere upstream from their location, or the like, but rather a set of policies that address the other components of their cluster of disadvantage. Issues like floods and storms and other natural disasters demonstrate the difficulties faced by governments in allocating scarce resources for the maximum benefit of society, particularly under the glare of an attentive media. The approach to understanding disadvantage discussed here together with the guidance for policy making supported by SDT should assist those tasked with this difficult challenge.

Further reading

Nussbaum, M.C. (2000) *Women and Human Development: The Capabilities Approach*. Cambridge: Cambridge University Press.
(Nussbaum's highly influential book on the Capabilities Approach.)

Sen, A. (1980) "Equality of What?" In S.M. McMurrin (ed.), *The Tanner Lectures on Human Values*. Cambridge: Cambridge University Press, pp. 195–220.
(Sen's classic essay on the Capability Approach.)

Wolff, J. (2009) "Disadvantage, Risk and the Social Determinants of Health," *Public Health Ethics*, 2(3), 214–223.
(How the social determinants of health might be used in the analysis of disadvantage.)

Wolff, J. (2011) *Ethics and Public Policy: A Philosophical Inquiry*. Oxon: Routledge.
(A philosophical assessment of central problems and controversies in public policy.)

Notes

1 For a recent complete list, see Nussbaum (2011: 33–34).
2 See http://www.selfdeterminationtheory.org/publications for a comprehensive listing.
3 Williams, Rodin, Ryan, Grolnick, and Deci (1998) "Autonomous Regulation and Long-Term Medication Adherence in Adult Outpatients," referenced in Ryan *et al.* (2008).

References

Boggiano, A.K. (1998). "Maladaptive achievement patterns: A test of a diathesis-stress analysis of helplessness," *Journal of Personality and Social Psychology* 74(6), 1681–1695.

Deci, E.L. and Ryan, R.M. (2000) "The 'What' and 'Why' of Goal Pursuits: Human Needs and the Self-Determination of Behavior," *Psychological Inquiry* 11(4), 227–268.

European Social Survey (2002) London: European Science Foundation.

Lane, R.E. (2000) *The Loss of Happiness in Market Democracies*. New Haven, CT: Yale University Press.

Marmot, M.G. (2004) *The Status Syndrome: How Social Standing Affects Our Health and Longevity*. New York: Henry Holt.

Mayer, S.E. (1998) *What Money Can't Buy*. Cambridge, MA: Harvard University Press.

Nussbaum, M.C. (2011) *Creating Capabilities: The Human Development Approach*. Cambridge, MA: Belknap/ Harvard University Press.

Rawls, J. (1971) *A Theory of Justice*. Cambridge, MA: Belknap Press.

Ryan, R.M., Patrick, H., Deci, E.L. and Williams, G.C. (2008) "Facilitating Health Behaviour Change and its Maintenance: Interventions Based on Self-Determination Theory," *The European Health Psychologist,* 10, 2008.

Walzer, M. (1993) *Interpretation and Social Criticism*. Cambridge, MA: Harvard University Press.

Walzer, M (1994) *Thick and Thin: Moral Argument at Home and Abroad*. Notre Dame, IN: University of Notre Dame Press.

Wolff, J. and de-Shalit, A. (2007) *Disadvantage*. Oxford, OUP.

38

FEMINISM AND WELL-BEING

Jules Holroyd

Introduction

All stripes of feminism endorse the following claim: that gender inequality damages women's interests, and is unjust. Should this damage be understood in terms of thwarted well-being? If so, what conception of well-being best enables us to both articulate how gender inequality damages women's well-being, and to ground social critique of existing inequalities? Do feminists need to make recourse to the notion of well-being at all to articulate the wrongs of gender inequality?

In setting out some of the central contributions from feminist philosophers, we see the distinctive challenges to various conceptions of well-being from a feminist perspective, and tease out the possible relationships between the notion of well-being and gender justice.

Some of the harms of gender inequality

Contemporary society is structured by various intersecting forms of inequality, one dimension of which is gender inequality. Women are more likely than men to be victims of sexual violence or domestic abuse[1,2]; in some parts of the world girls' access to education is more limited than boys', and women make up the majority of illiterate adults in the world,[3] whilst in the UK participation in different study subjects is strongly structured by gender[4]; women own only 1% of the world's wealth, and most contemporary society's have gender wage gaps which entrench women's economic inequality[5,6]. Women participate in the workforce at lower rates than men, with patterns of job segregation apparent, and more women in insecure part-time work.[7, 8] Women experience more sexual harassment in the workplace than men. Women are under-represented in roles of power and esteem, including in political office[9]; aspirations of girls are shaped by awareness of gender inequality, with under-representation affecting the perceived desirability of certain career options. Sexual objectification of women in various forms of media is rife, and women report higher levels of anxiety about their appearance.[10]

The statistics could go on, but the point is clear. In short, women suffer more sexual violence, have fewer opportunities for development of their capacities, less access to resources and opportunities afforded by employment, and less access to power; this shapes their aspirations and hopes for the future. Such inequalities (inter alia) disadvantage women, and are unjust. In what ways do these inequalities also impact on women's well-being, and how might this best be articulated? How might thinking about gender injustices shape our thinking about well-being?

In the following sections, I set out three key strands of thought about what well-being consists in, and show how feminist perspectives might shape our understanding of these views. Each has different implications for the relationship between gender justice and well-being.

Mental state views and psychological oppression

One kind of view of what well-being consists in focuses on the mental states experienced by individuals. The simplest version holds that a life is good for the person who lives it to the extent that it contains mental states of pleasure, and bad to the extent that it contains experiences of displeasure or pain.

It is not difficult to see how various dimensions of gender inequality would translate into negative mental states. For example, experience of gendered violence produces mental states of acute distress deleterious to well-being. Experience of sexual harassment or discrimination will produce mental states of distress that hinder well-being. However, there are limitations to this view in capturing the complexities of the mental experiences produced in a gendered society.

Oppressive pleasures

We might acknowledge the resources of the mental state view to capture certain well-being deficits, but contend that other well-being deficits are not adequately described. Consider, for example, the claim from Catherine MacKinnon that gendered social relations serve to (and indeed constitute) sexualized subordination, such that women (and men) take pleasure in women's subordination (1989: 113).

Or, consider Bartky's characterization of "repressive narcissism," whereby gendered socialization encourages women to take pleasure in their own objectification (via the various rituals by which women seek to live up to the stringent norms of appearance) (1990: 36).

These examples present cases in which women take pleasure—and thus experience the mental states characterized as constituents of well-being—in activities that are identified as in fact detrimental to their interests. The sexualized subordination of women, and the perpetuation of stringent and repressive norms of appearance, we might argue, negatively impact on women's well-being, notwithstanding the pleasure they take in such practices. But this cannot be adequately captured on a view which sees only pleasurable mental states as constituents of well-being, and thus sees the pleasures derived from such oppressive practices as contributors to well-being.

The proponents of the mental state view might offer the following responses. First, they might insist that, in fact, these pleasures *are* contributing to women's well-being; they might also serve to perpetuate an unjust state of affairs, and this injustice is bad for women in many ways—but not necessarily due to hindering their actual well-being. On this view, gender justice and women's well-being need not coincide.

Alternatively, the proponent of the mental state view might compare women's actual well-being (mental states of pleasure) with the possible mental states of pleasure that could be afforded in contexts that are not structured by gender inequality. Insofar as circumstances of gender equality afford greater pleasures (or a better quality of pleasure, perhaps) we might acknowledge that, whilst participating in some practices of gender inequality does contribute to women's well-being, a just society is preferable in affording more, or a better quality, of pleasures.

Ambiguous pleasures

Nonetheless, reflection on the ways feminists have articulated the dimensions of psychological oppression might prompt doubts about whether "pleasure" is an adequate metric for well-being. Feminist thinking here brings into relief a particular version of the familiar worries about how to characterize the relevant mental states that provide a metric of well-being (e.g., Dworkin 1981). One of the distinctive features that characterizes women's experiences under conditions of gender oppression, it has been argued, is that of conflict. Competing and conflicting norms (with conflict sometimes generated by feminist awareness) mean that experiences of some pleasures are conflicted or ambiguous. Here are two examples.

Consider again Bartky's description of the pleasure women might take in appearance-related activities of self-adornment. At once pressured to do this,[11] women might at the same time find themselves denigrated for such preoccupations being "trivial," or even self-chastising for enjoying rituals which perpetuate problematic norms, meaning that the pleasure taken in such self-adornment is not unequivocal.

Or consider the reports of women's experiences of pleasure in the development of their capacities in the workforce; at the same time, the force of the norm that assigns women (and not men) to role of home maker and mother means that such pleasures are not experienced as unequivocal. In a qualitative study of the experiences of parents, one UK mother, employed as a project co-ordinator, reported: "I enjoy the job I am doing . . . And I think there is a lot of guilt around it as well . . . Have I had a child just to give her away to somebody else and get them to look after her?" (420).[12]

Under contexts of gender inequality, where competing and conflicting norms govern women's lives, certain pleasures are equivocally experienced, or inflected by feelings of guilt. Mental state views of well-being which focus simply on whether an experience is pleasurable or not as the appropriate metric of well-being do not seem to have the resources to capture the complexities of these mental states as produced by contexts of gender inequality.

Structures of psychological oppression

These concerns might prompt mental state theorists to consider more generally the characterization of the mental states involved in well-being. For the experiences of psychological oppression described (first by Franz Fanon (1952), later by Sandra Bartky) involve a certain fragmentation of the psyche, a splitting of the self.

In a society where women are required to constantly self-monitor, and where they are required to conform both with specific gender norms and at the same time identify with supposedly universal cultural representations that in fact represent a male perspective on the world, Bartky writes, we find a problematic "splitting of the self." Further, women may find themselves feeling alienated from their bodies, and their capacities as human beings (1990: 32). These forms of psychological oppression, whereby women "may find [themselves] fragmented and the fragments at war with one another" (25), produce psychological disharmony of a sort deleterious to well-being.

This suggests that any adequate mental state view will appeal not simply to isolated and aggregated mental states of pleasure or displeasure, but should attend rather to the structure of mental life more broadly, and the ways that mental contentment of the sort relevant to well-being can be disrupted by the internalization of oppressive social structures. One route, then, is to develop these more complex accounts of the mental states and structures that are constituents of well-being in order to articulate the ways in which gender unequal societies hinder well-being.

On this view of well-being, however, the relationship between gender inequality and well-being is complex. For gender injustice does not wholly preclude the experiences that make up the constituents of a good life. Indeed, it might seem as though a feature of these views is that they would likely record well-being as higher in individuals who are not troubled by aspects of gender inequality. The unequivocal enjoyment of self-objectifying activities; the embracing of traditional roles and rejection of opportunities that give rise to conflict; the endorsement of inequalities that would otherwise produce unhappiness; we might think these attitudes stand at a far distance from those required in order to move towards equality; yet these might be the attitudes conducive to greater well-being under conditions of gender oppression.

Feminist defenders of mental state views might commit to the necessary emergence of the characteristics of psychological oppression under gender injustice, but this seems like a strong claim—we should not preclude that some women are genuinely able to take unequivocal pleasure, or avoid psychological fragmentation, in oppressive contexts. Thus, these views are committed to there being merely contingent connections between gender injustice and well-being deficits.

Summary

In summary: simplistic mental state views seem ill equipped to deal with the ways in which gender inequality can produce ambiguous pleasures and psychological fragmentation. Any mental state view that is able to capture the ways that gender oppression can undermine well-being will need to be sensitive to these more complex mental states. On this view, the relationship between gender justice and individual well-being is contingent: well-being is only hindered insofar as gender inequality produces these complex mental experiences, and there is reason to suppose that it may not always do so.

Preference satisfaction, adaptive preferences, and deformed desires

Mental state views have been famously criticized for failing to connect well-being up with the actual state of the world. As Nozick (1974) has remarked, we actually want to do something to be a kind of person, to leave some lasting impact on the world. Desire-satisfaction accounts of well-being seem to better fit the bill, by specifying that our well-being is constituted not by mental states of certain kinds, but by the satisfaction of our desires. This might be accompanied by some mental state of satisfaction, but need not be—our desires can be satisfied without us being aware of this, or be satisfied even after our deaths. For example, I desire that men and women secure equal pay. If this desire is satisfied, then with respect to well-being my life goes better, even if I am unaware of this momentous social and political achievement.

Clearly, on such views, much hangs on the desires or preferences of individuals—it is their contents that specify what state of the world constitute their being satisfied. However, in observing the effects of gender oppression on the formulation of preferences, feminists have marshaled powerful critiques of these views and the ways in which they have been developed.

Firstly, it is an obvious fact that people have all sorts of silly, mistaken, or erroneous desires. But focusing on preferences seems particularly problematic once we notice the role of oppressive social context in shaping the preferences people end up with: people often have desires shaped by their social circumstances, including circumstances of gendered oppression. In societies with traditional gender roles, should we take at face value women's preference for home making over participation in the workforce? Should we agree that the satisfaction of women's preferences for certain cosmetic procedures contributes to their well-being?[13] If women do not prefer more equal pay or power, should we say that social reforms to that end will not serve their well-being (even if it does serve justice)?

One thing we might say is that the satisfaction of those preferences *does* contribute to individuals' well-being, although it does not serve the purposes of gender justice. Once again, well-being and gender justice do not go in step, on this line of thought. It looks, though, that unless we suppose that something other than actual preference satisfaction is a constituent of well-being, we are unable to say that social reforms undertaken in the name of gender justice are in any way good for women.

Informed desires

Some of the most striking examples used to show the deficits of preference satisfaction views come from the work of Martha Nussbaum, who draws on her experience of activist work with poor women in rural India (1992).[14] Nussbaum describes the situation of the women of one village, whose levels of nourishment and general health measured as clearly worse than their male peers, but who reported that they had no complaints about either (1992: 230). They have "adaptive preferences" in that their preferences have adapted to the oppressive circumstances in which they live, in which women's role is to prioritize the nourishment and health of men. We would like to be able to say that increased health and nourishment is good for these women— that it will increase their well-being—but would be unable to say this if all that mattered were the satisfaction of actual preferences.

Defensible preference satisfaction views, however, don't attend to all, or only, actual preferences. Rather, a standard way of avoiding the problem of erroneous or mistaken preferences is to appeal to informed preferences—those an individual would have, if she had more information available to her. What further information must individuals have for us to specify their informed preferences? One option is to focus on the recognition of certain fundamental moral ideals. For example, Superson's (2009) solution to the "deformed desires" that individuals have due to oppression is to instead turn to the desires individuals would have if they fully recognized the equal worth of all individuals as agents with moral standing. Or, one might focus on more specific kinds of information (of the sort present in Nussbaum's discussion of adaptive preferences), such as that secured by having new experiences, or seeing a possibility as a live one. Thus, if individuals had more information about the health options available to them, if they were to experience more adequate nourishment, if they were to be afforded greater participation in the economic and political dimensions of their society, the supposition is, they *would,* with this understanding, in fact prefer those things. Thus the satisfaction of those informed preferences—for better health, nourishment, more political and economic power—is what constitutes their well-being.

This is an effective way of dealing with mistaken preferences of the ordinary sort: an individual who erroneously prefers to ingest the contaminated platter would prefer not to, if she had information about its toxic properties. Can the move to informed preferences explain why the satisfaction of adaptive preferences should not be determinative of individual well-being? This commits us to saying that if individual women recognized their fundamental moral equality with men, or if they simply had more information about or experience of the possibilities available to them—the opportunities for education, health care, economic independence, and political participation—we would find them with different—emancipatory—preferences (for broader education, for health care, for equal pay). The satisfaction of these informed emancipatory preferences is what constitutes well-being, then, and the problem posed by adaptive preferences seems to be avoided.

Hopelessness and distance

However, there are various concerns with this move to informed preference satisfaction. One worry, suggested by Julia Annas (1993), is that the context of gender inequality is such that we cannot suppose that individuals who gain more information—about their situation, its historical backdrop, the various obstacles in the way of securing gender justice, and so on—would in fact form the relevant, informed, preference. More information is likely to produce a sense of hopelessness, rather than the relevant emancipatory preference the satisfaction of which is supposed to contribute to well-being.

This objection turns on the articulation of the informed preference satisfaction account in terms of the preferences individuals *would have* if they had some further, or full, information. As such, the defensibility of this worry will turn on empirical matters about what preferences individuals would, with such information, have. In responding to Annas, Valdes (1993) has suggested that, far from producing hopelessness, more information can serve to politicize and encourage women to consider ways in which social change might better serve their well-being, and indeed, this seems to be the pattern reported in the work of Nussbaum (1992) with the women in rural India.

Even if we accept that the emancipatory preferences are ones that individuals *would* have, with further information, we might still doubt the claim that the satisfaction of these informed desires constitutes an individual's well-being. The informed desires are at too great a distance from the individuals' actual desires for this claim to be defensible. Considering the case of one of the women whose adaptive preferences do not motivate her to seek better nourishment or health care, Nussbaum observes that we should say, on the informed preference satisfaction account, that what would in fact contribute to her well-being is the provision of adequate nourishment and health care (what she would, if informed, desire). But can we really say that such provisions contribute to the well-being of an individual, even if she presently does not want such things? It is usually deleterious to the well-being of individuals to give them (for example) medical treatments that they do not in fact want (even if it is true that under different conditions, they would want it). The informed preference satisfaction view of well-being, then, faces a difficulty in bridging the gap between what individuals presently want, and what they would, if informed, want—but in fact do not. Without that part of the story, it is difficult to see how satisfying preferences individuals would have can *now* constitute a part of their well-being.

Authority

Annas provides as further grounds for dissatisfaction with preference-based views their unsuitability to justify social reforms of the sort required for gender justice. This will likely involve radical reform of social institutions and the norms that underpin them; considerable redistribution of wealth and power—in short, significant social and individual change. We need a notion that can authoritatively ground and justify such social reforms. Annas asks: can any conception of well-being grounded in individuals' preferences be sufficiently authoritative? What entitlement do we have to do so simply on the basis that it would satisfy (actual or informed) preferences (1993: 287)? From a distinctively feminist point of view, then, these preference-based accounts might seem to lack the requisite authority to underpin social critique and reform.

This is a difficult issue, and the force of this objection may rest on the role in which feminist philosophers are seeking to use the notion of well-being. If the claim is simply that things should be different because women's preferences (or informed preferences) are for states of affairs in which things are different, so much the worse for the authority of these views in grounding reform. But the critique of gender inequality need not have this form. The claim might rather be that there is a systematic gender inequality in levels of well-being: women's informed preferences are satisfied to a systematically lesser extent than men's. It is this dimension of inequality—and the injustice of such disparities in well-being—that grounds the impetus for social reform.

Whilst understanding the relationship between well-being and feminism in this latter way might avoid the concern about authority, there are other challenges for such a view. For instance, proponents of it must shore up the claim that there *is* a systematic welfare deficit whereby women's informed preferences are satisfied to a lesser extent than men's. The problem is, this is not at all clear if men's preferences are also shaped by gendered society: once we articulate men's fully informed preferences (presumably, informed preferences for a gender-just society and the things that would be enjoyed in it), we see that these preferences are not satisfied either, in our current gender-unjust society. For example, we might imagine a man who has an actual preference for adopting a "head of the household" role, as he believes men should, by working long hours to provide for his children who are cared for by his wife. Let us suppose that, were he more fully informed (about the contingency of work and family structures, about the problematic conception of masculinity that underpins his actual preferences), he would prefer quite different parenting and work roles. This man's informed preference is not, then, satisfied, although his actual preference is. If, as in this case, we think that men's informed preferences would be similarly different from their actual preferences, and would be presently unsatisfied, then both men and women suffer a well-being deficit under conditions of gender inequality. It might be quite difficult to firmly establish that women suffer from more unsatisfied informed preferences than do men.

Summary

Consideration of adaptive preferences or "deformed desires" helps us to see more clearly not only the need for preference-based views of well-being to be articulated in terms of "informed preferences," but also the difficulties such accounts face in explaining the relationship between the satisfaction of those desires and the well-being of the not-fully-informed individual. That is to say, the account needs to explain the contribution to well-being of the satisfaction of desires that an individual doesn't in fact have. Moreover, such views face challenges in explaining what authority preferences have in justifying social reform. However, they might justify social reform by pointing to inequalities in well-being between men and women; but it is not in the end at all clear that there are such inequalities in terms of satisfaction of informed preferences: a gender-unjust society might thwart the informed preferences—and well-being—of both men and women.

Flourishing and capabilities

Another way of dealing with the problem of adaptive preferences is simply to identify the objective goods that constitute well-being: irrespective of an individual's mental states, or actual or possible preferences, certain things contribute to well-being to the extent that they are in, or available in, an individual's life.[15] One of the most influential objective list views, and one explicitly motivated by feminist concerns, has been developed by Martha Nussbaum (1992, 2000a, 2000b).[16]

To start thinking about this kind of view, let us return to some of the ills of gender injustice, and consider what we might want to say: that it is bad for women to live in fear of violence; that it is bad for women to lack adequate access to education; that is bad for women that their choices of interests or careers are constrained by gender norms; it is bad for women to be economically dependent and made vulnerable by this dependency; it is bad for women not to have access to political participation or power; it is bad for women not to have adequate access to health care or basic nourishment, and so on. Insofar as these features are present in any one individual's life, she suffers a well-being deficit as a result. This is because certain goods—security, education, autonomy, economic independence, political participation, health care and nourishment—are constituents of a good life. We might list these items, amongst others, and specify that, independently of the pleasure they bring, and independently of whether they are wanted, these items are the constituents of a good life (of course, we should expect much contention about what is on the list). This would certainly enable us to say that women living in societies structured by gender inequalities such as ours are ones in which women suffer well-being deficits.

However, a simple "list" view seems unable to respect diversity across individuals in the following two ways. Firstly, whilst such a view is, by design, not susceptible to worries about preferences distorted by gender oppression, this means they are also peculiarly insensitive to the fact that, of the goods specified as constituents of a good life, individuals may differ with respect to whether they want those goods in their lives. Take the condition of fasting (an example from Nussbaum 2000: 44): some individuals want to eat and can, whilst others who can, nonetheless prefer a life of ascetic fasting. An objective list such as that we have sketched would say that, if this item on the list (nourishment) is not present in a life, it is to that extent bad, in well-being terms. If this seems problematic, and we seek to reflect this difference in preferences amongst available options, we should worry about this simple objective list view.

Secondly, such a view is not well placed to accommodate the fact that individuals may be in radically different positions regarding what they can do with these resources: how much of them they need to secure parity of well-being; whether they are in a position to take advantage of such resources. Formally securing economic or political participation, for example, will not permit individuals who are illiterate to benefit from these goods. Or, as Nussbaum points out, individuals may have different needs at different stages of their lives: a pregnant or lactating woman will be a less efficient converter of nourishment resources, and require more of them to achieve comparable well-being to non-pregnant individuals (2000b: 228). If all we look to is whether they have formal access to political participation, or nourishment resources, we may miss these differences in terms of what can be done with those resources.

Some of these concerns might be assuaged by specifying carefully the metric of the resources identified as constituents of a good life. But a better formulation of the view, Nussbaum argues, will articulate well-being not simply in terms of the presence of certain goods in a life, but rather in terms of their availability, and in terms of what individuals can do with those goods available to them. This is what is dubbed the "capabilities" approach. The capabilities view holds that the constituents of well-being include not simply what individuals do, but also the opportunities available to them.

The two central notions in this view are (a) functionings—things an individual does or is—and (b) capabilities—the things an individual is able to do or be. An individual's well-being is a matter of both what she is doing and what she could do. This allows us to speak to both of the concerns above: the fasting individual has the available option of nourishment, and this availability contributes to her well-being, even if she does not take it up. In focusing on what individuals are actually able to do, moreover, it goes beyond looking at what resources they have available to them, and focuses rather on what they are able to do with them. If a pregnant woman is not able to be adequately nourished, then the food she has available to her has not sufficed to secure this functioning (even if it would be sufficient for some other individual with lesser nutritional needs). In articulating an individual's well-being, then, we look at what they can do or be (capabilities) and what they actually do (functionings). To the extent that individuals lack capabilities—lack the freedom or opportunity to secure some of them—they suffer a well-being deficit; even if they would not presently take up that opportunity were it available to them.

Consider again the case of the malnourished woman. The informed preference satisfaction view had difficulties in making sense of how the satisfaction of her informed preference, for adequate nourishment or access to health care, would contribute to her well-being (given that she in fact does not now want those things). The capabilities approach observes first that she does not secure these functionings (they are not ways of being or doing that she currently enjoys), and secondly notes that it is not something that is presently available to her: so not only does she lack this functioning; she also lacks this capability. This puts her in a very different position from the ascetic faster, who does not have the functioning, but has available the capability, and so could secure nourishment if she wished.

So far we have talked about capabilities such as nourishment and access to educational resources, but clearly we cannot fully evaluate this account until we have a clearer sense of the capabilities that might be at issue. Not all capabilities are of equal importance. One way of utilizing the capabilities framework, which Sen suggests, is not to specify the capabilities of concern, as these are to be articulated as the outcome of democratic processes: we simply apply the analytical tools to that outcome, without building into our theory which capabilities are of crucial importance (Sen 2004).

However, Nussbaum suggests that the framework has critical power, and can better be harnessed for the purposes of justice, by articulating the central capabilities that any adequate life must contain. We look for universal features of human existence, and find common features which indicate to us that beings such as we are—human beings—are the sort of beings who require access to certain capabilities for a good life. Thus, whatever context we look to, we should be able to evaluate whether there are crucial functionings or capabilities missing, and make an assessment of well-being thereby. The list Nussbaum provides is one that is supposed to generate some "overlapping consensus," in that people who have radically different conceptions of a good life would nonetheless recognise that it posits goods the availability of which (if not their uptake) are necessary for a broad range of valuable lives. Her list (paraphrased) contains the following capabilities:

1. life: the ability to live a full life, avoiding premature death;
2. bodily health: being able to have adequate health, including reproductive health, and the nourishment and shelter needed to secure this;
3. bodily integrity: free movement, freedom from violence, opportunities for sexual satisfaction, reproductive autonomy;
4. senses, imagination and thought: to be able to use these senses, informed and cultivated by education; freedom of speech and religious exercise; freedom from non-necessary pain and availability of pleasurable experiences;
5. emotions: to be able to have attachments to things and beings other than ourselves, and to develop the capacities for such attachments;
6. practical reason: to be able to form a conception of the good and reflect on how to plan one's life;
7. affiliation: to be able to engage and associate with others, empathize with them, be able to engage in justice and friendship; being treated as a being with dignity, and being protected from discrimination on the basis of one's identity;
8. other species: the ability to have concern for other species, one's environment and nature;
9. play: being able to enjoy recreational activities;
10. control over one's political and material environment: being able to participate politically, being able to hold property, being able to seek employment on an equal basis with others, and be employed in meaningful work.

Nussbaum notes that this list should be considered open-ended, and that we should consider it revisable or to be added to in light of further cross-cultural dialogue about human needs and what constitutes a valuable human life.[17] But, to the extent that women's lives are lacking in some of these central capabilities, we should say that their well-being is to that extent lessened. The adding of capabilities—of the opportunity of adequate health care, better access to education, political participation, and so on—increases an individual's well-being even if she does not presently wish to take those opportunities up. This approach therefore captures the extent to which what is possible for us, as well as what we actually do, is a dimension of how well our lives are going.

Some have qualms about the appeal to human nature in articulating the central capabilities. For example, Louise Antony (2000) raises concerns about the legitimacy of extracting normative claims from claims about human nature; and about the dangers of giving centrality to a notion ("nature") that has so often been used against women's interests. Conversely, Julia Annas (1993) has argued that appeal to human nature is particularly well placed to explain what is wrong with organizing societies according to two norms (one set for men, another for women): namely, that it undermines the fundamental claim that there is a single ideal for human life. Moreover, she argues, the articulation of capabilities grounded in human nature provides an authoritative basis for social critique: one grounded in the idea that women's human nature is not being permitted to flourish. However, it is possible to endorse those listed items as goods without recourse to human nature: other arguments will then be needed to support the claim that these values are those constitutive of a good life.

Flourishing and justice

On a view which sees well-being as constituted by the flourishing of human nature, there is a tighter connection between well-being and justice. Insofar as gender injustice exists, and it exists in a way that limits important capabilities, and prevents women (and men) from flourishing qua human beings, then women (and men) will experience a well-being deficit. Even if individuals report themselves satisfied with their lives in various ways, their well-being will suffer due to the absence of the relevant capabilities; and the securing of gender justice, insofar as it secures these capabilities to a greater extent, will improve their well-being.

The idea that gender inequality is a hindrance to flourishing has been articulated in a subtle way by Claudia Card, who observes that the virtues that attach to the gender role "woman" under conditions of oppression are often traits that are, from a critical feminist point of view, in fact vices; they lead to a distortion of good character, and the stunting of personality. Traits such as attentiveness and self-sacrifice, which might in some contexts indeed be virtues, can serve to make women easier to dominate in contexts of gender oppression (1990: 202–204).

We might, by the same token, wonder whether men are capable of flourishing in the context of a gender-unjust society. Consider various traits encouraged by Western conceptions of masculinity to be the analogues of the gendered vices Card articulates: machismo, the discouragement of empathy, and so on. Would the presence of these traits damage the well-being of those who are privileged by gender inequality, as well as that of those disadvantaged by it? Lisa Tessman has pointed to two features of the position of privilege that might undermine the idea that gender inequality damages men's well-being (2005: 76–77): firstly, that their socialization is such that it inculcates a (misplaced) sense of moral goodness; secondly, that it promulgates a conception of the good that is consistent with their way of life, and obscures their complicity in entrenching the disadvantage of others.

Do these two features mean that those in positions of privilege can be said to flourish even whilst participating in relations of oppression? We might accept that such attitudes would sustain the self-deceptions that prevent discontents from being manifest in psychological experience. Indeed, as Friedman has argued, we might envisage a sort of "benign patriarch" who avoids typical masculine vices, demonstrates care, concern, sensitivity, courage (2009: 36–37), and finds himself happy and with satisfied preferences in his traditional role. Such an individual's subjective states are not those of an individual short on well-being.

However, if what is at stake is a conception of objective flourishing, which does not depend on the mental states or preferences of an individual, then we could articulate a well-being deficit even in those who do not experience discontent (much in the same way we proceeded to do so in diagnosing the problem with adaptive preferences). For example, if we endorse Nussbaum's list of capabilities above, we should conclude that men and women currently both lack the capability, in a large range of their personal and social relations, to engage in social relations of justice (capability 7, above), and perhaps also in various forms of friendship precluded by gender injustice. This would be one way in which the well-being of oppressors suffers, even if they do not experience any discontents or thwarted preferences as a result.

What is gained by this move? Friedman has raised doubts as to whether any argumentative ground is gained by being able to argue that men suffer well-being deficits under gender injustice: it is not obvious that the supposed gains in objective well-being would dislodge the attachment to the experiences of contentment and desire satisfaction available from the immediate and long-term privileges of gender inequality (2009: 37). If this is the case, then feminists would have no pragmatic reason to try to secure the sort of relationship between gender justice and well-being that falls out of the sort of objective well-being view considered here (but that, of course, does not engage the theoretical considerations that speak for or against it).

Preference-based capabilities?

One concern for capabilities approaches such as Nussbaum's, which remains unaddressed, is that of the commitment to objectivism. Whilst it has been argued that this feature of the view has advantages in providing an authoritative ground for social critique, it also comes with metaphysical commitments to objectivity of values that may make it unappealing to some. Harriet Baber (2010) has recently argued that this is not a necessary component of a capabilities approach, and that there is available to us a preferentist rendering of the capabilities approach.

On what she calls a "broad preferentist" approach, we attend not only to the actual preferences individuals have (which, as we have seen, might be adaptive or deformed in various ways), but also to possible preferences that, as Baber puts it, they could easily have had (preferences that are "relevant" to the individual). What matters for well-being on this view is not only the satisfaction or possible satisfaction of actual preferences, but also the possible satisfaction of (that is, the capability of satisfying) possible relevant preferences. And, the satisfaction of actual or possible relevant preferences is fruitful to the extent that it affords opportunities for the forming of other (fruitful, relevant) preferences, which could be satisfied.

For example, recall the individual who is satisfied with her inadequate levels of nourishment: her actual preferences are satisfied. But we need not resort to claims about human nature and the good to explain why more nourishment would be good for her. Rather, we appeal to the fact that she could easily prefer more nourishment; there is a nearby possible world at which she has this preference (nearby preferences are "relevant" ones (Baber 2010: 380)). Whilst her actual preferences are satisfied, she is unable—lacks the capability—to satisfy nearby possible preferences. And, she suffers a well-being deficit to the extent that her actual preference (though satisfied) is unfruitful (prevents a range of nearby preferences from being satisfied). Whilst it is good for her that at least one of her actual preferences is satisfied, it would be better for her if she had a wider range of preferences (as afforded by being more well nourished) *and* if those wider range of preferences could be satisfied, so as to open up the opportunity for the development, and satisfaction, of further preferences, and so on. Thus this "broad preferentist" approach, as Baber refers to it, can diagnose the ill of adaptive preferences.

The ability to do so, as Baber notes, will depend on (what we have referred to as) emancipatory preferences being "relevant" to the agent's well-being; that is, ones the person could easily have had—that the agent has in nearby possible worlds. Whilst this seems true of the women with whom Nussbaum worked in rural India, we might doubt that in all cases where preferences are shaped by oppressive gender norms, it is appropriate to consider the emancipatory preferences as ones that someone "could easily have had." Consider the strong preferences of a conservative woman for traditional family roles; it is not clear that preferences for equal parenting, participation in the workforce, economic independence, and so on are preferences she would have at a nearby world. In such a case, the broad preferentist may lose the ability to diagnose any well-being deficit. The broad preferentist must either persuade us that it is plausible that such individuals could easily have different preferences; or that the satisfaction of preferences so distant from an individual's actual wants cannot be defensibly identified as part of her good. Such an approach would also have to address the concern that an account based in preferences is insufficiently authoritative to ground programs of social reform in its cause.

Summary

Objective list accounts that are framed in terms of capabilities appear well placed to explain why having opportunities contributes to an individual's well-being. Whilst controversies remain over what should go on the list of goods, and how it is normatively grounded, it is claimed that such a conception has the authority to underpin social critique. Such a view would rule out the flourishing of both oppressed and oppressor. However, for those unpersuaded by the objectivism underpinning the capabilities view, preferentist construals of this approach may be available. Whether such views are able to adequately diagnose the problems of adaptive preferences, or provide sufficient authoritative ground for social critique, is something requiring further scrutiny.

Conclusion

Feminist perspectives help to identify a range of ways in which gender oppression can undermine well-being: by producing fragmented psychological structures; by producing deformed desires or adaptive preferences, by making unavailable certain goods that any good human life should contain. As we have seen, though, whether it is a desideratum for an account of well-being that it explains how gender oppression undermines women's well-being will depend on how one conceives of the relationship between well-being and justice. Mental state or preference-based views see well-being as thwarted only insofar as it leads to mental discontents or unsatisfied preferences, thus leaving open the (perhaps unlikely) possibility of lives high in well-being even in contexts of oppression. Meanwhile, views which focus on objective goods or flourishing generate the claim that individuals suffer well-being deficits given, and to the extent that, injustice hinders the attainment of such objective goods. Thus, we see that a further criterion by which we evaluate different conceptions of well-being can be whether we wish to see well-being as something that women might enjoy despite gender inequality, or rather as part of what gender justice would achieve for women.

Notes

1 For example, in the UK 30% of women (compared with 16.3% of men) experience some form of domestic abuse in adulthood: http://www.ons.gov.uk/ons/rel/crime-stats/crime-statistics/focus-on-violent-crime-and-sexual-offences–2012-13/rpt—chapter-4—intimate-personal-violence-and-partner-abuse.html.

2 WHO factsheet 239.

3 64% of illiterate adults are women. UNESCO report on gender and education: http://www.uis.unesco.org/Education/Pages/gender-education.aspx.

4 For example, recent data from Northern Ireland indicate that in subjects such as engineering and technology 80% of new entrants are male, in computer science 75.6%, and architecture 70%; meanwhile in subjects allied to medicine 83.2% of new entrants are women, in education courses 77%, and in language courses 72%. http://www.ofmdfmni.gov.uk/gender-equality-strategy-statistics-update-july-2013.pdf page 8.

5 http://www.undp.org/content/undp/en/home/ourwork/povertyreduction/focus_areas/focus_gender_and_poverty/.

6 For pay gaps by country, see http://www.weforum.org/issues/global-gender-gap. In the UK—ranked 18 out of 136 countries in the World Economic Forum 2013 gender gap index—these patterns of inequality in income and rates of poverty persist. http://www.weforum.org/reports/global-gender-gap-report-2013. In the UK, women in full-time work earn on average 84.5% of what men earn, whilst women in part-time jobs earn 65.5%. http://www.equalityhumanrights.com/sites/default/files/documents/research/gender_pay_gap_briefing_paper2.pdf page 5.

7 http://www.fawcettsociety.org.uk/2013/11/equal-pay/. See also http://www.ons.gov.uk/ons/dcp1717 76_328352.pdf page 11.

8 http://www.ons.gov.uk/ons/dcp171776_328352.pdf, page 1. Inequalities in individual income and patterns of employment are structured not only by gender, but by race, with rates of poverty particularly high for Pakistani, Bangladeshi, and Black African women. https://www.gov.uk/government/uploads/system/uploads/attachment_data/file/85528/ethnic-minority-women_s-poverty.pdf page 8

9 http://www.fawcettsociety.org.uk/wp-content/uploads/2013/02/Sex-and-Power-2013-FINAL-REPORT.pdf page 5

10 In a recent UK survey of attitudes amongst teenagers, 54% of the young women interviewed reported being put off careers in which women were underrepresented; 56% of 16–21-year-old women worried about the negative impact of having children on a career. In all, 75% of those who responded reported experiences of everyday sexism, and 42% that the influence of media left them unhappy about their appearance. See: girlsattitudes.girlguiding.org.uk/pdf/2013_Attitudes_EqualityForGirls.pdf pages 8, 12, 18–19.

11 See, for example, the following news story reporting that two-thirds of the British bosses surveyed said they would be more likely to hire a woman who wore make up: http://www.dailymail.co.uk/femail/article-2464409/Two-thirds-British-bosses-say-women-wear-makeup-want-successful-career.html.

12 Yerkes et al. (2010). The study looks at how women have experienced policies that aim to aid flexible working for parents.

13 See Chambers (2007) for a discussion of the complexities of culturally shaped preferences and how to address them in a theory of justice.

14 Nussbaum (2000a), pp. 33–34.

15 Woodard (2013) has noted that we might construe hedonism as a monistic objective list view, with one item on the list, to wit: pleasure.

16 See Sen (2004).

17 This list is from Nussbaum's (2000b) reference, and the items on the list vary slightly in other articulations of it (e.g., 1992, 2000a).

References

Annas, J. (1993) Women and the Quality of Life: One Norm or Two, in Nussbaum, M. and Sen, A. (eds.), *The Quality of Life*, Oxford: Oxford University Press, pp. 280–296.

Antony, L.M. (2000) Natures and Norms, *Ethics* 111(1): 8–36.

Baber, H.E. (2010) Worlds, Capabilities and Well-being, *Ethical Theory and Moral Practice* 13(4): 377–392.

Bartky, S. (1990) *Femininity and Domination: Studies in the Phenomenology of Oppression,* New York: Routledge.

Card, C. (1990) Gender and Moral Luck, in O.J. Flanagan and A. Oksenberg Rorty (eds.), *Identity, Character, and Morality: Essays in Moral Psychology*, Cambridge, MA: MIT Press, pp. 199–218.

Chambers, C. (2007) *Sex, Culture and Justice: The Limits of Choice*, Philadelphia, PA: Penn State University Press.

Dworkin, R. (1981) What is Equality? Part 1: Equality of Welfare, *Philosophy & Public Affairs* 10(3): 185–246.

Fanon, F. (1952) *Black Skin, White Masks*, New York: Grove Press.

Friedman, M. (2009) Feminist Virtue Ethics, Happiness, and Moral Luck, *Hypatia* 24(1): 29–40.

MacKinnon, C. (1989) *Toward a Feminist Theory of State*, Cambridge, MA: Harvard University Press.

Nozick, N. (1974) *Anarchy State and Utopia,* Oxford: Blackwell.

Nussbaum, M. (1992) Human Functioning and Social Justice: In Defense of Aristotelian Essentialism, *Political Theory* 20(2): 202–246.

Nussbaum, M. (2000a) *Sex and Social Justice*, Oxford: Oxford University Press.

Nussbaum, M. (2000b) Women's Capabilities and Social Justice, *Journal of Human Development* 1(2): 219–247.

Sen, A. (2004) Elements of a Theory of Human Rights, *Philosophy & Public Affairs* 32(4): 315–356.

Superson, A. (2009) *The Moral Skeptic,* Oxford: Oxford University Press.

Tessman, L. (2005) *Burdened Virtues: Virtue Ethics for Liberatory Struggles*, New York: Oxford University Press.

Valdes, M. (1993) Julia Annas: Women and The Quality of Life: Two Norms or One? in Nussbaum, M. and Sen, A. (eds.), *The Quality of Life*, Oxford: Oxford University Press, pp. 298–301.

Woodard, C. (2013) Classifying Theories of Welfare, *Philosophical Studies* 165(3): 787–803.

Yerkes, M., Standing, K., Waltis, L. and Wain, S. (2010) The Disconnection Between Policy Practices and Women's Lived Experiences: Combining Work and Life in the UK and the Netherlands, *Community, Work & Family* 13: 411–427.

Online resources

Equality and Human Rights Commission (2011) *Briefing Paper 2, Gender Pay Gaps*. http://www.equalityhumanrights.com/sites/default/files/documents/research/gender_pay_gap_briefing_paper2.pdf (accessed 4 October 2014).

Fawcett Society (2013) *News: Equal Pay*. http://www.fawcettsociety.org.uk/2013/11/equal-pay/ (accessed 4 October 2014).

Fawcett Society (2013) *Sex and Power 2013: Who Runs Britain*? http://www.fawcettsociety.org.uk/wp-content/uploads/2013/02/Sex-and-Power-2013-FINAL-REPORT.pdf (accessed 4 October 2014).

Girls' Attitude Survey (2013) *What Girls Say About Equality for Girls*. girlsattitudes.girlguiding.org.uk/pdf/2013_Attitudes_EqualityForGirls.pdf (accessed 4 October 2014).

Government Equalities Office (2010) *Ethnic Minority Women's Poverty and Economic Well-being*. https://www.gov.uk/government/uploads/system/uploads/attachment_data/file/85528/ethnic-minority-women_s-poverty.pdf (accessed 4 October 2014).

Office for National Statistics (2013) *Full Report: Women in the Labour Market*. http://www.ons.gov.uk/ons/dcp171776_328352.pdf (accessed 4 October 2014).

Office for National Statistics (2014) Chapter 4—Intimate Personal Violence and Partner Abuse, *Part of Crime Statistics, Focus on Violent Crime and Sexual Offences, 2012/13 Release*. http://www.ons.gov.uk/ons/rel/crime-stats/crime-statistics/focus-on-violent-crime-and-sexual-offences—2012-13/rpt—chapter-4—intimate-personal-violence-and-partner-abuse.html (accessed 4 October 2014).

Office of the First Minister and Deputy First Minister (2013) *Gender Equality Strategy Statistics: 2013 Update*. http://www.ofmdfmni.gov.uk/gender-equality-strategy-statistics-update-july-2013.pdf (accessed 4 October 2014).

Unesco Institute for Statistics, Gender and Education. http://www.uis.unesco.org/Education/Pages/gender-education.aspx (accessed 4 October 2014).

United Nations Development Programme. Gender and Poverty Reduction. http://www.undp.org/content/undp/en/home/ourwork/povertyreduction/focus_areas/focus_gender_and_poverty/ (accessed 4 October 2014).

World Economic Forum (2013) *The Global Gender Gap Report, 2013*. http://www.weforum.org/reports/global-gender-gap-report-2013 (accessed 4 October 2014).

World Health Organization (2014) *Violence Against Women, Intimate Partner and Sexual Violence Against Women*. Fact sheet N°239, http://www.who.int/mediacentre/factsheets/fs239/en/ (accessed 4 October 2014).

PART VI

Well-being and other disciplines

39

WELL-BEING AND THE LAW

Alex Sarch

Well-being is at least one of the things it is legitimate for the law to aim at. If a law would lead to a substantial improvement in well-being, and would not be overly detrimental to other things we value like equality or justice, then most would agree that passing the law would be permissible—even desirable. But what relationship, more precisely, does law bear to well-being? How does law aim at advancing well-being? And how should it? These questions are the focus of this chapter.

Distinguish two ways in which well-being might be an aim of the law. First, we might think law should aim to *promote* well-being. To say that law should promote well-being in the present sense is to claim that a law is more choiceworthy, all else equal, the more well-being it produces (the higher it causes people's level of well-being to be). This familiar idea figures centrally in the utilitarian tradition in moral philosophy, as well as welfare economics and the economic analysis of law.

Second, we might think that, rather than just aiming to promote well-being, the law should (to coin a technical term) *protect* well-being—i.e., defend against setbacks to well-being by imposing sanctions or liability[1] for actions that are detrimental to well-being. Note that a law can promote well-being at the same time as protecting it. After all, to protect a value like well-being might serve as a means to promoting it. But law can also promote well-being without protecting it outright (e.g., if the government were to set a minimum wage requirement to increase general well-being).[2]

Let me be more precise about what's involved in protecting a value. A law can protect a value, *V*, either (1) *directly*, by expressly stating that liability is to be imposed on the basis of setbacks to *V*, or (2) *indirectly*, by stating that liability attaches to actions that damage something distinct from *V* that nonetheless is closely connected to *V*. More specifically:[3]

> A law, *L*, *protects* a value, *V*, iff *L* states that civil or criminal liability (or some other relevant legal consequence) is to be imposed on the basis of either
>
> 1. infringements or setbacks to *V* itself or a constituent of *V* [*direct* protection], or
> 2. infringements or setbacks to something else, *V'*, that is sufficiently closely connected to *V*—as would be the case if *V'* were necessary for *V*, or typically useful as a means to *V* (even if not necessary therefor) [*indirect* protection].

Thus, for example, a law would protect well-being directly if it imposes liability in response to actions that lower the well-being of another (though there would be obvious practical challenges in applying such a law). A law might also directly protect well-being by imposing liability in response to actions that harm only a constituent of well-being (e.g., mental well-being)—though, in that case, well-being would be protected only *partially*, not as such or in general. By contrast, the law would *indirectly* protect well-being if it provided, for example, that the defendant is civilly liable for actions that harm interests of the plaintiff's that normally are *instrumentally linked* to well-being, such as freedom from assault or injury. Despite not expressly mentioning well-being, such a law would still indirectly protect it by defending against harms to things to which it is closely connected.

In the remainder of this chapter, I consider views about how the law might aim to promote or protect well-being. My goal is primarily one of arbitrage: I hope to point philosophers of well-being towards legal issues that might be of particular interest, in the hopes that this will lead to more contact between the two fields. In the first section, I discuss the law and economics movement, which supposes that law should promote well-being (perhaps exclusively). Then, I consider whether the law in general is concerned to protect well-being, and I suggest that, while the law plausibly aims to promote well-being, it only protects it in limited respects. In the final section, I take a closer look at tort law in particular, since one might think its practice of imposing liability for the harms we cause one another make tort law particularly concerned to protect well-being. Nonetheless, I argue that tort law for the most part only indirectly protects well-being, and even if it does offer some direct protection of well-being, this would still only be partial protection.[4]

Well-being and policy evaluation

The idea that law should promote well-being figures into many views about the question of policy evaluation, which legislators and regulators often confront. This question asks: of the different laws or policies we might impose on a given occasion, which one *should* we choose? Much has been written on how policy evaluation should be conducted, and I will not canvass the possible views here. Instead, I focus on one dominant approach to this question in the law: namely, the economic analysis of law. This approach takes it that laws or policies are to be evaluated chiefly by their effects on well-being. In this section, I sketch the economic approach and then discuss some common criticisms of it.

Starting in the 1960s, economic analysis of law grew into one of the most prominent approaches to the study of law in the USA.[5] It has also had a substantial impact on the reasoning in judicial opinions (Cohen 1985).[6] The movement was ushered in by the seminal work of Guido Calabresi and Ronald Coase (Calabresi 1961; Coase 1961), and was catapulted to prominence by an influential book by Richard Posner arguing that common law rules *are* economically efficient[7] (at least approximately) (Posner 1973). Posner subsequently argued that legal rules also *ought* to be economically efficient (Posner 1980).[8]

The economic analysis of law thus comprises two sorts of project, one descriptive and one normative. Arguably the most familiar of the descriptive projects is *predictive*. The aim is to use economic tools to predict how various legal policies will affect people's incentives, and thus their behavior (on the assumption that people are motivationally responsive to their incentives).[9]

For example, suppose a legislature is trying to decide whether some activity (say, hauling nuclear waste or operating a railroad) should be governed by a negligence rule or a strict liability rule. Negligence rules impose liability on those who cause injuries to others by failing to take adequate precautions (i.e., not acting with "due care"). Strict liability rules impose liability on those who cause injury regardless of the level of precaution they took (even if great care was taken). Law and economics provide the sort of predictive information the legislature will need to decide which sort of rule to adopt. Economic tools can be used to analyze the incentives that these two competing rules would create for participants in the relevant activity. After all, the question of when participants will face liability for injuries they cause, as well as how much liability, directly affects the level of precaution it is economically rational for participants to take. It also helps determine whether it makes economic sense to engage in the activity in the first place. Thus, by analyzing the incentive effects of legal rules, economic analysis can help predict how these rules will affect behavior.

The *normative* prong of economic analysis of law uses such predictive tools (or others) to evaluate policy alternatives. This amounts to applying the principles of welfare economics to law. The basic idea is to begin by determining how the policies on offer will affect incentives, behavior, and ultimately the satisfaction of individuals' preferences. Since preference satisfaction is taken to be either constitutive of or at least evidence of welfare, descriptive results about how various policies impact preference satisfaction are supposed to have normative implications about which policies are most choiceworthy.

To see how the normative project plays out, consider the most prominent recent defense of the normative prong of law and economics—offered in Kaplow and Shavell (2002) (hereinafter "K&S 2002"). K&S's main thesis is that "social decisions should be based *exclusively* on their effects on the welfare of individuals—and, accordingly, should not depend on notions of fairness, justice, or cognate concepts" (K&S 2002: xvii). Their preferred framework for evaluating policy involves several steps: "[t]he first is to determine the effects of the policy, [while] [t]he second step is to evaluate the effects of the policy in order to determine its social desirability" (K&S 2002: 15). The second, evaluative step itself proceeds in several stages.

The evaluative step begins by asking how the policy choice will impact the affected individuals' well-being, or equivalently, for K&S, their *utility*. As K&S note, "the primitive element for analysis of an individual's well-being is that individual's ordering of possible outcomes" (K&S 2002: 18, footnote 6). Thus, consider a policy proposal, P. It could lead to a range of outcomes if implemented: $O_1, O_2 \ldots O_n$. For each affected individual, S, we need to determine how she would rank these outcomes—i.e., what her preferences between them are. One common technique for generating these orderings (by no means the only one) is to read off the strengths of people's preferences from their market behavior—i.e., their willingness to pay for various goods (K&S 2002: 409–413).[10] Numbers are then assigned to the outcomes to reflect S's preferences between them, with higher numbers representing a higher position in S's preference ordering.[11] The utility number for each outcome is then multiplied by an estimate of the probability that this outcome has of occurring conditional on P's being implemented. These products are then summed in order to get the expected utility of P for individual S. K&S emphasize that their notion of utility or well-being "is comprehensive in nature": "[i]t incorporates in a positive way everything that an individual might value" (K&S 2002: 18). They also take on board "the possibility that individuals have a taste for a notion of fairness, just as they may have a taste for art, nature, or fine wine" (K&S 2002: 21).

Once this procedure has been carried out for all affected individuals to find the expected utility of P for each one, the next step is to aggregate these individual utilities to reach a conclusion about the overall desirability of P—i.e., its *social welfare*. As K&S explain,

> [a] method of aggregation is of necessity an element of welfare economics, and value judgments are involved in aggregating different individuals' well-being into a single measure of social welfare. [Moreover, it] involves the adoption of a view concerning matters of distribution.
>
> *(K&S 2002: 26–27)*

Aggregating the individual utilities is the job of the *social welfare function* (SWF). A simple utilitarian SWF would merely take the social welfare of *P* to be the sum of the expected utilities of *P* for all affected individuals.[12] However, the SWF might also be constructed to be sensitive to distributive equality. For example, K&S note that "the well-being of worse-off individuals might be given additional weight, as under the approach associated with John Rawls, wherein social welfare corresponds to the utility of the worst off individuals" (K&S 2002: 27). There are many other equality-sensitive SWFs as well.[13] K&S "do not defend any specific way of aggregating individuals' well-being [or] endorse any particular view about the proper distribution of well-being" (K&S 2002: 27). Rather, they argue only "that legal policy analysis should be guided by reference to some coherent way of aggregating individuals' well-being" (K&S 2002: 27).

Once an appropriate SWF has been selected, an overall ranking of the policy alternatives can be generated. For each policy *P*, the SWF would take as input the expected utility of *P* for each affected individual and then return as output a social welfare value for *P* (which may or may not be sensitive to distributive considerations). In this way, the policies can be ranked in terms of social welfare value and an overall policy recommendation can be reached.

K&S's defense of this framework for policy evaluation has received substantial criticism— especially their claim that policy evaluation should *only* be sensitive to how policies affect welfare, not what they call "notions of fairness" (K&S 2002: xvii). An initial worry is that K&S's distinction between exclusively welfare-based policy evaluation and evaluation based on notions of fairness is incoherent. On K&S's view, a notion of fairness is an evaluative principle "that accord[s] weight to factors that are independent of individuals' well-being" (K&S 2002: 44). As examples, they mention (i) corrective justice (the principle that one who wrongfully injures another must compensate or redress the wrong), (ii) the principle that promises must be kept, and (iii) retributive justice (the idea that one ought to be punished if, but only to the extent that, one deserves it) (K&S 2002: 39). However, if these principles are to be ruled out from the policy analysis framework as notions of fairness, one wonders why K&S are comfortable allowing considerations of equality or distributive justice to play a part in policy analysis—in particular, by incorporating such notions into the SWF.[14]

K&S are aware of this tension, and they respond that in fact,

> there is no tension because . . . [o]ur definition of notions of fairness includes all principles—but only those principles—that give weight to factors that are independent of individuals' well-being. [Thus,] distribution can play an important role even under a system of evaluation that is concerned exclusively with individuals' well-being.
>
> *(K&S 2002: 28)*

Their idea is to attempt to distinguish "factors that are independent of well-being" (like corrective justice) from distributive considerations on the ground that the latter, but not the former, are still "concerned" with well-being. Nonetheless, this does not fully resolve the problem. Suppose everyone has a right to a certain minimum amount of well-being. Such a right would be "concerned" with well-being at least as much as distributive considerations are, even though K&S see rights as a paradigmatic notion of fairness (K&S 2002: 5 and footnote 7).

A second, deeper worry concerns K&S's argument that justice and rights have no place in policy evaluation. A more moderate view would be that, while well-being and its distribution matter greatly to policy evaluation, avoiding injustice and preventing the violation of rights are also important. K&S reject such moderate views, however (K&S 2002: xvii). Their "argument for basing the evaluation of legal rules entirely on welfare economics, giving no weight to notions of fairness" is that "satisfying notions of fairness can make individuals worse off, that is reduce social welfare" (K&S 2002: 52). They continue that this point has "special force" because "fairness-based analysis [can lead] to the choice of legal rules that reduce the well-being of *every* individual" (K&S 2002: 52).[15] However, critics object that this argument cuts no ice, as it is trivially true that a concern for justice can conflict with promoting well-being (Coleman 2003: 1524).

Surprisingly, K&S themselves admit "it is virtually a tautology to assert that fairness-based evaluation entails some sort of reduction in individuals' well-being" (K&S 2002: 58). However, they respond that they "do not believe the full [cost] of fairness-based analysis for human welfare is appreciated" (K&S 2002: 58). Accordingly, K&S develop numerous examples designed to show how great the sacrifice to well-being might be if policy evaluation affords independent weight to notions of fairness (K&S 2002: chapters III–VI). Nonetheless, the worry persists. Even if there are some cases where preventing large losses in well-being might give reason to tolerate some degree of injustice, this is not sufficient to establish the *general* claim K&S want—namely, that justice should *never* be given any independent weight in evaluating policy.

One last set of concerns has to do with the notion of well-being used in K&S's framework. To start, one might question K&S's "comprehensive" notion of well-being, which incorporates "everything that an individual might value [like] social and environmental amenities, personally held notions of fulfillment, sympathetic feelings for others, and so forth" (K&S 2002: 18). One might object that the satisfaction of preferences that do not concern one's own life intuitively cannot affect one's well-being. For instance, it seems doubtful that one's well-being can be enhanced merely by the satisfaction of, say, a preference that things go well for the stranger on the train in Parfit's famous case (Parfit 1984: 494), or the satisfaction of a preference for sacrificing one's own well-being to benefit those one loves or to harm those one hates (Hausman and McPherson 2009: 6). Thus, we might want to restrict the preferences that can figure into policy evaluation so that only those concerning one's own life count.

More generally, one might challenge the apparent commitment of K&S's framework to a preferentist theory of well-being. After all, there are well-known objections even to restricted versions of preferentism on which welfare consists in the satisfaction of preferences about one's own life. For instance, when our preferences are manipulated or not autonomous, their satisfaction might not seem to enhance well-being (Sumner 1996, chapter 6). Moreover, it seems possible to strongly prefer things that intuitively make little or no positive contribution to well-being—as in certain cases of masochistic, antisocial, pointless, or otherwise defective preferences (Brink 1989: 227; Kraut 1994; Heathwood 2005; Bradley 2007).

One promising line of response for economic analysis to such problems for preferentism is the strategy defended in Hausman and McPherson (2009). They argue that welfare economics should reject preferentism about well-being, and instead insist only that revealed preferences are a *reliable source of information* about well-being—at least provided these preferences are well informed and self-interested. This would permit us to keep doing policy evaluation in the way economists recommend, without falling prey to the familiar objections to the theory that well-being consists in preference satisfaction.

Nonetheless, there are other sources of information about well-being besides preferences as revealed in the market (e.g., surveys, psychological information, happiness studies). Therefore, before Hausman and McPherson's strategy succeeds in vindicating economic analysis as currently practiced, more needs to be said to establish that revealed preferences are by themselves our *most reliable* source of information about well-being—or in some other sense our best (e.g., most practical) source of such information.[16] Only then can the evaluative project of economic analysis be placed on a more secure normative foundation.

The protection of well-being by law

Although more might be said about how policy evaluation might incorporate the idea that law should promote well-being,[17] let us press on. The other sort of question we might ask about the normative relationship between law and well-being concerns the role of well-being *within* the law. That is, we might ask whether law generally, or perhaps specific laws or legal doctrines, should *protect* well-being in the sense described earlier. Here I will mostly sidestep the normative question of whether law should protect well-being. Whether it should or not depends heavily on empirical questions about whether such protection is an effective and implementable strategy. Instead, my focus is the descriptive issue of whether and how existing law *does* protect well-being—whether directly or indirectly. I begin with some general observations, before considering tort law more closely in the next section.

In general, the concept of well-being does not seem to expressly figure into the content of US law very often. This, in turn, might suggest that US law typically does not protect well-being *directly*. Still, there may be exceptions. Here are some of the more notable references to well-being, welfare, or the like that appear in US law. (1) Art. I § 8 of the US Constitution states that "Congress shall have Power to lay and collect Taxes . . . to . . . provide for the . . . general Welfare of the United States."[18] (2) Decisions about child custody are generally made on the basis of what would be in the "best interest of the child."[19] This test plausibly involves a conception of the child's welfare. (3) To win a sexual harassment lawsuit under Title VII,[20] it is sufficient for the plaintiff to prove that the defendant's conduct "seriously affected" the plaintiff's psychological well-being (if there are no relevant defenses).[21] (4) The Supreme Court has held in the First Amendment context that there is a "compelling state interest" in protecting the physical and psychological well-being of minors, which can be sufficient grounds for curtailing the general right to free speech.[22]

Not all of these more or less overt references to welfare or well-being are examples of law directly protecting well-being in the technical sense introduced above. While (2) and (3) seem like plausible candidates, since they impose liability or other legal consequences in a subset of cases in which well-being is detrimentally affected, the same is not true for (1) and (4). (1) merely authorizes Congress to tax, and by implication to spend, in order to promote the general welfare, while (4) suggests that free-speech protections can sometimes be limited by a concern for child welfare.

Accordingly, US law only rarely makes reference to well-being in a way that suggests it is being directly protected. Indeed, there seem to be good practical reasons for this. There are many conflicting conceptions of the good life, as well as much intractable debate about what the correct theory of well-being is. Therefore, it might be prudent for legislators to formulate the law using concepts that are less hotly contested, not to mention easier to apply. Moreover, legislators might justifiably prefer laws for which there is an "overlapping consensus," i.e., which citizens can endorse despite having differing political ideologies or conceptions of the good life (Rawls 1987).

While the law thus does not often seem to protect well-being directly (probably sensibly), there is reason to think it frequently protects well-being *indirectly*. For example, the criminal law punishes (among other things) intentional or reckless attacks on bodily integrity. Since freedom from such attacks is at least normally of significant instrumental value for achieving high levels of well-being, the criminal law would seem to indirectly protect well-being.

Similarly, tort law often makes damages available to plaintiffs who can prove the defendant injured them at least negligently. Usually the relevant sort of injury here is physical harm, which is tightly connected to well-being. In some limited cases, tort law also makes damages available to plaintiffs who can prove the defendant's conduct caused emotional suffering (Kircher 2007). We see this most importantly in lawsuits for intentional infliction of emotional distress, negligent infliction of emotional distress, and assault (i.e., causing someone to reasonably fear for her safety) (Kircher 2007).

Finally, the law is frequently concerned to protect various property rights, contractual rights, and financial interests that collectively might seem to be necessary, or at least useful, for obtaining a high degree of well-being. The thought is that living in a society where property is secure, people perform their contracts and one's financial interests are protected will for most people be necessary for, or at least conducive to, achieving high levels of well-being. Accordingly, it's plausible that law often *indirectly* protects well-being.

Tort law

In closing, let's consider tort law more closely to get a clearer sense of the manner in which it protects well-being, as well as the scope of this protection.

Direct or indirect protection?

Tort law deserves special consideration because it might seem to be one of the few areas of law to *directly* protect well-being. The basic argument is this. On one prominent view, tort law aims to "redress the harms we inflict on one another" (Hershovitz 2006: 1149).[23] Harm, in turn, is often understood in terms of reductions to well-being. As a result, we might think tort law directly protects well-being. That is, it would seem to directly impose liability in response to reductions in well-being. (One might make a similar argument concerning criminal law. But since much of what I say here carries over to criminal law, I focus on torts for reasons of space.[24])

There are, however, reasons to doubt that tort law directly protects well-being. Start by noting that tort law does not allow just *any* harm to be the basis of a successful lawsuit. Instead, tort law takes only certain kinds of tangible injuries that are relatively easy to prove—e.g., bodily injury, physical or psychological illness, and sometimes emotional pain and suffering—to be actionable. "Historically, tort law compensated only direct and tangible injuries to persons or property," although over the past century it has started to provide limited "compensation of emotional . . . interests" (Levit 1992: 139–140).[25] Accordingly, tort law does not impose liability for reductions to well-being *as such*. Instead, it would count as directly protecting well-being only if the categories of harm it regards as actionable are reductions to things that qualify as *constituents* of well-being.

However, it's not clear that freedom from the kinds of harms that tort law regards as actionable would qualify as a constituent of well-being. Although it's not easy to say precisely what makes something a constituent of well-being, at least the following sufficient condition seems plausible:

(i)   *X* is a constituent of well-being according to theory *T* if *X* is identical to the instantiation of what *T* regards as a fundamental good-making property.[26]

But freedom from the injuries tort law protects against cannot plausibly be seen as an instantiation of fundamental *good*-making properties; rather, it at best involves the absence of fundamental *bad*-making properties. Thus, freedom from the harms tort law protects against can be a constituent of well-being only if (something like) the following condition is true:

(ii) X is a constituent of well-being according to theory T if X is identical to the absence of what T regards as a fundamental bad-making property.

If nothing like condition ii) is defensible, then freedom from the injuries tort law protects against would not be a constituent of well-being. In that case, tort law would not directly protect well-being at all. Thus, for the sake of argument (i.e., to charitably treat the claim that tort law directly protects well-being), I assume that something like condition ii) is correct. If it is, then the absence of pain, say, would count as a constituent of well-being on hedonism. By contrast, a painless surgery would not. Even though such a surgery would lack the fundamental bad-making property of being painful, it is not itself *identical* to the absence of that property. Constituents of well-being thus are to be distinguished from states of affairs that merely cause, *pro tanto* contribute to, or partially realize the presence or absence of a fundamental good-making or bad-making property. After all, merely causing something that in itself enhances well-being is not enough to count as a constituent of well-being, since that would allow an unbounded range of items (i.e., anything that causes an improvement in well-being) to count as a constituent of well-being. For the same reason, states of affairs that merely exemplify a fundamental good-making property (e.g., a pleasant massage), or lack a fundamental bad-making property (e.g., a painless surgery), cannot themselves be constituents of well-being. This would stretch the notion of a constituent of well-being too far.

If this two-pronged understanding of constituents of well-being is roughly right,[27] then it's doubtful that the absence of physical or mental injuries or illnesses would qualify as constituents of well-being.[28] According to most prominent theories of well-being, freedom from such injuries would not in itself constitute the absence of a fundamental bad-making property. On hedonism, for example, only *not being in pain* would qualify under prong ii) as a constituent of well-being. Freedom from physical or mental injury might help causally explain why someone is not experiencing pain right now, but it would not itself be *identical* to the lack of pain. A similar point holds for desire satisfactionism. On that theory, possessing desires that are unfrustrated is what would qualify under prong ii) as a constituent of well-being. While freedom from physical or mental injury might cause some of one's desires not to be frustrated, it would not itself be identical to avoiding the frustration of one's desires.

By contrast, freedom from emotional pain and suffering might well qualify as a constituent of well-being on some theories. This would most obviously be true on hedonism, and perhaps also versions of perfectionism that take human flourishing to involve freedom from suffering. However, desire satisfactionism would not regard freedom from emotional pain and suffering as something that itself constitutes the absence of a fundamental bad-making property. Granted, avoiding pain and suffering would satisfy the desire not to have such experiences. But this still would not make it a constituent of well-being on desire satisfactionism. After all, that theory only recognizes possessing desires that are satisfied, or at least remain unfrustrated, as constituents of well-being. Thus, theories will differ about whether freedom from emotional pain and suffering is itself a constituent of well-being.

Accordingly, the less controversial claim is that avoiding the sorts of injuries that are actionable in tort (perhaps except for emotional pain and suffering) is only instrumentally valuable for preventing the fundamental bad-making properties from obtaining in one's life. Avoiding physical injuries, mental ailments, and traumatic experiences is crucial as a *means* to avoiding that which in itself diminishes well-being. Thus, tort law would mainly protect well-being only indirectly.

If tort law directly protects any constituent of well-being, this would chiefly be freedom from emotional pain and suffering. Nonetheless, it is rare for suits to recover damages for emotional pain and suffering to succeed (Levit 1992: 143–144). Courts often "exhibit significant concern over whether claims for emotional or mental distress are legitimate" (in part due to the ease with which they can be exaggerated) (Levit 1992: 172). Thus, tort law's protection of this constituent of well-being appears tenuous.

Only partial protection

Even if tort law might directly protect what some theories of well-being regard as a constituent of well-being, it's clear that, no matter what one's theory of well-being, tort law at best protects well-being only *partially*. That is, it protects well-being (whether directly or indirectly) only in limited circumstances. In this subsection, I aim to clarify what these circumstances are in order to further elucidate the scope of tort law's protection of well-being.

One reason tort law protects well-being only *partially* stems from the harm–benefit asymmetry it embodies. While tort liability may be imposed in response to harms, it is rarely imposed for failures to benefit. First-year law students often are surprised to learn that there generally is no duty to rescue, such that tort liability is not imposed for failing to do so.[29] (There are some exceptions, the most notable being when one caused the danger from which the victim now requires rescuing.[30]) Thus, tort law is concerned with just one side of the well-being equation: it protects well-being if harmed, but not when merely unbenefitted. Since liability is not imposed for just any impediment to well-being, tort law clearly does not protect well-being as such— only partially.

A second way tort law protects well-being only partially has to do with the notion of harm it employs. There is a wide sense in which one is harmed by anything that detrimentally impacts one's well-being. Call this the *unrestricted view* of harm. It can be spelled out either comparatively or non-comparatively. The comparative version takes it that event E harms person P iff E lowers P's well-being relative to some baseline—whether this is the well-being P had before E (a historical baseline), or the well-being P would have absent E (a counterfactual baseline) (Hershovitz 2006: 1161–1163; Bradley 2012: 396–398; Klocksiem 2012). By contrast, the non-comparative version takes it that E harms P iff E causes P to be in an intrinsically bad state, where such states include "pain, mental or physical discomfort, disease, deformity, disability, or death" (Harman 2009: 139).[31] However the unrestricted view of harm is understood, it does not capture the conditions under which tort liability is imposed. To adequately capture these conditions, we must limit ourselves to harms that arose through a *rights violation*.

To see this, consider an example from Hershovitz (2006: 1165). Suppose I steal your TV and enjoy watching it for a time. Now suppose I'm hauled before the court and am sentenced to a term of one year in prison. In the unrestricted sense, the court's action harms me. My well-being is lowered, both relative to what it was before (when I was enjoying your TV) and relative to what it would have been were I not sanctioned by the court. Thus, I am comparatively harmed. Furthermore, supposing I experience mental and physical discomfort while imprisoned—the court's action places me in an intrinsically bad state. So I am non-comparatively harmed too. Nonetheless, the court's action (assuming it is procedurally valid) does not provide the basis for imposing tort liability on the court or any other government institution, even though I was harmed by its actions. Since I deserved (legally and morally) the punishment I received, the court's action did not violate any *right* of mine. Hence tort liability is inappropriate.

Accordingly, tort liability is not imposed in response to just any action that harms the plaintiff in the unrestricted sense. Rather, it is at best imposed only if the defendant's action (1) harms the plaintiff in the unrestricted sense (i.e., causes injury or damage) and (2) violates a legally recognized right of the plaintiff's.[32]

Not only is harm to well-being insufficient for tort liability, it is also unnecessary. One can prevail in some tort suits even if one suffered no perceptible injury, as long as one can show that one's rights were violated. In such cases, the plaintiff will simply be awarded nominal damages (e.g., $1).[33] If mere injury to well-being is neither necessary nor sufficient for tort liability, it seems the main factor on which tort liability depends is the violation of rights. One might question whether tort law should be this way. Perhaps it is an inefficient or otherwise objectionable system. Perhaps we should make compensation available for some injuries not caused by a rights violation. But this nonetheless is the institution we face.

Concluding remarks

This section has aimed to establish two things. First, it's controversial to claim that tort law directly protects well-being. After all, only some theories of well-being imply that tort law directly protects a constituent of well-being. Instead, tort law seems mostly to protect well-being indirectly. Second, even if tort law does directly protect some constituent of well-being, this would still only be partial protection. Tort law typically imposes liability only for harms (not failures to benefit), and moreover only when the harm involved the violation of the plaintiff's rights. Accordingly, the scope of tort law's protection of well-being (whether direct or indirect) appears limited.

One last question: is there work left for the concept of well-being to do in theorizing about tort law as it currently exists? The answer is "yes," at least when it comes to evaluating and reforming tort doctrine. As seen above, to understand the conditions under which tort liability is imposed, we need some notion of injury or damage that is deemed to be actionable, provided it occurred through a rights violation. And well-being can play a central role in determining what the relevant injuries should be. That is, we might appeal to our best theory of well-being to identify the kinds of injury or damage that should be actionable.

Currently, only limited kinds of injuries can be the basis for damage awards in tort—most commonly, medically diagnosable physical or psychological ailments. But perhaps existing tort law is too narrow, and a greater variety of injuries should be compensable.[34] Of course, practical difficulties will arise when it comes to proving in court the extent to which one suffered the more intangible injuries that a plausible theory of well-being might recognize, but which tort law currently does not. Nonetheless, in at least this way, well-being remains relevant to tort law: it matters in unpacking the best notion of injury or damage that tort law should take to be actionable, at least if that injury or damage came about through a rights violation.

Notes

1   Two forms of legal liability should be distinguished: civil and criminal. The former typically involves the payment of money damages, while the latter paradigmatically involves a term of imprisonment and/or fines. Other forms of legal relief include injunctions (court orders to perform or refrain from performing certain actions) or declaratory relief (a binding pronouncement of the parties' rights).

2   A law also might protect well-being without promoting it, as would be the case with an ill-conceived law that seeks to protect well-being but has the general effect of making people worse off.

3   There might be other natural ways to talk about protecting a value. For example, we might say the state should "protect" well-being by ensuring that all its citizens can lead lives with a certain minimum level of well-being (e.g., through social welfare programs). However, this would fall outside the technical sense of "protecting well-being" I employ here.

4   Throughout, I'll be focusing on US law, since that is where my training lies.

5   The influence of law and economics has been more muted in Europe (Dau-Schmidt and Brun 2006: 604).

6 See, e.g., *Wassell* v. *Adams*, 865 F.2d 849, 855–56 (7th Cir. 1989) (Posner, J.) (taking an economic approach to the issue of negligence). For an early precursor to this approach, see *United States* v. *Carroll Towing Co.*, 159 F.2d 169, 173 (2d Cir. 1947) (Hand, J.) (formulating the famous "Hand rule" for determining if a defendant acted negligently).

7 Economic efficiency is typically understood in terms of Pareto efficiency. A state of affairs, S, is efficient, or *Pareto optimal*, iff no available state of affairs is Pareto superior to S. S1 is *Pareto superior* to S2 iff at least one person is better off in S1 than S2 and no one is better off in S2 than S1 (Coleman 1992: 19). (Sometimes the principle is formulated in terms of preferences between states (Coleman 2003: 1516)). However, because most real-life policies create both "winners" and "losers," "very little efficiency analysis in the law actually invokes the Pareto criteria" (Coleman 2003: 1517). Instead, "[m]ost efficiency analysis relies . . . on the Kaldor-Hicks criterion. One state of affairs, S, is Kaldor-Hicks efficient to another, A, [iff] the winners under S could compensate the losers such that, after compensation, no one would prefer A to S and at least one person would prefer S to A" (Coleman 2003: 1517). For criticism of Kaldor-Hicks efficiency, see Hausman and McPherson (2006: Chapter 6).

8 For critical discussion of this normative claim, see Coleman (1980), Dworkin (1985), and Posner (1995).

9 Another project on the descriptive side argues that the *content* of the law is determined by efficiency. See Kraus (2007) for analysis of this sort of explanatory project.

10 For other options, see Adler (2012: 270–275, 297–302).

11 K&S emphasize that "utility numbers need not be interpreted as objective, measurable quantities, but rather should be understood as constructed, auxiliary numbers selected by the analyst to represent the underlying rank ordering of the individual" (K&S 2002: 18, footnote 6).

12 Another non-equality-sensitive SWF would involve ranking the outcomes according to Pareto superiority (or more likely Kaldor-Hicks efficiency). See *supra*, note 7.

13 For one particularly attractive equality-sensitive SWF, see Adler (2008: 27, 44–45). See also Adler (2012: Chapter 2); Hausman and McPherson (2006: Chapter 13).

14 This objection has been pressed by Dorff (2002: 849–850) and Farber (2003: 1793).

15 Perhaps letting preferences include a taste for fairness mitigates the tension between fairness and promoting well-being. However, this reply is insufficient. First, economic analysis could still recommend highly unjust outcomes—especially if the taste for fairness is not strong enough (Dolinko 2002: 359). Second, while K&S think fairness can have moral significance only in virtue of people having a preference for it, this is not how fairness is generally thought to get its moral significance.

16 I press this objection to Hauseman and McPherson in more detail elsewhere (Sarch 2015).

17 For example, Joseph Raz's perfectionist liberalism would take well-being to matter to policy evaluation, but would not understand well-being in terms of preference satisfaction.

18 The Preamble to the US Constitution also states that one aim of "establish[ing] this Constitution for the United States of America" is to "promote the general Welfare." But the Preamble is not "regarded as the source of any substantive power conferred on the Government of the United States." *Jacobson* v. *Massachusetts*, 197 U.S. 11, 22 (1905).

19 See, e.g., *Schult* v. *Schult*, 241 Conn. 767, 777, 699 A.2d 134, 139 (1997) ("'In making or modifying any order with respect to custody or visitation, the court shall . . . be guided by the best interests of the child . . . .' [which] include the child's interests in sustained growth, development, well-being, and continuity and stability of its environment.") (internal citations omitted).

20 42 U.S.C. § 2000e, *et seq.*

21 *Harris* v. *Forklift Sys., Inc.*, 510 U.S. 17, 22 (1993) ("Title VII bars conduct that would seriously affect a reasonable person's psychological well-being"). *Harris* also held that harm to psychological well-being is not *necessary* for such a lawsuit to succeed. *Id.*

22 *Sable Commc'ns of California, Inc.* v. *F.C.C.*, 492 U.S. 115, 126 (1989).

23 Hershovitz calls this "the model of harms," in contrast to "the model of costs" on which tort law aims to promote efficiency (Hershovitz 2006: 1147).

24 As Joel Feinberg observed, while "criminal law is not the state's primary tool for the reduction of harms," it still "is the primary instrumentality for preventing people from intentionally or recklessly harming one another" (Feinberg 1984: 31). Feinberg goes on to restrict the notion of harm relevant to criminal law in the same way as we'll see is needed in the torts context. Criminal law, he suggests, is largely concerned with *wrongfully* imposed harms (Feinberg 1984: 105).

25 Levit notes that "[t]hose incurring physical harms are readily compensated," while "[t]hose incurring psychic harms face skepticism" (Levit 1992: 175).

26 Fundamental good-making and bad-making properties are the ones that welfare ultimately depends on—i.e., whose instantiations completely and fundamentally determine how well one's life goes. See Bradley (2009: 19); Sarch (2011: 180–181).

27 Adopting a different conception of constituents of well-being may lead to different conclusions about whether tort law directly protects well-being.

28 The same holds for other kinds of interests that tort law protects, which may not be as tightly connected to well-being—e.g., privacy or property interests (Levit 1992: 139, 140–141).

29 Restatement (2d) of Torts § 314 (1965) ("The fact that the actor realizes or should realize that action on his part is necessary for another's aid or protection does not of itself impose upon him a duty to take such action"); see also *Osterlind* v. *Hill*, 263 Mass. 73, 76, 160 N.E. 301, 302 (1928).

30 Restatement (2d) of Torts § 321 (1965).

31 For more on the relation between harm and well-being, see Chapter 35 of this volume.

32 As Hershovitz notes, tort liability is conditioned on proof that "1) the defendant had a duty to the plaintiff, 2) the defendant breached the duty, and 3) the breach of the duty caused the plaintiff damage. Duties are the correlates of rights. Thus, to recover in tort, a plaintiff must show that the defendant invaded a right of hers, causing her damage" (Hershovitz 2006: 1168).

33 Nominal damages are available in suits for battery, libel, and the violation of one's constitutional rights, though notably not negligence, nuisance, or slander.

34 For example, Levit (1992) argues that tort law should be more willing to impose liability on the basis of emotional and other "intangible" injuries.

Bibliography

Adler, Matthew (2008) "Risk Equity: A New Proposal," *Harvard Environmental Law Review* 32: 1.

Adler, Matthew (2012) *Well-Being and Fair Distribution: Beyond Cost Benefit Analysis*, Oxford: Oxford University Press.

Adler, Matthew and Posner, Eric (2006) *New Foundations of Cost–Benefit Analysis*, Cambridge, MA: Harvard University Press.

Bradley, Ben (2009) *Well-Being and Death*, Oxford: Oxford University Press.

Bradley, Ben (2012) "Doing Away with Harms," *Philosophy and Phenomenological Research* 85(2): 390–412.

Brink, David O. (1989) *Moral Realism and the Foundations of Ethics,* Cambridge: Cambridge University Press.

Calabresi, Guido (1961) "Some Thoughts on Risk Distribution and the Law of Torts," *Yale Law Journal* 70(4): 499–553.

Coase, Ronald (1961) "The Problem of Social Cost," *Journal of Law and Economics*, 3: 1–44.

Cohen, George M. (1985) "Posnerian Jurisprudence and Economic Analysis of Law: The View from the Bench," *University of Pennsylvania Law Review* 133: 1117.

Coleman, Jules (1980) "Efficiency, Utility, and Wealth Maximization," *Hofstra Law Review* 8: 509.

Coleman, Jules (1992) *Risks and Wrongs*, Cambridge: Cambridge University Press.

Coleman, Jules (2003) "The Grounds of Welfare," *Yale Law Journal* 112: 1511.

Dau-Schmidt, Kenneth and Brun, Carmen (2006) "Lost in Translation: The Economic Analysis of Law in the United States and Europe," *Columbia Journal of Transnational Law* 44: 602.

Dolinko, David (2002) "The Perils of Welfare Economics," *Northwestern University Law Review* 97: 351.

Dorff, Michael B. (2002) "Why Welfare Depends on Fairness: A Reply to Kaplow and Shavell," *Southern California Law Review* 75: 847.

Dworkin, Ronald (1985) *A Matter of Principle,* Cambridge, MA: Harvard University Press, pp. 237–268.

Farber, Daniel A. (2003) "What (If Anything) Can Economics Say About Equity?," *Michigan Law Review* 101: 1791.

Feinberg, Joel (1984) *The Moral Limits of the Criminal Law. Vol. 1, Harm to Others*, New York: Oxford University Press.

Harman, Elizabeth (2009) "Harming as Causing Harm," in Roberts, M.A. and Wasserman, D.T. (eds.), *Harming Future Persons*, New York: Springer, pp. 137–154.

Hausman, Daniel and McPherson, Michael (2006) *Economic Analysis, Moral Philosophy and Public Policy*, 2nd edn, New York: Cambridge University Press.

Hausman, Daniel and McPherson, Michael (2009) "Preference Satisfaction and Welfare Economics," *Economics and Philosophy* 25(1): 1–25.

Heathwood, Chris (2005) "The Problem of Defective Desires," *Australasian Journal of Philosophy* 83(4): 487–504.

Hershovitz, Scott (2006) "Two Models of Tort (and Takings)," *Virginia Law Review* 92: 1147.

Kaplow, Louis and Shavell, Steven (K&S) (2002) *Fairness Versus Welfare*, Cambridge, MA: Harvard University Press.

Kircher, John J. (2007) "The Four Faces of Tort Law: Liability for Emotional Harm," *Marquette Law Review* 90: 789.

Klocksiem, Justin (2012) "A Defense of the Counterfactual Comparative Account of Harm," *American Philosophical Quarterly* 48(4): 285–300.

Kraus, Jody S. (2007) "Transparency and Determinacy in Common Law Adjudication: A Philosophical Defense of Explanatory Economic Analysis," *Virginia Law Review* 93: 287.

Kraut, R.H. (1994) "Desire and the Human Good," *Proceedings and Addresses of the American Philosophical Association* 68(2): 39–54.

Levit, Nancy (1992) "Ethereal Torts," *George Washington Law Review* 61: 136.

Parfit, Derek (1984) *Reasons and Persons*, Oxford: Oxford University Press.

Posner, Richard A. (1973) *Economic Analysis of Law*, Boston, MA: Little Brown.

Posner, Richard A. (1980) "The Ethical and Political Basis of the Efficiency Norm in Common Law Adjudication," *Hofstra Law Review* 8: 487.

Posner, Richard A. (1995) "Wealth Maximization and Tort Law: A Philosophical Inquiry," in D. Owen (ed.), *Philosophical Foundations of Tort Law*, Oxford: Oxford University Press, p. 99.

Rawls, John (1987) "The Idea of an Overlapping Consensus," *Oxford Journal of Legal Studies* 7(1): 1–25.

Sarch, Alexander (2011) "Internalism About a Person's Good: Don't Believe It," *Philosophical Studies* 154(2): 161–184.

Sarch, Alexander (2015) "Hausman and McPherson on Welfare Economics and Preference Satisfaction Theories of Welfare: A Critical Note," *Economics and Philosophy* 31(1): 141–159.

Shapiro, Scott (2011) *Legality*, Cambridge, MA: Harvard University Press.

Sumner, L.W. (1996) *Welfare, Happiness, and Ethics*, New York: Clarendon Press.

40

WELL-BEING AND ECONOMICS[1]

Erik Angner

Introduction

Since its early days as a science, economics has aimed not only to better understand the world, but also to improve it. The urge to change the world is perhaps most famously seen in the work of Karl Marx, who remarked: "The philosophers have only *interpreted* the world in various ways; the point is to *change* it" (Marx 1998/1845: 571). But economists from the left to the right have shared the sentiment. In the words of Paul A. Samuelson: "Beginning as it did in the writings of philosophers, theologians, pamphleteers, special pleaders, and reformers, economics has always been concerned with problems of public policy and welfare" (Samuelson 1947: 203). Friedrich A. Hayek agreed:

It is probably true that economic analysis has never been the product of detached intellectual curiosity about the *why* of social phenomena, but of an intense urge to reconstruct a world which gives rise to profound dissatisfaction. This is as true of the phylogenesis of economics as the ontogenesis of probably every economist.

(Hayek 1933: 122–123)

Hayek goes on to quote A.C. Pigou, who wrote: "It is not wonder, but rather the social enthusiasm which revolts from the sordidness of mean streets and the joylessness of withered lives, that is the beginning of economic science" (Pigou 1952/1920: 5). It remains standard for a journal article in economics to conclude with a section on policy implications—perhaps justifying its relevance by the potential to shape policy and thereby improve the world.

As Samuelson's choice of words indicates, the central normative concern of contemporary economists tends to be welfare or well-being—I will use these words interchangeably—and perhaps its distribution (Hausman and McPherson 2006: 97). Even economists who disagree sharply about economic policy frequently agree at least implicitly that policy is properly assessed by its welfare consequences. The subdiscipline that deals with normative economics is simply called *welfare economics* (Hausman and McPherson 2006: 97), and it absorbs a good part of both undergraduate- and graduate-level microeconomics textbooks. *The* standard graduate-level microeconomics textbook used in the English-speaking world, Andreu Mas-Colell, Michael D. Whinston, and Jerry R. Green's *Microeconomic Theory* (1995), explicitly identifies normative economics and welfare analysis (p. 80) and dedicates almost 140 pages to "Part V: Welfare Economics and Incentives" (pp. 787–925), while values other than welfare—including justice, freedom, fairness, dignity, and respect—do not even appear in its index (pp. 971–981). Pigou, author of *The Economics of Welfare* (1952/1920) and often described as the father of welfare economics, even considered economic welfare the very subject matter of economics (Pigou 1952: 11). A central part of the project of welfare economics is to provide criteria by which alternative policies can be assessed as better or worse with respect to welfare. Hence, as Tibor Scitovsky pointed out: "Welfare economics supplies the economist and the politician with standards, at least with some standards, by which to appraise and on the basis of which to formulate policy" (Scitovsky 1951: 303). Consistent with the ambition not only to understand but also to change the world, welfare economics was from the very beginning intended to be of practical use: "The goal sought is to make more easy practical measures to promote welfare—practical measures which statesmen may build upon the work of the economist" (Pigou 1952: 10).

From a philosophical point of view, the immediate question about the enterprise is: "What do they mean by 'welfare'?" The aim of this chapter is to explore what accounts (or conceptions) of welfare underlie contemporary welfare economics. (The second-most immediate question—"What does it take to measure well-being?"—will be completely ignored here, but see Angner (2011a, 2013a) for more.) As is customary, I will distinguish accounts of individual welfare (meaning the well-being of persons) from accounts of social well-being (meaning the well-being of groups, including entire countries). Moreover, I will follow Derek Parfit (1984: 493–502) in dividing accounts of individual welfare into three main classes: *mental-state accounts*, *preference-satisfaction* or *desire-fulfillment accounts*, and *objective-list accounts*. According to mental-state accounts, well-being is some subjectively experienced positive or desirable mental state. According to desire-fulfillment or preference-satisfaction accounts, a person is well off to the extent that her desires are fulfilled and/or her preferences are satisfied. And according to so-called objective-list accounts, a person's well-being does not depend on subjective factors like mental states and personal preferences; on such accounts, there is a list of things that are good or bad for people, independently in at least some cases of whether those things would make people happier, or whether they want those things. Parfit's tripartite division is not without its critics (e.g., Scanlon 1998), but it nonetheless serves as a first approximation.

My focus here will be on economic practice, that is, on what economists do when they make welfare judgments. I will explore three different approaches to welfare assessment: what I call standard economics, the economics of happiness, and the social-indicator/capability approach. These three approaches are not exhaustive, but they include the vast majority of practicing economists. For each approach, I will review briefly how economists working within the approach go about assessing welfare and proceed to discuss what accounts of welfare are reflected in their practice. I will argue that, roughly speaking, there is a one-to-one mapping between the three approaches to welfare assessment and the three philosophical accounts of individual well-being:

standard economics	—	preference-satisfaction accounts
economics of happiness	—	mental-state accounts
social-indicators/capability approach	—	objective-list accounts

Meanwhile, at least standard economics and the economics of happiness are based on some utilitarian social-welfare criterion, according to which social welfare is the sum or average of individual welfare (Mongin and d'Aspremont 1998: 415). The discussion underscores how economists both use and produce philosophy in their scientific practice, and how economists and philosophers may have much to learn from each other.

Standard economics

What I call "standard" economics—the approach first-year graduate students are taught in a mainstream economics department—in fact relies on a range of methods to assess welfare. Some are based on income or wealth. This kind of measure goes back to Pigou himself, who favored the *national dividend*—that is, "that part of the objective income of the community, including, of course, income derived from abroad, which can be measured in money" (Pigou 1952: 31)—as a measure of welfare. "The economic welfare of the country is intimately associated with the size of the national dividend, and changes in economic welfare with changes in the size of the dividend" (Pigou 1952: 50). Measures of this general kind, like *gross domestic product* (GDP) per capita, have well-known shortcomings but continue to be widely used as welfare measures for public-policy purposes (Nussbaum and Sen 1993: 2). The importance of the national product as a measure of well-being helps explain the widespread concern with economic growth: since "growth" is often used to refer to the first derivative of the national product, and "growth rate" to refer to the second derivative, high growth (or growth rate) can be seen as an indication of future well-being.

An alternative way to evaluate the welfare consequences of policy interventions is in terms of *consumer surplus* (CS) and *producer surplus* (PS). The notion of consumer surplus goes back to Jules Dupuit (1969/1844), who wished to determine the conditions under which public works can "be declared of public utility" (Dupuit 1969: 255). Dupuit's ideas were developed and popularized by Alfred Marshall (1920/1890), who defined the consumer surplus of a good as "[the] excess of the price which [the consumer] would be willing to pay rather than go without the thing, over that which he actually does pay" (Marshall 1920: 124). Total surplus, being the sum of consumer and producer surplus, is frequently used in economic practice to evaluate the consequences of public policy (Slesnick 1998: 2110). It is the tool preferred by many economics textbooks when evaluating the welfare consequences, e.g., of price ceilings and taxes.

Yet another set of measures revolves around the concepts of *compensating variation* (CV) and *equivalent variation* (EV). These notions were developed in a series of publications by John R. Hicks (e.g., 1943), who had noted certain technical difficulties associated with surplus measures. The CV is "the amount of money which, when taken away from an individual after an economic change, leaves the person just as well off as before," while the EV is "the amount of money paid to an individual which, if an economic change does not happen, leaves the individual just as well off as if the change had occurred" (Just et al. 2004: 9). CV/EV measures are used quite widely in cost–benefit analyses and other exercises in welfare economics to assess changes in welfare (Blackorby and Donaldson 1990: 471–472).

Though superficially different, one thing that these measures have in common is the fact that they are based on preference-satisfaction accounts of well-being. In the standard analysis, these measures are treated as measures of welfare because they can be shown to be *utility functions*. The proofs are available in any standard-issue graduate-level microeconomics textbook. Mas-Colell et al. demonstrate that, given a number of assumptions, e.g., about the rationality of individuals and the nature of the budget set, and holding prices fixed, utility is strictly increasing in individual wealth, which is to say that under certain assumptions wealth is a utility function (Mas-Colell et al. 1995: 56). Given slightly different sets of assumptions, they also show that consumer surplus as well as compensating and equivalent variation are utility functions

(Mas-Colell et al. 1995: 81–83). The significance of these proofs is that a utility function is an *index* or *measure* of preference-satisfaction. Thus, each proof establishes that a person with a higher score on the measure has his or her preferences satisfied to a higher degree—which, on a preference-satisfaction approach, is equivalent to saying that he or she is better off. John C. Harsanyi defends the standard approach by invoking what he calls *preference autonomy:* "the principle that, in deciding what is good and what is bad for a given individual, the ultimate criterion can only be his own wants and his own preferences" (Harsanyi 1977: 645).

Another thing these measures have in common is that they are based on a utilitarian social-welfare function, according to which social welfare is the sum or average of individual welfare. The significance of an income-based measure such as GDP per capita is that it represents an average value across the inhabitants of a country. On the assumption that individual income represents individual welfare, a utilitarian social-welfare function implies that average income represents social welfare. When it comes to surplus and CV/EV measures, economists construct aggregate measures by simply adding up the numbers for each individual in the group. On the assumption that individual CS/PS or CV/EV measures represent individual utility, the utilitarian social-welfare function implies that aggregate measures represent social welfare. Notice that, while contemporary economists sometimes express skepticism about the possibility of making interpersonal comparisons of utility, they routinely add up (or average) utilities across people, thereby implicitly assuming that utilities are perfectly comparable. The utility functions in question are often *money-metric* utility functions, meaning that they express welfare or welfare changes in dollar units (Mas-Colell et al. 1995: 81), but they are utility functions all the same.

The accounts of welfare underlying standard economics carry over in some domains where they would perhaps not be expected. Consider behavioral economics: the effort to increase the explanatory and predictive power of economic theory by providing it with more psychologically plausible foundations (Angner and Loewenstein 2012). Though behavioral economics represents a sharp departure from orthodox economics in certain ways, the normative foundations of behavioral economics are largely continuous with those of neoclassical economics. Behavioral economists too take their central normative concern to be that of welfare or well-being; thus, normative behavioral economics is often referred to as behavioral welfare economics (Angner and Loewenstein 2012: sec. 6.3). With some exceptions to be discussed in the next section, behavioral economists apparently continue to think of well-being in terms of preference satisfaction and of social welfare in terms of total or average individual utility (see, e.g., Camerer et al. 2003). As historian Floris Heukelom (2014: 199–200) has noted, the main difference is that behavioral economists emphasize more clearly than neoclassical economists that what counts are an individual's "true" or "ideal" preferences—the preferences he or she would have if he or she were ideally rational and perfectly informed—rather than the "manifest" or "actual" preferences revealed in his or her choices (Angner and Loewenstein 2012: 678–679). But this represents a shift in emphasis more than a disagreement. Philosophically sophisticated neoclassical economists like Harsanyi (1977: 55) already agree that well-being should be understood in terms of the satisfaction of true or ideal preferences.

Daniel M. Hausman and Michael S. McPherson (2006: 121–122) speculate that standard economists do not take the preference-satisfaction account they rely on literally and, in spite of appearances, adopt some mental-state account. The two offer no systematic evidence for the hypothesis, so it is difficult to assess. Nonetheless, the historical figures who were responsible for the neoclassical synthesis clearly rejected any connection to mental states (Angner and Loewenstein 2012: 647–648). Lionel Robbins's influential book *An Essay on the Nature and Significance of Economic Science* insisted that neoclassical economic theory "is capable of being set out and defended in absolutely non-hedonistic terms" and has no "essential connection with psychological hedonism, or for that matter with any other brand of *Fach-Psychologie*" (Robbins 1984/1932: 85). Moreover, with the rise of the economics of happiness (see next section), Hausman and McPherson's hypothesis has lost some of its appeal: these days any mainstream economist committed to a mental-state account can study happiness directly. At any rate, as long as we are engaged in unbridled speculation, it seems to me more likely that many economists are simply confused, in the sense that they take mental-state and preference-satisfaction accounts of well-being to be one and the same, when in reality they are distinct.

The economics of happiness

In the last few decades, economists have shown increasing interest in the scientific study of happiness, satisfaction, and other subjectively experienced positive or desirable mental states. The systematic empirical study of such states goes back almost 100 years, to a time when psychologists turned the tools of the nascent subdiscipline of personality psychology to the study of happiness and satisfaction (Angner 2011b). The economics of happiness as a self-conscious subdiscipline is largely due to Richard A. Easterlin (1974), who brought happiness studies to the attention of mainstream economists and whose results continue to attract attention from them (e.g., Stevenson and Wolfers 2008). The economics of happiness has benefited hugely from the concurrent rise of positive psychology within psychology (Seligman and Csikszentmihalyi 2000) as well as the endorsement of Nobel Memorial Prize laureate Daniel Kahneman (e.g., 1999) and other high-profile economists.

Welfare assessments within the economics of happiness are typically based on questionnaires with one or more straightforward questions, such as: "Taking things all together, how would you say things are these days—would you say you're *very happy, pretty happy,* or *not too happy* these days?" (Gurin et al. 1960: 411). Sonja Lyubomirsky and Heidi S. Lepper (1999) offer four prompts of the form "In general, I consider myself . . . " and invite subjects to respond on a seven-point scale, where 1 represents " . . . not a very happy person" and 7 " . . . a very happy person" (Lyubomirsky and Lepper 1999: 151). Others ask subjects "How do you feel about your life as a whole?" and give them response categories ranging from "Delighted," "Pleased," and "Mostly satisfied," through "Mixed (about equally satisfied and dissatisfied)" to "Mostly dissatisfied," "Unhappy," and "Terrible" (Andrews and Withey 1976: 18). In the past, participants were asked whether they satisfied descriptions such as: "Cheerful, gay spirits most of the time. Occasionally bothered by something but can usually laugh it off," "Ups and downs, now happy about things, now depressed. About balanced in the long run," and "Life often seems so worthless that there is little to keep one going. Nothing matters very much, there has been so much of hurt that laughter would be empty mockery" (Watson 1930: 81). Occasionally, researchers invite responses using graphic representations like horizontal lines (Watson 1930), ladders and mountains (Cantril 1965), or happy and sad faces (Andrews and Withey 1976).

A somewhat different approach has been developed by Kahneman and colleagues under the heading of *experience sampling*. Kahneman prompts his subjects every so often—e.g., with the use of handheld electronic devices—to judge the "quality of their momentary experience" along the "good/bad dimension" (Kahneman 1999: 7). The assumption is that, at every point in time, the brain rates the quality of experience in a manner that can be represented on a single numerical scale and which, furthermore, is accessible to the agent. What matters, at the end of the day, is the time integral (which Kahneman calls "objective" happiness) of the instant happiness rating (which he calls "subjective" happiness) (Kahneman 1999: 5). The effort to produce a dense record of an individual's affective state as a function of time was pioneered by Hornell Hart (1940), the inventor of the *euphorimeter*—a device that would permit the quick assessment of an individual's level of self-reported happiness. Though Kahneman and co-authors have since developed other measures, they insist: "Experience sampling is the gold standard" (Kahneman et al. 2004: 1777).

More recently, Kahneman and Alan B. Krueger have suggested the use of a measure they call the *U-index* (Kahneman and Krueger 2006; cf. Krueger 2009). Introduced under the heading of "A Measure of Society's Well-Being," the U-index is clearly intended to be a measure of social well-being. The "U" stands for "unpleasant" or "undesirable," and the index "measures the proportion of time an individual spends in an unpleasant state," where an episode gets classified as pleasant or unpleasant depending on whether the strongest affect experienced during the episode is positive or negative (Kahneman and Krueger 2006: 18–19). The U-index was designed to overcome several perceived problems associated with other subjective measures, above all, problems related to interpersonal comparability (Krueger 2009: 3).

Unsurprisingly, given their focus on mental states like happiness and satisfaction, these measures are all based on some mental-state account of individual welfare (Angner 2011c). Kahneman is explicit about using "happiness [and] well-being . . . interchangeably" (Kahneman 1999: 5). Some make it clear that they think happiness is what ultimately matters from the point of view of a person's well-being. Andrew Oswald notes: "The relevance of economic performance is that it may be a means to an end. That end is . . . the enrichment of mankind's feeling of well-being. Economic things matter only in so far as they make people happier" (Oswald 1997: 1815). The exact account presupposed differs somewhat across authors and over time and sometimes involves a combination of multiple mental states. Norman M. Bradburn and David Caplovitz (1965), for example, take well-being to be constituted by three irreducible components: positive affect, absence of negative affect, and satisfaction. Angner (2010) suggests that happiness economists can be understood as proponents of preference hedonism—an account according to which well-being is a matter of desired mental states (Parfit 1984: 493).

Perhaps more surprisingly, given the ways in which they try to gain distance from the standard economic approach, happiness economists typically maintain the very same utilitarian account of social welfare (Angner 2009). To construct a measure of social well-being for some group, it is customary for researchers to average the scores of the group members. As Rafael Di Tella and Robert MacCulloch note, "a large fraction of the happiness literature in economics is based on comparing average happiness scores for large numbers of people" (Di Tella and MacCulloch 2006: 29). When researchers compare different nations, for example, they typically compute the mean happiness or satisfaction score in each nation and compare and contrast those levels (Diener and Suh 1999: 435). To get a measure of social well-being based on the U-index, Kahneman and Krueger propose that the "U-index can be computed for each individual . . . and averaged over a sample of individuals" (Kahneman and Krueger 2006: 20). Richard Layard, one of the most visible happiness economists, vigorously and explicitly endorses the classical utilitarian approach: "[Bentham] proposed that all laws and all actions should aim at producing the greatest [total] possible happiness . . . I believe that Bentham's idea was right and that we should fearlessly adopt it and apply it to our lives" (Layard 2005: 111–112). The reference to Bentham supports the hypothesis that these economists commit themselves to some mental-state account of well-being and to a utilitarian social-welfare criterion. There are exceptions: some researchers use other measures of central tendency, such as the median (e.g., Angner et al. 2009) or the fraction of participants who answered "very happy" on a three-point scale (e.g., Easterlin 1974).

Social indicators and capabilities

The social-indicator movement, which emerged during the late 1960s in part as a reaction to the widespread adoption of what I call the standard economic approach, differs in at least two important respects (Campbell 1976: 117–118; Andrews 1989: 401). First, it uses a broader panel of indicators, which jointly give a fuller view of the nature and conditions of people's lives. Second, it aims to use "output indicators" that track directly how well off people are, as opposed to "input indicators" (such as income) that at best cause well-being. In practical terms, this movement encouraged the collection of data on life expectancy, quality of food and water, access to adequate medical care, level of education, quality of housing, and so on. As Angus Campbell notes: "It is reasonably argued that as the level of education rises, the adequacy of medical care improves, the amount of substandard housing is reduced, and the purity of the air and water is increased, the quality of life is therewith enhanced" (Campbell 1976: 118). Social indicators are sometimes referred to as *objective* indicators, since they do not depend on the individual's personal preferences or subjectively experienced mental states (Campbell 1976: 118). (Note that these "objective indicators" bear little resemblance to Kahneman's measures of "objective happiness.")

Quite arguably, the most famous outgrowth of the social indicator movement is the Human Development Index (HDI) of the United Nations Development Programme (UNDP). The HDI has appeared annually in the *Human Development Report* since 1990. Noting that "income is not the sum total of human life" (UNDP 1990: 9), the HDI is based on "three essential elements of human life—longevity, knowledge, and decent living standards" (UNDP 1990: 12). The UNDP explains that life expectancy matters because "a long life is valuable in itself" and because it is associated with important achievements such as adequate nutrition, and that literacy matters because it reflects access to education; the importance of decent living standards is treated as self-explanatory (UNDP 1990: 11–12). The summary HDI is the geometric mean of three normalized indices: one for life expectancy at birth, one for mean and expected years of schooling, and one for gross national income (GNI) per capita (UNDP 2014: Technical note 1).

In both conceptualization and execution, the *Human Development Report* reflects the influence of the *capability approach* associated with Amartya Sen (e.g., 1985) and Martha C. Nussbaum (e.g., 2000). The capability approach represents a shift away from what people succeed in attaining—whether evaluated in terms of happiness, preference satisfaction, or something altogether different—and toward the freedom they have in leading their lives (Sen 2008: 23). In this approach, the focus is on *capability:* the set of alternative functionings that a person can attain, where *functionings* are things that a person manages to do or to be in leading her life (Sen 2008: 24). Efforts to measure capabilities typically start with some list of central human capabilities and proceed to operationalize each element of the list. Thus, Paul Anand and co-authors (2009) take as their starting point the list provided by Martha Nussbaum (2000: 78–80): life; bodily health; bodily integrity; senses, imagination, and thought; emotions; practical reasoning; affiliation; other species; play; and control over one's environment. The authors then propose that life can be assessed by the question "Given your family history, dietary habits, lifestyle and health status until what age do you expect to live?," bodily health by the question "Does your health in any way limit your daily activities compared with most people of your age?," and so on (Anand et al. 2009: 132–137).

The social-indicator/capability approach (which for these purposes I will treat as one) is most plausibly interpreted as based on some objective-list account of individual well-being. The ambition to identify a panel of "output" indicators that directly track well-being is consistent with a conception of well-being according to which there is an objective list of things that are good for a person independently of whether they make her happy or whether she desires those things. The argument proffered in the *Human Development Report* to the effect that life expectancy data should figure in welfare assessment because life is valuable in itself similarly fits a conception of well-being according to which some things are good in and of themselves.

Moreover, the capability approach is explicitly based on a conception of well-being according to which having a large capability set is inherently good for a person. As Flavio Comim, Mozaffar Qizilbash, and Sabina Alkire (2008: 10) explain, "the capability approach is distinctive inasmuch as it stresses that capabilities and functionings have value in themselves: 'intrinsic value.'" Amartya Sen, who originally presented his account in response to mental-state and preference satisfaction accounts (Sen 1985: 14–15), traces the historical roots of the capability approach to Aristotle, who is often treated as the archetypical objective-list theorist (Sen 2008: 23). Given the commitment to objective-list accounts, it should come as no surprise that proponents of this approach often think of well-being as multidimensional, which means that there is no non-arbitrary way to construct a unidimensional index of well-being (Comim et al. 2008: 8).

When it comes to accounts of social welfare among proponents of the social-indicator/capability approach, the answer is more elusive. The fact that many indicators are constructed based on population-level data—such as average life expectancy—obviates the need for an explicit social-welfare function converting data about individual welfare levels into social welfare. Amartya Sen has long rejected the notion that economists need a social-welfare function of a kind that allows for the complete ranking of possibilities, like the utilitarian social-welfare function does. In Sen's view, "welfarism has much greater plausibility than the narrow perspective of utilitarianism, since utilitarianism pays no attention to the interpersonal distribution of happiness and utilities" but, even so, "welfarism is a very limiting approach, since it insists that nothing other than utilities or happiness matters" (Sen 2008: 26). That said, it is not uncommon for authors operating with a social-indicator or capability approach to average values across groups, just like economists committed to a utilitarian social-welfare function do. This is most obvious in the case of the Human Development Index, which is based on the (geometric) mean of three indices, one of which is the arithmetic mean of two other figures.

Discussion

This chapter has explored accounts of individual and social welfare in contemporary welfare economics. It has argued that, roughly speaking, there is a one-to-one mapping between three prominent approaches to welfare assessment and three philosophical accounts of individual well-being: while standard economics is based on preference-satisfaction accounts, the economics of happiness is based on mental-state accounts, and the social-indicators/capability approach on objective-list accounts. Moreover, I have argued that at least standard economics and the economics of happiness are based on some utilitarian social-welfare criterion. The discussion underscores how economists in their scientific practice, as Mario Bunge (1976: 137) puts it, "use and even produce philosophy." (It goes without saying that my intention here is not to assess or endorse approaches to measurement or accounts of well-being.)

There are caveats. As one would expect from any broad-brush treatment of a large and heterogeneous discipline like economics, every rule has exceptions. First, there are economists who are not welfarists, and who assign independent weight to values such as justice, freedom, fairness, dignity, and respect. Yet, values other than welfare have not so far inspired anything even remotely similar to welfare economics. Second, as I mentioned above, the tripartite division of approaches to welfare assessment is not exhaustive. And some economists who do adopt one of the three nonetheless fail to conform to the one-to-one mapping between approaches to welfare assessment and accounts of well-being. This should not be surprising, since there is nothing logically necessary about this mapping, and the fact that a given measure was developed and/or is typically defended with a particular account of well-being in mind does not mean that the very same measure could not be used and defended by an economist committed to another account. The HDI uses the standard metric of GNI per capita as one of its indices, in spite of the close historical and conceptual ties between the HDI and objective-list theories of well-being. Matthew Adler and Eric A. Posner (2008) defend the use of happiness-based measures for a range of purposes, though they explicitly commit themselves to a preference-satisfaction account. Even Amartya Sen himself agrees that happiness measures have important uses, arguing that "[the] perspective of happiness illuminates one critically important element of human living" (Sen 2008: 26). Third, not every economist is committed to a utilitarian account of social welfare. Representatives of the social-indicator/capability approach are particularly likely to reject such accounts, as signaled in the previous section. And some do attend to distributions: currently, for example, inequality is attracting increasing amounts of interest.

Why does it matter that economists use and produce philosophy? For one thing, the fact that economists operate with different philosophical accounts of well-being—even implicitly—helps explain important differences between them. A commitment to mental-state accounts of well-being helps explain why some economists measure well-being by distributing questionnaires asking people about their subjectively experienced mental states. A commitment to preference-satisfaction accounts helps explain why others favor indicators that assign higher numbers to people who have more options available to them and who get what they prefer. And a commitment to objective-list accounts helps explain why some economists argue that welfare is multidimensional and that welfare measures need to include a wide panel of "output" indicators. Moreover, the fact that economists operate with different conceptions of well-being helps account for the fact that many of their disagreements appear irreconcilable even in the light of rapidly increasing amounts of empirical data that, one might otherwise think, should help economists converge on one and the same approach to welfare assessment. Finally, the broad commitment to some utilitarian social-welfare function helps explain economists' history of relative indifference to issues of distribution in general and inequality in particular, since utilitarian social-welfare functions are entirely insensitive to the distribution of welfare when holding total or average welfare constant (Angner 2009).

The fact that economists use philosophy also matters to the assessment of their work. Even practically-minded economists' arguments often depend essentially on philosophical presuppositions, e.g., about the nature of well-being. For example, what I have called the underlying account of well-being will frequently appear among the premises in arguments to the effect that a given measure is valid, that is, that it represents that which it is supposed to represent. And any time premises about the nature of well-being appear (implicitly or explicitly) in arguments about welfare and its measurement, the truth of the former is relevant to the soundness of the latter. To Bunge, the fact that scientists use and produce philosophy entails that "they should be able to learn something from the professional philosopher" (Bunge 1976: 137). No doubt Bunge is correct: when economic conclusions depend on philosophical presuppositions, as they often do, economists have much to learn from the philosophers who have spent a great deal of time thinking about the advantages and disadvantages of alternative accounts.

The fact that economists not only use but produce philosophy also means that philosophers have much to learn from them. Over the course of the twentieth century, economists have arguably been decades ahead of philosophers when it comes to accounts of well-being. For example, philosophers' interest in preference-satisfaction accounts of well-being during the second half of the twentieth century lagged economists' (due to figures like Vilfredo Pareto and Robbins) by about half a century (Angner and Loewenstein 2012: sec. 2.2). When philosophers turned their attention once again to questions of happiness and satisfaction in the 1990s and 2000s, they lagged economists who had been working on the topic since the 1970s and 1980s, not to mention psychologists who had been at it since the 1920s and 1930s

(Angner 2011b). It is not completely unlikely that the next trend in accounts of well-being will similarly start among psychologists and economists, not philosophers. Moreover, philosophical conclusions—even outside of applied ethics—often necessarily depend on empirical presuppositions, which means that empirical research is highly relevant to philosophical conclusions (Angner 2013b).

In all, there is reason to think that philosophers and economists have much to learn from each other, when it comes to both philosophical commitments and empirical presuppositions. Although my goal here has been modest—I do not presume to determine who is right and who is wrong in any of these debates—I do hope the discussion will at a minimum permit deeper and more accurate assessments of the relative advantages and disadvantages of alternative welfare measures, as well as their suitability for public policy.

Related topics

Hedonism, desire-fulfillment theory, objective-list theory, happiness, the concept of well-being, the measurement of well-being, welfarism.

Note

1 Unless otherwise noted, all italics as in original.

References

Adler, Matthew D., and Eric A. Posner (2008) "Happiness Research and Cost–Benefit Analysis," *The Journal of Legal Studies* 37(S2): S253–S292.

Anand, Paul, Graham Hunter, Ian Carter, Keith Dowding, Francesco Guala, and Martin Van Hees (2009) "The Development of Capability Indicators," *Journal of Human Development and Capabilities* 10(1): 125–152.

Andrews, Frank M. (1989) "The Evolution of a Movement," *Journal of Public Policy* 9(4): 401–5.

Andrews, Frank M., and Stephen B. Withey (1976) *Social Indicators of Well-Being: Americans' Perceptions of Life Quality*, New York, NY: Plenum Press.

Angner, Erik (2009) "The Politics of Happiness: Subjective vs. Economic Measures as Measures of Social Well-Being," in Lisa Bortolotti (ed.) *Philosophy and Happiness*, New York, NY: Palgrave Macmillan, pp. 149–166.

Angner, Erik (2010) "Subjective Well-Being," *Journal of Socio-Economics* 39(3): 361–368.

Angner, Erik (2011a) "Current Trends in Welfare Measurement," in John B. Davis and D. Wade Hands (eds.) *The Elgar Companion to Recent Economic Methodology*, Northampton, MA: Edward Elgar, pp. 121–154.

Angner, Erik (2011b) "The Evolution of Eupathics: The Historical Roots of Subjective Measures of Wellbeing," *International Journal of Wellbeing* 1(1): 4–41.

Angner, Erik (2011c) "Are Subjective Measures of Well-Being 'Direct'?," *Australasian Journal of Philosophy* 89(1): 115–130.

Angner, Erik (2013a) "Is It Possible to Measure Happiness? The Argument from Measurability," *European Journal for Philosophy of Science* 3(2): 221–240.

Angner, Erik (2013b) "Is Empirical Research Relevant to Philosophical Conclusions?," *Res Philosophica* 90(3): 343–363.

Angner, Erik, and George Loewenstein (2012) "Behavioral Economics," in Uskali Mäki (ed.) *Handbook of the Philosophy of Science: Philosophy of Economics*, Amsterdam: Elsevier, pp. 641–690.

Angner, Erik, Midge N. Ray, Kenneth G. Saag, and Jeroan J. Allison (2009) "Health and Happiness among Older Adults: A Community-Based Study," *Journal of Health Psychology* 14(4): 503–512.

Blackorby, Charles, and David Donaldson (1990) "A Review Article: The Case against the Use of the Sum of Compensating Variations in Cost–Benefit Analysis," *The Canadian Journal of Economics* 23(3): 471–494.

Bradburn, Norman M., and David Caplovitz (1965) *Reports on Happiness: A Pilot Study of Behavior Related to Mental Health*, Chicago, IL: Aldine.

Bunge, Mario (1976) "The Relevance of Philosophy to Social Science," in William R. Shea (ed.) *Basic Issues in the Philosophy of Science*, New York, NY: Science History Publications, pp. 136–155.

Camerer, Colin F., Samuel Issacharoff, George Loewenstein, Ted O'Donoghue, and Matthew Rabin (2003) "Regulation for Conservatives: Behavioral Economics and the Case for 'Asymmetric Paternalism,'" *University of Pennsylvania Law Review* 151(3): 1211–1254.

Campbell, Angus (1976) "Subjective Measures of Well-Being," *American Psychologist* 31(2): 117–24.

Cantril, Hadley (1965) *The Pattern of Human Concerns*, New Brunswick, NJ: Rutgers University Press.

Comim, Flavio, Mozaffar Qizilbash, and Sabina Alkire (eds.) (2008) *The Capability Approach: Concepts, Measures and Applications*, Cambridge: Cambridge University Press.

Diener, Ed, and Eunkook M. Suh (1999) "National Differences in Subjective Well-Being," in Daniel Kahneman, Ed Diener, and Norbert Schwarz (eds.) *Well-Being: The Foundations of Hedonic Psychology*, New York, NY: Russell Sage Foundation, pp. 434–450.

Di Tella, Rafael, and Robert MacCulloch (2006) "Some Uses of Happiness Data in Economics," *The Journal of Economic Perspectives* 20(1): 25–46.

Dupuit, Jules (1969/1844) "On the Measurement of Public Works," in Kenneth J. Arrow and Tibor Scitovsky (eds.) *Readings in Welfare Economics*, Homewood, IL: R.D. Irwin, pp. 255–283.

Easterlin, Richard A. (1974) "Does Economic Growth Improve the Human Lot? Some Empirical Evidence," in Paul A. David and Melvin W. Reder (eds.) *Nations and Households in Economic Growth: Essays in Honor of Moses Abramovitz*, New York, NY: Academic Press, pp. 89–125.

Gurin, Gerald, Joseph Veroff, and Sheila Feld (1960) *Americans View Their Mental Health: A Nationwide Interview Survey*, New York, NY: Basic Books.

Harsanyi, J. C. (1977) "Morality and the Theory of Rational Behavior," *Social Research* 44(4): 623–656.

Hart, Hornell (1940) *Chart for Happiness*, New York, NY: Macmillan.

Hausman, Daniel M., and Michael S. McPherson (2006) *Economic Analysis, Moral Philosophy, and Public Policy*, 2nd edn., New York, NY: Cambridge University Press.

Hayek, Friedrich A. (1933) "The Trend of Economic Thinking," *Economica* 40: 121–137.

Heukelom, Floris (2014) *Behavioral Economics: A History*, New York, NY: Cambridge University Press.

Hicks, John R. (1943) "The Four Consumer's Surpluses," *The Review of Economic Studies* 11(1): 31–41.

Just, Richard E., Darrell L. Hueth, and Andrew Lee Schmitz (2004) *The Welfare Economics of Public Policy: A Practical Approach to Project and Policy Evaluation*, Cheltenham: Edward Elgar.

Kahneman, Daniel (1999) "Objective Happiness," in Daniel Kahneman, Ed Diener, and Norbert Schwarz (eds.) *Well-Being: The Foundations of Hedonic Psychology*, New York, NY: Russell Sage Foundation, pp. 3–25.

Kahneman, Daniel, and Alan B. Krueger (2006) "Developments in the Measurement of Subjective Well-Being," *Journal of Economic Perspectives* 20(1): 3–24.

Kahneman, Daniel, Alan B. Krueger, David A. Schkade, Norbert Schwarz, and Arthur A. Stone (2004) "A Survey Method for Characterizing Daily Life Experience: The Day Reconstruction Method," *Science*, 306(5702): 1776–1780.

Krueger, Alan B. (ed.) (2009) *Measuring the Subjective Well-Being of Nations: National Accounts of Time Use and Well-Being*, Chicago, IL: The University of Chicago Press.

Layard, P. Richard G. (2005) *Happiness: Lessons from a New Science*, New York, NY: Penguin Press.

Lyubomirsky, Sonja, and Heidi S. Lepper (1999) "A Measure of Subjective Happiness: Preliminary Reliability and Construct Validation," *Social Indicators Research* 46(2): 137–155.

Marshall, Alfred (1920/1890) *Principles of Economics: An Introductory Volume*, 8th edn., London: Macmillan.

Marx, Karl (1998/1845) "Theses on Feuerbach," in *The German Ideology: Including Theses on Feuerbach and Introduction to The Critique of Political Economy*, Amherst, NY: Prometheus Books, pp. 569–571.

Mas-Colell, Andreu, Michael D. Whinston, and Jerry R. Green (1995) *Microeconomic Theory*, New York, NY: Oxford University Press.

Mongin, Philippe, and Claude d'Aspremont (1998) "Utility Theory and Ethics," in Salvador Barberà, Peter J. Hammond, and Christian Seidl (eds.) *Handbook of Utility Theory, Vol. 1*, Dordrecht: Kluwer Academic Publishers, pp. 371–481.

Nussbaum, Martha C. (2000) *Women and Human Development: The Capabilities Approach*, Cambridge: Cambridge University Press.

Nussbaum, Martha C., and Amartya Sen (eds.) (1993) *The Quality of Life*, Oxford: Clarendon Press.

Oswald, Andrew J. (1997) "Happiness and Economic Performance," *The Economic Journal* 107(445): 1815–1831.

Parfit, Derek (1984) *Reasons and Persons*, Oxford: Clarendon Press.

Pigou, Arthur C. (1952/1920) *The Economics of Welfare*, 4th edn., London: Macmillan.

Robbins, Lionel Robbins (1984/1932) *An Essay on the Nature and Significance of Economic Science*, 3rd edn., New York, NY: New York University Press.

Samuelson, Paul A. (1947) *Foundations of Economic Analysis*, Cambridge, MA: Harvard University Press.

Scanlon, Thomas M. (1998) "The Status of Well-Being," in Grethe B. Peterson (ed.), *The Tanner Lectures on Human Values, Vol. 19*, Salt Lake City, UT: University of Utah Press, pp. 91–143.

Scitovsky, Tibor (1951) "The State of Welfare Economics," *The American Economic Review* 41(3): 303–315.

Seligman, Martin E. P., and Mihaly Csikszentmihalyi (2000) "Positive Psychology: An Introduction," *American Psychologist* 55(1): 5–14.

Sen, Amartya (1985) *Commodities and Capabilities*, Amsterdam: North-Holland.

Sen, Amartya (2008) "The Economics of Happiness and Capability," in Luigino Bruni, Flavio Comim, and Maurizio Pugno (eds.) *Capabilities and Happiness*, Oxford: Oxford University Press, pp. 16–27.

Slesnick, Daniel T. (1998) "Empirical Approaches to the Measurement of Welfare," *Journal of Economic Literature* 36(4): 2108–2165.

Stevenson, Betsey, and Justin Wolfers (2008) "Economic Growth and Subjective Well-Being: Reassessing the Easterlin Paradox," *Brookings Papers on Economic Activity*, Spring 2008, 1–87.

UNDP (1990) *Human Development Report 1990*. United Nations Development Programme. http://hdr.undp.org/sites/default/files/reports/219/hdr_1990_en_complete_nostats.pdf.

UNDP (2014) *Human Development Report 2014*. United Nations Development Programme. http://hdr.undp.org/sites/default/files/hdr14-report-en-1.pdf.

Watson, Goodwin (1930) "Happiness among Adult Students of Education," *Journal of Educational Psychology* 21(2): 79–109.

41

MEDICINE AND WELL-BEING

Daniel Groll

The connections between medicine—both its science and practice—and well-being are myriad. This paper focuses on the place of well-being in *clinical* medicine. It is here that different views of well-being, and their connection to concepts like "autonomy" and "authenticity," both illuminate and are illuminated by looking closely at the kinds of interactions that routinely take place between clinicians, patients, and family members.

In the first part of the paper, I explore the place of well-being in a *paradigmatic clinical encounter*, one where a competent patient interacts with a clinician. The main question here is how, or even whether, the pursuit of patient well-being—however we construe it—figures into a paradigmatic clinical encounter. In the second part, I consider what I will call a *marginal clinical encounter*—one where the patient is, as Agnieska Jaworska (1999) puts it, at the "margins of agency"—to theorize about the nature of well-being and to show how different theories of well-being can have dramatic consequences for clinical decision making.

Well-being and the ends of medicine

At first glance, the connection between clinical medicine (henceforth, simply "medicine") and well-being is relatively clear. We do not go to doctors to make ourselves worse off. Rather, we go to make ourselves better off or at least to stop things from getting worse (or, in some cases, to make the inevitable process of things getting worse as painless as possible). It seems, then, that a, if not the, goal of clinical medicine is to restore, promote, or protect a patient's well-being.

This claim is far from obvious, however. Promoting, protecting, or restoring well-being is far too broad an aim for medicine.[1] Medical professionals are not required to do whatever they can to increase a patient's well-being. This is not simply because time and resources are finite. There are all kinds of ways we might make someone better off that are clearly not *medical* in nature: giving a gift, offering a shoulder to cry on, or driving someone home to save her from a walk in the rain are not medical interventions. We do not think that medical professionals must do these things, at least not *as* medical professionals.

But the fact that not all ways of promoting, protecting, or restoring well-being are medical does not show that promoting, protecting, or restoring well-being is not the proper end of medicine. Rather, it suggests that the proper aim of medicine is to restore, protect, or promote well-being *via the tools of medicine*. Now just what makes something a tool of medicine is hardly clear, both sociologically and normatively speaking.[2] Even so, there is what we might call a paradigmatic core of interventions that are clearly medical and it seems plausible to think that these interventions aim at promoting, protecting, or restoring well-being.

But even this more limited claim faces several challenges. Robert Veatch has forcefully argued that clinicians are not well placed—and maybe are even especially poorly placed—to determine what is good for their patients (2009: 41). According to Veatch, this is true no matter what theory of well-being one is partial to (2009: 98).[3] The main concern for Veatch is that medical training, and the resulting expertise, doesn't equip clinicians with any special insight into what is good for their patients. As a result, clinicians should see themselves as "assistants for patients," who help the patient achieve well-being not "according to the *physician's* ability and judgment, but rather according to the *patient's* ability and judgment" (Veatch 2009: 62).

Veatch's deep skepticism about clinicians' ability to make judgments about their patients' well-being is unwarranted (Groll 2011). First (as Veatch acknowledges), clinicians *do* have expertise with respect to the medical *means* of achieving some aspects of well-being, even if they have no special expertise with respect to what ends or goals constitutively contribute to a person's well-being.

Second, and more important, there are cases where clinicians can plausibly be thought to know which ends are best for someone even if they do not know it *qua* clinician.

To see why, consider the case of Horace Johnson:

> Mr. Johnson is a forty-year-old, wheelchair-bound patient who has been suffering for the past ten years from type 2 diabetes mellitus. He has wet gangrene on his fifth toe. He doesn't visit the outpatient clinic for care of his diabetes and infection as he is scheduled to. The infection is so severe that his physician, Dr. Garcia, concludes that the toe cannot be saved and that if it is not amputated, Mr. Johnson could die. Mr. Johnson has been seen by a psychiatrist, who finds him eccentric but believes that there is no evidence of mental illness and that Mr. Johnson must, therefore, be declared competent to make his own health care decisions.
>
> *(Groll 2011: 27)*[4]

For reasons we'll get to shortly, one may think that at the end of the day Mr. Johnson's wishes must be respected. But if that is right, it is surely *not* because there is any real doubt about what is best for him. A clinician who respects the patient's wishes here does so despite justifiably and truly believing that it would better for Mr. Johnson to get his toe removed. But this knowledge—that (other things being equal) it is better to live minus a toe than to die—is not *medical* knowledge. It is, rather, a piece of common knowledge about what makes a life go well.

Even so, Veatch is surely right that, in arriving at a judgment about what is good for a patient, the clinician should take the patient's view of what is best very seriously indeed, even if not as wholly or automatically authoritative. This is because patients often *are* far better suited to know what is good for them than clinicians—at least when it comes to what ends or goals constitutively contribute to their well-being. One can think this is true without thinking, as Mill (1978) did, that people are generally the best judges of and most interested in their own good. For the nature of many clinical encounters—where a clinician has never met the patient or even thought about him prior to picking up the patient's chart minutes before having what is often altogether a very short meeting with him—are such that the clinician is often especially poorly positioned to make any informed judgment about which ends or goals are best for the patient.

Moreover, as the case above illustrates, even when clinicians do know which ends or goals are best for their patients, they do not know it *qua* clinicians. This means that any judgments clinicians make, let alone express, about what ends are best for their patients do not carry any medical authority.

But none of these points undermines the idea that the proper aim of medicine is to restore, protect, or promote well-being via the tools of medicine. Rather, they give us good reason to think that *determining* what goals or ends are good for patients is (i) not a medical task, (ii) not something clinicians are particularly well suited to figure out, and so (iii) something that should be a *joint* endeavor between clinician and patient (with the patient taking the lead).

Autonomy, authenticity, and well-being: the standard case

A closer look at the example of Mr. Johnson, however, complicates even this qualified conclusion about the place of well-being as an end of medicine. For, as we noted there, many people will think that if Mr. Johnson refuses to have his toe amputated, clinicians must, at the end of the day, respect that decision. Indeed, it is a tenet of contemporary medical ethics that if a competent patient refuses treatment, then it is almost always wrong for the clinician to *force* the treatment on him. Why? The short answer is that *respecting patient autonomy* is a central value of clinical medicine.[5] But what exactly does this mean? And is respecting autonomy an end that can be subsumed under the end of promoting, protecting, or restoring a patient's well-being?

These two questions are related. Indeed, part of what makes answering the second question difficult is that there is a sense of "autonomy" whereby respecting (promoting, protecting, restoring etc.) autonomy contributes to well-being, either instrumentally or non-instrumentally, or both.

Sometimes when we talk about an autonomous individual we have in mind someone who is doing something "her way": she is living her life in accordance with her conception of what matters. Ronald Dworkin (1993: 224) calls this living a life with "integrity." I will follow Daniel Brudney (2009: 32) in calling such a life an "authentic" one.

If we focus on autonomy-as-authenticity, then considerations of autonomy seem to be a subset of all welfare considerations. Why? What is the connection between leading an authentic life and your life going well for you?

First, we might think that individuals are best situated, in terms of motivation and knowledge, to actually pursue what is best for them (Mill 1978). Moreover, even if we have doubts about how well people know what is best for themselves or whether they are in fact more interested in their own well-being than anyone else's, we may doubt whether there are effective ways of making people do what is good for them that are not so coercive or invasive as to make the overall situation *worse* for the person who is the target of the intervention.[6] Consider our case above: even if it is true that it would be best for the patient to choose the treatment, it certainly doesn't follow that it would be best for the patient for us to *force* the treatment on him. The cure (forced intervention) might be worse than the disease when we tally up the psychological and physical costs to the patient.

The upshot is that it is plausible to think that living an authentic life, or at least letting people lead authentic lives, is *instrumentally* valuable with respect to well-being. But one might think that leading an authentic life is also non-instrumentally related to personal well-being inasmuch as it is a *constituent* of how well one's life goes. So, Dworkin (1993: 205) claims that, "integrity . . . has great independent importance in life." And while they do not use the term "authenticity," Valerie Tiberius and Alexandra Plakias have argued for a Value-Based Life-Satisfaction Account of well-being, according to which one's well-being is constituted by life satisfaction as a "response to how life is going according to certain standards, and these standards are *provided by a person's values*" (Plakias and Tiberius 2010: 420; emphasis added).

The common idea here is that living your life in accordance with what you take to be important is *part* of your life going well for you. Crucially, any plausible version of this idea will leave room for the idea that you can be mistaken about what is good for you. This might be because you are wrong about what will *lead* to your life going as you want to; or because you are wrong about what *counts* as living in accordance with your values on a particular occasion; or, more controversially, because your conception of how your life should go is distorted by misinformation. But even if we acknowledge the various ways we can go wrong in determining how to live or what to do, the idea is that doing things "my way" is part of my good even if "my way" is mistaken or misguided in various ways.[7]

So, leading an authentic life—a life that is lived in accordance with one's deeply held values—is plausibly part of what makes a person's life go well for her. If that's right, then it looks like decisions that might initially appear bad for the patient in fact are not inasmuch as they are part of the patient leading an authentic life. But now we might worry that we've lost sight of the phenomenon we're trying to give an account of, namely why there is a strong presumption in favor of respecting a patient's poor decision. For if it is best for the patient to act—or to be allowed to act—in accordance with his authentic self, in what sense can we understand the patient's decision as poor at all?

The answer is that our judgment that the patient is making a poor decision depends *on setting aside* the fact that the patient's decision expresses his authenticity. That is, we judge that *setting aside* the fact that the patient authentically wants (or refuses) X, wanting (or refusing) X is bad for the patient. But then, when we consider the fact that he authentically wants (or refuses) X, we conclude that *all things considered*, getting (refusing) X is best for the patient. So, we respect the patient's decision because, taking into consideration all relevant factors (including what the patient authentically wants), the patient is choosing what is best for him.[8]

This answer to the question, "Why respect a competent patient's autonomous (and apparently poor) decisions?" assimilates considerations of autonomy to considerations of the patient's good. According to this view, there really is nothing else to consider in a clinical encounter beyond the patient's well-being, provided we have a suitably broad conception of what counts as contributing to the patient's well-being.[9]

The problem with this approach, or indeed any approach that subsumes considerations of autonomy to considerations of well-being, is that it doesn't do justice to the *kind* of consideration a competent patient's decision with respect to an available treatment is. Consider again Mr. Johnson's refusal of treatment. When he says that he does not want a procedure performed, he is not *just* expressing a desire or value, authentic or otherwise. He is making a *demand*. Consider how odd it would be if, in response to this demand, Dr. Garcia said, "I completely understand. And we will consider that refusal as part of our determination of what is good for you." We can imagine Mr. Johnson being confused by this response. For surely whether to get the treatment or not is *his* decision and now, having made that decision, the clinician must respect it as a *decision* and not as a further consideration in determining what is good for the patient. This is not to say that clinicians cannot appropriately try to persuade a patient to reconsider. The point, simply, is that at the end of the deliberative day, so to speak, the decision belongs to the patient. So, when the end of the deliberative day is reached, the presumption is that the patient's decision settles the matter: further consideration of the patient's good, let alone acting for his good without concern for the decision, is (presumptively) inappropriate.

Respecting patient autonomy, then, involves respecting a competent patient's *right* to make decisions about his own care. And when patients assert this right, they are introducing a consideration that is not to be assimilated to judgments about what is *good* for the patient. The upshot, then, is that while considerations of *authenticity* are a subset of well-being considerations, considerations of patient autonomy are not. They are *sui generis*.

This doesn't mean that an account of *why* competent patients have the right to make decisions about their own care cannot ultimately be grounded in considerations of either patients' good or, more broadly, the good of letting patients make their own decisions. Indeed, we have already got on board the materials for how such an account might go: authenticity is deeply important to well-being, so important (perhaps) that on balance we promote patient well-being by giving competent patients the *right* to make decisions about their own care.[10]

Setting aside the fact that there are serious theoretical objections to this kind of account,[11] the central point remains: whatever grounds it, patient autonomy consists at least in part of a *right*, specifically the right of competent patients to make decisions about their own care. Consequently, a competent patient's decision in a clinical encounter provides a practical reason that is not a welfare reason (even if the existence of such a reason *is* to be accounted for by welfare reasons). When a patient demands that he not be treated, that demand is not further data for determining what is best for the patient. It is a (presumptively) authoritative reason to stop thinking in terms of what is *good* for the patient.

The upshot, then, is that a clinician's pursuit of her patient's good is constrained by the need to respect her autonomy, where this is something quite apart from promoting, respecting, protecting, or restoring her well-being. To say that patient autonomy constrains the clinician's pursuit of the patient's good does not entail that it is always impermissible to act against a patient's autonomy for her good. In other words, my analysis of the relationship between autonomy and well-being in a clinical encounter does not entail that clinician paternalism is always impermissible. But the idea that patient autonomy consists, at least in part, of a patient's presumptively having the *right* to make decisions about her own care means that acting against that right is at least presumptively impermissible.[12]

Autonomy, authenticity, and well-being at the margins of agency

So far, we've looked at how the pursuit of well-being figures into the ends of medicine and, more specifically, its place in a clinical encounter between a healthcare provider and a competent patient.

Oftentimes, however, patients are *not* competent decision makers, or at least not obviously so. This is clearest in cases where patients are not even conscious. Here, the patient has no right to make a decision for herself since she is literally not capable of making a decision. In these cases, a surrogate decision maker is the one with the right to make healthcare decisions for the patient.

Things are considerably more complicated, however, when the patient is able to express preferences with respect to how he wants things to go, either in a particular situation ("I don't want to eat!") or in general ("I want to live!"), but where he does not rise to the level of competence required for him to have the right to make decisions about his care. Once again, a surrogate decision maker is the one with the right to make healthcare decisions for the patient. But how should the surrogate go about making decisions? And what do we learn about the nature of well-being in answering that question?

The standard response to the first question—which is developed and explored in depth in Brock and Buchanan (1989)—is that there are three decision-making standards the surrogate can appeal to:

1. the advance directive standard;
2. the substituted judgment standard;
3. the best interest standard.

According to the standard view, surrogates should first check if the incompetent patient has an advance directive. An advance directive explicitly tells the surrogate or healthcare team what the then-competent, now-incompetent patient wanted done in the situation in which he finds himself.[13]

If there is no advance directive, then (according to the standard view) the surrogate should deploy the substituted judgment standard. This standard directs the surrogate to do her best to discern what the incompetent patient *would* choose were he currently competent enough to make a decision for his incompetent self.

Suppose, however, that the surrogate has no, or not enough, idea of what the now-incompetent patient would choose were he now competent (and deciding for his incompetent self). According to the standard view, the surrogate should make the decision that she thinks is in the best interest of the patient.

Why (according to the standard view) should the standards be deployed in this particular order (i.e., advance directive, substituted judgment, best interest)? The answer is partly found in our previous discussion about the relationship between autonomy, authenticity, and well-being. The advance directive standard is thought to respond to the importance of patient autonomy. The substituted judgment standard is thought to respond to the importance of patient authenticity. And, finally, the best interest standard is thought to respond to the importance of the patient's well-being.

But the discussion above also points to a problem for the standard account. For, as we saw above, considerations of authenticity are not *distinct* from considerations of well-being. They are, rather, a subset of well-being considerations. This means that if the substituted judgment standard really is meant to respond to the importance of authenticity, it is not conceptually distinct from the best interest standard. It is, rather, highlighting the importance of authenticity *to* well-being. A more conceptually coherent version of the standard view, then, would advise surrogates to first check (and then appropriately respond to) an advance directive and then, if there isn't one, to act in the patient's best interest, where this means taking very seriously what choice would be consistent with the patient's authenticity.[14]

But even with this amendment to the standard view serious questions remain.[15] Some are epistemic: how should surrogates *interpret* advance directives, which, in very many cases, will be too general to be straightforwardly applied? Are competent patients in a good enough epistemic position to make decisions *now* for a future self who will be in a position that the current self probably doesn't have a very good handle on? How can we reliably judge what a now-incompetent patient *would* want were she to suddenly become competent (and have to make a decision about her current situation)? Other questions are metaphysical: is it so clear that the person who made the advance directive is metaphysically identical to the person who is in front of the surrogate right now? And even if the now-incompetent patient is metaphysically identical to his former competent self, has the change in his mental status come with a genuine change to his authentic self (such that imagining what the old authentic self would choose in the situation at hand would be inappropriate)?

Finally, there is the following ethical question: what should the surrogate *do* when it appears that the patient's current best interest dramatically conflicts with the patient's previous authentic choice (via an advance directive, for example)? This is the question I will focus on in the remainder of this paper since, in addition to being practically very important, it highlights interesting issues in debates about the nature of well-being and also draws in some of the questions above.

To help grapple with our question, consider an example from A. Jaworska (1999: 105):

> Mrs. Rogoff was always an independent woman. Raised in an immigrant family, she was used to working hard for what she wanted. Most of her life she ran a successful business selling liquor. She also developed local fame as an outstanding cook and hostess. After her third husband's death she lived alone, enjoying what she considered, by

old-country standards, a luxurious lifestyle: keeping up a nice big house and indulging in restful leisure. She was an introvert, always carefully guarding the way she presented herself to others. Life interested her insofar as she could live according to her own sense of comfort, making her own mistakes and relying on her own strength and wisdom.

In her early eighties Mrs. Rogoff developed severe motor impairments, which could only be corrected by a risky neurosurgery. She decided to undergo the procedure, insisting that she would rather die than be immobile. She prepared a living will, requesting not to have her life prolonged if she became a burden to her family or if she could no longer enjoy her current quality of life. The surgery was successful, but shortly thereafter Mrs. Rogoff developed early signs of dementia: memory and word-finding difficulties. As she became more and more disoriented, her daughter hired a housekeeper, Fran, who moved in with Mrs. Rogoff. Fran takes care of Mrs. Rogoff the way one would take care of a child. Mrs. Rogoff enjoys the long hours she spends with Fran, and with her grandchildren whenever they visit, telling them somewhat disjointed stories about her earlier ventures. She watches TV a lot and her stories often incorporate the more exciting episodes from TV as if they pertained to her own life. In her more lucid moments, Mrs. Rogoff tells her grandchildren that she is scared to die, that "she doesn't want to go anywhere." She usually cries when Fran is away and when her grandchildren wrap up their visits.

[. . .] What treatments should [Mrs. Rogoff's daughter] authorize if Mrs. Rogoff develops a dangerous but treatable infection?

It seems here that considerations of autonomy tell in favor of *not* (aggressively) treating Mrs. Rogoff should she develop a dangerous but treatable infection. But by not treating her, we would effectively be allowing someone to die who has clearly expressed an interest in living. If we consider what Mrs. Rogoff currently wants, it looks like being treated is in her best interest.

How might we resolve this apparent problem? There are four broad strategies (the shades will be explained presently, and "AD" means "advance directive"):

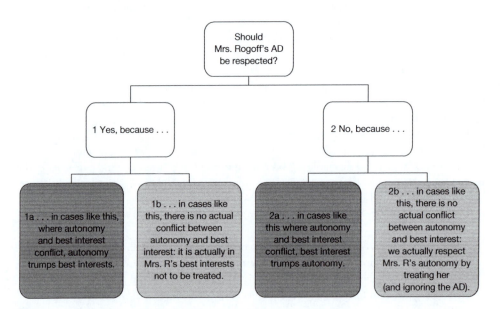

Notice that there is a sense in which 1a and 2a (shaded dark grey) belong together: both positions admit that there is a genuine conflict between autonomy and best interest in cases like Mrs. Rogoff's. They differ, however, in what should happen in the face of that conflict.

Likewise, 1b and 2b (shaded light grey) belong together inasmuch as both deny that there really is a genuine conflict between autonomy and best interest in this kind of case. They differ, however, in why they think this is so. 1b maintains that it is actually in Mrs. Rogoff's best interest for the advance directive to be followed. 2b, however, maintains that following the advance directive does *not* respect Mrs. Rogoff's autonomy on the grounds that Mrs. Rogoff still has (limited) autonomy to make medical decisions.[16] I want to focus on R. Dworkin's defense of 1b since it, and the replies it has generated, reveals significant fault lines in debates about the nature of well-being.

How could it be in Mrs. Rogoff's best interest not to be treated when she wants to continue living? According to Dworkin, the answer lies in appreciating the connection between autonomy and authenticity, or "integrity" as he calls it. The reason, according to Dworkin, that we think that competent people have the right to make decisions about their own medical care is because giving them that right allows for people to live authentically: they can shape their life in accord with the interests that reflect what really matters to them. Dworkin calls these interests "critical interests" (1993: 202).

Why should we care about living authentically (or with integrity)? We've already seen Dworkin's answer, namely that integrity is an independent constituent of a good life: "Integrity . . . has great independent importance in life . . . We admire the person who does it his way, even if that is very much not our way" (1993: 205). To put it in the terms I deployed above, Dworkin's view is that authenticity is a *part* of well-being and that autonomy—the right to make decisions about one's own care—stands primarily to protect this especially important constituent of well-being.[17] So, other things being equal, living a life that reflects one's values, or critical interests, is good for you and so in your best interest.

Suppose this brief account of Dworkin's view is correct. How does it help him to arrive at the conclusion that, contrary to appearances, it is in Mrs. Rogoff's best interest not to be treated despite her desire to continue living? The first claim Dworkin makes on the way to this conclusion is:

> *Narrative:* Having critical interests requires having a grasp of one's life as a whole or at least over a substantial stretch of time.

Dworkin's thought here is that our critical interests reflect our view of how we want our life to go as a whole (1993: 201). They provide a kind of structure for our whole life by marking out what really matters to us. They both give us a sense of where we're going (why we plan to do various things) and also where we have been (why we did what we did). To have critical interests, according to Dworkin, one must be able to take a kind of synoptic view of oneself and one's life.

Crucially, according to Dworkin, patients with relatively advanced dementia are not capable of thinking of their lives as a whole:

> By the time . . . dementia has become advanced, [its] victims have lost the capacity to think about how to make their lives more successful on the whole. They are ignorant of self—not as an amnesiac is, not simply because they cannot identify their pasts—but, more fundamentally, because they have no sense of a whole life, a past joined to a future, that could be the object of any evaluation or concern as a whole.
>
> *(Dworkin 1993: 230)*

The upshot then is that, assuming *narrative* is right, they are not capable of forming new critical interests.

But how does this get us to Dworkin's conclusion that we actually act in Mrs. Rogoff's interests by letting her die? The basic idea, recall, was that by following Mrs. Rogoff's pre-dementia wishes, we are thereby allowing her to live (or finish her life) with authenticity. But if Mrs. Rogoff cannot currently generate critical interests, it might seem that the issue of authenticity drops off the table altogether. So we don't help Mrs. Rogoff live (or end) her life authentically by allowing her die.

In response to this line of thought, Dworkin makes another claim:

> *Non-experiential:* Critical interests usually have non-experiential states of affairs as their objects. That is, the objects of critical interests are usually not that the holder of the interest *experience* something.[18]

Consider, for example, that if you ask a typical parent what he wants out of life he will probably rank the well-being of his children quite highly. To put it in Dworkinian terms, one of the parent's interests is that his children do well. This interest is not in the parent *experiencing* his children do well: the object of the interest is the children, not the parent.

Crucially, *non-experiential* does not claim that critical interests usually have someone other than the interest holder as their object. The idea, rather, is that critical interests don't have as their object the holder having certain *experiences*. This means that Mrs. Rogoff's pre-dementia interest in living independently is *non-experiential*: she actually wants to live independently and not just *feel* like she is.

Non-experiential moves us closer to seeing how it could be good for Mrs. Rogoff to not be treated for the infection. This is because the non-experiential nature of most people's critical interests means that the interest can be fulfilled without the interest holder knowing: a parent's interest in his child doing well might be met while the parent is on solo trek to the middle of Antarctica (suppose the child turned his life around during that time).

Likewise, Mrs. Rogoff's interest in not living in a highly dependent state can be met, without her knowing, by refusing to treat her. Moreover, in not treating her we are responding to an interest that is central to Mrs. Rogoff's living an authentic life. And living an authentic life is central to her life going well for her. So we arrive at Dworkin's conclusion: there is no real tension in Mrs. Rogoff's case between autonomy and best interest. Following Mrs. Rogoff's advance directive respects not only her autonomy but also is what is best for her.

Many people have rejected this conclusion. But they do so by rejecting different parts of Dworkin's view. Jaworska (1999), for example, rejects *narrative* (while accepting *non-experiential*). She claims that in order to have critical interests one needn't be able to have a grasp of one's life as a whole. As a result, patients like Mrs. Rogoff can have new critical interests, or at least new arrangements of critical interests, to which we must respond if we care about the patient's authenticity. And, inasmuch as Jaworska endorses Dworkin's "integrity-based" (1993: 224) view of the importance of autonomy, she argues that patients like Mrs. Rogoff have limited autonomy (based on current critical interests): they can make claims on providers about *ends* (such as being allowed to continue living) even if they are not authoritative with respect to how to actualize those ends (because they don't understand treatment options, for example) (1999: 136). So, she agrees with Dworkin that there is no conflict between best interest and autonomy here, but only because she thinks that Mrs. Rogoff has current critical interests that not only make it in her best interest to be treated but also ground a (limited) form of autonomy.[19] For Jaworska, both autonomy and best interest tell in favor of treating Mrs. Rogoff.

But suppose we accept both *narrative* and *non-experiential*. We might still resist Dworkin's conclusion. To see why, let's return to the comparison of the Antarctic trekker and Mrs. Rogoff. The idea there was that, just as the trekker's interest in his child doing well could be fulfilled without his knowing it, so too could Mrs. Rogoff's interest in not living in a highly dependent state.

There are at least three reasons we might reject the appropriateness of this comparison. First, to the extent that we have the intuition that the trekker is benefited by his child doing well during his (the father's) trek, this might be because we imagine that the time *will* come when he comes to learn about his child's success. But suppose now that the father *never* finds out. Even if there's a sense in which his interest is fulfilled, does the father *benefit* from that if the interest's fulfillment has *no* positive impact on his experience? Likewise, even if we admit that Mrs. Rogoff has a critical interest in not living in a highly dependent state, does it benefit her to not be treated assuming that, given the irreversibility of her dementia, this will have no positive impact on her experience?

Notice that if we are inclined to answer "no" to these questions we are not thereby committed to rejecting *non-experiential*. We can admit that the *object* of the trekker's interest is something non-experiential. The idea here is just that, in order for the fulfillment of an interest to benefit its possessor, the interest's fulfillment must have *some* positive impact on the interest holder's experience.[20]

Suppose, however, we side with Dworkin in thinking that the father is benefited by his child doing well even if he will never find out. We can still point to a difference between the trekker and Mrs. Rogoff that blocks the conclusion that Mrs. Rogoff is benefited by not being treated. To see why, notice how differently the trekker and Mrs. Rogoff *would* react to learning that their critical interests have been met. The father, presumably, would react very positively. Mrs. Rogoff, on the other hand, would not: she wants to live. The experience of not being treated, especially if we imagine that she is aware she's not being treated, will be highly negative for her.

This leads to the idea, which Jennifer Hawkins has recently argued for, that what is good for a person cannot be *alien* to her. What this means is that, "a person's good must enter her experience, if it does, in a positive way" (2014: 526). This *non-alienness principle* (Hawkins 2014: 526) does not demand that the good in question *actually* be experienced in a positive way by the person.[21] It must only be the case that *if it does*, it will be experienced in a positive way by the agent as she currently is. We have every reason to think that this is true of the trekker and every reason to think it is *not* true of Mrs. Rogoff. So, contrary to Dworkin, it is not good for Mrs. Rogoff not to be treated.

Finally, even if we reject the *non-alienness principle*, we might still reject the comparison between the trekker and Mrs. Rogoff by simply rejecting the claim that Mrs. Rogoff still has a critical interest in not being dependent on others in the way she now is. Imagine again that we stop our trekker and ask him if he is still interested in his child doing well. He will say "yes." But if we ask Mrs. Rogoff whether she would rather be allowed to die than to continue living as she is, she will say "no."

This test is clearly closely related to the *non-alienness principle*, but the emphasis is in a different place. The question here is not about Mrs. Rogoff's experience, actual or hypothetical. Rather, it's about whether she still even has the critical interest Dworkin attributes to her. And we might say "no" on the grounds that in order for someone to have a (non-instrumental) interest in something it must be the case that she would agree that she does if asked.[22] Let's call this the *endorsement principle*. If it is correct, then we are not responding to any interest of Mrs. Rogoff's in not treating her.

My goal here is not to endorse any of these ways of rejecting Dworkin's conclusion about how to deal with dementia patients whose current interests seem to conflict with their past interests. Each of the proposals above faces plausible objections which I leave to the reader to discover. There are, however, several broad conclusions we can draw from the above discussion.

First, Dworkin's own view and the possible responses to it highlight some major questions about the connections between a person's interests and experiences, as well as how they relate over time. Any compelling theory of well-being must answer these questions. Second, our discussion of Mrs. Rogoff shows that the kinds of cases that routinely arise in a medical context provide an excellent testing ground for theories of well-being.

But the third, and final, conclusion is perhaps the most important: how we answer the questions raised throughout the discussion—What is the relationship between well-being, authenticity, and autonomy? What is the role of actual experience in determining whether something is good for someone? What is the role of possible experience? What is involved in something being in a person's interest in the first place?— are of far more than theoretical interest. They can profoundly impact how we deal with those we love when they are at their most vulnerable.

Related topics

Autonomy and well-being, experience requirement, health, shape of a life, autonomy and paternalism.

Further reading

Beauchamp, T.L. and Childress, J.F. (2012) *Principles of Biomedical Ethics,* 7th edn. Oxford: Oxford University Press.
(This is the ur-text of contemporary medical ethics.)

Brock, D. and Buchanan, A.E. (1989) *Deciding for Others: The Ethics of Surrogate Decision Making.* Cambridge: Cambridge University Press.
(This is *the* classic text on the ethical and conceptual framework for surrogate decision making.)

Dworkin, R.M. (1993) *Life's Dominion: An Argument About Abortion, Euthanasia, and Individual Freedom.* New York: Random House.
(A very well-written text on ethical issues at the beginning and end of life. The discussion of decision making at the end of life forms the basis for much of the debate in the field.)

Jaworska, A. (1999) "Respecting the Margins of Agency: Alzheimer's Patients and the Capacity to Value," *Philosophy & Public Affairs,* 28(2): 105–138.
(A wonderfully written and deeply incisive response to Dworkin's views on advance directives and end-of-life decision making.)

Veatch, R. (2009) *Patient Heal Thyself.* New York: Oxford University Press.
(This is a provocative take on the proper nature of the clinician–patient relationship.)

Notes

1 Rather, it might seem that medicine is concerned with a particular *element* of well-being, namely health. Of course, whether "health" is more restricted than "well-being" as a category depends on how one construes the former. The World Health Organization's Constitution (1960), for example, simply defines health as "A state of complete physical, mental and social well-being." Leon Kass (1974) criticizes this conception of health on the grounds that it is far too broad and well beyond the purview of what clinicians should aim for.

2 What should we say, for example, about so-called "alternative medicine"? Talk therapies? Cosmetic surgery? Are these part of medicine? Or something else altogether? It's even more difficult to know what to say about certain social skills we expect clinicians to have, such as good bedside manner and a certain degree of empathy. Are these "medical tools"?

3 Veatch specifically mentions hedonism, desire-satisfaction, and objective list theories of well-being.

4 This case is a slightly modified version of one found in Veatch et al. (2010).

5 The classic discussion of this idea is in Beauchamp and Childress (2012).

6 Although, for a different view, see Thaler and Sunstein (2008) and Conly (2013).

7 This idea is nicely expressed in popular song. For example, in *My Way*, Frank Sinatra sings, "I've lived a life that's full//I traveled each and every highway//And more, much more than this, I did it my way." More recently, Kevin Barnes, the frontman for of Montreal, sings in *The Past is a Grotesque Animal*: "At least I authored my own disaster."

8 This idea is discussed in slightly different terms in Groll (2012).

9 This is basically the view of Pellegrino (2001).

10 This is basically Dworkin's view. I say a little more about it below.

11 There are, however, significant theoretical obstacles to providing a *good-based* account of rights or entitlements. In short, the problem is that there appears to be an unbridgeable conceptual gap between it being good or desirable that S is entitled to X and S actually being entitled to X. This idea is discussed in depth in Darwall (2006). Lott (forthcoming) argues that this gap is bridgeable.

12 I defend this idea in Groll (2014). Beauchamp and Childress (2012: 222) think there isn't even a *presumption* in favor of anti-paternalism.

13 This quick articulation of what an advance directive (AD) is glosses over the difference between an *instructional* AD and a *proxy* AD (Brock and Buchanan 1989: 95). The former gives guidance about what should be done in particular situations. The latter says *who* should make decisions for the patient when she is no longer able to make her own decisions. Of course, an AD might be both instructional and proxy. My emphasis here is on the instructional part of ADs (since a proxy AD on its own isn't very useful for the proxy decision maker!).

14 Dan Brudney comes very close to making this point, but does not suggest folding the substituted judgment standard into the best-interest standard as I am doing here.

15 These, and other issues, are discussed by Brock and Buchanan (1989).

16 The implicit assumption here is that an AD cannot bind a future self that still has autonomy. This idea is reflected in the very idea of the AD, which is meant to direct a *surrogate*. But of course a surrogate is only required in cases where the patient does not have the right (because she does not have the ability) to make decisions for herself.

17 Dworkin does contrast the "integrity-based view of the importance of autonomy" with a welfare-based view (1993: 224), but the welfare-based view he has in mind is one that does not construe integrity, or authenticity, as a *part* of welfare. Given what I said above about how considerations of authenticity should properly be seen as a subset of welfare considerations, I think Dworkin's view is accurately captured by saying that integrity is a fundamental and independently important constituent of well-being.

18 Dworkin's distinction between critical and "experiential" interests (as he call them) is not as clear as it might be. In some places (and as the name of the interests suggest), it sounds like he thinks that not having experiences as their object is *criterial* for an interest being a critical interest. But in other places, it sounds like the distinction is more about whether the person in question genuinely *values* whatever the object of his interest is or simply idiosyncratically enjoys it. The problem with the first way of making the distinction is that the dedicated hedonist would seem not to have any critical interests.

19 In other words, Jaworska occupies position 2b in the chart above. Shiffrin (2004) also occupies this position, but for different reasons than Jaworska.

20 Griffin (1988: 13) calls this the experience requirement.

21 Here is Hawkins' formal articulation of the principle:

NA says it is a necessary condition of X's being intrinsically good for A at T1 that either (1) A respond positively to X at T1 if she is aware of X at T1 or (2) A be such that she would respond positively to X at T1 if she were aware of X at T1 (2014: 527)

22 This is proposed as a necessary, not sufficient, condition.

References

Beauchamp, T.L. and Childress, J.F. (2012) *Principles of Biomedical Ethics,* 7th edn. Oxford: Oxford University Press.

Brock, D. and Buchanan, A.E. (1989) *Deciding for Others: The Ethics of Surrogate Decision Making.* Cambridge: Cambridge University Press.

Brudney, D. (2009) "Beyond Autonomy and Best Interests," *Hastings Center Report* 39(2): 31–37.

Conly, S. (2013) *Against Autonomy: Justifying Coercive Paternalism.* New York: Cambridge University Press.

Darwall, S.L. (2006) *The Second-person Standpoint: Morality, Respect, and Accountability.* Cambridge MA: Harvard University Press.

Dworkin, R.M. (1993) *Life's Dominion: An Argument about Abortion, Euthanasia, and Individual Freedom.* New York: Random House.

Griffin, J. (1988) *Well-being: Its Meaning, Measurement, and Moral Importance.* Oxford: Clarendon Press.

Groll, D. (2011) "What Health Care Providers Know," *Hastings Center Report* 41(5): 27–36.

Groll, D. (2012) "Paternalism, Respect, and the Will," *Ethics* 122(4): 692–720.

Groll, D. (2014) "Medical Paternalism—Part 2," *Philosophy Compass* 9(3): 194–203.

Hawkins, J. (2014) "Well-Being, Time, and Dementia," *Ethics* 124(3): 507–542.

Jaworska, A. (1999) "Respecting the Margins of Agency: Alzheimer's Patients and the Capacity to Value," *Philosophy & Public Affairs* 28(2): 105–138.

Kass, L.R. (1974) "Regarding the End of Medicine and the Pursuit of Health," *The Public Interest* 40.

Lott, M. (forthcoming) "Morality, Accountability, and the Wrong Kind of Reasons." *Utilitas.*

Mill, J.S. (1978) *On Liberty.* Indianapolis: Hackett.

Pellegrino, E.D. (2001) "The Internal Morality of Clinical Medicine: A Paradigm for the Ethics of the Helping and Healing Professions," *Journal of Medicine and Philosophy,* 26(6): 559–579.

Plakias, A. and Tiberius, V. (2010) "Well-Being" in J. Doris & the Moral Psychology Research Group (eds.), *The Moral Psychology Handbook.* Oxford: Oxford University Press.

Shiffrin, S. (2004) "Autonomy, Beneficence and the Permanently Demented," in J. Burley (ed.) *Dworkin and His Critics.* New York: Wiley Blackwell.

Thaler, R.H. and Sunstein, C.R. (2008) *Nudge: Improving Decisions About Health, Wealth, and Happiness.* New Haven, CT: Yale University Press.

Veatch, R. (2009) *Patient Heal Thyself.* New York: Oxford University Press.

Veatch, R., Haddad, A.M. and English, D.C. (2010) *Case Studies in Biomedical Ethics.* New York: Oxford University Press.

World Health Organization (1960) *Constitution.* Geneva: World Health Organization.

INDEX

Note: The following abbreviations have been used – f = figure; n = note; t = table